amazin'

Other Oral Histories by Peter Golenbock

amazin'

The Miraculous History of New York's Most Beloved Baseball Team

Peter Golenbock

St. Martin's Press ❧ New York

www.stmartins.com

Design by Michael Collica

Library of Congress Cataloging-in-Publication Data

Golenbock, Peter.
    Amazin' : the miraculous history of New York's most beloved baseball team / Peter
Golenbock.—1st U.S. ed.
        p. cm.
    ISBN 0-312-27452-1
    1. New York Mets (Baseball team)—History. I. Title: Miraculous history of New York's
most beloved baseball team. II. Title.

GV875.N45 G64 2002
796.357'09747'1—dc21

                                                                        2001048870

First Edition: April 2002

10   9   8   7   6   5   4   3   2   1

contents

list of illustrations

This book is dedicated to Rhonda Sonnenberg, who I met on the telephone while covering the story of a classmate who murdered his entire family. We fell in love before we even met, and through the years time has only increased my love and admiration for you.

acknowledgments

I wish to thank those friends, old and new, who were kind enough to share their time and memories with me or help me find sources or information: Ray Robinson, Larry Ritter, Jack Lang, Stan Isaacs, Robert Lipsyte, Charlie Einstein, Donald Hall, the late Joe Flaherty, the late Joel Oppenheimer, Bobby McCarthy, Billy Reddy, Kathy Shea, Jud Gould, Bernard Fishman, and Kevin McGrath.

Thanks to the Mets' longtime public servant, Jay Horowitz, always helpful, always kind; to the late Tony Salin, who constantly surprised me with interesting tidbits of information; to Scott Siebers and Eric Smith at ESPN; to longtime Mets fans Bernie Levy, David Brownstein, and Ken Samelson; to Mark Topkin, one of the best of the beat reporters; to the tireless Matt Lorenz, the one-man publications department for the Devil Rays; to my old St. Luke's School classmate Mike Greenwood; to longtime Mets icons Bob Mandt and Arthur Richman; to Charles Hurth III, the late Hazel Weiss, Frank Cashen, and to one of the finest managers in all the land, Davey Johnson. What happened to him in L.A. was a crime.

My fondest regards to the heroic men who performed on the ball fields across baseball land: Wally Backman, Gary Carter, Ron Gardenhire, Steve Henderson, Jim Hickman, Ron Hunt, Clint Hurdle, Rod Kanehl, Terry Leach, Al Leiter, Jon Matlack, Felix Millan, Amos Otis, Lenny Randle, Joe Sambito, Craig Swan, Ron Swoboda, George Theodore, Jerry Koosman, and Pat Zachry, who provided me with hundreds of hours of vital interviews. Despite the journalistic mantra to the contrary, these are men who played for the love of the game first, everything else second.

Thanks also to Neil and Dawn Reshen, my brilliant and caring watchdogs. To my editors at St. Martin's Press, Joe Veltre, who signed the book up, and Marc Resnick, a Mets fan all his life and a gentleman who is a joy to work with. And to my indefatigable and industrious fact checker, Bernie Levy: you are truly amazing. To Lia Pelosi, for her thoroughness and care; to my wonderful family: my wife, Rhonda, and our talented son, Charlie, and to our faithful bassett hound, Doris Day Duke Delilo, and to Fred, the gray squirrel outside my window clinging to the wild oak tree.

May your days be as rich as mine.

—Peter Golenbock
St. Petersburg, Florida

Baseball, from my prejudiced point of view, is the perfect game. Baseball demands and rewards teamwork, but at the same time, it highlights individual skills. On any given day, any player at any position can be a hero—or a goat.

—Tom Seaver

amazin'

o n e

The Original New York Metropolitans

In the summer of 1880, Jim Mutrie, the founding father of major league baseball in New York City, rode his bicycle on dirt roads, from a small town south of Boston to New York City with the intention of founding a professional baseball franchise in Manhattan. All he lacked was money.

Mutrie, who had played shortstop "of meager reputation" in small Massachusetts fishing towns like Fall River and New Bedford, arrived fashionably attired in gloves, spats, and a black silk top hat. The first potential backer he contacted was robber baron and financier August Belmont. Belmont listened to Mutrie's proposal and passed after deciding that pro baseball wasn't a solid enough investment.

Not long after, Mutrie was watching two amateur teams do battle when John Day, a wholesale tobacco merchant who had pitched that afternoon and gotten clobbered, sat down next to him. They started talking, and when Mutrie told Day what he was trying to do, Day surprised him by agreeing to bankroll such a team. Their team, they decided, would be called the Metropolitans, or Mets. The National League operated with eight franchises, but none played in New York. A New York franchise had operated during the initial 1876 season, but after a 21–35 record the team folded. The void remained.

In the winter of 1881 the American Association was being formed and Day and Mutrie were asked to take the New York franchise. Day listened to the sales pitch made by Oliver Perry "Opie" Caylor, a Cincinnati newspaper reporter and a founder of the upstart league, but in the end decided that the venture was too risky, and he demurred when asked to commit his money to it as did his partners, Mutrie and newspaper publisher W. S. Appleton. For a year the Metropolitans operated as an independent franchise.

Caylor knew the new league needed a strong franchise in New York to succeed, and was frustrated by their reluctance. He told Day and Mutrie the door would be left open for them to join in the future.

Rather than start from scratch, Day and Mutrie decided the best way to enter a competitive franchise was to buy an existing one and move it to New York. In October 1882 they bought the floundering Troy Trojans.

Troy, a town across the Hudson River from Albany, had been a landing point for thousands of Irish immigrants escaping the potato famine of 1846–48. Among these powerful sons of Erin who played for Troy were Hall of Famers Tim Keefe and Mickey Welch, each of whom had pitched for more than 300 wins during their careers; catcher and third baseman Buck Ewing; and Roger Connor, one of the great sluggers of the nine-teenth century. The team also had star catcher Bill Holbert and outfielder Pete Gillespie.

The Trojans had competed in the National League for four seasons, but the town was too small a market to support a major-league team. When the franchise closed down in December 1882, Day and Mutrie bought the team, moved them to the American Association, and renamed it the Metropoli-tans. That year they also bought a second team, the New York Gothams, and entered them into the more established rival National League.

Day, a shrewd businessman, was convinced the National League had a brighter future than the newly organized American Association, and he put fewer of his eggs into the Metropolitan basket than he did in that of the Gothams. When they divvied up the Troy players, Day and Mutrie kept most of their best players in the National League.

Keefe, for example, was moved to the Metropolitans roster, while Welch remained with the Gothams. Holbert and James "Chief" Roseman, good but not great players, went to the Metropolitans, while former Troy standouts Connor, Gillespie, and Ewing were left on the Gothams. Day made Mutrie, who had never managed professionally before, manager of the Metropolitans.

When Day was asked by American Association leaders to serve on the board, to their dismay, he declined. Instead, he spent his time helping to run things in the National League. American Association leaders rightfully were wary of his loyalty.

Since Day was leery of the financial viability of the American Association, he decided to run the Metropolitans on a bareboned budget. The team played at Metropolitan Park, one of the two fields located by the East River at The Polo Grounds, an enormous wooden ballpark boasting two fields. The land on which the Polo Grounds sat was owned by James Gordon Bennett, the publisher of the *New York Herald*. Bennett had originally held polo matches on the grounds, hence the ballpark's name.

The Southeast Field, where the Gothams played, was fancy with lush green grass and a fine grandstand. A short fence in front of the left-field bleachers was erected and a canvas barrier added to separate the two diamonds once the Metropolitans began playing on the West Field.

The West Field at 108th Street was so bad it was known as "The Dump" by New Yorkers because it sat on the old city dump. Commented pitcher Jack Lynch, you could "go down for a grounder and come up with six months of malaria." The noxious fumes from factories across the river wafted heavily into the nostrils of the players and the few fans.

Day provided the Metropolitans with so little equipment that the players had to resort to stealing bats from opposing clubs after they had emptied their equipment bags onto the playing field. The Mets players particularly enjoyed stealing equipment from Cincinnati, one of the league's richer teams. But despite these difficult conditions and a rookie manager, the Metropolitans surprised everyone when they finished fourth in the eight-team league with a 54–42 record. Their ten wins against Cincinnati in their fourteen meetings was a chief factor in keeping the Reds from winning the pennant.

The Metropolitans were led by pitchers Tim Keefe and Jack Lynch. Keefe, who was of the greats of baseball history, finished the 1883 season 41–27, pitching 68 complete games and with an era of 2.41, and 359 strikeouts in 619 innings. This was the first of six straight seasons in which Keefe would win 30 or more games. From 1880 through 1888, he started in 444 games and finished all but eight. His 342 wins is eighth all-time, and he is third all-time in complete games with 554. He was elected to the Hall of Fame in 1964. Lynch finished the season with a 13–15 record.

As for their hitting, only one Metropolitan, shortstop John "Candy" Nelson, hit over .300 with a .305 batting average. The entire team hit just six home runs all season long.

When the 1884 season began, no one had any reason to think the Metropolitans would be anything special. But, two months into the season, while

Day's National League Gothams were struggling, his stepchild Metropolitans were contending for the American Association pennant. The Metropolitans would win the 1884 championship by 6½ games over the Columbus Buckeyes. Three of the higher-rated teams in the thirteen-team league, Louisville, St. Louis, and Cincinnati, finished third, fourth, and fifth.

The individual Metropolitans' may not have had impressive statistics, but Mutrie turned out to be an excellent manager who had a knack for getting the best of his talent. His lifetime winning percentage of .611 is second in baseball history to only the legendary Joe McCarthy.

The wonder was that Mutrie could take a lineup of mediocre hitters and score a lot of runs with them. Left fielder Ed Kennedy hit .190. Catcher Bill Holbert hit .208, finishing his career as the only player ever to come to bat more than two thousand times without hitting a home run. John "Dasher" Troy, whom Day moved after the 1884 season to the Mets from the Gothams when he hit poorly, Candy Nelson, and Steve Brady hit only in the .250s.

The offensive star of the team was 250-pound first baseman, Dave Orr. In 1884 Orr hit nine home runs and led the league in hitting with a .354 batting average. Two years later he was the first player in baseball history to ring up 300 total bases in a single season. (Six years later Orr would suffer a stroke, ending his career at age thirty-one.) The other decent batsman on the team was suave and dapper third baseman Dude Esterbrook, who hit .314. (Esterbrook also met a tragic end when, seventeen years later, he jumped to his death from a moving train en route to a mental hospital.)

The heart of the 1884 champion Metropolitans was the pitching duo of Tim Keefe and Jack Lynch, each of whom won 37 games to tie for second in the league. Keefe was fourth in the league with a 2.26 era. Lynch was ninth at 2.67.

Providence won the 1884 pennant in the National League. The Grays were led by Gardner "Old Hoss" Radbourn, a legendary turn-of-the-century pitching sensation. That year Radbourn had his finest season, winning 59 games and losing only 12 with an era of 1.38. In mid-July Radbourn was suspended in midseason for drunkenness but when the other veteran pitcher, Charlie Sweeney, got drunk and quit the team after being threatened with suspension, manager Frank Bancroft knew he was in trouble, so he reinstated Radbourn and gave him a raise.

No World Series was played in 1883 because the National League's Boston Beaneaters had defeated the American Association's Philadelphia

Athletics in seven of eight exhibition games, and A's manager Lew Simmons refused to play for keeps.

When a clamor arose in September for the Metropolitans and the Grays to meet in a World Series in 1884, Mutrie challenged Bancroft to a two-game series. Bancroft declined. Mutrie turned up the heat by going to the New York papers and accusing Bancroft of being chicken-hearted. Bancroft finally agreed to meet in a best two out of three series. The three games would be played at the Polo Grounds. Each club put up $1,000.

The star of the series was Providence's Hoss Radbourn, who dominated the Metropolitans, winning the first two games 6–0 and 3–1. Since the championship already was decided, only three hundred spectators showed up for the third game. Radbourn defeated the Metropolitans easily in a 12–2 win, shortened after only six innings. In all, Radbourne gave up eleven hits and no walks in the three outings. One reporter wrote that "the Metropolitans played like children."

John Day, despite having won a pennant in the American Association, remained firmly convinced that his baseball future lay with his National League Gothams. Even though American Association tickets were cheaper and he could sell beer at American Association games, fans were few. The Metropolitans lost $8,000 in 1884 despite their success.

In November 1884 Day moved to further strengthen the National League Gothams. Impressed with the way Jim Mutrie had led the Metropolitans to the pennant, Day fired Gotham manager Jim Price and replaced him with Mutrie. Day also wanted to move his two best Met players, Keefe and Esterbrook, to the Gothams, but National Association rules forbade him, even though he owned both teams. Under the rules, he first had to release them, and then he had to wait ten days before re-signing them. During those ten days, any team owner could sign them. To prevent that, Day invited Keefe and Esterbrook to vacation with him at his onion farm in Bermuda. He issued their release, took off for Bermuda, and when the ten days were up, they returned to New York and signed their new contracts. With Keefe and Esterbrook onboard, the New York Gothams became contenders for the 1885 National League pennant.

The owners of the American Association were furious with Day. On April 29, 1885, twelve days into the new season, the board of directors met to consider kicking the defending champion Metropolitans out of the league. But, because they knew how important a New York team was to their survival, they backed down. Instead, they fined Day $500 for switching Keefe and Esterbrook, and they made Mutrie the scapegoat by banning him from ever managing in the American Association.

Without their manager and the two stars, the Metropolitans finished the 1885 season a dismal 44–64, seventh in the eight-team league. Jack Orr finished second in the league in hitting with a .342 average and led the league with a .543 slugging percentage, one of the highest in baseball history. But Jack Lynch couldn't handle the pitching load by himself, and he finished the season 23–21.

At the end of the season Day dropped the other shoe when he sold the Metropolitans to Erastus Wiman, the owner of the Staten Island Ferry, for $25,000. Wiman proposed transferring the team to Staten Island, but Association leaders insisted the team remain in Manhattan.

In December 1885 the league voted to oust the Metropolitans and replace it with a Washington franchise. Wiman got an injunction to stop the eviction and won in court to keep the team from being removed. But, the lawsuit only postponed the inevitable. When it appeared the franchise was going to fold, Dave Orr and outfielder Chief Roseman signed with Brooklyn. Brooklyn owner Charlie Byrne at first refused to return them after Wiman won the case for reinstatement, but was forced by the league to relent.

The Metropolitans were even worse in 1886. New manager Jim Gifford was fired after the team began the season 5–12. Their final record was 53–82, and despite Orr's .368 batting average, he lost his home run stroke. Pitcher Al Mays led the league with 28 losses. The Metropolitans suffered one of the worst seasons in the history of the game of baseball.

Some reporters blamed the failure of the Metropolitans on the ballpark, saying the trip was too expensive and too long. Others blamed it on the chancy New York weather. None laid the blame where it belonged, on John Day's machinations.

In 1887 the Metropolitans finished 44–89, seventh once again. They opened the season 1–12. Orr hit .368, and Mays again led the league in losses with 31. The Mets were bolstered by the acquisition of Joe Gerhardt, who had been released by the New York Gothams after the popular but paranoid Gerhardt blamed Buck Ewing and Monte Ward for turning his teammates against him. But almost as soon as he joined the Mets, Gerhardt suffered a bad back and then contracted malaria.

In early June, Jack Orr, who had replaced Bob Ferguson as manager, was hurt chasing a pop up. He decided he no longer wanted to manage, and he named catcher Bill Holbert as his replacement. However, president Walter Wattrous, with the approval of Wiman, vetoed Holbert and hired Oliver Perry Caylor, the cofounder of the league, to be the new manager. At the time Caylor was also working as a reporter for *The Sporting Life* magazine. When Watrous and Caylor tried to enter the league meetings in December, Caylor was tossed out for being a reporter.

Before the end of the 1887 season Wiman sold the Mets to the owner of the Brooklyn team, Charlie Byrne. Caylor quit, saying he could not work for the hot-tempered, Machiavellian Byrne. The Mets finished seventh amid the turmoil. Once again, the hitting of David Orr (.368) highlighted a dismal season. Al Mays lost 34 games.

Byrne's purchase of the team in September 1887 turned out to be the end for the New York Metropolitans. Byrne's stated intention was to turn it into a farm club for his Brooklyn team, but his real purpose became evident after the season was over when he cavalierly transferred the best Mets players—Orr, Paul Radford, and Mays—from New York to Brooklyn. This infamous act was the start of a century of bad blood between teams from New York and Brooklyn. New York fans never forgave Byrne for raping their team and building his Brooklyn franchise at their expense.

After Byrne denuded the New York franchise, he renounced ownership in the decimated team, and announced that he was giving it back to the league. The league transferred the Metropolitans franchise to Missouri, and in 1888 the renamed Kansas City Cowboys finished dead last. For the first time in almost ten years, there would be only one New York team, the Gothams (renicknamed the Giants), playing in the National League.

The loyal New York Metropolitan fans mourned the loss of their team. It would not be the last time New Yorkers would mourn for a lost franchise, and it would take almost seventy-five years for their Metropolitans to return.

t w o

The Emotions of the Giants Fans

When John Day sold the New York Metropolitans in the winter of 1885, he could now concentrate his efforts on his National League Gothams. With both Mickey Welch *and* Tim Keefe to pitch, and a lineup that boasted four more future Hall of Famers: first baseman Roger Connor, who at six-foot-three, 220 pounds, was the giant of Giants; shortstop John Montgomery Ward, and outfielder Orator Jim O'Rourke, who had played on pennant winners with Boston in 1877 and 1878, and was part of the championship Providence Grays of 1879, and catcher Buck Ewing, the first catcher ever to crouch behind the plate and ranked by many as the best player of his time. Ewing may well have been the baseball brains behind the operation, not Mutrie.

Mickey Welch, who died in 1941, once told *New York Times* columnist John Kieran, "Mutrie was what you would call today the business manager of the club. The real manager and leader on the field was Buck Ewing."

Ewing was an excellent hitter, a fast runner, and he had a great arm from behind the plate. He also had a flair for the dramatic. One time he singled to lead off the tenth inning of a scoreless game, stole second and third, and then announced that he would steal home. After he did so, a lithograph called "Ewing's Famous Slide" was made, and thousands were sold. Many were displayed behind the many saloons of New York.

Led by Ewing, Day and Mutrie had a solid team of veterans that would finish the 1885 National League season just two games behind Cap Anson's legendary Chicago White Stockings.

The players on the New York National League team were large men, and when they took the field for one of their early games at the polo field in 1885, from the stands Mutrie lept to his feet and was heard to brag, "These are my big fellows! These are my giants!"

Some fans heard him, and the nickname spread throughout the stands. The next day Mutrie was quoted in the newspapers, and they were the New York Giants ever since.

The Giants finished third in 1886 and fourth in 1887, and after the season Jim Mutrie orchestrated several trades and purchases that added pitcher "Cannonball" Ed Crane and outfielder "Silent" Mike Tierney.

In 1888 Tim Keefe, at his best, won 19 games in a row and led the league with a 35–12 record and a 1.74 era. Mickey Welch added 26 more wins, enabling the Giants to defeat Chicago for the 1888 pennant by nine games. Roger Connor, who hit fourteen home runs and drove in 71 runs, led a potent lineup that included stars Mike Tierney and Danny Richardson, in addition to Ward, O'Rourke, and Ewing. Although Ewing may well have been the leader on the field, it was Mutrie who had changed the makeup of the team and rebuilt it into a champion in 1888.

The Giants met Chris Von Der Ahe's St. Louis Browns in the 1888 World Series, winning four of the first six games behind Keefe and Welch. After losing in game seven, the Giants, behind Keefe, took an early lead and after a three-run home run by Tierney, ended up winning easily, 11–3. It was Keefe's fourth win of the Series, and the Giants' first World Championship.

Each member of the Giants got $200 as the winner's share. Jim Mutrie was credited with being the first manager in baseball history to win pennants in two leagues—he had led the Metropolitans to the American Association pennant in 1884.

In 1889 professional baseball fans were treated to their first New York subway series. After winning the National League Championship on the last day of the season, the Giants faced their interborough rivals, the Brooklyn Trolley Dodgers, first-time champions of the American Association. Brooklyn, also called the Bridegrooms, because several of their players had recently gotten married, had finally broken the chokehold held by the St. Louis Browns, winners in 1885, 1886, 1887, and 1888. Owner Charlie Byrne's attempts to build a winner finally had paid off, and the 353,000 fans that filled Washington Park in 1898 broke all attendance records.

The champion would have to win six games in the eleven-game series. Brooklyn won three of the first four games, but the Giants, behind pitcher Hank O'Day, who was stolen from Washington by Mutrie in July, Keefe, and Crane won the final five games in a row to take the title.

The 1889 season marked the high point of the nineteenth century for the Giants. It was the last great year for Day and Mutrie. The growth of upper Manhattan was responsible.

The Harlem board of aldermen in 1889 voted to cut a major thoroughfare right through the Polo Grounds. Day had so little notice he was forced to relocate for the 1890 season to the St. George Field on Staten Island. Most of the fans found the move inconvenient and refused to pay the nickel each way on the ferry to go to the new home.

Nationwide, there was a far worse development in baseball. When greedy, arrogant, and shortsighted owners decided to impose a salary cap on players in both leagues, the players, led by John Montgomery Ward, decided to start their own league and compete with their former bosses. Buck Ewing became manager of the Brotherhood League New York team, and Connor, Richardson, Whitney, Keefe, Crane, and O'Day defected as well. The three players who refused to jump were Welch, Tiernan, and Murphy.

Unfortunately for both sides, the owners learned they could not succeed without the players, and the players found out they could not run the business well enough by themselves to make a go of it. The result, not long in coming, was financial disaster for everyone.

With three players and no ballpark, Day purchased several excellent players including pitcher Amos Rusie and shortstop Jack Glasscock from the Indianapolis franchise, owned by John T. Brush, for $60,000.

Day, knowing he had to return to upper Manhattan to survive, invested a large sum of money building a new ballpark located farther uptown at 155th Street and Eighth Avenue. The new Polo Grounds was surely the grandest baseball venue in America. The large, horseshoe-shaped stadium sat under what was known as Coogan's Bluff, a steep rock face that seemed to shrink the elegant double-decker grandstand below it.

But despite the new pleasure palace, John Day's reign as owner of the Giants was coming to an end.

To his dismay, the Players League team built their stadium on grounds adjacent to his. In the war with the Brotherhood League, the competition from the New York and Brooklyn Players League teams proved too great for Day. Between the new players and his new stadium, all of his money was gone, and to make ends meet he was forced to borrow from Arthur Soden, an owner of the Boston team, and Ed Talcott, a New York financier. Making things worse, most of his old customers preferred to see his former players in the Brotherhood League than come to watch his team.

In 1891 Day was forced to borrow more money in order to survive. He went to Talcott who agreed to buy more of his stock if and only if he fired Mutrie, his longtime partner. Realizing Day had no choice, Mutrie resigned. Mutrie, who never again worked in the majors, was doomed to a life of poverty. Day's remaining days proved no better.

The Giants again lost money in 1892, despite the presence of four Hall of Famers, Rusie, O'Rourke, Ewing, and a little outfielder by the name of Willie Keeler, whose motto was "Hit them where they ain't." But the Giants still finished eighth in a twelve-team league, and Day, on the verge of bankruptcy, sold the rest of his stock to Talcott.

In the last years of the nineteenth century the New York Giants were in disarray. In January 1895, Talcott, who had bought the team primarily as an investment, sold them to Andrew Freedman, a politician of ill repute and dubious integrity who almost wrecked both the Giants and the league as well.

Freedman was a wealthy subway contractor and a close ally of Tammany Hall. He was the original Finley/Steinbrenner/Angelos, "coarse, vain, arrogant, and abusive," and if anyone got in his way, he would insult, threaten, or even assault him. He bullied newspapermen, and even had one fired. If he didn't like what you wrote, he'd bar you from the park. In 1895 Freedman hired and fired four managers. The fourth was Harvey Watkins, an actor and a Giant fan. The team finished ninth out of twelve.

There was another parade of managers in 1899, and that year Freedman rehired a financially desperate Day to manage. Day had failed at business and he badly needed the money. But Freedman treated him as shabbily as the others and on July 5, Day quit. His dignity was too great to continue to work for a madman. Day spent the rest of his days "in a bleak Bowery tenement so weak and inchoate that he was unable to attend to his wife, who lay dying in an adjoining bed."

Meanwhile, Freedman plotted to take over the league. He believed that the way to make the game more competitive was to have one man own all the teams, and to trade players around to control the competition. He was to be that man and he had the support of three teams—Boston, St. Louis, and Cincinnati. One more, and the ruin of the game would have been a certainty.

But Freedman was stopped cold by Chicago owner Albert Spalding, a businessman more ruthless and powerful than anyone in the game. Spalding, who had helped found the National League, made Freedman realize that he would never gain the control to implement his plan. In the spring of 1902 Freedman agreed to sell the team to John T. Brush, who had owned the Cincinnati franchise.

Freedman made two important transactions before he turned the team over to Brush. First, he traded a washed-up Amos Rusie to Cincinnati for a young pitcher by the name of Christy Mathewson. Brush knew how great Mathewson was going to be and he also knew he would soon own the Giants. When Brush completed the purchase from Freedman in the winter of 1902, Matty was on the Giants roster waiting for him. The other important transaction was to hire pugnacious John J. McGraw to manage the team. The twenty-nine-year-old McGraw, who ended Freedman's revolving door of managers, came in and fired nine of the players the first day he arrived.

He then began raiding other teams from the year-old outlaw American League. His raids brought him "Iron Man" Joe McGinnity, catcher Roger Bresnahan, first baseman Dan McGann, and outfielder Steve Brodie. He coaxed pitcher Dummy Taylor out of retirement. His staff of Mathewson, McGinnity, and Taylor became one of the best in the league.

McGraw would manage the Giants for the next thirty years, winning 10 pennants and three World Championships beginning in 1904 and making the Giants one of the most prestigious professional sports franchises in the world. Among McGraw's players who would be elected into the Hall of Fame were: Christy Mathewson, Joe McGinnity, Rogers Hornsby, Roger Bresnahan, Rube Marquard, Hack Wilson, Edd Rouch, Ross Youngs, Travis Jackson, Frankie Frisch, Freddie Lindstrom, George Kelly, Dave Bancroft, Bill Terry, Carl Hubbell, and Mel Ott.

After Freedman was forced to sell the team in the winter of 1902–3, Brush owned the Giants until January 1919. That year, bon vivant Charles A. Stoneham, a horseman and stockbroker, bought them from the Brush estate.

Stoneham had been a baseball fan as a boy, and Stoneham's love of his team and of the game marked his ownership. A fun-loving, free-spending gambler, who was known as a ruthless trader in the stock market, Stoneham couldn't have been less like Brush. But both he and Brush had one thing in common: they admired and trusted John McGraw who remained as manager under Stoneham for another 13 seasons.

On June 3, 1932, McGraw stepped down as manager, and Stoneham named Bill Terry to replace him. The Giants were in last place. McGraw had been in ill health and had been particularly irrascible, and the change to Terry brought the team emotional relief that brought Stoneham a pennant in 1933.

Charles Stoneham died on January 7, 1936, after sixteen years of ownership. His 33-year-old son, Horace C. Stoneham, succeeded him. The young Stoneham delegated a great deal of authority to Terry, who continued as manager, and eventually to his nephew, Charles "Chub" Feeney, later the president of the National League. Terry brought young Stoneham a pennant in his first full season. The team, led by Hall of Fame left-hander "King" Carl Hubbell and Hall of Fame slugger Mel Ott, won consecutive pennants in 1936 and 1937.

Then came the decline, which was rapid. By 1939 the team was in fifth place. The next year brought a sixth-place finish, and grumbling about Terry and the job he was doing.

Horace Stoneham was clueless as to how to improve his team. When a friend suggested he junk them and get a new one the way McGraw did in 1902, Stoneham answered, "Where are we going to get the players?" He didn't know.

Instead of getting new players, Stoneham made the easier move. He hired a new manager. At the winter meetings in 1941, Stoneham made Terry the general manager and named Ott the manager. The moves didn't improve things. Terry quit after a year, and Ott, it turned out, was unable to turn the Giants around. Giants fans would suffer through a pennantless decade of the 1940s.

Larry Ritter, who in 1966 authored *The Glory of their Times*, a recollection of men who played major league baseball at the turn of the twentieth century and perhaps the most important baseball memoir ever written, grew up a Giants fan. Ritter recalled his afternoons at the Polo Grounds watching Carl Hubbell and Mel Ott from the far reaches of his bleacher seat.

Larry Ritter: "I was born May 23, 1922, in Brooklyn, New York. When I was two years old, we moved to Hollis, Queens. My daddy was principal of P.S. 139 in Rego Park, Queens. He had gone to Boys High School in

Brooklyn, and he wanted me to go there, too, and therefore I grew up in both Queens and Brooklyn. I was, however, a Giants fan. Because my daddy was a Giants fan.

"My earliest baseball heroes were Bill Terry, Carl Hubbell, and Mel Ott. Also Jimmy Ripple and Jo Jo Moore. I really became a Giant fan in 1936, when they won the pennant. That's when I was most rabid. I was just the right age.

"On weekends I would go to the Polo Grounds all the time, at least one day of the two. I took a bus to the subway in Jamaica, and from the subway in Jamaica I wound up by transfers getting on the A train on the Independent Line that took me to 155th Street.

"The Polo Grounds itself was on 157th Street and 8th Avenue, although a lot of books mistakenly put it at 155th and 8th Avenue. Between 155th and 157th was a huge parking lot. There used to be two ballparks there way back at the turn of the century. The park where the National League Giants played and the Players Park, and one of them disappeared after the Players League folded, and the one that was left was the Polo Grounds.

"The Polo Grounds was a strange-looking ballpark, but it didn't seem strange to me. It was very short down the lines and it was 480 feet from the clubhouse in center field to home plate. So it was weird looking, and it was in the middle of Harlem, though it seemed that most of the audience was white. Most of the baseball audiences have always been white, and it's even more so today, which is strange, because a heavy percentage of the people on the field today are *not* white.

"I always sat in the same place in the bleachers, which in the Polo Grounds was a *long*, long ways from the batter's box. You gave the ticket, went in, and you could go either left or right, and there was a big entranceway to the bleachers on each side, and above the entranceway there were bleachers. If you could sit right above the entranceway, there was nobody in front of you. Nobody could stand up and obstruct your view, and I got one of those seats all the time, the most desired ones in the bleachers.

"All the games seem to meld together as one. When you're way out in the bleachers, you get general impressions instead of remembering particular infield plays. You're so far away.

"I remember I was there when Carl Hubbell's long streak of victories over two seasons, more than twenty, was broken. It was in May. Hubbell was my favorite, a great left-handed pitcher with a crooked arm, and Mel Ott number two. Ott was a big home run hitter with a big leg kick.

"Billy Terry was also a favorite. I didn't see Terry play. I named my dog Terry, I was such a big fan. Terry was the manager.

"I remember in the 1937 World Series Joe DiMaggio hitting a mammoth home run, unbelievable. It was at the Polo Grounds, and in my mind it was on a line and still going up when it hit one of the stanchions in deep left-center field. In my mind it was rising at the time it hit the stanchion, which holds the upper deck up. And I remember the day President Roosevelt came to the game. It was also a World Series game. Hank Lieber hit a ball way, way, way out, the last out of the ballgame, a ball that DiMaggio caught almost at the clubhouse, and he continued his run up the steps to the clubhouse, but stopped part way because, he said afterward, President Roosevelt had to be the first one to leave the field, so he stood on the clubhouse steps while the Roosevelt entourage left. That was a beautiful memory.

"The Giants didn't win for many years after the '36 and '37 pennants. That was the highlight for me. I then left New York and went away to college, the Navy, and then graduate school."

Stan Isaacs, who rooted for the New York Giants as a boy, is a longtime newspaperman who began his career covering sports for the *Daily Compass*, a leftwing paper valiantly attempting to make a go of it during the rightist McCarthy era. When he began working at *Long Island Newsday* in the mid-50s, the paper was small and regional. By the time he retired in 1989, New Yorkers from Brooklyn and Queens had moved to the Long Island suburbs by the thousands, and *Newsday* became a powerhouse in the New York Metropolitan area. Issacs loved the Giants through many years of bad baseball. His hero was Mel Ott. Most memorable for him was the Giant–Dodger rivalry. It burns for him still in memory, even after all these years.

Stan Isaacs: "I was born on April 22, 1929 in Brooklyn, and I grew up in Williamsburg. I began following baseball when I was seven. My father was a Giants fan, so I became one.

"My father was a truck driver and a taxi driver, and when I was a kid my father would drive us from Brooklyn up the West Side Highway on up to the Polo Grounds. He would park on the Speedway, which is what the street was called because it went up a hill above the Polo Grounds. The ride from Williamsburg took about forty minutes.

"Mel Ott was my hero the way Mantle and DiMaggio were to Yankee fans and Michael Jordan is today. I thought Mel was magical, because he had started at the age of 17. McGraw had brought him up from Louisiana, and he took one look at that peculiar, cock-footed swing, and the story was that McGraw decided that if he sent him to the minor leagues, somebody might mess with his swing, so he kept him on the bench for pretty much two years. When he started to play he was called 'The Boy Wonder.' To me, a game was successful if I saw Mel Ott hit a home run. All of it was magical to me. I can remember one time when Mel Ott got thrown out of the first game of a doubleheader, and I threw a peach at the umpire. I didn't come close to hitting him, but I *was* angry.

"Carl Hubbell, I recall, wore long pants, and he had that crooked arm from throwing the screwball, and he had terrific control. He was the ace of the staff, and there was something definitely heroic about him.

"And I can remember walking off the field after a game against the Chicago Cubs at the Polo Grounds. In those days you could walk on the field after a game all the way out to the center field exit under the clubhouse, and as we were walking Cub first baseman Rip Collins walked by, and my father said, 'Why don't you get his autograph?' And I said, 'Oh, no, he's not a Giant.'

"I was a kid when the Giants won pennants in '36 and '37. They were winning teams, and that solidified my being a Giant fan. I assume at that age if they hadn't been a winning team, I probably would have rooted for someone else. But by that time I was solidified, and of course, the next fourteen years were nothing but misery.

"After '38, the Giants were a losing team. They were just terrible. Mel Ott became the manager. He may have been a great player, but he was not a good manager. He didn't seem to handle pitchers well. He went for slugging rather than good pitching and good defense. One year the Giants set a record for home runs, hitting 221, but they lost a lot of games. I'm a great believer in defense because of rooting for the Giants and not seeing it all those years.

"In those days on Memorial Day it would almost invariably be a doubleheader between the Giants and the Dodgers. The rivalry between the two teams was intense, and the Giants used to get beat by the Dodgers in all sorts of ways. There was one year that not only did the Dodgers beat the Giants all eleven games in Ebbets Field, but monstrous games, where the Dodgers would come from behind—Giant outfielders would collide in the ninth inning to lose a game—so much so that Horace Stoneham, the owner of the Giants, never again went to a Giant–Dodger game at Ebbets Field.

"As a Giant fan, you got into it all the time with the Dodger fans. It wasn't fighting, but arguing, part of honing your polemical skills. Who was better, Mel Ott or Dixie Walker? Hubbell or Van Lingle Mungo? You'd argue how the game would have been different if the home run ball hit in the Polo Grounds had been hit in Ebbets Field, that it would have been an out. That kind of argument.

"To my mind, there never has been a rivalry to match it. They talk about the Yankees and Red Sox or Duke and North Carolina. I don't think it was the same. Not like the Giants and the Dodgers."

three

Yonkel! Yonkel!

The fierce rivalry between the Giants and the Dodgers that existed since the World Series of 1889, heated up considerably in 1914. Dodger owner Charlie Ebbets hired Wilbert Robinson, who had been Giants' manager John McGraw's right-hand man. Uncle Robby, as he was called, quit the Giants after a rift with the acerbic McGraw. Teammates as far back as the 1890s on the fabled Baltimore Orioles, McGraw and Robinson had been quarreling through most of the 1913 season. There was one final shouting match at the end of the World Series, which the Giants lost to the Philadelphia A's in five games. McGraw, who hated to lose, scapegoated Robinson, who was the pitching coach, and the rift led to an end of their friendship.

The rotund, tobacco-chewing Robinson managed the Dodgers for 18 seasons. He won pennants in 1916 and 1920, but lost both Series, to Babe Ruth and the Red Sox, and then to the Cleveland Indians when Dodger pitcher Burleigh Grimes gave up the first grand slam home run in Series history to Elmer Smith, and when a Dodger batter, Clarence Mitchell, hit into the first and only unassisted triple play in Series history to Bill Wambsganss.

When Dodger owner Charlie Ebbets died in 1925, the team went into bankruptcy, and the man who took control was George V. McLaughlin, president of the Brooklyn Trust Company, which held the loan. In 1937 McLaughlin, a devoted Brooklyn Dodger fan, decided he needed to hire a top baseball man to put the franchise back on its feet. He sought out the advice of National League president Ford Frick.

On Frick's recommendation in January 1938 McLaughlin hired Larry MacPhail to bring order from chaos. But MacPhail was a man who was uncomfortable with order. Fiery, unpredictable, brilliant, and often drunk, Leaping Larry, as he was called, created chaos and controversy wherever he went. Unlike Stoneham, who sat on his hands while his team slowly sank, MacPhail spent gobs of the Brooklyn Trust Company's money to rebuild the Dodgers. He was also a visionary who believed in the power of the then new medium, radio. When MacPhail left the Cincinnati Reds and came to Brooklyn, he brought with him a young broadcaster by the name of Walter "Red" Barber.

Barber gave the team an important marketing advantage over both the Giants and the American League New York Yankees. If you started at Borough Hall's epicenter and drew a hundred-mile radius outward—the distance that Red Barber's voice could carry on the Dodger radio network—you could find legions of Barber, and Brooklyn Dodger, devotees. Barber, one of the very earliest baseball broadcasters, captivated his listeners, both male and female, with his soft, dulcet tones.

Jack Lang, who had a glorious fifty-year career as a sportswriter first for the *Long Island Press* and then *Newsday*, was twenty years old when Larry MacPhail began to rebuild the struggling team. The move upward began with the hiring of manager Leo Durocher in 1939. Then came the flood of deals that brought the nucleus of players that would help the Dodgers win the 1941 National League Championship.

Lang had just begun his career as a newspaperman in 1941 when the next year MacPhail surprised everyone by joining the army as a lieutenant colonel. McLaughlin immediately replaced him with another promotional genius, Branch Rickey, who had made a name for himself in St. Louis by inventing the farm system. Rickey's innovative developmental program had brought a pennant to the Cards in 1934, and it would bring St. Louis pennants in 1942, 1943, 1944, and 1946.

When during World War II Rickey built the Dodger farm system during a time when the other teams were cutting back, Rickey's foresight would eventually bring Brooklyn pennants in 1947, 1949, 1952, 1953, 1955, and 1956. Such was the genius of the enigmatic, highly successful Mr. Rickey.

Yet, despite the pennants, there would be much Dodger heartache. Lang, who loved his Dodgers passionately, suffered along with all the other loyal Brooklyn fans when they lost the 1941 World Series in a most improbable manner. Dodger catcher Mickey Owen, normally sure-handed, could not catch a third strike thrown by Hugh Casey to Yankee outfielder Tommy Henrich. The ball got by him and rolled to the screen. After Henrich ran to first safely, the Yankees rallied to win the game, and then the series.

Lang then witnessed bad Dodger teams during the war and the heart-breaking losses of the 1946 pennant after two playoff games, the 1950 pennant on the final day, and the 1951 pennant on the final day after three playoff games.

The year with the highest drama proved to be 1947. Most Dodger fans rejoiced at the coming of Jackie Robinson, but at the same time had to suffer the suspension of manager Leo Durocher for the entire season for consorting with gamblers.

Jack Lang: "I was born in Brooklyn and raised in Jamaica, Queens. I started going to Ebbets Field by myself around 1936. I took four trains: the elevated from Jamaica to Eastern Parkway, then the shuttle to get over to to the Franklin Avenue line, which I took to the Brighton Beach line, and you went upstairs and got the Brighton Beach line. We got off at the Botanical Gardens and walked three or four blocks across to Ebbets Field. It only took about an hour.

"I went to a lot of games in 1941. I was twenty years old. I was a big fan of the Dodgers. My whole family were Dodger fans. In those days Larry MacPhail was building a team by buying players. He got Dolf Camilli in a trade with the Phils, bought Dixie Walker from the Tigers, he bought Pee Wee Reese from the Red Sox, he bought Ernie Koy from the Yankees. He put together the '41 pennant-winning team by buying players from clubs that were broke. The Phillies were selling off every player they had, and he got Kirby Higbe in a trade [for three players and $100,000].

"I can remember being at a semipro football game at Ozone Park on a Sunday afternoon when Mickey Owen dropped the strike. We were listening to the game on a portable radio. The Dodgers went into the ninth inning leading, Hugh Casey was pitching, and it looked like they were going to wrap it up and even the series. Then Owen missed the third strike, and the Yankees rallied and won the game, and all of a sudden the Dodgers' chances looked pretty grim. It was a heartbreaking defeat for the Dodgers. All of us in that part of Ozone Park were Dodger fans. We were disappointed. Their chances of being the World Champions were now a lot slimmer."

Joel Oppenheimer, who grew up in Yonkers, also was a boy during the 1941 World Series. The shocking loss scarred Oppenheimer in ways that would affect his entire life.

Joel Oppenheimer: "I was going to visit my uncle Morris and aunt Gus and I was walking with my cousin through the streets of Yonkers. It was a pleasant day. People had radios on listening to the World Series, so we could hear as we walked along. We passed a house and I'd hear someone strike out and pass the next house and hear someone singled. Understand I was eleven, and at eleven it was more important to visit Uncle Morris and Aunt Gus than to sit huddled over the radio. But I was paying attention. My cousin was a year younger. He didn't care.

"Finally, we're standing on the street in front of a house when I heard that things were coming to a crisis situation. And I was literally standing there on a street in Yonkers, and all streets in Yonkers are on hills, so I was at an angle, listening to a radio playing in somebody else's living room when I heard Mickey Owen drop the third strike. Years later I read that he hadn't really dropped the strike. What happened was the son-of-a-bitch [Henrich] had swung at a terrible pitch in hopes Owen would not be able to handle it. I don't know that that happened. All I know is, my heart leapt and I said, 'Ho, ho, more Yankee perfidy.'

"After he dropped the ball, I stayed there to hear, and I died with it there as the Yankees rallied. But the real memory was hearing him drop it, and knowing that all the magic is gone and nothing can stop the inevitable.

"I don't think I broke down and cried on the street. That didn't happen until years later. But I was certainly very upset and feeling that it was very unfair, that God had done it to us again, and give it to them, which was even worse. As I grew up in Yonkers, this became part of a whole aura I'm sure I constructed around myself. I mean, here I was a Dodger fan in a town full of Yankees and Giants rooters. A Royal Crown drinker in a town full of Pepsi and Coke drinkers. A guy who was interested in poems in a town full of louts. A Jew who insisted on running with the goyim in a town that was very, very rigidly stratefied. It all was one package, and I've always seen it as one package. I was a Brooklyn Dodger rooter because it was the loner's way and going against the tide. The notion that just fifteen miles away there was a borough full of people some of whom liked poetry and some who didn't, some who drank Coke and some who didn't and all of them were rooting for the Dodgers never really registered. What I knew was that I had this lonely mission in Yonkers."

Jack Lang: "You had to be made of tough stuff to be a Dodger fan, because they had so many things go against them over the years. Then along came the war, and Pee Wee Reese and other guys enlisted in the service, and from '43 on they were playing guys like sixteen-year-old Tommy Brown and 'Redneck' Bill Hart, anybody they could find who could play ball.

"But what I remember later about the Dodgers during the war years, when MacPhail went into the Army, Rickey came in in '43, and one of the first things he did was to get all his scouts together, and he ordered them to sign any kid who looked like he could run, throw or hit a baseball. The scouts said, 'A lot of these kids are going to be drafted. They might be killed or maimed in the war.' Rickey said, 'I don't care. Give them what they want to sign them.'

"I had been a copy boy at the *Long Island Press*, and I did some sports-writing too, but I went into the army the day after the World Series ended in 1942, and I was in the service until November '45. As soon as I came out, I was given a full-time job as a reporter and assigned to the sports department.

"When the war ended, in '46 in Sanford, Florida, an old naval base, Rickey had 600 ballplayers that he signed during the war. Half of them never got out of the camp, never made it, but out of that camp came Duke Snider and others. They were numbered one to one hundred in different colors on their back. Some had red letters, some yellow, some orange. There were so many ballplayers, it seemed that Rickey had cornered the market on young ballplayers. That was the start of the Dodger farm system. After the war the Dodgers had 28 farm clubs!

"In '46 I started going to ball games at Ebbets Field. I worked from seven until noon, and I'd get the train right there in Jamaica, and I'd go down to Ebbets Field every afternoon just to watch the ball game. I'd do an occasional feature on some kid from Long Island like Mickey Harris or Hank Behrman, and after a while my boss, Mike Lee, said, "'If you're going down there every day, you might as well do a story on the game.'

So I wound up becoming a sportswriter in '46 and covering the team until it left after '57."

Larry MacPhail brought the Dodgers a pennant in 1941, but it was Branch Rickey who brought greatness and historical significance to the Dodgers. In 1947 he brought the first black player to the major leagues—integrating baseball in an era when America was stubbornly segregated. Little was made of the move when it occurred in 1947, but more than fifty years later the innovation can be seen for what it was: a momentous occasion of vast social and political importance. That Jackie Robinson—and Roy Campanella and Don Newcombe—helped lead the Dodgers to pennants in 1949, 1952, 1953, 1955, and 1956 made them heroes among Dodger fans. That Robinson took the first steps to remove the stain of Jim Crowism from America made him a legend.

Lang was on hand to witness in 1947 the coming of Jackie Robinson to the Dodgers, to Brooklyn, and to America.

Jack Lang: "He played an exhibition game for the Montreal Royals, the Dodgers' top farm system, against Brooklyn, and that afternoon, a Friday afternoon, they announced his promotion to the Dodgers, and the next day he played an exhibition game with the Dodgers against Montreal. And two days later he made his major league debut with the Dodgers against the Boston Braves.

"I can remember that nobody treated Robinson any differently than if he was a white ballplayer. The fans didn't treat him any differently. The writers didn't treat him any differently.

"He didn't have a great first game. He got on on a bunt. And he was playing first base, which was not his natural position. He was a little awkward there. But he gradually fit in, and within a week he started hitting, and of course, he went on to have a good year.

"But it was not as big an event as it became fifty years later."

Donald Hall, the great American poet, grew up in Hamden, Connecticut, within reach of the Redhead, Red Barber. His love affair with the Dodgers began in the late 1930s and was an important part of his life and that of his father as well. The memories Hall cherishes most are those of the Dodgers of the early 1940s, the Leo Durocher-led team featuring Pee Wee Reese and Pete Reiser, Dixie Walker and Dolf Camilli. Hall especially revelled in the coming of Jackie Robinson.

Donald Hall: "Do you remember when Ronald Reagan in the debates said that when he was growing up, 'We did not know there wasn't any trouble about race?' Well, we didn't. The more fool we. All I had been talking about is white baseball. I didn't think about it. I didn't know. Then one read in the papers that there was a young man in Montreal, and that Rickey was going to try it. I do not remember anybody in my circle, or my parents circle, getting upset about it, except, oh, nonliberally worrying this might upset things. 'Will he get away with it?' Not regarding it as a moral issue but as a practical question. 'Will people be offended?' 'Will he be able to play in St. Louis?' Which was the most-Southern team. Then the relief and delight in the play of Jackie Robinson, and in the stealing of home. I can't say by that time I was a flaming liberal. I campaigned for Henry Wallace in 1948. I had a black roommate at college. I had no political problems with Jackie Robinson. I was just a knee-jerk young thinker.

"I admired Jackie enormously. I thought he was a marvelous ballplayer. And at that time he also had squeaky clean PR. He was Jack Armstrong— not human in the way he was presented. He changed in various different ways in different years, a complicated, complex character, an unhappy man. I recall Roger Kahn's portrait of him angrily driving white golf balls into Long Island Sound. I had no notion of the complexity of it all, what was going on, or the depth of the inequity toward the blacks. But, yes, I was all for Robinson, and I was a big liberal, and it was easy to be. No big mea culpa.

"And Rickey, whatever else about him, he was a courageous and decent man to do this. And then pretty soon came Roy Campanella, Don Newcombe, and Joe Black, all black stars on the Dodgers, which made a hell of a lot of difference!"

The writers and the white players certainly did not give Robinson's appearance in a Dodger uniform much import at the time. Of course, we know now that it was perhaps the most significant social event in the twentieth century, because it was Jackie Robinson's success that helped give Dr. Martin Luther King, Jr., both the impetus and the courage to fight his fight. When Robinson came to the Dodgers, he caused people to change alliances. Those who were committed to seeing fairness to blacks—

and Jews—became Dodger fans for the first time. Some rooters switched teams. Some added the Dodgers and rooted for two teams.

Ray Robinson was a New Yorker who, despite the presence of the Dodgers, Giants, and Yankees, as a youngster had no strong team allegiance. Instead he followed the careers of individual players. Then Jackie Robinson joined the Dodgers. Ray Robinson immediately became a die-hard Dodgers fan.

Ray Robinson: "I was born in 1920 in the month of December in New York City. I lived at 115th Street and Broadway. My father wasn't a baseball fan, and therefore I had to rely on the kindness of strangers. There was a fellow who lived in my apartment house, who I learned in later years was a bootlegger, who loved baseball, Giant baseball, and he happened to have a box near home plate at the Polo Grounds, and when I was seven or eight he invited me, the little neighbor, to go to a game with him.

"I became a baseball fan, but for a long time I didn't root for a team, but for individuals. I loved Lou Gehrig and Herb Pennock. I didn't have much feeling for Babe Ruth. It was a perverseness on my part.

"In 1947, I became a Dodger fan because of the presence in the lineup of Jackie Robinson.

"A year or two before Jackie even came up, I was in the army working for several air base newspapers, and I had written about the coming of a black into the major leagues. I was just a youngster. I praised Branch Rickey, and this accounts for my half-rooting for the Dodgers as well as half-rooting for the Giants. Not being a resident of Brooklyn, I really had no ties to the Dodgers. But I felt a black playing in the major leagues was long overdue. I had been aware of the tremendous prejudice against Hank Greenberg when he was with the Tigers in the late '30s. Hank was subjected to a lot of epithets. He even had battles with other players, and as an American Jew, I reacted to that.

"I remember an incident when I was in the army stationed at Barksdale Field, which was in Shreveport, Louisiana, in 1943. I was in the stands of a small high school football stadium, sitting near the top, when I heard a fellow in a real redneck accent saying, 'That goddamn Greenberg had a Jew-lover for an owner.' I was perhaps the only one sitting in the stands that day who knew the name of that owner of the Tigers, Frank Navin. Who was the fellow who was speaking? His name was Harry 'Stinky' Davis, and he had been the first baseman on the Tigers before Hank. He was a fine fielder, but a guy who couldn't hit, and here he was, boozy—he sounded drunk—and he was talking about how he had lost his job to this big 'Jew bastard,' Hank Greenberg. It was just coincidental that I was sitting near him, and many years later when I got to know Hank, I told him this story, and he was quite amused by it.

"'Oh, yeah,' he said, 'Davis was quite a redneck character.' Hank totally comprehended what Davis was saying, that his attitude was stuck back in the Middle Ages. I said to Hank, 'Somebody should have reminded Stinky Davis that the total number of home runs he hit in the major leagues was seven.'

"So when Robinson was playing in Montreal, we were following him closely. This was 1946. The postwar period was a tremendous period for baseball. The interest in the game, not only in New York City, but all over the country, was high. I followed it quite vigorously, and it was a day-to-day preoccupation, and here I am, eighty years old, talking to you about the same game.

"Robinson was a tremendously exciting ballplayer, an aggressive, angry black man. That made him as good as he was. And when I got into journalism professionally, I got to meet Jackie and got to know him fairly well, primarily through a guy named Alfred Duckett, who ghosted his autobiography, *I Never Had It Made*.

"Jackie was difficult. He was suspicious of people he didn't know very well. This is aside from his abilities on the playing field. He was an enormously appealing man physically. I'll never forget his blackness and he was a terribly handsome man, a physically impressive man. And when I got Jackie on the phone, I was always pleasantly surprised by his high-pitched voice that didn't quite seem to go with his general image.

"Even among ballplayers, Jackie was a cut above most of them in intelligence, and he married a remarkable woman, Rachel. She's still a fascinating person, a handsome woman. He was very lucky to be married to her. She helped steer him and guide him and keep him focused. I think she presided over a couple of would-be nervous breakdowns on his part.

"Over the years I got to know Jackie well enough to have a correspondence with him, where we argued politics. Jackie was, oddly enough, 'Progessive Republican,' who was quite involved with Nelson Rockefeller. When Jackie publicly came out for [Richard] Nixon against [John F.] Kennedy in 1960, I remember writing him a very critical letter, and he wrote me a lengthy letter back telling me why he was for Nixon, even though he said he didn't trust him very much. But, he said he didn't trust Kennedy either. It was typical Jackie, who had strong opinions. And he couldn't be easily dissuaded from them. He took a position, and by God, that was his position—which he was entitled to. And there was this underlying feeling—I always felt this about him—that no white guy, even if he was a good friend, was going to tell him what to think. He did his own thinking. Later, after we became more acquainted with what Nixon was all about, Jackie acknowledged that he had made a mistake in endorsing him."

Jackie Robinson

The coming of Jackie Robinson to the Dodgers would, in later years, take on a legendary aspect.

Joel Oppenheimer: "I was aware Robinson was going to be the first black to play. We had a vested interest in being on the liberal cutting edge. I doubt there wasn a Jewish family around who didn't have a member who was extremely active in either the labor movement of some left-wing organization, Communist or socialist. It had been a tough fifty years, culminating in the Depression. So given the time and place and my cultural background, I would have been surprised not to know.

"On the day Robinson was to play his first game, I was at my father's store. I was sweeping the floor, and maybe it was eleven in the morning.

"There are two kinds of fathers in this world to work for. There's the kind who makes his kid the president of the firm, and there's the kind who is convinced that he must bend over backward not to show favoritism. Guess which type of father I had? Not that Dad was mean. He just didn't want the other employees to think his son was getting away with anything.

"Dad was standing behind the cash register up front. He called me over, and I assumed he had another errand for me to do. Instead, he asked me, 'If you could do anything in the world today, what would you like to do?' I was so stunned I couldn't answer. He said, 'Isn't there something you want to do?' 'You mean like going to the moon?' I said. 'No,' he said, 'something real.' I couldn't think of anything to say. He asked me, 'Wouldn't you like to be at Ebbets Field today?' And I couldn't believe my ears. Of course I wanted to go. I knew Jackie Robinson would be playing his first game, and I was astounded that, one, my father was even aware of Robinson, and two, aware that I would want to go.

"So off I went, and when I arrived in the grandstand it was standing room only. I remember standing behind third base in a thick crowd of people, and for the first time in my life I was in a crowd of blacks.

"For years we used to hear stories about this fantastic black pitcher who once was supposed to have struck out all the Yankees. We didn't know his name—it was Satchel Paige—but we had heard about all the great black ballplayers and how they weren't allowed to play, and so for me Jackie was all those guys rolled into one, and he was going to lead my Dodgers to glory.

"During the game Jackie made a good play in the field, at which point everyone was yelling, 'Jackie, Jackie, Jackie,' and I was yelling with them. And suddenly I realized that behind me someone was yelling, 'Yonkel, Yonkel, Yonkel,' which is Yiddish for Jackie. With great wonderment and pleasure, I realized that here was this little Jewish tailor—I always assumed he was a tailor—the only white face in a crowd of blacks aside from me, and he's yelling 'Yonkel, Yonkel, Yonkel.' It was a very moving moment."

One result of the Dodgers' signing Jackie Robinson was the co-option of some Giants fans. No longer could they *hate* the Dodgers. They admired Jackie too much to feel anything but admiration for the player and the team that signed him.

Stan Isaacs: "The one thing the Dodgers' signing Robinson did was neutralize my dislike of the Dodgers. It changed me. Like most Giant fans, I hated the Dodgers. My politics were liberal, and when Jackie Robinson signed, I said to myself, 'I can't root against a team that all the bigots in the country are rooting against.' It was a dilemma for me, because I was still a Giant fan. It was ingrained. That was where my heart was. But where my head was: I told myself that the Dodgers are the team doing the social thing that I approve of, so I came to this conclusion: I would root for the Giants until they were out of the pennant race, which in those days was June! And then I would root for the Dodgers."

four

Leo Switches Sides

If Dodger fans were rightly gloating over the appearance of Jackie Robinson in the spring of 1947, they were troubled by the loss of their manager, Leo Durocher, who was suspended for the entire season by commissioner Happy Chandler. Charlie Einstein, whose book *Willie's Time* is the classic appreciation of Willie Mays and his legacy, could well understand why Durocher had been suspended.

Charlie Einstein: "In 1946 there was the Blue Ridge scandal. In this case the manager of the team was the pitcher, and he was supposed to throw a game, and he ended up winning it, and that's the reason it all came out. If he had lost, nobody would have said anything.

"But Durocher had a record as long as your arm for associating with unsavory people, and Chandler was on very safe ground taking a whack at him. And one of the things that appealed to Chandler was that no one was going to say no to him. There was one incident where Durocher was staying in George Raft's place at the Essex House in New York, and a pigeon got taken for a lot of money in a crooked dice game. And the pigeon complained. And here you have a new commissioner saying, 'How good is this for baseball?' An even bigger scandal was Phil Silvers getting taken in a gin rummy game at the Friar's Club. One of the perpetrators went to jail for it. This was during the time Silvers was Sergeant Bilko. The greatest con artist in TV history got taken in a gin rummy game.

"So when Durocher was seen with two known gamblers in a box in Havana, Chandler acted."

Though Dodger fans heard commissioner Chandler explain that Durocher was being suspended because of his association with gamblers, few could understand it.

Jack Lang: "That same spring training the Dodgers were in Havana, and Leo's picture appeared in the paper with Connie Immerman, who ran a Havana casino, and Memphis Engelberg, who was a race track gambler. Engelberg made his living at the race track, making smart bets. I remember him saying he would go to the track and there'd be eight races and he might not bet on but one race all day, but he knew the one he wanted to bet, and he was going to make money on that. But Engelberg wound up sitting in these box seats next to the Dodger dugout—the seats were given to him by Red Patterson, the Yankee publicity man. They were the only seats Patterson had left, and he gave them to Memphis Engelberg. So Leo had nothing to do with Memphis Engelberg getting into the ballpark.

"When baseball commissioner Happy Chandler suspended Leo for a year for consorting with gamblers, Leo was totally innocent. Leo may not have had the best of friends and acquaintances off the field, but when they had a hearing at Sarasota, Florida in the spring of '47, Larry MacPhail jumped all over Chandler and said, 'What are you crucifying this man for?' MacPhail even testified that Leo had nothing to do with the gamblers being at the ballpark.

"My feeling is that the real reason Leo ended up getting suspended was because the Catholic church in Brooklyn was against him. The CYO priests were claiming he was living in sin with Larraine Day. The Catholic paper, *The Tablet*, mounted a campaign against him. There were mumblings in the church that he was hardly the type to be a hero, to look up to, to be a leader. And so the priest at the CYO was probably just as much a reason for him being suspended as any.

"And when Leo was suspended, Rickey was totally shocked. He considered Leo a good field leader, the type to work a team up. I think Chandler was way out of line for suspending him. Burt Shotton had to manage the team in '47."

Ray Robinson: "When Leo was suspended from baseball in 1947 it all had to do with the Catholics over in Brooklyn incensed at Durocher's piccadillos, his constant running around with all sorts of women when he was married and his supposedly consorting with gamblers and with a character like George Raft, who was a good friend of his. The culmination was his getting involved in an odd divorce situation where he apparently wanted to marry the actress Larraine Day, and a judge named Duckweiler who made a charge that Durocher had somehow acted illegally in trying to break up her marriage, which then brought the strong pressure by the Catholic groups in Brooklyn to get rid of this man."

Under Burt Shotton the Brooklyn Dodgers won the pennant in 1947 though they lost the World Series to the Yankees. When the 1948 season rolled around, Durocher's suspension was over, and Branch Rickey again made Durocher his manager.

But during spring training Durocher got off on the wrong foot with Jackie Robinson, who came to training camp overweight after spending the off-season on the rubber chicken circuit. Leo was furious that Robinson hadn't stayed in shape. He wondered out loud why Robinson would do his all for Burt Shotton but be at less than peak performance for him.

Then when the Dodgers began the season badly, Leo lost interest. Durocher, a great manager when his team was vying for the pennant, was only mediocre when his team floundered. Making things more difficult for the Dodgers was the continued aversion to Durocher by the local dioceses of the Catholic church. Jack Lang was in his office on the day Leo Durocher moved from the Dodgers to the hated Giants. This was the shock of shocks for all Dodger and Giants fans.

Jack Lang: "The Dodger team was not doing well. Leo was not happy with Jackie, who came into camp overweight. Rickey felt Leo had lost some of his verve and desire in '48. It was his desire to get rid of him.

"Around this time Horace Stoneham called Rickey to ask him for permission to talk to Burt Shotton. Stoneham wanted to bring Shotton in to manage the Giants. He figured Shotton had done such a great job in '47 with the Dodgers that he'd be a good man to bring in to the Polo Grounds. And Rickey said, 'I got someone better for you.' And he talked Stoneham into hiring Leo, and he brought Shotton back himself."

Durocher's switch from the Dodgers to the Giants in the middle of the 1948 season sent the emotions of millions of New York baseball fans into turmoil. Some Giants fans, who had rooted against Durocher for so many years, hated the idea. Attendance dropped in 1948 as Giants fans boycotted. Some Dodgers fans who loved Leo switched along with Durocher to the Giants. Ray Robinson was were among the latter. Giants fan Stan Isaacs also was thrilled.

Ray Robinson: "When Leo came over to the Giants, that created a lot of mixed feelings in New York. It sure did. Because of Jackie I almost half-rooted for the Dodgers. I was not hostile to what was happening to the Dodgers. I think there were many Jews in New York who felt that way. But when Durocher came over to the Giants, I have to acknowledge that that's when I became a very vigorous Giants fan."

Stan Isaacs: "Leo Durocher had been the Dodger manager; as a Giant fan with a little bit of smarts, I saw how good a manager Durocher was. I hated him for being that good, and so when Durocher came over to the Giants, I was *delighted*. That was a big thing. Tumultuous. I knew Leo would change the Giants, make a winner of them, stress defense and pitching, which is what he did, and in only a few years they won the pennant. I know that some Giant fans hated the idea of Leo managing the Giants, but not me. I was delighted."

For Larry Ritter, unlike Robinson and Isaac, his love of the Giants was stopped cold with the hiring of Leo Durocher. Ritter, who by then had moved to the Midwest to pursue a career in economics, hated Durocher with such a passion that when he learned the Giants had signed the despised former Dodgers boss to manage, Ritter dropped his rooting interest in the team entirely.

Larry Ritter: "In 1948 I was gone from New York, but I remember that summer when Leo Durocher switched from the Dodgers to the Giants. I thought it was awful. I think my love of the Giants started to fade then, because I was not about to root for—I was very unhappy rooting for—the Dodgers' manager. I simply didn't like him as a human being. And there was a symbolism to the Dodgers' manager becoming the Giants' manager. And I didn't like the symbolism."

Dodgers fan Joel Oppenheimer, for one, was equally devastated. Now that Leo was the enemy, he absolutely hated his guts.

Joel Oppenheimer: "My father had always talked about Leo as a really smart manager, and a smart ballplayer before that, so I didn't pay any attention to the negative publicity until he left for the Giants. And then I really felt betrayed. Absolutely betrayed. Because when you're a kid and a player gets traded, trades hurt but you learn to live with them, like when Dixie Walker was sent to Pittsburgh, and even then we got Preacher Roe and Billy Cox, and so it wasn't long before I said, 'Wait a minute. That ain't such a bad deal. We got the best third baseman in the league and we got this pitcher I adore.'

"But when Leo went, it was like the boss went. Nobody traded him. *He* did that. And that really bugged me. That was a crushing blow. And I hated him thereafter, although I still hung over from my father's legacy and thought of him as a very smart manager.

"But, when it was announced that Leo was going from the Dodgers to the Giants, I couldn't believe it. I was absolutely stunned. And my feelings on that day took a complete one hundred-and-eighty-degree turn. The day before I might have been praising him to the sky, and now he was the worst son of a bitch who ever lived. And there was no doubt in my mind it was the biggest act of infamy ever perpetrated on anybody, and especially on me, in history. Little did I know that Walter O'Malley was already thinking of perpetrating an even greater act of infamy."

five

Willie Mays and Other Miracles

The years 1950 and 1951 would prove heartrending for Dodgers fans. For two years in a row the talented, appealing Brooklyn ball club would lose pennants on the final day of the season. In 1950 the heartbreaker was to the Philadelphia Phillies. The Dodgers would have tied for the flag had Dodgers outfielder Cal Abrams scored from second base on a single to center field by Duke Snider. But Philly center fielder Richie Ashburn, not noted for a strong arm, threw Abrams out at the plate by a wide margin, and when Dick Sisler homered in extra innings, the pennant was lost. Reporter Jack Lang was at the game, and he was witness to the anguish of Dodgers general manager Branch Rickey, who soon would leave the Dodgers and hand over the reins to Walter O'Malley.

Jack Lang: "Cal Abrams took a long trip around third base, or he would have been safe at the plate, and the Dodgers would have won the game and then the pennant. Ashburn was not known for his arm, but he was playing shallow on that play, and he made a perfect throw. If you look at the pictures, Abrams made a circuitous route around third base—he almost went into the visiting dugout to get to home plate. And the next inning Dick Sisler hit a home run, and the Phils won the pennant. That was a pretty devastating loss.

"I can remember after the game in a little anteroom off the press box, Branch Rickey was sitting in there and it was almost as though he had just recovered from a heart attack. His aides were fanning him, trying to cool him down, a devastating defeat for him because he thought he had the better team and they should have won it in regulation time. He was quite taken aback and quite depressed over the loss. That was his last game in Brooklyn too. He left after that, which was no surprise.

"We knew Rickey had been negotiating with O'Malley all year for the sale of his stock. He had a good friend in John Galbreath in Pittsburgh, so you know Rickey was going to get a job there. The big thing was Rickey getting Bill Zeckendorf to outbid O'Malley for the stock. Zeckendorf bid a million dollars—at the time the stock wasn't worth anywhere near that— but O'Malley had the first right of refusal, and he had to match any offer to get it, and so O'Malley had to pay Rickey one million and fifty thousand dollars, and O'Malley never forgave him for that. He never liked Rickey in the first place. You could tell that. It was Rickey's way to be in charge of everything, and O'Malley felt he should have had a little more power than he had, but Rickey was calling all the shots.

"But it was Rickey who wanted to get out, and O'Malley became the majority owner of the Dodgers. O'Malley, being born and raised in Brooklyn and Long Island, at least he was from New York, and he had been a very, very big baseball fan. He had borrowed the money from the Brooklyn Trust Company to buy his shares, and after he bought Rickey's shares and the shares of the widow of John L. Smith, the president of Pfizer, he was now calling the shots.

"The Dodgers began the 1951 season by winning the first ten games in a row. I still have a pewter mug on my mantelpiece that the Schaefer beer people gave out to all the writers, players, and team executives. A record-breaking ten in a row. That's how the season started."

At the same time Leo Durocher rebuilt the Giants into a contender and helped set the stage for one of the most momentous moments in the history of the game of baseball. When the 1951 season began Durocher predicted that his Giants would win the pennant. The Giants, after winning the opener, proceeded to lose eleven games in a row.

Bill Reddy: "The Dodgers had opened up in Boston, and their power was awesome, and they were hitting like crazy, and into my store came two Giant fans in the neighborhood. One of them said to me, 'How is anyone going to beat the Dodgers this year?' I smiled and said, 'No one is going to.'"

Stan Isaacs: "Part of what made Leo Durocher—and Casey Stengel—good managers was that they were the first two managers who didn't see color. And the black players knew that, and they played for them. That was part of what made Durocher and Stengel so good. Durocher and Stengel could rip a black player, and the player would know he was ripping him because he was not good, not because he was black. Other managers condescended to them, and the players knew that. All Durocher cared about was winning. It didn't matter what the color was.

"Durocher was so free of color he was not afraid to go after Jackie Robinson. They hated each other, but they hated each other as competitors."

Durocher had been so free of racism that once in the 1930s he was called on the carpet by baseball commissioner Kennesaw Mountain Landis for having the nerve to suggest that the Negro ballplayers he had barnstormed against were every bit as good as the whites he played with. Landis had Durocher travel to Chicago to meet him in his office so that he could tell the then Dodger shortstop to keep his left-wing opinions to himself. Only after Landis died in 1945 was Branch Rickey able to bring Jackie Robinson and other blacks to the big leagues.

Durocher got along just fine with his black players, Hank Thompson and Monte Irvin, and then in May of 1951 Durocher brought up a black player with such incredible talent that Durocher took him under his wing like a son as John McGraw had done with Mel Ott years earlier.

The boy's name was Willie Mays. He was the son of a sharecropper, nineteen years old and very shy. He had started in the Negro Leagues with Birmingham, was signed by the Giants, starred in 1950 at Trenton and in 1951 at Minneapolis, and was rushed to the majors. When Durocher called Mays to tell him of his promotion, the youngster told Durocher that he worried he wouldn't be good enough to play in the majors.

The boy told Durocher, "I can't hit the pitching up there."

"What are you hitting for Minneapolis?" Durocher asked.

".477," said Mays.

Durocher meekly answered, "Do you think you can hit two-fucking-seventy for me?"

He would play in all 121 games for the Giants in '51, hit .274 with 20 home runs, and be named the National League Rookie of the Year.

The kid greeted everyone with the same call, "Say hey," and it wasn't long before Russ Hodges, the Giants announcer, began calling him the

"Say Hey Kid." It took Mays three games before he got his first base hit, and it was a doozy, a home run against Warren Spahn, arguably the best pitcher in the league at the time.

When Durocher talked to the press, he made Mays sound like the second coming of Babe Ruth (it wasn't that much of an exaggeration). When Mays talked to Durocher, he called him "Mr. Leo." The love affair between the kid and his manager spread very quickly. Soon the adoration was between the kid and Giants fans through the five boroughs. Soon after arriving in New York, the boyish Mays captivated the press as well.

Stan Isaacs: "I was writing for the *Daily Compass* then. I knew about Mays and how phenomenal he was in Minneapolis. He came up with some fanfare, and I was there the night Mays broke his twelve at bat hitless streak by hitting a home run off Warren Spahn. With Durocher pumping him and talking about him and protecting him, cultivating this image of a 'natural man' who just loves to play ball, who even played stickball, he immediately became a magical figure. So it was instant. For the first time since Mel Ott, the Giants had this kid who was going to be a great ballplayer.

"And unlike Jackie Robinson, it was no social thing to bring up Willie. Mays was never a black figure. He was Willie Mays the ballplayer. I mean, he was black, of course, but you didn't think of him in terms of advancing the black race. The Giants already had black ballplayers. They had Hank Thompson and Monte Irvin. I rooted for Monte. Monte was a Giant, and he was a very nice guy."

Ray Robinson: "When Mays came up, I was immediately much taken with him, and after seeing him playing any number of games, I was convinced he was not only *the* center fielder in New York, but the best ballplayer I had ever seen, maybe even better than Lou Gehrig, who was a different type. He was certainly better than Joe DiMaggio, who never quite appealed to me. I knew Joe was a wonderfully talented ballplayer, but I never felt he was the player that Willie or even Mantle was.

"I remember when Willie came up from Minneapolis. Horace Stoneham took out an ad in the local newspaper and apologized to the Minneapolis fans for taking Mays out of the lineup and taking him to the Polo Grounds.

"And when he came up to the Giants, the one thing he injected was expectation. Once people learned about him—and they quickly learned about him despite an early slump in which he went twenty times without a hit—and the legend was that he went to Durocher and said, 'Mr. Leo, send me back. I can't play here.' They made him sound like a Stepinfetchit character. And it may be true. He felt he couldn't do it. He was just a kid, nineteen years old. And then his first hit was a home run off Warren Spahn at the Polo Grounds, and that began a tremendous career."

Charlie Einstein: "The reason that the Negro Leagues folded was not Jackie Robinson but Willie Mays. Because they could stand the loss of Jackie Robinson. They could even stand the loss of Satchel Paige. Mays was the first Negro Leagues star who was nineteen. When all of a sudden the bottom drained out and nothing was coming up because it was going straight to organized baseball instead, that's what killed them.

"After Mays went up, the Negro Leagues lasted four and a half years. They just folded. And it was one of the three existing black industries nationwide. The other two which have survived are publishing—black newspapers—and morticians—undertakers.

"Willie was different from Jackie. The blacks couldn't stay at the whites' hotels, and this was just as true in Chicago as it was in St. Louis. Now, how much of a traumatic blow was this to them? The answer was probably zero. Willie Mays loved staying with a black family or in a black hotel. Because he was getting the same money and the same perks but getting to pay half the price.

"The hotels desegregated sequentially. It didn't all happen at once. First you could stay in the rooms. Then you could eat in the dining room. Then you could swim in the pool.

"The Adams Hotel in Phoenix didn't integrate until 1960 or 1961. The Giants had been training there since 1954. Up to that time Mays had been living in a colored motel with a family. Now the news comes that the Adams will take you. To Jackie that would have been an enormous triumph. What did Willie say? 'Fuck them, I'm not going. They didn't take me then. They're not going to take me now.'

"Jackie played an enormous role. I also think Willie played an enormous role. If everybody like Jackie had said, 'Isn't this great! Now we can stay here,' it would have been death to the movement. You had to have the mix. You had to have the other guys like Willie who said, 'Thanks very much. Now go fuck yourself. I don't want to come.'

"Of course, what desegregated the hotels more than Jackie or Willie was the Bank of America, when it started issuing plastic and an 800 number for a guaranteed reservation. 'Yes, Mr. Robinson.' And what happens when you show up? They put you up."

Even with Mays, the Giants fell behind the Dodgers. Then, in June 1951, the Dodgers made a trade that seemed to guarantee them the pennant.

Jack Lang: "One of the big moves the Dodgers made was on June 15, 1951. For years the Dodgers had been the way the Yankees are now, shifting guys around in left field. They had Carl Furillo in right and Duke Snider in center, but they didn't really have a regular left fielder. They had had Luis Olmo and Dick Whitman and Dick Williams, Cal Abrams, Gene Hermanski, all kinds of guys.

"We were in Chicago on June 15, and Buzzy Bavasi, the new general manager, made what looked like the deal that was going to wrap up the pennant for the Dodgers for sure. He got Andy Pafko from the Cubs along with Johnny Schmitz, a left-handed pitcher and Rube Walker, a third-string catcher, and all he gave up were Eddie Miksis and Joe Hatten and a bunch of farmhands. Pafko had been a solid center fielder in Chicago, good for 25 to 30 home runs a year, a .285 lifetime hitter, and now the Dodgers had this guy in left field. I've said many times that the best team I ever saw were the Dodgers in the last half of the '51 season. They had an All Star at *every* position. They had Campanella, Hodges, Robinson, Reese, Cox, Furillo, Snider, and Pafko, all All Stars. And Preacher Roe, Don Newcombe, and Carl Erskine were all stars. And yet they did not win the pennant."

By late summer the Dodgers lead seemed insurmountable.

Ray Robinson: "In late August the New York Giants were thirteen and a half games behind the Brooklyn Dodgers. At this point I was an intense Giant fan, and my feeling was that they didn't have a chance, a feeling reflected by most people. Brooklyn had a wonderful ball club, and thirteen and a half games is a considerable margin by any standards.

"Then the Giants started winning games, day in and day out, many of them by one run, and a lot of them were won out of the bullpen with guys like Don Liddle and Marv Grissom. They had a starting staff of Larry Jansen, Jim Hearn, and Sal Maglie, and a very strong bullpen. Willie Mays came up from Minneapolis in May, and he and Monte Irvin and Don Mueller and Whitey Lockman were hitting, and Al Dark and Eddie Stanky anchored the infield, and they kept winning and winning.

"Still, it didn't seem that they'd be able to substantially cut into the Dodger lead, but it became increasingly exciting. And when the winning streak reached sixteen, that put them back into the race."

Late in the season the Giants, led by Willie Mays, began winning game after game.

Stan Isaacs: "When the Giants started winning, you started wondering, Can they possibly catch them? And they were playing terrific ball, and it seemed in those days—my memory begins to exaggerate—but every day there would be a ball hit that Mays would make a great catch on. I don't think I've ever seen as many balls hit to a ballplayer, giving him the opportunity to make plays. And he made at least two plays that were much better than the one he made against Wertz in the 1954 World Series.

"One was in Ebbets Field. Bobby Morgan hit a drive to left center field—more to left field. It should have been the left fielder's ball. Mays must have been playing Morgan in, so he began racing back to his right, seemingly overtook the ball, dove to his right, and he caught the ball, bounced on the dirt into the wall, and then lay prone and seemed unconscious. Whether he was, I don't know. But he lay there for a few seconds, and he never let go of the ball.

"I thought that was the best catch I had seen up until then, and then he topped it by what I thought was the greatest catch I've ever seen an outfielder make, against the Dodgers in the Polo Grounds.

"Billy Cox was on third. There were less than two out. Carl Furillo hit a short fly ball into right center field. Mays came racing from center to his left into short right field, caught the ball—which was a terrific catch in itself. That he could get there was amazing. It really should have been Don Mueller's ball. Then he spun around 360 degrees and threw the ball to the plate on the fly. The amazed Cox was tagged out standing at home plate. The ball wasn't hit that far, but the fact that he could spin and make the accurate throw and get him, it was phenomenal, topped only by Dodger manager Charlie Dressen, who would never give credit to anybody. He said, 'I'd like to see him do it again!' Nobody had ever done it before. But that was typical Charlie Dressen.

"Even during the last week of the season, it still looked like the Dodgers were going to win it. Cause the Giants had so much ground to make up."

Ray Robinson: "The last week of the season, Gosh, they were close, but it still looked to me like they wouldn't make it."

Jack Lang: "The Giants played up in Boston, and they won their game, and the Dodgers, who at one time had a thirteen and a half game lead, were now behind the Giants and had to win the final game of the season just to get a tie to get into the playoffs.

"In the twelfth inning Jackie Robinson made a great play behind second base. It was a sinking line drive that was going to score the winning run for the Phillies, and he dove behind second base, caught the ball, and fell on his stomach. There was some question whether he actually caught the ball. He insisted that he did. But he had to be helped off the field after jamming his elbow into his stomach and lying on the ground a few minutes. They got him up, and he walked off the field.

"And two innings later he hit a home run that won the game."

The Dodgers and the Giants would play a three-game series to decide the National League pennant. The first game, played at Ebbets Field, was won by the Giants by the score of 3–1.

Jack Lang: "In the first game Bobby Thomson hit a home run off Ralph Branca, a line drive into the lower left field stands, and Branca lost."

Stan Isaacs: "Jim Hearn of the Giants pitched an unusually good game for him. He wasn't that good a pitcher. He generally was wild, but he was the kind of guy who sometimes would pitch a good game and sometimes a bad one, and this was one of his good ones, and the Giants won easily."

The second game, played at the Polo Grounds, was a laugher for the Dodgers. Rookie Clem Labine, ignored by Dodgers manager Chuck Dressen down the stretch, pitched a shut-out in a 10–0 win.

Ray Robinson: "I was at the second game of the playoffs, which was the wrong game to go see if you were a Giants fan. The Dodgers won 10–0. It was no game. I went with my father-in-law. When I married Phyllis, as I did fifty years ago, she and her father and I would go. He was a Giants fan all his life, and he was a salesman. The games would start in those days around three in the afternoon, and he used to go up there.

"In the early '20s, when McGraw was the Giants' manager, a lot of theatrical people loved the New York Giants, because they could go to the games in the afternoon and perform at night. I remember Will Rogers, when he was in New York with the Ziegfield Follies, was a Giants fan.

"My father-in-law was a very excitable, very attractive man. He looked like John Barrymore, very theatrical looking. But unfortunately, he had a terrible temperament, which probably destroyed him in the end. He died young of a heart ailment.

"We went to this game, the second game, and we were sitting in very good box seats which my father-in-law had purchased. He immediately looked over and saw Sheldon "Available" Jones warming up for the Giants to pitch that day, and he started grumbling, yelling, 'How can Durocher do this to *me*? I brought them to this stage.'

"After the Giants had won the first playoff game with Jim Hearn on the mound, he took it personally that the Giants were starting this nondescript, journeyman pitcher. And he kept yelling and screaming, and he was right, because as the game developed, Jones had nothing, and Robinson and Hodges hit home runs, and by the sixth or seventh inning, my father-in-law was doing a good imitation of a raving maniac.

"My father-in-law, moreover, had claustrophobia. This meant that he never stayed at an athletic event or a theatrical event to the end, because he couldn't stand crowds hemming him in. So he had two reasons for leaving the Polo Grounds: the Giants were getting smothered and he was claustrophobic and had to leave. So with a mighty roar of anger, he got up and left the ballpark.

"Two people had been sitting behind me the whole game, and one of them tapped me on the shoulder. I turned around, and he said, 'Can I ask you a question?' I said, 'Sure.' He said, 'Who was the fellow who just left the park who was sitting next to you?' I said, 'That happened to be my father-in-law.' And this guy shook his head and said, 'You know my friend, you're lucky he's not your mother-in-law!'"

★ ★ ★

After the second game, a reporter asked Leo Durocher what had happened. His reply: "We got the shit kicked out of us. Does anyone else have a bright question?"

The third and deciding game was also played at the Polo Grounds. Don Newcombe faced Sal Maglie. This was for all the marbles. The ending, a three-run home run by Bobby Thomson to win the game in the bottom of the ninth, was perhaps the most dramatic in the history of the game. For those who were there, or who saw it on television, it was a memory of a lifetime.

Stan Isaacs: "It wasn't a full house [only 34,320 were there]. It was sort of a dark day. But I've never been able to understand why. It was an extra game, and people need to make plans. But it was surprising that the game didn't sell out.

"Don Newcombe started for the Dodgers, and he was pitching a great game. Newk was a tough guy to know in those days. He didn't get along with the press. Some of the reporters were particularly tough on him.

"I was in the press box behind home plate, and I was going to be covering the Giants' dressing room. It's a long walk to the clubhouse and normally about the eighth inning you make the long walk so you'll be outside the locker room when the game is over. And as you walk along the ramp, if you bend down, you can see between the upper and lower stands out onto the field. I was twenty-two years old, still a fan, and I didn't want to leave. I wanted to *see* what would happen, so I took a spot on the ramp in right center field, and by bending down, I could watch the game, and as the hits developed, the two singles and the double, I watched, and again, hoping against hope—because I'm always afraid the worst will happen, that we would fall short—so then when Bobby Thomson hit the home run, my first reaction was, 'Gee, I'm covering the *winning* dressing room.'

"After that, I raced down and got to the clubhouse long before anybody else, and I then waited outside a few minutes and then went inside into this tumultuous Giants' dressing room. I was as much thrilled as a fan as I was a guy writing. I talked to Thomson, who seemed dazed, and went and talked to Durocher, and enjoyed it on both accounts, as a fan and a writer.

"And then I went into the Dodger locker room and saw Ralph Branca lying prone over a few steps, the picture captured by Barney Stein of the *Post*, lying facedown. I looked at that, and looked for a quote from Dressen, which I knew wouldn't be very good because he was never any good. And then I went down and wrote my story."

Jack Lang: "With the Dodgers leading 4–1 in the ninth inning, myself and all the afternoon reporters—Bill Roeder, Mike Gavin, Sid Friedlander—headed for the Polo Grounds clubhouse where we were going to be when the winning Dodgers came in. By the time we got to the clubhouse, the score was four to two, and Branca was being called in. We never saw Thomson's home run because we were in the clubhouse and there was only one window, and sitting in front of that window was Senator John Griffin, the clubhouse attendant who weighed about 350 pounds. He was right in front of the window, and we couldn't see anything. So we were listening to Red Barber on the Dodger radio in the Dodger clubhouse when Thomson hit the home run.

"And as soon as that happened, they asked us to leave the room immediately. We were out in the hallway between the two clubhouses, and it was a New Year's Eve celebration in the Giants clubhouse and dead silence in the Dodgers'. Just dead silence. They couldn't believe what had happened to them."

Ray Robinson: "I was just beginning a job on a sports magazine, and I couldn't take another day off. Everybody was watching. My wife was at home in this little apartment on the East Side of Manhattan. She was pregnant with my daughter, our first child, and she was watching this game with the cleaning lady, and when Thomson hit the home run, the cleaning lady said, 'Ma'am, you're going to give birth right on the spot.'

"My boss was a guy by the name of Noah Sarlet, the owner of a group of magazines, and he was a big Dodger fan, as were most of the people working in our office. And when Thomson hit the home run, he punched a pane of window glass in his office and he was lucky he didn't break it. It was an impulsive thing he did as the ball disappeared into the left field stands.

"Those experiences were repeated all over the city.

"It was very exciting, and what made it even more exciting was that it was played in the afternoon. By five o'clock the tabloids were on the stands. Today you don't have that. I remember *The Daily News* and *The Mirror* and these other tabloids, they all came out with it in the evening, and we all rushed to buy them to see what we already knew. And there was Thomson on the front page hugging Durocher, and Stanky jumping on Durocher. You didn't have television to tell you about it. You had the tabloids."

Bobby Thomson

Joel Oppenheimer: "In '51 I was away at college, but I was back home during the playoffs. I went over to Herky's, an old high school friend's house to listen to the game with him, and they were all Giants fans.

"What I remember was sitting in front of the television drinking beer in a room full of Giants fans feeling very up, because we were going to win the game, and then getting totally destroyed. It was a repeat of Mickey Owen in '41. And every time I hear that scream, 'The Giants win the pennant. 'The Giants win the pennant,' I go crazy inside, like I'm back there,

Ralph Branca

and I'm twenty-one, and my world has been destroyed once more. Once again the Dodgers did it to me. It's one of those triggers that can absolutely return me to the situation.

"My friends went bananas. Absolutely bananas. They were jumping up. And I was sitting there. The image for me was Jackie standing by second base, making sure Thomson touched the bases. All I knew was these jibbering idiots were screaming and yelling, that they had undeservedly gotten this enormous bonus from life."

Ray Robinson: "As I look back at those very exciting times, those last few weeks of that season, including that final game when Thomson hit that final home run against Branca, there were only 34,000 people in the Polo Grounds, which could fit in about 57,000, so you had twenty thousand seats going begging.

"True, it was an overcast day, but their attendance all during the season was not that good. It wasn't. And one reason was that dominating the situation in New York was the Yankees. The Yankees were drawing. If the Giants couldn't pack in 57,000 people to see the third playoff game that would decide the pennant, something had to be wrong."

s i x

New York's Golden Age

The rest of the decade provided immense but fleeting joy for fans of both the Dodgers and the Giants as they experienced the Golden Age of New York City baseball. At Ebbets Field Dodgers fans would flock to witness a team that would become legendary. National League pennants would fly in Brooklyn in 1952 and 1953, as the names of the beloved Bums would pass into legend. Thanks to Roger Kahn the roster of Hodges, Snider, Furillo, Robinson, Reese, Campanella, Cox, Newcombe, Roe, Erskine, and Labine would become known as "The Boys of Summer."

The Giants, meanwhile, led by Leo Durocher and reinvigorated by the return of Willie Mays from the army, would go on to win the pennant in 1954. In the World Series the New York Giants would defeat the favored Cleveland Indians in four straight games. Overshadowing the triumph is the eternal image of a streaking Willie Mays, his back to the plate in deepest center field, catching a ball hit by Vic Wertz over his shoulder, then turning and firing a missile back to the infield.

Jack Lang: "I saw 'The Catch.' That was midway into the first World Series game. We all thought it was spectacular, but by then we had all become used to seeing Willie Mays do that.

"Willie will tell you that he didn't think that was his greatest catch. He thought his greatest catch was one he made on opening day in '54, when he went diving through the air in the first inning to catch a line drive hit by Bobby Morgan, went crashing into the center-field fence and was knocked out still holding onto the ball.

"So we were used to seeing Mays make great catches. The great thing about this one was the way he caught the ball, spun around and threw it back to the infield. He was just a great ballplayer. That was not the first one I saw him make going out to center field."

Willie Mays came to symbolize the New York Giants. For them, he was the greatest player who ever lived.

Ray Robinson: "First of all, Willie was a tremendously effervescent ballplayer. He could do anything. He could throw—he had a wonderful arm. He could hit and hit for distance. He played center field better than anyone I had ever seen. And don't forget, there was a lot of center field to cover out there.

"He could run. I can see him running around first base with that wide turn, and he was one of the great base runners I had ever seen in my life. In those years they didn't emphasize stolen bases, and for a big man he was an extraordinary base runner. If Willie was playing today, he'd steal 80 or 90 bases.

"And he could hit like hell.

"The competitiveness of the three teams emerged when you had these three wonderful center fielders: Mays, Snider, and Mantle. When these three emerged as the top three players in baseball, it was always a lot of fun to argue about the merit of these three men, who was better, Willie, Mickey, or the Duke. That's when the rivalry became an amusing constant."

In 1950s New York City the great argument was not whether or not the Rosenbergs had stolen nuclear secrets for the Russians, but rather who was the best center fielder, Willie Mays, Duke Snider, or the Yankees' Mickey Mantle. Giants fans, naturally, were convinced that Mays was the best. For them, the Dodgers' Duke Snider didn't even merit being part of the conversation.

Stan Isaacs: "Mays was in the army most of 1952 and in 1953. When he returned in '54, an aspect of Mays was, 'Would he be better than Mickey Mantle? We watched Mays and Mantle together. That was always a question.

"Snider had benefitted over the years by the fact that he was there when

Duke Snider

Mays and Mantle were there. In my mind, though others put the three together, Snider really didn't fit into their class. Snider used to sit down against some left-handed pitchers. He was a solid ballplayer, a marginal Hall of Famer. He was lucky to have made it. The other two were Titans."

Dodgers fans, who would begin their argument by citing the number of pennants Snider helped them win, were convinced their beloved Duke was the best.

Joel Oppenheimer: "The Dodger I fell in love most was Duke Snider. I just adored the notion that we had this incredible hitter and fielder and that he looked the way he looked. He didn't look like what a baseball player was supposed to look like. Snider was one of the first of the good-looking California guys, so alien to my experience.

"Of the three, Mays, Mantle, and Snider, I can prove with my version of statistics that for the five years they played against each other—you drop the years Willie was in the army, drop out the year Mantle was hurt—there were five years when they went head to head, and Duke comes out very well in those five years. If you add up his league leaderships in home runs, runs batted in, and hits, it seems to me that Duke either just edges out Mantle or runs dead even with Mantle, and Willie is a little behind.

"They kept saying that Duke wasn't as good a fielder as Willie or Mickey because he played in such a small field. What you have to do is use the reverse argument. With Duke in center, Brooklyn didn't need a left fielder. You could put a stick in left field, and some years they did, simply because Duke was there and Pee Wee Reese at short, great at going back. I would have to see someone clone Duke and put him at twenty-one in center field in Yankee Stadium or the Polo Grounds, for them to say to me, 'He isn't as good a center fielder as the other two.' Because from what I saw him do in the smaller park, there is nothing that says he wouldn't have been that great in the other fields.

"When the argument was raging, I just knew Duke was better. Mantle was always getting hurt. With Willie the Giants obviously weren't as good as the Dodgers, so Willie wasn't doing as much for them as Duke was for the Dodgers."

In 1955 the Dodgers, led by manager Walter Alston, regained the National League pennant as the Giants fell to third.

Stan Isaacs: "In '55 the Giants faltered, and by that time Leo had lost interest. He was a terrific manager with a contending club, but with a team that wasn't good, he would lose interest."

For Brooklyn Dodger fans, their most cherished memory came during Game Seven of the 1955 World Series. The Dodgers had lost the World Series in 1916 and 1920. Then came devastating World Series losses to the New York Yankees in 1941, 1947, 1949, 1952 and 1953. Dodger fans were convinced that they were doomed and perhaps cursed never to win a fall season classic.

With the Dodgers ahead 2–0 behind Johnny Podres, Brooklyn was knocking at the door. In the seventh two runners were on base with one out. Then Yankee catcher Yogi Berra hit a long fly ball to left field that surely appeared to be a home run.

But, wait! Left fielder Sandy Amoros races toward the left field stands of Yankee Stadium, reaches out his right arm at the last second, and catches the ball. After making the play, Amoros throws the ball to shortstop Pee Wee Reese, who then throws it to first baseman Gil Hodges to double off Yankees runner Gil McDougald. The play kills the rally, and the Dodgers survive to win 2–0. It is the happiest moment in Brooklyn Dodgers history.

Joel Oppenheimer: "When the Dodgers won in '55, it was almost disbelief. 'By God, it had finally happened, the thing I had been waiting for all my life.' And yet it was almost anticlimactic. They should have won in '41, should have won in '47. Somewhere before this they should have won. It was just too late to reverse this pattern. It was . . . they couldn't make up for all they had lost. It had its own wonder, but they should have won other times earlier.

"Then the next year Don Larsen pitched a perfect game against us. It was one more instance of God treating us badly. Why should Don Larsen, of all people. . . . Remember when Casey said, 'I got my drunk.' Why should he of all people? Why shouldn't Don Newcombe have had a perfect game? That would have been justice. Don Larsen? Never.

"I really believe with the Dodger fans that they got beaten down enough that there was an essential humility and an understanding which the Yankee fans never had. The simple fact is, as the world continually forgets, it is not a very nice place to live, and more bad things happen than good things. And that's how you learn to appreciate the good things, and two, once in a while you take it easy on somebody else. The Brooklyn fans are living proof of that. They are people who have learned to care about something other than winning: they care about excellence, and the proof is in the standing ovations Stan Musial got at Ebbets Field.

"There always seemed to me an essential meanness among a lot of Yankee fans, like God owes it to them. And if they ain't in the race, then it ain't a race, and if they ain't in the Series, it ain't a Series. I think because it came so hard to the Dodgers, because they had to fight so long for it, and they came so close so many times, they learned that, 'Gee, when it happens, it's wonderful, and when it doesn't, it's still baseball.' "

seven

Rumblings, Departure, and the Void

O nly in hindsight can one see that the year 1955 was the beginning of the end for the Dodgers and the Giants. When Giants owner Horace Stoneham didn't renew Leo Durocher's contract at the end of the '55 season, the air of excitement went out of the Polo Grounds as though a balloon had been popped. Giants fans were becoming disillusioned.

Stan Isaacs: "When Stoneham fired Leo, I didn't like it. Stoneham was a drunk, so you didn't know what was with him. Bill Rigney took over, but it wasn't much of a team. By '57 the talk was of the Giants going to Minneapolis."

Before that, as the Polo Grounds began to be viewed as an ancient, outmoded relic, there was talk of a new ballpark for the Giants. On April 10, 1956, Stoneham announced he was "very interested" in a proposal made by Manhattan Borough President Hulan Jack for the construction of a new stadium on Manhattan's West Side. It was to be a triple-deckered arena seating 110,000 fans to be built above the tracks of the New York Central Railroad yards. There would be parking for twenty thousand cars and a subway station under the stadium. The cost would be $75 million. (That same stadium, recently proposed for the New York Yankees, would cost a billion dollars today.)

There was one catch: the city was not offering to pay for it. Stoneham had decided that Harlem was becoming too black for him to stay at his current location, that with the advent of night baseball he was concerned that his fans would think it too dangerous to venture to upper Manhattan. Once he considered and rejected the notion of paying for this new stadium, he decided he had no choice but to leave New York. His first choice was Nordic Minneapolis, the lilliest of lily-white suburbs.

In Brooklyn, Walter O'Malley was making his own plans to escape the black and brown incursion and to get out of town. But first he had to pull two swindles. First, he needed to buy the rights to play in the Los Angeles area, then owned by the Chicago Cubs, who had a minor league team there. After that, he had to talk another team owner into moving out to the Coast with him. With two teams on the Coast, it would be more economical in terms of scheduling. To fly to the Coast to play but one team would be too expensive for the other owners.

O'Malley, a powerful man who got things done, ended up having no trouble at all either buying the rights to Los Angeles or getting another team to go with him.

Harold Parrott: "Walter O'Malley had been lucky enough to run into Phil Wrigley just when the chewing gum king was very angry at a whole city: Los Angeles. His team trained on Catalina Island and the grounds were not in shape for spring training one year. Wrigley vowed he would never bring his team back. 'A bush town,' Wrigley called it, and swore he'd never have anything to do with the place again, as soon as he could get rid of his minor league franchise, the Pacific Coast League Angels.

"O'Malley was drooling but trying hard to hide his interest."

Jack Lang: "The first move—we found this out later—came in January 1956 at the Baseball Writers' dinner. The writers were honoring Phil Wrigley, who owned the Chicago Cubs, and at the other end of the dais was Walter O'Malley. O'Malley wrote a little note and gave it to one of the waiters. He told him, 'Take this to Mr. Wrigley.' Wrigley opened it, and it said, 'I'll trade you Fort Worth for Los Angeles.'

"Wrigley was a big friend of O'Malley's. He was impressed with O'Malley's business acumen. At one point Wrigley either sold or gave O'Malley a very, very profitable business. Before he left New York, O'Malley bought Subway Advertising from Wrigley and made a fortune with it. He and Wrigley were pretty shrewd operators.

"What O'Malley was doing was getting his foot into California by buying the Los Angeles franchise. Wrigley, a big proponent of California—his family owned Catalina Island—wasn't about to move there from Chicago, and he foresaw the future of baseball in California as well. So he made the deal to swap the two minor league franchises. And so in 1957 the Dodgers' top farm club was in the Pacific Coast League in Los Angeles, and the Cubs moved to Fort Worth, Texas. And now that O'Malley owned the franchise in Los Angeles, he didn't have to pay any indemnities when he moved the Dodgers there.

"When the Dodgers started playing seven games in Jersey City in '56 and '57, one against each opponent, we knew that O'Malley was itching to get out of Brooklyn. If he was taking seven games out of Brooklyn, we knew eventually he was going to take out all seventy-seven."

Dodgers fans didn't know quite what to think when it was announced in 1956 that Brooklyn was going to play seven regular season games in New Jersey, of all places.

Joel Oppenheimer: "When it was announced that the Dodgers were going to play seven home games in Jersey City, the news was full of theories. I put the best face on it. 'Okay, they're playing in Jersey City. Why not play a couple of games there?' And I assumed that would keep O'Malley happy. I don't think it ever occurred to anyone that the Dodgers would go away. It was an immutable fact of nature that the Dodgers should be in Brooklyn. And it didn't much matter that the Boston Braves had moved to Milwaukee, the Philadelphia A's had moved to Kansas City, and the St. Louis Browns had moved to Baltimore. What did that have to do with me? Move from Brooklyn? That was crazy."

The fans, unfortunately, could not comprehend that for O'Malley baseball was less sport than a business, and after making overtures to the movers and shakers of Los Angeles, he quickly discovered that the Los Angelinos were prepared to grant to him a largess that few could turn down.

Jack Lang: "In the spring of 1957 O'Malley was entertaining the Los Angeles officials and writers in Vero Beach with the Dodgers. The smoke-screen was that they were there to cover the budding players in the Dodger farm system who would be playing in Los Angeles. But he was entertaining the Los Angeles people a year before he made the actual move."

★ ★ ★

Irving Rudd was the public relations director of the Dodgers at the time O'Malley left for California. He, for one, couldn't imagine anyone resisting the offer made to the Dodgers owner.

Irving Rudd: "Norris Poulson, the mayor of Los Angeles, showed up in Vero Beach one day, and he presented O'Malley with a laundry list— here's what I'll give you if you come to Los Angeles, including, 'You can sleep with my wife once a week.'

"Forget the emotion. O'Malley is a businessman. They say, 'This is what I'm giving you. The condominium is yours for life.' You say, 'But I got this contract.' They say, 'Two dancing girls and Jacqueline Bissette on weekends.' You say, 'Fuck the contract.' How many guys would say no? So what did Poulson give him? He condemned the land for him. They gave him the oil rights in case they discovered oil. They built him a stadium. Who needs Fort Knox to print money? That's why he went. Bye-bye Brooklyn."

Once O'Malley made the decision to move to Los Angeles, he decided he needed another ball club to go with him. He knew Horace Stoneham was thinking of moving to Minneapolis, and so he called Stoneham and proposed that they move to the coast together. Stoneham complied.

Horace Stoneham: "I had intended to move the Giants out of New York even before I knew Mr. O'Malley was intending to move. I was unhappy playing in the Polo Grounds. The ballpark was old, and it was darn near impossible to finance one in that area. I had intended to go to Minneapolis. We had a ball club there, so I had the rights to the area, and it's a big city in itself. Also, Minneapolis was well within transportation range of the league. Aviation at that time had been accepted by everyone.

"And then Walter called me up and asked me if I was going to move. I said, 'I think so. I think the league will give me permission.' He said, 'Why don't we both move and go to the far West together?' So we thought about it, and that's what we finally decided to do. When he asked me about moving West, I told him that I liked the San Francisco area, that I had worked there when I was a young fellow. I didn't even know he was intending to move. But when he saw I was, he saw we could make a rivalry on the Pacific Coast."

★ ★ ★

On May 28, 1957, the New York Giants and the Brooklyn Dodgers received unanimous approval from all National League clubs to move to San Francisco and Los Angeles.

Jack Lang: "There was more to it than just moving the team to California. At that time there was a guy named Marty Fox, who owned a cable TV company called Skiatron. Fox supposedly had the whole West Coast hooked up, or was going to get it hooked up, and O'Malley saw in his future not only the attendance in California but the future in cable TV as well. In New York he was giving baseball games away on TV; in California his future was to be Pay TV. O'Malley and Horace Stoneham each were given 50,000 shares in Skiatron.

"Stoneham had already agreed to go to Minneapolis. They even had the steel girders on the ground ready to erect a stadium there. He was all set to leave New York and go to Minneapolis. And then when O'Malley got the approval to go to California, he was told by the other owners that the only way he could go was if another team went out there, because the other owners said it didn't pay to go out to the Coast for three games and come back again. So O'Malley talked Stoneham into going to San Francisco. And they had a deal with Skiatron, which was going to make a fortune for them on cable TV. But it never came off. Skiatron went out of business."

On August 19, 1957, the Giants board of directors voted 8–1 to move the club to San Francisco from the 1958 season. The only dissenting vote came from M. Donald Grant, who represented minority stockholder Mrs. Joan Whitney Payson.

During a press conference announcing the vote, Horace Stoneham was asked, "How do you feel about taking the Giants from the kids in New York?" Stoneham answered, "I feel bad about the kids but I haven't seen many of their fathers lately."

In 1956 Giants attendance was 630,000. Only two years earlier it had been 1.4 million.

Jack Lang: "Stoneham was dying up there in the Polo Grounds. The stadium was in the middle of Harlem, and in the early fifties it was becoming more and more of a black area, and people just didn't want to go up into that area at night.

"It was different when they played day ball. It was a great place to go. They used to draw the show business crowd in the twenties and thirties when they played afternoon games, but then when they started playing night baseball, people didn't want to go all the way up there."

Despite the drop in attendance, loyal Giants fans were stunned to learn the Giants of McGraw, Mathewson, Ott, Hubbell, Thomson, and Mays were heading West.

Ray Robinson: "The first reaction to hear that the Giants were leaving was disbelief. As I said, the first inkling of the difficulty the Giants were having was that third playoff game in 1951, when only 34,000 people were in the stands. Twenty thousand tickets were uncalled for. That was an indication that something was wrong. After the most exciting pennant race in history, you had twenty thousand people staying away. And Stoneham, when he wasn't drunk was aware of that.

"And then, as we kept reading more and more stories, we got the feeling there was something going on *between* the Giants and the Dodgers to effect this move. Then we began to realize that this was really going to happen."

Stan Isaacs: "Once it was established the Dodgers were moving, we figured they wouldn't move unless the Giants were moving, too. O'Malley had to bring somebody out to the West Coast.

"So I blamed O'Malley for the Giants' leaving. I hated him. To my mind Horace Stoneham was a drunk who had run down the franchise in the first place. The Giants in the 1920s were the number one team in town, until the Yankees with Ruth, but even into the thirties, they were a good team, until Horace Stoneham took the team from his father, and he ran them down. Stoneham could have bought the railroad tracks out in left field at the Polo Grounds, which would have given him the parking he needed. He didn't do that. And by the time the Giants left, they were the third team in town. I, as a partisan Giants fan, blamed Stoneham for that. But the move West? *That* was O'Malley's doing.

"And when they actually left, I was disillusioned. This was the beginning of 'the business of America is business,' the Calvin Coolidge line. And now it was brought home: that they would actually move the teams in Brooklyn and New York.

"And it was a disillusionment that *never* went away. For my generation, there was tremendous disillusionment. And bitterness, which has never left. No, *never*."

Lou Larosa was a youngster who grew up in Brooklyn. When the Dodgers left, so did his interest in the team and the game.

Lou Larosa: "Ebbets Field wasn't fifteen minutes from where I lived. My father was a big Yankee fan, and he liked the Giants, too, but I liked the Brooklyn Dodgers because they were the team from the Borough. It was like a minor league team. The players mingled with the people. They weren't high and mighty like the players are today.

"I remember when I was ten years old the Police Athletic League took us to a night game at Ebbets Field, and the Dodgers lost, and we came out, and all of the players walked out, Roy Campanella, Pee Wee Reese, and we got their autographs. One big guy came out and pushed everybody out of the way. Really rude, rude, rude sonabitch, and I never forgot it, and I'm fifty-seven. It was Duke Snider. That stood with me forever and ever and ever. You can be intense, but when it comes to children, you should never be rude. Later I saw a movie, *The Boys of Summer*, and he apologized for being rude. There were hundreds of kids running around, and every other ballplayer signed.

"The Dodgers were great. Ebbets Field had a short left field, and when they had batting practice before the game, they'd hit the balls over the wall on purpose. They'd throw them easy ones, and boom, they'd bat them over the fence so the kids could get them, forty, fifty balls to the kids and to the people standing outside.

"I was a Dodger fan until 1957. I was fourteen. We were in Prospect Park playing baseball. One side was toward Ebbets Field, the other side toward Ocean Parkway. And a bunch of supporters came out and gave us T-shirts that said, 'Keep the Dodgers in Brooklyn.' They had a big parade, thousands of people marched. But the Dodgers moved anyway. And when they moved, that was the end for me because we didn't even have a television set until '58, as crazy as that sounds, and going to Yankee Stadium was just too far. It was a two-hour trip from Brooklyn. So I just kind of lost interest. I got interested in girls and cars."

Giants fans also turned their backs on baseball in droves.

Ray Robinson: "Arnold Hano and I went to the last game the Giants ever played at the Polo Grounds. That dreadful game, about 12,000 people there. It wasn't much of a game. The Pirates won 9–1, and we sat in the bleachers, which were cheap, fifty-five cents. I'm sorry we didn't pick up one of the seats. Everyone else ripped the place apart. They took the turf and home plate and God knows what else. Arnold was a lifelong New York Giants fan. He never rooted for another team."

When the Dodgers and Giants left New York, some of the beat writers were left with only the American League New York Yankees to cover. First-string beat reporters, their team having disappeared, suddenly became second stringers. Jack Lang was one of the luckier ones. George Burton, the reporter who covered the Yankees for the *Long Island Press*, decided to go to work for ABC, one of the major bowling companies. As senior man at the *Press*, Lang was next in line for the job. He remembers that even without the presence of the Dodgers and Giants, Yankee attendance suffered.

Jack Lang: "The first year the Yankees had New York City all to themselves [1958] their attendance went down from the previous year. People who were Giant and Dodger fans just didn't want to go to American League games. I'm not saying everybody. Some guys just wanted to see a ball game, but the Yankees did not benefit from having the city all to themselves. They were such staunch National League fans that they wouldn't go to American League games.

"I can remember when the Dodgers and Giants played in Philadelphia and Pittsburgh that first year, some of the local stations in New York would cover those games and have play-by-play. But it wasn't the same. The fans felt cheated and deserted. The line has been repeated many times: Pete Hamill wrote a column in which he said, 'The three most hated people in the history of the universe were Adolph Hitler, Genghis Khan, and Walter O'Malley."

Stan Isaacs was another of the handful of reporters who improved his standing after the Dodgers and Giants left. As a reporter for *Newsday*, Isaacs could not have known it at the time, but he and his paper would be a prime beneficiary of the mass white flight from the inner city to the suburbs.

Stan Isaacs: "I was writing for *Newsday*, and little by little we were going from a local paper to a big-time paper, so I was on the road covering the contending National League teams, and in '59 it was the Dodgers and Giants out on the Coast.

"I disliked both teams, because they had left New York, but I found when the Dodgers were playing the Giants, I was still rooting for the Giants, but clinically I was rooting more for my story. I was a little disgusted with Giant and Dodger fans who remained fans of the teams that had left. They were traitors. I could see rooting for Pee Wee Reese and Sandy Koufax. But not for O'Malley's Dodgers."

For a few years some fans, while continuing to hate O'Malley for taking the Dodgers and Giants West, refused to abandon their beloved players.

Joel Oppenheimer: "I know a guy who still spits three times when you mention O'Malley's name. But I must say that despite these feelings, until the Mets came into the league, it was very hard for me *not* to root for the Dodgers, because first of all, the thinking with a lot of New York fans was, we couldn't blame the players for what O'Malley had done, and if Koufax and [Don] Drysdale were having great seasons, or if the Davis boys were running wild, they were still our boys and you had to root for them. We had heard about Tommy and Willie Davis in the minors, so they still belonged to us, but slowly, as the players retired, and we had the new focus of the Mets, it became easier to let go. [In 1978] I went to a Dodger–Yankees World Series, and I sat on my hands the whole game. But I no longer had anything to root for in Los Angeles. There was nothing there for me. I had only gone because I had tickets and my kid desperately wanted to see the game."

Ray Robinson was another who could not abruptly cast aside his allegiance. The Giants were like family, even if they were now the black sheep.

Ray Robinson: "I was *very* angry when the Giants left, because I loved baseball and the Giants and Mays and Monte Irvin, and I wanted to be able to see games at the Polo Grounds. We were all very angry when they left, and then they brought in the Giant games late at night reconstructed by Les Keiter. I would sit up at two in the morning listening to that damn thing.

"I must say I kept following the San Francisco Giants, and they had a wonderful team with Willie, Orlando Cepeda, and Willie McCovey. But then I was also very eager for another National League franchise to come to New York. Because I half-rooted for the Dodgers and half-rooted for the Giants, what I wanted was a National League franchise. And that was the attitude of a lot of people."

eight

Bill Shea Performs a Miracle

Not long after the desertion of the Dodgers and the Giants in October of 1958, New York City's mayor, Robert Wagner, a savvy politician who felt the loss of the prestige to the city as much as anyone, formed a study group called The Mayor's Baseball Committee. Its express task was to try to persuade an existing franchise to pull up stakes and move to New York City—in other words to screw another National League city—just like New York had been screwed.

The panel consisted of men from New York City's baseball-loving high society, including Bernard Gimbel, the department store magnate, Jim Farley, the former postmaster general of the United States and chief fundraiser for the Democratic National Committee, and real estate developer Clinton Blume.

At its head was a hail-fellow, well-met attorney with social and political connections by the name of William A. Shea. A partner in a prestigious law firm, for many years Bill Shea had been a close personal friend and advisor to many politicians, and none more so than Mayor Wagner, who took advice from him at strategy meetings and who talked to him on the phone almost every day. Shea had raised great sums of money for Wagner's campaigns, and Wagner trusted him implicitly.

Among the other politicos who were Bill Shea's friends were New York governor Nelson Rockfeller, Connecticut senator Prescott Bush, and senate majority leader Lyndon Baines Johnson of Texas. An Irish charmer,

Shea, known for his wisdom and tact, had a stellar reputation and a great ability for getting things done. But as for bringing National League baseball back to New York, few thought that even a man of Shea's abilities had much of a shot.

Bill Shea was born in 1907 in upper Manhattan and after attending grammar school in Brooklyn, went to high school in Queens and upper Manhattan. At George Washington High School he won president of the student council by the largest margin on record at the time.

He enrolled at New York University, where he played end on the freshman football team and starred in lacrosse. After a year he switched to Georgetown University, where he would complete both his undergraduate and law degrees in four years.

Shea's family was solidly middle class until the Depression hit, and times became tough. His father, who was in the insurance business, had very few customers. As a result, Shea's father lacked the funds to continue to send him to college.

But according to Shea's daughter Kathy, Bill Shea's younger sister, Gloria, "a fabulously beautiful woman" who had modeled in the lace industy since she was sixteen, was offered a movie contract in California. During the four years she was out there, she made enough money to pay for her brother's education.

After passing the bar Shea returned to Brooklyn, where he went to work in the insurance industry for the state of New York. Almost immediately Shea began making friends, an ability that came naturally.

While in law school Shea had formed a small team of five fellow students with whom he conferred on a daily basis. They studied together, asked each other's opinions, and encouraged each other. All benefitted greatly. Such relationships would become the thread in Bill Shea's life.

And while he was in law school in Washington D.C., Shea met the love of his life, Nori Shaw, the daughter of "Long Tom" Shaw, a prominent "oddsman" at Belmont and other race tracks. Shaw had begun as a youngster at the turn of the century taking bets with a chalkboard and a soapbox, and by the mid-1920s he had become so successful he could take a bet of a million dollars on a horse. It was Tom Shaw who had lent Wellington Mara the five hundred dollars to found the New York football Giants.

Shaw also raced horses, and he became prominent in the upper-crust racing community. When pari–mutuel betting was instituted in the 1940s, the oddsmen were put out of work, and Shaw retired. He never did stop going to the track, until his death at age 99.

Once Bill Shea married, it was Nori who kept Shea focused on his family and his career as a man who could handle fifty things at once. Bill Shea loved politics, and with his personality easily could have been a U.S. senator or congressman, but his wife put her foot down. She told him, "Not as long as I am breathing."

"She didn't want to live that life," said their daughter Kathy Shea Alfuso. "She didn't think it would be good for the family or the marriage. She didn't want her husband gone all week and coming home on weekends, which is what senators and congressmen do, and if it was a state office, they would have had to move somewhere.

"She was raised in a different social strata. She was very happy and secure in one place. We lived in one house in Sands Point. She was very much into being stable, secure, and rooted. Politics does not afford that."

But, being an advisor to politicians did. It didn't take Bill Shea long to use his networking abilities to become one of New York City's powers behind the thrones.

After working for the state insurance commissioner in 1935 Bill Shea joined Cullen & Dykeman, the law firm that represented the Brooklyn Trust Company, which held control over the bankrupt Brooklyn Dodgers. The head of the bank was George V. McLaughlin, a gruff, red-faced banker who had been an important member of the Tammany Hall circle of politicans since the 1920s. McLaughlin, a sports fan who also headed the Equitable Life Assurance Society, was allied with New York governor Al Smith, the powerful urban planner, Robert Moses, publisher Herbert Bayard Swope, and the Catholic Church. McLaughlin would become Bill Shea's mentor and close friend. Soon, all of McLaughlin's friends would become Bill Shea's friends.

Shea worked under McLaughlin along with two other young lawyers, Walter O'Malley and Jim McLaughlin, no relation. The three became McLaughlin's proteges.

Shea left in 1940 to help found the law firm of Manning, Hollinger, and Shea.

In 1942, after Larry MacPhail enlisted in the Army, McLaughlin hired Branch Rickey to run the Brooklyn team. His other protege, Walter O'Malley, who had been watching over the Dodgers for McLaughlin and his bank since 1933, was given the opportunity by McLaughlin to buy a quarter share in the team along with Rickey, John L. Smith, a chemicals mogul, and relatives of Dodger founder Charlie Ebbets.

McLaughlin arranged a sweetheart deal for O'Malley, who got the stock for no cash down. McLaughlin, moreover, let him pay off what he owed from future profits, which, thanks primarily to Rickey, were considerable and came quickly.

"It was George V. who set O'Malley up with the Dodgers," said Shea. "He could have tapped any of the three of us for the Brooklyn job. O'Malley was the oldest and had more business experience, so he got the in—and gradually took over."

Bill Shea's daughter said Shea was never offered the job of watching over the Dodgers, and even if he had, Nori Shea would not have allowed him to accept it.

"That wasn't something he and my mother would have agreed to do," she said. "She wanted a broader scope for him. She didn't want him locked in to one single issue. He was a person who needed to be doing twenty things at once and could handle them."

For twenty years O'Malley's success in running the Dodgers was a source of pride for George McLaughlin. After O'Malley was able to wrest control of the Dodgers from Rickey, his fortunes grew as the Dodgers gained fame and favor in Brooklyn during the 1950s. McLaughlin could not have been prouder of his prodigal son.

But then, in the mid-1950s, O'Malley suddenly stopped calling and conferring with McLaughlin, as Shea had always done. Then in the summer of 1957, again without consulting McLaughlin, O'Malley announced he was taking the Dodgers out of Brooklyn and moving them to Los Angeles. McLaughlin was devastated and felt personally betrayed by O'Malley, who felt he had outgrown his former mentor. McLaughlin had appointed O'Malley to look after his baby, and instead the baby-sitter had kidnapped it and took it across state lines.

"It was [McLaughlin] who, as Walter O'Malley's closest friend, advisor, and council became his enemy the day Walter O'Malley decided to go to California without his consent and his knowledge," said Shea.

The job to replace the Dodgers and bring National League baseball back to New York, then fell to McLaughlin's other trusted associate, Bill Shea.

Shea embarked on this crusade as much to take the weight off of George McLaughlin's shoulder and bring him redemption, as for the citizens crushed by the loss of the two teams.

"I'm sure my father was upset that George was as hurt as much as he was about the Dodgers being gone," said Kathy. "My father was a very strong relationship man. If you were his friend, his attitude was: 'If we need to stand in the middle of the firing squad together, we will.' He meant it. 'If you go down, I go down.' "

And McLaughlin felt that by offering O'Malley a piece of the Dodgers, he had failed the city by handing "Judas" O'Malley the opening to exit New York. And so Shea felt a strong obligation to McLaughlin to succeed in his unlikely quest. And so, the committee's first mandate was to try to attract another National League team to move to New York—any way that it could.

Kevin McGrath, who was hired by Shea as an associate in his law firm in 1960, recalled how Robert Wagner got the ball rolling.

Kevin McGrath: "Robert Wagner was a mayor who ruled by committee. If there was a water crisis or some other problem, he would appoint a committee and get the best people who were qualified to handle the situation.

"When the Dodgers and Giants left, Mayor Wagner appointed Bill Shea, Barnard Gimble, Jim Farley, and Clinton W. Blume. Blume put together the parcel west of Rockefeller Center. Clint hired strawmen to buy properties west of Sixth Avenue; walk-ups, where there were a lot of Chinese restaurants. The straws then signed over the deeds to the developer. Nobody knew, but the developer was Rockefeller Center, which was expanding.

"Clint was not a guy who stood at a bar and told you how important he was. Blume was a rough, tough guy. He had been a ballplayer, an athlete.

"William A. Shea also was an athlete. He played a number of sports, once owned a football team out in Long Island, and he was a young and very vibrant young man in 1960."

One of the first tactical moves Bill Shea made was to call as many sports reporters as he could summon.

Kevin McGrath: "Mr. Shea had a very, very powerful ally, the New York press. I don't think there was a dissenter among them. The commissioner of baseball, for whatever shortsighted reason, did not want a National League baseball team in New York, and the reporters were furious.

"We had the *Trib*, the *Mirror*, the *Times*, the *News*, the *Herald Tribune*, the *Journal American*, the *World Telegram*, and *Sun*, and *Newsday*. We had Red Smith, Dan Parker, Dick Young, Jack Lang, and they were outraged by the National League not having a baseball team. With the help of the press, these men went about trying to get a [New York] baseball team. So Wagner must get credit for putting these people together."

At the beginning, says McGrath, no one gave Wagner's committee much chance of succeeding. "They were thought by major league baseball to be three clowns, one on canes and two lunatics," he says.

Jack Lang, who was working for *The Long Island Press* at the time, recalled the start of Bill Shea's long journey to bring National League baseball back to New York.

William A. Shea

Jack Lang: "As soon as the Dodgers and Giants left, Mayor Robert Wagner formed a committee to try to bring National League baseball back to New York. Wagner knew Bill Shea was a powerful Democratic supporter. He was very big in Tammany Hall with the politicians, and Wagner knew he was a dyed-in-the-wool New Yorker, baseball fan, and go-getter. There were other people on the committee, but the workhorse, the guy who did all the work, was Bill Shea.

"Shea kept me up on what he was doing. He was the most cooperative guy going. I had known Bill from years earlier when I was with the *Long Island Press*. He was a sportsman who lived in Port Washington, played basketball at George Washington High School and down at Georgetown. In 1948 he bought the Long Island Indians, a football team in the American Football League, They were a farm club for the Boston Yanks, an NFL team at the time, which was owned by Kate Smith. In the league with the Indians were Scranton, Pennsylvania; Lynn, Massachusetts; and Jersey City, the best team in the league. And I covered the Indians and got to know Bill then.

"So as soon as Bill was appointed to the Wagner committee, he got in touch with Dick Young of the *Daily News*, Barney Kremenko of the *Journal American*, and myself because he wanted to contact as many newspapermen as he could.

"We were very supportive of his efforts and wrote about them. Bill felt sure he had the Cincinnati Reds coming to New York. He really thought they were going to transfer the Reds here. And there was also some talk of the Pittsburgh Pirates moving to New York."

But even for a man as capable as Bill Shea, getting an existing franchise to pull up stakes and move to New York would not be easy. In 1958 there were eight National League franchises. Subtracting the Dodgers and Giants, that left six, and neither the St. Louis Cardinals nor the Philadelphia Phillies were going anywhere, because they had benefited from the departure of the American League Browns and A's. The Braves, league leaders in attendance and themselves transplants from Boston, were happy where they were, and the Chicago Cubs were fixtures in beautiful Wrigley Field.

That left the Cincinnati Reds and Pittsburgh Pirates. Neither owner had the lack of heart to do what O'Malley and Horace Stoneham had done. History and the passion of their fans made them both turn Shea down. He then made a proposition to the Phillies. They, too, said no way.

When no established major league team would agree to come to New

York, Shea embarked on a far grander but equally unlikely plan to push the baseball owners into a corner and twist their arms into giving New York City a National League franchise.

First he tried asking Major League Baseball for an expansion franchise. Though there were only eight teams in each of the two leagues, and at least a half dozen cities clamoring for major league baseball, every effort to force Major League Baseball to expand was met with a rebuff. Shea himself had called the men running Major League Baseball but had gotten no encouragement from the National League that it intended to return to New York.

Shea's scheme involved attempting the impossible—he intended to construct a whole new baseball league from scratch, enrolling franchises in large cities that didn't have a major league presence. He was counting on his new league putting the baseball owners in an untenable position: if organized baseball tried to crush the upstart league, Congress might lose its temper and take away baseball's sacred anti-trust exemption. But, if it chose to tread lightly, then the new league might succeed, and its impact on baseball's profits would be considerable.

This was Bill Shea's brilliant but elaborate plan. But Shea knew he needed someone inside baseball to help him, and so he went to McLaughlin for advice. McLaughlin suggested he contact Branch Rickey, who had written a magazine article saying that the best interests of the existing franchises would be served if baseball expanded and made the game truly national. Shea knew Rickey from the days when he ran the Dodgers, and when the two met, they agreed on the strategy to build a third baseball league, which they called the Continental League.

If a baseball executive had the Midas touch, it was the cigar-smoking, bible-quoting Mr. Rickey. With Rickey behind him, Shea's credibility was quickly established.

When Shea and Rickey went to Major League Baseball commissioner Ford Frick to ask for an expansion franchise, National League president Warren Giles informed them that there was no interest among the current owners to expand to New York.

"We don't need New York," was the message sent back.

Undeterred, Bill Shea began the time-consuming job of lining up political support to overturn baseball's long-held exemption to the Clayton Anti-Trust Act. Under that ruling, which the Supreme Court upheld in a lawsuit against Major League Baseball in 1922, baseball was not involved in interstate commerce and hence did not fall under federal jurisdiction. It was an idiotic ruling that had since gone virtually unchallenged. Once, in 1949 former Giant outfielder Danny Gardella sought to sue baseball after he had been banned for life for playing in the defunct Mexican League, but baseball offered him a $40,000 payoff to drop the suit, and needing the money badly, he accepted.

Bill Shea determined that if he could prove that Major League Baseball held an unfair monopoly, he could get baseball's anti-trust exemption lifted. To do that, Shea enlisted the aid of his powerful friends in Washington.

Kevin McGrath: "Bill Shea looked to senators and congressmen from states that didn't have teams. He became allies with the most powerful people at that time in Congress, Lyndon Baines Johnson and Sam Rayburn, who were from Texas. No baseball team there. He made allies with men from Washington D.C. No baseball team. From Florida, no baseball team.

"If you follow the powers of Congress, the cities he went after were places that didn't have organized baseball: Minnesota, Dallas/Fort Worth, Houston, Atlanta. Shea knew if they put teams in those towns, they would get the politicians to back him.

"He spoke about taking away from baseball the protection of the Clayton Anti-Trust Act. And on his side he not only had very, very powerful people, but he had Branch Rickey, a well-known baseball figure; the man who had done the impossible because he had brought a black player into baseball.

"They were well-received in Washington, and Shea and Rickey decided that the only way they could challenge the Clayton Anti-Trust law was to start their own league.

"Shea went out and gathered powerful people as owners of the Continental League franchises. In Washington he was backed by Edward Bennett Williams. In New York he got Joan Payson. He got Jack Kent Cooke to head the Toronto franchise. Bill had a long-standing relationship with Jack Kent Cooke, who was a Canadian. Bill ultimately got him his United States citizenship by getting a private bill passed for him.

"Their aim was to bring baseball back to New York. And this was the method. There was a method to their madness. This was all well planned out."

In addition to Williams and Cooke, Shea enrolled Bob Howsam, who would later become the general manager of the Cincinnati Reds, to agree to own the Denver franchise. Howsam's father-in-law was Colorado senator E. C. Johnson.

Amon Carter, one of the wealthiest men in Texas, agreed to own the Dallas/Fort Worth franchise. Wheelock Whitney headed a group in Minneapolis/St. Paul. Reggie Taylor owned the Buffalo franchise. Oil heir Craig Cullinan, who had offered $6 million to get the Cleveland Indians to relocate to Houston, owned the Houston team.

Houston and Atlanta were among the other Continental League franchises scheduled to open for business in 1959 or 1960. In addition, Shea and Rickey lined up investors for teams in New Orleans, Miami, Indianapolis, San Diego, Portland, Seattle, and San Juan, Puerto Rico.

In looking for investors for his New York franchise Shea turned to Dwight F. "Pete" Davis, a wealthy Long Island sportsman who was the son of the man who created the international Davis Cup competition in tennis. Davis agreed to invest, and he suggested that heiress Joan Whitney Payson, an immensely wealthy ex–New York Giants fan, be approached.

When Davis sought to interest Mrs. Payson, however, she at first declined, saying she didn't want to be involved in a second-rate baseball league. Rickey then flew down to Florida to confide in her that he and Shea were intending to use the Continental League as a sledgehammer to get the National League to expand to New York and that if they were successful she would become the owner of the New York National League franchise. Impressed, she quickly changed her mind.

Davis and Mrs. Payson were joined by Dorothy Killiam, a wealthy Canadian sportswoman (and a rabid Brooklyn Dodgers fan who had attended several Dodgers World Series games traveling in her own private railroad car), G. Herbert Walker, nephew of Connecticut senator Prescott Bush, and William Simpson.

When Mrs. Killiam made it clear that she wanted to run the franchise, Mrs. Payson and Pete Davis bought her out. Mrs. Payson then bought out Davis. Having spent $4 million the once-reluctant Joan Payson now owned an 80 percent interest in the nascent franchise. M. Donald Grant, her personal stockbroker, and Herbert Walker held the other twenty percent.

To prove to Congress that Major League Baseball held a monopoly in violation of the anti-trust laws, Shea and Rickey announced their intention to sign current major leaguers for their new teams. The effort, as they knew it would, proved fruitless.

★ ★ ★

Kevin McGrath: "They were only successful in getting one major league baseball player to sign, an infielder.

"They then went back to Washington, and told the congressmen, 'The reason we couldn't sign anyone was that Major League Baseball owners were not allowing them to sign.'

"And they built some credibility."

During the summer of 1960, the major league owners were unsure whether Shea and Rickey would be able to get their new league off the ground, but at the same time they were concerned that if they succeeded, the competition from the new league would cost them dearly in both players and large sums of money. Equally important, they feared the loss of baseball's anti-trust exemption. With Lyndon Johnson, Sam Rayburn, and other powerful congressmen lined up against them, and standing aside Shea and Rickey, baseball's moguls decided that the least painful and expensive tactic would be to give in to Shea's demands.

On August 17, 1960, four years after Mayor Wagner appointed Bill Shea to head his committee, the baseball owners met with Branch Rickey at the Conrad Hilton Hotel in Chicago, and agreed to add the Denver and Minneapolis Continental League clubs to the American League in 1961 and the New York and Houston Continental League clubs to the National League in 1962.

Kevin McGrath: "Faced with the tremendous adverse publicity of the Congress and the New York media, organized baseball decided to throw Shea a bone, and they threw it in the form of an expansion team, but they couldn't just throw a bone to New York, because Washington was all over them like a blanket, so they offered a franchise to Denver and Minneapolis, and also to Houston."

Jack Lang: "The American League owners didn't live up to their promise. They immediately jumped into Minnesota by transferring the Washington Senators there, so that eliminated the Minnesota Continental League people, and they gave the other franchise to Gene Autry in Los Angeles, and they became the Angels. That was proof enough you couldn't trust the baseball owners.

"But the National League remained true to its promise, and they took the Houston and New York Continental League franchises in '62."

After years of constant travel and gruelling hard work Bill Shea had accomplished what had looked like an impossible feat. He had brought National League baseball back to New York. Former Giant and Dodger fans were grateful to him and overjoyed.

Stan Isaacs: "I really liked Bill Shea. He seemed like a fan, and he *was* a fan, and I admired him for pulling it off. Branch Rickey was just as important. He knew the ins and outs, and he was shrewd. And Mrs. Payson had been a Giants fan.

"It had seemed outrageous that Warren Giles, the National League president, had said, 'We don't really need a team in New York.' It's no wonder Warren Giles was called 'Walter O'Malley's dancing bear.' We felt New York was a National League town, and as a citizen of New York it was a delight to have a National League team come back here. I felt that way, one, as a working journalist, and two, as a New Yorker."

But getting the new National League baseball team was only part of what Bill Shea did for the city. Shea also was the prime mover behind getting Harry Wismer the New York Titan franchise in the American Football League. The Titans first played at the Polo Grounds and later at Shea Stadium, where the name of the team was changed to the Jets. Wismer recalled Shea's role.

Harry Wismer: "Bill had once run a minor–league football franchise, the Long Island Indians, which had folded. He was the attorney for the NFL team owned by Ted Collins that was known variously as the Boston Yanks, New York Bulldogs, and New York Yanks. Collins dropped about $600,000 before calling it quits.

"Shea and I finally got together to discuss football at the Sands Point Country Club on Long Island. He noted that [George V.] McLaughlin and I were good friends, and that he and McLaughlin were good friends, and said he hoped we could work together with me heading a new football club in New York City. Shea named Lamar Hunt as his contact and inquired whether he could have Hunt look me up.

"Shea emphasized that a football as well as a baseball tenant was necessary to attract investors and financial support from the city, a war cry I soon began to know by heart. He advised me to start lining up important people. 'If you can't,' he continued, 'the mayor [Wagner], McLaughlin, and I, and other people in the community will come up with something. We know that it will take a lot to make it go.'"

Wismer, thanks to Shea, ended up owning the Titans franchise. And after that was accomplished Bill Shea helped bring in new basketball and hockey teams, the American Basketball Association New York Nets (later joining the NBA as the expansion team in New Jersey), and New York Islanders to Long Island's Nassau Coliseum.

Bernie Fishman: "Shea was the one who got the Nets and Islanders for Long Island. I was at the finance committee meeting [of the National Hockey League] as an alternative for Shea, voting to expand to give that franchise to the Islanders. Shea had said to the then county executive, a fellow by the name of Ralph Caso, 'If you will build a stadiumn [the Nassau Coliseum], I will get you the franchise.' And Bill delivered. Sure they had to pay for it, but it was a reasonable amount. It was before the craziness came to the sports teams."

When it came time to name the new stadium in Queens, Tom Deegan, who was the public relations head of the Triborough Bridge and Tunnel Authority, directed a campaign blitz to name it after Bill Shea. Thousands of letters flooded into Mayor Wagner's office recommending the new stadium be named for Bill Shea.

Kevin McGrath: "In 1963 Madison Avenue was still two ways. It was a smaller city if you compare it to today. There were some powerful movers and shakers, and the interlocking relationships were meaningful, so when you talk about reaching out to Brooklyn or to the Bronx, there were certain people you *had* to reach for, and you didn't have to reach very far.

"One of them was Tom Deegan, who was the public relations director for the Triborough Bridge and Tunnel Authority. In 1963 it was time to name the stadium, and Mr. Deegan came to Mr. Shea and said, 'The stadium should be named after you.' Mr. Shea said it was a terrible idea.

"Nevertheless, Mr. Deegan started a campaign blitz with penny postcards and letters to the mayor and others. He was the one who put the germ of the idea in the mayor's mind and Mr. Shea's mind, and he had the receptive ear of Mayor Wagner, and he was able to convince Wagner that there was this ground swell of support for placing Mr. Shea's name on the stadium.

"Mr. Shea really didn't want the stadium named after himself. He surely did not encourage Mr. Deegan at first. I don't even know whether Mr. Shea even thought Mr. Deegan was serious. There had never been a stadium named after a living person. So Mr. Shea was the first."

The question that begs to be answered is: who initiated Mr. Deegan's campaign? It wasn't Robert Moses, the head of the Triborough Bridge and Tunnel Authority. Moses, more than anyone, liked to have buildings and parks named after himself. But one of the commissioners of the Triborough Bridge and Tunnel Authority surely had felt most responsible for the Brooklyn Dodgers leaving town and was among the most grateful of men for what Bill Shea had done to rectify that: George V. McLaughlin.

For the rest of their lives, the two men remained close.

Kevin McGrath: "In later years Mr. McLaughlin was counsel to our firm. They were very good friends until Mr. McLaughlin died. Every morning Mr. McLaughlin would come into the office. He had an office next to Mr. Shea, and Mr. Shea made sure his office was as big as Mr. Shea's. When Mr. McLaughlin died, we divided that space into two offices, but while he was alive, Mr. Shea took care of Mr. McLaughlin in the respect that he always spoke very highly of him, and he admired him, and he was a true son."

Kathy Shea Alfuso: "I suppose it could have been George McLaughlin who spearheaded the campaign, but no one will really know, because things were done that way in those days. That was part of why my dad and Mr. McLaughlin got along so well. Neither wanted people to know all the things they were doing. They were very happy to be in the background, where they'd be more effective.

"When they first approached dad about naming the stadium after him, he said, 'You don't name things after people who are alive. What are you trying to do, kill me? Do I have to die first?'

"So [for him] it was like being dragged kicking and screaming to the front. And he was the very best person to name it after, because he really did the work. Bringing a team back to New York was a real unknown entity, and to rally people who could pull it off. . . . My dad had worked five to seven years for no pay, did it for the love of the sport, because he *really* loved the sport. Home was very important to him, but he was away a lot. He never traveled like he did during that period.

"So he was the first living person to have a building named after him. After a while it was, 'If you really want to do this . . . well, I'm really uncomfortable with it, but I really loved what I did, I loved the job, and you know, it wouldn't be bad for business.'

"I worked for a TV production company in Manhattan when I was eighteen, and I remember riding the train with dad, and we were going past the stadium, and we heard someone in the seat in front of us say, 'Who was this guy Shea?' And the other one said, 'I think he was a general in the first world war.' They came out with this antique man, dead and gone, and dad was sitting right behind them laughing hysterically saying, 'Listen to this.'"

"Dad was still dad. Having the stadium named after him didn't change him. My dad and mom never purported themselves to be any more than they were, or even what they were. My mom hated the social scene, refused to take part in it. She had lived it as a child, and she refused to get back into it.

"As a child I had no clue we were affluent. Every day my dad drove a Nash Rambler from the house to the train station. He loved his little Rambler, a little, square, ugly box. He was the president of the golf club, and he tootled off in it to play. That was the way they were. It wasn't important to try to impress people, even though dad was an advisor to presidents.

"Dad worked a lot with Lyndon Johnson. We went to dinner at the White House during Johnson's time.

"He stayed with the Democratic Party even when there was a major shift in the party in the mid-1970s morally and ethically, but he had friends on both sides. He wasn't limited.

"He was very close to George Bush, [Sr.], respected him, had known him for years. When my dad was ill, George Bush was president, and he would write dad notes. He wrote my dad a note on Easter morning that said, 'I'm thinking of you, my dear friend.'

"My dad was also friendly with Ronald Reagan.

"It was only after I went away to college that I would look in the newspapers and see all these people I knew that it dawned on me that no one else knew the presidents, world leaders, and heads of corporations."

★ ★ ★

The public will remember Bill Shea for his role in bringing various sports teams to New York, but the men who worked with him remember him most for his wise counsel and his humanity.

Kevin McGrath: "When I first met Mr. Shea in 1960, he had a law firm of fourteen men. It was called Manning, Hollinger, and Shea. Manning, who died in 1959, was a former FBI agent, and Hollinger had been a former assistant U.S. District Attorney in the southern district of New York. We represented the Catholic church. We represented the Yankees, the Jets, all sorts of banks, a bank at Bedford and DeKalb called the Brooklyn Savings Bank; we represented Security National Bank, a very big bank out on Long Island.

"I had gone to Fordham Law School. There were hard times. I went to work with him at $4,000 a year. My wife was making $4,800 as a teacher.

"They were making $7,000 a year in law firms down on Wall Street, but by the time I finished my first year I had made more than $8,000, because he shared the profits of the law firm with the associates as well as the partners, something nobody else did. Mr. Shea was what we called the 'savings bank for associates.'

"Our salary was modest, but he gave us two bonuses a year. This was very unusual. He said, 'Young men, I could give you another hundred dollars a week, and you'd get $5,000 more a year. But you'll spend that. If I give you $5,000 in bonuses, you can buy a car or put down a down payment on a house. This way it's forced savings, and if we do well, you'll do well.'

"He encouraged us to get clients, 'because,' he'd say, 'there is nothing sadder than a forty-year-old lawyer without a client.' He encouraged us and gave us financial rewards if we got clients.

"And when we were fourteen lawyers, we would meet once a year for dinner—no wives, no secretaries—just the lawyers. And we would talk about the future. He encouraged everyone to have lunch with each other once a week, so he built this true partnership. He also said, 'You shouldn't socialize with each other, because you can't get any business when you do that. Go out and socialize.' Everything he did was for the betterment of other people. He was not a selfish person by any stretch of the imagination.

"He was always available to you. He said, 'Putting together a law firm is just like a baseball team. You can't have four first basemen. You can't have a left-handed shortstop.' There are givens on a baseball team, and there are givens in a law firm. You can't have too many specialists who will hang around and not do any work. And if we needed something, a tax man, we got it. He put it together like a baseball team. What he was really saying was, There is a method to building an organization.

"While I was with him, our law firm never made less money the following year than we did prior, and he budgeted that way.

"He built the firm one step at a time, until the firm ultimately grew to 450 lawyers.

"I'll tell you a story about Mr. Shea. We were at 41 East 42nd Street, and he came in after lunch one day, and there was a woman running down the hall toward the ladies room, and she was crying. He went into his office and said to his secretary, Miss Cowan, 'There's a lady who just ran into the ladies room and she's crying. Would you please go in and find out why she's crying?'

"So Miss Cowan got up and went in and spoke to the woman, and she came back and said, 'She's crying because the senior associate was very rough on her. He was complaining about her work, and was verbally abusive to her.'

"I know who it was, because he told me the story, so I'm not going to mention his name. But Mr. Shea sat there for a few moments, and he called Miss Cowan back and told her to get the associate and bring him in.

"She brought him to his office, and he sat there a while while Mr. Shea was on the phone, and when he was finally finished—this man was sitting in front of him quite some time because Mr. Shea used the phone quite often—he said, 'You went to Harvard, didn't you?' And the associate said, 'Yes.' And Mr. Shea said, 'And you graduated quite high in your class, right?' And he said yes. And Mr. Shea called him by his first name, and said, 'If I needed to get a person who graduated higher in your Harvard class, all I would have to do is offer him more money, and I would get that person.' The guy looked at him like he was crazy. And Mr. Shea said, 'But you know, it's really hard to get good secretaries. No matter what I pay them, I can't get good secretaries. They have to want to work here. They can work anywhere in the city. Secretaries can get jobs any place.' And then he looked at the man and said, 'So the next time you make a secretary cry, you will be looking for another job.'

"Mr. Shea was a wonderful man. He was a generous, good person. He never forgot his faith. He was a Catholic and made no bones about it. He went to church every Sunday. He made no apologies for it. And yet, he was as comfortable with a rabbi as he was with a priest, and he was friendly with many, many, many, people of all faiths. He didn't care what you were. Nothing bothered him. He was a true New Yorker."

Judd Gould, the son of Shea's late law partner, Milton Gould, recalled Bill Shea fondly.

Judd Gould: "There's an ironic twist to Bill Shea. I couldn't understand most of what he said. Bill Shea talked in 'dos' and 'dees,' a 'ting der with a guy der with da red shirt.' You could be sitting in his office and he would yell out to his secretary, 'Get what's his name on the phone.' And I'd wonder, 'Who is he talking about?' And she would come back and say, 'What's his name ain't dere.' And I thought, 'Who's what's his name?' It was like an Abbott and Costello routine.

"This man had daily conversations with Jack Kent Cooke, who was not formally an educated man, was as literate as anybody, and as particular about the English language as anyone, and you would hear this conversation with split infinitives and dangling particables, and Cooke would overlook it, because he and Shea loved each other, they really did. They absolutely were in step with each other. And Cooke is woven into the Bill Shea story."

Bernie Fishman: "One client who would have filled you with stories, but he's gone, was Jack Kent Cooke. Bill and Jack were incredibly close, and Bill guided Cooke in his career because Cooke didn't know anything about sports, and Cooke wound up owning the [L.A.] Lakers, the [L.A.] Kings, and the Washington Redskins, and it was Bill Shea's guidance that took him where he went.

"Bill and Cooke and Edward Bennett Williams bought the Redskins from George Preston Marshall, and then Bill turned over his share at cost to Cooke.

"All I can tell you is that Cooke's praise of Shea was unlimited, and it was deserved.

"Bill was every bit a first-rate lawyer. Again and again clients came to Bill for his legal acumen. Sure he knew the judges, but they had a sense of his judgment. But Bill Shea had the reputation of being something else, a political operative and fixer, so to speak. I will dispel that.

"Every Monday by late morning every lawyer in our firm who had a case, who had anything of interest in Barron's or any of the other financial publications affecting his case, would find an article torn out, circled in pencil, with an illegible scrawl on it. Bill knew every case that was in the office, and he had a lawyer's instinct. Milton Gould, his partner, liked to belittle Shea's legal talent, which was absolutely unfair to Shea. Shea was a first-rate lawyer, and it's a great injustice when people refer to him as a politico.

"I can remember one day on a Friday Bill Shea met with Mayor Abe Beame, and Beame said to Shea, 'Listen, the Jets are threatening to hold a press conference on Monday at one o'clock to announce they are leaving Shea Stadium to play in the Meadowlands. Is there anything I can do about it?'

"Shea called me from the mayor's office to tell me this. Bill said to me, 'The city should sue for specific performance.' I said, 'Bill, a landlord can't get specific performance against a tenant.' A tenant sues for specific performance against a landlord, but no one ever heard of it being used by a landlord against a tenant. I told him, 'That's crazy.'

"At this point Bill said to me, 'Listen, there was a case in New Jersey where the anchor tenant of a shopping center was threatening to move. The owner of the shopping center went to court for specific performance and was successful in getting an injunction because if the anchor store moved, all the little stores would get killed.'

"It's the little stores from whom the shopping center developer really gets his money. The anchor carries itself, but the real money from a shopping center comes from the small stores.

"So Bill said, 'Find that case and call me back. I'll wait here in the mayor's office.' This was at the point where I had just finished telling him he was crazy and that he didn't know the law on this. Guess what? Not only did we find the case, but we found it had been cited by the Massachusetts Supreme Court, that in certain cases a landlord indeed could get specific performance, and so we reported back to Bill and the mayor. The theory that Bill was relying on essentially was that the hotels and restaurants and theaters were heavily dependent on people coming to the Jets games.

"The mayor said to me, 'Get out an order to show cause restraining them from announcing that they are leaving, and we'll present it on Monday.'

"We did that, and we got an order to show cause, and by a quarter to twelve on Monday they had called off their press conference and agreed to play out the balance of the term at Shea Stadium."

★ ★ ★

Even more than his political and legal skills it was Bill Shea's kindness and generosity of spirit that impressed his friends. His wife Nori also helped people on a smaller scale. If she read an article in the paper that a family lost its home in a fire and the children were left homeless, she would write them a letter and send them a check. If a friend or acquaintance became ill, she would drop glass jars of soup off at their doorstep.

Bill Shea also raised money for people in need but on a much larger scale. He raised millions of dollars for Catholic Charities and the Little League program in Harlem. He helped raise $300,000 alone to build a new ball field. The field is named after him.

When high school sports was dropped from the curriculum in Brooklyn, Shea was very supportive of the effort to raise money to fund those programs and get them back into the curriculum.

"He did all these things, but he never wanted people to know," said Kevin McGrath. "He never wanted to have anything written about him."

Arthur Richman was a columnist for the *New York Daily Mirror* when he first met Bill Shea, and Bernie Fishman was Shea's law partner. Both came to admire and cherish the man.

Arthur Richman: "Bill Shea was one of the finest gentlemen I ever met in my life. I loved him. It was such a tribute when they named the stadium after him. You couldn't meet a better guy. He was very strong in the church, very strong in the government. He had a lot of friends all over the country.

"He had a wonderful personality, and he took an interest in you. Just because he had a big name didn't mean he didn't care about you. He was good that way. I loved him very much."

Bernie Fishman: "Shortly after Shea Stadium opened, one of the nuns from a Catholic school in Queens called Bill Shea and asked if he would be good enough to contribute tickets for the students so they could attend Shea Stadium in the month of June. Of course, Bill said yes.

"Word spread among the other educational and [charitable] residential facilities. They all thought Bill owned the stadium, and one after another they used to call, and he would say yes, and he would buy tickets and give them away. This was in the early stages, and it wasn't a big, big deal.

"At a certain point he told one of the nuns he knew that he would only give her tickets on condition that each child who went to Shea Stadium be given two dollars in an envelope to buy food. He told the nun he remembered as a kid sneaking into Ebbets Field and seeing everyone eating hot dogs and other food and not having money himself to eat. He told her, 'There is nothing worse for a kid to attend a game and not be able to partake in the refreshments.' Bill told her he would donate the two dollars as well as the tickets for each child.

"The nun said, 'We will not let these kids eat this junk. That's the worst food in the world. The hot dogs and the Cracker Jacks will make them sick.' Bill said, 'Even if they get sick, that's part of the experience. If they can't eat, I won't contribute the tickets. I will not subject these kids to the feeling of being treated unequally.'

"And they had a stand-off. The nun wouldn't take the tickets, and Bill wouldn't give them except on his condition that they be able to eat what they wanted. She tried to negotiate specific foods, but Bill said, 'No, you gotta be able to choose your own.'

"Finally, the nun yielded, and so it became a tradition that each organization would get tickets and one of Bill Shea's checks that kept increasing as inflation crept along, until he was paying four dollars for each kid. It was all coming out of his pocket, the money for the food and the price of the tickets.

"And it became so automatic that the requests would go through his secretary Joan Cowan without even being cleared by him. But if a new organization called and asked for tickets, sometimes she would check out the organization.

"One day she called one of Bill's law partners to ask about a particular organization. It was a residential facility for retarded children. The partner checked it out and found it to be legitimate, and he said to her, 'They're a good group. Since it's mental retardation, I would like to share in the mitzvah,' which means joy in Yiddish. 'I will pay one half of the cash going to this group.'

"Joan said that Bill was out of town and she couldn't do that without his permission. The partner told her, 'I will guarantee you that you will not be subject to criticism for letting me underwrite this.'

"She agreed, and the partner sent a check for half the amount.

"Bill came back to the office, and she told him the story. Bill went over to the partner and he said, 'Ya shouldn'tna done it. You took away half of my mitzvah.'

"There are a hundred little stories that add up to the guy. For example, when he had his stroke that eventually led to his death years later, he was getting flowers delivered to the Rusk Institute in such abundance that first they filled the hospital room, and then the corridors, and then the lobby.

"The Rusk Institute has a policy not to give anyone a private room. They have four or five patients to a room. It's part of the theraputic mileau, and Bill was embarrassed because around his bed were all these flowers. So he said to his daughter Kathy, 'Take my credit card in the drawer next to my bed, go out, and I want you to send flowers to each of the people in this room.'

"Kathy said to him, 'Dad, I will go outside, and I will readdress the cards on some of these flowers. The place is flooded with flowers, and I will send each of the people in the room one of the beautiful bouquets that are out-side.'

"Bill Shea said to her, 'I don't give second-hand flowers.'

"Now you tell me if this isn't a person of character."

nine

Mrs. Payson Hires George Weiss

Joan Whitney Payson, who was born in 1903, had attended New York Giants games since childhood when her mother, Helen Hay Whitney, wife of Payne Whitney, the third richest man in America, took her to the Polo Grounds to watch her heroes, Bill Terry and Mel Ott. After suffering through fifteen years of desultory baseball, her interest heightened after Leo Durocher took over the team in 1948. By 1950 her children were grown and she was seeking a hobby, and so she purchased a single share of stock in the team. After Bobby Thomson homered off Ralph Branca to win the pennant in 1951, a moment she once described as "a highlight of my life," she kept buying shares until she owned 10 percent of the franchise.

When in 1957 the Giants board of directors voted on whether to leave for the Coast, Mrs. Payson cast the lone no vote. After Mrs. Payson offered to buy the team from Horace Stoneham in order to keep it in New York and Stoneham turned her down, she bitterly sold her interest. Mrs. Payton returned to a life of going from her Gold Coast Long Island home to the races at Saratoga during the summer and sitting on her veranda at her estate in Jupiter Island, Florida, in the winter.

When Bill Shea and Branch Rickey inquired who might best become owner of their New York Continental League franchise, Joan Payson was on the short list. She certainly had plenty of money. Mrs. Payson had inherited millions of dollars in 1927 when her father died. At the turn of the twentieth century papa Payne had owned 600 acres in Manhasset,

Long Island, and the home on which it stood was described as "unarguably one of the grandest residences in America."

Mrs. Payson was part of a group that one could properly describe as "American royalty." She was the sister of John Hay "Jock" Whitney, the former ambassador to the Court of St. James in England, and the owner of the *New York Herald Tribune*. Whitney also owned Greentree Stables whose prize racehorses every year ran for top stakes. Mrs. Payson's sister Barbara, who was a known beauty, married William Paley, the chairman of the board of CBS.

Charles Shipman Payson, her husband, had wealth of his own. He was a member of the wealthy Harriman clan and a close friend of Prescott Bush. In 1948 Payson organized a uranium refinery, and later he was chairman of a company that made parts for submarine-launched ballistic missiles and equipment for torpedo guidance.

Herb Walker, one of the original investors of the Mets, had helped get Charles Payson into the oil business. Walker was a close associate of his nephew, and Prescott's son, George Bush.

Mrs. Payson had been thwarted in her attempt to buy the Giants, but just five years later, she would own its successor. She wanted to call the team the Meadowlarks, a reference to the rolling meadows adjacent to the proposed ballpark being built in Queens. There were Orioles in Baltimore, Cardinals in St. Louis, and later there would be Blue Jays in Toronto. But Mrs. Payson, choosing not to wield her power, let the team hold a contest. Meadowlarks was one of the choices. So were Continentals, Skyliners, Jets, Burros, Skyscrapers, Rebels NYBs, Avengers, and Mets. The official name of the corporation had always been the New York Metropolitan Baseball Club, Inc. Dan Parker, the sports editor and columnist for the *New York Mirror*, had been calling the team "the Mets" from the beginning. So it was really no surprise when Mrs. Payson acted like she was pulling the name out of a hat and announced, "I like this one. The Mets."

"Okay," someone in the audience responded, "Let's go Mets."

The Mets needed someone to run the baseball operations. He would have to hire a manager, scouts, and a whole staff of ticket sellers, ushers, groundskeepers, and so on. Players would have to be selected from a pool of National League rejects.

Bill Shea suggested to Mrs. Payson that Branch Rickey be named the first general manager. Mrs. Payson was aware of Rickey's expertise—his St. Louis Cards and then his Brooklyn Dodgers had thumped her Giants year after year—and she was enthusiastic about the idea, until Rickey presented his terms: at 80 years of age he was far past retirement age. For him to take the job he asked for the moon: a $5 million budget and complete control of the team. Mrs. Payson declined, and she named her personal Wall Street stockbroker, M. Donald Grant, as president. Rickey chose Charles Hurth, his nephew who once ran Rickey's New Orleans franchise and later became president of the Southern Association, as the new team's general manager.

Charles Hurth III: "My grandfather was involved in the family business in Portsmith, Ohio, where Branch came from. They ran a hotel called the Hurth Hotel. After the Depression pounded the hotel, my grandfather went to New Orleans to work for Uncle Branch's New Orleans Pelicans. Eventually he became president of the Southern Association, which he enjoyed mightily. The fifties were the heyday of minor league baseball. After twenty-five years my grandfather moved to Manhattan to run the Mets.

"One thing my family talks about is that my grandfather took great pleasure in the fact that he talked Mr. Shea into adding a significant number of ladies' rest room facilities, more than Mr. Shea had wanted to put into that stadium. Because my grandfather had had some experience with that in other ballparks. Mr. Shea was trying to shave pennies off the deal. My grandfather told him, 'Listen, you have to let the ladies tinkle.'"

The name Charles Hurth is little-known, because on Oct. 17, 1960, one day after the National League awarded Mrs. Payson a franchise, the crosstown New York Yankees shocked the baseball world by firing its legendary manager, Casey Stengel, winner of ten pennants in twelve seasons, and two weeks later dropped the other shoe when they fired its dynasty-builder, George Weiss. Through M. Donald Grant, Mrs. Payson quickly offered the general manager's job to Weiss, putting Charles Hurth out of a job.

Weiss, whose entire life was baseball, eagerly accepted.

Jack Lang: "George Weiss was a great organizer. He had run the Yankee farm system for years, had developed all those great players and then took over as general manager of the Yankees and had good teams there for years. He always had money behind him.

"He put together a quick organization with the Mets. He hired good people. He had Johnny Murphy as an assistant. Look at his scouting staff. The first year he had Rogers Hornsby, Red Ruffing, Cookie Lavagetto, and Solly Hemus."

George Weiss was a Yalie from New Haven who possessed a brilliant business mind, and though he was low-key, had a flair for promotion. As a collegiate at the turn of the twentieth century, he fielded a team of semi-pro players who had played for his high school and had been outstanding. Joe Dugan, later a New York Yankee, and Chick Bowen, later a New York Giant, were members of the team, and Weiss scheduled major league and ex-pro opponents. His team drew more fans than the established New Haven team in the Eastern League.

Before he could graduate from Yale, his father died, and Weiss quit school to run the family grocery store. Weiss supported his mother, a brother, and a sister while continuing to manage his team. In 1920 the Eastern League club offered to let Weiss purchase it, and he sold the store and bought the franchise, shrewdly buying players and selling them to major league teams for large profits. That year Weiss conducted his first business with Yankee general manager Ed Barrow, booking the Yankees to play his team in an exhibition game. But when newly acquired attraction Babe Ruth was a no-show, Weiss refused to pay Barrow his guarantee. When Barrow ran to baseball commissioner Kennesaw Landis, the judge backed Weiss. Barrow was outraged.

In 1929 Weiss was hired to be the general manager of Baltimore in the International League, the top minor league. At Baltimore he continued to build his reputation as a shrewd operator. It was said that Weiss could squeeze a nickel so tightly that the ass of the buffalo on the coin had a permanent crease in it. It was this quality above all others that Ed Barrow admired about him.

In 1932 Barrow brought Weiss into the Yankee organization. Yankee owner Jacob Ruppert spent more than half a million dollars luring the best players from the Boston Red Sox in the 1920s, but by the '30s, in the depths of the Depression, purchasing players outright was becoming uneconomical. Ruppert had spent $35,000 for minor leaguers Lyn Lary and Jimmy Reese, neither one a sensation, spent $35,000 for Jim Weaver, who never made it big, and spent $150,000 for infielders Frank Crosetti and Jack Saltzgaver, the former a solid Yankee regular for ten years, the other another failure. Ruppert needed a cheaper way of obtaining talent.

Branch Rickey, the GM of the St. Louis Cardinals, had begun a farm system whereby a major league team bought several minor league teams to form a chain and then scouted the country for talent to stock these teams, paying prospects $75 to $90 a month during these hard times to play. Rickey's theory was to sign hundreds of kids in the hope that three or four would make it to the big leagues. He then sold others who weren't up to his standards to other major league teams. Rickey not only won a string of pennants, but he made hundreds of thousands of dollars selling his rejects. Ruppert wanted Weiss to set up a similar system for the Yankees.

Barrow chose Weiss because of his stellar reputation as a businessman. He remembered how Weiss had stiffed him the day Babe Ruth didn't show up for their exhibition game, and he nodded his head in admiration. Barrow and Weiss were two peas in a pod, hard-headed and ruthless.

Under Weiss the Yankees began buying farm teams, almost twenty in all, and Weiss and his four-man scouting staff signed thousands of players to Yankee minor-league contracts. For every player who reached the majors, twenty-five did not, but jobs during the Depression were scarce, and at the time professional baseball was a way out of poverty.

Weiss' farm system was a marvel of organization. The Yankees were spending less on talent than any other team except the Cardinals, but between 1932, when Weiss began his farm system, and 1943, when the war interrupted everything, the Yankees won the American League pennant in 1932, 1936, 1937, 1938, 1939, 1941, 1942, and 1943. During all those years the Yankees only purchased five players outright, two of whom were Joe DiMaggio and free agent Tommy Henrich. The five players Weiss bought cost the Yankees a total of $100,000. The players who Weiss signed and sold to other organizations netted the Yankees $2 million.

Weiss ability to evaluate player talent was sheer genius, and no one worked harder. When he made a deal often after thorough investigation he knew more about the opposing player than the team that owned him. Weiss would be making a trade, and he would say casually, "What's the name of that little fellow who plays third base for New Orleans? Oh, yes, Jones. If you throw him in, we'll call it a deal." And then Weiss would make money selling the throw-in.

A series of transactions he made in 1937 is a perfect example of how George Weiss operated. His scouts signed Willard Hershberger to a contract, and later Weiss sold him to the Cincinnati Reds for $40,000 and throw-ins Eddie Miller and Les Scarsella. Weiss then sent Miller to Kansas City, his own farm team where Miller excelled, and the next year Weiss sold him to the Boston Braves for $40,000 and five throw-ins, Vince DiMaggio, Johnny Riddle, Tom Reis, John Babich, and Gil English. DiMaggio then was sent down to Kansas City where he led the American Association in home runs. But because his fielding wasn't up to Weiss' standards, Weiss sold him to the Cincinnati Reds for $40,000 and Frenchy Bordagaray. After selling Scarsella, Reis, Riddle, Babich, English and Bordagaray to other major league clubs, Weiss had parlayed his original $500 investment in Hershberger into over $200,000.

After more than one such Weiss coup, Barrow would say to him in disbelief, "George, doesn't your conscience bother you?"

It never did.

When Dan Topping and Del Webb bought the Yankees in 1945 for $2.5 million, they gave Larry MacPhail a one-third share in exchange for his running the ball club as president. George Weiss remained as farm director. But MacPhail was a drunk who too often acted irrationally after having one too many, and Weiss attempted to purchase the Pittsburgh Pirates, a floundering franchise, just to get away from him. He came very close to completing the deal, but his penchant for arguing over every dollar ultimately cost him the team when Frank McKinney interceded and signed a deal before Weiss could complete his protracted negotiations.

Topping and Webb were as fed up with MacPhail as Weiss had been, and the two men negotiated to no avail to purchase MacPhail's share. On October 6, 1947, the day the Yankees won the seventh game of the World Series against the Brooklyn Dodgers, MacPhail held a lavish affair to celebrate, renting the entire penthouse of the Biltmore Hotel. The bubbly flowed.

Seated in a small side room, just off the main ballroom, MacPhail was drinking heavily with an old Dodgers employee, John McDonald, who had once been his road secretary. McDonald, still with the Dodgers, began praising his new boss, Branch Rickey, a man MacPhail disliked intensely. MacPhail began telling McDonald what a S.O.B. Rickey was. McDonald, loyal to his boss and perhaps miffed that MacPhail hadn't offered him a job with the Yankees, began defending Rickey.

"At least, Larry, he takes care of his own," said McDonald.

MacPhail arose, screamed, "You Judas," and with a heavy right hand swung his fist and struck McDonald flush in the face. McDonald sank in a heap, blood flowing on his suit.

MacPhail, blind with rage, his ego dented, felt that no one really appreciated his efforts, even after all he had done for the Yankees. George Weiss, he felt, had always been an Ed Barrow devotee. MacPhail, raging over Weiss being so damned independent, resented that he would barely even speak with him. As for Topping and Webb, those ingrates wouldn't give him a fair price for his stock.

MacPhail, a large man, came storming out of the side room like a wounded bull elephant, and a tipsy one at that.

Seated at a large round table in the middle of the large ballroom, Dan Topping, George Weiss, their wives, and several other organization officials, were eating dinner and chatting amiably. MacPhail charged toward this placid group fuming, weaving slightly, out of control and shouting obscenities. When he finally reached the table, he pointed his finger at Weiss and barked, "You are out. Out. You can pick up your check in the morning."

"And you," he yelled at Topping, "You weren't born with a silver spoon in your mouth like everyone says. It was eighteen carat gold." Topping rose to strike MacPhail, but others kept the two apart.

Del Webb, who was in another part of the hotel at the time of the incident, immediately rushed to Weiss' side to assure him he still had his job and that he was a most valuable employee. In a state of shock, the proud Weiss was inconsolable. He retired immediately with his wife and a cluster of friends to his hotel room, where the normally dispassionate Weiss cried over the shame he felt. All Weiss could mutter was, "How could he do this to me? How could he do this to me? I am disgraced."

"Don't worry for two minutes," Webb kept telling Weiss. "That son of a bitch will be out in the morning."

He was, and at Webb's price. Webb, a construction mogul and an extremely tough negotiator, refused to meet with MacPhail until the papers were signed. The Yankees then held a press conference announcing that George Weiss was going to be the new Yankee general manager.

With MacPhail gone from the Yankees, the emotional elements were purged. The flair and histrionics were replaced by the George Weiss model—efficient and unglorified somber work, work, and failing that, more work. If ever there was a dramatic example of the Protestant Ethic, the Yankee tradition as practiced by George Weiss was it.

Weiss's work brought the New York Yankees ten pennants in the next twelve years. Then, on November 2, 1960, his reign suddenly, shockingly, came to an end. Topping and Webb had plans to sell the Yankees, and they didn't want Weiss around to complicate things. Weiss was out, and there was no reprieve.

Even though he was fired, Weiss was gentleman enough to tell the press that he had retired. Weiss, a man so shy he was terrified to make a speech, handed out a statement and then added, "I want to thank you fellows. It's certainly been swell. See you around." The cold fish, the arrogant, and remote czar of the Yankees then started to cry.

Hazel Weiss, George Weiss' wife, recalled how they met and married. She witnessed Larry MacPhail's drunken escapades, and fondly remembered her husband's years in baseball.

Hazel Weiss: "George was the Class of '17 at Yale. Our senator, Prescott Bush, also was Class of '17. George didn't graduate. His father died, and he had to go to work.

"I met George through his sister when I was living in Boston. When I met him, there was nothing I liked about him. Nothing at all. I told his sister, 'I didn't know you had such a big, fat brother.' She went and told him.

"He was living in Baltimore with his mother. When George invited me to come down to New York to meet him, he did it beautifully. In the evening we went to all the best places. He knew all the speakeasys. One time Walter Johnson was with him. George had bought me a two–pound box of candy, a great big thing, and Walter wasn't drinking but he ate the whole box of candy!

"As time went on, I met his mother, who was very ill. She was such a dear, died in her nineties. George would be in Kansas City or somewhere, and my phone would ring, and he'd say, 'My mother has to go to the hospital.' It got so I was the only one around to take her.

"I had been married before and had a bad experience. When George asked me to marry him he was lonely. I had a son in prep school who was 11, and when I told him, he didn't say a word. The next weekend he said, 'I've been thinking about Uncle George. I think you better marry him because there are a lot of young pretty girls who would marry him.' And I did. That isn't very romantic, but it's the truth.

"I remember when the Yankees asked him to leave Baltimore to start their farm system. George Barrow wanted him. Two German squareheads. He watched George in Baltimore and said, 'That's the one I want.' If George had stayed in Baltimore, he would have had a very simple, very wonderful life.

"George said to me, 'I don't know what to do.' I said, 'You want to be tops in baseball, don't you?' He said, 'Yes.' I said, 'The Yankees are the place to go.' So he went. Branch Rickey had started the farm system, and that's what the Yankees wanted. And he built a farm system that nobody could beat. He had good scouts. His scouts found him material.

"George was so meticulous. Everything had to be just right. I remember when the man running the Newark team said to me, 'Hazel, I got him this time. He won't be able to find one single thing wrong.' I said to him, 'Wanna bet?' He said, 'Yup, ten bucks.' George did the inspection, looked at the grass, the stands, and as we were coming up the stairs to the office, there was a telephone booth. George said, 'Those windows in the telephone booth haven't been washed in I don't know how long.'

"I said, 'Give me the ten dollars.' See what I mean by details. I knew he'd catch him.

"I remember after we won the World Series in 1947, we had a big party at the Biltmore Hotel. After they won the game that clinched the pennant, Larry MacPhail said, 'George, this is the team that you built, not me.'

"Larry drank, and he had fights all the time. He was a wino, and he was worse when he drank liquor. Nobody ever got along with Larry. He was Peck's bad boy. You always wondered, what is he going to do next?

"Dan [Topping] was a drinker, too, but he never got that drunk. Dan wasn't against anyone having a drink. You couldn't be in baseball and not. But Larry was very difficult. And the players didn't like him. He'd even go down to the dugout and tell [Yankee manager Joe] McCarthy what to do.

"He was drinking champagne, and his daughter said to me, 'Look out for George. Keep George away from Larry. He's going to kick him out and put his son [Lee] in his place.' So Larry came in. Larry was always nice to me. Before he came over he had a fight with a Dodger official, and then he came to George and he said, 'You're out.'

"George went up to his room. Forty people must have followed him including Mr. Topping. But before that Dan went over to Larry and punched him in the nose. Anyone could have knocked him over, Larry was so drunk.

"Dan, Del Webb, everyone went up to George's room. And George was crying. He thought he was done. So they said, 'That S.O.B. is out in the morning. Nothing is going to happen to you at all.' And they said, 'And we don't want either of his kids either, anyone with the name MacPhail.'

"I said, 'Those two boys [Lee and Bill] have a wonderful mother, and they haven't done anything wrong. They are nice boys. They are not responsible for their father.' I don't think there was a better baseball man than Lee MacPhail. He said it in the paper, 'I don't give any credit for my baseball success to my father. I owe it to George Weiss.' After George retired from the Mets, he wanted Lee to come up and take over the Mets, but Lee's wife wouldn't leave Baltimore. That was George's man. Lee is a fine boy, quiet like his mother. You wouldn't believe he's Larry MacPhail's son.

"They took George and me and hid us in a suite of rooms in the Commodore incognito, while they tried to find MacPhail. Dan and Del didn't want anyone asking George questions which he possibly didn't want to answer. They found Larry in the morning in a turkish bath. That was that. Topping and Webb kicked him out.

"George was very shy. Nobody could get to *really* know George because he was so shy. He never used the word 'I.' I love everyone, and I'm social. If his friends and baseball people came here to the house, great. And he was the greatest host in the world. But you couldn't get him over to your house.

"God, he was shy. We'd go to Lou Gehrig's funeral or a great big, formal wedding, and he'd say to me, Don't you leave me.' 'Cause I'd bounce around the room, kiss everybody, go off. He didn't want me to do that. George never wore a bathing suit. He hated water. Wouldn't put his foot in it. George didn't know how to play. He had to leave college and take care of his sister and brother. How could he play? He wouldn't go to a tennis match. He just knew how to work. He took up golf. It was his only sport. He wasn't a good player, but he did it to be with his boys. If anyone else was standing around the first tee, he'd go out onto the course so no one could watch him. I guess he was born that way, and he married someone just the opposite.

"They wanted George to be the president of the American League, but he turned it down because he'd have to get up and talk at dinners. Word of honor. He said, 'You have to go all over the place and stand up and talk.' He wouldn't do it. If he didn't have to talk, he could have helped baseball so much. He had to make about three speeches in his whole life.

"I remember when he had to make a speech, for two weeks the man walked the floor. He'd say to me, 'I can't do it. What am I going to do?' And when he made it, it was short and perfect and to the point.

"When he was elected into the Hall of Fame, he wouldn't go because he was in a wheelchair. That was his pride again. He could have gone. He wouldn't do it. He wrote the speech, and Ford Frick delivered it. If you remember what he said was, 'Baseball was my whole life. It was my religion.' It was a beautiful acceptance speech. I think George would have worked for the Yankees or the Mets for no charge, just to be in baseball.

"His players called him long distance, and they all had something to say to him. Joe DiMaggio said to him, 'Remember the time in New Haven you fined me fifty bucks? I want it back.' That cheered him up very much.

"George will live forever in the Hall of Fame. He'll live in baseball.

"I'll give you some insight on George: Dan Topping had a football team, and he had no place to play, so he bought the Yankees. But the equipment for football is expensive, and the team wasn't drawing, and George was not making money. And either George makes money, or he doesn't play. He said to Dan, 'You get rid of the football team, or I'm going.' So football went.

"I entered a pillow-making contest, and I won second prize. Among thousands of pillows. I thought I had been a very smart girl to get that. I thought it was great to get second place.

"George said to me, 'There is no such thing as second place.'

"I said, 'What do you mean?'

"He said, 'You're first or you're nothing.'

"He wrote me two letters, and I didn't open them until he died. I think he loved me very much."

After Bob Mandt graduated from St. John's University, he went to work in a bank. When a St. John's classmate got a job working for the new National League baseball team, he contacted Mandt, who applied and was hired in the ticket department. His very first job was to contact everyone requesting tickets.

The first Mets ticket office was in the Martinique Hotel, off Broadway, about a half mile south of the Metropolitan Opera House. Outside the hotel there was a small sign that read: Mets Ticket Office. People would go up to the window thinking it was the MET ticket office and ask Bill Gibson, who had run the Brooklyn Dodgers ticket office, for two tickets to Traviata.

"Where would you like them?" Gibson would ask. "On the first base or third base side?"

Bob Mandt recalled his rudimentary beginnings working for the fledgling Mets.

Bob Mandt: "I started on the eighth of January 1962. The Mets business office and ticket department was in the basement of the Hotel Martinique, on Thirty-second Street on the West Side. Howard Clothes, one of our first sponsors, had a basement in the Martinique, and they let us use it. The main office, where George Weiss was, was on Fifth Avenue.

"There was a tremendous pile of paper of all sizes and descriptions with requests for schedules and ticket information. My first job was to put all that in alphabetical order so we could start calling these people back and organize a mailing list.

"It wasn't long after that that they needed someone to handle the ticket sales at Penn Station. We also had an office at Grand Central. I had never sold a ticket in my life, and they gave me a crash course, and I opened up an office.

"I worked there until June, and they called me up to the Polo Grounds. They were having some difficulties in their mail department. I did that, and toward the latter part of the season I began handling the VIP seats.

"When my boss went to the Jets the following year, I shared the ticket manager's job with a fellow by the name of Jerry Waring. In '64, Jerry got his wish, to run one of the farm teams. He went to the Williamsport Mets, one of our first farm clubs, and I was named ticket manager.

"I remember the first time I met George Weiss. The elevator at the Polo Grounds was the size of a small closet. We used to kid about it being the prototypical elevator. We'd say, 'This is where the elevator was invented.' When you got into that elevator with two people, there was a crowd. And it was very slow to boot.

"So I got on the elevator with, who else, but George Weiss. The thing was going up *so* slowly, and he was so reclusive and quiet, he was looking down at the ground, and I didn't know quite what to say. I'd never been introduced to him. So we rode up in silence. And he got off, and he went his way, and I went mine.

"His office in the Polo Grounds was behind the Rheingold sign in deep center field. In fact, when the Giants were there it was a Knickerbocker beer sign. Anyway, his office was behind that sign, and my office—I didn't have an office. We all worked out of a big area with a couple of nooks and crannies.

"This was a game day, and later on that afternoon, my boss said to me, 'Bring these club boxes to Mr. Weiss. Nobody ever uses them, but he likes them on his desk. Put them under the bottom right corner of his blotter. That's what he likes. Just put them there and leave.'

"So I walked in there, and Mr. Weiss has a napkin tucked in under his shirt, and he was eating an egg salad sandwich, which is not easy to eat. It was spilling all over the place, and he looked at me very startled, and I said, 'Hiya, Mr. Weiss.' I put the four tickets under the blotter at the proper place, and I walked out. So now he has seen this guy who he's never seen before twice in one day.

"Later that afternoon there was a ladder outside his office, and if you climbed the ladder, you could look out the window from center field and watch the game we were playing. I figured that Mr. Weiss was down in the seats, so I climbed the ladder and began looking at the game. I didn't know he was in his office with a bunch of people. He came out of his door, and he looked up at me, and now he has seen me for a third time.

"I had to laugh. I said to my boss, 'He's going to wonder who the hell I am.' He was such a shy man.

"But I liked him. I thought he was a pretty good guy. He used to say, 'For heaven's sake.' He was not a cursing man. Not in front of me. And I never had any experiences with him where he lost his temper. But people were afraid of him. I never could understand why.

"I remember being at an Old Timers game one time, and afterward we went to Toots Shor's for a party afterward, and he was sitting with Ford Frick and Gene Mauch and a couple others telling stories about rail travel and ballplayers and personal things I thought were very funny. I was in awe.

"But Weiss was also the kind of guy who would say, 'How do we know that Toots Shor is really giving us what we are paying for?' There would be a wild party with everybody drinking, and the bill would say 'eighteen bottles of Scotch, ten bottles of rye, six bottles of gin.' Weiss asked, 'How do we know?'

"So I remember he called Hank Kelly, who was in the ticket department, and assigned Hank the job of counting the whiskey bottles that we used. So Hank was at the party, but he had to keep an eye on the whiskey!

"Arthur Richman and I got to know him extremely well after he left the Mets. He knew he could trust us. He used to call us up to find out what was going on.

"He and his wife had no children, and they lived in Greenwich, and he would ask me to bring my wife and children to visit him. I never did go.

"One day I was on the phone with him, and he said, 'I really want you to come. What's your favorite team?' I said, 'The 1955 Dodgers.' He said, 'Come on up. I have barrels of autographed baseballs. I'll give you the 1955 ball. I have extras.'

"Then he asked me, 'What's your other favorite team? What other ball would you like to have?'

"I said, 'The 1927 Yankees.' He said, 'Come on up. I got it.' I never went. I never made it up there. True story. And I heard that when he died, his wife turned everything over to the Hall of Fame."

Arthur Richman, who was named director of promotions of the Mets in 1963, began his newspaper career as a copy boy in the sports department of the *New York Daily Mirror* making $12 a week in 1943. He worked there writing features, and then in 1958 William Randolph Hearst called Harold Weissman, the executive sports editor of the paper, and said, 'I want Arthur Richman to have his own column with his picture in the paper.' Weisman told him, 'We don't have any room for another column.' Said Hearst, who owned the *Mirror*, 'Make room.' And after that Richman's column, "The Armchair Manager," appeared every day.

The *Mirror* folded, and after he worked in an ad agency for a year, George Weiss hired Richman to work for the Mets.

Arthur Richman: "The *Mirror* had folded, and I was working for Gray Advertising when George Weiss called me and asked me if I'd like to join him with the Mets. I had made a tremendous amount of money working for Gray. I'll tell you something: if you want to make money, go work for an advertising agency. I traveled with Del Shofner for Old Gold cigarettes.

They sponsored the NFL championship film, and we'd have a tremendous expense account, and when we'd go to cities like Omaha, we'd go to the track to try to lose some money. And guess what would happen? The horse would win!

"But Weiss called me and asked if I would like to join him. I said I would. He said, 'What kind of money are we talking about, young man?' I said, 'George, suppose I work for you for nothing?' He said, 'You're hired.' And he ended up giving me a salary of $20,000, which at the time was a hell of a salary, and every year he'd give me substantial raises—they talked about him being cheap, and maybe he was with the ballplayers, but George Weiss was the best boss I ever had in my life.

"He was a very hard-nosed guy, and everything had to be to the letter. He watched expenses very carefully. But if he hired you, he kept his word in everything he said.

"I'd be in my office, and my phone would ring at five o'clock, and he'd say, 'Young man, come right in here.' I said, 'Yes sir.' I'd walk in, and he'd say, 'Close the door. Sit down. What will you have?' And we'd start having a few toddies. He wasn't close with hardly anybody, but he did like to have a toddy once in a while. And if he had too much and he was driving, I wouldn't let him drive home. I would drive him to his home in Greenwich.

"And after he was out of the office as president, when he was in a nursing home, Bill Murray and I would go visit him, and when he died, we were the only ones invited to the private funeral along with Mel Allen.

"I have his picture hanging in my office inscribed to me. It's like part of my life to look at it every day."

t e n

The Return of The Old Perfessor

As soon as George Weiss became Mets' president, he knew who he wanted to manage the new team: the man who had won ten pennants for him with the Yankees: Casey Stengel. But Stengel was seventy years old, and his wife Edna wanted him to stay home and slow down. So at first Stengel turned Weiss down. When the Detroit Tigers offered him a job, he turned them down as well.

But Weiss persisted. The owners had stacked the deck against his finding any real gems. He knew the players he would be getting would be retreads and rookies with dubious potential. He needed the one man who would take the focus off the team and put it on himself. Weiss needed a manager who would be the center of attention. Stengel was unique in that he had a gift of gab that allowed newspaper reporters to fill long columns with his words. Most managers were afraid of the press, or at best wary. Stengel wined and dined them and enjoyed their company.

When Stengel first said no, Weiss hired Cookie Lavagetto and Solly Hemus as coaches. If Casey remained recalcitrant, he would have backup choices. But Weiss and Joan Payson wanted him badly, and they persisted.

With Stengel on the Mets, the team would gain a great public relations coup. The hated Yankees had fired him, and he had became a martyr, as had Weiss, though to a lesser extent. With Stengel onboard, even before a single player had been chosen, automatically the Mets would become good guys.

In the end, despite his wife's objections, Casey Stengel could not stay away. Like Weiss, baseball was his whole life. Stengel had no hobbies whatsoever. He didn't even play golf. He was being offered an arena where he could talk, live, and breathe baseball. It was only a matter of time.

Once Casey agreed to manage the team, he embraced the challenge with all the vigor of a man thirty years his junior. Stengel soon would coin the catch phrase that would define the Mets for the next ten years: Amazing. But, in fact, the most amazing facet of the Mets in the early years was the man who coined the phrase, Casey Stengel himself.

George Weiss had hired Casey Stengel to manage the New York Yankees back in 1949. Stengel was fifty-nine years old, with deep lines crisscrossing his pliant face and pronounced creases on his cheeks which flowed toward a jutting jaw. He had palm-leaf ears and a broad nose, and his legs angled oddly, and when he talked he waved his arms and made exaggerated gestures. He looked comical, like an elderly gnome, though the New York sportswriters were not amused. He had been a National League manager since 1934 and never a very successful one in the nine years he managed Brooklyn and the Boston Braves. His reputation was one of a clown, not that of an astute handler of men.

Weiss had known Stengel for many years, going back to the Eastern League in the mid-1920s. Yankee owner Del Webb and Stengel, both West Coast residents, had also been acquainted for many years. Weiss had hired Stengel to manage the Yankees' Kansas City farm club team in 1945. Kansas City didn't finish very high that year, because while the majors were weak from wartime attrition, the minors were even weaker, and with Stengel leading a team so woefullly thin that the second baseman was a left hander, Weiss had nevertheless been impressed with Stengel's ability to teach his players and work with them and his ability to maneuver his limited forces.

A year earlier Milwaukee had hired Stengel, and he led the team to the American Association pennant, and when he was fired after the Milwaukee management changed hands, Webb and Weiss helped him land the manager's job in Oakland in the Pacific Coast League. At Oakland in 1948 Stengel led "Nine Old Men" to the club's first Pacific Coast League pennant since 1921. Webb and Weiss then hired him to manage the Yankees.

Charles Dillon Stengel was born in Kansas City in 1890, or maybe 1889, or possibly even earlier. No one knows for sure. After graduating from high

Casey Stengel

school he enrolled in Western Dental College in Kansas City for two and a half years, but after a scout from the Aurora, Illinois, team scouted and signed him, he never did complete his studies. While playing for Aurora, Stengel was discovered by a Brooklyn Dodgers scout, and after the Dodgers bought him, he joined the team a year later in 1912. He was a regular Dodgers outfielder for the next five years.

While still a Dodger, Stengel injured his arm during spring training of 1914, and while incapacitated, he agreed to coach baseball at the University of Mississippi for a few weeks when his old high school coach, who had become the UMiss athlete director, asked him to help out. Stengel was appointed a full professor for his short stay at UMiss, and he returned to the Dodgers team just as spring training ended. His nickname, The Professor, remained with him the rest of his life. In later years he became known as The Old Professor, or Old Perfessor.

Stengel, however, did not have the demeanor of a professor. He was a hard-nosed brawler who loved his liquor, and though he preferred to spend his evening hours on the town, Stengel always hustled and showed great desire on the field, developing an excellent reputation as a dependable and entertaining player.

Some of his performances are now legendary. After he was traded from Brooklyn to Pittsburgh in 1918, he returned to Ebbets Field with the Pirates, and just before his first at bat as the formerly Brooklyn faithful booed him as vociferously as they had once cheered him, he bowed low to the ground, removed his cap, and underneath the cap perched on Stengel's head was a sparrow, which flew away. Stengel had found the small bird dazed in the outfield during batting practice. He knew the Brooklyn fans were going to boo him, so he figured that if they were going to give him the bird, he would give them one in return.

Before another game with the Pirates, Stengel stood in center field, rigid and stock-still. When the manager ran out to find out what the matter was, Stengel told him that he was too weak to move because he wasn't getting paid enough to eat.

On to the Philadelphia Phillies in 1919, he was suspended when he demanded more money, and was traded in July of 1921 to the New York Giants. Under the legendary John McGraw, the left-handed Stengel platooned in the outfield with the right-handed Bill Cunningham. Stengel, a lifetime .284 hitter during his fourteen-year career, batting .368 in 1922 and .339 in 1923, and in the World Series Stengel hit two home runs, including one inside the parker in the ninth inning to defeat the Yankees. Rounding the bases after hitting the other, Stengel is remembered for taunting the Yankees bench by raising his middle finger, enraging Yankees owner Jacob Ruppert.

After the series McGraw traded Stengel to the Boston Braves for better-hitting Billy Southworth. Stengel finished his major league career early in 1925, retiring and becoming the president, manager, and right fielder of the Worcester, Massachusetts team in the Eastern League. Unhappy there, Stengel again made history that year by giving himself his release as a player, firing himself as manager, and then quitting as president. He continued to manage in the minors in 1931 when he was hired by McGraw to manage Toledo. He was then hired by the Brooklyn Dodgers as a coach, and in 1934 he replaced Max Carey as manager, inheriting a team of mediocre bumblers. Stengel managed there for three seasons, finishing sixth, fifth, and seventh, and at the end of the third season, though he had another year left on his contract, the Dodgers fired him, thus paying him in 1937 *not* to manage.

While with the Dodgers, Stengel made himself visible on the third base coaching lines, delivering impromptu orations, conversing with the opposition, performing an occasional soft shoe, and badgering the umpires, providing more entertainment than his players did. Stengel drove his players hard and tried to instruct them, but most had neither the talent nor the intellect to take advantage of his guidance.

It is said that Stengel invented a pickoff play that he taught his team, a play to be employed in a situation with a runner on third and a right-hander at bat. Stengel instructed the pitcher to throw at the head of the batter and then yell, "Look out" as he released the pitch. Stengel's ruse was that the runner on third would be so concerned about the welfare of the fallen batter that he would freeze in his tracks, allowing the catcher to pick him off third. Stengel finally had to discard the play because his third baseman also froze, allowing the throw to whiz by his head into left field where the left fielder ended up having to chase it.

"Managing the team back then," Stengel would say years later, "was a tough business. Whenever I decided to release one of them, I always had his room searched for a gun. You couldn't take any chances with some of them birds."

While managing Brooklyn, Stengel's most important personal gains were monetary. A player from Texas, Randy Moore, convinced him and three other ballplayers, Al Lopez, Van Lingle Mungo, and Johnny Cooney, to invest money in an East Texas oil field. Stengel's wells began gushing in 1941 and continued to do so for many lucrative years afterward. A Dodgers stockholder also touted Stengel on a firm that was beginning to produce a new miracle drug called penicillin. He made a killing. He was becoming almost as wealthy as his wife, Edna, whose father was a successful banker.

After sitting out the '37 season while being paid by the Dodgers, Stengel signed a contract to manage the Boston Braves, another collection of ragtags and has-beens. He bought a small piece of the club when he took the job. Again he became the center of attention in order to divert the minds of the fans from the poor quality of the baseball being played. One dreary, rainy afternoon Stengel appeared on the field to exchange the line-up cards with the umpires wearing a raincoat and holding an umbrella in one hand and a lantern in the other. It was classic Stengel, and most of the writers loved him for his antics, his colorful stories, and his congeniality. Once Stengel was relating to a group of writers an incident concerning a pitcher who had once played against him back in the '20s. The catcher's nickname was Horseface.

"When Casey showed how the catcher used to look," said a writer who was there, "he not only looked more like a horse than a catcher, he looked more like a horse than Whirlaway!"

"For us," wrote Boston sportswriter Harold Kaese, "it was more fun losing with Stengel than winning with a hundred other managers. Unfortunately, the Boston fans did not have the benefit of Stengel's company." In his six years in Beantown, Stengel's teams never finished higher than fifth. When he was accidentally struck down by a taxi cab in the spring of '43, breaking his leg and missing the first two months of the season, Boston Record sportswriter Dave Egan, a cruel man who for years tried to run Ted Williams out of town, voted the cabdriver as "the man who did the most for Boston in 1943."

At the end of the year Stengel was released, travelling to Milwaukee, where he won the American Association pennant in '44, to Kansas City, where he impressed Yankee owner Del Webb, and to Oakland where he won the pennant in 1948.

When the Yankees fired Bucky Harris at the end of the 1948 season, Weiss's first and only choice was Stengel. Stengel was a man Weiss trusted, someone he could work with and who would work with the younger players, and he was the perfect buffer to keep the press from Weiss.

When the announcement of his appointment was made at the press conference, Stengel was unusually serious and closed-mouthed. He knew he was on the spot, because of the firing of the popular Harris and because of his tarnished reputation.

"I didn't get this job," he said in a low, gravelly voice, "through friendship. The Yankees represent an investment of millions of dollars. They don't hand out jobs like this because they like your company. I got the job because the people here think I can produce for them."

And produce he did. In the years he managed the Yankees between 1949 and 1960, he failed to win the American League pennant only twice, in 1954, when Cleveland won a record 111 games, and in 1959, when his pitching staff suddenly grew old.

For a record five seasons in a row, from 1949–1953 and again in 1955, 1956, 1957, 1958, and 1960, the Yankees took the flag. Stengel managed some of the greatest players ever to perform for the Yankees—DiMaggio, Tommy Henrich, Phil Rizzuto, Vic Raschi, Allie Reynolds, Whitey Ford, Mantle, Gil McDougald, Billy Martin, Hank Bauer, Yogi Berra, Elston Howard, and Roger Maris.

The Yankees won the World Series under Stengel in 1949, 1950, 1951, 1952, 1953, 1956, and 1958. He became the symbol of Yankee superiority. And then, at the end of the 1960 season, he was fired, much to the chagrin of the reporters, who revered him for providing them with reams of good copy. Rarely did a reporter come away from an interview with Stengel without a story and a great quote. Stengel favored the everyday beat writers, whom he called "my writers," but he would talk endlessly to any writer who came calling. Casey Stengel may well have been the most interviewed man in the United States.

And so when Casey Stengel was fired by the Yankees, the New York writers felt sorry for both Casey and themselves. They felt loyalty to Casey, who had been told by Topping and Weiss to tell everyone he had resigned. He dutifully made a statement to that effect, but the writers who were close to him knew better.

At his press conference the first question asked to him was, "Casey, an AP article said you resigned. Is that true?"

Casey answered, "What did the UPI say?" That day UPI sportswriter Milton Richman had written the truth: he had been fired. Topping and Webb had asked him not to say the words, "I was fired," and he had obeyed. But anyone who had a copy of Richman's article could read the truth.

Two years later, Casey Stengel was unretired and became the manager of the New York Mets. Said Casey, "It's a great honor for me to be joining the Knickerbockers." No one was happier about that than the reporters covering the team.

Jack Lang: "When Casey came over to the Mets, he was the same as he had been with the Yankees. Absolutely. He never changed. He was the most wonderful man you'd ever want to meet. He was a great guy.

"I remember we were in spring training in '62, and the team was working out at Miller Huggins Field, and the fans were hanging out behind the screen, and somebody told Casey, 'There's an old guy over here who claims you knew him in Keokuk, Iowa, when you played out there.' It was Casey's first team. Somebody took him over to the screen, and Casey said hello to the guy, and he introduced himself, and the old guy said, 'I ran a restaurant in town in Keokuk. You used to buy a meal ticket and eat your meals in my restaurant.' In those days during the Depression you could buy a weekly meal ticket for $3.50, and you got three meals a day, and they punched your card. And Casey said, 'I remember you. You ran that restaurant, and the league folded in the middle of the week, and I still have three days left on my meal ticket!' And this eighty-year-old geezer didn't know what the hell he was talking about!

"During the season we played a night game in Los Angeles and flew up to San Francisco, and when we arrived, the Women's Republican Club of California was holding its convention at the same hotel we were staying, and we arrived at the hotel about two in the morning, and when we got there, all these old dowagers had waited up for him. They were standing in the lobby, and he stood there regaling them with stories for another hour. Until three in the morning. He was a charmer with everybody. He really was.

"Casey did nothing but preach, 'Mets, Mets, Mets. I remember watching one of his television interviews. He said, 'All the kids in New York are growing up, and they want to see the Metsies, the Metsies, the Metsies.' He was a great publicity man for the ball club.

"Casey would stand and talk to anybody. He made [the Mets] lovable."

Stan Isaacs: "Stengel was a comedian, and he was bright, and he had total recall so there wasn't hardly anything that didn't happen that Stengel couldn't refer to, one way or another. He had played at Kankakee, played everywhere, and it didn't matter, if there was a news event and in the morning we'd mention it, Stengel would have a reference to it, even if it had nothing to do with baseball.

"I was always amazed by him. Stengel loved newspaper people because he grew up with newspaper people. He was suspicious of radio and television, hated Howard Cosell, probably because he saw him as a phony, and he didn't like people putting their hands on him. Cosell was a horrible man. He was brilliant, but he was horrible. He had a way of putting his arm around you when he wanted to interview you. Stengel didn't like that, and he didn't like Joe Reichler of the AP, who put hands on people. Stengel was very loyal to newspapermen and very good with young newspapermen. I liked him for that. When a new reporter came around, most of the time he was ignored. Stengel would make a point of talking to a new reporter to bring him into the group. I saw him do that a lot, and I admired him for that."

One of those new reporters was Robert Lipsyte who was plucked from obscurity by the sports department of the *New York Times* to cover the Mets in the spring of 1962. Lipsyte fell under the aegis of Stengel and came to admire the seventy-two-year-old manager for his brilliant mind and his quick wit.

Robert Lipsyte: "When the Dodgers and Giants left, it left the Dodgers' and Giants' writers—Roscoe McGowan and Louis Effrat—also known as Louie F. Rat—kind of high and dry. So when the Mets were brought back through the wonderful machinations of Bill Shea and Branch Rickey, among others, there was a great excitement and a lot of drum beating led by Dick Young, who was thrilled to be back in action.

"We knew that whatever the Mets did we were all going to be thrilled and happy, so, as it was later with Cassius Clay, the *Times* saw the Mets more as a feature story than as a real baseball story. This was a time when Jim Roach had taken over the *Times'* sports department, and sports was devalued at the *Times*—nowadays that would never happen—but in those days sports was not highly regarded—it was the *Times'* version of the comics, and so they decided to send a twenty-four-year-old feature writer down to spring training in 1962, which totally scandalized the real reporters like McGowan and Louis Effrat. The idea was that I would cover the first half of spring training and write feature stories, and Effrat would cover the second half when the games began.

"I went down there believing all the hype about what a bad team they were. I even brought down, along with my Olivetti portable, my glove. I was no great athlete, but I figured, who knew? Maybe they would need a backup second baseman.

"And that's where my education began, because I had covered some Yankee games, writing sidebars, but I really hadn't been up close. Early on I went out onto the field, and I took batting practice against Solly Hemus, a coach. Everything was a lot looser than it is today. He threw a couple of pitches, and I realized I had no business having a bat in my hand. I had never seen anything so fast. I took a couple of pitches, and I walked away. I bailed out. It was just too fast.

"There was an attempt, especially when George Weiss was around, to make it a big league camp, but Casey Stengel was kind of crazy out of his mind, and covering the Mets was a very tough assignment, because I was scared of missing anything, so I would get there early, and then part of the deal was that you didn't go to bed until Stengel did, and every night he closed the bar at the Colonial Inn, which was on the main strip on St. Petersburg Beach, where we were staying.

"I couldn't drink along with him, obviously, but I didn't want to leave early, just in case he said something. So there was a lot of hanging out with Stengel, and the one thing that happens when you hang out long enough with Stengel, you realize that he makes absolute sense.

"The columnists who drifted in and out would get chunks of what sounded like jibberish repeated as Stengelese and then leave, but if you stayed there long enough, you got to know who the pronouns were about, and then you could follow the course of the conversation and you'd have very interesting stories about baseball, and great discussions of strategy and technique, none of which I remember, because I was drunk. I really thought he was a genius. I didn't think he was a blithering old man like a lot of people did. I really thought he had a lot to say.

"I also think he was mean. He could be kind of cruel to talentless young players, of which he had a number, and he would make fun of them. He wasn't always kind in the press to young players who sometimes needed that. But I thought he was a great baseball mind, and that he was very bitter. I think that he was not all that happy to be back with a shitty team, something he realized early on. But for me it was a wonderful situation.

"Everyone was staying at a place called the Colonial Inn, and there were families there. This was 1962, before the Civil Rights Act. The rule was that no Met was allowed to swim in the pool. They had this huge pool, with this restaurant and kids. It was very nice.

"The official explanation was that swimming used a different set of muscles and that swimming would be deleterious to playing baseball. I kind of didn't buy it, and the rumor was that part of the deal to have the team as an integrated group there at the Colonial Inn was that blacks wouldn't mingle with the paying customers, who generally tended to hang around the pool. So I asked Stengel one time, 'Casey, is it true you are keeping all the ballplayers out of the pool so that black players wouldn't be there and scandalize. . . .'

"And it was as if for the first time he really recognized who I was.

Because he looked at me very coldly, and he said, 'None of them are allowed to swim, and I've also given them instructions that none of them are allowed to fuck. Now you put that in your *New York Times*.' And that was the end of the discussion. His stock really shot up in my mind as a smart man. He really knew just how to handle me.

"And I always felt he had this kind of sense of how to manipulate people, because the hardcore, crusty things he would say to Dick Young, whom he read as a 'hardcore, right-wing sportswriter,' was very different from what he would say to me. He read me as a 'liberal child.' He would include me privately in moments where a blind man would show up, and he'd let the blind man feel his face.

"I remember one incident, it really knocked me out, where a grizzled old guy showed up with his grandson, and you could tell from the body language that they were not getting along at all, and he dragged the boy, a teenager, down to meet Stengel, and he said to Stengel something like, 'Remember me. We played at Kankakee. I was a pitcher.' And Stengel kind of looked at him, and I had been around him long enough to know that he didn't know who the hell the guy was, but he read right away that this surly teenager was pulling away from his dad, so he looked at him and said, 'Yeah, I remember you, the fireballer himself. I couldn't get a hit off you. Man, I was glad when you left the league.' And you know, in that moment you saw something happen between father and son. The kid kind of took a step closer to his dad. He wasn't pulling away from him any more.

"Stengel was unerring. He could read people. But, of course, the other side was how selfish and manipulative he was.

"The phrase Casey used a lot was 'horseshit.' That was a big baseball word in those days. He used it when talking about the team in general. 'Horseshit.' And he used another phrase a lot, 'Mrs. Payson and the attendance wuz robbed.' At first we kind of thought of it as charming eccentricity of this crazy old man rather than the honest appraisal, which it really was. But it was hard to cover him in that way, because editors had marked him as a nutty old fart, a sort of court jester, and they thought that's what people liked to read about, so you were kind of pushed into that kind of coverage.

"I got to know George Weiss, but he was not accessible or friendly to me. There was a former relief pitcher, Johnny Murphy, who was a really good, patient guy. He was very helpful. One of the big stories I jumped on was a kid named John Pappas, who came down from New York City—

this is a measure of my ignorance—with a story about how he had practiced all winter under a bridge and he really wanted to pitch for the Mets. It was the perfect story for me—Pappas was another young guy from Queens. And Stan Isaacs and I bedevilled the Mets into giving him a try out. He threw three or four pitches, and Murphy slapped him on the back and said, 'Nice try, son, but we don't have anything for you.' And I remember afterwards interviewing Murphy and not really knowing who he was [John Murphy pitched thirteen years in the big leagues, twelve for the Yankees. His record was 93–53, with 107 saves, and he appeared in six World Series.]—this was my lack of background—saying, 'Who are you to make a judgment like that?' I cringe with shame when I think of that. I keep things like that in mind whenever I think I know something about anything—but Murphy was very kind and gentle, and he was even patient with me.

"But that was the atmosphere of the camp.

"There was a mission in all of this. It was a brand-new team. Everything was up for grabs. It was New York. Casey Stengel was getting good media attention. So people were kind of up for it.

"There were some crusty old veterans. Richie Ashburn had a lot of enthusiasm for an old guy. [Ashburn was 35.] He was particularly warm and friendly, and I remember once sitting between him and Dick Young, and Young was giving Richie a speech about how important he and the other sportswriters were, because 'we are the conscience of baseball,' and Ashburn said, 'Are you serious?' And Dick said, 'Very serious.' And Ashburn fell out of his seat laughing. And it seemed like such an honest expression of hilarity.

"Ashburn was warm and friendly, and he was accessible. He answered questions. He just seemed like a very nice guy, and in that group he was an All Star. Gus Bell, for instance, was grumpy. Gus was not happy to be there. And Frank Thomas was even grumpier than Gus Bell.

"But Richie seemed happy to be alive. Richie was an enthusiast, and he just lifted everybody's spirits. This was not a kid looking for his break. This was the guy, if he thought it was appropriate for him to be there, then hardly anyone else could complain.

"Gil Hodges was there. He was a good one. He didn't talk a lot, and you remember Casey's famous line about him, 'Be careful. He can tear your earbrows off. He's that strong.' We thought he might have meant 'eyebrows,' but he said 'earbrows.' Gil was solid, pleasant enough.

"There was no sense of circus about this. These were solid ballplayers. I don't think they were happy to be there, but it was great fun. I had a wonderful time. It was that kind of team, and Stengel was a great story. There was a nice group of people down there who were terrific to me as a young reporter who really didn't know what he was doing. That group included Dick Young, who could not have been more supportive and more helpful. There was nothing I ever wrote that he agreed with. He always thought I was a liberal fool. But he could not have been more personally warmer or more collegial. He was great. So was Jack Lang, who handled the charters for the press. Anywhere we had to go, by bus, train, or plane, Captain Jack made the arrangements. He was great. Captain Jack was the man. Also Milton Gross and Lenny Shecter, who was really terrific, Stan Issacs, and Maury Allen. So it was a wonderful group. I was the child in all of that and the least experienced. It was a very early meaningful experience.

"After a month down there I met Louie Effrat at the airport. We had to exchange some material, a typewriter or credentials, I can't remember what. The only thing he said to me was, 'Everybody is talking about you in New York, kid. You can really write, but you don't know shit about baseball.'

"And I had a very bad plane ride home after that. But then I got back to the office, and everybody said I had done a good job, so I felt better."

eleven

A Shortage of Talent

On October 10, 1961, the day after the New York Yankees defeated the Cincinnati Reds in the World Series, the National League held its expansion draft. That season the American League expanded into Los Angeles and Washington. Each existing team was allowed to protect the forty players on its major league roster. Anyone else could be drafted. As a result, a handful of outstanding youngsters were made available to the new teams, including pitcher Dean Chance, infielder Jim Fregosi, and catcher Bob Rodgers.

Having seen what their American League counterparts lost, the National League owners decided to make sure that didn't happen to them. Instead of making their best prospects available, the National League owners gave themselves the flexibility to reshuffle their forty-man rosters before the Mets and Houston Colt .45s made their picks. Instead of allowing their best prospects to be plucked, they replaced them with players in their system either too old or not talented enough.

Said columnist Jimmy Breslin, "It really was robbery in the daytime."

Joan Payson paid $1.8 million for elderly or incomplete players whose futures no longer were ahead of them. The sharp-tongued Breslin was outraged that the men in power could be so shortsighted as to leave the Mets and Houston Colt .45s woefully shorthanded.

Jimmy Breslin: "It was the kind of a scheme only some sneak business-man could come up with. Baseball has plenty of these. What makes it worse is that the scheme was obviously designed to harpoon money away from Joan Payson. She was coming in with millions, and everybody thought it would be smart to grab some of it. Here was a lady coming into baseball for sport. More important, she was coming to stay. She would be an important addition to the game. So what do they do? Why, rob her?"

The first player ever drafted by the Mets was catcher Hobie Landrith, who had been in the league a dozen years without ever establishing himself as a starter. According to Stengel Landrith was the first pick because "you have to have a catcher, or you'll have a lot of passed balls."

George Weiss, having to choose between has-been old-timers and mediocre younger prospects—the Houston Colt .45s took most of those—chose the old-timers. He figured that the best way to bring fans into the old Polo Grounds would be to draft players who were familiar. And if they were former Dodgers or Giants, so much the better. Among the veteran players acquired by the Mets were Richie Ashburn, Frank Thomas, Gus Bell, Gil Hodges, Don Zimmer, Clem Labine, Charlie Neal, and Elio Chacon, Felix Mantilla, and Roger Craig. Had the Mets taken these men in 1957, they might have had a contending team. By 1962, though, most of them were on the cusp of retirement.

Ashburn, the fleet ex-Phillie center fielder, still had one solid year left in him, but it would be his last. Thomas would finish the season with 34 home runs, but would be a defensive and base running liability. Craig, a superb relief pitcher, would be pressed into service as a starter and have two consecutive twenty-loss seasons; Hodges would be injured so badly they could barely make it out onto the field; Zimmer would start the season virtually hitless before being traded away, as would Landrith; Chacon couldn't hit, but was kept because he was the best the Mets had to offer; and Labine would be cut shortly after the season began.

The job of picking a starting lineup fell, of course, to manager Casey Stengel, who right up to game time on opening day at the Polo Grounds was wrestling with his lineup. Before the game *Post* columnist Lenny Shecter asked Stengel what it would be. In a booming voice Stengel stood in the little dingy office once occupied by John McGraw and Leo Durocher, and he began:

"Neal. He's first. Then Chacon."

"Chacon?" asked Shecter.

"Mantilla," said Stengel, making it sound like it rhymed with scintilla. "I mean Chacon. I mean I said Chacon but I meant Mantilla."

He paused. "I don't know who to hit third. If it's a right-handed pitcher, which it is, I might go with Bell in right field."

Then he turned angry. "You asked me for a lineup, and I can't give it to you."

Shecter and the other reporters could see that the challenge was eating at him.

"I got two center fielders," he said, "Christopher and Smith."

But Stengel had just told the reporters that Christopher had been sent to the minors.

"Christopher?" he was asked.

"Ashburn," he said. "Smith and Ashburn. Whichever one I play I'll put leading off."

But Stengel had said that Neal was going to lead off and play second and that Mantilla would bat second and play shortstop. Gus Bell was batting third playing right, and now he was batting Ashburn leadoff.

"Didn't you say that Neal was going to lead off?"

"Well, put Neal third and Mantilla second."

Stengel stared into his locker as he dressed. "Let's see. You can put Hodges fifth. No, put Bell fifth. Hodges sixth."

Stengel walked over to one reporter and looked at the notes he was taking down. "Better write it down so I'll remember it. And put [Jim] Marshall along with Hodges. Maybe I'll put Hodges in for a while and then Marshall."

"Who are you hitting fourth?"

He looked puzzled. Another reporter said, "Thomas. That right, Case? Thomas in left field batting fourth."

"That's right," said Stengel. He sighed. Two slots remained. A reporter asked whether Zimmer would bat seventh and play third base. Stengel nodded yes.

"One more thing," asked Shecter. "Who's the catcher, Landrith or Ginsberg?"

Stengel said, "It's Ginsberg or Landrith. Ginsberg caught him [Roger Craig] pretty good. I'll decide when I get there."

Leonard Shecter: "This was the process by which Casey Stengel made up his lineup every day. But usually, it happened inside his head."

★ ★ ★

All season long Casey Stengel entertained the reporters and the public with his running commentary. Sometimes it was humorous, other times sharp, and still other times undecipherable. Always it was entertaining. It was an irreverence that was picked up by the Mets fans.

Stan Isaacs: "The Mets in the first spring training had a whole bunch of ragtag guys, some of whom never made it to the opening day lineup. One of them was a guy by the name of Butterball Botz. Butterball was his nickname. They got him in expansion. And he didn't make the club. A lot of guys during spring training don't come north. Botz didn't.

"It was early in the season at the Polo Grounds, may have been the first game, and the Mets are losing, and I happened to be walking out of the press box to get a soda, and I heard a fan yell, 'Bring back Butterball Botz.' That was the personification of Mets fans."

After the Mets lost their first nine games in a row, Met pitcher Jay Hook defeated the Pittsburgh Pirates 9–1. Elio Chacon had three hits. Said Stengel about Chacon, "He looked like he owned Venezuela." He added, "Ninety-nine more wins, and we got the pennant."

But as upbeat as he was, Stengel also was realistic. His team was talent-thin. He was also aware that even a team with minimal talent could improve if the players did the little things, the fundamentals, required to win ball games. When they didn't, Stengel noticed but rarely did he go to the player to deliver the critique. He preferred instead to let the players read his acerbic comments in the newspapers.

After that first win he told reporters, "I'm glad we did good. It's good for the club. But we ain't so great. My pitcher didn't throw the ball over to first base so they got down and broke up two double plays. It was a good game, but we still did the same thing with men on base [not hit]. I don't know when they're going to learn."

When a reporter asked Stengel where he thought the Mets would finish, he replied, "We'll finish in Chicago."

By May Stengel decided to shed some of the older players whom George Weiss had purchased in favor of younger less–well-known players. Among those sent away was third baseman Don Zimmer.

Early in the season Stengel stood by the batting cage watching the former Brooklyn Dodgers utility infielder hit.

"Swinging too hard," he said. Then he watched Jim Marshall. "See, he turns his head. If he don't turn his head he hits a line drive. [Yankee first baseman Bill] Skowron is the only one I know who turns his head and hits the ball anyway."

Zimmer began the 1962 season going 0 for 34. When a fan said to Stengel, "That Zimmer's the guts of the club, isn't he?" Stengel replied, "Why, he's beyond that. He's much more. He's the perdotious quotient of the qualificatilus. He's the lower intestine."

On May 4, Zimmer ended his hitless streak with a double. Two days later he was traded to Cincinnati.

Don Zimmer: "We're in Philadelphia after finally winning our first game. I'm in the shower and Casey is standing in the middle of the clubhouse. He starts winking at me. Just winking. I can't figure out why, so I towel off quickly and come over to him.

"He puts his arm around me. 'You'll love the center field fence,' he says. 'You'll love the left field fence.'

"I'm completely baffled. 'What are you talking about?'

"Oh! We just traded you to the Cincinnati Reds!'"

It was Stengel, perhaps before anyone else, who saw that the future of the franchise lay in the signing of young prospects. By early May 1962 Casey Stengel launched a protracted one-man effort to attract young talent to the Mets. At a luncheon in Pittsburgh honoring Pirate manager Danny Murtaugh, he stood up before the audience and congratulated the Pirates on having a great team, "a fine team with wonderful men at every position." He added, "The Pirates are so good, how can you play for them? You can't. But you *can* play for the Mets. If you want rapid advancement, play for the Mets. We've got the bonus money. We'll even buy you a glove. So join us. Take the bonus money. Play a year or two. Then you can go back to school."

It would not be too many years before "the youth of America," as Stengel called them, would turn the franchise around. But in the meantime, Stengel would lose a lot of ball games, and Mets heroes would come from unlikely sources.

twelve

Hot Rod

Of the originals, the player who first captured the hearts and minds of the Met fans was an unknown Double A ballplayer from the New York Yankees organization by the name of Rod Kanehl.

Stengel remembered him from the time when the kid was a rising minor league star with the Yankees in the mid-fifties. He was a center fielder then, and in 1954 during an instructional league practice at Miller Huggins Field in St. Petersburg, a batter had hit a ball over the wire fencing in the outfield. Kanehl, who had been a high jump standout in high school, effortlessly leaped over the five-foot-high fencing, retrieved the ball, and leaped back over. Stengel, who didn't impress easily, took notice of his athleticism.

When Stengel told George Weiss he wanted to bring up Kanehl for the Mets from the Syracuse farm club, Weiss, who also knew Kanehl's talents, demurred.

"He can't field," Weiss told Stengel.

Replied Stengel, "But he can run the bases."

Kanehl began spring training behind better-known, more seasoned second basemen such as Neal, Mantilla, and Ted Lepcio. He hadn't been expected to make the team, but Stengel loved his intensity. He was brash and outspoken, he loved to party, and he played with all-out abandon. The veterans thought him a show-off, but he ignored them. At age twenty-eight the career minor leaguer had nothing to lose.

The writers also loved the kid, who they would call "Hot Rod," because his was a story about an ex-Yankee—the only ex-Yankee—coming to the Mets.

In the very first game televised from Florida back to New York, the Mets faced the Los Angeles Dodgers. Sandy Koufax was cruising along in the seventh inning with a 3–1 lead, when the Mets managed to put runners on second and third. Stengel called Kanehl in to pinch hit.

Kanehl ducked away from a pitch and hit it down the right field line for a two-run double to tie the game. When the Mets won 4–3, the fans had themselves a favorite Met.

Who was this guy, they wondered, and where did he come from?

As a boy Rod Kanehl's first love was track. In high school he was the Missouri state champion in the outdoor pole vault and the indoor high jump. His father was track coach and athletic director at Drury College in Springfield, Missouri, and after enrolling there he entered the Kansas Relays in the decathalon and finished fifth in the country as a freshman. If he had completed college, he could have been a favorite in the 1956 Olympic decathalon, but when he failed physics his freshman year, he became ineligible for spring track, and he decided to quit school and give professional baseball a try.

Kanehl had starred in American Legion ball, and New York Yankee scout Tom Greenwade, the man who gained fame from having signed Mickey Mantle, told Kanehl that anytime he was ready, he should call.

In January of '54 Kanehl called, and the next month the Yankees signed him for $4,000. At the time if a player signed for a penny more than $4,000, he had to stay on the major league roster for two years. The Yankees had signed first baseman Frank Leja and Notre Dame shortstop Tommy Carroll to large bonuses, and both sat on the Yankee bench two years and rotted. It was a terrible system, but it was designed by the owners to keep bonuses low, and in that respect it did its job very well.

When Kanehl signed, he agreed to go to a special rookie camp that manager Casey Stengel inaugurated in February 1954. Like all the players back then, he took the train. Riding the rails from Springfield to St. Petersburg, Florida, was an experience Kanehl never forgot.

Ron Kanehl: "When you signed your contract, it provided 'first class' transportation, and first class transportation in 1954 was the Pullman car.

Rod Kanehl

The way of the train was an art form. You had to learn to tip the porters, and I learned that to order your meals you had to fill out an order form and write down what you wanted.

"The train line started in Kansas City, and it was like a tributary. All the baseball players heading to spring training from every team who came from Nebraska, North and South Dakota, Iowa, and Kansas would go to Kansas City, and they'd get on this train. It would go through Springfield, and we had a lot of ballplayers from Springfield, and it would then go to Memphis, and all the players from up around St. Louis or Chicago would come down to Memphis and get on this train. Then the train would go to Birmingham, and all the players from the Ohio Valley would get on, and then on to Atlanta. It was like a river. It just started filling up. And by the time it left Atlanta, it held practically all ballplayers going to Florida.

"Even players from California hit this train. They would come in from

San Diego. George Delfino was on the train. After a week in spring training he disappeared. He went home. I later played with him in the minors. Deron Johnson was one on it. He joined the train at Jacksonville after riding along the southern border states from California.

"We had to change trains in Jacksonville to catch the Seaboard Line coming down from New York, and when it left Jacksonville, there were nothing but ballplayers, from all different teams, going to spring training.

"I met a bunch of the Yankee players: Ralph Terry, Jerry Lumpe, Jack Urban from up in Nebraska, and Fritzie Brickell, the little shortstop from Wichita. The guys played cards and craps.

"I remember one poker game. I was an observer: I never had enough money to play. Leroy Thomas, who is now called Lee Thomas, who later became general manager of the Philadelphia Phillies, was in the game. Along came this other little guy, Fritzie Brickell, who wanted to get in the game. They told him, 'Kid, you aren't old enough.' Fritzie was short and he had a baby face, but Fritzie was tough. He didn't take anything from anybody, and Fritzie got in the game.

"Today they fly. You don't get the same camaraderie."

When Kanehl arrived in camp he was joined by the cream of the Yankee rookie crop, promising youngsters such as Tony Kubek, Bobby Richardson, Johnny Blanchard, Marv Throneberry, Leja, Lee Thomas, Brickell, Gus Triandos, Woody Held, and Bob Grim, who was promoted to the Yankees and became the 1954 American League rookie of the year.

It was at that first camp that Stengel took notice of Kanehl.

Ron Kanehl: "Casey was developing the Yankee system. He wanted everybody to learn how to take signs one way, how to lead off first base, how to lead off second, and how to round the bases, how to make throws from the outfield, how to pivot to make the throw to second. He wanted the corps of players they expected to finally make the big leagues to be able to advance from D ball—to C, B, A, Double A, and Triple A—with everybody doing the same thing.

"Casey had a lot of the minor league managers at this advance camp so they would know what he was teaching so that if you ever got a shot at the big leagues, everybody would be on the same page. That was the Yankee system. And Casey had a routine he would start the first day of spring training.

"He'd take you from the bench to the on-deck circle to home plate, and then go one by one around the bases. This was a routine he would do every spring training, year after year after year.

"I was only nineteen when I signed, but when I arrived at the advance camp, I was awed, and I discovered that everybody was awed—a lot of people down there were in the same boat. Even though Bobby Richardson had played the year before, and Kubek, too, they were in awe.

"Casey noticed me that first camp. I was green as a gourd from Springfield, Missouri, and we were playing at Miller Huggins Field in St. Petersburg. There was a big lake in the back. They didn't have chain link in those days. The fence was made of barbed wire. Balls would run under and through the fence, and the kids would chase the balls down and run off with them.

"I was out in the outfield, and a ball rolled under the fence, and being a high jumper, I hopped this five-foot fence. No big deal for me. I beat a kid to the ball, then hopped back over and threw the ball in. I didn't hear that Casey had noticed until the next winter at the Hot Stove League dinner in Springfield.

"Tom Greenwade came over to me and said, 'You know, you really impressed Casey with that,' and he told me the story. Nobody made anything of it at the time, but Stengel saw it, and he remembered it.

"And during that first spring training, Casey would sit and talk to me. Casey and I always hit it off. Cause he was from Missouri also. He's from Kansas City. That's why they called him Casey. He knew my dad was a coach and a teacher, and he had been a coach and a teacher. My dad and Casey were from the same area of Kansas. Casey was from Westport. We'd sit and talk. Apparently I played like him. He would point out things on the field. I was like his bobo."

After two weeks of advance camp, the Yankees sent Kanehl to Birmingham, their Double A team. The team trained in Ocala, Florida. At the end of spring training Kanehl was sent to McAlester, Oklahoma, D ball, for the '54 season. Two of his teammates were Roy and Ray Mantle, Mickey's younger twin brothers. They were tall and imposing, but neither could hit the curveball.

At McAlester, Kanehl set a league record by hitting in 33 games in a row. He hit 11 home runs and drove in 99. The team finished third but reached the finals of the playoffs.

His performance spurred the Yankees to invite him back to the advance rookie camp the next February. Stengel had a surprise awaiting him.

Rod Kanehl: "Phil Rizzuto was retiring soon, and so when I arrived Casey took all the center fielders—me, Tony Kubek, and Woody Held, and he started making shortstops out of us. That's how Kubek ended up a shortstop, and Woody played shortstop for Cleveland for years.

"Stengel was always filling the Yankee roster with young blood. That was a great attribute of his. Bob Grim was a pitcher at that first rookie camp in '54, and he came to the team and went on to be the Rookie of the Year in the American League. Then Johnny Kucks made the Yankees from the '55 rookie camp.

"Gil McDougald once told me, 'Casey's greatest attribute was that he loved to sit a proven veteran on the bench and play a kid.' And that's why Casey had so many great rookies year after year after year. And he always had young pitchers coming up to his staff.

"A lot of people said, 'Stengel won because he had all those great players.' Well, Casey developed those great players through the organization, and he kept young blood coming all the time. And it's not easy to sit there and deal with a player who can't speak English or a temperamental center fielder in the twilight of his career [Joe DiMaggio], bringing in young blood and platooning Hank Bauer and Gene Woodling and dealing with all those personalities, and dealing with Whitey and the carousing of Mickey [Mantle] and Billy [Martin] without ruining the team. It took some talent for him to deal with all of that."

After rookie camp in '55, the Yankees sent Kanehl to Monroe, Louisiana, C ball, to play shortstop in the Cotton States League. Along with Roy and Ray Mantle, the team won both halves of the split season.

To reach the majors, a kid has to be lucky. He has to avoid serious injuries. At Winston-Salem, Kanehl broke his hand the first week of the '56 season sliding head first into second base. He was out a month. When he came back, he made a lot of errors at shortstop and was sent back down to Monroe.

By '57 he was promoted to Class B Peoria in the Three-I league, but by then his star had fallen. Billy Davidson was the regular shortstop. Rod was only a utility player filling in where needed.

By this time Kanehl was married with four children, making $450 a month, and he only was paid for the five months he played. He poured concrete in the off season so he could afford to play baseball in the summer.

By '58, the Yankees no longer had a place for Kanehl in their organization. He wanted $600 a month, and they refused to pay it. They sent him on loan to Monterrey in the Mexican League, a Cincinnati farm club.

When he arrived at the Monterrey training site, he didn't run into too many other players on the team who spoke English. Without telling anyone, he instead played with Cincinnati's Albuquerque team. When Cincinnati general manager Gabe Paul noticed Kanehl, he asked Kanehl how much he wanted to play. When Kanehl told him $600 a month, Paul also said no.

For Kanehl it looked like the end of the road, until he had a few too many and mouthed off. Had he not done so, it's likely his career would have been over back then.

Rod Kanehl: "I was to go to spring training in Laredo, Texas, the armpit of the world. I joined the Monterrey club, only to discover that the Cincinnati Reds organization was all fucked up. There was no organization down there. I got down there, and nobody knew who I was, because I was coming from the Yankee chain. They had a big hospital where all the players in the Cincinnati minor league organization lived. I knew I was supposed to have a Monterrey contract. But I hadn't signed anything. I took one look at the Monterrey team, and I could see that everyone spoke Spanish but me. I said, 'The hell with this,' and I went and started working out with Albuquerque. Jimmy Brown was the manager, and I started taking ground balls, and they just assumed I was on their roster. So I made their team as the shortstop.

"The owners, real rich people, threw a big party for us over the border in Nuevo Laredo. The writers were writing about me, I was having a good spring, and all of a sudden Gabe Paul came to me and said, 'Rod, you're not even signed.' I said, 'Yeah, I know.' He said, 'What are you asking?' 'Six hundred a month.' 'Oh, Jesus, we can't pay that. We just can't.'

"I said, 'Well, I guess that's it. You've got to pay my expenses back to Springfield, Missouri.' He said, 'Okay, come in in the morning, and we'll have your ticket home.'

"And so I went out that night and had a few cocktails. I came in after curfew, and Paul happened to be walking in. We started chatting and went to his office.

"I told him, 'I've always hit behind the runner, given myself up, but if I ever had a kid, I'd tell him, "Look out for yourself and forget about that team play," because it doesn't get you anywhere.'

"The next morning I was in line eating, and Gabe Paul said, 'Rod, are you still the ballplayer you were last night?' I laughed and said, 'What do you mean?' He said, 'I talked to Dallas of the Texas League, and they'll sign you on a ten-day look, and if you make it, they'll give you the six hundred a month you're asking for. They are opening in Austin tomorrow. If you're interested, here's your ticket.'

"I joined Dallas. It was an independent, owned by a guy named J. W. Bateman, a big contractor. Davey Williams was the manager. He had played with the Giants when Jackie Robinson busted him up. Freddie Martin, an old-time pitcher, was on the team, and Tommy Carroll, one of the Yankees' big bonus babies, was the shortstop. He had size-12 feet, and he was from Notre Dame.

"I sat for two days. I went to Davey Williams and I said, 'I'm on a ten-day look, and two of those days are gone. I need to play.' So Davey played me three days at shortstop. I made a play in the hole and got some hits and looked pretty good. And then it started raining, and it rained for five days. So they saw me for three days, but they decided to sign me.

"So I ended up in Dallas, and I started at shortstop. Our center fielder was Sam Suplizio, who was supposed to take Joe DiMaggio's place. Sam had had a great year at Binghamton and was dubbed 'the next center fielder' for the Yankees, but then he ran into a fence and wrecked his throwing arm.

"When Sam got a sickness, jaundice or something, they put me in center field, and I ended up hitting .295, had a good year, and made the All Star team.

"And then the Yankees invited me to spring training in '59. I went from being on my way home from Laredo in '58 to going to spring training with the Yankees in '59.

"And I had a pretty good spring. Casey played me. He moved me to second. And when we broke camp, I went to Richmond. Going north the Yankees played us in Richmond, and I got a couple of hits off Jim Coates, and I was really expecting to play, but they had a second baseman by the name of Curty Roberts, a great Triple A second baseman, and we also had Dick Sanders and Deron Johnson, so I wasn't playing much.

"We went to Buffalo, and between innings I went to the bullpen and warmed up Bob Wiesler, a left-handed pitcher, and he threw a slider, and I split the middle finger of my right hand. As a result, I didn't get to go to Havana, and that was the last team to play in Havana before the Cuban revolution.

"I was back at Richmond with this knocked-down finger, and I got a call from Jerry Coleman, who the Yankee personnel director. He said, 'Rod, we want you to go to Binghamton. We want you to learn how to become a slap hitter.' I had hit .295 at Double A. I refused to go back there.

"I said, 'Coleman, last year at Dallas I had 154 hits and 178 total bases. You're going to teach me to be a slap hitter? What are you going to teach me?'

"That was the way I hit anyway. But that sealed my destiny with the Yankees. Jack White, the Richmond general manager, said to me, 'You just stay here in Richmond. I'll make sure you get paid, and we'll see what happens.'

This time his big mouth appeared to have ended his Yankee career for good. The Yankees lent him to Houston in the American Association, another independent team. The Continental League was being formed, and everyone thought that Houston and Dallas were going to be part of it.

Kanehl didn't hit well that season, and in 1960 after starting with Dallas/Fort Worth, he was sent to Double A Nashville. He hit .275 but was just hanging on. It was better than laying concrete in the summertime.

In '61 Kanehl still had a Richmond contract, and he went to spring training in Fort Lauderdale, where the Yankees' Triple A team had moved. The next year the Yankees would move their major league spring training base from St. Petersburg to Fort Lauderdale. In 1961 Fort Lauderdale became the magnate for the college crowd during spring break. Kanehl was on the "B" team, which meant he got to take long bus rides to towns like Lakeland and Homestead. It was a memorable spring for Kanehl. At the end of spring training he was glad to leave Fort Lauderdale. Another couple weeks of booze and broads, and he might not have survived the spring.

Rod Kanehl: "This was '61, the year of the limbo. It was also the year of *Where the Boys Are*. All the chicks from up north were coming down. This was the year that started it all. We stayed at the old Broward Hotel, which was downtown. My roommate was a guy by the name of George Risley, who had gone to Boston College and played Triple A ball. I thought lemonade was the greatest drink in the world, but George introduced me to Cuba Libres. We would work out, and there was a liquor store next to the Broward Hotel. We'd get a pint of rum and a six-pack of Coke, and we'd go up to our room and take the glass pitcher that was on our hotel dresser and fill that with ice, and we'd cut up the limes, and we'd sit there and finish that pitcher of Cuba Libres. We did this after every workout!

"And after we finished that, instead of going to dinner, we'd hit the beach. The hell with dinner. We're gone! And Fort Lauderdale had some wild clubs with midnight licenses like Randy's Roost, Omar's Tent, The Elbow Room, The Three O'Clock Club, and The Four O'Clock Club. I hit them all. But I would get my sleep on that bus going to Homestead or going to Lakeland or going to Vero Beach playing all those B clubs. And I had a great spring.

"I've always resisted being sent out. I hit well over .300 during spring training, had a great spring, and so when they called me in to tell me they wanted to send me down, they said, 'Rod, they want you back in Nashville, and the season starts tomorrow.' I gave them no resistence. I said, 'Where's my ticket?' I needed to get out of Fort Lauderdale. I was beat!

"I arrived in Nashville for opening day. Lyndon B. Johnson, the vice president, threw out the first ball. He needed a glove, and I lent him mine. We played in Sulphur Dell, the oldest ballpark in baseball, and I was one of only two players to play in every game in the Southern Association that season. It was a tough bus league in those days. You'd drive from Little Rock to Atlanta to play the next day, then drive all night.

"I hit .304, played every game, and with expansion coming, I figured you'd never know, and that winter I was drafted by the Mets. The Yankees had left me on their Double A roster, and I was drafted by Syracuse, which had a partial working agreement with the Mets and also with Minnesota. When Syracuse drafted me, Minnesota figured it was for them, but it was actually for the Mets, and the commissioner had to make a ruling. So when I went to spring training with the Mets in '62, I had a Syracuse contract."

When Rod Kanehl arrived for the Mets' inaugural spring training he was greeted by his old mentor, Stengel, and by hitting coach Rogers Hornsby, whose lifetime .358 average ranked him as one of the great hitters of all time. It had been years since Kanehl and Stengel were together, but Casey, who never forgot a face even when he couldn't remember the name, used him to his advantage.

Rod Kanehl: "I really enjoyed that spring training with the Mets in '62. It was great. Our hitting coach was Rogers Hornsby. Nobody could hit like Hornsby, and Casey would tell us that, but Hornsby was just a figurehead. He would make comments about hitting, but he didn't coach anybody.

"Hornsby's theory of hitting was to hit up the middle, which is one theory. Casey was a very observant person, and Casey's theory of hitting was to put the ball in play down the lines. Here was Casey's thinking: Where do they put the worst fielding ballplayers? On the corners and in left and right field. He said, 'Why play with the best players on the diamond, which are the pitcher, the catcher, shortstop, second baseman and center fielder?'

"Casey held a meeting one time. Hornsby wasn't there. He said, 'Hornsby preaches, "Hit up the middle," but Hornsby could hit up the middle because he could hit home runs hitting straight away. He could do that. If you guys show me you can do that, you hit up the middle.'

"Casey was also very practical. In spring training that first year I heard Casey tell Ray Daviault, 'You were 5 and 13. You don't have a third pitch. You don't have a change-up. If you had a change-up, you might have won three more games, so instead of being 5 and 13, you'd have been 8 and 10, and instead of making $10,000, you'd be making $20,000.'

"I never saw him purposely put someone in a position to look bad. Because he always tried to create a value. He would play marginal players, players he knew they were trying to get rid of, in positions so they could look good. He always tried to increase your value.

"He put things in dollar and cents. If you were going to a speaking engagement, he'd always ask, 'Are you going to get paid for this? If you get paid, go. If not, tell them no.'

"I was the only American Leaguer drafted and the only guy out of the New York Yankee chain. Because it was National League expansion, the only players offered were National Leaguers. And so no one else knew anything about Stengel except me.

"Here were old pros like Gil Hodges, Don Zimmer, Roger Craig, Clem Labine, Joe Ginsberg, Frank Thomas, Richie Ashburn, Gus Bell, and here I am, coming from Double A, and when Casey started teaching his system, he knew I was the only one who knew what he was talking about.

"So he started out and went through his routine. He intended to teach the Mets the Yankee system, and he said, 'Kanehl, go to first base and show them how to lead off.' Then I'd go down to second. 'Kanehl, show them how to lead off second.' We'd go down to third. 'Kanehl, show them how you take the signs.' We went to bunting. 'Kanehl, show them how to bunt.' Those guys were veterans. They were thinking, who is this fucking Kanehl? They didn't know me from Adam. I was the only one from the Yankee chain, and he was using me as his mouthpiece to show them the fundamentals.

"I grabbed a bat and went up to the plate to bunt. Roger Craig was on the mound and he was supposed to be lobbing the ball in to me so I could show them how to bunt. Well, he turned one loose and knocked me on my ass! He decked me! And I grabbed the ball and jumped up and fired it right back at him. I said, 'Get the ball over, Meat.' Later Richie Ashburn told me he was wondering, 'Who is this brash fuck from Double A ball?' Ashburn was just as brash as anyone. He loved it. *Loved* it. I didn't give a shit. I was twenty-eight years old. I either make it, or I go home.

"And so I caught their eye, and during batting practice I would always work on my skills in the outfield, playing the ball off the bat. These other veterans would be standing around, telling war stories about the National League. One time Ashburn, Bell, Frank Thomas, and Roger Craig were standing around in a little circle, and a ball was hit in their direction. I bolted over for it, and I called it, and Ashburn stepped out of the circle and said, 'I got it,' and he dropped it. I told him, 'If you call it, catch it.' That's the way I was. Because I was out there working, and they were just farting around. Later Ashburn told me, 'I knew you were going to make it.'

"Late in spring training Casey sent me up to pinch hit in a game against Sandy Koufax and the Dodgers. It was the first ball game televised back to New York. All day I had sat in the bullpen at Al Lang Stadium, and there were two outs in the last of the ninth inning, and a runner on second. We were losing 3–1. The game was about over, so I was inching up from the bullpen toward the dugout, because you wanted to race to get a cab back to Miller Huggins Field, where we dressed. So I reached the dugout. I could see there were shadows coming across between the pitcher's mound and the catcher. It was pretty tough, and Koufax was pretty tough anyway.

"Casey said, 'Kanehl, grab a bat.' John Roseboso was catching. I went up there, and Koufax threw one right down the middle. Strike one. I didn't even see it. He threw another one. Strike two. I didn't even move my bat.

"Stengel started hollering, 'Butcher boy, butcher boy.' I knew that meant to swing down and try to make contact. So I was striding as he was releasing, and I saw it was going to be high, so I checked my swing, and it was this big curveball, and the ball hit my bat, and I hit a line drive between Ron Fairly and the first base line, a double down the right field line. The ball had eyes, and the tying run scored, and I ended up on second base. And then Felix Mantilla, the next hitter, got a base hit, and I scored the winning run. And that was it. I made the team.

"At the last moment they sent Joe Christopher to Syracuse, and that made room on the roster for me. Ted Lepcio had been penciled in as the utility man. But I could also play outfield, and I could bunt better and probably hit a little bit better. So I got the last spot.

"But my making the team killed George Weiss. George Weiss never did like me, for the same reason he never liked Billy Martin. Neither one of us looked like we had any talent, but we won ball games. We made things happen, and we always made Casey look good. But Weiss always wanted to get rid of me, and now he couldn't because I had become a hero in New York. All of New York was asking, 'Who is this guy?' and the front page of the *Daily News* had a picture of Stengel pulling me out of a hat like a rabbit.

"The season began in St. Louis. We were staying at the Chase Hotel. We were going up to our rooms, and I was in the elevator with a bunch of other players, and it was packed, and Harry Chiti jumped in there, and that's what did it: the elevator went about three floors, and it stopped. We were in there thirty or forty minutes!

"We lost the opener, but when we came back from St. Louis, they had a ticker tape parade down Broadway, and that was great. We ended up at City Hall, and Mayor Wagner was on the steps, and he gave Casey the key to the city. It was quite an experience.

"When the season started we were full of confidence. We had veterans at every position. Gus Bell, Richie Ashburn, and Frank Thomas were in the outfield, and Hobie Landrith, the first player drafted, caught.

"In the infield Don Zimmer was the third baseman, and Felix Mantilla was at short, Charlie Neal at second, and Gil Hodges at first. Charlie was a good second baseman. Felix could play, and Elio Chacon could play. We could all play.

"Hodges was a friend of mine. We would sit around and talk baseball. I was one of those guys who would sit in the locker room and talk baseball with Zimmer, Ashburn, and the guys.

"I remember one time Gil and I were talking, and during the conversation I referred to my father as 'my old man.' He pulled me off to the side and said, 'Ron, when you're around me, never refer to your father as your "old man." Always refer to him as your father.' The phrase bothered him as being disrespectful. He just didn't like to hear it. That's the kind of guy Hodges was.

"One time we were going to Pittsburgh. We left out of Newark Airport, and we were flying a Caravelle, a short-hop plane. Casey was in the habit of calling Gil 'Gilly,' and so people started calling him 'Gilly,' and as we were boarding, people were saying, 'Good luck, Gilly,' and my son, Phil, who was eight or nine at the time, said, 'Good luck, Gilly,' and they shook hands.

"We got on the plane, and after we got airborn and leveled out, Hodges came over to me and said, 'Rod, don't you think your son ought to call me 'Mr. Hodges?'

"We returned home. Casey had a rule that our families could only come into the clubhouse after a game if we won, and so it was two or three weeks before we won a game, and I watched Phil come into the clubhouse after the game we won, and he went right over to Gil, and he said, 'Nice game, Mr. Hodges.' And Gil looked at me and winked. Hodges loved those things.

"But we had absolutely no pitching. And we had no bullpen. We had one of the finest relief pitchers in the National League, Roger Craig, as a starter. He would have set all kinds of relief records had he been able to be used as a reliever. Roger was a good five-inning pitcher, had a good pick-off move, and he had a good sinker/slider. He could come in and get a ground ball, and boom, it's over. He was perfect for relief. But we had to use him as a starter.

"We would be in the game through the sixth or seventh inning, and then it was over. We lost our first nine games, but we were in a lot of those games. We just didn't get off the ground.

"Even though we lost, we were still upbeat. And so was Casey, who was leading the parade down Broadway. A lot of people identified with the Mets—underdog types, not losers—quality people who weren't quite getting it together. And Casey was always a draw. Casey would fill the [newspaper] columns. He could fill them. That's why Yogi never made it as a manager. He couldn't fill the columns. And you've got to do that in New York. You have to give them something to write about. Casey always had print for the writers, and that's why the writers would go along with him. People loved Casey Stengel. And they didn't like the way he had been dismissed from the Yankees.

"If it hadn't been for Casey, we'd have all been buried. What Casey did was keep the writers off our backs individually. They could write all the bad things they wanted collectively, but Casey wouldn't let them pick on individual players. I think he must have made an agreement with them early in the season, or else it just evolved that way.

"And even though we lost a lot of games, Casey had the knack of keeping us in position to win at the end. You know, the "Let's Go Mets" thing. We were in a lot of the games until the ninth inning, and he always had Hodges, or Woodling, or Throneberry, somebody to send to the plate to give the fans hope. They would have to hit a home run to tie it or win it, and Throneberry did that a couple of times.

"We started the '62 season with nothing but veterans, because that's what George Weiss wanted. He wanted to attract the National League crowd. And Casey didn't want that at all.

"I was hitting .330 in early May. I went up to Casey in his office in the Polo Grounds, and I said, 'I'm hitting .330, leading the team in hitting. How come I'm not playing regularly?' And he asked me how much I was making. I said, 'Eight thousand.' He said, 'You're not making enough money to be playing regular.' He said, 'I'm going to give the Old Man upstairs,' meaning Weiss, 'the walking dead til he's sick of it.' He meant he was going to play these old guys until Weiss got sick of it.

"And then Hodges went down, and Zimmer was gone, and we traded Bell to Milwaukee. Before the season was over, he started playing the younger guys, but we didn't have any prospects. We had Marv Throneberry to play first. A lot of people think Marv Throneberry was an original Met. They also think he was a Met forever. But we didn't get Marv until May, and he didn't hardly play in 1963. He was just there that '62 year and the first part of '63. He was acquired to be the left-handed platoon with Gil Hodges at first.

"Marv had been at that Yankee rookie camp in '54. He was agile, and he looked good. He wore the cuffs of his pants just like Mickey Mantle. He had power and he was going to be I-T. But he spent all his time in the minor leagues. One year he drove in 150 runs and hit 45 home runs at Denver. He did this two, three years in a row. And then he was traded to Baltimore, where he sat on the bench behind Jim Gentile. So he sat on the bench, and when he came to the Mets, they expected him to be able to play. Marv was my roommate in '62. He never was twinkletoes, but he always looked good in the lobby! Marv was a country boy, but he had the taste of the big city. He loved New York.

"The writers wrote about Marv's misplays. I remember one time he chased Musial across home plate in a rundown. I was involved in that play. It happens. Sometimes you get caught in a situation where there's a point of no return. You have to let the guy go. Marv was unconscious that way. Things he did were magnified, but he did win some games with home runs. Marv was a great guy. He was like a teddy bear. He would laugh it off. He laughed off the criticism. He would recite the saying, 'Rasberries, strawberries, we want Throneberry,' to the fans.

"If it hadn't been for Richie Ashburn, Throneberry never would have become as famous. My locker was across the room from them. On one side of me was Ken MacKenzie, and next to me on the other side someone was always coming or going. I never knew who that was. But I had a good seat to watch what was going on. The writers would come in, and Ashburn would tell them, 'Throneberry says, "Blah, blah, blah, blah,"' And they would quote Throneberry. But it was Ashburn's glibness that put the words in Throneberry's mouth. And it was Ashburn who schooled him on the fact, 'Accept the notoriety, good or bad.' I roomed with him. Marv didn't take it badly. He was a celebrity, and he liked his celebrity, and he got along with it. He signed autographs. Mentally he was in good shape.

"I heard a great story about him and the Miller beer ad he did. They called him up and said, 'We want you to come to New York and make this commercial.' Marv laughed and hung up the phone. He thought this was a prank. They had to call him three times before they could convince him they weren't kidding. And this is where he got so much of his notoriety, from the Miller ad. That brought him back. That's why a lot of people think he was around a long time.

"We signed Ed Kranepool the first year. He just came up, and then he went out. He came back at the end of the year. Ed was brash. He was cocky. He was a New Yorker, and he knew he was going to make it because they gave him a lot of money. Ed had had a good high school career at James Monroe High School. I remember he came over to take batting practice with us for a look, and he hit balls out of the park. He hit the shit out of the ball. And everybody thought he was going to be a big home run hitter.

"I was in the on-deck circle when he got his first base hit. He came up, and he got a little slap hit into center field. And that's the way he hit. He was a slap hitter all the way. Ed was all right. He lasted a long time.

"Frank Thomas loved New York. He was happy there. Ashburn was all right, but he hated to lose, and we lost a lot. But he got a lot of notoriety and press that he never got in Philadelphia, and he survived because he was a sportsman. Roger Craig survived. Jay Hook didn't take it too well, and neither did Craig Anderson, Bob Moorhead, or Ray Daviault. They didn't survive. Jay Hook had a great arm, but he threw some of the longest home run balls I've ever seen thrown. Willie Mays would hit them into the lights in left center at the Polo Grounds on the dead fly. And Frank Howard would hit golf ball–like balls. One time Elio Chacon jumped for a ball Howard hit at the Polo Grounds and it hit off the Listerine sign in left-center! The ball caromed clear around to Ashburn in right field!

"One player who was unhappy in New York was Jim Hickman. He was a country boy, and he was in the city. He was miserable. His wife was miserable. His kids were miserable. We lived in the same apartment building one year over in Jackson Heights. We lived in a fourplex with Al Moran and Galen Cisco, but Shea Stadium didn't get built on time, and we had to play another season in the Polo Grounds.

"Hickman couldn't stand playing on the Mets. He took the criticism personally, and he'd get his dobber down. He'd duck writers. He hated writers. And Casey couldn't get him motivated. He looked like he was going to sleep all the time. But he had a live bat, and when he popped it, the ball jumped off his bat. But Jim was a straightaway hitter, and the Polo Grounds was not his ballpark. After he went to Wrigley Field, he went crazy. But before he joined the Cubs, he played a season for the Dodgers, and he couldn't hit there either. Then he went to the Cubs, and in '69 he had a great year.

"Charlie Neal was another one who wasn't a happy camper, but I don't think Charlie ever was happy. I played with him in '65 with Wichita when we won the national semipro tournament. He was always grumbly.

"In May Charlie got hurt. Charlie had a bad hand, a bone spur, so I started playing regularly at second base, and when Charlie got well, Casey put him at short, and Charlie and I made more double plays in a two–week period than anybody. We had a lot of pride and confidence in making the double play. I was hitting good and playing a regular second base, and Charlie was playing short.

"I got a few hits. The Giants came to town, and there were 50,000 people at the Polo Grounds, a Sunday doubleheader, and Gil Hodges had a bad knee and couldn't play, and Billy Pierce was pitching for the Giants, so

Casey came to me and said, 'Can you play first?' You know you gotta say yes. I'm a utility man, right? I had never played first base in my life, except goofing around in the infield. Casey said, 'Get a glove. You're in there because Hodges can't play.'

"I hit a home run off Pierce, and we got beat 6–1. Juan Marichal pitched the second game. He had to play me, so he played me in right field, and I went two for three against Marichal, and I was the toast of the town! Who's this Kanehl? No one had ever heard of me, other than that spring training hit off Koufax. And through June I was hitting over .300, even though I had only been up a hundred times. They were touting me for Rookie of the Year. Once I started reading that, then I went to hell!

"You know, I hit the first grand slam in Mets history [off Bobby Shantz of St. Louis], and the first banner ever flown in the Polo Grounds said, 'We love the Mets. Hot Rod Kanehl.' I was on the bench, and Ashburn called me over, and he said, 'What did you pay those kids?' It was up in the deep left field upper deck in the Polo Grounds. About a month into the season.

"In May, we beat Cincinnati, and we beat the Braves at home, we were playing well, but then we went on the road and lost 17 games in a row. We sure could dream up ways to lose. We hated to go into LA. We couldn't beat LA. Maury Wills would drive us crazy. Stengel used to get up on the bench and holler to our catcher Chris Cannizzaro, 'Throw it to third.' Meaning, if Wills attempted to steal second, just throw it to third. Because Cannizzaro would hurry the throw, and the ball would go into center field, and Wills would end up on third. I don't know how many times that happened. So Stengel yelled, 'Throw it to third.' It wasn't a joke. He meant it.

"Against the Dodgers we faced Koufax, [Don] Drysdale, and Johnny Podres. And Ron Perranoski in relief. The Giants had Jack Sanford, Mike McCormick, and Juan Marichal. And Stu Miller in relief. In late June Koufax pitched a no hitter against us.

"With one out in the ninth Casey called Gene Woodling up to pinch hit, Gene went crazy. They almost had a fight on the bench. He called Casey every name in the book for sending him up against Koufax, his being a left-hander. Woodling said, 'You got young, right-handed guys, and you're sending me up, you no good. . . . ' I was on first base. I could hear every word.

"And Koufax struck him out, and I made the last out, and that was the end of it.

"We were eliminated from the pennant the first week in August. Casey called a meeting. We were in LA, and he said, 'You guys can relax now.

We're mathematically eliminated from the pennant.' He was half-joking, but he called a meeting to say that. 'You can loosen up now.' So we loosened up. We won just eleven more games in the last two months!

"Richie Ashburn hit over .300 in '62. And the greatest comment he ever made came when he would get on our pitchers. He'd say, 'I'd be leading the league if I got to face you guys.' He was the greatest. In his last play in the big leagues, he was the third out of a triple play!

"We were in Chicago, and it was a Saturday game. It wasn't even the last game of the season. And it wasn't the ninth inning. He was on first, and Sammy Drake was on second, and Ken Hubbs was playing second base for the Cubs. Joe Pignatano hit a looper over Hubbs, and he caught it running away, and he turned and threw to second to get Drake for the second out, and then they threw back to first to get Ashburn for the third out. Richie had that little come-up slide, and he popped right up, and our dugout was right there and he took two steps into the dugout, grabbed his glove, and he said, 'That's a fine-fucking-finish to this year. I'll see ya next year.' And he went right on up the ramp to the clubhouse. And by the time the game was over, he was packed and gone. We thought we'd see him the next spring, but we never saw him again. That was his last play in the big leagues.

"Richie was one of the best. He was from Tilden, Nebraska, and he won a sailboat, and Marv Throneberry won a sailboat. But Ashburn didn't have to pay taxes on his, cause he won his in a contest, and Marv did, because his was a gift.

"I was going good until the first part of August. They were talking Rookie of the Year, and then my knee started acting up, and I didn't play a whole lot after that. I was worn down. We ended our season playing in front of three hundred people in Chicago. And Bob L. Miller finally won a game [after losing 12 in a row]. This was the next to last game of the season, and there was a big horse race, and all the writers went to the track!

"Miller said, 'All year every time I'd lose a game, ten writers would want to know what went wrong. Now I win the game, and there's nobody here.' Bobby was a great guy. He took it well.

"We lost 120 games. It was a long season. After the last day of the '62 season at the Polo Grounds, they awarded Casey Stengel home plate. He hobbled from home plate all the way across the field out to center field to the dressing room while they played 'Auld Lang Syne,' and I sat up there in his office and cried like a baby. Most everybody cried. If you play 'Auld Lang Syne,' I'll cry every time."

thirteen

Ron Hunt

Despite the 40–120 record in 1962, the New York Mets drew close to a million fans to the Polo Grounds. Stengel, analytical as always, found the rousing support of his terrible team "amazing." And, as usual, his depiction of the Met fans, made two years later, defies description.

Casey Stengel: "I wanna say that the Mets fans have been marvelous. And they come out and done better than we have on the field and I'm glad we got 'em. If we could do as well as them it'd be better and we're tryin' 'cause in supportin' us the attendance has got trimmed. You'd think we'd do better and without all these people turnin' out to help us we wouldn't but they come out with the banners and the cheers and it's 'Metsie, Metsie, Metsie.' When the little children first start to speak they once said, 'Mamma' and 'Papa' but with the fans we got they say the first thing, 'Metsie, Metsie, Metsie.'

"I'm glad to see that we got so many of the ladies turnin' out to see our team 'cause it proves that we got effeminate appeal which is the result of my charm school which I run as chief instructor in effeminate appeal and we got 'em turnin' out with their dates, the young 'uns and the old 'uns, and I wish we could do it better on the field.

"And you might wanna say wasn't it the World's Fair that drew the people into the park and I'd hafta say no maybe it was we halped out Mr. Moses and his Fair across the street because if you'll remember we drew over a million people at the Polo Grounds which was fallin' in and they didn't have no Fair across the street and you couldn't park it, unless you drove on the subway and there's no place to dine."

In January 1963, 500 Mets fans flocked to the Garden City Hotel on Long Island where Stengel congratulated them for surviving the first season. A hand from the audience was raised. "What will the Mets fans have to look forward to this coming season?" Stengel was asked.

Replied Stengel, "We have this big new scoreboard that is going to be just magnificent. Oh, it's huge. Grand. Nothing ever like it before." Then he added, "But it's not going to be so useful to us if you don't get the man to home plate."

By the start of 1963 the people of New York were growing fonder and fonder of the Old Man. He was becoming a folk figure.

As Stengel and Weiss tried to refigure the team, many of the first-year players fell by the wayside. First baseman Marv Throneberry, who had kicked away a passel of games only to be cheered by the fans for his ability to lose ball games, had been awarded the Good Guy Award by the writers at the end of the season. Throneberry then tried to convince assistant general manager, Johnny Murphy, that as a result of the notoriety that stemmed from his futility, he deserved a raise in 1963.

Throneberry told Murphy, "People came to the park to holler at me, just like Mantle and Maris. I drew people, too."

Answered Murphy, "You drove some away, too."

"I took a lot of abuse," said Throneberry.

"You brought most of it on yourself," Murphy told him.

"I played in the most games of my career."

"But you didn't play well in any of them," said Murphy.

Said general manager George Weiss, "Marv got the good guy award mixed up with the most valuable player award."

Early in the '63 season Throneberry was sent to the minors, never to return. Weiss never understood Throneberry's importance to Mets fans. In the same way he never understood why they could be so rabid about one of the worst teams in baseball history. The relationship between Weiss and the young fans anticipated the split in America's culture ten years hence. Weiss and his assistant, Johnny Murphy were akin to Richard Nixon and his teutonic duo of John Erlichman and John Haldeman, while the Mets fans were more in tune with Yippie funsters Abbie Hoffman and Jerry

Rubin. So, even though the fans loved him, Weiss shipped Throneberry off to Buffalo without a second thought.

Banners were hung proclaiming: "Bring Back Marvelous Marv," and for a while the *New York Post* wrote of his exploits at Buffalo. Weiss, however, never brought him back.

By the start of the '63 season the only starters left from the year before were infielder Charlie Neal and left fielder Frank Thomas. Everyone else was new: Tim Harkness at first, Larry Burright at second, Al Moran at short, Duke Snider in center, phenom Ed Kranepool in right, and Clarence "Choo Choo" Coleman behind the plate. Harkness, Burright, Neal, and Snider were ex-Dodgers.

In the season opener at the Polo Grounds, the very first Cardinal batter hit a dribbler to Charlie Neal at third. He raced in, picked it up and threw it into right field. The Mets lost 7–0.

Stengel stormed into his office, threw his cap down and shouted, "The attendance was robbed. We're still a fraud."

In a game against the Cardinals, the Mets held a 3–0 lead going into the ninth and blew it. Said Stengel, "Can't anybody play this here game?" Jimmy Breslin changed it to, "Can't anybody here play this game?" It was the title of a book he wrote and the team's catch phrase for the next few years.

One highlight of the '63 season was the team's June 24 victory over the New York Yankees in the Mayor's Trophy Game. Most of the 50,000 fans who flocked to Yankee Stadium were Mets fans. When the Yankees played that afternoon it was for fun. For Stengel, it was war.

After Jay Hook pitched five excellent innings, Stengel called down to the bullpen. He inquired of pitching coach Ernie White, "Who ya got ready, Mr. Weiss?"

"Ken MacKenzie's throwing," said White.

"Mr. Weiss," said Stengel, "ain't we got somebody better than that?"

"Carl Willey," who at the time was one of the best on the staff.

"Heat him up, Mr. Weiss."

Willey pitched four shutout innings, and the Mets won 6–2. Stengel was out to prove that the Yankees had been wrong in firing him. He told one reporter about Yankees manager Ralph Houk, "That fella said I hollered at the players too much, but I notice he's playing the players I hollered at."

The win over the Yankees was a highlight of 1963. Most of the rest of the season was about losing games. The Mets had one streak where they lost 29 of 31.

When the Mets won two in a row in early August, Stengel told reporters, "I don't think we can catch the Dodgers—unless we play winter ball."

During one game Stengel kept saying to Duke Snider, "They're mahogony and we're driftwood." His head started to droop, and he said to Snider, "Look kid, I'm tired. You know the signs. You run the club." Stengel dozed off. A couple of innings later he awoke. The Mets were losing 9–0. Snider said, "I'm sorry, Casey." Stengel replied, "That's all right. I told you they were mahogany and we're driftwood."

Later that season Tracy Stallard gave up two long home runs into the right field seats. After the second one, Stengel came to the mound to talk to his pitcher.

"Doctor," Stengel said, "at the end of the season they're gonna tear this joint down. The way you're pitching, that right-field section will be gone already."

Rod Kanehl recalled that even though the Mets won ten more games in 1963 than they did in '62, the team wasn't as good as it had been the year before.

Rod Kanehl: "I always was a utility player. I just had streaks of playing regularly at second or in center field. But I played over a hundred games as a utility man, which is saying something. In '63 I thought I was going to have the second base job, but I had a knee operation in the off-season.

"I got a chance to start the first Old Timers Day game the Mets ever played, because Ron Hunt's wife had a miscarriage in St. Louis and he had to fly back.

"We never played an Old Timers game in '62. The first one got rained out, and they rescheduled it, and it rained. But I got a chance to start the one in '63, and I got a couple of hits against the Yankees. On a hit-and-run play I pulled the ball because the shortstop was covering, and I made them look bad, and we won the game.

"And the Mets fans came to Yankee Stadium with firecrackers and signs. The Yankees had never seen this before. The Yankee fans had never seen this parading of signs and the throwing of firecrackers. We had to stop the game because someone had thrown a cherry bomb onto the field. It was great!

"And I got a little ink after the game. I got a couple hits, and in the locker room the writers came over, and I said, 'You know, when I signed with Tom Greenwade, he said to me, "Rod, sign with me and you'll end up a winner in Yankee Stadium."' And I said, 'After ten years, I finally made it. I'm a winner at Yankee Stadium.'

"But, aside from that, things really disintegrated in '63. We were worse in '63. We won more games, but we were bad.

"In '63 Felix Mantilla was gone. Elio Chacon was gone. They got Larry Burright from the Dodgers and Ted Schreiber out of the Boston chain, and Al Moran at short. We got Cliff Cook, and he had a back operation. We had a shortstop out of the Dodger chain, Chico Fernandez. He got the last hit in the Polo Grounds. I got the last pinch hit. Our first legitimate prospect was Ron Hunt in 1963.

"Al Moran couldn't do anything. Who wants to go see Al Moran? Who wants to go see Ted Schreiber? Tim Harkness had his streaks. Cliff Cook was in and out, and later we had a guy named Charlie Smith, and they didn't know where to play him. He would get his dobber down. He was bad. And then we had the Joe Christopher situation. God, he was terrible in the field. Joe was into himself so bad, but he could swing the bat. And in '63 we got Jimmy Piersall, and that was a total disruption. Jimmy was crazy like a fox. He was known for being a nut, and he played it like a nut. But he would go on *The Tonight Show*. He got a lot out of New York.

"Piersall said a lot of nasty things about Casey. He sure did. Until Casey got rid of him. Howard Cosell would pump guys to say bad things about Stengel. Cosell did the pregame and postgame radio with Ralph Branca, and he and Stengel had a running feud for years. Cosell and I were good friends. If I needed tickets to the shows, he would get them for me. He was good that way. Cosell would have me on his TV show downtown, and he'd always try to get me to say something bad about Stengel, and I would never go there. The show would be over, and he'd say, 'Well, you did it again. You just won't say anything bad about that man.' I said, 'Hell no, I'm not going to.'

"But he got Tim Harkness on there one time, and he got Tim to agree with what Snider had said and what Jackie Robinson had said about Casey sleeping on the bench, and Harkness was gone within five days. Who needs it? You're gone. It's all over. In those days a team could do that, and nobody questioned it.

"After Robinson had blasted Stengel, I loved what Stengel said: 'He's chock full of nuts!'

"Casey was so quick and witty. When the season started, he held a meeting, and he would tell us, 'The bar in the hotel is mine.' So you never saw him drinking. The writers would say, 'He'll drink anything you put in front of him. He'll drink a Manhattan, then drink a beer, then drink a Scotch. He'll drink anything, and he'll drink every one of us under the table. He's the last one to leave, and the first one at the ballpark.' He was great.

"I did my share of carousing. Well, Casey had this trick. It didn't dawn on me until after I was out of baseball. But if we were flying, just before takeoff Casey would walk up and down the aisle, and he would see which guys pulled pillows before we taxied. If you pulled a pillow before we taxied, he knew we were carousing. He *knew*. Because he had been a carouser in his days.

"I roomed with Ron Hunt, and we both pull pillows, and we taxi. We play a game in Chicago, and the locker room attendant comes over to me after the next game, and he says, 'Stengel wants to see you in his office.'

"So I went in the office, and Casey said, 'Kanehl, do you think you've been staying out a little too late, a little too much partying? It's affecting your play. I want you to think about it, and try to curtail some of your activities.' And before I could answer him, he said, 'And that goes for your roommate, too.'

"All he was doing was telling me to tell Hunt. He dressed me down, and before I could even answer him, he said, 'And tell your roommate the same thing.' He didn't want to call Hunt in and get on him, because Hunt was tempermental. But Casey knew we were roommates, and he knew I'd tell Hunt. He didn't give a shit about me. My career was over. I was a suspect. Hunt was a prospect. Honest to God. Casey was cute that way. Stengel was good."

Second baseman Ron Hunt turned out to be the one bright spot for the 1963 Mets. Hunt, who had not been expected to make the team, put the bat on the ball and ran the bases intelligently. His trademarks—a chaw of tobacco in his cheek and a dirty uniform from a head-first slide—made him the kind of hard-nosed player Stengel loved: cocky and fearless.

When Stengel offered his players cash for every time they got hit by a pitch while batting, Hunt made a closet industry out of it. His rookie year

Ron Hunt

he was dinged thirteen times. In 1971 Hunt set a major league record when he was hit by pitches 50 times. The next year he broke Minnie Minoso's then–career record of 192.

Hunt rode the bench early in the '63 season while the Mets lost their first eight games. Frustrated because he wasn't playing, Hunt, who was assigned the job of being the Mets' bullpen catcher, stopped Stengel in the runway in Connie Mack Stadium. The kid told Stengel he deserved to play over Larry Burright and first-round draft choice Ted Schreiber. Stengel gave him that chance. Against Milwaukee, Hunt singled off reliever Claude Raymond in the ninth to win the game 5–4, the first Mets' victory of the season.

After the twenty-two-year-old rookie won a game with a late-inning hit, Casey Stengel went on television and used Hunt as the perfect example of a youngster who gets to play in the major leagues quickly because of the talent shortage on the Mets.

Casey Stengel: "It's young ballplayers like Ron Hunt that have a great chance with the New York Mets, and if you're anybody who wants to play baseball, you want to get to the major leagues in a hurry, just sign up with the New York Mets because the New York Mets can get you to the major leagues quicker than anyone else, and if there's anybody out there lookin' in on the television that thinks they can play baseball in the major leagues, get in touch with the New York Mets."

That night the Mets' switchboard was swamped with calls from kids who wanted to play for the Mets. A special crew of operators stayed at their stations until well past midnight.

While Hunt played second and Al Moran shortstop, Stengel tried Elio Chacon in the outfield. The experiment failed.

"What the hell is the difference where you play him," Stengel sneered. "He's still gonna knock in twenty-seven runs for you."

With Hunt and Moran up the middle in place of Mantilla and Chacon, the pitchers felt more secure. Instead of losing 12–5, the Mets would lose 3–2.

In 1964, Hunt was the first New York Met to be voted onto the All Star team. At the end of the year he finished second to Pete Rose for Rookie of the Year. Characteristically, Hunt felt passionately that he, not Rose, deserved the honor.

Ron Hunt: "I was born on February 23, 1941, in St. Louis. My dad was a butcher. I grew up in a city, St. Louis, played ball in the alleys or the sandlots, any place we could find. I played Corey League ball, high school ball, Legion ball, and I played basketball. That was before all this weight lifting when you were able to keep your flexibility and participate. If I got injured, I kept playing. In those days you played with injuries, you didn't sit out.

"The scout who took an interest in me was a guy by the name of Richard Keeley, with the Milwaukee Braves organization. He said he had been scouting me since I was twelve. I don't see how that was possible but that's what he said. I had never seen him before.

"He didn't sign me out of high school. He wanted me to get a scholarship and play football and baseball at Northwestern or SIU Carbondale, cause that was the only way I could get a full ride, and I couldn't afford to go to college. But I was only five-ten-and-a-half and one-seventy, going against six-foot-four, two-twenty, and they could run as fast as I could. I couldn't see over them, and I said, 'Self, you've got no goddamn business playing football here.'

"So I went home and got on a summer team, and then Keeley asked if I was interested in playing pro ball, and I said, 'As long as the money is good enough.'

"We spent about a week negotiating. It all came down to a double-header. If I did well, I'd get what I was settling for, and if I did bad, I was going to take what he offered. It was a shake of the hands, which meant something in those days. And I went seven for nine. So I got about $20,000, and a train ticket to McCook, Nebraska. McCook was a nice town, and the people were nice, too. The whole league of Nebraska was just farmers and good, hardworking people.

"Then I went to Cedar Rapids, Iowa, for two years. Red Schoendienst [the Milwaukee Braves second baseman] had TB so they changed me from a third baseman to a second baseman. I played for Jimmy Brown, who was the kind of ballplayer I was trying to be, and he and Solly Hemus helped me as much as anybody to get me a look-see as far as getting to the majors.

"In '62 I played for Austin, Texas, where Solly with the Mets was scouting the Texas League for a second baseman, and in the winter of '62 the Mets picked up my contract.

"I didn't want to go down to South America. It was just too far for my wife Jackie and me to go. We've been going together since we were sixteen, and we got married September 16, 1961, the happiest day of my life, which she tells me to tell everyone. That winter I went to St. Petersburg, Florida, for the winter league.

"It was great. Paul Waner was my manager. All he did was teach hitting the ball where it was pitched, hitting it solid, and a quick belly button, and that all fit into my profile. His technique of hitting was just super.

"Eddie Stanky and Solly Hemus were down there. Solly taught me to take pitches, to get on base, and to not be afraid to get hit by the ball. Eddie the same thing. Eddie was a hard-nosed player who wouldn't give you an inch, wanted to beat you any way he could. That fit into my profile perfectly. Just about everything down there I could listen to and understand without changing a lot of things.

"And then Casey Stengel came down, and they brought in Jesse Owens to teach running. He taught that everything should go forward instead of winging your feet or arms. Just keep everything together so you don't have that air flow. And I teach my kids the same thing today: You can't run with your elbows or toes sticking out.

"To me, going to spring training with the Mets was no big deal. It was just getting a chance to play more and better baseball, and knowing that Cookie Lavagetto was there and Solly Hemus was there, and Eddie Stanky, who took a liking to me because he liked to hit ground balls and I liked to take them, so it wasn't as though I was going someplace where I didn't have somebody to talk to.

"I never was too much on getting star struck. My idols when I was young were Red Schoendienst and Alvin Dark, who just went out and beat you. Besides, in spring training who would have thought a kid from Double A would jump all the way to the majors? So I was just there. I was number seven of seven second basemen: Charlie Neal, Rod Kanehl, Larry Burright, Elio Chacon, Ted Schreiber, and one other. I was on the bottom of the list.

"Casey liked me. He liked young kids who liked to play and hustle. If you got on Casey's shit list, man, you didn't get out. You may not have known why you were in there, but by God, you didn't get out of it.

"I remember spraining my ankle pretty bad. We were playing a game in St. Petersburg, and Casey came by and said, 'Can you hit?' I said, 'Yeah.' He poked my ankle, and it hurt like a son of a bitch. He said, 'Aah, go on up there and hit. If you get to first base, I'll get you a runner.' I got a base hit, and I came back to the dugout, and he winked at me.

"Nothing else was said. I broke camp as a bullpen catcher behind Neal, who was still there, and Larry Burright, the starting second baseman, and Kanehl was playing the outfield.

"I remembered what Casey had said in spring training about coming to him if you were dissatisfied rather than going to the press. I didn't feel I was a bullpen catcher, and Larry Burright wasn't doing very well at all either offensively or defensively, and I ran across Casey in the dugout there in Connie Mack Stadium in Philadelphia. There was a long runway between the field and the clubhouse, and Casey was coming one way, and I was coming the other.

"I said, 'Casey, can I talk to you?' He said, 'Yeah.' I said, 'Ron Hunt, number thirty-three. Second base.' He said, 'Yeah.' I said, 'I remember what you said in spring training about coming to you rather than going to the press. I want to be ready to play, when and if you need me, and I can't do that in the bullpen. I'd like to have a chance to play.'

"He said, 'You want to play that bad?' I said, 'Yes, sir.' He said, 'You'll play tomorrow.'

"We went into Cincinnati, and I went four for four against Jim Maloney and Joe Nuxhall, and I made a couple of good plays in the field. That's how I got my start. And after we lost eight in a row, we beat the Milwaukee Braves at the Polo Grounds when I got a base hit off Claude Raymond, the little left-hander, with runners on second and third. I hit a slider, high and inside. I got him. And after the game Mrs. Payson sent my wife and me a dozen roses. That was a surprise, and besides that, I was allergic to them. It was a small apartment, and we couldn't put them in a corner far enough away for me to stop sneezing. But we didn't throw them away either.

"I was making $7,000, the minimum. Casey called me in and he said, 'Son, you need a raise.' I said, 'Yes sir.' He said, 'How about five hundred bucks?' I said, 'Is that a month?' He said, 'Fuck no, that's for the year!' I went home and told my wife, and she said, 'We'll take it.'

"We had to take my salary over the course of the season, because if I took it over the whole year it wouldn't have been enough to live on. But Jackie and I worked during the winter. I'm a Teamster. I drove a tractor-trailer, and I loaded them and unloaded them, and Jackie was a secretary. We didn't sit around. We worked during the winter because we couldn't afford not to.

"I was the Mets first All Star voted on rather than designated. I played the game hard, and I played it well, I thought. I gave it everything I had. Some of the guys who you run across in the majors may be content just being in the majors. I wasn't a contented player. I wanted to beat you any way I could. And I wanted to play. I didn't want to sit. So whether I was injured or not, I wanted to play. I didn't want somebody to take my job. That's the way it was.

"When I got up to bat, I crowded the plate. I didn't give the inside or the outside of the plate away. And if I got hit, I got him. I wore a blousy uniform anyway, and I just kind of learned to give with it. It didn't hurt quite as bad.

"I remember one time when Elio Chacon ducked out of the way of a ball with the bases loaded, Casey told him, 'Stand up and get hit with the damn thing. I'll buy you a new neck.' And I found that by getting hit, I could steal first base, which they said you couldn't do. And I found this was a way to give me some longevity. I had to have as many pluses as I could, because I didn't think I was that outstanding of a player, although I did make myself a pretty damn good player.

"Casey talked to me about getting hit. He said I would get fifty bucks or a suit of clothes. I didn't want the clothes. I didn't want to go to his tailor! I took the fifty bucks!

"I look back at Casey, and I probably didn't appreciate him as much as I should have when I was there. What I remember most about being a rookie in a major league camp was that the sportswriters really didn't want to talk to us much. They wanted Casey's stories. Looking back during the two-and-a-half years I played for Casey, he surrounded himself with good coaches on the field, and he took care of the press. So it wasn't a constant hammering of what you're doing or not doing or 'Why did you make this error?' like in the papers today. Hell, today all they want to do is write bad stuff when they get a chance. I don't remember the sportswriters hammering us that bad. In fact, they wrote about baseball. You're talking about Dick Young, Jack Lang, Barney Kremenko. I didn't think they were that bad. I don't think I ever got nasty with them, or them with me.

"Where are you going to go after a ballgame except to a bar. It's got food. And if you run into a sportswriter today, I imagine the ballplayer is going to turn around and walk out. In our day, if you ran into a sportswriter in the bar, you bought him a drink. Or he might buy you a drink. That's as far as it would go. You didn't have to read about it in the paper the next day.

"For us ballplayers, if you did the best you could and hustled for Casey, Casey was a pretty lenient manager. If he thought you were loafing or bullshitting around, he'd hammer you. He took care of business. He took care of Howard Cosell when Cosell was yapping his jaw too much. I remember Cosell yapping and sticking Casey every time he could, and Casey stuck it up his ass. He blackballed him from the field, and Cosell tried *every way* to get in to that field, and he couldn't. That's the way Casey was. He'd shoot straight. He'd give you that Stengelese, but you ask the sportswriters, he'd eventually answer your question, but maybe you weren't paying attention when he did. I think Casey was as dumb as a fox.

"Casey was beautiful to me. He was like another Dad to me. Shit, he gave me a chance. Just getting a chance to play and getting someone to like you is the difference between making it and not making it. You gotta get a chance, and when you do, you gotta do the job and you gotta have some-one who will stick with you through hard times, cause he has the feeling or knows you can do it. Casey was good to me that way.

"I remember we played the Yankees in an exhibition game in late June at Yankee Stadium. I didn't walk out to center field to see the monuments. I was there to play. It was evening, because a couple of us commented on the lighting being kind of poor. It was foggy.

"I didn't like playing exhibition games too well. I had a reason. It wasn't that I was trying to snub the fans. I was programmed to get hit. When balls came inside, I didn't flinch from them, so when I was playing in an exhibition game, whether it was at Yankee Stadium or some minor league park, I worried that a pitcher would come inside on me and break my wrist. For an exhibition game? Because I'm programmed not to get out of the way. I just get hit and think about it later. That's the reason for me not liking exhibition games.

"In '63 our shortstop was Al Moran. I didn't know Al at all. He didn't hit well, but if you can't do one thing well, then you have to do another thing very well to make up for the shortcomings and then have the guts to work on your shortcomings to try to make yourself as good as you can, just so you make sure you have more pluses than minuses. And Al, even though he was struggling with the bat, it didn't effect him in the field. He was a pretty good fielder.

"Off the field I was a loner. I didn't run with too many people. I can look back and say, 'I didn't want them to know too much of my business.' Maybe I'd be traded and I'd have to play against them. If they knew too much about me, that was a plus for them and a minus for me. I heard Bob Gibson felt that way, too. But, Bob Gibson is a piece of shit. He doesn't like nobody, and I don't like him. So as far as my opinion of him, you got it.

"We lost a lot of games [111] in '63. Roger Craig was a twenty-game loser. But he didn't do it all by himself. We helped him a hell of a lot.

"We weren't very good, but by God, we tried to do the best we could. Roger knew the score. You had to have a strong constitution, bud. He'd go home and say to himself, I did the best I could. Baseball is a funny sport. It's a team sport made up of a bunch of individuals. Take a round bat and a round ball and try to hit it square. It's not like football, where the backs get all the glory, but without the guys up front, they wouldn't run for shit. In baseball the individual is more exposed. In those days we played a team sport. We might not have won, but we tried to do the right thing. We played with Casey, and even though we lost more than we won, we played fundamental ball, gave ourselves up, hit behind the runner, advanced him even if it meant a time at bat, tried to get a runner in from second base, or from third even though it was giving yourself up.

"If you want to know whether I found it hard to play on a team that lost so much, the truth is I never thought about it. I was in the majors. I was playing baseball. We tried to win. We didn't go out there trying to lose. I can look back at it now and think, What the hell, so maybe I wasn't playing for the best team in the National League, but I sure was playing for the best fans in the National League, and you owed them something, and I never did forget the fans in New York.

"When I was a rookie, the rookies did all the freebies, and the veterans did all the pay dates. But, doing the freebies, though I didn't always enjoy them because it meant giving up my day off, I found that doing them helped me to reflect back on the things in baseball I took for granted, like the fundamentals, which helped me for twelve years. I only had a starting job for five of those years. The rest of the time there was a kid who had more power or more speed or something, someone I had to beat out.

"I never missed a Banner Day. I always sat in the dugout and watched the fans parade by. I thought, by God, if they could do something like that, I could pay them a little respect by sitting there and watching. Some of them were so clever. I was amused by it. Anyone who wasn't had to be dead or stupid.

"I loved the Polo Grounds, loved the old ballparks. They were homey. Crosley Field, Wrigley, the one in Philadelphia, [Connie Mack Stadium] even though the Philadelphia fans treated you badly, but that's their right. Even Forbes Field in Pittsburgh, as shitty as that old ballpark was, there was still something about it when you walked in. Maybe it was the idea of someone being here before, but also the fans who were there. They were close, on you, and you knew exactly what they were saying. They gave you a little constitution, a little backbone, a little grit. The New York Met fans were good to me on the field, and they were good to my family off the field.

"You hear a lot of things about New York, but [those] people don't know New York. They want to read the dirt, and there's that in every city, but the people treated me and my family very well, and I don't think I snubbed the fans.

"When I started doing free clinics fifteen years ago, after I had accumulated enough money from making speaking engagements and Old Timers games, the first people I thought of doing the free—that's free, F-R-E-E—clinics for were the people of New York and New Jersey.

"At the end of the year the fans thought I should have beaten out Pete Rose for Rookie of the Year. I thought I should have finished first, too. Because we didn't have a very good team, so if one guy is doing well, you can pitch around him. On Rose's team it was very hard to pitch around one guy, because you have someone else who can whack it. Look at the home run hitters on that team. So statswise, positionwise, secondwise, yeah, I thought I should have been number one."

fourteen

Kings of Queens

At the end of the 1963 season it was time to say good-bye to the Polo Grounds after more than seventy seasons. For the second year in a row Rod Kanehl grew teary eyed as the fans bid *adieu* to the home of McGraw, Mathewson, Ott, Hubbell, and Terry.

Rod Kanehl: "At the end of '62 it was discovered that Shea Stadium was sinking into the bog, so we had to play in the Polo Grounds another year, so at the end of '63 they did the same thing they did in '62, they presented Casey with home plate, and they played 'Auld Lang Syne' as he walked all the way to our clubhouse in center field. And I cried again. I cried two years in a row."

After Bobby Thomson's dramatic home run off Ralph Branca to win the 1951 pennant, Giants fans would never forget Russ Hodges' electrifying call, 'The Giants win the pennant. The Giants win the pennant. The Giants win the pennant.' But the site where it happened would fall to the wrecker's ball. Nothing would remain but an iron staircase that would climb to nowhere. Giants fans would shed many a tear over the loss of what once was a baseball shrine.

Leonard Shecter: "There's a housing project on the site of the Polo Grounds now, red brick and ugly. People don't pour out of the subway, full of bustle and excitement there any more. There are no flags, no peanut vendors. There is no Polo Grounds, and we are all the poorer for it."

The new stadium in Queens, named after Bill Shea, was designed by a team led by Robert Moses, New York's master builder. Moses, who made over his city as dramatically as Caesar transformed Rome, years earlier had built a commerce center on the west side of New York he called The Coliseum, but few noticed the Old World connection. With a second opportunity to get it right, Moses designed a stadium in Queens across the highway from LaGuardia Airport that on the outside was designed to be a modern reflection of Rome's Coliseum. It cost $20 million and was financed through the issuance of New York City bonds.

The Queens subway line ran nearby, but there were also spaces for twenty thousand automobiles in the surrounding asphalt parking lot. With the move to Shea, the majority of fans would go to the games in their cars. The team was located in a borough of New York City, but George Weiss knew his target audience were the men and women who had fled the inner city for the Long Island suburbs to escape the hoards of immigrants and blacks flocking to take their place. It was the same constituency Walter O'Malley was courting three thousand miles away in Los Angeles.

On April 14, 1964, the day their regular season opened, the Mets sold Duke Snider to the San Francisco Giants. They no longer needed the old names to draw fans. The opener at Shea drew 50,312 fans. The parking lot was a sea of automobiles. The traffic jam that choked the Brooklyn-Queens Expressway and the Long Island Expressway was monumental.

In 1964 the Mets, despite only winning 53 games, began to outdraw the Yankees, who had won pennants the last four seasons in a row. In a panic, the Yankees tried to counter the Mets success by moving the skilled but colorless manager Ralph Houk into the front office and hiring popular Yankees icon Yogi Berra to be manager.

But the Yankees hired Berra for the wrong reasons. He turned out to be patient and understanding of his players, but the Yankees didn't hire him for his managerial skills. Rather, they were hoping he'd be entertaining like Stengel.

Berra had been with the Yankees since 1946, but apparently the top brass didn't know him very well. As loquacious as Stengel was, that's how mum Berra tended to be. Sure, he was known for his bon mots, like "It ain't over til it's over," but most of Yogi's wit had been manufactured by his close friend Joe Garagiola, who enjoyed recounting so-called Berraisms on his "Game of the Week" show.

When Yogi turned out to be silent and sullen with the press, especially after the team faltered during the summer, Houk himself panicked and hired a replacement even before the season was over. When Berra ended up winning the 1964 pennant and then getting fired, the Yankees once again looked like ingrates and bumblers.

In contrast, the hapless Mets had become an institution. In their first year at Shea, 1,732,000 fans flocked to Queens to watch them. And in ballparks across America one could hear the chant of "Let's Go Mets."

Among the highlights of the 1964 season was a Memorial Day weekend Sunday doubleheader that took almost ten-and-a-half hours to play. Rod Kanehl recalled it fondly.

Rod Kanehl: "I played the first game, and Casey started me in the second game, and for some reason he pinch hit for me in the second inning. Why? I don't know. Maybe something came down from the front office where they wanted to show off somebody.

"But that night, Jim Lowe, the disc jockey who wrote 'The Green Door' and 'Gambler's Guitar' for Rusty Draper, invited me for dinner. He lived in Manhattan. He wanted to know when the doubleheader would be over, and I told him, 'Six or seven. Eight o'clock at the latest.'

"The second game went twenty-three innings. I ended up delivering hot soup to the bench during that second game, and then about midnight, when the game was over, I called him. He said, 'I turned it off in the ninth inning, and you guys were getting beat.'

Another magic moment in 1964 was a brawl between the Mets and the Milwaukee Braves. Kanehl and Ron Hunt were participants, of course.

Rod Kanehl: "It was in Milwaukee. It was the last out of the game. Ron Hunt was on second base, one out, men on first and second. A ground ball was hit to the shortstop, Dennis Menke, and Frank Bolling, the second baseman, came across and took the throw for the force at second. Hunt was rounding third, and he figured Bolling was going to go to first automatically to try for the double play, so Hunt figures he'll go on home.

"Bolling doesn't throw to first; he throws to Bailey at home, and Hunt doesn't have a chance. Hunt comes barreling in, and Bailey just really unmercifully hits him. Hunt went one way, and Bailey got up, and the game was over.

"Well, Bailey started for Hunt. Hunt and I were roommates, and I came running off the bench, and I grabbed Bailey by the shoulder and threw him off balance, and I kept going toward the Milwaukee bench. In '62 Gene Oliver was with the Cards, and Oliver used to come into second base and just rip ya, even though there was no play at all. Even if it was a little force out, a hopper to the middle of the infield, he'd still come at you. One time he slid across my shins.

"Roommates always discuss things like, 'If a fight breaks out, who are you going to get?' And Oliver had gotten Hunt, so Oliver was our number one target. And we'd been waiting for over a year.

"And the first guy off the Milwaukee bench was Gene Oliver, and I hit him right in the nose. Blood splattered everywhere, and there was a big pileup. I was on the bottom of the pile, and I looked up between all the legs in the pile, and I could see Stengel on the back of Dennis Menke! And Menke threw him off. Menke didn't know who it was. And Stengel went flying on his ass. And Menke ran over, and started saying, 'Oh, God,' and he apologized, and he picked Stengel up, brushed him off. I saw all that from the bottom of the pile.

"Anyway, the pile broke up, and the fight was over. Bobby Bragan was the Milwaukee manager. The writers came in and said, 'Bragan says you're just a bunch of pop-offs and showboats and you can't play ball so you have to fight instead.' They asked me about it, and I said, 'You don't see any blood in this locker room, do you? Go over and check their locker room?'

Reporters first began to mumble about getting a younger manager in 1964. Led by Howard Cosell, the criticism was that he was too old, that he sometimes slept on the bench. Kanehl realized the talk was premature.

Rod Kanehl: "There was talk about Casey stepping down, but there was no one to replace him. There was no talk of anyone in particular at the time. Who? Wes Westrum? Are you crazy? Don Heffner? What kind of deal was that? There was nobody. You kind of figured Solly Hemus might be the next manager, but he had disappeared. He must have pissed off Weiss."

Rod Kanehl's last hurrah turned out to be 1964. After the Mets final home game, there would be a couple of days off before the team left to go west on its final road trip. During those two days Kanehl celebrated in style in Manhattan, partying hearty with his hero, Mickey Mantle.

Rod Kanehl: "We played our final home game in '64 on a Sunday, and we had an off-day Monday, and then on Tuesday we were scheduled to fly to Milwaukee and then St. Louis, where we finished out the season. Well, I had a girlfriend with me, and we went to Jilly's on Fiftieth Street, and the maitre d' knew me, and he said, 'John Blanchard is back there with a girl. He might be embarrassed if he saw you with your wife.' I had known John since the Yankee rookie camp in '54 and '55. I said, 'Hey, this isn't my wife, but pretend it's my wife, and I'll *really* embarrass him.'

"We went and sat down with him, and he was hiding his head like he didn't want me to recognize him, and then when I went over, we were laughing and giggling, and John said, 'Mickey is so envious of you.' Mantle loved me. I knew him because I had played with his brothers and we were from the same part of the country.

"I said, 'What do you mean?' He said, 'The writers tell us you go to town, screw around, have more fun than any ballplayer in New York, travel by subway, go anywhere.' He said, 'Mickey can't go anywhere. If he does, Dorothy Kilgallen will write about him. He cannot go anywhere.' I said, 'Where is he now?'

"Blanchard was rooming with Mickey at the Essex House on this Yankee homestand because it was the last week of the season. John said, 'He's up there now with some airline stewardesses. Let's go up there.'

"They had a suite, two bedrooms. I had this gal with me. It was midnight. We went up there. We were there damn near all night. It was daylight before I left. The six of us were drinking, having pissing contests, throwing paper bags of water out the window on people! We were having the time of our lives, a great time with Mickey.

"I had about two hours to go to my apartment, get all of my things and get to Shea Stadium to catch the plane to Milwaukee. With no sleep. So my last night in New York was with Mickey. Little did I know it was going to be my final day in New York."

★ ★ ★

In 1964 the Mets became a factor in the pennant race for the first time. The St. Louis Cardinals were fighting the Cincinnati Reds and the Philadelphia Phillies for the pennant, as they hosted the Mets for the final three days of the season. When the Mets won the first two games, all of baseball was talking.

Rod Kanehl: "Al Jackson beat Gibson 1–0, and then we won 15–5, and then Sunday, if we win it's a three-way tie for the pennant. I was sitting on the bench. We're playing in St. Louis. I live in Springfield, and my season is over. My wife was there from Springfield. I had brought all my stuff from New York, and as soon as the game was over, I was driving home while everyone else was going back to New York and dispersing from there.

"There were two outs in the ninth, and Barney Schultz was pitching, and Stengel says, 'Kanehl, get a bat.' Christ, it's over. We're losing big. I went up to the plate, congratulate Tim McCarver, and he says, 'We haven't won yet.' Those guys were so ready to choke they could hardly even speak. So I got a base hit and drove in a couple of runs, and Eddie Kranepool came up. I went down to first, and Bill White was the same way. He can't hardly talk. After I congratulated him, he said, 'We haven't got the last out yet.' And then Kranepool popped to McCarver, and the game was over.

"There was bedlam in St. Louis. It was just crazy. We went to the locker room, and all the guys were packing up to go to the bus. I let everyone shower first, let them get out of there, because I was driving to Springfield.

"Everyone left, and in came Bing Devine. Bing had been fired by the Cards in August and had come over to us. So after I shower I looked up and Bing Devine was sitting on the bench. And in St. Louis the Cards' locker room was right over our head, and I could hear corks popping and the cheering. The Cards were going crazy upstairs in their locker room.

"I turned to Bing and said, 'You know, that's your team. You should be up there.' And he looked at me and said, 'Thanks, Rod. I think I'll go up.' And he left me.

"As soon as '64 was over, I went home. I expected to return in '65. I had never gone to camp with a Mets contract, always a minor league contract. But I'd go down there and make the team. Because they had young guys to protect.

"In the winter of '64 they sent me a Buffalo contract and did not invite me to spring training. I had eight years in the minors, and I wasn't going back. I was thirty, had four kids, and they were in school. So when it came out in the paper that I wasn't going to return, Johnny Johnson of the Yankees called and said, 'Would you be interested in managing in the minor leagues?' I said, 'Well, sure.' The Yankees had always touted me as managerial material. He said, 'I'll call you right back.' I thought it would be one of those deals where I'd never hear from him again. He called me back within an hour. He said, 'Rod, I got bad news. George Weiss wants two ballplayers for you.'

"So I stayed in construction. I didn't get my official pink slip until five years later. Talk about the old system!"

fifteen

Soboda

The year 1965 was a watershed for the Mets. The winter before they had lost one of their top prospects, outfielder Paul Blair, because he had been left unprotected, and the Baltimore Orioles had drafted him. Rather than take such a risk again, in 1965 George Weiss decided to promote some of the best minor-league talent to the big club. Among the rookie prospects kept on the Mets roster in the spring of 1965 were pitcher Frank Edwin "Tug" McGraw, shortstop Bud Harrelson, and outfielder Ron Swoboda, who had first come to Stengel's attention during spring training in 1964 when the former University of Maryland star hit a ball over the center field fence at Miller Huggins Field in St. Petersburg. No other Met had done that.

Swoboda, young and naive, had a lot to learn. He always kept his eyes open, and he recalled how so much was new to him.

Ron Swoboda: "I was born on June 30, 1944, in Baltimore, Maryland, in what is really Edgemere. My dad was in the automobile business. He was always my hero. He spent World War II as a waist gunner on a B-29 at Tinnian. We had no ballplayers in our family before me. My dad was a pretty good athlete. He boxed a little while he was in the service. He didn't seem to want to pass that along, and he hasn't. I've never been a fist-fighter and never wanted to be, though there are times having a couple of people on the team who go out there to bust somebody's head is pretty important.

"I was okay in high school. My senior year we played eight games. That was the whole schedule, and we won the county championship. Somewhere during that year I remember feeling that my baseball career was pretty much done. Not that I didn't have dreams of going on, but I didn't know. I can remember this pitcher for Towson High School in Baltimore County throwing me a couple of curve balls, and I didn't hit them, and I remember running in the outfield, and I was standing there, and I just started crying. I was blubbering because I was thinking, After all I've given up in the summer, after what I've dedicated to this game, I can't play. It's over.

"And after my senior year I had a very ordinary summer, struggled pretty much. I played a lot of baseball during the summer, played on a couple of different teams. But at the end of that summer I didn't feel I had anything to offer.

"I went to the University of Maryland on a baseball/work scholarship. I cleaned the dorm, polished the floors. For your room and board I would sweep the floors every day and once a week polish them. No big deal. There were no baseball scholarships. Back then, they didn't sell tickets to college baseball games. Very few people came to watch. The only person who was important who came out to watch me play ball at the University of Maryland was my future wife, Cecilia.

"After my freshman year, that summer I played for the Leone Boys Club, which was coached by a guy named Walter Youse, who was an area scout for the Orioles. He was very in tune with the professional game. We played every day and twice on Sunday all summer long. We played ninety games. We played *all* the time. You found out two things. You found out if you wanted to play, and you found out if you could play. Youse coached like he was coaching a minor league team. You were expected to do things correctly and conduct yourself in a professional way. Our team went to the Triple ABA tournament in Johnstown, [Pennsylvania], and we lost in the championship game to the Brooklyn Cadets, which starred Matty Galante, who is now the bench coach for the Houston Astros.

"I might have signed with Baltimore, but they signed a pitcher by the name of Wally Bunker and gave him a lot of money, and apparently they didn't have a lot of money. But another coach I played for, name of Sterling Fowble—they called him Sheriff because his father was a sheriff—he was a bird dog scout for the Mets, and he got together with Wid

Ron Swoboda

Matthews, the full-time scout. Wid had scouted for the Cardinals and signed Stan Musial, among others. One night at the end of that summer Wid waltzed into my front room and offered me $35,000 to sign.

"Considering the fact my mom and dad probably barely made $13,000 a year between them, $35,000 seemed like a *lot* of money. But it always bothered me that I wasn't more business-minded. In other words, if someone waltzes in and offers you $35,000 and they make it sound like, 'Take it or leave it.'—what he said was, 'This money may not be here tomorrow.'—anybody else sitting there might have said, 'Really? Let's call a couple other clubs and see what they think?' I had a few cards from a few scouts. But I didn't do that. Matthews had suggested that I might get to the big leagues a little earlier with an expansion team, and I took the money. And it turned out to be true.

"And when I signed, I bought myself a car, I bought my brother a car, I paid off what was left on the house, and I bought my parents a washing machine and other things they needed. I pretty much spent it on the people around me who had been part of the support system all my life and who I felt deserved it. And I've been comfortable with that. You always wished you could have been smarter about things, because you could have done more for more people if you had been smarter about money, but we never had anything, so that's what I did.

"In the spring of 1964 the Mets invited a bunch of their younger players, guys who had just signed, like myself, and first-year players, to an early camp in St. Pete with the big league coaches. It was a hell of an idea. It was a pre–spring training workout camp. They took a look at you. Tug McGraw was there, Jim Bethke, Danny Napoleon, Rob Gardner, Dick Selma, players like that. Casey Stengel and the coaching staff were there. I roomed with Sheriff Robinson, one of the coaches, for God sake.

"It was all so new. I was still nineteen. We went to Miller Huggins Field, where the big club worked out, and I did pretty good in this camp, and they kept me around for a few weeks for the regular spring training.

"I played a game against the Pirates. I saw Roberto Clemente swing at a ball and fall down. I thought, This is Clemente? Gus Triandos, who used to play with the Baltimore Orioles, was there. When I was a kid, Triandos once worked with my father at Luby's Chevrolet in Baltimore. My dad was a service salesman, and Gus worked in the sales department, and my father invited him over to dinner one night. As a kid it was incredible to have Gus Triandos walk into your house! He was huge anyway, and he had dinner with us, so he was always my favorite player, and once when I was fourteen or fifteen he even handed me a trophy at a sports dinner. So here I was in spring training as a nineteen-year-old kid, and Gus was catching with the Phillies, and I walked up to home plate, and Dallas Green was pitching, and I hit a ball over the center field wall at old Al Lang Stadium. Center field was 390, they had a big screen, and it was a home run, and I touched them all. And Gus Triandos was behind the plate when I did it! This was pretty heady, pretty awesome. I was so inexperienced.

"I remember it was my first year, and I was trying to get my throws down from the outfield. I was missing some cut-offs, and Casey was talking about 'bending over and picking up grass.' You follow through low, bend over, pick up grass. 'That will help you keep the ball down.' Made sense.

"And I was practicing it early one day with Carlton Willey at Miller Huggins Field in St. Pete. He was hitting me some balls, and from the outfield I was coming up with them and throwing them back in, only I was throwing toward the clubhouse, toward the locker room. I let one go, and I was doing it at speed, and it was way over Carlton's head, and as I stood there, I realized it was going through the glass window of the door of Casey's office. There were three panels of horizontal opaque glass. I hit the middle one. From where I stood I could see Stengel's silhouette stand up. I could see him walk over, and see his silhouette bend down, and I see his eye looking through the hole where the ball went through. I thought, This is it. I'm done. What's going to happen now?

"He opened the door, and he said, 'Throw the ball the other way, dammit.' He closed the door.

"Another time I was in the outfield, and Dave Nicholson was the hitter. They had a sliding pit in left center of the old Al Lang, where nobody was supposed to hit the ball, and it was full of sand, and Dave hit one of those monumental fly balls. I never saw a fly ball hit higher. I went after the damn thing, and I hit that sliding pit, and I went down, and the ball kept going, and I hit the wall, and I knocked myself silly. They had to come out and get me. God knows what happened to that ball. All I know is, I got up and didn't know where I was, and I was embarrassed as hell. It wasn't long after that that I got sent to Triple A, but I had gotten a little big league experience.

"Elio Chacon, who was with Buffalo, pulled something on me in spring training that showed you how completely naive I was. We worked out on this terrible diamond where high school teams played. I didn't know Elio Chacon. We came out together after practice one day, and we were getting ready to leave the park, and Elio was standing next to an old, open-top Jaguar. I said, 'Hey, that's a nice-looking car.' He said, 'You want to take a ride in it?' I thought, Sure, this is neat. The keys were in it. I jumped in and off I went, running around Dunnedin. I took a pretty good spin, and when I came back a kid was standing there saying, 'Where the hell did you go in my car?' He said, 'I was calling the police. You stole my car.' And I proceeded to explain the whole thing to him. Aw, man, don't trust the veterans! Elio completely hooked me. You need to learn that.

"I started on the Triple A club, Buffalo, which was the most depressing place I have ever walked into. We played in War Memorial Stadium. It looked like a prison. It certainly wasn't a baseball field. It had a short right field and was huge in left field. They had converted it for baseball. It was just this big, unwieldy, ugly looking place. The only thing missing from the clubhouse was bars. The manager was Whitey Kurowski, the old third baseman for the St. Louis Cards. He had played with Stan Musial.

"We opened up on the road. We pulled into Richmond, and the black guys and the dark-skinned Latins: Pumpsie Green, Choo Choo Coleman, Elio Chacon, got off at another motel. I was like, 'What? Excuse me?' We had been training with these guys, laughing with them, showering with them, and they gotta go to another motel? This was 1964. It seemed so strange to me, and yet I had grown up in what was technically a segregated community in Maryland. We had a black section. The black kids didn't go to school with us. They were right behind the elementary school I went to. And I never thought to ask why. When we played ball on the school field, some of the black kids would come out of their section, and they'd play with us. We needed guys. They played with us. And there was next to zero trouble. 'You want to play? Let's go?' Never had any trouble.

"In fact, one time coming home from the playground, three white guys wanted to kick my ass for some reason. They corralled me. I didn't know these kids. They were bigger than me, and they were going to hammer my ass, and a couple of the black kids came out from their section and made sure that didn't happen. And I always wondered, Why did they care?

"I was taught that you have no right to look down on anybody. You respect everybody. It was a lesson and that made sense. And it was also because I was a certain kind of sensitive. I knew what it felt like to be embarrassed. I had terrible skin problems when I was going through puberty. It was so humbling. Those scars never leave you, and that just changes you about certain things. So I tried to be sensitive to other people's feelings. So when the black players got off the bus, I asked, 'What is this all about?' And I was told, 'This is how they do it down here.' I didn't make a deal out of it. I was a nineteen-year-old kid, the youngest player on the roster. And it was interesting, because I always had black friends on the Mets, players like Al Jackson and Cleon Jones.

"My first ball game was in Richmond, Virginia, against the Richmond Yankees. My mom and dad and my uncles came down from Maryland. In that game I went three for five with a home run, and got picked off first base on a hidden ball trick! We won the game. The next day Mel Stottlemyre struck me out four times. And looking back on it, that's about how my career went! That was it in a microcosm! Only I didn't know it then.

"In the spring of 1965 I was invited to spring training with the big club. There was a reason for this. Earlier the Mets had let Paul Blair get away because of the first-year rule. Basically, if you played one year of professional baseball, they had to protect you in some way, either moving you up in the organization or designating you as the one first-year player they could send out. In 1965 they signed a pitcher by the name of Dennis Musgraves, and he got a bunch of money, and they designated him as the player to go out. And so the Mets kept me, Tug McGraw, Jim Bethke, and Danny Napoleon all on the big-league roster as first-year players. It had nothing to do with what we could contribute or how we had played in the spring. We were simply there.

"In spring training I remember Casey brought in Jesse Owens to try to teach us how to run faster. Of course, we all thought that was amusing as hell. Jesse was a great guy, and probably everything he said was valid, but once you've swung at a ball and dropped the bat, you're going to run the way you're going to run. He could make you think about running a little better, but by and large spring training was about baseball. You did a little loosening up, jumping jacks, sit-ups, and then you started doing baseball things.

"It was my first chance to watch Casey Stengel from up close. Here's the thing: I didn't know anything about him as a player. I knew he played, knew he was an outfielder, but I didn't know he was a right fielder. And I was pretty much oblivious to his history.

"One of my earlier memories had to do with Casey and a player by the name of Duke Carmel, who was having a pretty good spring. History was going to judge him as a journeyman ballplayer, but he was going to make that Mets team.

"We went on a trip to the East Coast of Florida, over to West Palm Beach, where the Whitney Estate was, and the tradition was for Joan Payson to throw a big party for the team. It was a big steak dinner, and there was Lancer's wine all over the place, and a lot of it.

"Casey was up at the podium issuing forth on a variety of subjects to the Mets players, and much of it was good advice. He was saying, 'Don't try to spend all the money you make. Try to invest some of your salary during the summer in annuities so that down the road you have a little something.' He told us, 'When you're going out after a game, don't go out with five guys, go out with two or three. If you go out with five guys, by the time everybody buys back, you're drunk.'

"The room was tittering with laughter, and about the time he made that comment we could hear Duke Carmel from the audience say, 'I've seen you out with ten guys,' because Casey often would entertain all the writers.

"Well, Casey just glared at him, and the whole room went quiet, and you got the terrible feeling that somebody had just made a big mistake. Casey said to Carmel, 'Look here, I've seen you out when you didn't see me, and you haven't made this baseball team yet.' And it was like a thunderclap. Uh, oh.

"Well, when we got back to St. Pete, Duke's locker was empty, and he was in Triple A, and he ain't gonna see the big leagues. That was it for Duke. And it was because of that, I believe. You didn't show the Old Man up. While he's got the microphone, he's got the microphone, and your job was to sit there and laugh and listen. And man, you talk about sobering. The effects of that Lancer's wine left that room like a big exhaust fan turned on.

"My experience with Stengel was always, *always* good. I listened to him. I used to listen to him talking to writers. He told stories, regaling the writers. If you've ever tried to interview an athlete, if he doesn't want to tell you something, most of them will just not tell, or give a 'no comment,' or tell you to fuck-off. Stengel would take your question, start an answer, and he'd spin you around the park a little bit. He'd wind around a few corners and duck and dive, and by the time he brought you back fifteen minutes later, you couldn't remember what you asked him, and he didn't answer anything. It was kind of like the USSR. They censored by deprivation. Casey censored by inundation! He hit you with so much you'd be hard-pressed to tell the truth from the bullshit, because you can't filter that much.

"And his stories were amazing. Here's a guy who went back fifty years. He'd always say, and it was the title of a book, 'You can look it up.' He always knew. I have subsequently looked up some of the teams Casey played on. He came up in 1912 with the Dodgers. He was in the 1916 World Series against the Boston Red Sox, who had an interesting pitcher, a guy named Ruth. Ruth pitched a six-hitter, won it 2–1 in fourteen innings. Ruth pitched all fourteen. [Casey didn't face Ruth because he was a lefty.]

"I loved that guy. Goddammit, Casey was good. He used to get the rap for not dealing with young people very well. Well hell, when you're managing the Yankees and you're supposed to win, what are you going to do? When you're managing the Mets—and Stengel figured out that his job was to coach this team, that he couldn't manage it—it was like managing the unmanageable. Like the steering wheel was not attached to the front wheels. There was no connection there.

"He had a bunch of has-beens and never-will-bes, and he knew it was important for him to entertain the media guys, his press, he called them, 'My writers,' and he'd take them out and regale them and liquor them up and keep a smile on their faces so they didn't turn on the franchise. He knew that's what his job was, and as a result of that, more than anything else, his legacy gets skewed a little from what it really was because his image was tarnished in the eyes of people who mistakenly thought he was some kind of clown. Because out of the Mets publicity about him came all the stories about Casey as a player, how when he was a Dodger he went to home plate, tipped his cap, and a bird flew out. But Casey was a serious ballplayer. Look, if you were a human being at the turn of the century, you had to be made of sterner stuff, because there was no penicillin, no miracle drugs. If you got influenza back then, you died. You were in a sport where you were tearing up your knees and getting gouged and spiked. Infection could kill you. The animals that survived through that period were pretty tough, and Casey was a tough animal.

"But he had this entertaining side to him that came out with the Mets, because that's what was called for.

"One time I asked him about the story of his going to dental school, back when dentistry was like plumbing. In the off-season you could get a certificate and start drilling on people, for Christ's sake, and one year management was giving him trouble, and he took a dentistry course as leverage. That's all. It was just leverage. Smart. So I asked him about it. This was after he had retired. It was one of these Welcome Home Mets dinners. Casey was off from the dais, sitting there waiting for his ride, and I walked up and sat down next to him, and we started shooting the shit. I loved the guy, loved to talk to him, loved to listen to him. I said to him, 'Casey, you think you'd have had as much fun if you'd have gone on and become a dentist?' Which I thought was a funny line. And Stengel said, 'If I was going to be a dentist, I'd be an orthodontist.' I said, 'Why?' He said, 'Because parents will buy things for their kids that they won't buy for themselves.' I thought to myself, That's sagacious as hell. That's wisdom.

"I never would have thought that was the answer that was going to come out of his mouth, that he would even think of something like that. But Casey was a banker. Obviously, if you're running a bank you have a little sense of money. It just impressed upon me that this guy was so much smarter than this thing he was doing, so much smarter than the life he was leading.

"I remember seeing him at an Old Timers game. He was an old man, a *really* old man as he stood in the tunnel, and then when he came up those steps and headed onto the field, he lost thirty or forty years. He came alive. He was clicking his heels. I thought to myself, If there isn't something about that crowd that makes you come alive, if you can't live a little bigger in front of that crowd and absorb that energy and do something with that energy, I don't believe you can play the game. You have to get something from that, not in terms of ego, but being able to take your clothes off and be naked in front of people and do what you do, and let that energize you in a way that wouldn't happen if you were somewhere else. That was fun. I was always conscious of that. And I was very lucky, because I was so flat-fucking ordinary, and I was allowed to do that. For the meager things I accomplished as a player, I got a benefit from that, and I was a better player in game situations. I got up for that. And so did Casey.

"I was in no position to judge Casey Stengel. In *no* position. On what basis do you say, 'He can't manage this team?' Nobody could manage that team. But who do you know who's seventy-five years old and is managing in the big leagues? Nobody. So I would maintain that there was nobody *more* qualified to manage *that* team. Nobody. What he lost in the process was historical imagery. And you know what, if you asked Casey, he would say he doesn't give a shit anyway. His history was made, and anybody who bothers to look it up. . . . The truth is, you ain't as good a manager as you are when you're managing the Yankees, and you ain't as bad a manager as you are when you are losing a hundred games four years in a row with the Mets.

"You want to know how bad we were? They should have put a disclaimer on the tickets to the effect that, 'Anything resembling major league baseball is purely coincidental.' Ed Kranepool used to tell me, 'We used to celebrate rainouts.' "

In spring training in 1965 Swoboda skulled a photographer with a thrown ball. Pitching coach Ernie White warned Stengel that Swoboda would kill somebody before he was through. "Somebody's in danger every time he moves," said White. But Swoboda was not Marv Throneberry, who was twenty-eight and no longer a prospect. Swoboda was twenty, enthusiastic, well-meaning, and earnest.

His first home run, against Houston at Shea Stadium, traveled 550 feet over the left field fence and the bullpen and into the parking lot. He hit long home runs, but he had trouble hitting the curve ball.

Mets fans were crazy about him, as they had been for Throneberry. They cheered him whether he did well or not. On Banner Day, one wag wrote: SWOBODA IS STRONGER THAN DIRT.

Swoboda was proud of being a fan favorite.

Ron Swoboda: "Most of us players, not all, came from a lower-middle class socioeconomic level. The kids working the games selling peanuts and programs were fans, and they would come down, and we'd spent a lot of time talking to them and to the special cops. Freddie Amadeo was a special cop, and Tug [McGraw] and I used to go over to his house over in Brooklyn and then we'd go to Coney Island. He'd have fabulous Italian meals with six courses. We'd see him and his whole family at the ball game. You knew them all. That's the kind of friends I had.

"Our family's best friend was a Nassau County cop named Charlie Blanchfield and his wife Gertie. They helped my wife when I was on the road. My wife was in this strange place with two babies. If we needed anything, they were there. Friends like that are friends forever. And the kids who worked at Shea Stadium were fun because they were hip. There was no barrier. We happened to be playing ball in front of them, and they happened to be selling peanuts and popcorn. Hey, these kids were cool and smart.

"The Mets were the biggest baby-sitting operation in the city. People would give the kids five bucks and send them to a ball game. And you didn't worry about them. They were going to be all right. The crowds in the summer when school was out was largely kids. Me and Tug—Tug was the same way—dug the kids. You didn't feel like you had to be something different in front of them.

"I also loved the writers. To me writers were interesting people—they were good writers for the most part. You learned something from Red Smith, for instance. There weren't too many writers better than Red Smith.

"One day, after I left the Mets and signed with the Yankees, Ralph Houk and I were talking about the merits of keeping your throws to the infield down. With a runner on first and a base hit to right field, we discussed how the most important thing is to keep the throw down at head level, because the runner coming around first base can only read height. He can't tell whether it's ten feet either way, but if it's down, he can't tell whether it's going to go through or not, so he has to hold up. If the throw is high, it

doesn't matter whether it's right on, left, or right, it's over the head of the
cutoff man, and he's going. Ralph and I were talking about this, and Red
made a whole column out of it, and at the end he wrote, 'Baseball is full of
a lot of little things that fans, even the good ones, wouldn't imagine.'

"My first at bat was opening day against Don Drysdale. We were playing the Dodgers, and I had a pretty good seat. I thought, This is *good. Don
Drysdale. The Dodgers.* I'm sitting on the bench. Casey Stengel is down at
the other end. This is nice. I crossed my legs and leaned back, digging it.
Man, I was digging it.

"We were behind about the seventh inning. I had made the team because
of the first-year rule, right? I had no sense that I had arrived in the big
leagues. I'm feeling like I'm on the bus and I had bought a ticket, and I have
a great seat here! And I was watching the game, and I could see Stengel start
to look down the bench for a pinch hitter. So I kind of leaned back, like
'Don't pick me,' like I could hide from him. He said, 'Soboda get a bat.' And
man, my heart started pumping, because Drysdale was still out there. It was
like, Holy shit, I have to hit off Don Drysdale! But if ya gotta go, ya gotta go.

"I went and put on a helmet and walked up to the plate. I walked in the
batter's box, and I can remember vividly—because your first at bat in the
big leagues is like getting laid for the first time. You're never going to forget it. And I was a lot more nervous about my first at bat. It was Drysdale,
for Christ's sake.

"I was really worried that I was visibly shaking, that people could actually *see* me shaking. So Drysdale winds up, and he threw me a fastball, and
the ball comes in, and I thought to myself, Jesus God, I never saw it. I
didn't. I thought, If the next one's a strike, I'm going to swing. He threw
me another fastball, and I swung, and I had no better idea where the ball
was. I knew it was in the strike zone. I knew it was up. I knew I missed it.
But really where it was, I had no idea.

"I was 0–2, and I figured, Well, this isn't going to take long. He threw
me an 0–2 slider, out over the plate, and I saw it pretty good, and I hit a
line drive to Jimmy Lefebvre at second base. I thought, Wow, that was the
nicest out I ever made. I couldn't save the game in that at bat, and I didn't
strike out against Don Drysdale. Wow!

"That was pretty cool, and my second at bat was a pinch hit against
Turk Farrell, and I hit the ball over the back wall of the left field bullpen at
Shea. I hit a fastball. And then in the first game I started against the Giants,
I hit a home run off Juan Marichal. I got rolling pretty good. I had four

home runs in my first sixteen at bats, and I was thinking, This is *too* easy. And the first half of the season I had fifteen home runs. But then the pitchers started throwing me sliders. I wasn't a bad breaking-ball hitter, but the slider was tough. It gave me trouble, and there were no hitting coaches then. There were just a bunch of people trying to figure out why I can't hit this slider. I could figure it out: because it was sliding! It's breaking, fast and down, and I haven't seen a lot of these, and I can't hit it.

"But the truth is that is was more of a discipline problem. I was a free swinger. Always was, always will be. This is where I could have learned in the cooler environment of the minor leagues, out of the glare. The key to everything: I needed to be more disciplined with the strike zone. Just like when a pitcher gets behind, he's at a disadvantage. A hitter needs to know how to get ahead in the count, and you do that by *not* swinging. What you *don't* swing at early in the count has everything to do with what you get to swing at later. I hadn't learned that lesson. That was nowhere near any part of the program. All I heard was, 'To hit the slider, change your technique.' Go the other way. 'Take the ball to the opposite field.'

"What they succeeded in doing was taking a pretty good fastball hitter and changing all that, and after that I was never as good hitting home runs. I changed to a thirty-five-ounce bat, which was probably a mistake. And even the year I hit .281 was a distortion. I had five bunts that year, a fifteen-point swing. Truth be known, I hit .265 and bunted five times to hit .280. For me to be a better power hitter I needed to think *less* about home runs and *more* about the strike zone. And I needed to understand more about my swing, which I never did either. I didn't understand the baseball swing. Fuck, I just practiced it. And in '65 I only hit four more home runs the rest of the year."

Nineteen home runs was a record for a Mets rookie. But for every wonderful moment, for the sensitive Swoboda there were also humiliations. On May 10, 1965, Stengel broke his wrist from a fall during a visit to West Point for an exhibition game. The reporters, some of whom were arguing for his dismissal, wanted to know if he could still manage.

Casey Stengel: "Whatta ya mean, can I still manage?" he asked. "If I wanna take a pitcher out I can hit him over the head with my cast to convince him.

"I didn't fall on my head, so I don't think I'll handicap the club if I manage with one arm. It's not the first time I had a broken bone or two or six in my arms or legs and ya would if ya played the game hard the way ya should. I been up there before with McGraw so I know they'd do something to me because they always wanted to show up the big leaguers, those very smart college army boys and I expected it but not the fallin', which was my own fault 'cause I didn't look."

The next day Stengel was at his post in the dugout. Vain to the end, he removed his sling whenever he went out to the mound. Swoboda recalled that what Stengel said was true: the broken arm didn't slow the Old Man down a bit.

Ron Swoboda: "We played at West Point every year. One year I hit a home run, and the catcher shook my hand! I thought, This is odd.

"In '65 Casey fell during the trip and broke his wrist. He had a cast on his hand. I'll tell you why I remember that: We were in St. Louis, and I was playing right field, and we were leading 3–0, and it had been one of those days when it had rained two or three times, and the Sportsman Park ground crew was pretty old, and they had put the tarp on and off twice, and the third time they took it off they barely got the thing rolled up in foul ground, and it was heavy, so it was kind of sitting out there.

"In the bottom of the ninth, the bases were loaded, and Dal Maxville was up. The sun started to peak through between first base and third base. I was in right field with no sunglasses. Now I saw the sun, and I felt, Nah, I don't need these glasses. I don't call time out. I don't get glasses. Larry Bearnarth—the late Larry Bearnarth, what a sadness—was pitching. He jammed Maxvill, who was a little Punch-and-Judy hitter anyway, and he flared a ball over second, a little fly ball I should have caught, except for the fact it went straight into the sun. And I had no glasses on. I not only don't catch it, but it got by me, and all three runs scored.

"So I was feeling awful about this, and I was angry, embarrassed, the gamut of negative feelings. The next inning I was up second, and I tried to hit one out to put us ahead. I popped up, and I was out.

"I dropped my helmet on the top step of the dugout, came down the steps, and I was steaming and trying to act macho. We got out three up and three down, and now I started heading up the steps to the outfield, and I was livid. We should have been in the locker room having a beer celebrating our win, but I've fucked this game up. So I started up the steps, and there was my helmet, still sitting up there upside down, one of those old fiberglass helmets, and I saw it and took a leap at it, and I stomped it. The helmet cracked like an eggshell, and it sprung back onto my foot.

"So now I had a helmet stuck on my foot, and I was shaking my foot trying to get away from this helmet, and Stengel saw this display, and I bounded up the steps, and he said, 'Goddamit, when you missed that fly ball, I didn't run into the locker room and throw your watch on the floor. When you pop up, I don't want you breaking up this team's equipment.' He had me by the front of my shirt, and his other hand had the cast on it, and I was thinking, This is beautiful. I'm standing on my helmet, and he's going to crack me right on the top of my head with this cast.

"He jerked me out of the game, and I was disconsolate. I went into the locker room, and I sat down and cried. Cause I had fucked up this game, I had fucked up my career, and Casey had jerked me out of the ball game. This was beyond embarrassment. Beyond. I was sure the veteran ballplayers were looking at me and practically pissing themselves, because I was taking it to heart. This got to me big-time.

"And Casey was entirely right, and I was entirely wrong. It was just a lesson of what happens when you overexpose somebody emotionally.

"My emotions ran in so many different directions. The least thing under control about me was my emotions. Shit, I was emotionally unprepared for the big leagues. I should not have been in the big leagues that early. In truth, the biggest mistake you can make with a ballplayer is premature exposure to the big leagues, because it can damage your self-confidence to an extent that your ceiling becomes lower. Because you get overmatched to an extent that you can't accomplish as much, and in some ways I was affected by that. Had I stayed in the minor leagues another year or so and played at that level and learned a little bit more about the game before getting bounced into prime time with writers approaching you for your opinions after the game, and you start thinking you have something valuable to say because these are intelligent people.

"It was the most traumatic thing that ever happened to me on a ball diamond ever. And it happened my rookie year, but it happened with Casey Stengel, who I always thought had my interests at heart. He did what he had to do. There was nothing else for him to do."

Beginning in June, the Mets lost 20 of 23 games, and the grumbling about Stengel grew louder.

On July 23, 1965, New York City Mayor Robert Wagner proclaimed

"Casey Stengel Day." At City Hall the mayor presented the seventy-five-year-old Stengel with a scroll. Stengel got up to talk, and during a long, rambling speech he said, "When I go home this fall, I hope to leave a young team."

The reporters interpreted these words to mean that he was retiring, and the next day headlines reflected that. But Stengel denied that had been his intention.

"I've been going home to California for a long time, but I'm still active, ain't I?" he grumped. "What they interpret ain't in my mind. It's in theirs. I can't help that." Then he added, "I didn't go to City Hall to retire. The mayor's retiring, and I'm not competing with him. I went to City Hall to get a scroll. Also to hear the mayor proclaim "Casey Stengel Day." I never had a day before."

The next day, July 24, was Old Timers Day. Former Brooklyn Dodgers and New York Giants were invited. That day Casey Stengel wore a Dodgers' uniform. When he was introduced, he received a loud ovation. It would be the last time he would be introduced to a crowd as an active combatant.

That night there was a big party at Toots Shor's restaurant. Shortly before midnight Stengel, who as always had been drinking, walked into the men's room, slipped on the wet floor, and fell.

He felt a twisting pain in his side, struggled to his feet, and said nothing about it. Joe DeGregorio, the comptroller for the team, took Casey to his home in Beechhurst, Queens.

Casey couldn't sleep. The pain in his left hip was too severe. X rays taken in the hospital showed it was broken.

The next day, July 25, while the Mets were publicly celebrating his seventy-fifth birthday—they would be on the road on July 30, the exact birth date—Casey was on the operating table at Roosevelt Hospital. Dr. Peter LaMotte put a metal ball in his hip.

Casey called George Weiss to say he wanted Wes Westrum to be the interim manager. He could have picked Yogi Berra, who for years on the Yankees he had called "my assistant manager," but instead he chose Westrum, in part because he was assuming he was coming back.

But five weeks after he fell Stengel announced he was retiring. He blamed his walking stick.

"If I can't run out there and take the pitcher out, I'm not capable of managing."

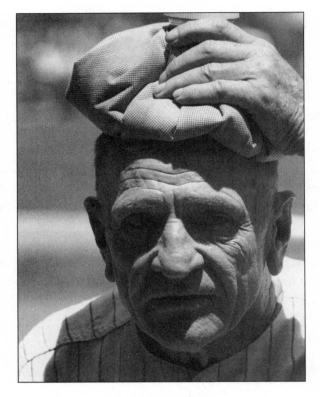

Casey Stengel

Fifty-five years after starting in Kankakee, Illinois, Casey Stengel's incredible career in baseball had come to an end.

On September 2, 1965, in a quiet ceremony three hours before the game before 50,000 empty seats, the Mets retired his uniform number 37. Stengel was informed that it would be put in a glass case in the stadium's Diamond Club.

Said Stengel, "I'd like to see them give that number thirty-seven to some young player so it can go on and do some good for the Mets. I hope they don't put a mummy in the glass case."

After standing on the mound and having his picture taken, he hobbled into the Mets clubhouse and made a final speech to the players.

Casey Stengel: "I've been fortunate in being able to watch some of you men on television, where you can see some things you can't see from the bench. And if you could see yourselves, you might be surprised at some of the improvement you're making in which was possibly some of your weaknesses.

"You've got a month to go, and I think you can still do something. Your manager and coaches have been doing splendid work, and you see now that a baseball season is a long time, and that some of those good clubs can't win in August and September, especially when they play each other. The season is too long for some of them.

"But you've made progress, and I mean the green men as well as the others, and if you keep on you can be here four or ten years. Now, that's it."

Galen Cisco, the player representative, spoke for the players when he told Stengel, "You got us off the ground, and I think we can go on."

Stengel then appeared on Ralph Kiner's pregame television show, where he noted the lack of syntax in Cisco's brief remarks. Said Stengel, 'That Cisco from Ohio State University seems to have picked up some Stengelese somewhere along the way."

He sat in the stands and watched a few innings of the game, and then he was gone—forever. In his wake, baseball lost much uniqueness and color.

Ron Swoboda: "It happens to old people, doesn't it? And it had nothing to do with his drinking. Hey look, Casey drank. But he wasn't a drunk. But when you get old, you're brittle. I guess it made all the people who said he was over the hill feel correct. And it made it a lot easier to make the move to replace him.

"But they replaced him with Wes Westrum, and Westrum came in with the idea that he could create a different attitude and get everyone in line. If Wes could come in there and get this team in shape, get them thinking, playing better baseball, get them focused, whatever, that would be some credentials for him to get the job permanently. But Westrum was a damned good coach—he could read pitches from a pitcher. They tell me he called a bunch of home runs for Willie Mays on the Giants by reading pitches. But as far as being a manager and handling people, I don't think Westrum had the stuff.

"I remember one thing Westrum tried. Bob Gibson could shut you out in about two hours, and Westrum devised a strategy against him. Gibson liked to pitch, get the ball back, get on the rubber, and throw. He worked very fast. Our strategy against him was to step out, call time out, get the pine tar, take our time getting there, step out, let him stand out there and wait. So we employed this strategy, and it took Gibson two-and-a-half hours to shut us out. The net gain was that we spent a little more time out there getting shut out!

"And Wes had a worst winning percentage than Stengel in '65. And Westrum was awful copy. He tried to turn around a losing attitude, and I don't blame him for trying. He left us slogans in the locker room, but what happens in a situation like that, when you know you're horseshit, your grin becomes a little sarcastic. 'Nice try, pal.' It doesn't fit. Only after we learned we could play did we think we could. But even though I never felt a particular lift there with Westrum, that team wasn't going anywhere, though I did have my best year for him in '67. But I played because I was hitting the ball.

"Westrum was not a bad guy. He just had strange little ways about him. He was a strange little man. He would say things like, 'It makes sense in the daytime and it makes sense at night.' That's the only one I can remember. He'd say things like that. But under Westrum we weren't going anywhere. He managed all of '66, and in '67 we reverted to 100 losses, and he resigned when the Mets wouldn't rehire him."

s i x t e e n

Bing

One of the most important events leading to the marked improvement of the New York Mets came in August of 1964 when St. Louis Cardinals owner Gussie Busch lost the little patience he had and fired general manager Bing Devine. Through a series of brilliant trades, Devine had acquired for St. Louis, Lou Brock, Dick Groat, Bill White, and Curt Flood, building a team that would win pennants in 1964, 1967, and 1968.

But in August 1964 the Cardinals were not yet in contention, and Busch, needing to release his frustrations from having never won a pennant since he bought the team in 1953, fired Devine. The Mets signed him, with the promise that he would take over from George Weiss when Weiss stepped down as president at the end of the 1965 season.

While serving under Weiss, Devine made some very important decisions in the history of the franchise. He began in the scouting department, and he was involved in the drafting of future Mets players Ken Boswell, Jim McAndrew, and Nolan Ryan. While working for Weiss, Devine stopped his boss from releasing prospect Jerry Koosman, and when Weiss was dead set against the Mets signing pitching prospect Tom Seaver for $50,000, it was Devine who insisted and got his way.

Devine also was the man who hired Whitey Herzog when everyone else on the Mets wanted to let him go, and Herzog turned out to be an important cog in the front office.

In December of 1966 Devine took over as general manager. He would return to the Cardinals after a two-year tenure, but during his short stay was largely responsible for assembling the players who led the Mets to pennants in 1969 and 1973. Devine recalled the events leading up to his hiring by the Mets and the stories behind some of his best signings.

Bing Devine: "After I was let go by the Cardinals, there was a local public relations man, Al Fleishman, who was very close to me and very close to George Herbert Walker, [one of the Mets' minority stockholders], and knowing what was happening with me, I know there was a push from Al Fleishman about my coming to the Mets. Herb Walker got in touch with me and talked to me about coming to the Mets. My immediate reaction was thankfulness that somebody wanted me. I had young children and never had been out of a job before.

"I really didn't know how to negotiate my own contract at the time. I didn't know what it was worth, and I was in limbo, not knowing what I would do. And one day Al Fleishman called me and said, 'If you don't make up your mind pretty quickly now, they are going to go in another direction. So decide quickly what you want to do, or forget the Mets.' I thought, There's the only people I'm talking to. The job is there to have. I better take it.

"I don't think George Weiss was involved in my hiring. When I came, he was there, and it was supposed to be his last year. It was indicated to me they didn't want to kick George Weiss out arbitrarily. He had devoted so much to the Yankees and then to the Mets, so they wanted to do it properly and on a reasonable schedule he could live with. The group of owners let me know pretty quickly that George Weiss was there, and obviously I had to work out a proper relationship with him, but I was to understand that when George Weiss left at the end of 1965, I would become the president.

"George Weiss, like Charlie Finley, was an all-powerful president. He knew where all the bodies were buried and what was going on everywhere. He was a big man, a very impressive man, never loud, very soft-spoken, but you always knew exactly what he thought, and you tried to relate to that.

"And I did work out a relationship with him. I like to think that's one of the things I've always done. In this case I don't know if I felt sorry for George Weiss—I don't think he needed my sympathy, but I recognized he should go out on his own terms and on a gradual basis, so I worked with him. Whatever he wanted me to do, I did.

"The one thing he really wanted me to do, I was to be one of the first double assignment double-checkers. They call them cross-checkers now. Each scout has his first-round draft choice in his area, but the scouts can't make comparisons or evaluation between their man and the first-round choices of the other scouts, so George Weiss wanted me to go out and check them all and put them all together and see if I could come up with a plan of who should be number one, two, and three. Since then I've always jokingly said, 'I think George wanted to get me out of his hair, and that was an easy way to do it,' but I'm not sure that was true. It may have come into play, but who knows?

"In June 1965, the teams held the first player draft. Rick Monday was the first player taken by Oakland, and we had the next pick and took Les Rohr. He was high on my list. I remember him as a big left-handed pitcher who had an exceptional amount of talent. I certainly knew he was a great prospect. But he never materialized into what we thought he would be.

"We also drafted Ken Boswell, Jim McAndrew, and we took Nolan Ryan in the tenth round. That was the most amazing story of the whole draft. [He was the 295th player selected.]

"I can tell you the story of Nolan Ryan from my cross-checking. Red Murff was a very dedicated scout who recommended him. He was one of those scouts who really pressed for his people, and to see this number one pick of his, I flew into Houston, and he picked me up, which was a common practice. Rather than spend a lot of time getting a car and finding a place to live, the scouts would pick me up and make it easy for me. I guess I was kind of a visiting dignitary.

"Red raved about him even in the car on the way out to watch him pitch. We got out to see this game in Alvin, Texas, not an impressive base-ball field, a typical small-town high school baseball field. The two teams were very unimpressive, and Nolan Ryan had a heck of a time. In the first place, he was wild. And the second place, the other team hit him. You think, how can a second-rate high school team make a dent in Nolan Ryan that they did? But they did.

"And after the game, I was on my way to the airport to go see another player in another area, and Red Murff was really down. He said, 'Aw, jeeze, I know that fellow is better than that, and I know you got a bad reaction to him. I sure wish you could see him again.' And I was either smart enough—or lucky enough—to say, 'Look Red, you've been around a lot longer than I have as a scout. You pitched in the big leagues. You go ahead and make the biggest case for Nolan Ryan you can. Don't let this change your approach. It's one ball game, and I recognize that. You go ahead and put Nolan Ryan just as high as you want, and when the discussion comes as to who is going to be our number one, I can't affirm what you say, but I won't negate it. I promise you that.' And that's what happened, but it still moved him down to the tenth round.

"And what I always think about that: all the clubs had several chances to draft him and didn't. And if I were some of the other clubs, I'd ask, 'What's wrong with us?'

"At the end of 1965, Mr. Weiss was supposed to retire, but he didn't. He had an option year remaining on his contract, and he chose to exercise it. I can't say I was disappointed, certainly not as disappointed when I was hired by the Cardinals to be the general manager, only to have one of Mr. Busch's people outside make a case for Frank Lane, and have Mr. Busch hire Frank Lane. I ended up staying, and I became the general manager after Mr. Lane was fired. So I had seen this before.

"But I will say this about Mr. Weiss. If I made a strong case for wanting to do something, he would give in and gracefully do it. I'll give you an example. The Mets were going to release Jerry Koosman because he owed the club money. And Mr. Weiss did not like players who were not able to pay off what they owed. He didn't like the fact we had to lend money to a minor league player. And he wanted to release Koosman.

"And having seen Koosman pitch—that first year I got to see a lot of the Mets minor leaguers play, so that was a benefit too—I made a big case, and Joe McDonald, who was my right-hand man, convinced him, too. 'We can't just let Koosman go like that.' It would have been an outright release. As a result, we kept him.

"We got Tom Seaver in the spring of 1966. I don't know all the details, but in effect, the commissioner made a decision that the Braves had made an illegal signing. They signed him while he was still at the University of Southern California. At that time the rule was you couldn't sign anybody while they were in college. He was supposed to wait until the end of the school year.

"So the commissioner decided that any club that wanted Seaver could sign him for what the Braves had offered—$50,000—pin money now. It sounds silly to say they were debating over something like that. Joe McDonald and I went through the thing pretty thoroughly, and we really felt that Seaver was a key. And scout Nelson Burbrink, who I brought over from the Cardinals, pushed him as much as Red would push a prospect.

"We felt he could be a great addition. I don't know if we felt he'd become as great as he did. I don't know if anyone knows for sure when they make what looks like a great pickup and becomes one. Who knows if he's going to mature?

"The rule was, you had to match what the Braves had offered. Any club who wanted to draft him had to agree to take on his contract. They didn't want to get in a position where Seaver would sue.

"And George Weiss was against it. Yes, he was against taking Seaver. Let's be honest about it: he didn't know anything about him. And so he just said, 'We can't do it,' and Joe McDonald and I had a private meeting, and we agreed I had to make a case for that. I made a big case, and I recall it was only hours before we had to make a decision and agree to that, and George Weiss finally shook his head, I'm sure not wanting to do it and said, 'If you people make such a big case of it, go ahead.'

"So we went into the draft, and we were one of three clubs, Cleveland, Philadelphia, and the Mets. And we were the one who won the drawing. I got a call from Lee MacPhail, the deputy commissioner, saying, 'You just won Tom Seaver in the draft.' I thought it was good. More than anything else, I was thinking that George was feeling, If we were as high as we were on Seaver, there would be more clubs interested in him. He thought, I wonder now just how good Seaver is.

"After you get through telling the story of these successes, there are bad choices, too. In that same June 1966 draft, we had the first choice in the draft, and it was between Reggie Jackson and a high school catcher by the name of Steve Chilcott. We took the catcher, and there are a lot of things that go into it. We felt we were really short on catching in the organization at the minor league level at the time, and we needed catchers on the big league club, so we kind of made up our minds as we went through the draft to get a catcher, and Chilcott was the best of the lot.

"And I remember going to the West Coast to see Chilcott pitch, and the Mets were playing in Los Angeles, and I said to Casey Stengel, 'How about taking a ride with me? There's a doubleheader of a high school player we're looking at. Take a ride with me and see what you think. Give me your opinion.'

"Well, Casey was like he always was. 'Let's go,' and he talked all the way up there, and I had the pleasure of hearing all his stories, and we watched the doubleheader, and I don't recall the results, but I do recall that Chilcott hit well. We had to leave before the second game was over to get back to the ball game in Los Angeles. I got in the car and I said to Casey, 'All right, you've seen him. We have to make a decision. What do you think of Chilcott?' He said, 'He got six out of eight, didn't he? That's all I need to know.' That didn't push me over the line, but I had a lot of help. A lot of people agreed, 'Take the catcher, period. We obviously went the route we were looking for, to get the catcher who would help the organization immensely and quickly come to the big leagues, and Chilcott never really did anything because the first year out he hurt his back. I've often thought how the course of baseball history would have changed if the Mets had taken Reggie Jackson. We could have, and we didn't. So if you want to give me credit for Ryan and Seaver, put that one against me!

"Unless you have to you mention the good ones, but not the bad ones. But since it was such a good story, I went and told it to you.

"While Casey was still the manager, he wanted to make some coaching changes, and Whitey was one of them. And in my capacity of walking a thin line of myself and George Weiss and the future, they let me know that Casey wanted to get rid of Herzog. I said, 'Don't fire Whitey Herzog. Give him to me, and I'll use him in player development.' And they did. And Whitey has said that that was the decision that put him in a front office capacity and led him to the career he had, where he became general manager and manager.

"If I hadn't spent two years with Frank Lane in St. Louis, I would have been the conservative general manager that a lot of people speculated I would be. I sat with Frank Lane and listened to all the talk about deals almost every day. I recognized you don't want to deal just to make a deal, but at the same time it made me recognize you couldn't stand still. You had to have movement. You had to do something. Even if your club was good, you couldn't say, 'That's fine.' The other clubs were all moving and changing, perhaps not as much as they are now with free agency, but they are changing, and you better change with them. And the way we were with the Mets, you better try to change *ahead* of them. So I was always in the mode of, 'How can we help ourselves and with whom?' And 'don't get yourself too excited with who you have to give up.' I learned that from Frank Lane. He would even have dealt Stan Musial. I don't think I ever would have done that. I'm sure I wouldn't. But I was rolling the dice. Let's face it, it's easy to roll the dice when you're losing a hundred games a year.

"Jerry Grote was an important pickup. We got him from Houston. We knew he could catch. We were impressed with the way he caught and the way he ran a ball game. He didn't knock down the fences and make a big impression as a power hitter, but he could really catch and handle a pitcher, call a ball game, and throw. When we got him, I don't think anyone else had that big an opinion on him. There was no great hurrah about him. This was just another pickup.

"Jerry was withdrawn and had a negative personality, but he knew how to catch a ball game and how to handle pitchers, and maybe that very thing helped him to deal with the pitching staff. He was great. I know he surpassed our expectations.

"I got to know Jerry pretty quickly. I recognized his importance in the whole picture of building a team.

"The field staff seemed dedicated to getting rid of Cleon Jones, but I wouldn't do it. And the thing that always existed in my mind, and still does: don't pay attention to what goes on with the player personally. Take John Rocker. He antagonized people. He talked too much. He left himself open and was his own worst enemy. But if Rocker had come available and I was a general manager somewhere, I would have had interest in Rocker from what I knew of him as a pitcher.

"It's like when I got George Hendricks in St. Louis. Very few people thought it was a good deal because George had been a pain in the neck at Oakland. He was *persona non grata* mostly because he wouldn't talk to the media. So what? I don't think it's right, but I didn't negate getting players I thought would be helpful because of what they did personally.

"As a result, we kept Cleon, and he eventually played enough to become an important part of the club.

"And from spending my first year in the minor leagues, I knew there were some pretty good prospects down there. From cross-checking to see your minor league clubs extensively, I had a pretty good handle on the personnel. I didn't need to sit with two or three people. They would confer, make it easy, but I had seen it all myself and been in that capacity where I was pretty free to not worry about what went on with the Mets proper and what was going on in Shea Stadium. I could go ahead and see the people targeted for the future."

seventeen

Tom Terrific

Of all the moves that Bing Devine made, none was more important than convincing George Weiss to change his mind and pay the $50,000 for Thomas George Seaver, one of the finest pitchers ever to play the game. That the Mets had a shot at signing him was a stroke of luck. That Weiss considered passing on the boy because he had been used to paying $4,000 bonuses is too grim to contemplate. But thanks to Devine, Weiss took a deep breath, grumbled, and agreed to sign the check.

Tom Seaver was a late bloomer. In his senior year at Fresno High School, Seaver had a 6–5 record. Though he made the All City team as the third pitcher, he was not approached by a single scout.

When he graduated high school, he was five-foot-ten and weighed 165 pounds. Fresno, California, is one of America's vegetable and fruit centers, and during the summer, he worked for the Bonner Packing Company, where his father, who once played on the Walker Cup amateur golf team, was vice president. For $2.05 an hour Tom toted heavy boxes packed with raisins.

Vietnam was on the horizon, and to get his military obligation out of the way, he spent six months as a reservist in the Marines, his last two at Twenty-Nine Palms in the Mojave Desert. When he came out, he was six-foot-one and weighed 195 pounds.

He wanted to go to the University of Southern California, but he wanted to pay for it himself. To that end he decided to go to Fresno State College for a year, play baseball, and win a scholarship. Fresno State cost him ten dollars a semester for tuition. He won his last eight games and finished the year at 11–2. He also met his wife-to-be, Nancy McIntyre, on the last day of the semester.

Rod Dedeaux, the USC coach, asked Seaver to play in the fast Alaska summer league before he would offer him a scholarship. He played for Fairbanks, Alaska, with a lot of the USC players. They played games at night and worked day jobs.

Seaver pitched mostly in relief. Among the other future major leaguers on the club were Graig Nettles, Danny Frisella, Rick Monday, Curt Motton, and Gary Sutherland. Almost every member of that team would sign a major league contract.

In August 1964, his team competed in the National Baseball Congress tournament, and he was named to the NBC tournament All Star team and won his scholarship to USC.

Like Stengel, Seaver intended to be a dentist. But as a sophomore at USC, Seaver compiled a 10–2 record, and in June 1965 he was drafted by the L.A. Dodgers. When Seaver asked for $70,000, however, the Dodgers passed.

In the summer of '65 he rejoined the Alaska Goldpanners. They entered the ABC tournament again—their pitching staff had Andy Messersmith, Frisella, Al Schmelz, and Seaver.

Ex-pro ballplayers who batted against him told Seaver he had a major league future. He returned to USC for his junior year, and in January 1966, the Atlanta Braves drafted him number one. In late February he signed a contract worth $51,500.

Seaver was supposed to report to Triple A Richmond the first week in March. But on March 2, baseball commissioner William Eckert ruled the contract invalid. USC had already played two exhibition games when Seaver signed on February 24, and even though he hadn't pitched in either game, Eckert ruled it had been illegal for Atlanta to sign him.

Seaver took it in stride, intending to return to USC and finish the 1966 spring season. But because he had signed a pro contract, the NCAA then ruled him ineligible. Now Seaver was stuck, and his father began talking about a lawsuit. He called Commissioner Eckert to complain how unfair the situation was, and Eckert, intent on keeping baseball from getting sued, agreed to act.

Within two weeks, Eckert ruled that any other major league team had until April 1 to match Atlanta's offer. If more than one team wanted him, Eckert would conduct a drawing.

Cleveland, Philadelphia, and the Mets agreed to match the offer. On April 3, 1966, Lee MacPhail, the assistant to the commissioner, phoned Seaver to tell him "the commissioner is going to draw the name of the winning team—right now.

"And the name is," said MacPhail, "the New York Mets."

Seaver says he was glad it was the Mets. His close high school friend, Dick Selma, was playing in New York, and his brother Charles was living there. But after the lottery, when the Cleveland Indians informed Seaver that they would have given him as much as $80,000 to sign, Seaver tried to get the Mets to give him more money only to be rebuffed.

"Very frankly," said Nelson Burbrink, the Mets' chief scout in California, "you can either accept what we agreed to give you, or you can wait until the next draft."

The youngster decided not to wait. Seaver figured: I took it before. I might as well take it now. Why try to get a few thousand more? The main thing is to get to the big leagues."

With his bonus money, he bought himself a 1966 Chevy and as an indication of how different he was from most of the hotshot bonus babies, he put the rest into an investment plan. Two days later he reported to the Mets' minor-league training camp.

At Jacksonville, he immediately impressed manager Solly Hemus. With three different fast balls, plus the slider, Seaver was able to throw pitches that would start toward the center of the plate and hit all four corners of the strike zone. And he could throw all three fast balls at varying speeds. Hemus saw he was a young kid with the mastery of a grizzled veteran.

But Seaver was having trouble living away from his steady girl Nancy, who was back in California. Seaver was living at Jacksonville's Roosevelt Hotel, which he says, "was horrible, very, very depressing." After winning his first three games, he then lost his next five.

He called Nancy on the phone and said, "Get down here, we're getting married. This is driving me nuts. I'm getting to the point where I don't even want to play baseball and that's absurd. My heart is in California." She flew in, and the next day they were married. Seaver finished the season with a 12–12 record.

In the spring of 1967 Bing Devine knew he had to promote Seaver to the Mets. He was the only rookie to make the Mets team.

Tom Seaver

Bing Devine: "There was a lot of discussion about him. I recognized—with a lot of help and agreement—that we were short on pitching. We had to make some dramatic moves, and Seaver impressed me. We were lucky getting him, and I thought we could take advantage of it, and the thing to do was go ahead and take the gamble. It paid off very quickly and to an extreme.

"What I remember about Seaver is he was a student of the game and a student of pitching. He was a very smart guy. He could have done anything else. I recognized that about him, that he had a lot of things going for him that a lot of young ballplayers didn't and probably never would—this was aside from his ability to pitch and the stuff he had on the ball."

Ron Swoboda: "Seaver had Hall of Fame written on him when he walked into camp and pitched his first game in '67. He was a finished product when he came there. I don't ever recall the sense of him being a rookie. He came out of the box a big league pitcher, and there was this golden glow about him. This was clearly *big* talent, intelligent, capable, controlled, and awesome stuff.

"Look, you knew Seaver was special. Were we tight? No. We weren't tight. I would have been smart had I hung around Seaver more often. Because I probably could have learned something from it. Buddy Harrelson and Seaver were tight. They were California guys. And more than anything, Seaver came from a different socioeconomic level. Not that he looked down on anybody. His awareness of things was greater as a result of that. He was a younger, more aware person. Also, he had come out of the Marine reserves. He had done that bit."

After the Mets lost the 1967 season opener, something the Mets were in the habit of doing, Seaver pitched the second game and beat the Pirates 3–2.

Tom Seaver: "Some people, who'd watched the Mets stumble through their first five seasons, cracked jokes after the game; 'Break up the Mets. They've reached .500. From here on, it's all downhill.'

"I didn't laugh. I hadn't been raised on the Met legend; I wasn't part of that losing history.

"I never did find defeat particularly amusing."

Seaver's attitude rubbed off on the others, as did the attitudes of shortstop Buddy Harrelson and catcher Jerry Grote, two fierce, young players who worked to discard the "lovable loser" attitude, though "it was definitely there when I first joined the club," said Seaver.

By early June of 1967, Tom Seaver had become a sensation in New York. The players performed better behind him than they did the other pitchers. He inspired their confidence. By the All Star break Seaver had a 6–5 record and a 2.68 era. He was chosen for the game.

When the twenty-two-year-old arrived at the ballpark for the game, he was dressed in a sweater. St. Louis star Lou Brock mistook him for the bat boy. Brock asked the cherub-faced Seaver, "Hey, boy, would you get me a beer?" When Brock found out that Seaver was going to play in the game, he still couldn't get over how young he looked. Brock jokingly asked him, "Does your guardian know you're out so late?"

The All Star game went fifteen innings. Tony Perez homered to give the

National League the lead in the fifteenth. Walter Alston called Seaver in to save it. He retired Tony Conigliaro, walked Carl Yastrzemski, induced Bill Freehan to fly out, and then struck out Ken Berry to end the game.

No Met had ever done so well in such an important ball game.

Seaver finished the 1967 season with 16 wins. He had 18 complete games, 170 strikeouts, and a 2.76 era, all Mets records and he was named the National League Rookie of the Year.

Despite Seaver's heroics, on August 20 the Mets sank into last place and never climbed out. With the team's drop in the standings manager Wes Westrum worried about his future. He knew he wasn't popular with his bosses. And according to Jack Lang, his lack of recognition gnawed at him. Westrum worried that the better-known Yogi Berra, one of his coaches, would take his place at the end of the season.

In late July Westrum and Berra were sitting in the lobby bar of the Hilton Hotel in Los Angeles when a fan asked Berra for an autograph for his son. Then the man asked the famed ex-Yankee star, "Is the guy next to you anybody?" Westrum fumed.

Making Westrum's life equally difficult was his inability to fill the columns of ink in the many New York dailies. Westrum was a thoughtful baseball man, but he was not a storyteller, definitely not an entertainer, except when he didn't mean to be.

Jack Lang: "Westrum was full of malaprops. We were in the press room one night, and Casey was regaling us with stories, and all of a sudden he got up and left, and Westrum just sat there shaking his head. He said, 'Boy, when they made him, they threw away the molding!'

"I remember during spring training we beat the Cardinals, and Westrum went back to Miller Huggins Field where we got dressed, and we called him from the press box. Dick Young made the call. We went into extra innings before we won the game. Wes told him, 'That was a real cliff dweller, wasn't it?'

"He knew what he wanted to say, but sometimes it didn't come out right. But he was a very, very nice man who wasn't cut out to be a manager. He was a nice man who should have been a coach, which is what he was."

On September 1, 1967, the Mets were 51–79. Fans, no longer the rebels they once were, and no longer interested in lovable losers, stayed home in droves. Without Stengel these Mets no longer were lovable. Under the colorless Westrum, they were just another bad ball club.

Westrum had been looking for assurances he would return as manager in '68, and when Bing Devine made it clear it wasn't forthcoming, on September 21, 1967, Westrum walked into the clubhouse and announced he was resigning. His friend, San Francisco manager Herman Franks, hired him to be his third base coach.

The front runners for the job were Berra, Bob Scheffing, and Whitey Herzog, Devine's special scout who would have been wildly successful had the Mets allowed Herzog to pick his team and manage.

But M. Donald Grant, who was still calling the shots for Mrs. Payson, had another idea.

e i g h t e e n

Gil's Kids

With Wes Westrum's abrupt departure Bing Devine intended to search for a new manager for '68. His search was halted when a group of the Mets owners led by M. Donald Grant, the Mets president, asked Devine to consider hiring Gil Hodges as manager. Hodges was managing the Washington Senators at the time.

Bing Devine: "The ownership: Donald Grant, Herbert Walker, and Luke Lockwood, quickly came to me and said, 'We want you to do whatever you want to do, but we would like you to take a long look and think about Gil Hodges.' I don't know that I ever would have thought of Hodges in that capacity. At the time it sounded strange to me, but they were so strong about it I didn't think I could ignore it.

"I was at a point where I didn't want to agitate or irritate the ownership, so I said, 'We'll take a look and see what we can do.'

"One of the owners had talked to top level Washington ownership, and he said to me, 'We've paved the way, but to have it happen and to make it legitimate, we'd like you to make a deal with Washington to get Hodges. Give them something of value, money, a player, whatever.' The guy who really keyed that, who was very important in getting agreement from Washington on the deal was Johnny Murphy, who worked for me. I knew that Murphy and George Selkirk, the Washington general manager, had once been roommates playing on the Yankees, and that's why I put Johnny Murphy in the position of talking to Washington. Incidentally, I knew

George Selkirk well, though I did not get involved in that deal talking to him personally.

"[Washington owner] Bob Short was nice enough to let Gil come back to New York. Because the deal as it was made wasn't something so breathtaking that Washington had to take it. Maybe Hodges hadn't made that much of an impression.

"Johnny Murphy and Selkirk worked out this deal. We gave them pitcher Bill Denehy and $100,000. Denehy was considered a prospect, but he wasn't anything we were really disappointed about losing. He obviously had something, but it wasn't someone where we said, 'Oh, my Lord, how could we give him up?'

"My next mission was to sign Hodges as manager and get him announced. I met him in St. Louis at the World Series, of all places. I remember sitting with him in the stands and discussing this between things happening in the game, and coming to a virtual agreement that I ran by ownership, and they agreed. Then after the series went back to Boston I got in touch with Hodges, and I went to Boston and made the deal, and we announced it in Boston. We had a press conference. Very strange. People try not to take something away from the World Series, but we had a press conference in a hotel in Boston and made the announcement.

"Hodges was outstanding, and the ownership—the people who knew him and liked him, they were right. Give the ownership a plus for that. And once we acquired Hodges—once I met him in St. Louis and began to spend some time with him—he was immediately impressive. He was great to relate to. It didn't take long to make friends with him. And I trusted him.

"After I got to know Gil, and I have never made this comment before, I'm thinking that Gil Hodges as a manager reminded me a great deal of Johnny Keane in St. Louis. When you asked Gil Hodges a question to get his opinion, he gave you his opinion. You didn't get a half-baked, 'This is good but who knows? . . . ' I didn't get that from Keane and people like Harry Walker, Eddie Stanky or Bob Kennedy, and I never got that from Hodges."

Ron Swoboda found the imposing Marine to be a fascinating character.

Ron Swoboda: "Gil's approach was entirely different from the year before. His approach was serious and all business, man, and he was a big,

Gil Hodges

imposing guy, scared the shit out of you. My problem with Hodges was that I had just hit .281, and I thought I was a big fucking deal, and he came in with his authority, and I thought I approached the game pretty seriously myself. I had certain things I liked to do—Eddie Yost would hit me balls from a hundred and fifty feet away, line drives left, right, over my head, ground balls in front of me, whatever came off the bat, so I could read the ball as it came off the bat. I wanted to read the ball where the differences were subtle. Because if you can catch those, it's a piece of cake on balls where you know they're left or right or deep. You can't get enough balls off the bat in batting practice, but Gil wanted me to take my outfield with the rest of the guys, when I had thrown already after working out with Eddie. But Hodges didn't see that. We grated there.

"It was just this thing I had with authority. One time [on] opening day, we were in Pittsburgh, and Hodges got the team together in a meeting. He said, 'All right, we're going to set curfew, and since you guys have to live with it, I want you to decide it.' Somebody said, 'Two-and-a-half hours after the ball game.' And Gil said, 'That's too long.'

"I said, 'Gil, why don't you just tell us what you want, so we can end this meeting?' My big fucking mouth, you know?

"Another time Gil was giving Eddie Kranepool some trouble, and I stuck my nose into that. It was like, Why did I do that? What did you do that for? And don't get me wrong. I respected the guy. He was a *good* baseball man, knew how to manage, made decisions quickly, *always* ahead of the game. Always.

"But, it was just this thing I had with authority. In other words, I could take the authority, but don't say we're going to pick a time, and then it turns out we're not. I don't need the guise of democracy. It ain't a democracy, and that's fine with me.

"But, I seemed to do these things where I knew if I was the manager and somebody else was the player, I'd have said to myself, 'What in the fuck is this guy's problem?'

"I did those kind of things with Hodges, and yet I liked him.

"Gil Hodges was as decent as managers come. If he was guilty of any of the things I made a deal out of, it was certainly within his prerogative, and it certainly wasn't cruel or unusual, and it certainly would have been smarter for me to swallow that shit and just go on and be a ballplayer. Because he was not a bad guy. He was a great guy. He really was.

"He was from another generation, but he was so solid a baseball man, and I chastise myself for not understanding that better and respecting it more. It turned into a little bit of a battle of wills, and it was so immature and stupid on my part, I could thrash myself over that.

"And Hodges managed in a very interesting way. He could be very creative when he thought the situation called for it. In '68 we played a twenty-three-inning game against Houston, and there was a point in the game when the pitcher was up in a bunt situation with a runner on first. I was playing right field, and he called me in and he said, 'Just play first base. Stay here. Don't move. Catch the ball if they have to throw it to you.' And he had the first baseman and the third baseman walk up to the pitcher's shoe-tops, daring him to swing at it. Hodges was taking the bunt away, and it worked. It was a pitcher who he would rather swing the bat because he knew if he did that, we had him.

"So Hodges did these titillating little things where you said to yourself,

'Goddamn, that was interesting. And it lifted you. 'Interesting.' That got my attention, and it got to where you said, 'That's pretty sharp. Why not do that?'"

But hiring Gil Hodges was one of Bing Devine's last moves as the Mets general manager. His wife and kids were living in St. Louis and he was flying home for the weekends. When Stan Musial quit as general manager of the Cardinals at the end of the 1967 season, Gussie Busch decided he had made a mistake when he fired Devine in August 1964. When Busch asked Devine if he would come back, Bing jumped at the chance.

Devine is emphatic in denying that he left because of interference from M. Donald Grant, as Whitey Herzog charged in his book *The White Rat*. (Herzog remained with the Mets until 1973, when he no longer was able to stand Grant's meddling.)

Bing Devine: "When I was general manager, I never had any interference from Donald Grant or any of the other owners. The only thing you had to do if you wanted to trade certain players who had standing on the Mets was to run a deal by them so they didn't get surprised. I don't think I was ever stopped from doing anything I wanted to do with the Mets."

When Devine told Donald Grant of the offer, the Mets did everything they could to get Devine to stay.

Bing Devine: "Donald Grant was the liaison to Mrs. Payson, the same way that Dick Meyer was with Mr. Busch in St. Louis. And Donald called me and said, 'I have to be honest with you. I'd like to talk you out of this. We would like to keep you. I don't want to say you're making a mistake, but we think you are, and we'd like you to meet with us and give me a chance personally to discuss this with you.' He was on vacation in Boca Raton, Florida, and he asked me to fly down to see him.

"I got on the plane and went to Boca Raton, found his house and talked to him. And he was very kind, very nice about what I had done and what he thought the future held. He said, 'If you change your mind and come back here, I can't guarantee how we'll do it, but I think I'm strong enough to get you a piece of the club.' Wow! If you look at what happened to the value of the franchise, I say to myself, Think what would have happened if you had hit the jackpot! And that would have been the jackpot. So how smart am I? Nobody in my family has ever second-guessed me. I'd be more likely to second-guess myself.

"But in the end I decided to go back to St. Louis, and when I did, I wanted to go see Mrs. Payson personally before I left. She was about as nice as you can get for an owner. She was part of the Mets success because she didn't get in the way of the part that made them successful. She was a shadowy figure because she always stayed in the background. And I remember calling and setting up an appointment with her downtown in New York in midday in her office during the Christmas rush.

"I got downtown and I was driving, and I couldn't find a place to park. I parked in a garage about twenty blocks away, got outside, looked for a cab, couldn't find one, and ended up virtually running the twenty blocks. Because I wanted to see Mrs. Payson for sure before she got away, and before I got away.

"I explained what I was going to do and why. She was very nice about it, understanding. It was with a great deal of sorrow. There were no negative reasons with the organization or with her, but I wanted her to hear it from me personally."

It would turn out to be a dark moment for the Mets. Devine's successors as general manager would not have the unfettered reign that Bing had. Donald Grant, impatient for victory and always willing to trade his very talented farmhands for better-known but often less-talented quantities, would extend more of an influence. As great as the Mets farm system turned out to be under Devine and Herzog, the Mets would only win pennants in 1969 and then in 1973. If Grant hadn't traded away such nascent stars as Nolan Ryan, Amos Otis, Tim Foli, and Ken Singleton, the dynasty that Bing Devine had begun to build may well have come to be.

Devine left the Mets on December 5, 1967. To succeed him, the Mets board of director selected fifty-nine-year-old Johnny Murphy, who had run the Boston Red Sox farm system before joining the Mets organization. According to Jack Lang, Murphy's biggest task was to blunt potentially harmful decisions made by Donald Grant.

Jack Lang: "His biggest plus, perhaps, was his willingness to dispute Grant on baseball matters. Grant, a fan, thought he knew baseball as well as the baseball men he hired. He sat in one front office strategy sessions and did not hesitate to express his views. Those views did not always match those of the professionals he hired, but few people were willing to argue with him. More than once Herzog told Grant he didn't know anything about baseball."

If Murphy was feeling the pressure from Grant, who had his pet players, he was also getting it from below from Herzog, who did things his way, no matter what Grant thought.

Whitey Herzog: "When [Devine] left the Mets, they made John Murphy the general manager. John was a fine man, but his nickname was 'Grandma'—he just couldn't seem to make a decision. That was fine with me, since I moved in to make all the tough ones for him. All Murphy really cared about were the bonus babies and the big pitchers. He let me run the organization pretty much as I wanted.

"One morning in spring training I released about $400,000-worth of bonus babies without bothering to check with him. Players like Steve Chilcott and Les Rohr.

"'Oh, my God,' John said when I told him what I'd done. 'Tell me you didn't really do that.'

"'Yeah, John,' I said, 'I can't look at them any more. We're better off getting them out of here. They're just taking up space. We've got to get this organization moving. If any of them ever makes the big leagues, you can have my job.' None of them ever did."

After Devine left, Herzog was the best man in the organization when it came to making personnel decisions. Devine had recognized his talents from the start.

At the end of the 1966 season Herzog, the Mets' third base coach, decided to go home to Kansas City and take a job with Charlie Finley's A's. When Devine learned of this, he raised his pay and hired Herzog to be his special assistant. In 1967 Herzog scouted other big league teams, minor league prospects, and free agents.

Herzog missed being in uniform, and at the end of '67, right before Devine left, Herzog and Bob Scheffing switched jobs, making Herzog director of player development. That job was to assess the talent in the Mets organization and to decide which players should move up or down. But when Herzog decided to make a personnel move, he discovered that too often he was being undermined by Grant.

★ ★ ★

Whitey Herzog: "The only real problem in working for the Mets was working with M. Donald Grant, the one who ran the team for Mrs. Payson, the owner. He was a stockbroker, a guy who didn't know beans about baseball but thought he did. I've run into guys like Donald Grant a lot in my career, and everywhere they show up, they're trouble. They figure, 'Hell, I always wanted to be a baseball player, so I'll just pretend I know what I'm doing.'

"No manager likes to be second-guessed, but it comes with the territory. I figure that being second-guessed is part of the territory, and I don't mind it—as long as I don't have to pay any attention to it. That was the problem with Grant. We had to pay attention to him.

"Grant had his 'pets,' and no argument on earth could convince him that they weren't worth keeping. One of his pets was a left-handed pitcher named Don Shaw—'my Donnie Shaw,' Grant called him. He won a total of thirteen games in the big leagues, but Grant was convinced he was a great prospect. In the winter of 1967–68, we went down to Mexico for the winter meetings and had a deal all set with the White Sox. We were going to give them Shaw and outfielder Tommy Davis for Tommy Agee, a young outfielder everyone in the Mets' organization was hot for. Gil Hodges wanted him. Bing, Scheffing, and I wanted him, and we had the deal set. But Bing said we'd have to wait until Grant flew in to approve it.

"The deal leaked to the papers, and when Grant hit town, he was furious. 'How could you think about trading my Donnie Shaw?' he asked.

"And he killed the deal."

The Mets were eventually able to acquire Agee anyway. When Herzog left Donnie Shaw unprotected in the next expansion draft and Montreal took him, Herzog says it almost cost him his job. He finally left in 1973 after he could no longer stand Grant's meddling. He went to Texas to begin a managerial career that one day will land him in baseball's Hall of Fame.

It was no coincidence that two years after Herzog took the job, the Mets won the World Series, as Herzog tossed the deadwood and began promoting the young players.

As the 1968 spring exhibition got underway, in the outfield besides Ron Swoboda were left fielder Cleon Jones and centerfielder Tommy Agee, two talented youngsters who grew up and played high school ball together in Mobile, Alabama.

★ ★ ★

Ron Swoboda: "I liked them. I still like them. Everybody wanted to try and make Cleon and Tommy Mobile boys. But Cleon came from a much rougher background. Tommy's people were religious. There was a lot more structure in Tommy's family. Cleon grew up a little rougher.

"There was a tendency back then for whites to grant black athletes their due as physical athletes, but reluctant to recognize them as intelligent athletes. And Cleon was a very studious hitter. He understood hitting. He would look at film. He would be in the back looking at the little loops of film we had of hitting. He studied that and understood it. I didn't. He would be a good hitting coach today. He could transmit what he knew about hitting to today's young players, no doubt in my mind. I've seen him talk hitting. It's illuminating.

"Tommy understood himself as a hitter very well, too.

"A couple of years ago, Cleon and I were talking, and he mentioned to me for the first time that he used to go to barbecues at Louis Armstrong's house 'all the time.' He said that Tommy Agee sometimes went, but that he went more often. He said Louis was not at the peak of health and that he spent much of the time sitting down. Louis was very much a baseball fan, watched the Mets on TV, and he wanted Cleon to brief him on what was going on. And that's what Cleon did. I'm a big music fan. I've studied the history of New Orleans music a bit, and I would have loved to have gone with them. But I was not part of that, I'm sorry to say. It would have been wonderful."

Behind the plate crouched a surly Texan by the name of Jerry Grote. He wasn't likeable to anyone, except his teammates, and even some of them weren't so sure.

Ron Swoboda: "The writers never respected Grote, but fuck, the guys who played with him could barely stand him. He was a red-ass Texan who loved to fuck with people but who didn't like anybody to fuck with him. It was a one-way street, it seemed like, but we've all grown-up and gotten a little older. Grote is Grote, and we would not have been as good without him behind home plate. Because we were so much of a pitching staff that it was utterly key who was sitting back there handling them.

"When you talk to the pitchers, they will tell you he was one of the better handlers of pitchers. He wasn't easy to get along with, but the pitching staff respected him. He was outstanding. If you weren't trying to pitch to him, you would have no way of knowing that. He had great tools as a catcher, and an ability to call a game. Seaver and I talked about Grote's arm. I said I thought he threw better than Johnny Bench. Seaver said, "I wouldn't go that far.' But he was pretty damn good. He threw out a lot of guys. If you gave him half a shot, he'd throw him out. He could hold down a team's running game. He and Lou Brock had some classic battles.

"Talk to Seaver, Koosman, McGraw, talk to them. They will wave his flag. They will burnish his apple. And rightfully so."

In addition three young pitchers became important members of the cast. One was a flaky lefty by the name of Tug McGraw.

Ron Swoboda: "He was California all the way, man, full of all these different expressions about things. He had four or five different words for titties, you know, very much a California mentality. He and Buddy Harrelson had an entirely different perspective on things. I thought, Whoa, man, they've been in the sun too much.

"Tug was interesting, fun, real. Tug can delight me more in five minutes than anybody I know. And there's so much more to him than I thought when I first met him. Much more drive. And he had more fun playing baseball than anybody I knew. He could take more delight in some of those situations he found himself in as a relief pitcher as he fell into that role. He was so much more able as a player than I thought he would be. I did not think he would be a successful pitcher. He threw pretty good, had a curveball and change-up and a fastball that was pretty straight, but then he came up with a screwball and about the time people thought that was his story, he developed a slider, and he became more competitive and more confident. Tug could pitch. Tug always had runners on base, *always*. Always let the shit get close to the fan. And the majority of the time he came out unscathed. Which was amazing. And Tug looked like he was having fun, looked like he had a broader view of the game that he was in, and I always enjoyed people who projected that. My scope was much narrower. The guys who saw more seemed to be having more fun. Tug was what I wanted to be more like."

Tug McGraw, born Frank, was given his nickname by his mother who called him her "little Tugger" while breast-feeding. The name stuck.

McGraw grew up in Vallejo, California, twenty-five miles from San Francisco. His father had been a fireman until he hurt his back. While Tug and Hank were in high school, he took a job as a plant operator with the water department working midnight to eight in the morning so he could watch his boys play baseball.

When he was a freshman in high school, he was four-foot-eleven and weighed ninety-eight pounds. As a kid he was an attention seeker, a "show-off," a wisecracker" a "brat."

Despite his size, McGraw wanted to pitch. But the coach of the JV team, Father Freehan, an elderly priest whose eyesight was failing, wanted Tug to play center field.

Tug, a sophomore, came up with a mischievous solution, as he tells it. His teammate Bobby Hay, who pitched, wanted to play the outfield. So Tug and Hay switched uniform tops, McGraw pitched in his place, and Hay played center in Tug's place.

Tug began pitching regularly his junior year. His brother Hank, a senior, was the catcher.

At the end of the 1961 season Hank signed with the Mets for $15,000 and used the money to pay off his father's debt.

After high school, Tug went to Vallejo Junior College. He played end on the football team, and in the sixth game of the season hurt his back, suffering a cracked vertebra and a concussion. Always a wild and crazy guy, when the baseball season began he dislocated a finger on his pitching hand when he did a flip from a hayloft into a pile of hay and missed. He missed the first five weeks of the season. When he returned he still pitched well enough to attract the scouts.

The St. Louis Cardinals asked him to play on a team in Canada during the summer. He was coached by Ray Young, the Stanford baseball coach. He got $300 a month. McGraw was such a rube that when he saw "prime rib" on the menu, he asked one of his teammates what that was. The teammate thought he was kidding.

McGraw took his team to the state championships his sophomore year. In the finals he got knocked out in the third inning. In left field he made a damaging error, dropping a fly ball. When the season ended, the Cardinals were no longer interested.

Tug called Mets scout Roy Partee who had signed his brother, and Partee gave him a try-out. After a second try-out, the Mets gave him $7,000.

After one season in the minors McGraw received a big league contract and in February 1965, McGraw reported to spring training. Casey Stengel was there. McGraw couldn't figure out why Stengel didn't pay a doctor to fix his gimpy leg.

Tug McGraw: "My first impression was that he was shorter than I'd thought, but not as old. You used to get the idea in those days that Stengel was ancient. When I met him in the locker room, he didn't have his uniform completely on, and I could see where the taxicab had hit his leg in Boston about twenty years earlier when he was managing there. I couldn't believe anybody could walk around with a leg like that, all bent and sort of gnarled. He *was* Casey Stengel, and I didn't understand why he hadn't had it, well, fixed.

"There was nothing wrong with his voice though. He was talking and jabbering away, to nobody or anybody or everybody, and even to me, and it was a blast just meeting him."

McGraw's first three seasons were spotty. There was his win over Sandy Koufax, but only three others. Part of it was that the team was bad. The other part was that he was.

When McGraw came to spring training in 1966, he tried too hard and his left elbow became stiff. By May, he couldn't throw at all. He had tendonitis and went on the disabled list. That year his record was 2–9 and he was shipped to Jacksonville.

While he was in Jacksonville playing in the Instructional League, he learned to throw a screwball from former Yankee pitcher Ralph Terry, who had been picked up by the Mets. But when he tried it, coach Sheriff Robinson told McGraw to concentrate on getting his fastball and curve over the plate.

In 1967 he didn't have a good spring and was sent to Jacksonville. That year he started throwing his screwball in earnest. His record was 10–9 with a league leading 1.99 era. Bill Virdon was his manager. In the fall McGraw went back up to the Mets, but he and manager Wes Westrum didn't get along, and he didn't pitch much.

In a game against the Dodgers in LA, he pitched well for four innings, then got in trouble in the fifth. Westrum took him out.

After the game McGraw went into his office and complained. His next start was against the Astros in Houston and this time Westrum left him in the game to absorb a real beating. McGraw gave up eight runs in five innings.

"Just like I'd demanded," said McGraw. "But, I thought it was horse-shit, sort of you-pop-off, you-take-the-consequences sort of thing."

After a group of players spent an afternoon in Disneyland and were later that evening beaten badly by the Dodgers, Westrum announced that Disneyland was off-limits for the players. Said McGraw, "Get that, Mickey Mouse was off-limits because he made you too tired to play ball, but Joe's Bar was all right."

Before the 1968 season, McGraw apprenticed at a barber shop on the Bowery. Most of his customers were the homeless and down and out.

McGraw, a free spirit, hated authority. In spring of 1968 the coaches tried to get McGraw to stop throwing the screwball, and he had a bad spring, and was sent back to Jacksonville. Tug's older brother, Hank, who was also playing down there, accused manager Sheriff Robinson of not knowing what he was talking about.

"Why don't you just leave him alone and let him do his own thing?" Hank McGraw yelled at him. Hank's career ended shortly after that.

1968 Hodges still didn't like the way he was pitching and he sent McGraw back to the minors. In Jacksonville, McGraw, going against his nature, decided to do what management wanted; he threw only curveballs, and hurt his shoulder.

The Mets didn't protect McGraw during the 1969 expansion draft, but after three rounds, they pulled him back and he returned to play with them in the spring of 1969. This time everyone left him alone, and he started getting batters out.

That spring Hodges told McGraw he had a choice. Since the starting rotation was set, he could either go back to Tidewater and start, or stay on the Mets and relieve. McGraw chose to stay in the big leagues and become a reliever. It was a decision that would soon make him a star.

The second young pitcher was a hard-throwing Texan from a little town called Alvin. His name was Nolan Ryan, and though he threw gas, he often wasn't quite sure where the ball was going.

Rich Wolfe had gone to Notre Dame, where he roomed with Mets prospect Shaun Fitzmaurice, an outfielder who ended up playing nine games with the Mets in 1966. Wolfe drove to New York to watch his roomie and

Nolan Ryan

at the same time got to see Nolan Ryan pitch in his very first game as a Met. Wolfe had seen Ryan pitch in the minors and had known all about him.

Rich Wolfe: "When I first saw Shaun play in Williamsport, everyone talked about Nolan Ryan, but I never got to see him pitch. I asked, 'Who is this guy?' They said, 'He's the phantom. He's in military service all the time, or he has blisters and can't pitch. But when he pitches, he's phenomenal.'

"And then I saw him pitch in Williamsport, and he just blew everybody away.

"It was September of '66, and Shaun and Nolan were called up to the Mets from the minors, and I saw Nolan make his first big league appearance. He was the starting pitcher against the Braves, and Eddie Mathews was the third batter, and after the first pitch, he backed out of the box, looked at Jerry Grote, and you could see him mouth the words, 'What the fuck was that?'

"Ironically, Nolan didn't strike anyone out until the pitcher, Pat Jarvis, came up, and that was his first strike out.

"At Williamsport everybody talked about what nice people he and his wife Ruth were. The last time I saw Ryan he was the very same nice guy he was way back then, just a total class act."

Ron Swoboda: "I remember seeing Nolan for the first time, either right before the Mets signed him or right after. Red Murff brought him in to the Astrodome. They brought him out onto the field before everyone went onto the field. Nolan was throwing to John Stephenson, who is now managing in the Mets organization. Johnny was warming him up, and he was throwing these fastballs in the empty Astrodome—a skinny little kid—and it sounded like someone was shooting skeet in there. 'Pow. Pow!' It was resonating, filling up the dome. 'Pow. Pow!' They used to have pigeons in there, and someone told me someone went in there with a .410 shotgun and shot them; an indoor pigeon shoot. That was what it sounded like, somebody shooting a gun.

"Nolan started throwing curveballs, and without telling John Stephenson, he went back to throwing fastballs. Stephenson rightfully expected a curve, and he was thinking down and away, and this ball came up and in, and drilled him right in the chest. Boom! He didn't break anything, but he could have stopped his heart. He just flat drilled him, and he was hurt. He didn't play again for another three weeks.

"That was the first time I ever saw Nolan Ryan. Stephenson will never forget it, and probably neither will Nolan.

"Nolan's biggest problem was that he was a high-ball pitcher in a low-ball league. In the National League, the umpires had the inside gear, and they umpired on the inside corner, down low by the catcher's face. In the American League umpires were still using the big life raft, exterior gear, a big balloon, and they umpired behind the catcher over the top of his head, so they couldn't get close and see that low strike, so the strike zone was different and higher in the American League by virtue of the technique of umpiring.

"Nolan was about as naive and frightened of New York as anybody I've seen. His wife Ruth was especially intimidated by it. New York scared the hell out of those two people. They were kids from a little town, and here was New York. Nolan was never comfortable in New York and neither was Ruth.

"Ryan was young and raw and completely out of place in New York City. Not that any of us were really up to New York City, because we were all so young. Very few of us were up to New York City in those days. Dick Stuart came through, and he was up to New York City. He was savvy. Phil Linz was, because he had been around it awhile. Art Shamsky had lived in the city. Ken Boswell was an Austin, Texas, boy, but Austin was a big city. Alvin was a one-horse town. Boswell lived in the city. But Nolan came with his wife, and I don't suppose they cultivated a whole lot of friends, and basically they mistrusted the area, never felt right.

"I never hung with him. He didn't go out and run around and drink beer like the rest of us. He wasn't into that, and you never saw that. Nolan knew how he wanted to behave and didn't need any of that.

"Nolan was Nolan. There wasn't a lot of artifice about him. When you were with him, you were around a completely authentic person. One time when I was with the Yankees and he was with the Angels, I went over to his house and had barbecue. He cooked some hamburgers on the grill at his apartment."

The third important young arm belonged to that of Jerry Koosman, a left-hander who, like Nolan Ryan, was signed in Texas by scout Red Murff. Koosman was a Minnesotan who Murff had scouted as a high schooler. When Koosman ended up in Texas during the service, Murff was invited for a second look. Koosman and Seaver would team up to produce the most effective tandem since Koufax and Drysdale.

Koosman made a splash on opening day of 1968 before 52,000 fans at Shea. Ron Swoboda, who played that day, has never forgotten it. Koosman started the afternoon by loading the bases in the first inning with nobody out.

Ron Swoboda: "Jesus God, what a display. I was playing in that game. I was in the outfield, and I was thinking, 'Oh, shit, we're in trouble.' Four, five, and six were up, Willie Mays, Jim Ray Hart, and Jack Hiatt, who was a little bit of a drop-off. And Koosman retired all three of them, and in a hurry it became, 'Oh, shit, *they're* in trouble.' You know what I mean?

"Tom Seaver was the number one starter, and he certainly deserved to be that, which meant that he was the guy they tried to keep in the regular rotation as much as possible, and then everyone else kind of had to make due. Also, over the years, Koosman got a lot of the tough matchups. If you have a choice in the matter, why would you burn your number one guy against the other team's number one very often? You want to give your number one a chance to win a ball game for you. Koosman was number two, and he got some of the tougher matchups.

"Jerry was just wonderful, wild and crazy, and fun. He and Gary Gentry were kind of fearless. Jerry had good stuff, and he knew he had good stuff. He should have signed a contract with Louisville Sluggers. They should have paid him for all the bats he broke. This guy sawed them off.

"Jerry had a fastball, and he came off the side of the mound, and he could get that fastball in on right-handers, and I mean he ate them up. And he kind of cut it a little bit, too. It ran in on right-handers. Boy, you talk about eat them up! Jerry made a science out of it.

"At night we'd all end up at the same bar. There was a group of fun-loving boys. Like I said, we saw each other on the road a lot. We enjoyed each other."

Jerry Koosman was an engineering student as well as a baseball player. After two years of study, he was drafted into the army. He would have gone into helicopter training if an influential friend hadn't gotten his orders changed to a base in Texas where he was assigned to the baseball team. Without the change, Koosman would have been flying choppers in Vietnam where the casualty rate for pilots was very high. Instead, Red Murff scouted him (for a second time) while he was pitching at Fort Bliss, and Koosman became an important member of the Mets pitching staff.

Jerry Koosman: "I was born in Appleton, Minnesota on Dec. 23, 1942. My dad was a farmer. We had livestock, cattle, and hogs, and we raised them and did everything that's involved. Most kids would rather play than work, and I had two brothers, and we would play whatever we could with three guys.

"The high school I went to didn't have baseball, but I started playing semipro ball on Sunday afternoons when I was thirteen. And then I played a year of American Legion ball when I was fifteen, and I played semipro ball up until I went into the service. The Mets' Red Murff scouted me back then.

"I went to the University of Minnesota, Morris branch, the first year they had college there, so they didn't have a baseball team. Then when I transferred to the State School of Science in Lofton, North Dakota, I was ineligible.

"Then in 1962 I was drafted into the army. I took basic training at Fort Leonard Wood, and after that I went to Belleview Air Force Base for two weeks, and then got assigned to a Nike Hercules site in Grafton, Illinois. I was stationed there at the Pierre Marquette State National Park on the top of a hill. There wasn't a even flat spot to have a baseball field, and I couldn't see myself spending twenty months there and not be able to play.

"I came home on leave and I asked my dentist, Bob Miller, who was the commanding major general of the Minnesota National Guard, 'Bob, can you get me transferred some place where I can play baseball?' He said; 'You'll have to go south, the Fifth Army. I'm in the Fourth Army, and I don't know if I can get you transferred.' I said, 'I appreciate whatever you can do.'

"It didn't sound good, so I went and took my OCS test so I could go to officer's school and become a warrant officer and train in helicopters in Texas, because I liked to fly. I knew they did that in Texas, that it was warm enough there to play baseball.

"I passed the test, and two weeks before my orders came through to go to officer's school, they transferred me to El Paso, Texas. My orders were to play baseball down there, and I played for seventeen months.

"So, if it wasn't for Bob Miller, I'd have been flying choppers, and I would have been sent to Vietnam, and most of those guys didn't come back. So you might say I was two weeks from having my destiny changed.

"I began pitching in the army, and my catcher turned out to be the son of a man who was an usher at Shea Stadium, and the story goes that he told his dad he was catching a good pitcher and the Mets should send a scout to see him. And because of that connection, the Mets sent the same scout, Red Murff, back to see me again.

"I signed on August 28, 1964, and when I got out of the army in October, I went back to college for a quarter. I could go back to school again because I had to go to spring training, which for the minor leaguers was held in Homestead, Florida.

"I heard that the Mets were going to release me, but Frank Lary, who was our minor league pitching instructor, taught me how to throw a slider, and I caught on to it right away, and he said that because my slider was so good, he thought they should give me another opportunity.

"And so they didn't release me, and my second year I went to Auburn, New York. [He led the New York-Penn League with a 1.38 era.] On that team was Steve Chilcott, who was really a good-looking catcher. He had a great arm. But he threw it out up there in Auburn. I went up to the big leagues the next year, and we never saw each other again.

"I also played with Les Rohr. I don't know what happened to him. He was six-foot-five, a strong kid with a great arm. He just never mastered all the things you have to do to get to the big leagues.

"I made the Mets club starting in 1967 along with Tom Seaver. Back then you went north with twenty-eight players and after thirty days they cut three to get down to the twenty-five-man roster. Ralph Terry, Greg Goossen, and I were cut, and I was sent to Jacksonville under Bill Virdon. I stayed there all year, had a very successful year, and was called back up in September. My first big league manager was Wes Westrum, and he was very kind to me, and so I was pretty downhearted when he got released.

"Gil Hodges was hired in '68. He was excellent, a gentleman's gentleman. We were anticipating that he would be a strong disciplinarian the first year because of a book Hawk Harrelson had written, but when he came to the Mets he was happy-go-lucky, and we had a lot of fun. There was a lot of laughing going on. Looking back, he was feeling the club out and learning the organization and the players.

"Then after '68, he made some changes, and in '69, once he had his own club put together and knew the personalities, he became strict.

"A week before the '68 season was to begin, Martin Luther King was killed. We went to San Francisco, and they had a day of mourning for him, so all the big league games were cancelled, and that was the day I was supposed to pitch, our last day in San Francisco, so I was moved back to open up in Dodger Stadium, and I shut out the Dodgers 4–0.

"We returned to Shea for opening day, and I started against the Giants. To set the stage a little, we left Los Angeles and went to Houston, and we played a game there that went twenty-four innings, and we lost it 1–0 on a ground ball hit to Al Weis. It hit an irregular spot in the infield, bounced over his head, and we lost the game. That was before they dragged the infield every five innings. And during that long game everybody on our staff was used except Nolan Ryan and myself. Nolan had pitched the night before, and I was pitching the next game in New York.

"And so going into New York it was an afternoon game, and I loaded the bases in the first inning with nobody out.

"Willie Mays was up to hit. So I struck out Willie Mays on fastballs, and Jim Ray Hart, the third baseman, was up next, and I popped him up to

Jerry Grote, and the Giant catcher, Jack Hiatt, was the next hitter, and I struck him out. And I went on to shut them out 3–0.

"My next start I pitched five more shutout innings for a total of twenty-one, and then Bob Aspromonte hit a low-and-away fastball to left center to drive in a run, and I won that game 3–1.

"By early June 1968 no one on the team was hitting very much. Our feeling was this: if you got four runs, it was a laugher. If you got three runs, you'd win. If you got two runs, you had to win half your games, and some of them you should win one to nothing. We just knew we'd have to win with one, two, or three runs.

"One of our pitchers that year was Nolan Ryan. He was a relief pitcher with us. He threw hard but was wild. He was trying to get the feel and control his pitches.

"Everyone's skin is a little different. I callous real easy, and he didn't callous hardly at all. And so consequently the end of his big power finger would blister.

"Nolan and I used to drive together to the ballpark. Nolan is a farm boy from Texas, and I'm a farm boy from Minnesota, and neither one of us was comfortable in New York. It was way out of our realm of upbringing. Neither one of us was used to the lifestyle. Going from the farm to New York City, I don't know of any other extreme a person could have as a young person. Look at the change in the pace of life. You go from the farm to the tension and the crowd, something neither one of us was used to.

"You have to adjust. It was tough on a lot of us young guys. It had been tough on some of the veterans. Cause you are scrutinized by every radio, TV, magazine, and newspaper there is.

"Tom Seaver also was on our staff. He was a friend. He's younger than me. We came up to the big leagues the first year in '67, and we made a little pact between us that our goal was to win twenty games each year, and get five years in the big leagues so we could qualify for the pension plan. He was a college graduate, well-spoken, well-read, a man who handled himself real well with the press.

"Our catcher was Jerry Grote. If you looked up 'red ass' in the dictionary, his picture would be in there. Jerry was the guy who you wanted on your side, because he'd fight tooth and nail 'til death to win a ball game.

"If you didn't throw the ball where you were supposed to or if you bounced a curveball when you weren't supposed to, Jerry had such a great arm that from a squatting position he could throw the ball back at you as hard as you threw it up there. But he could throw it with great control and handcuff you right in front of your belt buckle. He used to do this to Jim McAndrew a lot. McAndrew would never challenge hitters according to where Grote wanted the ball; so Grote kept firing it back and handcuffing him in front of the belt buckle, and we would kind of laugh about it, because we knew what Grote was doing. And when McAndrew would bounce a slider or curveball, it used to tick Grote off.

"During a game in New York he did it to me and I called him out there, and I told him, 'Grotes, if you throw the ball back at me one more time like that I'm going to break your fucking neck.'

"And I turned around and walked back to the mound, and he never threw it back at me again. We always had respect for each other after that.

"Grote had a red ass with the media, but Grote didn't care. All he cared about was what he did on the field. If you didn't get your story from what he did out there, you either talked to him nicely or he wasn't going to give you any more story. I'll tell you, if I had to do my career over again, Grote is the catcher I want behind the plate.

"After the '68 All Star game, we slumped. Buddy Harrelson needed a knee operation. Ken Boswell and Nolan had reserve duties, and then he had to go on the DL because of his blisters. I didn't realize it until a game in Atlanta, which I was pitching, but in the fall of 1968 Gil was starting to get chest pains.

"It was a very hot, humid night, toward the end of the year with my second to last start. I got knocked out in the sixth inning, and I went into the clubhouse, and Gil was laying on the trainer's table, and his complexion was real blushed. I asked him, 'Gilly, are you okay?' And he said, 'Yeah, I'll be all right.'

"I was concerned about him as he was laying there. I felt bad. I got knocked out, gave up six runs in an inning, the worst outing I ever had.

"And he went to the hospital afterwards and stayed there for two weeks while we left and went on to finish the rest of the season.

"We didn't know whether Gil was going to come back in '69. We heard he had heart problems and that he had had a mild heart attack. But we were certainly hoping he'd come back. He was our leader, and we thought a lot of him.

"I had one more start against Philadelphia at Shea Stadium. I won my nineteenth game 3–1. Johnny Callison hit a pinch hit home run off me. But before that outing in Atlanta my era had been in the ones all year, and after that game it went up to 2.12, and then after the last game that I pitched in Philadelphia it went down to 2.08. I won nineteen games, but I didn't win Rookie of the Year, Johnny Bench did. He caught a lot, hit fifteen home runs, and Tom Seaver had won Rookie of the Year the year before. And so a writer in Chicago by the name of Enright decided that he didn't know who to vote for, so he split his vote, and I lost by half a vote."

In addition to Koosman's 19–12 record in 1968, with his gaudy 2.08 era, Tom Seaver was 16–12 with a 2.20 era. Despite their brilliance, the Mets finished the year with a 73–89 record and a ninth-place finish. The team hit .228 as a team. When Hodges had a mild heart attack toward the end of the season, the Mets' future appeared to be cloudy.

nineteen

1969

During the 1968 season the National League owners met to engineer another expansion. Two more teams, Montreal and San Diego, were being added. The question was how to split up the teams. When the owners arbitrarily (and illogically) placed Chicago and St. Louis in the NL East with the Mets, and Atlanta and Cincinnati in the NL West, the stage was set for an undreamed of finale in '69.

After spending four weeks in the hospital in Atlanta, manager Gil Hodges was released. In November 1968 he conducted the Mets' Instructional School in St. Petersburg, Florida, and after spending the month of December cooped up in his home in Brooklyn, he returned to St. Pete to get some exercise. In an interview he said he fully intended to manage in '69.

"What if the doctor gives you a bad diagnosis?" he was asked.

"I'd change doctors, that's all," he said.

Hodges gave up smoking, and his weight dropped from 225 to 201. In February of 1969 he was cleared to manage.

A player boycott, however, threatened the start of the season. The players wanted better pension benefits, and the owners didn't want to give them. The players' union had hired a wiry, mustachioed former steel organizer by the name of Marvin Miller. Sitting on the other side of the negotiating table was a tall, bespectacled Wall Street lawyer by the name of Bowie Kuhn, who had replaced General Eckert as commissioner in early

February just as the job action was getting under way. The players were impressed with Miller's savvy and smarts.

Ron Swoboda: "When I first came into the game, Judge Cannon, who was really an owner's guy, was running the players' union. The owners' attempt to placate the players was so feeble, Cannon's advice was all preapproved by the owners, because the pension plan was really *no* pension plan, it was bullshit. Then Marvin Miller came in and the owners warned us about him, saying he had come from the Steel Workers' Union and that we'd be carrying placards and walking picket lines.

"When they told us this, of course we ignored it. Marvin talked to you, and you listened. Before Marvin Miller came in, the pension plan had been contributory, and it was never going to amount to anything. Marvin came in and started licensing. He had the players' union create a logo and start licensing merchandise and selling goods 'approved by the Players' Association.' Well, Major League Baseball was starting to get a little more savvy about marketing, and they knew they had a competitor here. As soon as Miller came in, the pension program doubled the amount it could pay out and now you paid nothing. It became noncontributory.

"Back in 1969 we were talking about nickels. There were nickels and dimes on the table, and we still had to hold out. It was finite sums of money, and we weren't changing the system, just improving the dollars in the system that existed.

"But to suddenly have a job action was traumatic. It was pretty scary, but Marvin knew about these things. We never walked any picket lines. Because it wasn't about keeping anyone out, because there wasn't anybody coming in. And replacement players were a bad idea anyway.

"You didn't do it lightly, and you felt these issues could be important, and the only way we're going to succeed is to withhold services. That was the *only* way, even though the net gain was very little. We weren't going to break the game, but that was never Miller's intention. He understood those situations. Marvin was a very smart man, and very reasonable.

"Spring training was postponed, and all of us who were living in New York went and worked out at a high school field."

Jerry Koosman: "We went to Florida to start spring training in 1969, but because there were no organized workouts, we worked out informally with some of the Pirates and Cardinals, and we held our own workouts, throwing and running and taking ground balls.

"We didn't settle the strike until the end of February, and so the pitchers all lost time, and it was very unsettling for a young guy like myself. You're looking at what's going to happen with your career. I didn't know the workings of the major leagues and the Players' Association as well as I do today. We had been told by Marvin Miller in our meetings that, 'Hey, you gotta stick together.' He was big on getting the players to stick together, and ultimately we did, and we got what we needed."

The new pitcher added to the staff in 1969 was a tall, lanky college kid by the name of Gary Gentry. Gentry would have been drafted after high school, but his father insisted he go to college for at least two years. His father, an elementary schoolteacher, stressed education to his son, so when the Orioles, Astros, and Giants sought to draft him, he said, no, and went to Phoenix Junior College. In his first season at Arizona State he had a 17–1 record and won two games in the College World Series. He struck out 229 batters in 174 innings. When the Mets made their bonus offer, Gentry accepted.

Gentry pitched two seasons in the minors, and in 1969 came to St. Petersburg hoping to make the team. At age twenty-two he had drive and maturity, like Tom Seaver. In fact, the media wags called him "the new Tom Seaver."

Ron Swoboda: "His stuff was every bit as good as Seaver's. Aw, shit yeah, man. He had just as live an arm. When I wasn't playing I used to warm him up in the bullpen just to keep my reflexes sharp. I'd go down to the pen rather than sit in the dugout when I wasn't playing.

"I remember warming this guy up a few times, and let me tell you something, his ball was all over the place. It just jumped and ran. Gary was this western guy who just wasn't afraid of anything. He was a cowboy, a skinny kid with a tremendous arm. He was great.

"Gary demonstrated his fearlessness out on the mound where he made his living. Here was a kid, a rookie, who wasn't intimidated by anybody. He just let you have it.

"You can tell when a pitcher wants out of there. Sometimes Jim McAndrew would want out. Jim was a great guy, threw hard, but he was on the timid side. He didn't get the nickname 'Moms' for nothing. And look, this is a macho world, and I ain't the most macho guy in the world, you know? I don't run around looking for bar fights either. This was a macho world, and everybody was judged by very macho standards.

"And the way you conducted yourself out there and how you dealt with certain situations led people to come to certain conclusions about whether you were a tough guy or not. And being tough was an important thing. And some guys were tougher than others. I consider myself about in the middle. I think Gentry was at the high end. He was cold.

"What he ended up having was an arm that went bad. I don't know if his technique wasn't any good, because he threw differently, with a little more arm than Seaver or Koosman, who used their hips and legs, or maybe his luck was just bad. You don't know. But I do know that his arm was as good as any of them."

The Mets brass decided that they needed more power in their lineup, and rather than trade for a third baseman, they opted to move outfield prospect Amos Otis there.

Like Tommy Agee, Cleon Jones, and Hank Aaron, Amos Otis grew up in Mobile, Alabama. At age ten he was playing ball with eighteen-year-olds, when people told him, "If you can play with those guys, you'll probably be a major league ballplayer one day."

Scouts began to follow him when he was thirteen. By high school they were coming in packs. He was invited to a three-day Mets tryout camp in May of 1965, just prior to the fist amateur player draft. The Boston Red Sox took him on the second round as a shortstop. He got $20,000 to sign, tax free.

His first year he was sent to Harlan, in the boondocks of Kentucky. One of the things his parents, country folk, warned him was that when he got into his hotel room, he should make sure to check the room carefully before he settled in.

Amos Otis: "For a guy who had never been more than twenty miles away from home by himself, Harlan—those mountains and those people in the hills with the jugs slung over the shoulder with the shotguns—was frightening, but I survived it.

"When I went away my father and mother said, 'Make sure when you go into your hotel room check behind the shower curtains, in the closet, under the beds, and I did. I checked the room, under the bed, and there were a pair of shoes standing straight up. And there was a guy lying under the bed—dead. So I left the hotel! I was frightened, but I survived."

Otis moved up the Red Sox minor league ladder to the New York–Penn league where he played for Oneonta. He played first base, third base, and outfield. The Sox decided to protect a thin, rangy outfielder by the name of Bobby Mitchell and put him on their forty-man roster. They sent Otis to A ball, trying to hide him. But the Mets had had their eyes on him. They drafted him and sent him to Jacksonville where he played under manager Bill Virdon. In September Otis was called up to the Mets.

In 1968 although Otis had a fine spring, he was cut the day the team was getting ready to head north. The choice was between Otis and outfielder Don Bosch, and manager Gil Hodges chose Bosch, a more experienced switch hitter. The following year, however, Otis finally made it. But Hodges was insistent that Otis fill the gaping hole at third. Otis fought him bitterly.

Amos Otis: "Gil Hodges was the manager. I wanted to play the outfield, and he wanted to keep me at third base.

"He was stubborn and I was, too. He didn't get his way. I wouldn't play no third base. I only played four games there, and I was considered one of the failures of the Mets hundred-and-something third basemen. But he wanted me at third and I wanted to play the outfield. I could outplay all their outfielders, out-throw them, out-run them, but I didn't have the experience, so they kept me on the bench until they got mad enough, and they sent me to the minor leagues for a month. [He played 69 games in the outfield and hit .320.]

"They called me back September 1, just in time to go into the record books when Steve Carlton struck out nineteen. I was something like numbers 3, 7, 12, and 19!

"Then on December third, my father's birthday, I got traded to Kansas City along with Bob Johnson for Joe Foy. And my career took off from there.

"Gil was the boss, and so he got his way, and I got traded."

Jerry Koosman: "The New York press had always been on the Mets about getting a home-run hitting third baseman, and gosh, when I was with the Mets, they had tried thirty-some third basemen, looking for that person, and Otis wasn't really a third baseman. He was a better outfielder, but they tried so many people there because of the pressure from the media to get a home-run hitting third baseman. And that pressure ultimately led to the trade of Amos Otis for Joey Foy and Nolan Ryan for Jim Fregosi. We traded away a lot of talent to try to get a third baseman."

Ron Swoboda: "I didn't know Amos very well. He was kind of quiet, kind of cool. He was one of those guys if you looked at him play, you wondered if he gave a shit. But he looked like that when he was having his great years with Kansas City. George Hendricks with the Cardinals was the same way. So Amos obviously gave a little bit of a shit.

"Amos never got a chance with the Mets. He was sent back to Tidewater in June. The organization might have been looking at me and thinking, We have Cleon in left and Agee in center and Swoboda and Shamsky in right, and they're looking at Amos Otis and thinking, He's hitting .151 for the year, and they're wondering, Can this guy play in the big leagues? Well, he's twenty-two years old. How do you know? They tried him at third base, and he didn't want to play there. He *really* didn't want to play there. And I guess that's what made them decide to let him go, before they really knew what kind of player he could be. That's not a *huge* mistake, but rather a failure to read a guy. In '69 they didn't look wrong. Who did they trade him for? Joey Foy. They got a third baseman."

During spring training Gil Hodges announced that the goal in 1969 was to win eighty-five games. Hodges added that he intended to do a lot of platooning.

Ron Swoboda: "I was never unhappy with the way Hodges platooned me and Art Shamsky. Shamsky could swing that bat. If you look at what Art and I produced in right field—I drove in 52 runs; he drove in 47, and if you add Gaspar, he had 14 rbis, and he played in 118 games, and a lot of those games were as a defensive replacement for me, and boy, I hated that.

"Boy, that frosted my nuts. Because I had worked so hard to make myself better. Rod might have been a little faster, and he was certainly a good outfielder, but I didn't feel I needed a defensive replacement.

"I never told Gil. I just made Eddie Yost hit me thousands of balls. He was tired of seeing me come to him. I wore him out hitting me balls. And

I felt I turned myself into a pretty good outfielder. I could cover some ground. I got good jumps on balls, because I worked on ball recognition. That's what the drill with Yost was all about.

"And eventually Gil stopped taking me out, but it took a long time."

Hodges was a man of strong beliefs. For example, when he learned that Don Cardwell threw a spitball, he ordered him to stop on principle. According to Tom Seaver, it was because "it wasn't a fair pitch." The players noticed Hodges' stubbornness about certain things. They also noticed he knew more about baseball than most.

Jerry Koosman: "We were playing an exhibition game in New Orleans against the Twins. They put a makeshift mound in there. It wasn't packed, and there was a huge hole in front of the mound, and I was having trouble pitching out of the hole.

"Gil came out there and said, 'Cover the rubber up with dirt and pitch ahead of the hole.' So I gained a foot or two, and I didn't have to pitch in the hole any more.

"Two stories, both in Pittsburgh. The umpire threw a ball out there that had no seams on it and was shiny, and I didn't want the ball and threw it back, and the umpire threw it back out again. He wouldn't exchange balls. So Gil came out and said, 'What's the matter?' I said, 'I don't like this ball. I can't throw a curveball with it.'

"He said, 'When I leave the mound, drop it in the hole and stomp on it with your spikes. The umpire will change the ball.' Gil left, I dropped the ball and stomped on it with my spikes, and the umpire called for the ball and changed it!

"Another time I was pitching against Pirate catcher Jerry May, the eighth-place batter, and I threw him a slow curveball, and he hit a line drive back off my left elbow.

"The trainer and Gil came out right away. I was perturbed that I got hit by the ball to start with—I got hit hard—and they said, 'Take a couple of pitches and make sure you're all right.' I was hot. I said, 'I'm not going to give them the pleasure of letting them think I'm hurt. I'm all right.'

"Gil said, 'You better be.' Then he said, 'Here's what I want you to do: I want you to take one throw and throw it up at the press box and then say you're all right.' So I did that. I threw it at the press box behind home plate, and I said, 'I'm okay.' Well, that gave me an edge on the next hitter.

"There were times when our hitters thought the pitchers should be throwing at opposing batters. Gil said, 'It's not their job. There are other ways. If you want to get a hitter, you drag a bunt down the first base line, and when the pitcher comes over to cover it, you run right up his back. Get him yourself.

"There were a lot of things like that Gil would do."

Under Hodges' strong leadership, some of the players began to believe that the team just might have the talent to go a long way. How long, they didn't know. How could they? The Mets had never won much of anything.

Tom Seaver: "During training camp in the spring of 1969, Bud Harrelson, Jerry Grote, Nolan Ryan, and I often went fishing at night. We went fishing for sheepshead and silver trout off one of the causeways in St. Petersburg. We brought along coffee, beer, and doughnuts, and while we fished, we talked about almost everything, including baseball.

" 'You know,' one of us said, early in training camp, 'we could win our division if we play up to our potential.'

"The other three of us didn't disagree.

"We didn't talk that way too loudly, because we knew that if the sportswriters heard us, they'd scoff, and if the average baseball fan heard us, he'd laugh.

"But the four of us really didn't care if the sportswriters scoffed and the fans laughed. We wanted to win. We felt we could win."

Seaver, Ryan, Grote, Harrelson, Koosman, Jones, and Agee were all in their early to mid-twenties. They had played on winning teams in high school and college, knew what it was like to win, and wanted to feel that way again.

"We knew that our best days were in front of us," said Seaver.

But despite their promise, the 1969 season did not start well. The Mets lost seven of their first ten games as the Chicago Cubs, under Leo Durocher, raced out to an early lead. On May 4, the Mets record was 9–14, eight games behind the Cubs. At Wrigley Field before 40,000 fans, in the first game of a doubleheader the bad blood that would mark the rivalry between the Cubs and Mets began early when Tom Seaver low-bridged the Cubs star third baseman, Ron Santo, in the second inning. The Cubs led 1–0 in the third when Cubs pitcher Bill Hands retaliated, hitting Seaver between the shoulder blades. Then, when Hands came to bat, Seaver hit him in the stomach. When the smoke cleared, the Mets proved themselves the victors, 3–2, and in the second game Tug McGraw started and defeated Dick Selma 3–2.

The Cubs–Mets rivalry would simmer and blaze up throughout the '69 season.

Jerry Koosman: "The Cubs had an excellent ball club, just top notch. And whenever they would win, Santo would jump up in the air and click his heels, and it was an intimidating antic that he did for the opposition to see. Those kinds of things make you want to beat them worse; make you really try extra hard against them. Leo Durocher was a manager who tried to intimidate umpires, and it became a great rivalry.

"You would have thought it foolish to throw at us when we had Tom and myself and the other guys, who could throw hard, but we weren't that well-known yet. Tom had had a good year, but they talked about the sophomore jinx. You don't prove yourself in just a year or two.

"But they helped get the fire going. They generated a lot of energy. That was one club you loved to beat."

On May 15, Gil Hodges was stewing. After a game against the Braves where the Mets played sloppily, Hodges closed the locker-room door to the press.

Ron Swoboda: "I can tell you this: he didn't scream at us. He quietly reminded us that we were a better ball team than this, and that we needed to make sure we were doing all the things we needed to do to be a better club.

"And then right after that, we had an eleven-game winning streak. We plowed through the West Coast. I remember playing some great games against the Padres. Winning eleven in a row tells you something. It tells you you can play some ball. It was an eye opener.

"Again, you educate yourself. It was like at the meeting Gil saying to us, 'Don't set low standards for yourself. It's not acceptable. You're a better team. It's unacceptable to throw games away."

The Mets got hot.

Jerry Koosman: "We won ten games in a row. We won at Shea Stadium and went on the road and made that West Coast swing, and when we came home after that we proved we could beat the best clubs, that we could beat anybody. We had confidence. Our confidence was so high we felt, Hey, we can beat anybody. We really started to jell as a ball club."

On June 15, the punchless Mets acquired thirty-four-year-old first baseman Donn Clendenon from Montreal for three young minor leaguers, including pitcher Steve Renko and infielder Kevin Collins. Clendenon had been a star for the Pirates from 1962 through 1968, and he agreed to go to Montreal in the expansion draft. But, when Montreal traded him to Houston, he refused to report. Houston's manager was Harry Walker, a man he didn't like from his Pirate days.

Clendenon told Montreal he intended to retire. A lawyer, he had a job waiting for him from the Scripto Company in hometown Atlanta, and he was thinking of starting a restaurant there.

Commissioner Bowie Kuhn stepped in and ruled that Clendenon didn't have to go to Houston, and he resumed his career in Montreal. He told the Expos he would agree to go to New York, and when the deal was made, the Mets player rejoiced. The offense needed him desperately.

Jerry Koosman: "Getting Donn Clendenon meant a great deal. We finally had a legitimate home-run hitter. He hit tons of home runs in batting practice, plus he hit a few for us during the games. With one swing of the bat he could put us in the game or put us ahead. So it was a pleasure to see him there, somebody who could swing the big bat."

Ron Swoboda: "Donn was not only a clubhouse lawyer, he was a [real] lawyer. He was a member of the bar, an off-season lawyer for Scripto. Donn was a very educated guy. And he had a big mouth, he was always talking, always giving you shit about something, but it was wonderful, all good shit.

"He came in and played right away because he had not been playing much. He didn't want to play in Montreal, and he engineered the trade that got him here. He could do that because he had a job—he was a lawyer. And he threatened to do that, and the Expos came to him with a deal.

"So Donn was operating on a different level from most ballplayers. This was before Curt Flood. Back then players didn't refuse to report. My naive perspective had no notion of what was going on with him and his career and how he was engineering this trade at the time.

"And when we got him, it was a big deal."

★ ★ ★

The Mets went West and came home sporting an 8–4 road record. The fans were beginning to buzz about this team. Then the St. Louis Cardinals came to town, and the Mets took three out of four from the defending champions. Koosman won the finale 1–0.

Ron Swoboda: "When we came home, things had changed. How about our pitching staff was giving up nothing. And we had a pen that could do it: McGraw, Ron Taylor, and Cal Koonce. Hodges had a lot of buttons to push, and he understood all of them.

"We were coming out of the weeds. There is no discounting the fact that we were a surprise, that we came from off the pace. And now we have Clendenon, and Clendenon was the key acquisition. We might have been better and done good, but I doubt we win it without Clendenon.

"Ed Kranepool could play, but against left-handed pitching Clendenon was able to generate runs for us. [Reading from the *Baseball Encyclopedia:*] He had twelve home runs and drove in thirty-seven runs in seventy-two games. Now this was back when guys didn't drive in a lot of runs. If you had 100 rbis, you had a hell of a year. And the next year he drove in 97 runs in less than 400 at bats, which was amazing.

"We were a tight-knit team. Cleon [Jones] and Tommy [Agee] were pretty close in New York, and I just liked them as guys. Al Jackson was there in '68, and he was another guy I liked. My wife and I had the three of them over to our house. My folks would bring steamed crabs from Baltimore, and we'd sit around, drink beer, eat crabs, and tell stories. We had a good time.

"I just thought it natural. I judge people based on people, not that I'm the greatest at it. We didn't always hang together. We'd have drinks on the road. And our team was like that. That team was young and close.

"Clendenon was a lawyer, for Christ's sake. Ron Taylor was an electrical engineer, and he went on to become a doctor. Incredible. But Taylor didn't flaunt his education and his erudition. *Never.* He was capable of communicating with us on a level that was not condescending. He had fun being around the guys.

"The world was a different place then. Think about '69. You had the Vietnam War and you had the protests—they were big in New York and pretty influential people were coming out and taking stances against the war. Of course, New York was a liberal, intellectual city. That summer was Woodstock. And man walked on the moon. Jesus God, what a time. What an incredible time!

"We were in the airport in Montreal when they first walked on the moon. We viewed it live because our airplane wouldn't work! There was something broken in our airplane. It was a charter flight. I mean, the irony of being in the airport because we couldn't get from Montreal to New York in an airplane, so we were standing around in the bar in Montreal airport watching a man step on the moon! I loved it.

"There was, in every way, a fabulous sense that all things were possible. God, it was exciting, stimulating. Way more than now. Will there be anything more boring and banal than the Presidential race of 2000? And when you're fifty-six years old, the truth is that the Neilson company doesn't give a fuck about what you watch. We should be very worried about that."

The Mets held second place much of the month of June, but could not creep close enough to Chicago to be considered a legitimate contender. Then, in early July, the Cubs visited Shea Stadium, and strange, wonderful things began to happen.

The Cubs were beating the Mets 3–1 in front of 55,000 fans at Shea. Second baseman Ken Boswell, who was in Gil Hodges' doghouse, pinch hit and sent a weak fly ball to center fielder Don Young, who got a late break on the ball. He let it fall for a double.

After Tommy Agee fouled out, Donn Clendenon hit a high drive to center toward the outfield fence. Young raced back, got a glove on it, and then dropped it as he crashed into the fence. Boswell ran to third. Clendenon was credited with a double. When Cleon Jones, the hottest hitter in the league, followed with another double, the score was tied. After a walk and a fielder's choice, there were runners on second and third. Cubs manager Leo Durocher chose to pitch to Ed Kranepool, who lined an outside fastball over the shortstop's head to win the game.

After the game Durocher and third baseman Ron Santo loudly and publicly castigated Don Young. When Durocher was asked why he didn't walk Kranepool and pitch to J. C. Martin, he huffed out of the room.

Ron Swoboda: "They never had a center fielder. Don Young played it, and they tried to make [centerfielder] Adolfo Phillips into a lead-off hitter, but he couldn't handle that. Psychologically, it made him too nervous to lead off. He wanted to hit eighth. 'Please hit me eighth.' What kind of shit is that?

"So we were losing to the Cubs, and Bossie hit a short fly ball, and Don Young dropped it. And then Clendenon hit one up against the wall that he should have caught. Those were two balls that were catchable that he didn't catch. So your center fielder has just screwed you. If he makes the plays, we lose. And they should have been made, to be honest. They should have been caught.

"And the Cubs began imploding, which was good for us. We were winning games because things were happening. And we were platooning, and we were fresh, and Leo Durocher was playing the same guys every day. I have a friend, Tom Gamboa, who is the manager of Albuquerque. Tom is a very interesting man, and he loves to talk baseball. He was talking with Billy Williams, and Billy Williams admitted to Tom that he felt that the Cubs had choked in '69. They have been accused of that, and what Billy might have been talking about was what would have happened if they had won some of those head-to-head games with us.

"What happens if they win the Young game? What effect does that have on us? Do we have enough gas?"

The next day Shea Stadium attracted the largest crowd in its history, 59,083. From the first pitch a loud roar emanated from the fans. If Woodstock was a happening, so were the Mets, game after every wonderful, energy-filled home game.

Ron Swoboda: "Shea is a great big bowl, and when you filled it up, it resonated in a way that you can't hardly describe. But when you are in this great big triple-decker horseshoe, the way the sound came out of there, it was a generator. Imagine being at home plate, which is the focal point of it all, or being in the field somewhere with the stadium vibrating. It literally vibrated. It was awesome."

Tom Seaver, who had some stiffness in his shoulder, struggled the first few innings against the Cubs, but he managed to keep them from getting any hits. By the third inning pitching coach Rube Walker could see he had his best stuff, and he told a teammate, "Tom could pitch a no-hitter tonight."

Seaver had a perfect game going through eight innings. There had only been ten such games in baseball history, eight since the turn of the century. Cy Young, Don Larsen, Jim Bunning, and Sandy Koufax were among the precious few.

When Seaver batted in the bottom of the eighth, the roar that arose from the stadium could be heard in Astoria.

Tom Seaver: "The noise gets in your system. I could hear my heart pounding, feel the adrenaline flowing. My arm felt light as a feather. It was like being in a dream."

In the ninth inning Cubs catcher Randy Hundley bunted, trying for a base hit, but the ball rolled toward Seaver, who threw him out. Two outs to go.

Bernard Levy: "I sat next to [former major league catcher] Moe Berg the night that Seaver had his perfect game going against the Cubs. When Hundley tried to bunt for a hit in the top of the ninth and Seaver threw him out, Moe told me that Grote ought to call time out and go to the mound to talk to Seaver. He didn't, and on the first pitch Qualls got a hit."

Jimmy Qualls was playing center field because Don Young had played badly the game before. Qualls, a left-handed batter, was playing in only his eighteenth major league game. His batting average was .243. Mets outfielder Bobby Pfeil, who had played with Qualls in the minors, told Seaver to throw him fastballs.

Qualls had hit Seaver hard his first two times up, pulling the ball each time, so Seaver started Qualls off with an outside fastball. Qualls reached out and hit a line drive into left-center field. The perfect game lay in ruin as the fans stood and applauded and hoorayed for what seemed like ten minutes. After Seaver got the last two outs and earned another big win, the fans cheered him some more.

Ron Swoboda: "There was one out in the ninth, and this kid Qualls hit a line drive to left-center. It was a base hit. There was no way it wasn't. And it was a shame. You ask, How much worse is a one-hitter? It's the difference between being a virgin and not. There's not very much, but there is.

"I remember after the hit Grote went out to Seaver and said something, and Tom went right after the next two hitters and got them. I'm sure there was huge disappointment, but when you talk about Seaver, you're talking about someone whose emotions and skills were always under control. You had to pretty much go out and beat him. He wasn't going to give you much."

The pain was greater than anyone realized.

Tom Seaver: "I smiled, but inside I still hurt. I couldn't measure the disappointment. Never in any aspect of my life, in baseball or outside, had I experienced such a disappointment.

"At twenty-five, I was too old to cry. Will I have another chance? My answer had to be yes. I couldn't have gone on playing without that thought, without that goal. Someday I'll pitch a perfect game."

On June 16, 1978, Tom Seaver finally achieved a no-hitter, defeating the St. Louis Cardinals. He was with Cincinnati at the time.

Ron Swoboda: "Why Tom never threw a no-hitter with the Mets I'll never know. He was so consistent with such great stuff. I remember a game he pitched against the Cardinals. No hits. We were way ahead, and Orlando Cepeda hit a little pop fly down the right field line. I just ran as hard as I could trying to get this ball, and I couldn't. I overran it, but it didn't matter."

Jimmy Qualls was also responsible for helping to beat Gary Gentry and the Mets 6–2 in the series finale.

After the game a reporter asked Leo Durocher, "Were those the real Cubs today?"

Durocher responded sarcastically, "No, those were the real Mets today."

But Leo was whistling in the wind. For the rest of the season he and the snakebit Cubs would spend the rest of the season looking over their shoulders and checking the scoreboard.

t w e n t y

Amazin'

After pitching an almost perfect game against the Chicago Cubs on July 9, 1969, Tom Seaver developed a stiffness in his right shoulder and lost four of his next five starts. The pain became so bad he could not tuck in his shirt behind him with his right hand. The Mets ace tried to pitch without altering his style, but for almost a full month, the stiffness persisted. Though petrified that his career might be over, he didn't let anyone see his angst. He didn't even tell his wife Nancy because he didn't want her to worry. Working hard to stay calm, Seaver told himself, You're twenty-five years old, you've got your whole life ahead of you. You're intelligent enough to do something else if you have to give up baseball. Then, as mysteriously as it came, the stiffness went away, and Seaver didn't lose another game all season long.

There would be other uncomfortable moments for the Mets that year. The worst came on July 30 during a doubleheader against the Houston Astros, two games that New York lost by football scores of 16–3 and 11–5. In a single inning of the first game the Astros Jimmy Wynn and Dennis Menke each hit grand-slam home runs as the Shea fans booed loudly.

In the nightcap Johnny Edwards sliced a double to left field. According to the way Gil Hodges saw it, Cleon Jones half-ran after it, and then he lobbed the ball back into the infield.

Hodges called time and walked out to left field to ask Cleon if he was hurt. Hodges then walked Jones all the way back to the dugout. Ron Swoboda was the player who took Jones' place.

Ron Swoboda: "I remember it very well. If you talk to whoever the pitcher was that day, he thought Hodges was coming to get him, and if you talk to Bud Harrelson at shortstop, he thought he had done something and Hodges was coming his way. And it was the slowest, longest walk out there to the outfield. Jonesy really hadn't hustled after the ball that got by him. He kicked it, and he didn't exactly kill himself recovering the ball.

"And Hodges and Jonesy had a rocky relationship. Cleon had trouble with Hodges like I had trouble with Hodges, because Cleon wouldn't go out there for outfield practice or sometimes Cleon wouldn't take batting practice. But he'd be in the clubhouse watching film. And Cleon suffered somewhat from the country-boy image in that he had this country Alabama accent, and people misjudged his intelligence. He stepped over lines here and there.

"This was a transgression as serious as Gil wanted to make it. And Gil decided to make a *big* deal out of it, and that's why he did the slowest walk. It took forever. And so the pitcher [Ryan] thought he was coming out to get him, but he went all the way out to left field, and he started talking to Cleon. And they had this long discussion, and the next thing I knew, he was waving me into the game, and I went out and played left field, and I played a whole lot the next three weeks. In fact, I got half my rbis playing for Cleon while he was in Hodges' shithouse. I wasn't half the hitter Cleon was. The message was, 'We're going to play all these games all the way.' It was probably not unrelated to getting our asses kicked a little bit by Houston, and without ever saying a word to anyone but Cleon, that was the message. Was it harsh on Cleon? Should Cleon have been playing more and me less? Probably. But I didn't mind. I got to play against a bunch of right-handers. It was an opportunity. Cleon and I got along, so it wasn't as though I wished him any bad luck. And we didn't stop being friends after this happened. It resonated a lot more than that clubhouse meeting in May."

Jerry Koosman: "Houston was the toughest club we faced. They had a great pitching staff with Larry Dierker and Don Wilson. We had a heck of a time beating them.

"But, I didn't see what Gil saw. I didn't see that Cleon didn't hustle after the ball. And so when Gil walked out there, we all thought maybe Gil saw that Cleon had hurt himself. And then they walked in together. None of us knew why Gil took him out. We thought Cleon was hurt or wasn't feeling well.

"You don't slough off when you play for Gil Hodges. You give him a hundred percent all the time. It sends a message to the rest of the club."

The next day Hodges benched Jones, and Houston pitcher Tom Griffin shut the Mets out 2–0. The Mets were six games behind the Cubs. Jones sat three more days. The reporters wondered whether he would sulk or respond with inspired play. It was August, and at this point everyone was willing to concede the pennant to Chicago.

But what no one could anticipate was the dominance of the Mets' top two pitchers, Tom Seaver and Jerry Koosman. To the end of the season Tom and Jerry were virtually unbeatable.

Jerry Koosman: "As late as August 19, we were still nine-and-a-half games back, but then we started to make our move. Seaver and I won our last fifteen starts. I asked him how come he didn't win that sixteenth start, too. I told him he was the load, that he wasn't keeping up his own end!

"We had so much confidence at that time, Tom and I started to get cocky between ourselves. If Seaver struck out ten the night before, and if I was pitching the next day, I tried to strike out 11. Or if he got a base hit, I tried to get two base hits.

"We started making little bets as to who could get the side out with three pitches. And if we accomplished what we said we were going to do, I'd look into the dugout at Seaver, and he'd acknowledge me. If he said he was going to saw off somebody on a certain count and he did it, I'd acknowledge him. That's the kind of confidence we had. At that point the press were calling us 'The Tom and Jerry Show'—after the cartoon."

Ron Swoboda: "Journalistically it's conventional to want to look for turning points. In a one hundred and sixty-two-game season there's no single turning point. There are a collection of things that turn you in another direction, and for us, the collection was Cardwell, Koosman, Gentry, and even McAndrew getting physically well. Look at their first half, and then look at their second half. Koosman, Gentry, Ryan, McAndrew were having trouble in the first half. They all had little things bothering them, and they didn't pitch very well in the first half of the year. Everyone but Seaver. Seaver was the same; dead steady.

"The rest of the starting rotation all got better in the second half, and when you start winning ball games like we were winning, you don't need 'Go get em' signs in the locker room. Because that's all bullshit. If you're not good enough, they become a parody of the gesture. If you win ten or eleven in a row once you've played everyone, you go, 'Christ, we can play with all these people.' You are very much in the here and now. You say to yourself, 'Right now we can play with all these guys.' "

On September 4, 1969, the Mets flew from Los Angeles back to New York. The rest of the games would be against teams in their division, and the Cubs lead was down to five games. After the Mets won three of four from the Philadelphia Phillies, the lead was down to two-and-a-half. With Leo and his Cubs coming to town, Mets fans were infused with pennant fever.

Though it was a cold and nasty night, 43,000-plus braved the weather to root on their heroes. Jerry Koosman started for the New Yorkers and retired the side. In the bottom of the first inning Tommy Agee led off against Cubs right-hander Bill Hands. Leo Durocher wanted Agee to feel fear, and he had Hands throw at Agee's head on the very first pitch. While the fans emptied their lungs with boos, Tom Seaver screamed a promise of revenge from the dugout. Agee glared. Koosman bided his time. From the dugout Ron Swoboda wondered whether riling the Mets like that was such a good idea.

Ron Swoboda: "[I said] 'Hey, Leo, with your pitching staff, do you really want to get into one of those contests with us?'

"You had to be crazy to want to get in one of those deals with us. We had the arms. Bill Hands was a sinker/slider pitcher. Jerry Koosman threw a ninety-plus fastball, and when he hit you, you stayed hit. And Koosman would *hit* ya. Koosie would fucking *hit* ya.

"In the second inning Ron Santo came to bat, and Koosie drilled him real good. No one moved. I think it scared the living shit out of them. They made a gambit, and we fucking trumped it, and it was 'Ooh, ooh, I don't think we want to do that.'

"We already knew we belonged on the field with those guys. And I'll tell you something, some things changed when that happened: the way you

look at them, and the way they look at you. Impressions are always tran-
sient, based on what you have going and what they have going at that point
in time. And there was a shift. You started thinking, they ain't so tough.

"It's the same thing if you get into a fight with someone on the field,
and you have a couple of thumpers hammering people, and you start
thinking, boy, do you really want to get in one of those? It's an aspect of
the game."

Jerry Koosman: "It was a cold and nasty night, and Bill Hands started the
game throwing at Tommy Agee's neck, about neck high. Agee naturally
hit the dirt, and he got Agee out, and Bill got us out.

"I pitched the first inning and got them one, two, three, and he got us
out in the second inning, and I went back out the top of the second, and
Ron Santo was the first hitter, and I went to drill him in the ribs, and he
got his arm in there, and I hit him in the middle of the forearm.

"Nobody told me to throw at Santo. Hodges didn't say a word. It's just
something you learn. It's how the game is played. It was something that
was taught by everyone I ever worked for. My feeling was, I wasn't going
to let Bill Hands intimidate my hitters. And the best way to prove it was, I
had the clean-up hitter, so let's stop it right now. I was telling them, Here's
what happens if you throw at my hitters. And that stopped it.

"When I came up, after my first at bat, Bill Hands was still out there,
and the first pitch he threw at my head, and I spit back at him and hollered,
'You pussy! You don't throw the ball hard enough to hurt anybody.'

"And he threw at me three more times! He missed me, and I walked.

"And Agee hit a two-run home run, and then later Agee doubled and
Wayne Garrett drove him in, and Agee slid under Hundley's tag, and we
won the ball game and the whole series. That pitch getting Santo let them
know, You're *not* going to intimidate my players.

"It gave our hitters more confidence to stand in there and say, 'Hey,
thank you for protecting us and we know if they do throw at us again,
you're still going to protect us.' So they stood in there with more confidence and started whaling on Hands."

Ron Swoboda: "With the score tied, Garrett singled, and Agee came
around third and scored as Hundley was tagging him, and Agee was called
safe. He *could* have been called out. Understand? He could have been
called out. To this day Hundley will go to his grave thinking he tagged

him, and Agee will go to his grave thinking he was safe, and nobody will know what the truth is, because you can look at that film a hundred times."

Agee's run allowed the Mets to win the game 3–2, and they were now only a game-and-a-half back. In the second game Seaver faced Fergy Jenkins in a battle of Hall of Famers. The game was a rout, as the Mets won 7–1. During the contest the Shea Stadium organist played "Good Night, Ladies," as the Mets fans chanted, "Good night, Leo." It was also a game in which one of the Shea Stadium stray cats came onto the field and hexed the Cubs.

For the first time Mets fans gloated after a victory.

Jerry Koosman: "This was a sold-out crowd again, amd the fans all pulled out handkerchiefs and started waving them up and down, and singing that song, 'Good night Leo.' Fifty-three thousand five hundred people waving their handkerchiefs, all standing and singing! The house was rocking! They were stomping on the floor, and the whole stadium was shaking. And while this was happening, we had some junkyard cats who lived underneath the stadium, and one of these cats was black, and it got scared and came out onto the field between the Cubs dugout and the stands where there is an opening. And when it came out, naturally it saw the fans and right away ran away from them, and it ran across their dugout toward the outfield. It got to the far end of the dugout, and saw all the fans waving the handkerchiefs, and it ran back the other way, got to the other end, saw the fans, and ran back the other way.

"Our pitcher was taking his warm-up throws, and the fans are seeing this cat, and it was going back and forth, and the hitters were on deck swinging bats taking practice swings. You had this black cat running back and forth, and the Cubs must have thought we had that black cat trained! It was fabulous and it was wild."

Ron Swoboda: "That was the series with the black cat. Where in the fuck did the black cat come from? Central casting was my guess. This cat was trained. How do you train a cat? This cat came out from under the stands, looked like he was right off a Halloween poster, had the hair up on his back, and it ain't gonna tell you anything, and he's running back and forth in front of *their* dugout! And we're dying, and the fans see it, and it's like the Cubs can't buy a break, and here comes the black cat, as if you didn't get the point! This was like Hollywood. This happens in movies about baseball games. You know what I mean?

"We played so well against the Cubs and Leo was playing the same guys all the time. All the time. They had to be tired. And they only really had Phil Regan out of the pen. I felt we had the advantage, that we could handle the pressure, that we had more guys ready to play, and that we could matchup with them on any given day. Billy Williams told my friend Tom Gamboa that had it been any other team in the Eastern Division, like the Cardinals, the Cubs might have been on their toes a little more, might have been better prepared, but that the Mets truly surprised them, and when they tried to turn it around and turn it up in September, it wasn't there. We beat them in head-to-head matchups, and they had some holes in their game, like center field and the lack of a bullpen, and the fact that they played with that lineup every day, every day, every day in the heat of the Chicago summer. They were an older team and they played every day, and it showed.

"I felt that by us winning those head-to-head games with the Cubs and then playing .650 ball down the last six weeks, we set a standard that was untouchable. I felt what happened was we hit a passing gear that they couldn't keep up with."

Every Mets fan wondered: Could this long-suffering franchise climb into first place for even a single day? On September 10, 1969, the Mets faced Montreal in a doubleheader. If the Mets could win both games, first place was theirs.

They won the first game in 12 innings on a single by Ken Boswell with two outs. Fans were literally dancing in the aisles. Nolan Ryan got a start in the second game, and after trailing 1–0 in the third, the Mets scored six runs, plenty to win. When it was announced that the Cubs had lost to the Phils, the fans at Shea were beside themselves with joy. Madness and mayhem ruled. The *New York Times* ran a front-page headline: METS IN FIRST PLACE.

There were twenty-one games left to play.

Ron Swoboda: "It was getting real heady. The scary part is that you know that the peak is slippery. When you're on the peak, it's just you. You're not sneaking up on anybody. You're in the middle of the bull's-eye, and you've never been there before. So it's exhilarating and scary at the same time. All those elements are wrapped up in the trip.

"The other side of the coin is we were playing pretty good. Too many things had already happened that made it pretty clear that something was in the wind for us, and it all seemed good, and we knew we didn't have to do anything but play the way we were playing. We were up on a wave. We were surfing. It was so exciting to feel like we were on a board and riding this wave pretty good.

"We knew we had played everybody, and we had beaten everybody, so we just had to keep doing it. You felt a sense of, 'It's 1969, we've landed on the moon, we've had Woodstock, and all things are possible, including the New York Mets winning the National League pennant.' Which to us would have been the most fantastic of all."

Jerry Koosman: "We were elated to be in first place. We had come a long ways to get to where we were. We had momentum going for us, confidence. None of us starters wanted to be the guy who would end the winning streak. And so you went out and pitched your heart out.

"It was amazing. Sure, it really was. We knew what we could do. I'm not saying we were the smartest pitchers, but we certainly had the arms to go out there and do just about what we wanted to do. I'm sure if we had had six more years under our belts we would have won more games, given up fewer runs. Our average age was twenty-six years old.

"Everything was going our way, but also, our confidence was so high."

On Friday, September 12, Jerry Koosman and Don Cardwell started in a doubleheader against the Pirates in Pittsburgh. Each game ended 1–0 and in each game it was the Mets' pitcher that drove in the run! [It was Koosman's only rbi of the season.] The next day Tom Seaver started and won 5–2. Ron Swoboda won the game with his first grand-slam home run. It was the Mets' tenth win in a row.

Ron Swoboda: "It was off Chuck Hartenstein. I played in all four games that series. I got four base hits in that series. I went 1–4 in each game, and all four base hits were off Chuck Hartenstein, and he started one of the games. Is that weird? That's weird. And that last base hit was a checked-swing double down the right field line. Shit like that was happening, and it was strange."

★ ★ ★

The strangest happening of all involved Swoboda, and it occurred against
Steve Carlton of the Cardinals. On September 15, the Hall of Fame left-
hander struck out nineteen batters—and lost. Swoboda hit two two-run
home runs to beat him 4 to 3.

Jerry Koosman: "Carlton had great stuff that night. God, he was just
untouchable. But Swoboda went up there and hit two two-run home
runs. Swoboda was just up there swinging. I don't think he was out-
thinking Carlton. I just think he was looking for a pitch in a zone and
swinging. And unbelievably, he ended up beating Carlton that night.

   "Lefty had great stuff. He was intimidating. He intimidated everyone—
except Swoboda. Swoboda was looking for a fastball, and he's swinging.
And it did the trick. Everything was falling into place that year. It was
amazing."

Ron Swoboda: "Is that weird or what? Usually I didn't hit Carlton worth
a shit. He was tough. But before he hooked up with that Tae Kwan Do
guru, he would make mistakes, and guys who shouldn't have hurt him
would hurt him. One time I watched him beating the shit out of the Cubs,
when Kenny Holtzman drove a ball down the third base line and beat him.
And I thought, How do you let *him* beat you? It was one of those things
that didn't make any sense.

   "And it didn't make any more sense than me hitting two two-run home
runs off of him, and beating him 4–3 in the greatest game that he's ever
pitched in his life to that point. In terms of strikeouts, it's the greatest game
anybody's pitched up to that point in the history of baseball. Is that strange?
And you know something, St. Louis was one of the few stadiums with batting cages. Busch Stadium had them out behind the left-field wall in the
old configuration of the new Busch Stadium. Ralph Kiner, who broadcast
our games, went down there with me, and there was a pitching machine,
one of those old versions of the two rubber wheels, and it had a big box
mechanism, and it would throw breaking balls, and Ralph fed me some
balls and talked about hitting with me. I would ask him, 'Ralph, how does
this look?' He'd say, 'Move your hands back a little bit. That looks good.
Let's try that.' And we monkeyed around a little bit, and I walked out of
there feeling comfortable, that I had something working. And that was the
day that I took Carlton deep twice.

"I can't to this day figure it out. And there is no video record of it. That game was not on TV. But that game he struck me out twice, and I had two strikes on me when I hit each of those home runs. One was a slider down and in. It was not a bad pitch. I just got the head of the bat out, and I hit a line drive that just made it over the wall in left field. And the other home run was fastball kind of up and out over the plate that I hit upstairs in left field. I really crushed that one.

"And after the game Harry Caray had me and Carlton on together in a little room, and Carlton was so baffled as to what happened, he couldn't talk. I don't know that we said anything to each other. Carlton looked like someone had just run over his dog. What else could he feel? To have that much going and have this palooka take you deep twice? What else could he feel except that the stars had conspired against him? It's like being the pumpkin in someone else's Cinderella story. You know what I mean? You ain't the princess. You're the pumpkin!"

When Montreal beat the Cubs, the Mets' lead was now four-and-a-half games, and Chicago was toast. It was only a matter of time before the Mets would clinch, and that came on September 24, 1969, at Shea Stadium when Gary Gentry allowed only two hits in eight innings and defeated the St. Louis Cardinals 6–0. The final out came with two on and one out on a Joe Torre double-play grounder that zipped from Bud Harrelson to Al Weis to Donn Clendenon.

A month after Woodstock, the Mets' seven-year famine was over. The fans flooded onto the field and grabbed anything that wasn't tied down, including hundreds of patches of sod. The infield looked like a World War I battlefield. Hundreds, maybe thousands, of others just sat on the outfield wall, dangling their feet and emoting a combination of joy and tears. They sat quietly and watched the scavengers strip the stadium bare of everything except first base, which was wedged too tightly into the ground to be moved.

After the game, George Weiss, the Mets' first architect, went into the clubhouse and hugged manager Gil Hodges, who had played for him in the team's initial season.

"Nineteen sixty-two," said Weiss.

Hodges grinned. "Nineteen sixty-two," he said back.

M. Donald Grant told reporters, "Our team finally caught up to our fans. Our fans were winners long ago."

After clinching, the Mets continued to win. Down the stretch the Mets would win 38 of their last 49 games. A nine-and-a-half game deficit would magically turn into an eight-and-a-half game lead. They swept the Phillies four games before returning for the last time to a doleful Chicago where the Wrigley faithful could only taunt emptily.

Ron Swoboda: "Earlier in the season when we realized we were gaining on these guys, we talked about the possibility: 'Wouldn't it be nice if we could come into Wrigley Field with a four-game lead and three to play.' And you know what, we went in there with a lot more than a four-game lead! So it was even better.

"Wrigley Field was one of those places where cute little young girls would yell awful stuff at you, where they would say vile words, and you'd think, 'Jesus God,' and they threw pennies and hit you out in the outfield, and yet I still loved playing there. I *loved* Wrigley Field. Wrigley is a shrine of baseball. It should always be. You felt the history when you went in there, and the fans were so close and biased. Chicago is a wonderful town anyway, a big-hearted town. A great town worth going to.

"We went into Chicago, and the Chicago fans pulled a purple funereal crepe—a funeral cloth—stretched it out and dropped it over our dugout. It was a gesture, but our attitude was, 'You're too late. We've clinched. You can't do anything. You're pissing in the wind, and the wind is blowing in your face! It's over.' Security came and took it away, and we thought it was funny as hell.

" 'You can't hurt us now. It's too late. History has passed you all by.' "

twenty-one

Champions

The Mets finished the 1969 regular season with a 100–62 record, eight games ahead of the Chicago Cubs. Tom Seaver compiled a 25–7 record with a 2.21 era, and Jerry Koosman finished 17–6 with a 2.28 era. The staff boasted 28 shut-outs, and the relievers had 35 saves.

But, because of expansion and the new two-tiered playoff system, the Mets still had to defeat the Atlanta Braves to win the National League pennant. Led by Hank Aaron, Rico Carty, Orlando Cepeda, and Clete Boyer, the Atlanta wrecking crew out-slugged San Francisco and Cincinnati in the National League West. Atlanta, who had won 17 of their last 21 games, were heavy favorites over the unproven New Yorkers.

Ron Swoboda: "Our attitude going into the series was that we just didn't want to get embarrassed. I had no idea how we'd do—for me it was completely foreign ground—all I knew was that the Braves had a tough-ass lineup—Hank Aaron, Felipe Alou, Rico Carty, Orlando Cepeda, Clete Boyer,—and they scored some runs against us, but our little nobodys, our no-names out-hit them."

Jerry Koosman: "Everyone said it was going to be a pitching-duel series, and it turned out to be just the opposite. It was a hitters' duel."

Ron Swoboda: "Look at the scores of those games. They were slugfests, and we out-hit them! We won the first two games, 9–5 and 11–6."

★ ★ ★

In the second game Koosman had an 8–1 lead after four, but he couldn't finish the fifth inning and pick up the win.

Jerry Koosman: "The Braves were a tough ball club. I gave up a home run to Henry Aaron, the only home run I ever gave up to him, and then Cepeda doubled, a single to Millan, Boyer singled, and Gil took me out. I just wasn't able to get the job done that day. I never wanted to come out of a game. I'm sure I was peeved, but he had a reason to take me out."

In game three Gary Gentry started and had some trouble, and Hodges brought in Nolan Ryan in relief in the third inning, the first time in the Series he had used him that way.

Ron Swoboda: "When he brought him in I thought, This is interesting. Ryan came in, pitched seven innings, gave up three hits, and he got the win.
"Wow!"

Jerry Koosman: "There were runners on second and third, and we were winning by two runs, and Gil brought Ryan in, and we wondered, 'Why is Gil bringing Nolan in?'
"The whole bench said, 'If he's bringing Ryan in, Gil has given up.' Because Ryan could be wild. [The game he pitched] just before Nolan had walked the ballpark. We thought this was really going out on a limb. Gil had never used Nolan in this situation before.
"Ryan came in with ungodly stuff and a great curveball, and he was controlling the ball. He had it down. He wasn't wild! He retired the side—without giving up a run.
"We went, Holy God! You talk about an uplifting inning. That certainly was it right there. It lifted our whole ball club. He dominated that day. He was untouchable. It was a laughing matter. Every pitch he threw was intimidating.
"And that game won us the National League pennant.
"We felt we were pretty lucky to win that series, because we had never scored those kind of runs, and we had never given up those kinds of runs. I mean, we just felt God was with us. We couldn't do anything wrong. We couldn't lose a game.

"We never had a star on our ball club. We had a different star every day. Every day somebody was going to be a hero, and you didn't know who it was going to be."

With the score tied 4–4, Wayne Garrett, who had not homered since May, hit the right field foul pole to give the Mets the lead. The Mets would go on to score two insurance runs, as Ryan finished his shut-out performance with seven strikeouts in the seven innings he pitched.

In the clubhouse after the game, a gracious Henry Aaron commented, "The Mets really are amazing."

Atlanta general manager Paul Richards commented, "We ought to send the Mets to Vietnam. They'd end the war in three days."

The next day the Mets were the toast of the town.

Ron Swoboda: "We were being hosted by Mayor Lindsay, Governor Rockefeller, and it was exciting. Everything was happening at Shea."

Jerry Koosman: "We were so elated, and so was all of New York. The tension of the world was on us. Everybody wanted to be on the bandwagon. Rockefeller and Lindsay and numerous big names were suddenly appearing in our clubhouse.

"I just wish it had happened later in my career, so I'd remember it more. There was so much happening you couldn't take it all in. If you were in one room, you were missing what was going on in the other room. It was that huge."

The Mets went into the World Series as they had against the Braves, as a decided underdog to the American League victors, the Baltimore Orioles. The O's had won 109 games and then defeated Minnesota three straight to win the pennant. Jack Lang commented, "In the eyes of the Orioles the Mets were a bunch of virtual unknowns, while the Orioles' own lineup was studded with established stars." In the Baltimore dugout the players spewed contempt for the Mets' chances.

After Mets reserve Rod Gaspar had predicted that the Mets would win in four games, O's slugger Frank Robinson commented, "Bring on Ron Gaspar."

Said teammate Merv Rettenmund, "Not Ron. That's Rod—Stupid."

"Okay, bring on Rod Stupid," said Robinson tartly.

★ ★ ★

Ron Swoboda: "I had to believe the Orioles were really hoping it was us. Based on all the options they had to feel glad about that. They had Frank and Brooks Robinson, Boog Powell, Davey Johnson, and a pitching staff of Jim Palmer and two twenty-game winners, Mike Cuellar and Dave McNally. And they had Earl Weaver, who was one of those guys like Leo and Gene Mauch, who took such obvious glee in beating you and worked so hard at it. You loved to beat him because you knew how much he burned inside. You knew Earl had no graceful acceptance of losing, that it ate him up. So, it was more fun beating Earl, because you knew he died a little inside.

"I had played against Earl when he was the manager at Elmira in Double A ball, my first year. He argued a lot and got thrown out a lot. That was his intensity. So, I knew Earl, and what kind of competitor he was.

"Did I think we were going to beat them? *Fuuuuuuck.* I didn't take any of that 100-to-1 action. And I knew I was going to play in this series because they had two left-handed pitchers, and I hadn't played much. I felt real rusty going into it, because I had sat and watched the playoffs."

And yet, the Mets also went into the series feeling that the National League was a tougher league, and that they could play with anybody. Gil Hodges called the troops together and told them what they needed to do to win the World Series. His words made an impression.

Ron Swoboda: "As we were going into the World Series I distinctly remember what Gil told us. He said, 'You guys don't have to be anything but what you've been.' Which was interesting. He was saying, You don't have to play any better than you've been playing, so don't try to be better, just play the game. And by then, we knew that. We had convinced ourselves. But that was his message. I thought, Why not do that?"

Tom Seaver started the first game against Mike Cuellar. Seaver had not lost a game since August, but when a quality fastball to the first batter, Don Buford, was hit over right fielder Ron Swoboda's head for a home run, he was shaken.

Tom Seaver: "On the second pitch I came inside with a fastball, a good fast ball. Buford got his bat around quick and lifted a fly ball to right field, as easy fly ball, I thought at first.

"Then I saw Ron Swoboda fading back, and back, and back, and I wondered what in the world was going on. And then I saw Ron leap and saw the ball sail over his glove and saw it bounce on the far side of the fence. I couldn't believe it. I had faced one batter in my first World Series game, and I had given up one home run."

Jerry Koosman thought that if Swoboda had had more experience playing Baltimore's moveable fence, he could have caught the ball.

Jerry Koosman: "The key play that day was a fly ball Buford hit to right field to Swoboda. They had gates out there—there was a big gate in right field, and Swoboda went back and the ball went over his head. If Swoboda had gone back right away, he'd have seen that you can push those gates back. They were chained in the middle, and you could push them two or three feet. And had he known that, he could have gone back and caught that ball.

"And that was kind of a demoralizing run they got. If he had had more experience in that ballpark, Rocky would have caught that ball."

Swoboda himself was upset that he didn't catch the ball.

Ron Swoboda: "Don Buford led off the game against Seaver, and the first ball he hit was over my head. He hit it pretty good, and I look at the film now, and I look like a mechanical man going after the ball. I turned the wrong way, I stutter-stepped, drifted back to the fence, and I jumped late, and the ball came down next to my glove, outside of my glove, but certainly within reach, certainly catchable, and I let the damn thing get over the fence, and I felt, Jesus, I just couldn't have fucked it up any worse.

"But I was so nervous being out there. I wasn't in the flow, and here I was challenged on a pretty difficult play. It was not an easy play, but shit, you ought to be able to get back on the ball. There wasn't any doubt it was deep, but I misjudged it and misplayed it, let it get over the fence for a home run. On the bench I was pretty upset about it. I was railing at myself, and Ed Kranepool came by and said, 'Shut up. Get the next one.' He was right. 'Shut up.' I liked that.

"Cuellar beat us 4–1. Cuellar was pretty good, threw a lot of screwballs. He was good, and we lost, and I felt like, Whoa, this isn't going to take long. I didn't feel very good at home plate. I didn't feel I was ready to play. After the game it was kind of quiet, a strange feeling.

"I grew up in Baltimore. It was my home. I had all kinds of relatives who I had gotten tickets for. I went out with my parents. It was the World Series, and *woo*, baseball of this magnitude is *very* different."

This was Tom Seaver's first loss after ten straight wins, including one against the Braves in the playoffs, but he was such a pro that after the game he was neither upset nor depressed. When he analyzed it, he told himself that not many players get to pitch in a World Series game. Upon reflection, he felt "cheerful."

He may have been the only one. The Orioles had given the Mets' wives tickets in Siberia, way out in the right-field bleachers. The Mets players were ready to mutiny.

Jerry Koosman: "Here it was, our first World Series, and our wives were all there, and the Orioles gave them tickets in the upper deck between first base and the outfield, and that ticked us off.

"We said we weren't going to play that second game if they didn't give our wives better seats. And they moved our wives down to where the Oriole wives sat."

In game two Koosman started against Dave McNally. As it was for Seaver, pitching in the World Series was a dream come true for the Mets lefthander. His goal, however, was a bit more grand.

Jerry Koosman: "My goal from when I was sixteen years old was to pitch a perfect game in the World Series. Don Larsen had done that already, but my goal was to do that and get a hit every time up to bat, which Larsen didn't do.

"So I had a perfect game going into the seventh inning [the Mets led 1–0 on a home run by Donn Clendenon], when Paul Blair got that first hit between third and first. Being that I gave up my first hit, I lost my concentration a little bit, and rather than hold Blair on, he stole on the first pitch. So that caught me by surprise, too. And Brooks Robinson hit a ground ball single up the middle to score him to tie the game 1–1."

Jerry Koosman

McNally retired the first two Mets in the ninth, but Ed Charles singled past Brooks Robinson and went to third on a hit-and-run play executed by Jerry Grote. Supersub Al Weis, who hit .215 during the regular season, was up next.

Jerry Koosman: "In the ninth Al Weis came up. Here was a guy who was a singles hitter. And he hit a ball off the wall in left field and drove in a run to put us ahead 2–1.

"I went out to start the ninth, and I got two outs, and then I walked Frank Robinson and Boog Powell, a left-handed hitter.

"The next batter was right-handed, so Hodges brought in Ron Taylor, and Taylor got the last out on a great play by Ed Charles. I nicknamed him 'The Glider,' because everything he did was slow. He got the ball, and his throws to first were always alley-oop throws, like he had to throw it over a building. You could count to twenty waiting for his ball to get to first base, but he got him on a bang-bang play, a great play, a hell of a hard-hit ball to Charles that he grabbed.

"So that was a great win for us to leave for New York knowing we could beat the Orioles."

Ron Swoboda: "Al had something going, and a lot of it came from when he played every day for the two weeks during the season when Bud Harrelson was away doing his military service. He got to play a bunch, and Al did very well. He fielded well, got some hits. We didn't lose anything. Al was a pretty good player. He hit only two home runs during the season, but hit one in the World Series. See, that's the thing about the World Series: It is a segmented experience so you aren't as bad or as good as you show. Anything can happen, and it is an ideal opportunity for lesser athletes to shine, because you don't have to do it for three months in a row. You just have to get on a roll, and good things can happen.

"The real accomplishment is in not allowing the aura of the World Series to change you in a negative way. To just be ballplayers, which is exactly what Hodges said. 'Don't try to be anything different than what got you here.' And of all the things Hodges said during the year, that was the one that made the most sense to me, because there's a lot coming at you, a lot of hoopla, a million things happening to tell you it isn't business as usual. But part of it is what starts and stops when you go out on and off the field, and that should be business as usual, and in that element you succeed by trying not to be more than what you are. You succeed in the World Series by doing what you can do and making yourself oblivious to everything else going on around you. And that's the only way to do that.

"And after we won the second game, we knew that it was going to be more than a four-game series. We were going to be around for more than four games, and that ain't a smart-ass answer. That's what we knew. That was the bottom line. And it was like, Well, we can play with these guys."

With the series tied at one game each the team returned to New York. Out on the field at Shea Stadium before the third game Jerry Koosman was slighted by Orioles pitcher Jim Hardin, who had once been a teammate in the minors.

Jerry Koosman: "After batting practice that first day in New York as we were going to the outfield to shag for our hitters, I met Jim Hardin, who used to be in the Mets organization, and as I was going out, he was coming in, and he said, 'What are you doing here?' I said, 'What do you mean?' He said, 'You guys don't belong on the same field with us. What are you doing here?' I said, 'You'll see.'

"So after batting practice, I went into the clubhouse and I told everybody that. Which really helped charge the ball club more."

Gary Gentry had to face Baltimore ace Jim Palmer. In large part because of the fielding skills of center fielder Tommy Agee, Gentry was able to shut out the Orioles for six and two-thirds innings in what would be a 5–0 Mets victory.

In the fourth inning Elrod Hendricks hit a ball hard and deep that sliced toward left center. Agee stuck out his glove backhanded and caught the ball. He bounced off the fence but held on. The white of the ball could be seen through the webbing of his glove. People said they hadn't seen a catch like that.

Then an hour later he did it again. In the seventh inning with two outs Gentry walked the bases loaded, and Hodges brought in Nolan Ryan. Paul Blair hit a long drive to the warning track in right center. It looked to be a three-run triple. Agee ran and ran, only to see the wind push the ball downward. Just as it was about to hit the ground he dove, skidded along the ground and caught the ball. Blair might well have had an inside-the-park home run had he not caught it.

Jerry Koosman: "Agee would catch anything that was hit out there. He had an unorthodox running style. He was fast, though he'd go after the ball with a kind of wobble. But, he always caught up with the ball. We loved him.

"Gary threw hard. His fastball was kind of straight, so they rackeytacked a couple of good ones, and Agee was our savior."

Ron Swoboda: "The first time up Tommy Agee walked up and hit a home run, boom. Ed Kranepool hit one in that game, too. But the highlight was the two catches Tommy made. I've seen those many, many times. There is one ball he catches in left-center, where he starts in right-center. And the ball he catches in right-center, he's playing in left-center. He had to come a tremendous distance each time.

"The first one that Hendricks hit that he caught in left field was going through his webbing. He backhanded it, and it hit him square in the web, and his web was stretched, and the ball got stuck coming out the back of his web.

"Paul Blair hit the one in right-center. Art Shamsky was playing right that day, and I always felt that if I had been out there that I would have caught that ball. Tommy came a *long* way. And on that play Tommy pounded his glove with his fist before he dove for the ball. I never saw anyone do that before. When you pound your fist, you are sure you're going to get it, but the wind took the ball away from him, and he realized after he pounded his glove that he better get prone, which he did, and he made the catch.

"Tommy made those catches with two outs and five runners on base. If he doesn't catch those balls, five runs score and they take a 2–1 lead in [the Series]. And I don't think I want to be down to the Orioles."

With two outs in the seventh inning Gil Hodges, as he did against the Braves, brought in Nolan Ryan to close out the Birds. With two outs in the ninth inning Ryan allowed a walk, an infield hit, and another walk to load the bases, but Hodges stuck with his fireballer. Ryan struck out Paul Blair looking to end the game.

Ron Swoboda: "Gil brought Ryan in game three, which to me was a stroke of genius."

October 15, 1969, was a beautiful fall New York day. It was Vietnam Moratorium Day and once again Tom Seaver's turn to pitch. Outside the ballpark protesters were handing out leaflets announcing that Seaver was urging the United States to get out of Vietnam.

Before the series Seaver had announced that if the Mets won the series he would take out an ad in the *New York Times* calling for the end of the Vietnam War. But the antiwar movement had enraged Seaver when the Chicago Seven, led by Yippies Abbie Hoffman and Jerry Rubin, used Seaver as an example in an antiwar message without his permission. Seaver certainly was antiwar, but almost as surely his corporate executive father's friends were not, and neither were many of the sponsors of the Mets. Tom Seaver had to walk a fine line, because public figures find themselves in hot water if they are too controversial.

Before the game Seaver refused to comment on the leaflets. Unflappable as always, he pitched eight scoreless innings. Clendenon homered in the second to give the Mets their only run, and Tom Terrific made it stand up. Seaver nursed that 1–0 lead going into the ninth.

Ron Swoboda: "Tom Seaver was pitching, and I'm watching, and he's behind a lot in the count, and they still aren't doing anything with him. His stuff was so good [that] when he made a pitch, it was a tough pitch.

"One time he said to me after watching a replay of the game, 'How did I win with that shit?' I said, 'You were pitching to the Baltimore Orioles. That's a pretty good team. And you were pitching behind in the count, and they still weren't doing a hell of a lot with it.' That's what impressed me. That's not the way you're supposed to pitch, especially to good hitters, but he did, successfully."

Out in the field to start the ninth Swoboda was positioned in right field. Seaver was surprised to see him there. Hodges often substituted Rod Gaspar for Swoboda in the late innings. Not this day.

Jerry Koosman: "Under Gil, we all knew our positions. When Ken Boswell was put in for defense, he knew when he was going to pinch-hit. When Wayne Garrett was put in for Ed Charles on third, he knew that. We all knew our situations.

"And so when Gil *didn't* do something, there was a reason for it, and it was probably because if they had tied the game, Swoboda was coming up to hit, and Cuellar was the pitcher, and he had the screwball, and so the best hitter to face against a screwball pitcher would be a right-handed batter. You took the screwball away from him. It was his big out pitch, and that was probably Gil's thinking.

"Gil never explained his moves to us. After we thought about it for a while, we usually could figure it out. But he was always *way* ahead of us and two or three steps ahead of the opposing manager."

Paul Blair was the first Oriole hitter. He flew out easily to Swoboda. Seaver then tried to blow a fastball past Frank Robinson, who singled to left field. Had the ball been a fraction of an inch lower on Robinson's bat, the ball would have gone out of the park.

Boog Powell, the large first baseman, was next to hit. Seaver threw him an offspeed pitch that Powell drove for a hit into right field. Robinson ran to third.

With one out, the dangerous Brooks Robinson was the batter. Hodges came out of the dugout.

"How do you feel?" the manager asked.

"All right," said Seaver. "A little tired, but nothing serious."

Hodges trusted what Seaver was saying and left him in the game. Hodges told him, "If he hits the ball back to you hard, go for two. But if it isn't hit hard, forget about the double play. We don't want the tying run to score. Go to the plate if Robbie tries to score, or, if you can hold him, just get one out at first." The meticulous Hodges had covered all the bases.

"How do you pitch to Brooks?" Hodges asked Seaver.

"Hard stuff in," he told him. "That's the only way we can go now. Let's go with my strength."

Hodges nodded his okay.

Brooks Robinson had gone 1 for 15 in the series. Seaver knew he was due. Seaver wanted to show Robinson he wasn't scared of him. He threw him a pitch in, trying to move him off the plate.

But Seaver didn't get the fastball in enough. It was up and across the plate, and the Oriole legend hit the ball to right field, a low line drive that appeared certain to be a hit. From his vantage point, Seaver fully expected the ball to roll to the fence. Seaver knew he should be backing up the play behind either third or home plate, but he stood in the middle of the diamond watching right fielder Ron Swoboda sprinting to his right after the ball. And at the last moment, there was Swoboda stretching full out making a desperate dive in an attempt to snag the ball before it could touch the ground.

Jerry Koosman: "From my vantage point in the dugout it was, 'Here's a base hit. The game is tied.' Swoboda was breaking in on it all the way. Throughout the year he had charged balls he shouldn't have, letting them get by him instead of getting them on one hop, and all of a sudden here comes Swoboda—and it was pure instinct right off the bat, and in a split second I was thinking, Here comes another misplayed ball. It's going to go back to the wall.

"Well, he made this marvelous catch, and it was like, 'God!' These type of things were happening all year long. Here's another hero. You didn't know who was going to be that hero out of the twenty-five guys."

★ ★ ★

Ron Swoboda: "Recently I watched the tape on the Classic Sports channel, and I caught game four of the '69 World Series, and it was interesting. That was the one I made the catch in. I was curious how it played in the context of that broadcast.

"They broadcast the games differently back then. The high shot behind home plate was their principal shot—rather than from behind the pitcher, which is so much better. You lose the sense of where and what the pitch is. You can replay a stolen base. I hate that shot from behind home plate.

"Boog Powell was the runner on first, and Frank Robinson was on third, and I don't know what the hell I was thinking at the time. I knew Brooks could hit the ball my way. He would come to right center. He had power that way.

"When I looked at the replay from behind home plate, I could see the pitch was a nasty pitch, a hard fastball sinking away from him down and away. Tom was running it over the outside corner, sinking it back over the outside part of the plate, and Brooksie fucking smoked it to right center.

"If you look at that play, it's a base hit. You say to yourself, That's a base hit. And then all of a sudden in the frame comes this maniac, diving, backhanding, and somehow coming up with the ball, and I would say to myself, 'This doesn't make any sense either.'

"But I got it. And then I try to put myself in that frame and recall what was in my mind, and what was in my mind was: 'Shit, this ball is *by* me. I don't think I'm going to get this. But I'm going to run. I'm going to chase it.'

"I chased it, all right, and made a mad lunge, a dive, whatever you want to call it. I was laid out, way out backhanded, and the ball hit right in the best place it could hit, the web of my glove. And I still have that glove. It's the best glove I ever had.

"I recall after making the backhand, diving catch, I thought to myself, *Geez, you just made one hell of a catch.* I didn't need anyone to tell me that. And I had done it in the middle of the World Series, and it was like, 'Wow, this is just too much.'

"People have asked me whether I should have played it safe. I've heard the discussion. I honestly believe the way that ball was going if I had taken a different angle I might not have gotten it and the ball would have been up against the wall.

"Look, I was a pretty decent outfielder. I worked hard at ball recognition with Eddie Yost, and I don't think I could have made that catch without thousands of balls from Eddie Yost. This was as pure a reflex action as you can imagine. It wasn't intellectual. I wasn't thinking about anything when I made that play.

"Gene Rogas, a former football player for Tulane, who is now an artist, got three sequenced pictures of my catch and combined them into three overlapping images, a big wonderful drawing, and when I sit down at my computer I look at it a lot. The theory is that when you're relaxed in a zen sort of way, the world around you slows down, and that's true. Keeping the waters of your brain calm is another expression they use. All of which was very difficult for me over a prolonged period of time. I never managed it because my emotions were always stirring up the waters. But in that situation, I had incredible calmness, a purity of reflex and reaction into a white space that I don't get in very often."

Some people remember Swoboda's catch as an inning ender, but it wasn't. It was only out number two, and from third base Frank Robinson tagged up and scored to tie the game 1–1.

Ron Swoboda: "The next batter was Elrod Hendricks, and I ran pretty far in right center to get his hit, but I was going to catch that one all the way. I caught all three outs in that inning. People forget that.

"They interviewed me after game four about my catch, and I told the writers, 'I worked hard in the outfield to get better, and when I was out there I really wanted the ball hit to me.' And I read in the paper that Agee told them, 'He said he wanted the ball hit to him? *We* didn't want the ball hit to him!' "

As Swoboda ran in from right field after the Orioles were retired in the ninth, the cheers for him were deafening.

The Mets went down in the ninth leaving two men on base. Seaver wondered whether he would get to pitch the tenth, but Hodges never said a word. Seaver crossed the white line and headed back to the mound.

The Mets had to sweat out the tenth. Davey Johnson led off and reached first when third baseman Wayne Garrett couldn't field his ball cleanly. Mark Belanger, who was trying to bunt, popped out to Jerry Grote, but pinch hitter Clay Dalrymple singled to left-center, and Johnson stopped at second.

Rube Walker, the pitching coach, went out to the mound. Seaver had thrown more than 140 pitches but insisted he had a few more good ones left in him.

Don Buford flew out to right field for the second out. Johnson tagged and went to third. The tension was high. Paul Blair was the next batter. Seaver got him swinging on three pitches. The inning was over. Seaver was done. Could the Mets score a run?

The bottom third of the Mets order was coming to bat. Dick Hall came in to pitch in relief for the Orioles. Jerry Grote hit a fly ball to shallow left field, an easy chance, except that left fielder Don Buford lost the ball in the sun. He started back instead of in, and by the time center fielder Paul Blair and shortstop Mark Belanger could get to the spot, it was too late, and Grote ended up on second.

Hodges sent in Rod Gaspar—"Rod Stupid"—to run. Hall then walked Al Weis intentionally to set up the double play. Seaver was the next batter. Seaver figured that Hodges would send the left-handed Ed Kranepool to hit, but Hodges wanted a bunt, and instead sent in backup catcher J. C. Martin. The Orioles brought in lefty Pete Richert. The wheels were turning, and the crowd at Shea was on its feet.

Ron Swoboda: "Gaspar was on second base, Weis on first, and J. C. Martin was up. Everyone knew it was going to be a sacrifice, and it was a perfect bunt. Pete Richert, who went to Vietnam with me in '68 [as a visitor], a good guy, an old school guy, and refreshing, picked up the ball and threw it to first, and J. C., running to first, was not in the box all the way in foul territory. And the throw wings J. C. in the arm, and the ball goes down the right field line, and we knew at that point that Gaspar was going to score. And he scored standing up.

"How odd was that play we won it on?"

Jerry Koosman: "There was a big argument over where J. C. was running, but the umpires ruled he was running where he was supposed to be, though replays showed otherwise. It was another break we got. And J. C. was the hero!"

But he wasn't as big hero as Ron Swoboda. His catch of Brooks Robinson's line drive would make him one of the most renowned of World Series heroes.

Ron Swoboda: "To make what is physically the greatest play you ever made in the World Series, the greatest arena you could ever be in, to do that as an average ballplayer—if I even was average—to have that happen to you, and to have it make sense in terms of the work that you put into being a better outfielder is interesting to me. We're not remembered for much, and if you're an average player and you do something memorable in the World Series, you do leave something, like when they discover dinosaur footprints. This thing that I did keeps coming up, even thirty years later. And that's fun. Hell, it's been a small annuity, because otherwise I ain't doing any card shows. For people to carry that memory in their minds is so neat, because I live a much quieter existence now, and the hubris of those athletic days are gone, and it's fun to know that you've inscribed something on the permanent record of baseball that's probably going to be there awhile, just like my name in the *Baseball Encyclopedia* having nine lines, and that's cool. It's one of the things I say to the minor leaguers when I'm invited to camp: 'Whether you get a whole paragraph or a whole page, I would wish that for you, because you are in that continuum, and that's a neat thing.' Yeah, it is."

After the game Tom Seaver's brother, Charles, a sculptor who had taught in the black public schools of Bedford-Stuyvesant, left for Bryant Park near the New York Public Library in Manhattan for an antiwar Moratorium rally.

In the clubhouse Tom Seaver turned to Koosman and said, "Wrap it up tomorrow. I don't want to go back to Baltimore. That place makes Fresno look like Paris."

"I'll get 'em," said Koosman. "I don't want to go back there either."

But, Koosman didn't start out very well. The day had dawned cold and cloudy, and the Mets pitcher was feeling the pressure.

Jerry Koosman: "I was very anxious to get the game underway. It was like time was slow, one second was a minute. I was just really biting at the bit to get rolling. I was nervous. We did not want to go back to Baltimore. We wanted to end it right there.

"I was in the bullpen, and I was pacing down there waiting to start warming up. If I had warmed up then I could have left my whole game down there. While I was pacing, Pearl Bailey came down to the bullpen. She was going to march out with the flag-carrying group and sing the National Anthem, and she was a big fan of ours. She had ESP and had predicted a lot of our outcomes. She said to me, 'Jerry, just relax. You're going to win this game, and I can see the number eight. I don't know what it means, but I know you're going to win.'

"It gave me a little consolation, but not a lot. I knew I still had to do my job.

"I warmed up and went out there and got 'em out. And then in the third inning the eighth-place hitter got on, and Dave McNally was up, and it was a bunting situation. We were all playing for the bunt. Gil was, too. My job was to throw a high fastball, hoping to get him to pop up, do the trap play, and turn the double play. But McNally swung away and hit the ball to left field for a home run. And then Frank Robinson hit a home run.'

Ron Swoboda: "In game five, Koosman gave up a two-run home run to McNally and another home run to Frank Robinson. He came in to the dugout and he said, 'I'll hold them there. You guys get some runs.' You ask him."

Jerry Koosman: "I was *really* perturbed now. I was really angry. I was so mad, when I came into the dugout, I said, 'Let's score some runs, boys. They will not get another run off of me.'

"We went to work after that."

In this game the Mets got all the breaks.

Jerry Koosman: "The next time Frank Robinson came up, I drilled him for hitting that home run off me. And Shag Crawford was the umpire, and he called it a foul ball. I hit him right below the cup on his right leg. The ball came off his leg and hit his bat, and the umpire called it a foul ball! Believe it! I don't think anybody could. Cause it was a slider, and he kind of took a checked swing, and maybe Grote blocked Crawford out because the pitch was inside.

"Anyway, it took about twenty minutes before I threw the next pitch, and I struck him out on a curveball."

Ron Swoboda: "Koosman drilled him pretty good. The ball was right on his hip. But it didn't show up very well on his dark skin, and they ruled it didn't hit him."

Then came a play that Oriole fans have grumbled about since it happened. Turns out, they've had every right to complain.

★ ★ ★

Ron Swoboda: "In the sixth inning McNally hit Cleon in the foot. Back then we wore black shoes, and they were polished every day, and if you were the manager it makes sense for you to keep a ball with shoe polish smudges on it in the dugout somewhere, and as soon as a pitch is close, toss that sucker out there and say, 'Here's shoe polish on the ball.'

"But that *was* the ball. Grote got the ball and handed it to Hodges, and Hodges went out there and made his case. There was the evidence."

The only person on earth who knows the real story is the person who put the black spot on that ball. That person was not Jerry Grote, but Jerry Koosman.

Jerry Koosman: "After the ball bounced, it came into our dugout. The ball came to me, and Gil told me to brush it against my shoe, and I did, and he came over and got the ball from me and took it out there and showed the umpire, 'There is shoe polish on the ball.'

Ron Swoboda: "Anyway, after Cleon was awarded first base, Clendenon got up and hit a home run, and then in the seventh inning Al Weis hit a home run to tie it.

"Cleon led off the eighth with a double against right-hander Eddie Watt. Clendenon grounded out and Cleon had to hold on second. I was the next batter, and it was curious to me that Hodges didn't pinch hit for me with Shamsky. I knew Eddie Watt was a three-quarter arm pitcher, and I said to myself, I'm going to hang in there the best I can. And he threw a slider away, and I adroitly jerked it down the third base line, and here's more irony: Don Buford was playing left field, and I had let his ball get over the right field wall to start the series. Now I hit a ball to him, and he was a *bad* outfielder, and he didn't make the play that some outfielders would have, because I didn't hit the ball hard. I did jerk it, but he didn't make the play, and Cleon scores, and I end up on second base,

"After Charles flew out to Buford, Grote was up next, and he hit a ball to the right side of Boog at first, and I'm running to third and watching this, and Boog didn't catch it—he kicked it, and he kicked it pretty far, and he threw to Watt at first, and Watt dropped it—Powell and Watt were given errors on the play—and I scored standing up easy."

★ ★ ★

Jerry Koosman: "I grabbed Swoboda when he came across home plate toward the dugout and hugged him. There's a picture of me doing that in *Life* magazine."

Ron Swoboda: "So we're ahead 5–3, and we got them now. *Now* we have a chance to win the thing."

Jerry Koosman: "So we were up by two runs when I went out to pitch the ninth, and that was the toughest inning I ever had. It was so noisy at Shea you couldn't hear yourself think. And the cops and specials were already coming down the first row so people couldn't mob the field. It was so noisy you couldn't even hear the bat hit the ball.

"I was nervous. I noticed during my warm-up that I couldn't control the ball any more. I couldn't throw it where I wanted to. I couldn't throw it in and out, or up and down. Because I was *so* nervous and excited. So, all I tried to do was throw the ball with everything I had on it for strikes. I was just trying to throw it down the middle of the plate with everything I could throw.

"I walked Frank Robinson, and then I got Boog to ground into a force play. They pinch ran for Boog, and I was concerned about them stealing, but it was 5–3, so I decided that they weren't going to steal at that point, and I got Brooks out, and then Davey Johnson hit a fly ball to left field.

"With all the noise, you couldn't hear the crack of the bat. I didn't think it was going out, but the fans were going *nuts* when the ball was in the air, and I thought it was going to be a home run, but when I turned around and looked at Cleon, I knew right away . . . he started to go back, but he caught the ball on the grass. He wasn't even on the warning track. I thought, Oh, my God, whatever you do, just don't drop this ball. And when he caught it and went down on one knee, it was, 'Oh, my Gosh.' "

Ron Swoboda: "Davey Johnson was the last batter, and I'm going to tell you something. Even though the ball he hit barely made it to the warning track, I thought he hit that ball pretty good. What stopped it from going out? He had some power, and he thought he hit the ball pretty good. And it barely made the warning track, where Cleon caught it."

Jerry Koosman: "I turned around, and here comes Grote, and I jumped up on him. I just was so elated, and here come the fans. They came right through the cops, and my mind immediately went from celebration to running for your life!

"I remember taking my cap off my head and clenching it in my fist as hard as I could and just bolting for the dugout. By then the fans were coming over the top of the dugout, and I remember going down the steps fighting my way through them. Already they were falling on top of each other going down the steps, and you had to walk over the top of them to get to the clubhouse.

"I remember stepping on the side of one guy's leg and just tore his leg up with my spikes as we fought our way and got to the clubhouse."

Ron Swoboda: "We had had a couple of celebrations at this point. We had had trouble with fans trying to grab your glove and hat, and after the game ended some of the players ran in through the bullpen and went in that way. I didn't join in the celebration on the mound. I ran into the dugout, and I had my hat and glove in my hand. I wasn't losing either one of them.

"I got off the field pretty fast. At one point we went back into the dugout and watched what was going on, fans picking up the grass and digging up the mound and picking up home plate. It was the most appropriate loss of institutional control I can ever recall. The fans had a right to do that. Besides, they had to resod the field for football anyway. What difference did it make? Let them go out there and have some fun."

Jerry Koosman: "It was jubilation for an hour, talking to the press, and pretty soon things started to slow down when the media got their stories, and then we all became so choked up, we couldn't talk.

"I remember Grote and Cardwell and five of us pooled up in front of Grote's locker, and we were going to talk, and we sat and looked at each other, and we were so choked up with emotion we couldn't talk."

Only a player who had struggled with some of the early Mets teams could fully appreciate what it meant to win the world championship. Ron Swoboda was such a player.

Ron Swoboda: "I had been on the teams that lost a hundred games a year, and it was wonderful to see [the Mets] come full-circle with this championship team, feeling the way I felt about the fans, entirely in touch. I spent most of my off-seasons in New York, and we did appearance after appearance. That's how we lived during the winter. I never really worked a job. I did appearances for money, big money like fifty dollars here and an occasional seventy-five dollars there. That's how I paid the rent, so I went *everywhere*. I went to New Jersey and to Connecticut and all over Long Island. Not just me. *All* the Mets who lived around there.

"Christ, I played my rookie year in New York for $7,500. It was actually $6,000, the minimum, and then I got $1,500 more for making the big league roster. God. And I was living off that money. The next year I got married, and I wasn't making more than $10,000 or $12,000 the next year. Incredible. And I was saving money.

"Where I came from, my mother and father were barely making $13,000 between them when I signed a couple of years before. From my perspective, I wasn't complaining. I didn't have it bad. I *loved* doing this.

"I was making $13,500 when I hit .281 in 1967, and I talked to Johnny Murphy a couple of times, and he was going to offer me $28,000, and I remember saying to him, 'Johnny, $30,000 sounds like a nice round number to me.' And I told him, 'That $2,000 is the different between my having to live in this cheesy apartment and maybe being able to buy a home.' And he coughed it up. I thought, Holy shit!

"This was January 1968, and I didn't start collecting that money until April, so I didn't get to see it for a while, and I thought, Holy shit, I'm never going to live that long!"

The Met's World Series victory in 1969 brought joy to New York City during a period of antiwar and race riots. Throughout that glorious summer, all New Yorkers could focus on the one institution that could unify them: baseball. There were three ticker tape parades in '69. First came the one for the New York Jets's Super Bowl victory over the Baltimore Colts. The Jets, led by Willie Joe Namath, were feted during a confetti-shrewn ride down Broadway. The next parade, even bigger, was for Neil Armstrong and the *Apollo II* astronauts after they landed on the moon. New York went wild to see both parades. But neither outpouring compared to the third one, the gala celebration for the World Champion New York Mets. Their host, Mayor John V. Lindsay, had been reelected campaigning on the "I Love the Mets" ticket. He greeted the team at Gracie Mansion after the parade. The city government was in shambles around a bloated, bankrupt bureaucracy, but he won anyway. Amazing.

Donald Grant and GM Johnny Murphy rewarded Gil Hodges with a

three-year $70,000-a-year contract. Right after the series the Mets released
veteran third baseman Ed Charles. Hodges, who held it against Amos Otis
that he would not move from the outfield to third base, pushed Murphy to
trade him. Otis was sent to Kansas City for third baseman Joe Foy. Hodges
was told that Foy was having "personal" problems, but felt he could handle him and made the deal anyway.

On December 30, 1969, Johnny Murphy suffered a heart attack at his
Bronxville home. He was taken to the hospital. Two weeks later, on January 14, 1970, he suffered a second massive heart attack and died. Ideally, his
replacement should have been Whitey Herzog, whose ability to judge
players was peerless. But Whitey was the sort of person who hated that
Donald Grant thought he knew something about baseball, and had once
too often called Grant an idiot to his face. Five days after Murphy's death,
Grant hired Bob Scheffing, a mild-mannered man who had been the special assignment scout. Scheffing really didn't want to leave his home in
Arizona to come to Queens. Grant lured him back.

Herzog, meanwhile, was realistic about the state of the ball club.

Whitey Herzog: "I still don't know how we won the World Championship, but we did. I've never seen a young pitching staff that could equal
the one we had that year. The players who won the Championship were
all in the Mets' system before I got there, but I like to think I helped move
them along, put them in a position where they could play in the big
leagues as quickly as possible."

The way Herzog saw it, as long as M. Donald Grant stuck his nose where
it didn't belong, for the Mets to win another pennant it would take a
fluke—or a miracle.

twenty-two

Vietnam

While America continued to function as usual back home, thousands of young boys were fighting a police action in a Southeast-Asian country called Vietnam. Though it was an undeclared war, the fight to keep the country from the Communists was fierce, and the U.S. death count grew every day.

Ron Swoboda had the opportunity to visit the fighting troops twice, after the '68 and '69 seasons. His remembrances are a reminder of a war that would ultimately split the country in half. At one time Swoboda believed that President Nixon was sincere about ending the war. But as the fighting dragged on and on, Swoboda's allegiance to Nixon and his strategy waned.

Ron Swoboda: "In '68 I went to Vietnam with Bing Devine, Larry Jackson, and Ernie Banks. We went into all kinds of places. We had dinner with Creighton Abrams, who was a general, to little bases where they wouldn't even leave a helicopter on the ground.

"You flew to bases. They dropped you in the middle of fucking nowhere, and you'd walk around and visit guys. You saw kids out there conducting the war, kids saddling up with their M-16s, walking into combat. An eighteen-year-old gave me his good conduct medal and cried in front of me, and you wished you could hide this guy in your luggage when you left. I had a doctor working in the hospital at Tonson Ute who just poured out his guts, his frustration with all of it. He just spit it out, and I was flabbergasted. I was expecting 'rah-rah.' And he went on a rant. You'd also meet hardcore guys.

"We went to visit this A camp with special forces guys, and we got into this little boat, a Boston Whaler, with a 30-caliber machine gun mounted on the front, the old Browning with the pistol grip, and he gave Larry Jackson an M-16 to hang onto.

"We went up a canal, and we could see villagers fishing in this canal. They dropped a counterweighted net into the water. We could see the net in the water, but no one was around, and the special forces guys gave us a heads up. Jackson, in the front of the boat, jacked the chamber of his M-16 open and put a shell in it. My whole being tightened. Then a villager came over, lifted the net, and off we went.

"I still run into guys I saw over there. Recently I was at an event, and a guy got up and said, 'I was in Vietnam when you showed up, and we had the general impression that people had forgotten about us or were against what we were doing, and I can't tell you what it meant to us.' I was embarrassed as hell. It was thirty years later. But I appreciated that.

"In '69 I went back over to Vietnam, this time with Joe DiMaggio and Bowie Kuhn. It was a three-week tour, and Joe was there for about ten days, and Joe was amazing. He didn't need to be there. He had a bad back.

"Joe was fun to be around. If you were sitting there just with Joe, he told great stories. We talked about Las Vegas and Frank Sinatra getting his teeth knocked out. Of course, he hated Frank Sinatra. He hated anybody he felt had taken advantage of Marilyn [Monroe]. Like Joe, Marilyn also was damaged property. Her sense of worth was zero. It was the wrong package for that, with the Kennedys around, and he hated the Kennedys. You could tell in his behavior.

"Joe happened to be in the same club the night Frank got punched out by the owner, and cried like a baby. Joe enjoyed the shit out of that. Frank was giving some lip and the club owner had had enough of this skinny little shit and popped him. Frank always walked around with goons and talked big, like he could do anything without the goons. Joe was interesting when you got him alone, but that was hard to do.

"Joe had dark corners, but the thing is, he was very protective of his image. If you tell enough people to introduce you as 'the greatest living ballplayer,' and you insist upon that, and insist on all these other perks—he needed to be treated like royalty. He needed to be deferred to—if you were going to be around him on a regular basis, you had to bow and scrape, and that's what Joe had around him.

"In '69 Jack Lang's son Craig was over there, and I ran into him. He was outside An-Khe, and when I saw him, I got scared, because his skin was gray and his boots were rotted from operating in the jungle. They brought him in from the jungle to see me, and we immediately went to the sergeant's club and began drinking beer.

"This was during the day, and it got toward dusk. The bachelor's officer's quarters, where we were going to stay, was up a hill. The sun was going down as we got into our Jeep, and as we drove up this hill, and we looked back toward the front gate, and I could see something blow up. And then something blew up again! Boom! You talk about sobering your ass up in a hurry!

"Craig said, 'We better start looking for shelter.' And it turned out to be a diversion. They had infiltrated sappers, guys with little satchel charges. They had slipped under the wire, gone over to the helicopter pad, and blown up nineteen helicopters.

"We reached the command bunker, and I could see the gunships come over, and they were shooting electrical cannons and fired a stream of red tracers, which makes an eerie noise—just a terrible noise—and they came around and dropped flares and lit up the whole perimeter. As they were shooting off rounds, we could watch the helicopters go up. Boom! Boom! It was like the Fourth of July. One American died, but nobody ever heard about it back home because it wasn't significant enough. It is my only war story.

"I felt we needed a much better strategy for withdrawal, because I thought we were spinning our wheels. I've read a lot about the war. I've had some good discussions with David Halberstam. McNamara didn't get it then and he didn't get it with his hideous attempt at expiation, which I hated because I've known too many people who were so fucked up by that experience. He should have stayed in his rathole and not come out.

"By the time he *did* get it, it was too late because we had lost our will over here, and [the government] started withdrawing troops and funds, and so Abrams tried to conduct the war in the right way, getting concrete results, but it was too late.

"That war is the preeminent piece of history in my life. I don't think anything has changed us as a country more in terms of squandering our living capital and our living assets—young people, and not just the 25,000 people who died—but the money we wasted that could have gone somewhere else. And look what we did to a fairly worthy population over there. The Vietnamese are really intriguing, and we just decimated their culture. I feel a big guilt about that.

"Go to the Vietnam memorial. It's the most incredible structure, an architectural response to the war, because of exactly the way we snuck into the war, and the way that thing is constructed, from one angle you can't even see it, and even when you walk up to it, the names start with one, and then there's two, and then three and four, and it builds up, just the way the war built up, slowly and gradually, to a peak, and then it builds down. It's too perfect for something sponsored by the government.

"Go there and read the notes left behind. People go there and leave notes and flowers. They are still trying to resolve issues, because we made it so hard. It was just so hard.

"I didn't fight the war. I just went and watched it and met some guys. It made me feel like I didn't do enough. When I came back I felt the way to get out of there was to support the government's attempt to get out of there. And I went on the *Tonight Show* with Joe Garagiola and said so. Looking back, I'm not so sure. I felt Nixon prolonged the war because he wasn't ready to accept terms, and he escalated, and by escalating he took more lives. At that time, I felt a little betrayed.

"And when he ran for reelection, I got a call from some of his people. They were having a rally in New York, and they wanted me to stand there and be counted with Nixon, and I refused. The guy's last statement to me was, 'You know who's going to be President, don't you? You know who's going to be elected?'

"I said, 'Yup, but not with my help.'"

twenty-three

Gil's Untimely Demise

At the annual Governor's banquet in St. Petersburg during the winter of 1970, Governor Claude Kirk got up and made a speech about how great it was that the Mets players were not long-hair hippies, that they wore coats and ties unlike the unwashed rabble protesting the war in Vietnam.

The speech angered pitcher Tug McGraw. "It was the wrong time for anybody to go giving me lectures about my lifestyle or anybody else's." His brother Hank had been dropped from the Phillies' organization for refusing to cut his hair shorter. Also, four kids at Kent State had been killed by national guardsmen that spring, and that greatly bothered him.

Tug McGraw: "These guys in the Ohio National Guard were no different from me and my teammates, and yet [students] were being shot by them—it was that simple and cruel. When we heard the news, there was no way to absorb it and still go on doing the usual routine. I never could believe that the country had reached the point where the National Guard would shoot people.

"The one thing I was never able to shut off in my mind, or even to explain to myself, was Kent State. I couldn't get myself to go to the ballpark and enjoy myself, for God's sake, playing a game of baseball. It didn't seem fair that I could be happy or even safe after the Guard had been called out and started shooting at students."

★ ★ ★

When it came time for Tug to come to the podium to say a few words, he turned around to Governor Kirk and gave him the "peace" sign. The next day dozens of writers sought out McGraw to ask him about his political views.

During the spring of 1970, the reporters didn't know it, but Tug McGraw was having a nervous breakdown. His parents had gotten divorced and were no longer civil to each other, and the country was in great turmoil over Vietnam. Not long after the Kent State killings, McGraw went to Hodges to tell him he couldn't function any longer, that he was cracking up.

Tug McGraw: "I went in to Gil, not so much because he was the boss but because he was the real strength of the outfit, physically and morally sort of immovable. And that was one of those times when he opened up and did a lot of talking.

"'Listen,' he said, 'I was in the service, too.' I was younger and it was a different situation, a hell of a lot more clear-cut. Now the only thing I can tell you, or tell myself, is that life can be bitter, the way it is today. Adversity comes and goes, bitterness comes and goes. But the thing that stays is your committment to what's right. Think of where it all starts—your family and your sense of right and wrong, even your job, if it's good. If you let the worst in us ruin the best in us, you'll never find the answer. We'll look for it together, no matter how much we want to cry over the question.'

"Hodges was sweet to me, gentle and sort of fatherly, and I could see that he didn't know exactly what to say either. [But] he was reaching out to me as personally as he would reach out to me impersonally during a ball game when he'd get on the bullpen phone and say: 'Get McGraw ready.'

"When Gil was running the ball club, you always felt that things were sane, even if you were kind of insane, the way I felt during the spring of 1970. There never was a time when he meant more to me. Hodges was a man of a few words—all of them effective. Sometimes he would just look at you and deliver the message. Other times, he would put it on the line in a fairly long bit rapping, one on one. There were even times when he'd watch me pull one of my stunts and say nothing."

Hodges was certainly a rock, but once the 1970 season got underway, even he couldn't bring to the team the cohesiveness and dominance of the year before. Part of the problem lay in the fact that most of the Mets players hadn't spent the winter getting in shape. Quite the opposite. They had spent it earning extra money entertaining their fans and putting on pounds.

Jerry Koosman: "We had guys who were on the circuit all winter long, who really never got away from the game. So they talked baseball every day and never got away from it to rest.

"And we came out, and we were probably in the worst shape, because we were on the rubber chicken circuit and we didn't get a chance to work out.

"We had a lot of injuries that year. They began right after spring training. And because there were so many injuries, the guys who all knew their roles got all upset because they had to play out of position. Our top talent wasn't always available.

"Plus everyone was out to beat us. Things just did not work out."

Ron Swoboda: "We had been spoiled in 1969. But the next season was very difficult baseball. We were in it—we won 83 games, and then the Pirates came from behind and beat us.

"This wasn't a terrible year. We just couldn't make it happen. The year before *everything* happened, and in 1970 we couldn't make anything happen. It was a very tough act to follow. People played you tougher, because they knew you were the defending champs, and we didn't understand what that was all about. It had happened to us so quickly. And there were all the questions, 'What's wrong with the Mets?' "

One of the things wrong with the Mets was Joe Foy. The Mets had acquired him for Amos Otis, who would go on to have an All-Star career. Foy would return to his boyhood friends and almost immediately get hooked on drugs, destroying his career.

Jerry Koosman: "Joy Foy was from the Bronx, so now he was back in town with his old cronies, and pretty soon he started walking down the wrong sidewalk again.

"We saw it gradually coming on. I remember a doubleheader in New York. The first game Hodges didn't play Foy, and you could tell in the dugout he was high on something. One thing you didn't do was walk in front of Gil Hodges during a pitch. Foy not only walked in front of him, he stood in front of him, cheering. We could see right away that this was a no-no. Here was a disaster about to happen. We could see he really wasn't in his right mind.

"Well, Gil put him in to play third base for the second game. And we knew he wasn't capable of playing that day. I remember the first batter hit a hard ground ball by Foy, and after the ball went by him, he was still patting his glove and saying, 'Hit it to me. Hit it to me.' He never even saw it.

"We were looking at each other and saying, 'Oh, my God, you gotta get him out of there.' But Gil left him in a little longer just to let everyone see that he didn't fit on that ball club.

"And it was not long after that that Joe was gone."

Despite their slow start in 1970, the Mets were able to climb into first place on July 11, but a loss to Montreal dropped them back again. They regained first on September 9 and 10, but two weeks later dropped into third behind the Pittsburgh Pirates and the Chicago Cubs. The Mets were eliminated during a typical Mets low-scoring performance—Dock Ellis defeated Jim McAndrew 2–1.

Ron Swoboda: "We just had no magic. We didn't have a bad pitching staff, Jim McAndrew was 10–14, and everybody else was pretty ordinary, and we scored more runs, but we still didn't score a lot of runs."

On the last day of March 1971, general manager Bob Scheffing decided he would play rookie Ken Singleton in right field and trade Swoboda, whose career was on the decline. Swoboda was understanding but distraught.

Ron Swoboda: "I had asked for it. I had run my mouth to Gil. I had had a blow up with Seaver the year before that was stupid. I did so many stupid things.

"In 1970 I was feeling vulnerable. I could feel it slipping away. The players took up a collection for the clubhouse guy, and someone said to Seaver, 'Get the money out of Ron's pants pocket.' This was money I was going to give. But Tom then stood in the doorway at Miller Huggins Field and announced to everyone that he had gone into my pockets and gotten it.

"And I started screaming back to him, 'You don't go in my fucking pockets. . . . ' Stupid shit, and in the earshot of the writers, and it was so stupid and immature and all my fault.

"In 1970 that was the toughest baseball I've ever played. I played 100 games in the outfield, had 9 home runs, 40 rbis, and hit .233. Shamsky had 403 at bats, hit .293, had 11 home runs and 49 rbis, and Ken Singleton came up, and he was playing and looked pretty good. He was a switch hitter, was young and had some ability. It was very difficult baseball.

"And then in late September came the the the question: What's wrong with the Mets? Larry Merchant, who now does the fights on HBO, came around. He was doing a piece on why the Mets weren't winning, and I spilled my guts out to this guy: 'I want to be playing more,' and I made a stupid comment that 'it would be fine if they traded me.' So I sort of asked for it. And it was just stupid. I could understand why the organization said to itself, 'Let's get this guy out of here. We've seen enough.' It probably made all the sense in the world. 'Just get him out of here because he ain't doing nothing anyway.'

"It was like, Why the fuck did you do that? But I had a little burr under my saddle. I was feeling kind of betrayed. I was inventing shit in my brain, and I got myself traded at the end of the 1970 season. I went to Montreal for half a season. I was traded with Rich Hacker for Don Hahn.

"It's a shame that it works that way. I didn't understand the value of playing in New York and how much I should have guarded that. I didn't understand that if you run your mouth and get traded, it ain't going to be better anywhere else and that other people are going to wonder, 'What happens when *we* get him?' And the next little outburst people are going to say, 'He hasn't changed.'

"So I spent a half a season with Montreal, and then Ralph Houk brought me back to New York with the Yankees for the last two-and-a-half years of my career."

But in 1971, the Mets did even worse than in '70. They won the same number of games and finished tied for third. Tom Seaver had a spectacular year, winning 20 and during one streak pitching 31 consecutive shutout innings. His era was 1.76. Gary Gentry did next best with 12 wins.

Jerry Koosman, who finished the year 6–11, was pitching on a cool June night in San Francisco's Candlestick Park when he heard a "pop" in his back.

Jerry Koosman: "I was pitching in Frisco, and in the eighth inning Willie Mays hit a home run to tie the game at one. I ended up pitching 11 innings, but there was a wind at my back, and it was 40 degrees the whole game, and I tore my rhomboid muscles—the ones that go between your shoulder blades and backbone. About an hour after the game I really started noticing the pain back there.

"They put me on the disabled list for six weeks. Then I went through a three-year period of tearing those adhesions loose so I could get my fastball back. I had a real struggle after that."

The other starting pitcher who was continuing to struggle was Nolan Ryan. He was an enigma if ever there was one. On April 18, 1970, he pitched a one-hitter against the Phillies, striking out 15. But he finished the year at 7–11, and in 1971 was 10–14 with a 3.97 era. In retrospect, had the Mets shown more patience with their young flamethrower, Ryan might have ended up the winningest pitcher in the history of the franchise.

But after Foy had failed at third base, and Bob Aspromonte had only 5 home runs, 33 rbis, and a .225 batting average, Dick Young and Jack Lang were clamoring for a home run–hitting third baseman. So was Gil Hodges.

On December 10, 1971, they got one. The Mets traded Ryan, Francisco Estrada, Don Rose, and Leroy Stanton to the California Angels for Jim Fregosi, a hard-hitting shortstop who Hodges planned on moving to third base. Though Fregosi had been injured most of 1971, the year before he hit 22 home runs, drove in 82 runs, and scored 95 times.

Though at the time the trade looked like a good one for the Mets, history has shown it to be one of the worst ever. Ryan would go on to win a total of 324 games, strike out 5,714 batters, and earn acclaim that even surpassed Tom Seaver. He played for 27 seasons, retiring in 1993, and he was voted into the Hall of Fame in 1999.

But, back in 1971, Nolan Ryan was a question mark during a period when the Mets wanted answers.

Ron Swoboda: "Ryan was a wild high-ball pitcher in a low-ball league, which is like being a pair of brown socks in a room full of tuxedos."

Jerry Koosman: "Nolan was a high-ball pitcher. He threw so hard, and he had a hard curveball. His fastball was around the belt or letters, and he had a tough time getting it down. And in the National League you had to throw the ball to the bottom of the belt to get the high-ball strike.

"And Nolan just had a tough time in that strike zone. So I could see [why] the Mets felt he was never going to get his pitches under control, and the media was also pressuring the Mets to get a home run–hitting third baseman. And so Ryan became available.

"But, you have to understand in that organization at that time they had a ton of pitchers who threw ninety-plus. We had a scouting staff that was pitching oriented, led by Red Murff. If you didn't throw ninety-plus in the Mets organization, you got released to the minor leagues. We had Dick Selma, Dick Rusteck, Les Rohr, and you could go on and on about players we had in the minor leagues who could throw hard."

The trade may well have occured because of the pressure put on Donald Grant by reporter Jack Lang.

Jack Lang: "The annual winter meetings were held in Phoenix that December. Most of the major league officials and baseball writers were headquartered at the plush Arizona Biltmore Country Club. It developed into one of the most active winter sessions in years. Clubs made fifteen separate trades that winter. The Mets, after two disappointing finishes, had made none."

Bob Scheffing was playing golf with Donald Grant.

Jack Lang: "Their affinity for the game brought them that much closer together, but it wasn't getting the Mets any hitters. Late in the afternoon of the final day of the meeting, I encountered Grant as he came off the course. I decried the lack of trading activity on the part of the Mets, pointing out the deals made by many other clubs.

"Don, you've got to make a trade," I pleaded, sounding like a fan but in reality looking for something to write about that would give Mets fans at home something to cheer about.

" 'I know,' he replied, 'We're trying.'

"Nothing happened that night or the next day. The New York press corps went home that weekend moaning about the Mets' lack of action."

Five days later the Mets announced the Nolan Ryan for Jim Fregosi deal. Fregosi was slated to be the ninth starting third baseman in as many years. Fregosi was only twenty-nine, and the Mets were expecting him to hold the job for the next five or six years.

Gil Hodges, who initiated the disastrous Amos Otis for Joey Foy trade the year before, knew of Fregosi's skills from his years managing the Washington Senators.

For the Angels to give up their regular shortstop, the team demanded one of the Mets starters. They didn't care which one. Gary Gentry, who would be traded at the end of the '72 season, was one possibility, but Hodges believed that Nolan Ryan was the most expendable. Mets management also rationalized the trade by citing the fact that Ryan and his wife were unhappy living in New York City and were afraid he might retire if he weren't traded, as preposterous as that might sound.

Bob Scheffing, for one, was excited about getting Fregosi.

Bob Scheffing: "We really thought we had a chance to win the pennant if we could get a third baseman. Fregosi had been one of the outstanding offensive shortstops in the American League for years. We didn't think he would have any trouble shifting to third."

But in the spring of 1972 when Fregosi came to camp to learn his new position, he was chunky and out of shape. At third base balls rocketed past him.

Hodges saw his new acquisition needed to lose weight and to practice taking ground balls at his new position, the Mets manager personally involved himself in his training. Hodges hit Fregosi hundreds of ground balls every day.

The morning of March 5 was rainy and wet. When there was a break in the clouds, Fregosi and Hodges returned to their ground-ball regimen. Before a scheduled spring training game that was eventually rained out, Hodges swung his fungo bat and hit a hard shot that skipped off the wet grass, bounced up, and struck Fregosi on the right thumb, breaking it. The rest of spring training his thumb was in a cast.

Fregosi would go on to play in 101 games that year, hitting .232 with 5 home runs and 32 rbis—Bob Astromonte numbers. By July 1973, Fregosi was gone, sold to the Texas Rangers for cash, while Ryan pitched superbly for the next two decades.

"This may well have been the worst trade in major league baseball history," said Jack Lang.

Unless you count Amos Otis for Joey Foy.

A year later, after Fregosi's dismal failure, Donald Grant accosted Jack Lang and accused him of being responsible for the trade.

★ ★ ★

Jack Lang: "One night, as he strolled through the back row of the press box following a few cocktails and dinner in the Director's Room, Grant stopped and looked at me. I got out of my seat, and soon we were engaged in a heavy conversation in the doorway that separated the press box from the television booth, where Lindsay Nelson and Ralph Kiner were announcing the game. Our conversation quickly turned into an argument.

" 'You've been blaming us for the Fregosi deal, and you're the one who made us make that deal,' said Grant.

" 'What are you talking about?' I demanded.

" 'When we were in Phoenix, you told me we had to make a deal. So we made a deal and now all you've done is knock it.'

" 'I told you you had to make a deal,' I said, 'but I didn't tell you to make *that* deal.' "

On Monday March 31, 1972, Gil Hodges, Don Grant, Bob Scheffing and the Mets players flew from Tampa to Fort Lauderdale for a couple of final exhibition games against the Yankees and Montreal, before heading north to start the season. Hodges, Grant, and Scheffing were working on a blockbuster trade.

Hodges had ignored his doctor's orders and resumed smoking. At the airport his wife Joan's last words to him before he left were, "Watch the cigarettes."

Pitchers Tom Seaver and Ray Sadecki were not on the plane. They flew to Dallas to meet with Marvin Miller and other player representatives to discuss the owner's reluctance to increase the players' pension and medical benefit fund.

While the rest of the players went home, Jerry Koosman was the only player to stay behind in West Palm Beach.

Jerry Koosman: "It was my day to throw on the side. Gil and the coaches were golfing right there behind the hotel, and Jack Sanford [the former New York Giants pitcher] was the pro there. They decided to go golfing, and since it was my day to throw, I was trying to figure out how I was going to do it. I had nobody to throw to. I went and caught Gil and the coaches when they got to the ninth green. I went over and talked to Rube Walker.

"I said, 'Rube, it's my second day to throw. Will you catch me when you're done playing golf?' Rube went over and talked to Gil on the other side of the green, and Rube came back and said, 'No, Gilly won't let us. We're not allowed to do anything with the players because of the strike.' Rube said, 'Go get a catcher's mitt off the truck and some balls and go throw against the back of the hotel wall. Get your workout in.'

"I got the glove and the baseballs, and I was walking through the pool area, taking a shortcut, when I ran into [Minnesota Viking football player Mick] Tinglehoff and his family. He wanted to know what I was doing. I said, 'I don't have a catcher. I'm going to throw against the back of the wall.'

"He said, 'I was a catcher. I'll warm you up.' He came back behind the hotel, and a block away we could see Jack Sanford. I started throwing, and the looser I got, the more trouble Tinglehoff had catching me. I was hitting him in the chest and the knees.

"Finally Jack felt sorry for him. He came over and took the glove away from him and finished warming me up.

"I then went to my room and showered, and I heard sirens outside. I thought to myself, There must have been an accident somewhere in the area. I got dressed and went downstairs, and Red Foley, the writer, said, 'Hey, did you hear what happened to Gil?' I said, 'No, what happened?' He said, 'I don't know, but the ambulance was here and took him to the hospital.'

"I said, 'Which hospital?' He told me and said, 'I'm going to go up there. Want a ride?'

"We went, and I got inside, and I said, 'I'm here to see Gil Hodges.' And the woman at the desk said, 'Are you with the ball club?' I said, 'Yeah.' She said, 'In what capacity?' 'I'm a player.' They let me in, but they wouldn't let Red in, and when I went up, there were the coaches and Arthur Friedman, the statistician, and Jack Simon, the TV director. I said to Arthur, 'How's Gil?' and he just looked at me and turned away.

"So I asked Rube, 'How's Gil?' And he said, 'Gil's dead.'

"That was a real shock. It was like a stone fell and hit your heart.

"What had happened [was] they had finished golf, and they were walking back to the hotel to take showers and then go out to dinner. Piggy [Joe Pignatano] hollered to Gil, 'Hey, Gilly, what time are we going to meet in the lobby?' And as Gil started to turn around, he fell and hit his head on the pavement. They said he was dead before he fell from a massive heart attack.

"I don't even remember what happened after that. I was in shock. The next day we all flew up to New York. My wife was already up there with the car. She had driven up already. The other players flew in, and we went to the funeral. In my car was my wife and I, Rube, Pee Wee Reese, Joe Black, and Carl Erskine.

"I remember that Joe Black, who was a big guy, got in the back of my car, and when he got out he ripped his pants way down the back, and he said, 'Now what are we going to do?' 'You go in first,' we said, 'and the rest of us will go in behind you and block the back while we go into the pew.' We did the same thing leaving the pew again until we got back into the car.

"I don't remember too much about the funeral. We were all still in shock."

"The big change came when Hodges died. He was a person on the field who really made some great decisions. And when he left, we didn't have that strength of person making those good decisions. It was more by committee.

"Oh, man, it was a huge void. [But,] you had to go on. Everybody went through the motions, trying to do what we thought Gil wanted us to do. They named Yogi Berra the manager. Yogi was in charge, but every manager has his own mind. The same guy wasn't making the decisions any more. And yet no matter who the manager was, every player was trying to live up to what Gil expected of you. It didn't make any difference who the manager was, whether Yogi or anyone else. Those shoes would have been impossible to fill."

twenty-four

Yogi Takes Over

A fter Gil Hodges' funeral on April 6, 1972, the Mets players had to put aside their grief and go forward. So did management. Two hours after the end of the somber ceremony, Donald Grant and Bob Scheffing announced that Yogi Berra had signed a two-year contract to manage the Mets. Berra said he accepted the job only after he was assured that Hodges' coaches all agreed to stay on. Whitey Herzog had been hoping to get the job. When he didn't, he left the following year to manage the Texas Rangers. The loss of the brilliant Herzog from the organization haunted the team for a generation.

Whitey Herzog: "For some reason Grant always thought a former Yankee or Dodger [or Giant, Westrum] should manage the club. Grant's people even ordered me to stay away from Gil's funeral just so there wouldn't be speculation that I'd be the new manager. I've never forgiven them for that."

At the same press conference, Grant and Scheffing announced the trade Hodges had been working on had been completed, one that Herzog would have stopped cold. For the third time Hodges had pushed for a trade of blue chip youngsters for a proven veteran. This time the kids sent away were three of the very best in the Mets farm system: shortstop Tim Foli, outfielder/first baseman Mike Jorgensen, and outfielder Ken Singleton. In exchange, the Mets received former Houston Colt .45 prodigy, Rusty Staub, who after six years with the expansion Colt .45s had gone to Montreal where he became a hitting star known as Le Grand Orange, a tribute to his reddish-orange hair. Staub was a quality bat, but a painfully slow runner. Foli, Jorgensen, and Singleton would all go on to have long productive careers. Foli would play sixteen years, and play more than 1,500 games at shortstop. Jorgensen would play 17 years for six teams, including a three-year stint with the Mets over decade later. Singleton would play fifteen years, hit .282, with 246 home runs, and drive in 1,065 runs.

The twenty-eight-year-old Staub played for the Mets for four seasons, the last three very productively. He would hit .423 in the 1973 World Series. Later in his career he would return to the Mets for five years in another productive stint. But the loss of three quality youngsters would come back to haunt the team. Whitey Herzog blamed Grant more than Hodges.

Whitey Herzog: "We made a terrible deal with Montreal, giving up three fine players for Rusty Staub.

"Here I was busting my tail to develop young players, and Don Grant says he doesn't trust minor leaguers, that we need big names. We had guys in our system who could have helped the Mets dominate baseball in the 1970s—players like Foli, Jorgensen, and Amos Otis—and we gave them up."

In addition to Staub, the Mets roster for 1972 featured a twenty-two-year-old farm-system prodigy, Jon Matlack, brought up to take Nolan Ryan's spot in the rotation. Matlack, who signed out of high school, was the fourth player chosen in the 1967 draft. After Matlack had an excellent stint pitching in Puerto Rico during the winter of 1971, Gil Hodges added him to his staff in '72. When Hodges died, Berra kept him in the rotation with Seaver, Koosman, Gentry, and McAndrew. The rookie finished the season 15–10 with a 2.32 era. He was named National League Rookie of the Year.

Jon Matlack: "I grew up in West Chester, Pennsylvania. In high school we had very good teams. We were undefeated for forty-one straight games over a three-year period. We lost the final playoff game my senior year. It was a record at the time. In high school I was 22–1. I had six no-hitters, and I had a perfect game against Great Valley High School.

"It was real cold day in early spring. In high school you play seven-inning games, and I struck out seventeen or eighteen, so there weren't many balls hit. It was a real thrill, but it wasn't just me. We had a tremendous ball club. Quite a few guys got scholarships or were drafted off that team.

"And yet I always felt I was doing it by the skin of my teeth. Yeah, I was winning and I struck people out, but I wasn't overpowering then. I relied on control and a fairly good breaking-ball, and every pitch was a challenge. It wasn't like walking out there and sailing through. It was like I had to work for it, every pitch, every out, all the way down the line. It seemed that every time someone swung the bat, that one could leave the ballpark.

"Late in my junior year my high school coach, Charles Perone informed me that all the guys behind the backstop with stop watches were there to see me. They started asking all sorts of questions, trying to figure out what sort of person you were. 'Did I have plans to go to college? Did I want to play proball?' That type of thing. It was all more or less a dream to me.

"None of it hit home until June 6, 1967, draft day. We were out on the athletic field practicing for graduation when Coach Perone came racing out of the school waving his arms and yelling that I had been drafted the fourth pick in the country by the New York Mets. I felt someone was going to pick me, but I had no inkling it was going to be that high. It was really a very special day.

"I couldn't sign immediately. I was playing American Legion ball, and Legion and Major League Baseball had an agreement that they wouldn't sign a player as long as he was still playing American Legion ball. We didn't lose. We won our league, went into the playoffs, continued to play. The season normally ends in mid-July, but it wasn't until sometime in August that we finally got knocked out of the state playoffs, and I was able to sit down and negotiate a deal with the Mets.

"With very little time to play, they sent me to Williamsport, Pennsylvania, Double A, the Eastern League. I was sent there because it was so close to home. I was seventeen and my roommate was thirty-one. I was *way* over my head. I pitched twice, and when I went out there, I got clobbered.

"I went from there to instructional ball, and continued to learn that professional baseball was a different game from what I had been playing. This was now a business, and it became apparent fairly early on that this was a serious business. You saw guys get thrown at, guys rushed the mound, guys did whatever it took to win a ball game, [they'd] run over a catcher if the play was close, as opposed to sliding or giving up and not risking an injury. Guys went all out to make every conceivable effort to make the play to win the ball game. That was something I really hadn't seen before, an eye-opening experience.

"After Instructional League [3–2 with a 2.00 era] I went to college at the University of Pittsburgh. The school was on a trimester system, and I was given permission to miss spring training the first year. I worked out with the college team, and after finishing school I went to Raleigh/Durham, A ball. We had a split home season, playing half our games in Raleigh and half in Durham, and the rest on the road, so we were really never home.

"I was eighteen. Mike Jorgensen played on that team with me, and Mike had a GTO Pontiac. I had an Oldsmobile, and we used to drag-race back and forth between Raleigh, where we lived, and Durham. The cars were loaded up with players. We'd dress at home, throw your stuff in the truck, jump in the car and race to the Durham ballpark, which was twenty miles, open-road pretty much, and we used to see who could get there first. Thank goodness we never blew a tire, never had a wreck. We were flying.

"We had a teammate who had a Corvette but we never let him race us because he had us outmatched. One night he decided to outrun a cop who had him blocked for speeding, and he just kept making turns and accelerating, and the last turn he made was into somebody's driveway, and he shot through their cyclone fence into their backyard. There was quite a lot of hoopla about that, trying to get the car back through the fence and him out of jail. It was a lot of fun.

"Pete Pavlick, the manager, was more hardnosed than I was used to. I was young and I never really got to understand where he was coming from or what he was trying to do. He used to go on tirades, and one of the jokes was, [since] his index finger had been broken somewhere along the line and was crooked, you never knew who he was pointing to because it was curled.

"The next spring I went to spring training with the big club, and I made the jump to Triple A, Portsmouth, Virginia, in the International League. It was a year prior to the Mets opening up their stadium in Tidewater.

"A ball to Triple A was a big jump. In A ball I was 13–6 with a 2.76 earned run average, a decent year. The next year the record was about the same [14–7], but the earned run average was over four [4.14].

"We had quite a talented group there, and it was a tremendous experience for a nineteen-year-old kid to play on a team like that and watch how they were able to come back from adversity, come back from being down, not give up. We won the league. Amos Otis did not want to play third base, and he and our manager, Clyde McCullough, went round and round, and there were numerous shouting matches between the two of them over third base and various other things that were going on.

"Choo Choo Coleman was the catcher on that team. It took me half a year to be able to have a conversation with Choo Choo. He spoke another language, various slangs and sayings I never heard before. It took me quite a while to understand what Choo Choo was talking about. Thank goodness, when he put his signs down, I could still read his fingers.

"I learned a lot that year. It was the only time I ever got fined in my career. One night we had a game in Portsmouth, where Clyde was certain the opposing team was throwing at our hitters. He was equally certain it was the catcher who was making the calls.

"The catcher was leading off the next inning. Clyde took me aside and told me, 'I want you to hit the son of a bitch.' He had a real deep voice. I had never in my life thrown at anybody. I wasn't afraid of doing it, I just didn't know *how* to do it. So I walked back out to the mound and threw the first pitch at the guy, and he jumped out of the way. It went to the backstop. Ball one. I figured, I missed, I better try again.

"I do this two more times, and I miss him two more times. He's jumping, diving, throwing the bat. I've got his attention, but I haven't hit him. And Clyde has ordered me to hit him.

"Now I'm in a mess because I'm 3–0 on the batter. He's leading off the inning, and I don't know what to do. I don't want to walk him. So I figured I'd better pitch to him, and I threw a couple of strikes, and he ended up breaking his bat and getting a bloop single.

"The inning ended, and when I came into the dugout, Clyde had me up against the wall, reading me the riot act. He told me it was going to cost me fifty bucks, and he wanted it the next morning, and fifty bucks back then was a whole lot of money.

"It was my turn to throw on the side in between starts, and all I did was practice throwing at hitters. We had a player coach by the name of Wilbur Huckle who dressed up in catcher's gear, and Clyde stood him up there as a batter, and for fifteen minutes he had me do nothing but throw balls at Wilbur.

"Turned out, you gotta zero in on a spot just behind the batter. It's the natural reaction to back away from the pitch. It's the first move, and if you make it backward, you walk into it.

"After that I never had trouble throwing at guys or throwing inside again. When you think back, you think, Jeez, how in the world did I ever get through that?

"In 1970 I went back to Triple A and played for Chuck Hiller and then for Hank Bauer in 1971. I had to watch Hank in the clubhouse because he had a fetish for taking a fist which was the size of a cardboard box and planting it just under your ribs as a way of saying hello. And five minutes later when you got your breath back, you maybe could say hello back. He had the short burr haircut, a big imposing guy. He was good to play for though. He never went off the deep end. He never lost his cool. We didn't win the league either year, but we had representative teams and played well.

"Each year I started the season in the major league camp, but I was told, 'We're pleased with your progress, but you're not quite ready and need a little more seasoning.'

"And when I looked around at who was in the Mets starting rotation, I still came up short, in my mind. They had Seaver and Koosman, Don Cardwell, Gentry, McAndrew, and Ryan. They had won in '69. There weren't going to be too many changes. I never really had enough game experience in spring training to feel comfortable that, 'Hey, I can get big league hitters out.'

"In '69 my first spring training Seaver pitched three innings, and Ryan pitched three innings, and they gave up one run combined, and I was going to pitch the last three innings in Winter Haven against the Red Sox, and I got through the first inning without any problems, and in the second inning I gave up three home runs. Every other ball was flying into the orange groves that used to surround the ballpark in Winter Haven.

"I came off the field, and Hodges was the manager, and he shook my hand and said, 'Welcome to the big leagues, kid.'

"I had been called up at the tail end of the '71 season, pitched eight innings and gave up one run against the Pirates, did not get the decision, and they asked me to go to Puerto Rico and pitch during the winter and fine-tune my game. Which I did.

"I played for San Juan. Bill Virdon was the manager, and we won the league and lost in the playoffs. We had a good rivalry with the Caguas team, and a couple of times as we were leaving Caguas the local residents thought it would be fun to see how many windows in our bus they could break. Glass was flying all over the place, and everyone was ducking as we were trying to get out of town. I started the season in the bull pen, and I got back into the starting rotation and finished 7–2.

"I felt I pitched pretty well, and pitching in Puerto Rico gave me an edge when I came to spring training in '72. I could have pitched nine innings opening day. That was a big plus.

"The other thing that happened was that the Mets traded Nolan Ryan in the off-season and obtained Jim Fregosi. So that opened up a spot on the staff, and I was able to make the team. I was the tenth man [on the pitching staff], starting the season working out of the bull pen.

"Gil Hodges was my manager during spring training. The Mets were on the road the last day of spring training and came back to Miller Huggins Field in St. Pete, and I knew there had been some cuts made, but I did not know who. I knew there were twenty-five lockers full of uniforms—that we were down to the limit—and I was trying to sit in my locker getting my uniform off while I quietly counted around the room to see how many bodies I came up with. And I didn't know it, but Hodges was standing in the hallway watching me do this. And when I completed my count and realized there were only twenty-five left and I was one of them, I was sitting there sort of smiling, and he walked by and said, 'That's right, kid. You made it,' and went off to his office. And I just wanted to crawl under the carpet.

"We broke camp, played a game, and went to West Palm for two games, and it was in West Palm that he had a heart attack and died at the golf course.

"The manager dies. I make the team. But then that year there was also a ministrike at the start of the season, and everyone was told to go home and wait for instructions. I went back to Pennsylvania.

"And I was lost. I was very young, inexperienced and impressionable, and at that point Gil was the only manager-type person I had come into contact with at that level. To this day I don't think anybody I played for had better tabs on the game than he did.

"I had spent a little time with Gil in '71 when Koosman injured some rib muscles. I replaced him in the rotation for five or six weeks, mostly sat on the bench and watched things expend during the ball games. Gil would tell guys to get loose for a possible pinch-hitter role two innings before it happened. He just seemed to be totally in tune with what was going on, anticipating every possible thing that could happen in the game. He kept *you* in the game. Gil would be down at his end of the bench, and you'd be where you were, and at some point during the game he'd lean down and

Jon Matlack

say, 'Matlack, what's the count?' Oh, my God. Even if I did know it, it was all I could do to get it out.

"He did things like that from time to time, always kept you alert during batting practice and other drills. He'd have a pocketful of baseballs, and he'd walk behind the cage, and if a left-hander was hitting and most of the balls were going to right field and you were out in left field standing with some other guy talking, and you might have a couple of rockets come your way off his fungo. He'd yell, 'You guys want a lounge chair out there?' He hit me in the chest on a one hop more than once.

"Gil was a unique guy. I was scared to death of him to the point where if I saw him in the lobby, I'd go the other way rather than go by and say good morning. But by the same token, if there was anything that came up that I needed to talk to him about, I knew the door was always open, and he'd be fair.

"I drove to Gil's funeral. It was the passing of a great baseball man.

"Yogi had been a coach on the staff, and when we came back he was the manager. I really didn't have any understanding of what the strike was all about. We had a system worked out where certain guys had other guys to call, and I was on somebody's list. It only lasted a few days, and I got a phone call. 'We're going to play.' That was the key thing to me: We were going to play.

"Yoge couldn't have been more different from Gil. Night and day. Yoge was good people. Yogi was more of an even-keeled guy than anybody I've ever seen. He was the type of manager who said, 'Here are the bats and balls, guys, here's the lineup. Go do your stuff.'

"Yogi was Yogi regardless.

"Over the years a lot of Yogisms have come out. This is the funniest one I remember: We had just gotten off a plane, and we were coming through the terminal to get to the bus, and Yogi ducked into the men's room to go to the bathroom. I had been walking near him, and he hollered at me to make sure the bus didn't go until he got there. I thought that was strange, because why would they leave without the manager? I said, 'Okay, Yoge, no problem.'

"When he got to the bus, his pants were soaking wet. Everyone was sort of laughing and said, 'Yogi, what happened?' He said, 'You won't believe what happened to me.'

"Apparently he had gone into the rest room and was standing there going to the bathroom, and somebody came in next to him and was going to the bathroom as well, and he looked over at Yogi, and realized who he was, and he turned around toward him and said, 'Hey, You're Yogi Berra,' and he peed all over Yogi's leg!

"So Yogi was my first full-time manager, and it was all brand-new to me. My first two appearances followed Gary Gentry out of the bullpen. And then we got to a point where we needed a fifth starter, and I got out of the chute real good, started the season with a 5–0 record with an earned-run average under two. I was throwing the ball very well, and I was just sort of locked into my little niche. I was facing guys who I had never faced, trying to study the box scores and see who was swinging the bat, who I was likely to face, trying to get prepared for each game. So I was in my little cocoon trying to get myself going, and I was relating to Yogi, watching what he was doing.

"And I was also learning from the other pitchers. We had a real good staff, Seaver, Koosman, Gentry, McAndrew, McGraw, and Danny Frisella. Not bad.

"I learned a lot from Tommy, who was a consummate professional. Pitching is a science and an art, and Tommy was a master. There were so many different ways he was able to win. So many times he walked out onto the mound, and you watched him start a ball game, and you'd say to yourself, man, he's never gonna make it. His stuff wasn't there, the ball was up a little bit, things just weren't clicking, but somewhere around the third or fourth inning it was as though the early innings had just been a get-ready. Everything would come together, and they might as well put the bats away, because they were not going to score now. And it was all over for the rest of the game.

"He would find a way with whatever stuff he walked out there to be successful, until he could find the missing link that was keeping him from competing on that hard basis, and it was 'Close the door, turn out the lights, the party's over.'

"I watched him pitch a one-hitter against San Diego, an afternoon game where he struck out the last ten batters. I don't think there was a foul ball. And he didn't throw anything but fastballs. It was the most awesome display of sheer power and location pitching I've ever seen. They guy was just phenomenal.

"Tommy was a student of the game, and he was a tremendous worker. He talked about it, analyzed it, pushed himself regardless of the weather. If it was his day to throw, somehow, someway, he was going to find a way to get his throwing in. He was one of those people come hell or high water who was going to be the best he could be. And he wasn't selfish about it. If he had knowledge or wisdom to impart on someone else, he was willing to share that.

"If I had a ball club [that] for some reason I couldn't find the key to, [in order to] get through the lineup, I knew if I asked Tommy about it, he'd spend as much time as was needed to hash it around and come up with some different ideas. He and Jerry were both invaluable along those lines in my early years to help me with my questions both about opposing lineups and also positioning, game-day preparation, diet, sleep habits, all these things that hopefully have you as totally prepared on the day you have to pitch.

"As a staff we were very competitive. It was almost as though a good performance from one of the pitchers warranted a better one from the next guy. Seaver would pitch and win, and Koosman would go out behind him and pitch an equally good game, and if you had the next assignment, God forbid if you do anything different. The inner competition to keep the thing going was really great.

"I learned an awful lot from having my locker stuck between Koosman and Seaver. It was a very, very good location to be in. For the first two, three years Tom, Jerry, and I had a competition among ourselves as to who would get the most hits during the course of the season. The losers bought dinner for the winner. There was some friendly competition plus a whole lot of help for me early on from those guys.

"Our catcher Jerry Grote was quiet off the field, fun, a totally normal nice guy. Put the uniform on him, and he was totally different. He'd turn into an animal.

"I roomed with Grote for a little while. He had a tremendous mind for the game. He never entered into a late-inning problem without having as much knowledge as anybody could have. He would come out to the mound, and you might have first and second and one out, and whoever you were facing, he'd relay to you exactly what had happened the previous at bats, pitch by pitch by pitch by pitch, exactly where the guy hit the ball, and he'd sit and look at you. 'What do you want to do?' I'd say to him, 'You're putting down the fingers. Let's go get him.'

"Grotes was very quick on the uptake. He did most of the noticing about guys shifting their feet in the batter's box, any little thing that might help us. If a batter tried to peek back to try to see where he was setting up, I can remember on more than one occasion when he'd lean out from behind the plate and say to me, 'If this son of a bitch looks back here one more time, hit him in the head.' He was a tough player.

"Grote used to scare me to death when I'd be pitching to him, because if I bounced the ball with nobody on base, he was just as liable to knock me off the mound as not. But if there was somebody on base, he'd block it, snag it, do something to catch it, and just flip it back to you, no big deal.

"The way I approached a game, I would pick the four batters who I was not going to let beat me. They were definitely going to have to hit my pitches all the way through the count if the game is on the line. Grotes and I would have the usual charts and scouting reports and we'd sit down with a staff member, sometimes Rube [Walker, the pitching coach], sometimes Roy McMillan, depending on who was assigned to do it, and we'd go over the overall stats, who was hot the last two weeks, talking in general how we were going to pitch everybody, and after we were done doing that, then Grote and I would take it a step further and say, 'We are not going to let these three guys,' boom, boom, and boom, 'beat us.'"

twenty-five

Willie's Return

On May 2, 1972, the day J. Edgar Hoover died, Jack Lang of the *Long Island Press* was told by a confidential source that the Mets were about to acquire Willie Mays from the San Francisco Giants. Lang called Donald Grant, who tried to stop him from running the story. "It could kill the deal," Grant told Lang. But Lang had this blockbuster story all to himself, and he was not about to sit on it.

Perhaps because of Lang's story, the Mets did not complete the Mays deal for another six days. But when it finally was announced, all the former New York Giants fans, those millions of New Yorkers who had been deprived of watching the wondrous Mays since his departure to the Coast in 1958, were ecstatic.

Poet and Mets lover Joel Oppenheimer, who never employed capital letters in his musings, commented, "all i can say is that losing mr. hoover and gaining mr. mays are two of the best reasons for doing without opiates."

Ken Samuelson: "I remember the hype that surrounded his coming. *The Daily News* sold buttons with Willie's picture on it. Even though we were getting Willie Mays, we realized we really weren't getting *the* Willie Mays. The season before Willie had begun to slow down, and so the idea [of him] was probably more than the reality. But I was real excited. It was just the idea of him coming back and having such a magical player in our lineup."

★ ★ ★

In a twenty-year career starting in 1951, Mays, who was born on May 6, 1931, had starred in 2,857 games, batted over .300 lifetime, hit 646 home runs, and drove in 1,859 runs. On April 30, 1961, Mays hit four home runs in a game against the Milwaukee Braves.

He also was one of the great base runners in baseball history. He stole 336 bases (a hundred more than Ruth, Musial, and Williams combined) and scored more than 2,000 runs. In a night game at Connie Mack Stadium against the Phils in 1961, he scored from first base on a single to left.

He was, moreover, the greatest-fielding center fielder in the history of the game. Not even the great Tris Speaker had his range and arm. In one game in Los Angeles in 1961 Mays almost threw for the cycle—throwing out a runner at home, another at third, another at first, and on another play he threw to second, but second baseman Tito Fuentes, his back turned, swung the wrong way and missed the tag.

In 1962 Mays led the Giants to a pennant, and in 1965 he was named the National League's Most Valuable Player for a second time. [The other year was 1954.] In January 1970 he was named Player of the Decade by *The Sporting News.*

In 1971 Mays helped lead the Giants to the National League West division title. By season's end he was exhausted. In 1972 the season began with a player's strike. Mays wanted a long-term contract, but Giants owner Horace Stoneham was running out of money. Years earlier Mrs. Payson had tried to buy Mays from the Giants for $1 million, but Horace Stoneham turned her down. But, in '72 with Stoneham in debt and Mays' best days behind him Stoneham decided to send his longtime superstar to a team that could better take care of him financially. Bob Scheffing was able to acquire the Hall of Famer for young pitcher Charlie Williams and $50,000. Mays received a ten-year contract at $175,000 a year, and after he retired, he was to get $50,000 a year for life.

But at age forty-one, Mays was in the twilight of his career, with retirement just over the horizon. How much he had left remained to be seen.

Some of the players were as excited as the fans. Jerry Koosman, long a Mays worshipper, was ecstatic to see the Great One playing out in the field behind him.

Jerry Koosman: "The day we signed Willie Mays was another great day in Mets history. Here was my hero—Willie had always been my hero—coming to the Mets.

"I was thinking it would only be a short time before he retired, but luckily, he was with us for two years. Having Willie Mays as your center fielder/first baseman—talk about giving you a pump! To turn around and see him out there, he was like God, like having three extra players behind you. And he was another legitimate home-run threat on the ball club."

"He was a guess hitter 98 percent of the time, and I had good luck pitching against him, because I saw a little flaw which told me what he was looking for.

"I discovered it pitching against him my first time in Palm Springs in an exhibition game. If he was looking for a fastball, he had a closed stance. If he was looking for a breaking ball or off-speed pitch he had a more open stance. But that only varied by an inch. I had to look close, but I could see what his stance was. I told Grote about it. He couldn't see it because it was so minute. But I could."

Koosman and Mays became good friends.

Jerry Koosman: "Willie was a guy in big demand. He was like Michael Jordan walking around the street, so Willie spent 98 percent of his time in his room, and I got to be friends with him. He didn't want to go out into the public. We'd go to his room, and we'd talk baseball about every night. He always had room service. He'd squeeze a rubber ball or exercise in his room every night.

"We talked about how to play the game, what to do in certain situations, what hitters to look for, what he looked for against certain pitchers."

Mays joined the team on a Friday night. Two days later on Mother's Day, Mays played his first game as a Met against his former teammates. In the fifth inning Mays hit a home run to put the Mets ahead. New York rejoiced.

Pete Hamill: "Willie Mays ran the bases, carrying all those summers on the forty-one-year-old shoulders, jogging in silence, while people in the stands pumped their arms at the skies and hugged each other and even, here and there, cried. It was a glittering moment of repair, in a city that has been starved too long for joy. Don't tell me New York isn't going to make it. Willie Mays is home."

Willie Mays

Joel Oppenheimer: "In the first inning, he walked to start the game. And then he scored and got thunderous applause for every step. Out in the field he took a throw and he caught a fly, also to thunderous applause. Then, in the fifth inning, with the rain getting heavier and the score tied, he hit a home run to put the Mets ahead, and if the heavens had opened up at that moment to put the game away officially there would have been an awful lot of immediate conversions to all faiths. Later on he walked and then was out on what certainly looked like a steal, but on The Kiner Show he said it was a hit-and-run—we did things different on the Giants'—and he wasn't stealing at all.

"So he went from aging hero to myth to ballplayer in one easy game, which is the best way to do it, and the measure, I would say, of a human being."

★ ★ ★

Ken Samelson: "It was a storybook moment. In one of his first games, he hits a home run to win a game against the Giants. And then the Mets got hot after that for a while. Shortly after he joined them, the Mets went on an eleven-game winning streak. They had the best record in the National League for a while. *Sports Illustrated* put Willie on the cover: The A-Maysing Mets. It was like he had brought them magic."

Mays played well the first month. He got on base and scored a lot of runs. The Mets finished the month of May with a 21–7 record, and when it reached 30–11, the Mets were five games in front. Yogi Berra was being hailed for his leadership.

Ken Samelson: "But then the whole team got injured, and that whole year went downhill."

On June 3, 1972, the Mets' fate was sealed when Rusty Staub, who was hitting .311, was hit on the right hand by a pitch thrown by Atlanta's George Stone. X rays at first showed no break, but X rays later revealed he had been playing with a broken thumb. He was operated on July 20 and didn't return until September 18. His season was ruined.

In June there were injuries to Ken Boswell, Tommy Agee, Cleon Jones, and Mays, who pulled a hamstring muscle. When John Milner got hurt, Berra began using Mays every day. He wasn't up to it, and his play suffered.

Behind the scenes friction began to grow between manager Yogi Berra and Mays. With the Giants, Mays had been allowed the privilege often given to longtime aging superstars to dictate when he would play. With the Giants if Mays felt logy or banged up, he took himself out of the line-up. But Yogi had been criticized in 1964 for losing control of his Yankee ball club, and he adamantly refused to let Mays dictate anything.

Tug McGraw watched Mays handle himself during the two years he played with the Mets, and never lost his admiration for the fading star.

Tug McGraw: "I guess I learned as much from Willie Mays as anybody, and maybe it'll settle me down into a better guy, maybe even a better pitcher.

"You know, Willie was forty-two, and he was hurt a lot. He got down on himself after a while because he knew he was going to retire and he wanted to help the club and also not embarrass himself. Sometimes he forced himself to play, and then he'd get hurt again while trying to do it. He also knew that Yogi was taking a lot of guff, and he didn't want to get involved in making things worse. I know he and Yogi had a tough time as far as the lineup went, and a lot of times maybe Willie didn't want to come to the park at all—so as not to cause trouble about whether he should be in the lineup.

"He was even afraid his 'retirement night' might disrupt the club when it was going good at the end.

"So, he didn't go around second-guessing anybody in the clubhouse, and on the bus and plane he really made himself fit in. I mean, he was with us only two years and he was twice as old as some of the guys, but you'd think he'd spent his whole twenty years in the bigs with them."

In June of '72, an upset Mays disappeared for a few days. By September he was loudly complaining that Berra was using him too often and that his play was suffering because of it. The proud, disgruntled Mays finished the season hitting .267 with only eight home runs. The Mets finished third in '72, behind the Pittsburgh Pirates and the Chicago Cubs.

That winter Donald Grant and Bob Scheffing sprung into action, trading away Tommy Agee for Rich Chiles and Buddy Harris, two minor leaguers who never made it to the team, and then sent Gary Gentry and Danny Frisella to Atlanta for a second baseman by the name of Felix Millan and left-hander George Stone, who had earlier ruined Staub's season.

The Millan—Stone trade turned out to be a good one. Millan would help anchor the Mets infield for the next four-and-a-half seasons. In 1973 Millan would go to bat 638 times and only strike out 22 times.

Millan had grown-up poor in Puerto Rico. Baseball was his way out and a means for him to help support his large family. He was first scouted when he was fifteen years old by Felix Delgado, a scout from the Kansas City farm system. After two years in special services in Fort Gordon, Georgia, he signed with the A's for $2,500. After two more years, he was drafted by the Atlanta Braves. At Richmond in Triple A he was tutored by manager Lum Harris. Harris knew he would be the Braves manager the next season in 1966, and he told Millan, "Next year I'm going to be the manager, and you're going to be my second baseman, no matter what."

Millan hit .275 for Harris and was a regular for the Braves until Eddie Mathews took over as Atlanta manager the last month of the '65 season. Millan had an injured finger on his throwing hand, and he couldn't play. Mathews traded him to New York. Millan was thrilled.

Felix Millan: "I knew I was going from a club that didn't draw too many people to a club that drew a lot of people, and a lot of Latin American people. I thought, Maybe this will be a good break for me."

It was. Millan hit .290, scored 82 runs, and was one of the most valuable performers on the team. He and shortstop Buddy Harrelson would rate among the best double-play combinations in New York Mets history.

Jerry Koosman: "Felix brought a strong bat into the lineup. He didn't strike out. He put the bat on the ball and hit a lot of line drives. And in the field he was a great defensive second baseman. Felix was a great asset to us.

"And Buddy at shortstop caught everything, and he knew the pitchers so well and how we pitched the hitters. If we did make a mistake, Buddy caught it, and if we didn't make a mistake, it was a can of corn. If it was a ground ball anywhere toward short, he was a vaccuum cleaner out there."

The 1973 season began with a player lockout that closed the training camps and hurt the players' ability to get in shape. When some of the players began the season overweight, and others didn't seem to be hustling, once again the critics accused Yogi of not being enough of a dictator, saying he ran such a loose ship that the players took advantage of him.

Jerry Koosman: "Gil had a strict weigh-in. We had to weigh-in every week, and we had to be at weight, and if you weren't, it cost you a hundred dollars a pound, a day.

"After Yogi took over that went by the wayside, because Yogi wasn't as strict as Gil, and some guys took advantage of that. And because there was no weigh-in, some guys got too heavy. Under Yogi we just didn't have the discipline that a strict hand can dictate. Like in the army. If you don't have strong discipline in the military, more people go their own way. We had some of that."

★ ★ ★

Perhaps because Berra was allowing his players to fall out of top shape, or perhaps just because of sheer bad luck, the team suffered a devastating rash of injuries for the second year in a row.

Tug McGraw: "At first, I remember we'd come to the park every day and everything was cheerful, the guys were doping around, and everybody was anxious for the warm weather to come. We were looking for hot weather—and we got injuries instead. They kept piling up."

First baseman John Milner pulled a hamstring muscle and was lost. Jerry Grote was hit on the right wrist by a pitch and was out until July. After the Mets purchased catcher Jerry May from Kansas City to replace him, he suffered a sprained wrist in his first game. He caught only four games. By the end of April fluid had to be drained from Willie Mays' knees. Rusty Staub continued to play with an injured hand.

Cleon Jones hurt his right wrist diving for a ball and missed almost all of May. Then, in early June, Bud Harrelson broke his left hand when the Reds' Bill Plummer crashed into him trying to break up a double play. He didn't play again for a month.

With Mays ailing, Jones hurt, and Agee having been traded away, a gangly outfielder by the name of George Theodore got a starting nod in the outfield.

Nicknamed "The Stork" because he was so tall and thin, Theodore had been told at the start of spring training that he had no chance of making the team. But Theodore, who was drafted in the thirty-first round, was a long shot from the beginning. A college grad, "The Stork" was educated and erudite. He could also hit.

George Theodore: "I was really born in 1946. The *Baseball Encyclopedia* says I was born in 1947, and that's because when I signed my contract, I was told, 'You'll have a better chance if you're 21.' So I became a year younger, which I assume happens, whether [you're] in the Dominican Republic or not.

"I come from Salt Lake City, Utah. I didn't see a scout until my senior year of college at the University of Utah. I was Western All-American my senior year and All Conference for a couple of years.

"In 1969 I was drafted by Roy Partee of the Mets. Roy signed three kids from Salt Lake City, Tom Gilfore, who was a friend of mine, a high school boy, and me.

"I was one of the last people drafted. It seems like I was the 715th player picked, and there weren't many behind me. I would have signed for nothing, but we negotiated a price on what it would cost to go to graduate school for a year.

"I said, 'I'd like to sign, but I would like to go to graduate school.' They gave me three thousand dollars.

"After a week-and-a-half at Marion, Virginia, I was sent to Pompano Beach, in the Florda State League. It was the only team in the league without lights, and it was *hot*. I figured I would play the season, see how I did, and go to grad school in the fall. And without any expectations, I started doing quite well, hit .283. I asked my manager, Joe Frazier, if I could skip spring training to go to school and he said, 'No, you *have* to do to spring training.' So I did and I put school off. And Joe the next year went to Visalia, California, and I went with him, and I had a pretty good year there.

"Joe was kind of cantakerous and a little bit mean, but he was a real scientist. He got you thinking about different ways of hitting, how to use your hands and your arms, how to get the bat through. He got me thinking a lot about hitting, and I enjoyed that.

"He was a great manager for me, a good motivator. He might pull you out of a game or embarrass you or just yell at you a little bit. I got along real well with him. He didn't get real close to his players, but he was an excellent manager.

"The next year I went to the Instructional League. I never saw Gil Hodges. We saw Whitey Herzog a lot because he was in charge of the minor league operation. He did some instructing. Boy, he was great. Whitey was a no-nonsense guy, but he was fair, too.

"In 1971 I went back to Visalia to play for Joe Frazier. I had gone to Memphis, but the manager there, Johnny Antonelli—not the pitcher— didn't like the way I played. He wanted slash-and-run hitters, and the Mets were about to release me when Joe asked them to send me back to him.

"So that's where I went, and I ended up the Most Valuable Player in the league. In 438 at bats, I had 113 rbis, and we won the championship.

"Then in '72 I skipped Double A because of my contract demands. If I couldn't make it in Triple A, the Mets had to release me. I went to Tidewater with Hank Bauer. Hank was kind of grumpy, but he was the kind of manager who didn't say too much to anyone. He just kind of put you out in your position. His feeling was, 'Do your job and we'll get along just fine.' And we had a good team, and we ended up winning the league. We had a bunch of older players to fill the team up, Jim Gosger, and Jose Morales on loan from Oakland, a great bunch of guys.

"And then in the winter of '72 I went to the Dominican Republic for winter ball and I played with the greatest pitcher I'd ever seen in my life, J. R. Richard. I was at San Pedro de Macaris, the little city where all the major league shortstops come from, the poorest place on earth. They had an agreement with Houston, and so I played with a bunch of Astro players, Larry Yount, Robin's big brother, Cesar Cedeno, Rico Carty, and J. R. Richard, who in his prime could throw that slider faster than anyone could throw his fastball. And under the lights down there he was just unbelievable. He was great until he burned his foot cooking fried chicken in his room and missed the last three weeks of the season.

"We won a playoff series against a team from up north. I didn't think it was such a big deal but I remember we didn't go through the town on the way out because the people from the losing city were going to stone the bus. As I think about it, it was surreal.

"We arrived back in San Pedro at four o'clock in the morning, and the whole village had lined the streets, yelling and screaming. What a wonderful experience! They had such emotion and affection for their baseball team.

"We finally lost to a team that had Steve Garvey and several Dodger players before they became great. And then the next spring, just when I had a chance to make the Mets, the owners locked out the players, so we went to spring training late in '73, but because I played winter ball I had a jump on some of the other players.

"I was invited to spring training with the Mets with the implicit understanding there was no room for me. But I was in shape, and they had me in the outfield, though my best position was first base, and I was catching the ball and throwing the ball better than I'd ever done, and I hit well, which was unusual, because I was more of a summer hitter. I made the team with the understanding that if they needed another pitcher, I was the one who would go. So I was prepared for that. I got to play a few games with the Mets and did well, and I just absorbed every experience.

"And I did quite well, so they kept me. When they needed another pitcher, they sent out Rich Chiles, and when they needed another pitcher, they sent out someone else, and there reached a point where I became a starter, a regular."

The player who Theodore looked up to the most was Willie Mays.

George Theodore: "Willie was very happy-go-lucky, very down to earth and approchable, even though he was one of the greatest superstars. Even at his age you could feel the magnetism when he came to bat. It was just unbelievable.

"Willie was really a nice guy. He'd joke around. You would think, In his position he doesn't have time for rookies, but he would be nice to me and the younger players.

"Willie had the constitution of a horse. He was really a dynamo. I once asked him, 'I'm a little tired. How do you stay strong? Do you lift weights? Do you take health foods?'

"He said, 'Here, I'll show you.' He said, 'When I get kind of tired, I do this' and he rocked from his heels to his toes, just going up and down to build his calf muscles, after ten or fifteen times. He said, 'I do that a little bit, and I'm just fine for a few weeks.'

"Willie had the constitution of people who don't usually have it like that. For him he didn't need to lift weights. He didn't need to do any exercise. He could just go and go."

Mays was able to go and go until April 1973, when the Mets medical staff had to regularly drain fluid from Mays' knees. He had hurt his left knee, and when he favored his right one, that one went, too. At age forty-two, Mays' legs were suddenly starting to go, and he no longer had the range he once had. Then, during a game he misjudged his leap against a wall and injured his right shoulder. Hurting, his hitting began to suffer.

As for Stork Theodore, his season and ultimately his career would come to a disastrous end before it ever had a chance to begin. On July 7, 1973, he crashed into center fielder Don Hahn and dislocated his hip. Two weeks earlier Theodore had dreamt he was being carried off the field on a stretcher with McGraw holding one end and Koosman at the other. Eerily, his dream turned into reality. He was in the hospital in traction for a month and then on crutches for another month. He wasn't reactivated until September. He played in 60 games in 1974, hit .158 and sank from the majors forever.

In the first week of July 1973, Jack Lang reported in the *Long Island Press* that Donald Grant was considering firing Yogi Berra. The Mets were in last place, eleven games out of first. Some of the players, especially those passionate about Gil Hodges, were upset that Yogi didn't seem to have Hodges' ability to anticipate managerial moves during ball games.

Tug McGraw: "In baseball, you hear guys horsing around, asking questions like, 'What's the difference between Gil Hodges and Yogi Berra?' And some joker can always get a laugh by answering: 'six innings.' [Because] in the third inning, Gil was thinking about what he was going to

Yogi Berra

do in the sixth; in the sixth, Yogi was thinking about what he *should* have done in the third."

In mid-June in New York, Yogi had brought in a relief pitcher and then tried to remove him before he faced a single batter, which is against the rules. This happened a second time in Montreal.

In his column Lang criticized Berra, accusing him of not knowing the rule book. The next day Yogi had harsh words for Lang. But, when Berra's wife Carmen handed Lang a quarter and told him it was all he was worth, Yogi was embarrassed.

"Aw Carm," he said, "don't say that."

It was a measure of Yogi's humanity that he never stayed angry at anyone very long. Though Yogi may not have been a disciplinarian, which bothered some of the players, and kept too tight a reign on Willie Mays, which bothered others, those same players full-well understood that the injuries to so many of the starters hadn't been Yogi's fault.

Jerry Koosman: "Yogi was always a very positive person, and easy going. It took a lot to make Yogi mad. Yogi was a players' manager.

"It was just that things didn't work out for Yogi. We had a lot of injuries. Had we been a healthy ball club for Yogi, yeah, maybe we would have won it a couple more times. But a lot of the time it was tough for Yogi to put nine healthy guys on the field. It seemed like one thing after another. People had to play out of their normal positions. We had right handers having to hit against right-hander pitchers. It seemed to be a struggle. We just got some wrong hops. We lost a bunch of close games."

twenty-six

"Ya Gotta Believe"

One player whose performance suffered greatly during the first half of the 1973 season was relief pitcher Tug McGraw, who was unhappy with the way Yogi Berra managed.

In a game against the Cincinnati Reds during the first part of the season Berra brought McGraw in to save it. He gave up a walk, a single to Pete Rose, and then Rusty Staub made an error on a fly ball. McGraw threw a wild pitch, and then pitched carefully to Joe Morgan and walked him.

When Yogi pulled McGraw out of the game and brought in Phil Hennigan, McGraw was furious. Johnny Bench, the next batter, hit a home run against the journeyman Hennigan to win the game.

Tug McGraw: "Some of us were getting down on Yogi for the things he did. Then more injuries came, our luck kept getting worse, and the guys started griping a bit."

M. Donald Grant was asked whether he was going to fire Berra. "Only if the fans demand it," was his reply. Grant adamantly wanted to fire Berra but was afraid of the fan backlash.

Jack Lang: "Grant could not get Scheffing to go along with him. In fact, insiders later revealed that when Grant asked Scheffing to drop Yogi, the general manager refused. 'If you want to fire Yogi, you do it. I won't,' Scheffing told Grant."

The *New York Post* took a poll as to who was most responsible for the poor play of the team, Grant, Scheffing, or Yogi. Berra continued to be a fan favorite as most fans blamed Scheffing, followed by Grant. Shortly after the poll, McGraw pondered who would get fired first, Yogi or Richard Nixon? (It turned out the first to go was Spiro Agnew.) For his part, Yogi kept telling everyone to be patient, that a hot streak was coming. Few took him seriously.

In early July against Montreal, McGraw gave up seven runs in less than an inning. First, Bob Bailey hit a grand-slam and then he gave up a double, another home run, two walks, and he was finally taken out. McGraw was feeling desperate.

Tug McGraw: "I didn't have any feel for the baseball at all. I didn't have any idea how to throw the baseball. It was as if I'd never played before in my entire life. I just felt like dropping to my knees and saying, 'Shit, I don't know what to do. Don't know what to do. Can't hack it any more.'"

Though McGraw went into the clubhouse and acted as though nothing had happened, he admitted he didn't have the "foggiest idea what in hell to do."

When the team returned home to New York, McGraw went to see a close friend, Joe Badamo, an insurance salesman who had also been close to Gil Hodges before his death. Badamo believed in self-actualization— picturing something happening in your mind before it happened. For a pitcher, the way it works is, if you intend to throw a fastball on the outside corner of the plate, first you see that happen in your mind, and then you go and throw the pitch. A lot of other ballplayers find this technique very helpful as well.

Jon Matlack: "There was a certain amount of brinksmanship in Tug's personality. He lived to be in tight situations with the game on the line. And he seemed to be at his best and most relaxed when that situation occurred.

"At one point he was very much into the power of positive thinking, visualizing what you had to do each pitch before doing it. He had me doing it, too, and it does work. It's pretty powerful. You can do it in a flash of a second. The key to the whole thing is believing it. Once you get to that point, I know I was making pitches on a consistent basis that a couple years before I wondered if I'd ever make.

"Tug had a friend, who used to come to the stadium early on occasion and meet with Tug and me, and a couple other players in the little waiting room right outside the locker room. He was a mentor to Tug. It was a big plus."

In mid-summer 1973, though, Tug was anything but confident. McGraw told Badamo what was bugging him, and Badamo told him that before he could succeed on the mound he had to get his confidence and concentration back.

"The only way to do that, Badamo kept saying, was to *believe* in yourself." McGraw pondered what his friend was telling him and responded, "You gotta believe."

Said Badamo, "Yeah, you gotta believe, start believing in yourself."

The desperate McGraw didn't have any other solutions to turn to. He decided that he was going to believe.

After he left Badamo, McGraw drove to Shea Stadium. He arrived at the park early and was greeted by a group of fans waiting for autographs.

"What's wrong with the Mets?" he was asked.

McGraw responded by hollering, "There's nothing wrong with the Mets. Ya gotta believe."

Once inside the stadium McGraw stood with pitchers George Stone and Harry Parker in the outfield, and lightheartedly he gave them the "Ya Gotta Believe" speech.

"I was just screwing around having a good time that day," he said.

After batting practice it was announced that Donald Grant was going to have a meeting with the players. During the meeting Grant pointed out the large number of serious injuries, and he told the players that management didn't think they were a last-place ball club. Grant said, "I believe when you guys get healthy, there'll still be time left for you to get healthy on the field and win this thing."

Grant's speech struck a chord with McGraw, who began running around the clubhouse hollering at guys, "Ya gotta believe."

Some players laughed because they thought McGraw was making fun of Grant. Others kept solemn because they were afraid Grant would think they were making fun of him.

Jerry Koosman: "We had a meeting in the clubhouse. Don Grant, our chairman of the board, came down. It was a low point. We had lost a few games, and Grant gave us a speech. He raised one finger and said, 'Number one, you have to have heart. Number two, you have to have . . . ' whatever. He tried to give us a pep talk.

"When he was done, he turned around and headed for the door, and Tug came off his stool, and in a Hulk Hogan–strongman stance, he said, 'Ya gotta believe.' It kind of broke the air a little bit, loosened some of the tension, and that was where I first heard it.

"Some of us thought he was making fun of Grant a little."

McGraw contends he wasn't making fun of Grant at all, but rather just expressing what he had been feeling all day.

When Ed Kranepool, his roommate, told McGraw that he was afraid Grant thought McGraw was mocking him, McGraw made it a point to phone Grant and assure him that wasn't the case.

Once again Grant stressed to McGraw that everyone in the front office was confident that as soon as the team got healthy, the club would start winning and would win it all.

McGraw told Grant he agreed with him.

Yogi Berra decided that in an attempt to get McGraw out of his funk he could give him a start against the Atlanta Braves. On the first pitch of the game Ralph Garr hit a ball over the center field wall. McGraw gave up seven runs in six innings, but the Mets won the game when they scored seven runs in the ninth inning.

In his next start against St. Louis, McGraw only gave up a couple of runs. Berra decided he was pitching well enough to return him to the pen. These were savvy managerial moves that would prove most beneficial to the Mets in 1973.

When McGraw relieved against the Giants, he kept putting men on but would then get out of the jams. The game should have been over in the thirteenth inning, but Wayne Garrett—playing short for the injured Buddy Harrelson—let a double-play ball go through his legs.

With runners on second and third, Yogi elected to walk a rookie batter and pitch to Bobby Bonds with the bases loaded. Bonds singled to left to win the game.

McGraw had lost, but he was feeling that he was coming out of his slump. Meanwhile Berra kept repeating *his* best-known line, "It ain't over til it's over."

In August, shortstop Buddy Harrelson returned and so did catcher Jerry

Grote. Felix Millan played great at second, and Don Hahn replaced Willie Mays in center field and began playing excellent defense.

On August 22, 1973, the tide turned for McGraw. With the Mets losing 3–2 against the Dodgers in the eighth inning, Yogi brought McGraw in to pitch. With two outs in the ninth, Felix Millan singled to drive in Cleon Jones with the tying run. Rusty Staub singled, and then John Milner singled in the winner, giving McGraw his first win of the season.

After the game McGraw came into the clubhouse screaming, 'Ya gotta believe."

In his next nineteen appearances, Tug McGraw allowed a total of four runs, and never more than one run in any one game. He didn't blow a single lead the rest of the way.

A week later the Mets were still in last, but only six-and-a-half back. To win it, in September they had to get past the Pirates. Could they do it?

"Ya gotta believe."

twenty-seven

The Miracle Mets

The big names on the Mets' pitching staff were Tom Seaver, Jerry Koosman, and Jon Matlack, but the star pitcher during the month of September was the little lefty, George Stone, who won his last eight games in a row, all *big* victories.

He beat the Cardinals 4–1, the Expos 3–0, the Pirates again 7–3, and when the Mets swept three games against the Pirates at home behind Stone, Ray Sadecki, and Seaver, the Mets incredibly found themselves in first place.

Jon Matlack: "It was a strange division that year. Every team in the division spent some time in first place. When our time came, it was at the end, when it counted.

"We just put together a real strong last six or seven weeks that was enough to get the job done. It wasn't one or two individuals, it was an overall effort where everybody pitched in. Whatever was needed to be done, somehow it got done that day."

On September 19, 1973, Willie Mays, suffering from cracked ribs, revealed he was going to retire at the end of the season. Everyone, including Mays, had tears in their eyes. Some of the players pleaded with him to reconsider. Mays said that if the Mets made it into the World Series, he would "be there to help."

The writers tried to make it sound like Mays had been a detriment to the team, that he was only window dressing to draw old New York Giants fans, but his teammates made it abundantly clear that wasn't the case at all.

Jerry Koosman: "He was still our best player. I begged him not to retire. He said, 'Koos, I'm tired.' "

Tom Seaver: "There's no question he was beneficial to us, especially in [1973]. He taught our young players quite a bit—he taught John Milner, for one, and the outfielders how to play and where to play. He was a tremendous asset all the way around.

"Many of the New York writers made him out as a load that we had to carry, but, quite the contrary, he helped us *carry* the load we had all the way down through the season, especially the last month-and-a-half when we got hot, and put it all together."

The night of Mays' announcement the Mets played Pittsburgh in a game that went to thirteen innings. Ray Sadecki was pitching in relief of Jerry Koosman with a Pirate runner on first when Dave Augustine hit what appeared to be the game-winning home run to left field.

They say baseball is a game of inches, and it certainly was in this case: the ball hit the very top of the outfield fence and bounced back into Cleon Jones' glove. Jones threw to cutoff man, Wayne Garrett, who threw to catcher Ron Hodges, who tagged Richie Zisk out at the plate. The Mets won it in the bottom of the thirteenth.

After Seaver beat the Pirates 10–2, the Mets' record was 77–77. Though the record was only .500, miraculously, they were in first place with eight games remaining to the season.

After Jon Matlack and George Stone beat the Cardinals, on September 25, 1973, before a game with the Expos at Shea Stadium, the Mets held "Willie Mays Night," a farewell to the "Say Hey Kid." Mays was showered with gifts for over an hour.

As tears streamed down his face, the beloved Mays announced to the 43,805 Shea faithful that he would retire at the end of the season. He talked of his teammates' pluck and made his moving farewell.

Willie Mays: "I hope that with my farewell tonight, you'll understand what I'm going through right now. Something that I never heard: that I were ever to quit baseball. But, as you know, there always come a time for someone to get out. And I look at those kids over there, the way they are playing, and the way they are fighting for themselves, and it tells me one thing . . . Willie, say good-bye to America. Thank you very much."

Mays wept as the fans applauded.

In the dugout after the ceremony, manager Berra walked over to Mays and said, "I may need you to play tomorrow. Okay?"

"Fine with me," said Mays."

The last four games of the season were scheduled against the fifth-place Cubs at Wrigley Field. After rains beat down on Chicago all Friday and Saturday, the Mets were forced to play two doubleheaders in a row on Sunday and Monday.

The rain continued to fall on Sunday, but not hard enough to wash out the games. The Cubs beat Matlack in the opener 1–0, but Koosman beat Fergy Jenkins 9–2 in the nightcap. The Mets still had to win one game on Monday, the final day of the season, to win the division title.

On Monday it was still rainy, and only 1,913 fans showed up at Wrigley Field for the final-day doubleheader. Berra started Seaver in the opener, and the Mets led the Cubs 6–2 going into the seventh. When Rick Monday hit a two-run home run, Yogi called McGraw into the game.

The Mets needed nine outs to win the division title. After McGraw pitched a perfect seventh and eighth, Ken Rudolph singled in the ninth inning. McGraw struck out Dave Rosello, and when Glenn Beckert lined out to Milner at first, Milner stepped on first to complete the double play, and the improbable division title was theirs.

The Mets players weren't sure how to celebrate, because they still had to play another game, but when the umpires ruled that wet grounds made it impossible to play the second game, the regular season was officially over, and a real celebration could begin.

Tug McGraw: "We stopped being restrained and poured it on, hollering and screaming and wondering what all the people who'd counted us out of the human race a couple of months earlier must have been thinking.

"They tell me that I jumped up on one of our equipment trunks with a bottle of champagne and kept screeching, 'Ya gotta believe,' with all the guys yelling back at me."

★ ★ ★

Jerry Koosman: "Our celebration in '73 was nothing like it was in '69. Not at all. It was like, 'We couldn't believe we had won it and that nobody wanted to win it.' It got dumped in our lap."

Counting their final win, the Mets finished the last month with a 20–8 record. Their margin over the second-place Cardinals was a game-and-a-half.

On the plane ride home from, Chicago, Koosman grabbed the intercom phone and announced to all the passengers, "The starting pitchers on the Mets baseball team give their 'Bullpen of the Year Award' to Tug McGraw—because we would have won by twenty-five games if he hadn't screwed up all those games early in the season."

Cheers and good-natured ribbing filled the airplane.

The Mets had four days to rest before playing Cincinnati in the National League playoffs. Beating the Reds, led by Pete Rose, Johnny Bench, Joe Morgan, and Tony Perez would be a daunting task. It was a Reds team that would one day become known as the Big Red Machine.

Jon Matlack: "The Reds could come from nowhere, absolutely nowhere. I did have a number of occasions where I was leading going into the sixth, seventh, or eighth inning with a no-hitter or a one-hitter or a two-hitter and maybe a one-run lead, but you were never safe. They could manufacture runs out of nowhere."

In the series opener played in Cincinatti, Tom Seaver was spotless through seven innings, when the Reds struck. Pete Rose homered in the eighth and Johnny Bench in the ninth. Seaver lost the game 2–1.

Jon Matlack: "The playoffs were more fun and exciting than the Series. Seaver pitched one of the best games I ever charted. He gave up two home runs, one to Rose and one to Bench. He struck out thirteen. Other than those two pitches he had an overpowering day.

"After we lost I sat there in the clubhouse and reviewed that chart I don't know how many times and thought to myself, 'My God, how can you pitch this good and come away getting beat?'"

In the second game Jon Matlack threatened to pitch a no-hitter. A Rusty Staub home run gave the big lefty all the runs he needed in a 5–0 victory.

Jon Matlack: "I had a better-than-average day for me. If it hadn't been for one guy, Andy Kosko, who hit two ground-ball singles, I would have had a no-hitter. That was all the Reds got. They were a *very* tough club. That was a real good experience.

"We were facing Don Gullett. Before the game Rusty told me, 'I've got his pitches.' Rusty was the best at knowing what pitchers were going to throw. He said, 'Before the day is over, I'm going to get him, so you keep them close, because I'm going to hit you at least one.'

"We had an early lead, and in the fourth inning he hit a three-run home run off Gullett to put the game away.

"We ended up winning 5–0.

"Joe Morgan, believe it or not, was one of the easier guys for me to handle, but the rest of them was a flip of the coin. They had a whole bunch of real good hitters and tremendous speed, especially in that park with the AstroTurf. It was *very* tough keeping those guys off the bases. They were a tremendous team. To this day I'm not sure how we got by them."

If Rusty Staub had Gullett's number, he also had Ross Grimsley's, who started game three played at Shea Stadium. The redhead homered his first two times up to give Jerry Koosman a 9–2 win.

Jerry Koosman: "Grimsley had been tough on us during the season. He was a little left-hander who always gave us trouble.

"I knew that when I went out there not only was the club depending on me, but I had my work cut out for me because this guy was stingy giving up runs. I knew I'd have to pitch a good ball game to beat him."

With the Mets leading 9–2 in the fifth inning of game three, Rose tried to light a fire under the Reds. He slid hard into shortstop Buddy Harrelson, and when the two started to fight, a brawl broke out. According to Koosman, he had been the one who had angered Rose into action.

Jerry Koosman: "I started it. Usually I threw fastballs down and away to Pete, and I could see he was charged that day, and certainly I was, and I threw him a slow curveball, off-speed, just trying to keep it down and away. When you're pitching against a good hitter like him you have to remember all his other at bats and how I had tried to get him out with nobody out and runners in scoring position. And this was a little bit different pitch. And he went after it and popped it to the infield.

"He knew I threw a lot harder than that, that I had a good fastball, and as he got back to the dugout he reached the second step, and even though the stadium was full and it was noisy, I could hear him holler out to me, 'Throw the ball, you big, dumb, fucking donkey.'

"I didn't look over there, but with my peripheral vision I could see him hollering at me.

"I just said to myself, Wait till the next time you get up, you son of a bitch. And so the next time he came up I tried to drill him four times with a good fastball. He got away every time. And so he took first base with a walk, and when he tried to break up the double play, he went into second base with a hard stand-up slide and took it out on Harrelson. It was a beyond fair-play slide. And so that caused the ruckus out there.

"Buddy wasn't going to take that, not in that situation. Here we were in the playoffs. We weren't going to let them show us up. You're not going to let them intimidate you.

"We were David going against Goliath, which was what the Mets were going up against Cincinnati. And maybe we didn't have the strength that Cincinnati had, but we weren't going to back down, and that's what Buddy was proving. 'I'm half your size, but tell you what, I'm not going to take it.'

"And the fight had kind of dispersed before the bull pen got there. It was real short, just a couple guys beating on Rose, and it was broken up.

"When the bull pen finally got there, it started again, because they realized it was about to be stopped and they wanted to get their swings in. Pedro Borbon blindsided Bob Apodaca. And it was broken up, and all the caps were lying on the ground upside down, and if you turn them upside down they all look alike because they come from the same company, and so you can't tell if it's a Cincinnati cap or a Mets cap. Borbon picked up Apodaca's cap and put it on, and one of his teammates said, 'Hey, that's a Mets cap,' and he took it off and looked at it, and he took a bite out of the bill! You have to have a pretty good set of teeth to take a chunk out of the bill of a cap!

"And after that, I became even more intense. If I'm pitching, there is less chance of them scoring than before. After all, I was the one who started it."

★ ★ ★

Rose gained his measure of revenge the next game when he homered off Harry Parker to beat New York 2–1.

Jerry Koosman: "I don't know of one guy in the National League who didn't want Pete Rose on his team."

The series was now tied at two games apiece. The rubber-match pitted Tom Seaver against Jack Billingham. It was one of those games where Seaver started without his good fastball.

Tom Seaver: "Jerry Grote realized that right away. He made me change my whole game. He made me change my speeds."

With the Mets leading 3–2 in the fifth and the bases loaded, Willie Mays, pinch-hitting for Ed Kranepool, hit a ball into the dirt near home plate. It bounced thirty feet in the air. Pitcher Clay Carroll had to wait until it came down, and he threw home, late. The run scored, and Mays had the last regular season hit of his career. A groundout and a single by Harrelson raised the score to 6–2, as the out-of-their-minds fans pushed toward the edge of Shea stadium for the on-the-field celebration.

By the ninth inning the mob was out of control.

Manager Berra took Seaver out with one out in the ninth and brought in McGraw. When McGraw got the final two batters to win the game 7–2 and the National League pennant, he and the other Mets had to run for their lives as the fans ripped the field to pieces.

Despite all the grumblings about the way he managed, even his worst critics had to admit that Yogi Berra's patience had been crucial in allowing the players to regroup and come back to win. Berra would go down in history as only the second manager (along with Joe McCarthy) to win pennants in both leagues. Four months earlier, Yogi almost had been fired.

After beating the Reds, the Mets flew to Oakland to face the American League champions. Oakland had defeated the Reds in the 1972 World Series. The A's were an experienced, veteran ball club. The A's outspoken outfielder Reggie Jackson sniffed, "The Mets have no name players."

The Mets certainly had no firepower to match the A's lineup of Jackson, Bert Campaneris, Joe Rudi, Sal Bando, and Gene Tenace. The A's, moreover, had three twenty-game winners on the mound, Catfish Hunter

(21–5), Vida Blue (20–9), and Ken Holtzman (21–13), more than a match for the Mets' trio of Seaver (19–10), Koosman (14–15), and Matlack (14–16).

The Mets went into the World Series as decided underdogs.

Jerry Koosman: "Going into that series I had the same feeling as us approaching Baltimore. We were the underdogs again, mainly because of our regular season won–lost record. The playoffs had been no easy series and Oakland had their big guns."

Beating the Reds had taken a lot out of the Mets players. For them, all the pressure was getting into the World Series. Matlack started the opener in Oakland against Holtzman in a battle of left-handers.

Jerry Koosman: "Matlack was a perfectionist in the way he dressed and the way he worked out and the way he pitched. I can still picture his motion, bringing his arms up in front of him, just far enough that he could see through the vee in the bottom of his two hands, and that's the way he pitched.

"He didn't have an overpowering fastball—not as hard as Seaver and myself, but he was still in the nineties, and he had an excellent curveball and real good control. Putting that all together, Jon was tough to hit."

Jon Matlack: "The World Series was almost anticlimatic. There was such tension and pressure in the playoffs that the series was almost matter-of-fact by comparison.

"We opened in Oakland, a late afternoon start. The sun was bad in the outfield. That Oakland ball club was a good ball club.

"Felix messed up a ground ball, I gave up too good a fastball to the pitcher, cost me a double, I gave up two unearned runs, and we got beat 2–1. I could have easily won 1–0. That day it wasn't in the cards."

In game two McGraw blew a two-run lead, and the game went into the twelfth inning when Oakland second baseman Mike Andrews made two costly errors to give the Mets four runs in a sloppy 10–7 win. In that game Willie Mays had trouble with two balls in the sun. At forty-three, Mays was the oldest position player ever to appear in a World Series. He won the game with a base hit.

With the score tied, two out and two on, Mays batted. Oakland's star reliever, Rollie Fingers, threw a fastball. Mays yelled in despair, "I can't *see*. The background is terrible."

Catcher Ray Fosse signaled for another fastball. Mays had been play-acting. Fosse threw a fastball, and Mays hit it up the middle on one bounce over Finger's head as the Mets scored the winning run.

After the split, the series moved to Shea Stadium. Game three also went extra innings, and this time the A's won it, 3–2, when Bert Campaneris drove in the winner against Harry Parker. Seaver struckout twelve batters in eight innings. Mays pinched hit once and grounded out.

Matlack won game four when Staub homered off Holtzman in the first inning, and when Koosman shut out Oakland 2–0 in game five, the Mets were sure the Series was in the bag.

For game six Yogi Berra had to decide whether to start Seaver or Stone. He picked Seaver. Some players, including McGraw, were quick to second guess. They thought Berra should have given Seaver an extra day's rest.

Tug McGraw: "Some of the guys wondered why we pitched Seaver in the sixth game and Matlack in the seventh. They felt Seaver was tired and could've been held back a day, and maybe Stone should have started the sixth game instead. He'd pitched super all season and deserved a shot. But, Yogi went with Seaver. The club stopped hitting anyway."

Seaver pitched excellently, giving up only two rbi doubles to Reggie Jackson. Catfish Hunter allowed the Mets just one run, and the A's won 3–1.

In game seven Jackson, who a few years later would become known as "Mr. October," with the New York Yankees, hit a long home run to help defeat Jon Matlack and the Mets by the score of 5–3. Matlack, who didn't get through the third inning, felt he hadn't pitched badly; rather the A's had risen to the occasion.

Jon Matlack: "The way I look at it, the true Oakland team never really surfaced until the seventh game. Whether our pitching held them down or what, in the seventh game they looked like the Oakland club we had heard about all year following them in the papers.

"I gave up a home run to Bert Campaneris. I couldn't believe he could hit an outside curveball that far. He hit a fly ball to right field that proceded to carry all the way over the fence for a two-run home run.

"I hung a curveball to Reggie Jackson, which he just absolutely powdered for another two-run home run.

"We got beat 5–3, and I gave up four of the five. But really, it wasn't as if I was worn out or I made bad pitches. I made the one bad one to Reggie; the rest of it was just the A's rising to the occasion. Maybe they had seen enough of me that they anticipated the type of stuff I was going to use, where they had a better idea of what to look for. I don't know. They were a very good ball club."

During that seventh game, Koosman was warming up in the bull pen. His presence in the game wouldn't have changed the outcome, but he was pitching so well it frustrated him that Yogi never called him into the game.

Jerry Koosman: "In game seven they had me warming up in the bull pen, and I was throwing the best I had thrown all year. I was just bringing it, knee high, peas, a great curveball, everything was really working for me, and I'm telling Rube, 'Tell Yogi to bring me in. They will never get another run.'

"And that switch was never made, and I never got into that ball game. It was the third inning when Matlack got in trouble, and there were no other games after that one. And I never got into that ball game, and that perturbed me. That's the game I remember most, being in the bull pen and just so ready to come in, and that switch wasn't made."

When it was all over and done with, the player who made the biggest impression on the Mets players all series long was Reggie Jackson.

Tug McGraw: "Ninth inning, the A's had us, 5–1, and we had only three outs to go in the whole unbelievable season. Yogi called down: 'Get McGraw ready.' So I started throwing on the grass in the bull pen down the right field line.

"Reggie Jackson came out to take his position for the last time in 1973, unless we got hot and scored four big ones.

"When I was warming up, he called over and said, 'Tug, don't bother warming up, we got you now. You might've had an edge on us before, but we got you now.' Then Milner walked, Grote flied out, Hahn singled, and, with two down, Krane pinch-hit a grounder that Tenace booted behind first base. Now it was 5–2, and the Amazin' Mets were stirring around, and I was warming up faster. And I shouted over to him, 'Hey, Reggie, we're going to get you now.'

"And Reggie kind of took a breath. He didn't exactly say, 'You gotta believe' or anything like that. But he sort of conceded the point that a lot of us had started to believe, and he called over, 'You might, at that.'"

Manager Berra, two runs down, decided to pinch-hit Wayne Garrett and hold Mays back in case Garrett got on.

Tug McGraw: "But, then Garrett popped a little fly behind shortstop that Campaneris caught in his cradle and it was over. I quit throwing and headed for the dugout while all hell broke loose, and I looked around for Reggie Jackson. But by then he had disappeared in the crowd."

At the end of the Series the Mets came away with a strong respect for the Oakland players. After the finale, A's outfielder Joe Rudi came into the Mets' clubhouse to chat.

Jon Matlack: "The unsung hero of the whole Series was Rudi. He was one of the toughest hitters I ever faced and a phenomenal outfielder. You never heard too much about Rudi prior to that Series.

"When the final game was over, we were in our clubhouse, and I was sad we had lost. A lot of guys were just so glad it was over so it wasn't the morgue-like setting you'd expect. But after the game Rudi came into our clubhouse and sat down with Seaver, Koosman, myself, and Cleon Jones, and we talked about the various plays, the pitch sequences, just talking baseball. He must have spent fifteen or twenty minutes before he went back to his locker room to celebrate, which I thought was a class act."

twenty-eight

The Seaver Fiasco

During the winter of 1973 Donald Grant rewarded manager Yogi Berra with a two-year extention to his contract. But through the off-season the Met front office did nothing to bolster the team. The Mets pitchers begged the front office to get them players to beef up the offense. The Mets desperately needed more scoring.

Jerry Koosman: "When we didn't win in 1973, we needed another power hitter, especially since '73 had been Willie Mays' last year. We *needed* a power hitter. I know Tom Seaver had been propagandizing the Mets—it was said in the press—that we needed another power hitter, and they never got one, and so in '74 we were playing a lot of the guys we had brought up from Triple A. We needed someone strong in that lineup hitting with Cleon and Rusty and Milner. That was it. And they never went and got that other player for us, and that hurt. We didn't score many runs."

Whitey Herzog: "A baseball team is like an organism which is constantly changing, one cell replacing another. You hang on to the old players too long, and rot sets in. That's what happened to the Mets. We looked around, and the team we had counted on for the future wasn't there any more.

"The Mets won the pennant again in '73, with a club that was only three games over .500. They took the A's to seven games before losing the World Series, but I think they gave up too much for that one year of glory.

It was a long time before they even got close to winning again. And by then I was long gone, trying to beat their brains out."

When Herzog left to manage the Texas Rangers in 1973, the Mets players were acutely aware that over the years there had been a constant front-office brain drain. In 1974 the exodus continued when Bob Scheffing departed as general manager. Scheffing had taken the job as a favor to Donald Grant, and after five years wanted to be back home in Arizona.

Replacing Scheffing was Joe McDonald, the Mets' farm director. McDonald had been raised in Brooklyn, where his father had been an usher at Ebbets Field. He was hired in 1962 to be the statistician for the Mets' broadcasters. The next year he became secretary to Whitey Herzog, who ran the farm system. Many wondered whether McDonald had enough experience to take the GM job.

At the time the players didn't focus on the hiring of McDonald. Rather, they rued the loss of Herzog. They also wondered what would happen to their team.

Jerry Koosman: "When they lost Whitey and Red Murff, [they lost] two huge people in their minor league system. You talk about a loss. That was unbelievable.

"Whitey had the respect that was incomparable to anyone. Him and Hodges were the two most respected people in the organization. But Red and Whitey had a falling out with Mr. Grant. They didn't have a strong front office, and somebody had to make some calls, and Don Grant didn't have the baseball education to make them, and he made some bad ones. If you let the baseball people go. . . .

"The people we had there had been through the grind: Bing Devine, Hodges, Rube Walker, Joe Pignatano, Eddie Yost, Whitey Herzog. These guys were veterans of the big leagues, and they got replaced by people like Joe McDonald, who started out as a statistician with the Mets. So you can't have too many of those guys making decisions. We didn't have the on-the-field experience making those decisions."

In 1974 the Mets sank to fifth with a record of 71–91. The team hit .235. John Milner and Rusty Staub supplied most of the power. Jerry Koosman was the top winner with a 15–4 record, but Tom Seaver finished only at

11–11. Only a stellar year by pitcher Jon Matlack saved the team from falling further.

Jon Matlack: "Seventy-four was probably the best year I ever had. Statistics would bear that out even though my 13–15 record wouldn't. I had a 2.41 earned run average and led the league in shutouts with 7. There were only three games in which I allowed more than three runs. One statistician took ten pitching categories, and when he compared all the pitchers in baseball, he said that if I had played for Cincinnati or Oakland, my record would have been 33–3.

"It was a frustrating year. There were a lot of games where you went out and pitched your tail off and got beat 1–0 or 2–1. It was just the way things were going. We were just coming up short."

At the end of the '74 season it was the Mets turn to represent Major League Baseball and participate in a three-week goodwill trip to Japan. Several of the regulars, Harrelson, Grote, Jones, and McGraw, refused to make the trip. One of those who did go was Koosman, who enjoyed seeing Japan although he desperately wanted to go home and get some rest.

Jerry Koosman: "The season was long and hard, with not a lot of success, and now we were supposed to go to Japan when all we wanted to do was go home and relax. Some of the guys didn't go, but I figured we had to go and it was an opportunity to see Japan. I had never been there, and so I figured, let's make the most of it, and most of us took our wives along for the first two weeks, then they flew home and we finished up.

"It was not a lot of fun, though we had many moments of joy. But overall it wasn't. It was great going into a country and seeing the culture, but if you were a tall guy, you were always bumping your head in places that normally you wouldn't, you were riding buses with little seats, everything seemed crowded all the time, and after games we were served vegetables and fruit, which was rare for us, and we couldn't speak the language.

"I remember four or five of us went to a movie and saw it dubbed in English, and after the movie we were hungry. We went to a restaurant in a hotel, and I ordered a cheeseburger with lettuce and mayonaise, and this took forever, and when the waiter brought out the order my plate had four saltine crackers on a leaf of lettuce. That's what the waiter understood from me. Everyone burst out laughing.

"But we did have fun. It was a great experience, even though it seemed like it was a long, long time."

In December 1974, new general manager Joe McDonald dealt away one of the spiritual leaders of the team, Tug McGraw, who had had arm trouble that year and saved only three games.

When McDonald called McGraw to tell him about it, they cried. When the Mets fans heard about the next day, they wept even more.

McDonald traded Mr. "Ya Gotta Believe" to the Phillies along with Don Hahn and Dave Schneck for outfielder Del Unser, pitcher Mac Scarce, and catcher John Stearns. Unser would play a season and a half with the Mets and Stearns would play ten seasons with the Mets, only three as a regular. McGraw, after getting proper treatment for his injuries, would become the spiritual leader of a Phillies team he would lead to division championships in 1976, 1977, and 1978, and in 1980 he would help bring a World Championship to the City of Brotherly Love. In other words, losing the charismatic McGraw hurt the Mets badly.

Jerry Koosman: "Tug had a bump on his back between the backbone and the top of the shoulder blade on his left side, and the Mets were concerned about that because it was bothering him. I remember looking at it in the trainer's room. I think that's the reason they traded him: he was an injured product, and they figured they should get something for him while they could.

"And when he got to Philadelphia, they took the cyst out, and he was fine."

That same winter the Mets finally made a bold move to try and bolster the team's sagging offense. Bob Scheffing, having retired, was playing golf in Arizona when he heard that Giants' owner Horace Stoneham was once again strapped for cash. Scheffing told the Mets who offered to buy power-hitting outfielder Dave Kingman for $150,000. Grant authorized the deal.

During spring training of 1975 Kingman hit eight homers and hit .310. The rest of the Mets team hit six home runs.

For some of the Mets players Kingman was something of an enigma.

Jon Matlack: "He was different. He would walk to the beat of a different drummer. He was difficult to get close to. I never could. Never did. Our

Dave Kingman

relationship was one of necessity, very congenial and all that good stuff, but except for a couple rare instances, he was one of the few who had that kind of relationship. I really don't know a lot about the real Dave Kingman, cause I don't think we saw the real Dave Kingman in the clubhouse or on the field."

Jerry Koosman: "Dave was a moody player. He loved to hit. He was strong. Jeez, he could hit home runs to left field with one hand. He could pull the outside pitch one handed.

"But unfortunately the guy couldn't hit an off-speed pitch. The only thing he could hit was a fastball. If you pitched to him, you could get him out."

The Mets started the 1975 season 1–5 and quickly slid into the cellar. During one of those early games manager Yogi Berra took Tom Seaver out of the game after only six innings, angering his pitching star. Seaver criticized Berra for his quick hook to reporters after the game.

Jerry Koosman: "When you have your star player criticizing your manager, what are you going to do, get rid of the star player or get rid of the manager? So, yeah, that was probably the start of the end for Yogi."

By mid-July of 1975 the Mets were ten games out of first. Some of the players were grumbling about the lack of discipline on the team and about Yogi's mediocre game strategy. Cleon Jones, benched in favor of Dave Kingman, was one player particularly angered by the manager's moves.

On July 18, 1975, Berra asked Jones to go out to left field as a defensive replacement for Kingman. Sulking because he wasn't starting, Jones refused to go. An angry Berra ordered him into the clubhouse.

Yogi insisted that Jones apologize to the team for his insubordination, but players were shaking their heads, because for years Yogi had brought no discipline to the team whatsoever, and now all of a sudden he was coming down with all his weight on Jones.

Jerry Koosman: "Yogi was making moves that didn't set well with the team. They didn't seem to be the proper moves, though the players probably didn't have all the information Yogi had. Right or wrong, Yogi had a reason for what he was doing, but the players didn't agree with it, so there was some dissension toward the manager. Players didn't always know their right place.

"And with Cleon, Yogi was trying to make the point that Cleon had put on a couple of pounds and he thought he should be in better shape. That's what Yogi was getting at. Hodges had ruled the club with an iron hand, had weigh-ins all the time, and Yogi didn't, and consequently even though we were adults, some of us stretched the rules a little bit, and Yogi let it go by.

"Gil always said, 'We have one set of rules here,' and what he meant was that the stars weren't going to get treated any different than the twenty-fifth guy on the club. 'If the plane is leaving at two o'clock, you better be on it. We're not waiting five minutes for the star.' Those were Hodges' rules. And Yogi's famous line was, 'Next time it's gonna cost ya.' So if somebody made a mental error where Gil would fine you immediately, Yogi would say, 'Next time it's gonna cost ya,' and it became a saying. 'Next time it's gonna cost ya.' And you'd get away with it over and over."

Donald Grant called in Berra and Jones to try to resolve their differences. Yogi wanted Cleon suspended. Grant didn't. But Yogi refused to back down, and on July 26, 1975, Cleon Jones was released. It was, however, a Pyrrhic victory for the Mets manager, just over a week later, on August 6, 1975, Yogi himself was fired. He was replaced by coach Roy McMillan.

Jon Matlack: "To a certain degree you shrug your shoulders and say, 'So long.' There was definitely a certain amount of sadness. Yogi was a likeable guy. He was not a detriment by any means, but the team wasn't producing, wasn't winning, and I guess it was felt that part of that was his responsibility and they needed to make a change."

Jerry Koosman: "Roy was a great guy. He really was, a really outstanding person to play for, and I was surprised that they didn't hire him full-time."

Donald Grant hired McMillan because he felt he was another Gil Hodges, silent but forceful. But McMillan was not comfortable in the limelight, and he decided he didn't want the job full-time.

Said Jack Lang, "Grant had simply misread his personality."

In 1975 the Mets finished the season 82–80. Rusty Staub had a terrific year, hitting 19 home runs and driving in 105, and Dave Kingman, despite a .231 batting average, struck 36 home runs, some of them tape-measure blasts, and drove in 88 runs.

Tom Seaver won his third Cy Young Award, finishing the year at 22–9, with a 2.38 earned-run average. He struck over 200 batters for his eighth straight season with a league-leading 243.

Jon Matlack won 16 games by August 29, but because of poor hitting support didn't win in his last six starts. Once again, the Mets had difficulty scoring runs.

When it came time to pick a manager for 1976, the man Joe McDonald chose was a career minor leaguer by the name of Joe Frazier, who had won two pennants managing for McDonald at Memphis and Victoria in the Texas League and who later led Tidewater. Frazier was almost unknown, but McDonald reminded everyone that Dodgers Hall of Famer Walter

Alston had been equally unknown when he began managing the Brooklyn Dodgers.

Some of the Mets had played for Frazier in the minors, and the pitchers especially appreciated the way he handled them.

Jerry Koosman: "Joe Frazier worked well with me. In 1976 I went out and won 21 games for him. Because he left me in there. He didn't jerk me out for a pinch hitter like Yogi did. The Mets had a tough time scoring runs, so a lot of times if there was a runner in scoring position in a close game, Yogi felt, 'We have to get that run *now*.'

"When Frazier came in, he handed me the ball and said, 'You know what you have to do, take care of it.' He put more of the responsibility on the starters than Yogi did.

"Plus my dad died that spring, on March 30, 1976, and I felt his spirit was with me all year. My concentration was great—I was never, ever able to reach that level of concentration again—I finished 17 games that year. That was my greatest year."

The Mets managed something of a rebound in the 1975 season. With Kingman hitting 37 home runs, and Koosman, Matlack, and Seaver continuing to pitch well, the team finished in third place with a 86–76 record.

The following year was make or break. The team could have gone either way. But two important events conspired to send it spiraling downward. The first was the death of Mets owner Joan Payson in September of 1975.

Jerry Koosman: "I thought she was great. She was an owner everybody loved to have and bragged about. She was *our* owner. She hired people to run the ball club for her. Through the years you see owners who never grew up in the game make decisions. She never interfered with the ball club."

The second event was a ruling binding on major league baseball issued by arbitrator Peter Seitz on December 23, 1975. Andy Messersmith of the Dodgers and Dave McNally of the Orioles had decided to challenge baseball's long-held interpretation of the reserve clause, which bound a player to a team for perpetuity.

The two pitchers would not sign a contract, but instead played unsigned to the end of the year and then argued they were free agents the next season. Why not? There was nothing written in their contracts to bind them for additional years, only the owners' self-serving interpretation and base-ball's long-standing tradition.

The baseball owners—stupidly as it turned out—allowed the issue to go to arbitration, and picked Seitz to decide. The arbitrator set baseball on its ear when he ruled that the end of a contract was truly the end of a contract. The reserve clause was dead. Long live free agency.

As soon as Seitz made his ruling, the owners fired him. In a panic, they twice appealed to the courts, and twice lost. Marvin Miller and the Players' Association had won a landmark victory that would change baseball's landscape. The owners were now screwed—the era of "take it or leave it" salaries was over—but arrogantly and stubbornly they refused to accept their brave, new world, pretending instead that nothing had changed.

Seitz' ruling totally disrupted the negotiations for a new basic agreement between the players and owners. When no agreement was reached on February 20, 1976, the owners shut down the training camps.

Mets players began working out on their own with players from the St. Louis Cardinals at the Eckerd College ball field in south St. Petersburg. But, when the owners continued to balk at settling, Marvin Miller told everyone to stop working out and to close up the makeshift camps.

Jerry Koosman: "I felt bad that we had to do that. But we knew we had to. Marvin Miller was a great leader, and he told us we had to make a point with the owners that, 'Hey, we're not going to be working out for your good if you're not going to settle. So when you finally do agree, we're still going to need some weeks to get in shape. Not on our time, but on your time.'

"When the camps finally did reopen, a lot of players were not in shape. It takes a pitcher six weeks to get his arm in shape, two to three weeks to get his body in shape. So when you go north, you know you're only going to pitch five or six innings, and that's it, and the next time you may be stretched a little more. So the relief pitchers got a lot of work at the start of that season."

The new agreement and the start of the 1976 season did not lessen the acrimony between owners and players that was a by-product of the Seitz ruling. Beginning in 1977, according to the agreement, a small group of star players would be eligible to be offered contracts by multiple teams. The owners should have made *everyone* a free agent, but as usual Marvin Miller was smarter. Because only a handful of top players became free agents, each received huge offers that set the standard for everyone else. The era of the $100,000 superstar was over. Million-dollar contracts were in the offing.

With Mrs. Payson dead, the person who took charge of the Mets was M. Donald Grant, a creature of Charlie Comiskey/John McGraw-era reserve-clause era economics, who began a slash-and-burn campaign to keep salaries at their former levels. It was a strategy guaranteed to end in disaster for the Mets team.

Jerry Koosman: "Free agency was the best and worst thing that ever happened to baseball. At the time, I didn't realized what the Seitz decision would mean.

"But, I can remember in those days when you signed a contract, you were their property for life, and the only thing you could negotiate was your salary. After my second year in pro ball at Auburn, I wanted a $200-a-month raise, and they offered me $100, and I wrote two or three letters to Johnny Murphy, and they weren't going to budge. So I either accepted their contract or stayed home as property of the Mets.

"So when Seitz made his decision, that's what I thought about, that I wouldn't have to go through that again, that I could play the year out and I could go to work for someone else. I wasn't thinking about it in terms of making more money, but at least I knew that if the Mets didn't want to pay me, I could get a job someplace else.

"I was still making $60,000 in 1976, and after I won the 21 games, my salary went to $100,000. That was my goal, to make a hundred thousand in the big leagues. And after the '76 season I held out and signed a three-year $100,000-a-year contract. That was huge for me. I felt I was in the ballpark with other pitchers of my caliber."

Tom Seaver, winner of 182 games in ten seasons, Tom Terrific, the player who brought the Mets franchise into the Promised Land, announced in the papers that even though free agency was coming, he wanted to stay in New York. But for him to stay, he wanted a long-term contract for new-era money. Joe McDonald, Donald Grant's mouthpiece, used Seaver to test Grant's antagonistic strategy—he chose to ignore Seaver rather than have to pay him what he deserved.

Tom Seaver: "This was the way they were treating me after ten good years with the club. Why couldn't they have had the courtesy to give me a yes or a no? They were trying to intimidate me if I didn't sign.

"One day I just decided to speak to McDonald, face-to-face. You know what he said to me? He said, 'No one is beyond being traded. I have one deal I can call back on right now.' I was livid. I said, 'Pick up the fucking phone and make the trade.' But he never moved. Suddenly it began to dawn on me. Everything I had done, everything I had meant to the team could go out the window with one phone call."

According to Jack Lang, McDonald almost made that call. On March 28, 1976, McDonald met with Larue Harcourt, the agent for Dodgers pitcher Don Sutton. The Seaver-for-Sutton deal was a go if McDonald could satisfy Harcourt who told Grant that Sutton wanted to become a broadcaster once his playing career was over.

Lang spotted McDonald and Harcourt talking and wrote of what he was sure it meant in the *Long Island Press* the next day. The Mets fans were furious and outspoken. Trade Tom Seaver? Never. The public furor led McDonald to back off from the trade.

A week later Tom Seaver signed a contract for a $225,000 base-pay, plus incentives. Historically, this was a small fortune for a professional baseball player. But Tom Seaver's timing was bad. When in the spring of 1977 he saw how high the owners were going to acquire some of the free agents, his deal began to look puny.

By the end of June 1976 the Mets were 14 games behind Tug McGraw and his Phillies. In July, Joe McDonald made another terrible trade. He shipped two productive players, Del Unser and Wayne Garrett to Montreal for Pepe Mangual and Jim Dwyer.

Meanwhile, Dave Kingman, the team's lone gate attraction, was making a run at beating Hack Wilson's National League home-run record of 56. In mid-July he had 32, but then on July 19 he dove for a fly ball against Atlanta at Shea Stadium, tearing ligaments in his left thumb. He would be out for six weeks, and when he returned he would hit but five more home runs.

Without Kingman, the Mets had no drawing card other than Seaver, and attendance in 1976 dropped to the worst in team history. The team drew one million fans fewer than the year before. When the Mets had their best month in September, they finished the 1976 season with a record of 83–76, respectable, but 15 games behind the Phillies.

Despite the turmoil caused by the new economics the Mets players were optimistic about the team's future. The Mets had acquired Joe Torre from St. Louis, and Torre had hit .306 and proved his leadership on the field. With Torre and Kingman playing together in '77, the players felt, all management had to do was add a couple of free-agent hitters, and the Mets could make a run for the pennant. And since the Mets had a lucrative TV-radio contract, the team certainly had the money to do it.

The players asked Donald Grant to sign Gary Matthews, among the first group of free-agent players. Matthews was a power-hitting outfielder. But Grant's offer to Matthews was considerably lower than Ted Turner's, and Matthews signed with Atlanta. It was the beginning of Atlanta's slow but steady rise from patsy to powerhouse.

Jerry Koosman: "That was the start of collusion. The owners hated the Seitz ruling and they weren't going to fall into this free-agency thing and start paying big salaries. But, some owners did, so owners were mad at owners.

"Charlie Finley saw the beginning of the end, and he tried to get rid of all his players, and he got called on the carpet for it.

"Evidently, in the beginning the Mets were one of those teams who were not going to sign free agents."

Events were conspiring against Donald Grant, McDonald, and the Mets. Ted Turner wasn't the only owner to show his willingness to spend money to improve his ball club. During the winter of 1976, George Steinbrenner, owner of the Yankees, rocked the other baseball owners when he shelled out $2.7 million over four years so Reggie Jackson could flee Baltimore (after Oakland traded him there) and stir the pot in New York. All spring long Dave Kingman, who had hit 36 and 37 home runs in two previous seasons for the Mets, despite his injuries, demanded Reggie money. Donald Grant offered him $200,000. When Kingman kept holding out, Grant decided that Tom Seaver was behind Kingman's intransigence, as though Kingman couldn't figure out for himself that Grant's offer was insulting in comparison to the Jackson jackpot. Kingman announced that he would play out his contract and at the end of the year become a free agent.

When the 1977 season began, the Mets were racked with disharmony over salaries. Kingman was furious. Seaver was furious. The others couldn't believe Grant hadn't signed at least one more hitter.

In late April, McDonald signed infielder Lenny Randle, a free-agent infielder placed on waivers by Texas after he punched Rangers' manager Frank Lucchesi, who had been taunting him, calling him "boy." When Randle, a bright and decent man, came to the Mets, he was struck by how much discord there was among the players.

Lenny Randle: "There was a lot of turnover in personnel and management. Seaver was having contract troubles and Matlack was having contract troubles. Kingman was having contract troubles, and it was a bad time. Harrelson was debating retirement. Felix Millan was going to retire. It was still the nucleus of a decent club on paper. If everybody had been content and happy to play in New York, that team would have been okay. That was the key.

"But Grant was *not* willing to pay anyone. He still had a 1918 mentality about the game. Seaver had a 1977 approach to the game, and Koosman had a '77-and-beyond approach to the game. Because the Yankees were taking a different approach, the Mets players felt, 'Here we are in New York, we're underpaid, we've done all these great things.' So Steinbrenner was pretty much in control of New York. Chemistry was important and he built a winner."

The player Randle recalled most vividly upon meeting the other Mets players was Seaver.

Lenny Randle: "The first day in the clubhouse, Grote and Seaver came over. I was going to be playing third, and Seaver said to me, 'You're going to need a bigger cup, kid.' I had this little cup, a spongy cup. I wasn't worried about getting hit. I said, 'I have good hands.' He said, 'No.' So I knew right away we had a good rapport. He was telling me how he was going to pitch guys. He said to me, 'I'm glad we got somebody who will dive for a ball. I like your hustle and your effort that you give.'

"But Tom ended up getting traded."

That was because the Tom Seaver–Donald Grant feud continued through the spring and summer. Seaver didn't want to leave New York, but he was making $225,000 a year, and George Steinbrenner had given Reggie Jackson $2.7 million for four years. Seaver felt grossly underpaid and underappreciated, a fact that was evident to everyone—except Donald Grant.

Seaver had signed his contract before the Seitz decision came down and he wanted it adjusted. Grant called Seaver "an ingrate." The news media took sides.

In his column in the *Daily News*, Dick Young took up the Met management hardline position that a contract is a contract is a contract.

Jack Lang, who had joined the *News* that year, wrote that Seaver deserved better pay. Lang also advised Seaver to go see Lorinda de Roulet, Mrs. Payson's daughter, the inheritor of the ball club, and Grant's boss.

Newspaper reporters are not supposed to get involved in their stories, but Lang was smart enough to know how much Seaver meant to the Mets and their fans, and Lang sat down with Seaver and suggested he stay if they extend his contract. Seaver then worked out a deal with de Roulet to stay in New York calling for the pitcher to get $300,000 in 1978 and $400,000 in 1979.

On the morning of June 15, 1977, Dick Young in the *New York Daily News* wrote a scathing harangue against Seaver and his wife Nancy. His article accused Nancy Seaver of being jealous of Ruth Ryan, Nolan's wife, because Nolan was making more money than husband Tom. The charge was ludicrous. Later Young would say he got the information directly from Donald Grant.

When Seaver learned what Young had written, he called the deal off. He phoned Arthur Richman, the Mets' PR director, and told him, "Get me out of here."

Seaver wrote a message to Mrs. de Roulet that read: "Tell Joe McDonald that everything I said last night is forgotten. I want out. The attack on my family is something I just can't take."

Seaver flew home to Greenwich, skipping the Mets–Braves game. The Mets then announced they had traded Seaver to the Cincinnati Reds for Pat Zachry, Steve Henderson, Dan Norman, and Doug Flynn.

When Young endorsed the trade the next day in his column, he became the most reviled journalist in America. For years Young had been a respected, almost revered reporter. After the Seaver incident, he was marginalized and shunned until the day he died.

Jerry Koosman: "I never talked to Tom about it. Tom never brought his personal problems to the ball club. He kept it between himself and his agent and McDonald.

"I don't know if I should be talking about it, but Dick Young carried a powerful pen in New York, and there was a lot of talent in Dick Young. He wrote some great articles. I remember an article he wrote about the time I hit Ron Santo in '69. That was the retaliation for Bill Hands hitting Tommy Agee.

"After the game the reporters all asked me if I had thrown at Santo, and I said, 'No, I was throwing a pitch inside and it got away.' After repeating that two or three times, all the other writers left and wrote that.

"I was taking a shower and I was in shaving, and Dick Young came to me, and he was the only reporter in the clubhouse, and he came up to me in the washroom in back, and he said, 'Hey, really it's your job to protect your players. I'm not going to believe it was a pitch that got away.'

"I said, 'Dick, off the record, just between you and me, yeah, I drilled him. I did it on purpose.'

"The next day in the papers the headline on the back of the *Daily News* said, KOOS: I HIT SANTO. Now I was really perturbed. The next day I saw him in the clubhouse, and I said, 'Dick, what I told you was supposed to be just between me and you.' He said, 'Koos, it's my job to tell the truth.'

"And so I really respected him after that, *really* respected him, because I knew he was honest and doing his job.

"But then his son-in-law, Thornton Geary, was given the job of go-between between the Mets and the media. And I have nothing bad to say about Thornton Geary. He's a great guy. But Dick Young helped get him the job, and after that happened, Dick Young became pro-ownership. He didn't write unbiased articles any more. He went turncoat against the players and went all-pro ownership. It was so obvious in the paper. We all felt he sold himself out. I had respected him so much as a writer, and I felt it was my duty to talk to him about it, in part because of that incident where he told me, 'It's my job to print the truth.'

"I even got in a debate with him one day. I said, 'Your job is to report the truth. Talk about both sides of the issue, not just the owners' side.' He turned red in the face while I was talking to him, because he knew I was right. I said, 'You are not an objective reporter any more. [Your column is] biased. You're pro owner.'

"And he denied it up one side and down the other, but I said, 'Dick, you are not going to fool me. It's obvious. You're not fooling anyone.'

"And it was after that that he wrote that article about Seaver. He came out with an article where he singled out Tom and Nancy as being jealous of Nolan and Ruth.

"And so, yeah, he was on Grant's side. I felt the Mets had bought him off. They gave his son-in-law a job, and they got Dick Young to write for the owners.

"And getting Tom traded became Dick Young's legacy. All the great things you do in your career, and you do one thing that's not correct, and you get remembered for it. He's never been forgiven for it in New York. He was so powerful at the time.

"I know that article really ticked off Tom. That was the quick start to Tom's departure. He then demanded a trade, and he had certain clubs he could go to, and he ended up going to Cincinnati.

"It was a tough thing to see happen. I remember the day he was traded. We were in Atlanta, and there were a lot of tears shed.

"How could they trade him? Tom was one of the first, and after Tom we kept dropping like flies. McDonald was making trades that just did not make sense. We were not getting better. We were getting worse. It was like every general manager in the league was taking advantage of us.

"And the Mets got so bad, we couldn't throw anybody out. If a batter hit a tweener single, he went to second, no hesitation. And if there was another base hit the same way right at the guy, the runner on second would go home. Constantly. Our outfield arms were just sorry. So it was home to second, second to home, constantly.

"We were competing in the National League with Double A and Triple A ballplayers."

Lenny Randle: "The impact was awesome. [For] the fans, the team, and media-wise, it was tremendous. I had no idea a player could have that much impact on a city, since Joe Namath, I guess. And management was going to be the butt of the whole thing. It was a bad move."

Jerry Koosman: "We lost somebody who shouldn't have been traded, and we were in mourning. He was somebody who was really important to us. It was as though we had lost our leader, our spokesman. You might say

Buddy Harrelson

for the first time we were just floundering. As far as running the infield, Buddy was the on-field leader, but even Buddy couldn't step up and fill Tom's shoes. And all of a sudden we were playing with guys we hadn't played with before, and you have to play a long time with people to know what they are going to do in certain situations, and we had to relearn each other again.

"I remember the first time Tom came back to New York with the Reds, we were matched up, and here we are, a Triple A ball club, facing the Big Red Machine, and he beat me 5–1, and the next time I beat him 4–2.

"It was fun to see him even though he was in a Reds uniform. It was really hard to see him walk from the mound to their dugout. Tom told me after getting our three guys out in the first inning, his first inkling was to walk toward our dugout."

Jon Matlack: "It was Dick Young. He had M. Donald Grant's ear, and that was it. This is my opinion, pure and simple. I don't know why the Mets would trade him. I don't think anybody could give me any reasons that would explain what happened in '77 but nevertheless did happen.

"Tommy went through a whole lot of hell, and to me much of it unwarranted. He couldn't get things worked out with the Mets, and all kinds of dirty stuff was being brought out in the press. And subsequently he was traded, and that was it. It was ridiculous, utterly ridiculous."

twenty-nine

Into the Abyss

The same day that Donald Grant solved his Tom Seaver problem he also resolved his Dave Kingman problem—trading the moody slugger to the San Diego Padres for infielder Bobby Valentine and pitcher Paul Siebert. He also shipped Mike Phillips, a utility infielder, to the St. Louis Cardinals for infielder/outfielder Joel Youngblood. The New York press called it the "Midnight Massacre."

As a result, Mets fans lost not only the best pitcher in franchise history, but their one offensive draw as well.

In 1977 Dave Kingman tied a record: he played on four different teams that year, going from the Mets to the San Diego Padres to the California Angels to the New York Yankees in one season. Even George Steinbrenner couldn't sign him.

Jerry Koosman recalls Kingman's struggles that year.

Jerry Koosman: "When the Mets saw they were getting him out on pitches away and on off-speed pitches, they wanted him to start hitting the ball to all fields. He started concentrating on that, but it was an impossible challenge for him.

"He was traded to San Diego, and soon afterward we went there to play, and they were taking batting practice, and some of us were teasing Dave—we called him 'Dave-O.' We said, Dave-O, can you hit the ball to right field yet?' 'Cause the Mets had tried to make him do that, and he couldn't. And so we said, 'If you could hit the ball to right field, you wouldn't have been traded.' We started to rub it in a little bit. Our strategy was to try to get him to hit the ball to right field.

"So in batting practice he was trying to hit the ball to right field. And in the game he was going to prove to us he could do it, and four times he made out trying to hit to right, so mentally we won the game on him, because we didn't want him to pull the ball. We knew he could hit it out of the ballpark if he pulled it."

Lenny Randle remembers how difficult it was for the players who came from Cincinnati in exchange for Seaver to hold up under the pressure of playing in New York. They were not, Randle recalls, the only ones.

Lenny Randle: "I became good friends with Joel Youngblood, Steve Henderson, and Pat Zachry. They had no idea of the impact of playing in New York. Until you come and play in New York, you don't know what the impact is. It takes a certain player to be able to play in New York. Some guys just couldn't handle it. *Period*. A bunch of them.

"It was, 'God, these people really expect a lot.' On and off the field, just being out there, the comments, the insults. 'Yea. Boo.' You heard a lot just going to get your car. Youngblood did what he could as an outfielder and a utility player. Lee Mazzilli went through a lot of stuff, too. He was the Broadway Joe of the Mets, the Italian Stallion. Pat Zachry was very much affected, because he's a very sensitive guy. I think it really had a negative impact on his life after playing there. Hendu, too. There was a lot of pressure. Hendu wasn't your spokesperson for the media. He was more, 'Leave me alone and let me play. Ask Lenny. Go see Mikie.' Cause the writers would follow you around like ants.

"Grote used to come over and say, 'Leave the Goddamn guy alone. He's trying to work. He's trying to concentrate. Get out of his locker. He can't even get dressed. What do you think this is, for Christ's sake?' And they'd run. Not too many guys could do that, but Grote could.

"Jerry had his way of easing tensions if the media was too much. Guys respected that.

"Kingman didn't talk. The media wanted him to say more, do more, and someone rubbed him the wrong way for him to just close and close and close. He wanted to hit, show up, do the best I can, have a rapport with the players. The media wanted him to be like Mazzili or Joe Namath, and he wasn't. Dave wasn't outspoken or controversial. He'd hit you 40 home runs, but 'leave me alone.' [It] wasn't his style to talk, and that hurt him. That's why some guys can't play in New York. Dave was one of them."

Pat Zachry was the one pitcher from Cincinnati in the Tom Seaver trade. In 1976 he compiled a 14–7 record with the Reds and had a 2.74 era. He was named co–Rookie of the Year (with Houston catcher Butch Metzger). Zachry had also won games in the playoffs and the World Series that year, and he looked forward to a long career pitching for the Big Red Machine. But the monetary panic gripping the baseball owners also struck in Cincinnati, where general manager Dick Wagner would subsequently dismantle the Big Red Machine.

Before the dismantling, though, he traded for Tom Seaver. The pitcher the Mets wanted was the big Texan, Pat Zachry. Great things were expected of him when he came to New York. But, Zachry discovered that no matter how well he did, he couldn't take Seaver's place. He was a good pitcher, but a Tom Seaver only comes along once in a generation.

Even though Zachry put tremendous pressure on himself to perform, he didn't pitch badly. Zachry was 7–6 as a Met in 1977 and won 10 games in 1978 and made the All Star team. Then in anger he kicked the steps of the dugout, broke his foot, and he was never the same pitcher again.

Pat Zachry: "I was twenty-four years old going to the World Series, and then going to Hawaii for the Super Teams competition, and all of a sudden there you are, not even twenty-five fully, and you get traded from the penthouse to the outhouse. You go from first to last.

"I was Rookie of the Year in the National League in 1976. We beat the Phillies in the playoffs and won the World Series.

"Against the Phillies I was scared to death. I had an 0–2 pitch on Greg Luzinski in the fifth inning, and I tried to come up and in, and I didn't get it there, got it out over the middle of the plate, and he almost hit it out of Veteran's Stadium. He hit it into the upper deck. In fact, if you see those chairs with the bull's eyes on them, I have three of them up there, one in right and two in left. One from Schmidt, one from Luzinski, one from Jay Johnstone.

"Then we came back and scored six runs in the top half of the sixth and seventh, and I was spitting that hook. And I got a win out of that, and we played the Yankees in New York, and I pitched the third game there, and won. That Reds team won seven straight playoff and World Series games.

A good ball club. Beat the Yankees in four straight. It didn't matter who the Yankees put out there. Everyone on our club had that same feeling— could have been guys in steel helmets carrying five-foot-long swords, we would have kicked their ass. It was something that seemed destined to be, that that ball club was going to beat the crap out of anyone on that field.

"We went to Hawaii in January with the Super Teams, and that was fun. I met my wife my rookie year. I was twenty-four years old and I was on top of the world. I was looking forward to staying in Cincinnati for a while and I got traded to New York on June 15, 1977. The Reds had a chance to get Tom Seaver and they took it.

"When I got traded I was 3–7. I was the winningest pitcher on the Reds staff in '77. That's how bad we were. They were screwing around with Pete Rose's contract, and Don Gullett had left as a free agent because they wouldn't give him any money.

"All of a sudden they decided, 'After winning two back-to-back World Series, we're not going to pay you guys.' Why wouldn't they pay the people? Here was Don Gullett who was going out there hurt. Some of the time he wasn't able to pitch, but when the guy was healthy he went out and played, and a lot of times he wasn't always a hundred percent, and he was still a seventeen-game winner. He was a good pitcher, a good athlete, and never said anything. It was strictly money. They didn't want to pay him.

"They ran an ad in the Cincinnati papers explaining why they couldn't pay Pete Rose. The guys saw that and thought, 'Hey, look what this guy is doing. When it comes my time to get a contract, what are they going to do to me?' Everybody did a lot of soul searching. On the other hand, they took care of Johnny Bench like he was the mayor. It was strange. They broke the whole team up. They traded Rawley Eastwick, traded Mc-Enaney, traded Santo Alcala. Rose went to the Phillies.

"With the Reds it was fun. The Mets were fun, but we didn't win very many ball games, which was the bottom line. That was all we really cared about.

"My managers in New York were Joe Torre and then George Bamberger. Some of the things Joe did I didn't agree with. But he was good to me. He left me alone and said, 'Here, all you have to do is pitch, kid.'

"When I first got to New York, they were trying to cut back on everything. They would have put us on a wooden airplane with a rubber band for a propeller if they could have. Mrs. Payson had died. Her daughter, Mrs. deRoulet, was the owner. One of the nicest ladies I ever met. A lot of charm, elegance, and in her own way had a lot of personality, but it made as much business sense for her to be around that ball club as it would have for me to have been moving in her circles wearing earrings at one of her parties or in a tux with brown shoes.

"When she was on the team flight, boy, she'd hear all kinds of things. We'd do it on purpose. We'd talk about how horseshit the meals were. Every meal. Every meal now, we were getting fillets that weren't always cooked, sometimes were cold in the center. Every time they put us on a flight—and when you're on a two-week road trip, you're on a lot of flights—they's send us fillets with a twice-baked potato, green beans, and cake. This was airline food. We were on Allegheny Airlines—we called it Agony Airlines—now it's U.S. Air. The stewardesses were nice and tried to take care of us, but it was one of those poor periods in life when the Mets didn't try to splurge very often. But we weren't walking and we weren't taking a bus.

"Speaking of which, I remember a day in St. Louis when it was 136 degrees on the AstroTurf. Mark Bomback went eight-and-a-third innings. Then we come out, get on a nice city bus. It was air-conditioned when it had all the windows opened. The diesel fumes came in. We went to the airport. We had a charter flight. The Allegheny gate was locked. We sat there for twenty or thirty minutes waiting for someone to come and unlock the damn thing. We're all in suits and ties. We got on the airplane and had to wait another half-hour for them to get it ready. And by the time we started back to New York, everybody had icicles hanging all over them from all the sweat drying on them from the air-conditioning of the airplane. You could have hung meat in that thing.

"It was one of those crazy days.

"I feel terrible talking about Dick Young because he's dead now—but better him than me. Better him than *anybody* I can think of. He was not my favorite person, and he only got on me a couple of times. I didn't like the way the guy went about his business. Most of the time the stuff he was quoting he could not have gotten from anybody in our clubhouse because nobody talked to him. Especially after he went to so much trouble to stress that he was not the same as the ballplayer when he switched jobs for more money. He was *above* that. And he never came in there. Somebody was giving it to him. One of the people we thought of was his son-in-law, who was in the Mets front office.

"That spring I was talking contract with Joe McDonald on the phone, and I could hear someone else breathing on the phone. Joe had called, and I said, 'Hi, Joe. Hi, M. Donald.' I could hear him. I got no response. When it was all said and done, we were debating the difference of five grand.

"I said, 'Mr. Grant, what is this? We're talking five grand.' He said, 'Hi, Pat.' It was no big secret he was there. He was just waiting for the right time. So we settled that.

"In 1978 I was 10–3 at the break and made the All Star team. I was pitching real good. And a couple games later I got mad when I was taken out of a game against Cincinnati. That was the team that traded me, and I always tried to do a little extra against them—everybody thought I was mad because I gave up a hit that let Pete tie the [consecutive game hit] record, but that wasn't the case. I gave up the hit to Pete, then walked Joe Morgan, and George Foster hit one of those dying quails over Frank Tavaras' head, and when I came out of the game I was pissed off about not doing well against my old teammates, and I walked over and kicked a helmet, and I missed it, a spike caught on the wooden step, and I busted the mehickular bone in my foot. I was out the rest of the year.

"When I kicked the step and broke my foot after a game, they wanted to take twenty grand from me.

"And the next year I came up with an elbow problem. When I went down to instructional ball and tried to throw after I got the cast off, my arm was fine, but I tried to run, and I did too much the first day, and I really came close to exploding my achilles tendon. I could hardly walk for about a week. And it got to where it was okay, and maybe I changed my motion unconsciously, and for whatever reasons I came up with elbow problems the next year with the ulnar nerve and had to have surgery. And after that I was fine. I never had any problems the last five years I played. Just getting to play was the problem.

"When you get traded there is always so much hope and promise. I was the only pitcher in the Seaver deal. And I was not able to reach that potential everybody tagged me with. That Met ball club was bad.

"I'm sure everybody who was there at that time and who have since gone to different organizations, like Hubie Brooks, Neil Allen, Jeff Reardon, Stevie Henderson, Matlack, they had a degree of success in New York, a pretty good degree of success. Myself, Joel Youngblood, some of us, we didn't. I always felt there was unfinished business there, maybe I didn't do enough.

"I don't like to back to Shea Stadium for that one reason. I just don't feel comfortable going back to that stadium. Hopefully, the people's hearts have softened a bit.

"I had a chance to go free agent, and I chose to sign and stay there. I felt that up 'til then, I had been part of the problem, and I wanted to be a part of the solution. But, they didn't feel that way, and [in 1983] the Dodgers wanted me, so good. But it turned out the Dodgers didn't want me either." [Two years later he was traded to Philadelphia for Al Oliver.]

When Houston native Steve Henderson arrived in New York as part of that Seaver deal, he was totally out of his element. Hendu, as his friends called him, had been the big star in the American League when he learned he had been traded to the Mets. Hendu assumed he would be going to Tidewater, the Mets' Triple A team. But he quickly found that the trade was his ticket to the major leagues. On the plane ride to New York, a frightened Steve Henderson resorted to prayer.

Steve Henderson: "In 1977 I went to Indianapolis, Triple A, and I didn't start the season because in spring training I hurt my knee. But once I got well, I got hot. I was Player of the Month. They had been talking about a trade, Zachry, Flynn, and Norman—another minor leaguer going to the Mets, but they wouldn't say who, for Tom Seaver.

"When I went to spring training in '77 I knew I wasn't going to make that Reds club, because they had Cesar Geronimo, Ken Griffey, and George Foster, but I was the top prospect at the time. Sparky Anderson one time said, 'I don't care if the kid hits .400, he's not going to make this ball club. He needs to go down and play.' When he said it, I didn't like the way he said it.

"He cut me on the first round. And when he cut me, I was leading the Reds in everything. Home runs, rbis, batting average.

"I didn't say anything, went down, got ready, did everything I needed to do at Indianapolis, so they kept talking about this trade. Cincinnati was playing, and we were playing the Omaha Royals. We played them in a doubleheader, and after the second game was over with, I was in the shower, and the guys had the radio on, and they said, 'Hendu, you're gone.' I said, 'What are you talking about?' They said, 'You and Dan Norman are gone.' 'What do you mean? I got traded?' 'Yeah, man, for Tom Seaver.'

"I had been with these same guys all these years. Same guys. They became like brothers to me. Now came the phone calls. I was still in the clubhouse getting ready to leave, I was thinking I was going to Triple A Tidewater and they said to me, 'We'll see you in New York.' Me and Danny. I said, 'We're driving to Tidewater, Danny.' But, everybody kept telling me, 'You're going to New York.' I said, 'What?' And so I got on the plane and went to New York, and I was excited. I was going to be on a major league team, and I hadn't even known it. I didn't sleep that night. I shot baskets all night by myself at the apartment complex.

"I remember one thing when I got on the plane to New York, I asked the Lord to just take care of me.

"I was flying over the city, and looked down, and the buildings all looked nasty. I thought, 'I'm going to play here?' Because I wasn't used to seeing big old dirty buildings like that.

"I got there, and there were cameras. 'What the hell is going on here?' I had never been in the big leagues. I had never been to New York. Houston and Dallas were the biggest cities I had ever been to.

"I walked in the clubhouse, and I was sitting at my locker, and sitting right next to me was Lenny Randle. I met Lenny, John, Koosman, Kranepool. I talked to Joe Torre. He told me, 'We're glad you're here. Relax. I want to work you in kind of slow. I'm not going to play you that much at first. You're going to be my left fielder.'

"I got in there, and the first game I pinch-hit for somebody, and it was pitiful. I was so nervous, I swung at one ball, and the ball was on the ground. I got a standing ovation when I came up to bat, and I got a standing ovation when I struck out. I thought, 'Oh, Lord, that's embarrassing.'

"After a while I started relaxing, and my first hit came off Floyd Bannister with Houston. It was a broken bat hit. And then I started to relax and everything hit the fan. I pinch-hit and we were losing, and I remember I was supposed to be a fastball hitter at the time. Don Collins, a left-hander, was pitching for Atlanta. He threw me a fastball first pitch, I took it. Next pitch he threw me a curveball, and he got it up, and I hit it up in the left field deck. I crushed it. And I'm running around the bases, and the fans are hollering. I had never played in front of a crowd like that before, and that's when everything started clicking. I started hitting the ball.

"Everything was going right, and the season was over with, I went right to Tampa, got an apartment, and the lady I met in Tampa, Pam, she and I started dating on a regular basis, and they wanted me to go to the Instructional League and work with Willie Mays on charging balls.

"That was awesome. Willie was one of the nicest people I ever met in my life. And I learned a lot from him. That was great. I remember the next year I didn't have a glove contract, and Willie had been working with McGregor, and he had a high pitch in his voice, and he told the McGregor rep, 'You get this man a contract,' and he said, 'Willie, we'll take care of him.' Willie said, 'You have to take care of him. Give him eight gloves.' What was I going to do with eight gloves? 'And they signed me for a five-year deal for eight gloves and $700 a year. I said, 'Willie, I don't need all those gloves.' He said, 'Sign it. They'll take care of you.'

"And that was Willie Mays. That was something. And during the games I didn't play, Willie and I would sit on the bench and we would discuss things, and this guy was amazing, man. It was awesome. We'd talk about how guys would charge the balls. He'd tell me pitches that guys were going to throw to a batter because he already knew from experience. He would be sitting there, and guys would be in the outfield, and he'd see guys not getting jumps on balls, and he'd say, 'Look at this guy in center field not moving.' He would tell me things like that, and it was awesome. He knew the game, and he was a very nice person. I don't care what anybody says about him, I really liked that guy."

After the departure of Seaver and Kingman, the Mets promotion department came up with a new slogan, "Come bring your kids to see our kids." The campaign featured a picture of all the new, young faces. But many of the newcomers weren't ready for prime time, and the rest of the '77 season was marked by one loss after another, as the team finished dead last, 37 games out. When on August 31 the Mets traded Jerry Grote to the Dodgers for two kids who never made it, all remnants of the 1969 Champions were gone.

Mets fans couldn't understand why their old favorites, pitchers like Matlack and Koosman, were traded away. In Matlack's case, he couldn't understand it either. In Koosman's case, as one of the last ones holding onto the bobbing flotsam of the gurgling *Titanic*, he no longer could tread water and demanded a trade.

Jon Matlack: "When Seaver was traded, a couple of us voiced our opinions to Joe Torre and Joe McDonald together about our desire to see the club do something constructive to bolster a bad situation. And if they weren't prepared to do that, then I for one—and there were a couple of other guys—preferred to play somewhere else.

"I was gone shortly after that. For me that was the lowest point in my association with the Mets. They were at rock bottom.

"A month or so before the '77 winter meetings, I had a conference call with Torre and McDonald, and after the pleasantries were out of the way, one of the first questions I was asked was, 'Do you still want to be traded?' I said, 'I never said I wanted to be traded. What I said was I wanted to see you guys do some constructive things and was asking if you intended to do something constructive over the winter to help bolster the ball club.'

"They said, 'Oh, well, we're thinking about this guy and we're looking at this guy,' mentioning a couple of free agents who were listed. It was a very strange conversation.

"When I hung up the phone and reflected on the conversation, the more I thought about it and talked to my wife, the more I realized they wanted me to say I wanted to be traded, because they intended to trade me, and that way they could say they were acquiescing to my wishes. I told her, 'Honey, we need to start reading the papers and listening to the radio because something's fixing to happen.'

"It was ironic because we had bought a house in Bedford [N.Y.], had a three-year plan to renovate it to exactly what we wanted. The day I finished painting the screened-in porch—I was in the basement cleaning the paint brushes when the call came from Hawaii.

"'This is Joe McDonald. We have good news and bad news. The good news is we acquired Willie Montanez, Tom Grieve, and Ken Henderson. The bad news is in order to get them you are now a Texas Ranger.'"

The Mets traded Jerry Koosman to Minnesota on December 8, 1978, for minor-league-nobody Jesse Orosco, who would turn out to be one of the great relief pitchers in Mets history. If the Mets hadn't traded Koosman, he would have quit and walked away. Pitching on this team wasn't fun any more.

In 1977 the Mets record dropped to 64–98. Joe Frazier was fired as manager at the end of the season, and Joe Torre was hired to replace him. In 1978 the record was 66–96. Once again, the Mets were doormats. Jerry Koosman remembers what it was like pitching on those teams.

Jerry Koosman: "It was sad, really sad. We had *no* offense, and *terrible* defense. The next year [1978] I was 3–15. And to show you how bad our ball club was, I was throwing as good as I was when I was winning.

"Joe Torre was the manager, and he was a hitters' manager, and I can remember five occasions when the score was 0–0 in the fifth, two outs and a runner on second, and I'm coming up to hit, and Torre pinch hit for me. I said, 'Joe, why?' He said, 'We don't score many runs. I have to take advantage of every run we can score.' I said, 'Let me throw a shutout. Maybe we'll score one in the ninth.' And that upset me a lot. He just would not allow me to stay in there long enough to throw a shutout. And so, it was bad. I wanted to do more for Joe as a manager. He was a good buddy of mine. I played my butt off for him.

"I had already started to plan my life after baseball. I was going into the air freight business. I had already started working extremely hard on it. And I told the Mets if I wasn't traded, I was going to retire from baseball.

"I gave them ten ball clubs I'd accept a trade to. It didn't happen, didn't happen, didn't happen, and I narrowed it down to five, and it didn't happen, and finally I just said, 'I'm narrowing it down to one, the Twins. Either trade me to the Twins or I'm out of here.'

"They traded me on December 8, 1978, to the Twins for Jesse Orosco and another player [minor league pitcher Greg Field]. My mother was visiting, and we had a bottle of champagne in the house, and we celebrated. We were so happy to be coming home.

"I hated to leave the Mets. It was just that the front office wasn't doing anything. I didn't want to waste my years while they were rebuilding. I just couldn't stomach that any more, all the mistakes we were making.

"But it was so embarrassing, I was having chest pains. And that's when I said to myself, If I want to play for a losing club, I can play for a losing club at home, which was the Twins. Because the front office of the Mets did not want to win, and I just couldn't stomach that.

"We were living on our minor league system, and it wasn't strong enough. You can add one or two players a year, but not a dozen. The front office moves caused the whole general picture to deteriorate. Players made bonehead plays and mental mistakes. The team was put out there by the front office, and it wasn't the best team we could have put out there. To do that, we had to deal from strength, and instead they decided to rebuild. When they traded Seaver, it got to be a rebuilding period, and that was the beginning of the end. And ironically, the Seaver for Zachry, Flynn, Norman, and Henderson was the *best* of the deals. They were four really good players. They really helped build the ball club. But, the process didn't continue that way. For everyone traded after that we didn't get all top-quality players.

"It was sad. Gosh, I had my heart and soul and blood in the Mets, and I wanted to do everything I could to make them succeed. We had a ball club that was rich in the front office and in scouting, and that deteriorated first. We had a lot of pride in what we had accomplished, going from a ninth-place finish in '68 to winning the World Series in '69, and then hanging on to win in '73. But our top form was so short-lived. Only five years, from '69 through '73, and now here we were, struggling.

"Where did it all go? How could it happen so fast?"

thirty

Swannie

In 1978 the crosstown New York Yankees, who had fallen fourteen games behind the Boston Red Sox in August, won the American League pennant on a playoff home run hit by Bucky Dent off pitcher Mike Torrez. It was a year of turbulence in the Bronx, a year that saw the firing of Billy Martin, the hiring of Bob Lemon, and the stellar play of one of the most exciting teams in baseball history.

It was an entirely different story over in Queens at Shea, an edifice that felt more like a morgue. Under strong-but-silent manager Joe Torre, the 1978 Mets, bland and lackluster, finished last in the Eastern Division with a 66–96 record.

The Mets' top performer was young pitcher by the name of Craig Swan, who while pitching for Arizona State set the record for most wins during a college career with 47. Appendicitis and a stress fracture to his pitching elbow inhibited his progress, but he made it to the Mets to stay in 1976. After winning 9 games in 1977, Swan surprised everyone when in 1978 he led the National League with a 2.43 earned-run average, despite only a 9–6 record.

Swan had the misfortune of having his best years during a period when the Mets were at their worst. The following season he led the staff with 14 wins but his success didn't gain much attention because Mets attendance was at rock bottom and the press had pretty much stopped paying attention to anything the Mets did.

★ ★ ★

Craig Swan: "I was born in Southern California, in Van Nuys, in 1950, and I lived there until I went off to Arizona State. The next-door neighbor got me playing in Little League at nine years old. My dad wanted me to be the quarterback he never was, so we threw a football from the time I was two until I was eleven, almost every day. It got my arm to where I could throw a baseball, because if you can make a football spiral, your timing on your body mechanics is pretty good for a pitch.

"When I was about eleven, I got my head beat in [playing football], and I said, 'Dad, I really don't want to play that,' and I was doing pretty good in baseball, so I don't think he minded.

"When I was fourteen my team won the Pony League World Championship. I pitched that last game, and I got to throw out the first ball of the fifth game of the 1965 World Series between the Dodgers and Twins. The assistant coach of the Pony League team took me around to play Instructional League ball in Southern California, and I got to play against some Rookie League and Double A players. I was a big boy at fourteen. I was six-foot-two and it was an advantage.

"In high school we vied for the CIF championships my junior year, and I was offered a full scholarship at Arizona State and at Long Beach State. My family went through turmoil my senior year—my parents were starting to go through a divorce process—and I blew up sixty pounds and had a terrible year. Recently during Halloween I said to my girlfriend, 'See these pound bags of M&Ms. I used to eat one of those a day!' I blew up pretty fast. I was drafted on the twenty-first round by the St. Louis Cardinals, but chose to go to Arizona State.

"Bobby Winkles, [the Arizona State head coach], had heard about me from the scouts after my junior year, and he still offered me the scholarship. Playing for Winkles was the best for me. He treated me hard, but he treated me well. I did a lot of running, but he would run with us, so you really couldn't complain too much.

"I was successful. I was first in career college wins. It was my claim to fame. I had a lot of real good college seasons. I won 10 my freshman year, and we won the College World Series. I won 8 my sophomore year, and then I got kicked off the team for Fall ball. He didn't think I tried hard enough. It was one of those years where you kind of lose it for a year. I wasn't going to class my sophomore year. I thought I had it made. Winkles kicked my ass in more ways than one, so I got back on track. That was Winkles. After I flunked out of school, he got me a job during the summer in Phoenix working outdoors under a tin roof busting tires off cars at a Goodyear place, sweating ten hours a day. It just about killed me. Then they had me out doing tractor tires in 120 degrees heat. I could eat anything I wanted and not gain a pound.

"Halfway through Fall ball, he let me come back on, and my junior year in the spring I won 16 games and made second-team All American.

"After my junior year Winkles took a job coaching the Angels, and I was crushed when he left. Jim Brock came in. He was fine. He knew we were seniors who had played for Winkles, and he kind of did his thing and let us do ours. No one was upset with anyone, but it was still a hard adjustment. That year I won 13 games, but we lost in the finals of the College World Series. I won a couple games, and then in the final game

Craig Swan

Jim Crawford, a big left-hander who pitched for Detroit and Houston, lost 1–0 on a passed ball.

"In June of 1972 I was drafted in the third round by the Mets. We were in a hotel in Phoenix, and the moment I put the pen to the contract, a lightning bolt struck a palm tree right out my window and blew it to smithereens. I put the pen down and said to Buck Elliott, the scout who signed me, 'I need a beer.' That scared the hell out of me.

"I had no leverage because I was so young, I couldn't sign until my senior year. So after two years of being All American, and a right-handed pitcher in the College World Series, I got $15,000. I often told my parents, 'God, you could have had me ten years later! You fools!' Oh, well.

"I got to start at Memphis in Double A ball. John Antonelli—not the Giants pitcher—was my manager. He was great, kind of a Southern man, easy going, older, had a bad stomach. He had to take Tagament all the time. Every time I threw my change up, he'd come over and say, 'Swannie, please don't throw that pitch any more. I have to take these pills.'

"Because of the College World Series I only pitched half a season, and I was 7–3, and I got to go to the Instructional League right from Memphis. Whitey Herzog got to see me throw down there. Whitey was great. I loved Whitey. He was a players' guy like Winkles. He would tell you directly what you needed to do to improve your game. He'd tell you what to do in certain situations or about the pitch itself. 'Got to be a little sharper.' Very specific mechanical things.

"Whitey took a liking to me, so I got to go to the big league camp in '73 with Seaver, Koosman, and Matlack. Those guys could throw! Seaver and I got to be friends, and Koosman was a great guy to be around. Koozie gave me more mechanical tips than anything. Seaver gave me more of pitch selection to certain hitters. And I played bridge, so I was in the bridge group with Seaver, Koozie, and Ken Boswell. Seaver was the best of the bridge players. He tried the hardest at it, but that's the way he was with everything. He seemed to know a little more about it, or at least he let on that way.

"I was in awe of Seaver for a while. He was six years older, and I was a right-handed pitcher like he was, and he was just teaching me.

"During that first spring training I was in awe of everybody, of course. I dressed for the first game, and I was seeing all these players I've read about all these years like Brock and Flood, and Bob Gibson was pitching against us at Al Lang Field. John Milner was up, and it was the first or second inning, and Gibson nailed Milner in the ribs.

"As Milner was trying to grab his breath, Gibson walked three quarters of the way to the plate and yelled out, 'Just practicing for the season.'

"And I was awestruck. I thought, My God, this is the big leagues.

"At the end of spring training I went down to Tidewater with John Antonelli, who had come up. John never got any higher because his stomach was pretty bad. He *couldn't* have gone any higher his stomach was so bad. I pitched there for two months, was really starting to get going, had thrown the ball well the last three or four games, and I had an attack of appendicitis and missed two-and-a-half months.

"I came back, and I was actually called up to the Mets in September 1973. I started one game against the Phillies. Willie Montanez hit me in the ass with a line drive in the second inning. I gave up four runs in four innings before they got me out of there. I remember M. Donald Grant saying, 'Send the fat kid back to Tidewater.'

"In '74 I made the team in the spring, broke with the team as the fifth starter, but with the rain outs I didn't get to pitch for a month-and-a-half. I pitched two or three games, and I broke my pitching elbow. When your elbow locks, the lower arm fits into a place in the upper arm. I snapped that end off when I didn't follow through properly. I kind of snapped it off. It's not a break you have after one pitch. It's a stress fracture. Runners get it in their feet.

"I was in pretty severe pain, but the doctors couldn't find anything wrong. X rays didn't reveal it because it was too small of a break. They sent me down to Tidewater.

"I pitched down there for another six to seven weeks in incredible pain thinking it was the end of my career. And then the strangest thing happened. I was taking a leak and Dr. Canton came in, and he was taking a piss next to me, and I started telling him about my symptoms, and he said, 'You know, Swannie, it sounds like your arm is broken.' I said, 'No, doc, they took X rays.' In September after the Tidewater season was over the Mets called me back up to check my arm, they x-rayed it again and this time they found the break. It had been broken the whole time.

"The cast came off in early November 1974. I decided to strengthen my arm, so I went to a strength trainer by the name of John Cole in Scottsdale. He had been at Arizona State when I was there, and he opened his own studio. I started hitting the light weights, and when I came to camp it was the strongest my body had ever been, and I went out and I won 13 games in about three quarters of a season at Tidewater in '75.

"My manager was Joe Frazier. He loved me. He used to put me in in relief on my throwing day after my start. He was great. He was fun. During a bad streak he would tell us to go out and get drunk, that he didn't want to see us in before 5 A.M. He could be a little harsh but he seemed to forgive and forget. He was fair. Joe and I both would make the Mets in '76.

"But, Joe lost something when he went up to the Mets. He was a little more careful. He lost some of his spunk. It was New York. He was from the South. That kind of overwhelmed him. It's hard for a lot of players to play in New York. Playing in New York is extremely hard. In fact, I started having stomach problems again playing in New York. I held all the stress in my stomach, and I had had stomach problems since I was nine.

"I was showing signs of promise playing with the Mets in '76, starting to get people out. I had refined it a little bit, just got better. And we had a decent team. We had Seaver, Matlack, and Koosman, and Jerry Grote was our catcher. He could be trouble if you didn't do what he said. He wanted you to throw the pitches he called. He made it very simple.

"I would shake him off now and then, and he would shake his head back at me. If a guy hit a home run, he wouldn't let me hear the end of it.

"Actually, we got along great. He was only testy on the field. Of course, if you ever drove with him, you just closed your eyes and hung on! Other than that, he was a great guy. I really enjoyed my time with him. In fact, when my wife and I drove to Texas from Scottsdale for spring training, we used to stop in Texas and stay at his house on our way to Florida.

In '76, the Mets' attendance was at a new low. I don't know why. I have no idea. That kind of stuff was not my concern. I was just trying to just stick in the big leagues. But I used to know all the fans by name.

"Dave Kingman was our hitting star, I loved Dave. We played against each other a little bit in college. He played at USC. He also played in Fairbanks one summer while I played for Anchorage. I remember we played the Midnight Sun game against each other. On the longest day, June 21, they start at midnight in Fairbanks with no lights. Fairbanks let Dave pitch. He could throw the hell out of the ball, but he was wild. Nobody on our team wanted to go up to bat.

"I enjoyed playing with Dave on the Mets. He was a toys guy, like me. I had been raised on the water, too, so we befriended each other. He did like to play. He liked his boats, liked his jet skis, and he was talking about buying a bus. He sure liked his toys.

"Ed Kranepool was on that team. Krane had been there for a while. He was a nice guy all the time. Buddy Harrelson was at shortstop. He had been there a long time and was winding down. He had about had it. He had to arc the ball over to first base. John Milner was our first baseman. We called him Hammer. You would have thought he'd have been better, but it's hard to tell. There were guys in college who I would have thought would have made the pros for sure and they didn't get out of A ball. You never know. People's lives change and whatever.

"They fired Joe [Frazier] early in '77. Joe said something to us, nothing very much, and he was gone. We were so used to people getting traded and moving. There was nothing traumatic about it. You felt bad for the guy, especially if he didn't have another job.

"Joe Torre came in [as manager] and he was just a player, but he was super. All the players loved him. I understand I'm hanging on a wall in Yankee Stadium because I pitched his first managerial win in the big leagues. He's got that lineup card framed.

"Torre handled the players well. He used what he had. There are only so many things you can do during a ball game, and it seemed he did those things.

"We didn't have much hitting in '77. Koozie was 8–20, that year was tough on him. If you looked at the batting order, it didn't seem too bad, but they all just had bad years. Steve Henderson was our best hitter. He sprayed the ball around.

"Those were my garden days. I used to go out to the bull pen during the games and tend my garden. Piggy [bull pen coach Joe Pignatano] had started it. It was a tomato patch when I took over, and then I started farming. I had all sorts of things, green beans growing up the wall, pumpkin and squash running down the runways, had all sorts of vegetables. This was what I was doing during the games. If the couple thousand fans made some noise, I'd look through the Plexiglas to see what was going on. I knew the hitters, and the day before I would keep the chart, and I got what I needed from that.

"In 1977, I was making $35,000, and I was totally ecstatic, just trying to make my four years so I could get a pension. Some of the other guys were really unhappy about their salaries, but I didn't pay much attention to it.

"I did know Tom [Seaver] was unhappy. He never really talked to me about it, so I didn't know how much, but I would see him in the clubhouse, and you could see the stress on his face. In '77 the Mets and Tom carried on a feud. I remember Tom being really upset with Dick Young. It seemed that Dick Young took Grant's side and just pummeled Tom in the press.

"But in '77 they traded Tom away and Dave, and it was shock. Seaver seemed like he was going to be a Met until he died. That's what it felt like. That was really a shocker. He was really upset. I remember he did a lot of crying. He was *very* upset.

"As for Kingman, he had his toys—his boat and jet skis. He went home to Frisco and played with them. He was probably just as happy there.

"And then Grant traded Grote. These were the best players we had for years.

"Joe McDonald was the general manager who made the deals, but it was really Grant. All GMs—there is no GM that does anything without the owner's permission—just do what they're told. They have no power.

"I remember Grant was pretty scary then. It seemed he could do anything he wanted. And free-agent spending was not going to be what Grant was going to do with the Payson money. So the team really hit the skids there in the late 70s because of it, and it took a *long* time to recover.

"It really affected my morale. Absolutely. I didn't feel that the team was going to be a winning team, so it kind of turned me in on myself. For a couple of years I really lost that team concept that I so enjoyed about baseball. It got more like, Okay, just do what you can do. And I pitched some good games in '78 and '79.

"In '78 I only won 9 games, but I had the best era in the National League. I was 1–5 in the first half with a 2.50 era. I was hoping to get losses the first half of the season, because I was still leading the league in earned-run average, but to make the papers so my relatives could see, you had to have a certain number of decisions, so I was willing to take the losses just to be able to make the 'era leaders,' which they published all over the country.

"If I gave up one run in eight innings and got the loss, I didn't care. I figured, That will get me in the papers, and the relatives can follow me. It was the only way I was going to get in the national papers every week.

"We didn't score. I was begging Joe to let me hit in front of Doug Flynn. I wanted to hit eighth. Doug could hit ninth. Joe wouldn't do it. I could hit harder, but he was our second baseman, and it would have been a real slap in the face.

"I did pitch some pretty good games. I remember a night game we played at Dodger Stadium. We had been renting a house on Long Island, and I had a garden and my corn had grown up to four, five feet, and it was getting ready to pop. We were out in LA, and that morning my wife called to say there had been a thunderstorm and she said, 'The corn is gone. It's flat as a . . . ' Before that Dodger game I was so irritated about the corn, I was in a zen place, and I took it out on the Dodgers. They had Garvey, Cey, Russell, and Lopes, and I mowed those guys down. They didn't come close to me. Jam city all night. I pitched a three-hit shutout.

"In another game where I struck out 13 Phillies, it was 1–0 in the 9th, and I got the first two outs and then Bob Boone cued one out at the end of the bat, and it just made it over Willie Montanez' head. Jose Cardinal came up next, and on the next pitch he hit a two-run dinger, so we lost 2–1. That was tough. But, I had a lot of good games. I'd give up a run or two over seven innings and then I was always lifted for a pinch hitter because we were down by one or two. There were a lot of those.

"In '78 Koosman was 3–15 with a 3.75. That was unbelievable. We never scored. Koozie and I used to throw good game after good game and get nothing out of it. He used to get the losses. Pat Zachry was the pitcher who took Tom Seaver's spot. Pat was pretty mellow, though I remember a few times when he got so upset he would hit or kick something, and one time he broke his foot. It was embarrassing for Zack.

"In November 1978 Mrs. de Roulet got rid of Donald Grant. I thought possibly it was going to get us into the free-agent market, but they didn't.

"Those were funny years. They were my best years, but it was weird the way the ownership was. The de Roulet girls had this mule Met-Al and they would have it on the field sometimes, and poor Pete, the grounds crew guy, had to take care of it. That was very strange. It was like the circus.

"They would parade the mule around the field when we weren't out there.

"The de Roulet daughters were kind of fun. They were in their twenties, and they were dating some of the players. Mrs. de Roulet's daughters had the pick of the litter. If you own the stable, you should be able to ride the horses. The boys who did that got rewarded.

"In '79, we lost 99 games. Our star was Lee Mazzilli. *Rocky* was playing then and Maz had that kind of appeal. The girls loved him. He was a nice, shy kid. He was wonderful.

"Maz was fast and he had a couple of good years.

"We had Joel Youngblood. Blood, we called him. He was a very good friend. He was definitely a character. He was from Houston, a hunter, a big-time hunter.

"I hunted with him one time. I had never been hunting, and we went out to shoot a deer. We were sitting on top of this hill, back up in this valley, freezing our asses off. Blood sees the deer and he starts pointing to me. He's motioning for me to swing around, and right before I started to swing my gun around to take a shot, he stood up and pumped three shots into the deer, with the shotgun shells falling on my head!

"I said, 'Blood, this is my only time. What are you doing?' He said, 'I didn't think you could make the turn!'

"We were walking out of this place in South Salem, and he spied some turkeys. He said, 'Swannie, go behind the bush over there, work your way over, and flush those turkeys to me.' He was treating me like I was his dog. I said, 'I'm not flushing any turkeys to you. Go flush your own turkeys.'

"And I never hunted with him again.

"Our catcher during those years was John Stearns. Stearns and I had a real strange relationship. Our personalities clashed. We fought a lot off the field. He just rubbed me the wrong way, and I would call him names. That was our relationship. He used to strut around like a rooster, like he was a bad dude. I'd get on him. 'Who's that bad dude?'

"But on the field John and I were great.

"I won 14 games in 1979. No one else won more than 6. They couldn't with that team. I had actually pitched better in '78 when I only won 9. For some reason '79 was a payback year from the year before. I had a 3.30 era in '79. I just got a few more runs when I pitched that year. I just got lucky with the 14, at least compared to the year before, when I got no runs.

"We didn't have a bad staff. We had Dock Ellis, Pete Falcone, Neil Allen, Dale Murray. But we didn't win because we didn't score.

"I thought I would end up as a free agent. I didn't think they wanted to sign me, even though I was throwing well. In fact, I heard that Joe Mac almost traded me to the Angels for Willie Aikens and Dicky Thon.

"In November of 1979, Mrs. de Roulet announced she was selling the team. Thank God. And when Doubleday and Wilpon came in, everything changed."

thirty-one

Doubleday and Wilpon Rebuild

On November 8, 1978, Lorinda de Roulet, the daughter of the late Joan Payson, announced that she was kicking Donald Grant upstairs and taking over. Her father, Charles Payson, had inherited the majority of her stock, and heartsick over the sudden decline in the team, he blamed Grant, whom he had resented for years for having too much influence over his wife.

"The time has come, more or less," said Mrs. de Roulet in her understated way. At a press conference she announced grandly that the Mets were prepared to improve their lot by signing free-agent Pete Rose to a lucrative multiyear contract. Rose, she said, was just the gate attraction the team needed.

It wasn't a bad idea, but she obviously didn't know Rose. Pete had received offers from a half dozen teams, including a whopper from Ted Turner and the Atlanta Braves, but Rose, who cared a great deal about money, cared more about winning. His intention was to go to the team that had the best shot at a pennant. The Mets weren't even a consideration.

After Rose turned down Mrs. de Roulet and Turner, he signed with Philadelphia, National League Eastern Division champs in 1976, 1977, and 1978. Rose correctly intuited that he and his leadership was all the Phillies needed to go all the way, and in 1980 he led the Phils to the World Championship. Having lost Rose, the Mets of 1979 were fated to look and play like the Mets of 1978.

At spring training in 1979, Charles Payson announced that the team was not for sale. But owning a team and running it well are two different animals, and Payson's bank account was hemorraging badly. He was pinching pennies so tightly that the Mets front office barely had the operating funds to open the gates of the stadium.

At one executive meeting Payson was looking for ways to save money. Granddaughter Beebe piped up, "Couldn't we take the used balls and wash them?" She wasn't joking. The joke instead was on general manager Joe McDonald, whose hands were tied and whose mouth was taped shut to prevent him from calling other general managers and making deals. When he failed to make free-agent pitcher Nelson Briles an offer, the rest of the pitching staff realized just how up the creek the Mets were. The staff was so thin that manager Joe Torre was forced to add three rookies, Mike Scott, Jesse Orosco, and Neil Allen to the roster.

The Mets were in last place before the end of April. The team lacked skill and interest. By then Mrs. de Roulet needed a $1 million loan from her father to pay the bills. At that point Charles Payson decided it was time to get out. By year's end the Mets record fell to 63–99, more typical of the Polo Grounds days, and attendance sank to 788,905, far worse than it had been even back then. As her final act, Mrs. de Roulet signed Joe Torre to manage for another year.

On November 8, 1979, Mrs. de Roulet announced that the Mets were for sale. More than twenty different groups were bandied about in the newspapers. The winning group, led by Nelson Doubleday, the owner of Doubleday publishers, and Fred Wilpon of Sterling Equities, a real estate corporation, bought the team for a record $21.3 million.

Fred Wilpon, who began his quest to buy the New York Mets in 1978, soon after Joan Payson died, grew up in Bensonhurst, Brooklyn, the son of a funeral-home operator on Coney Island Avenue. At Lafayette High School, Wilpon pitched on the baseball team, which wasn't unusual in itself, except that his first baseman was a kid by the name of Sandy Koufax, whose greatest talent seemed to burst forth on the basketball court. The Koufax kid threw 100 miles an hour then, but he never was able to throw three strikes to any one batter, so Wilpon did a lot of the pitching for Lafayette.

Wilpon went to the University of Michigan on a baseball scholarship, but during his sophmore year, he tore up his arm and was forced to turn in another direction to find his life's work. Business was what interested him most. After taking real estate courses at night, he began with a real estate investment firm. After a year he and his brother-in-law began making acquisitions, often enlisting other partners. He began Sterling Equities in

1971, and by the end of the decade the company had grown into a nation-wide business with holdings worth more than $200 million. He owned properties in Atlanta, Chicago, Kansas City, Houston, Jacksonville, and St. Louis, as well as in New York City.

When it was finally announced that the Mets were for sale, Wilpon contacted his friend John O. Pickett, the chairman of the board of the New York Islanders and of Nassau Sports Productions, which produced the telecasts for the Mets, Nets, Islanders, and Yankees.

Wilpon learned that Pickett, forty-seven, and Nelson Doubleday, forty-six, were attempting to buy a 40 percent share in the Mets. But when that deal fell through and they saw they would have to buy the whole thing, Pickett, who had his hands full with the Islanders, suggested to Wilpon that he should partner with Doubleday, the grandson of the founder of the publishing company that bears his name. Since Wilpon, Pickett, and Doubleday all were friends (they all were members of the board of the posh Greenvale School on Long Island), the switch was made easily. (A silent investor, City Investing Corp., bought the remaining 6.5 percent.)

Nelson Doubleday Jr. grew up in Oyster Bay, Long Island, and attended the prestigious Deerfield Academy. He enrolled at Princeton, where he wrote his senior thesis on "The Impact of the Paperbound Industry on the Publishing Industry." After serving in the Air Force, he joined Doubleday & Co. in 1958, was named vice president in 1963, and was elected president in 1978.

Having trust funds and investments worth millions of dollars made him a logical candidate to be approached by friends seeking to invest in sports franchises. His first two forays into professional sports, investments in two hockey teams, Charlie Finley's California Golden Seals and Roy Boe's New York Islanders, were disasters. After investing in 11 percent of the Islanders, the team sank into a $22 million morass of debt.

Eventually his investment paid off and Doubleday watched as his friend Pickett rebuilt the laughingstock hockey franchise into four-time Stanley Cup champions. After he discovered how profitable and how much fun owning a team could be, Doubleday allowed Pickett and Wilpon to talk him into buying the Mets. (Wilpon and City Investing Corp. bought their shares from Doubleday.)

Doubleday who described himself as a shy, private person, has rarely been heard from during his reign. Like Mrs. Payson, he has preferred to stay in the background and let Wilpon and others do the promoting and talking.

In one of his rare public statements, he discussed why he bought the Mets. Said Doubleday, "There are still a lot of National League fans in this town. If you can show them a clean stadium where they can get a beer and a hot dog and have a good time, you've got a good thing going."

Wilpon, who was made president and chief executive officer, was perfect for the job. Wilpon's specialty was buying distressed properties and resuscitated them. A full quarter of the properties he purchased had gone bankrupt. Wilpon then developed the sites and made them profitable—he had the same plan for the Mets.

Wilpon said a great deal about himself when he told a reporter in an interview, "Sports teaches you something about competition, playing within the rules, and the desire to win. Sports teaches you never giving up when it seems impossible: You can be behind and all of a sudden the momentum changes and starts to go in your direction. The same things are true in life and in business."

Clearly these were men used to getting their way and who would not be satisfied until the Mets once again won a World Series. When they took over, Mets fans everywhere wondered whether the two would put their money where their mouths were. Quickly, Doubleday and Wilpon showed they would.

Doubleday and Wilpon fired Joe McDonald as vice president of operations and began asking baseball executives for names of a replacement. One name that kept coming up was that of Frank Cashen, who had brought pennants to the Baltimore Orioles before going to work for a brewery and then–baseball commissioner Bowie Kuhn.

On February 21, 1980, Frank Cashen signed a five-year contract to run the Mets. He also brought with him a lot of baseball executive talent, Al Harazin, Lou Gorman, and Joe McIlvaine. Joe McDonald left the Mets to work for his old boss Bing Devine who was then with the St. Louis Cardinals.

Cashen, who habitually wore a bowtie, was a methodical, analytical man. In 1980 he spent the season observing. He made but one trade, acquiring outfielder Claudell Washington from the Chicago White Sox for a minor leaguer.

He signed Craig Swan to a five-year contract. Since the Seitz decision freeing all the players, general managers found that the best way to build their teams was to give their best players five-year deals. It insured stability and protected against salary inflation, which grew at an alarming rate. The one drawback to five-year deals is that a serious injury to a player, especially a pitcher, dooms the general manager to nights of angst and sleeplessness. Cashen gave Craig Swan $3.20 million for five years guaranteed. A month into the season Swan tore his rotator cuff and missed most of the rest of the season.

Craig Swan: "In 1980 I started the season 5–2, and boom, I felt something in my shoulder. I tried to pitch a little bit with it, but after they shot dye into it. Dr. Parkes found my rotator cuff was torn."

In an attempt to convince the fans that the future held promise, Doubleday and Wilpon hired an ad agency that came up with the slogan, "The Magic Is Back." But Joe Torre's Mets started poorly in 1980 and quickly fell into fifth place, 24 games behind. When early in the season the St. Louis Cardinals rode by bus into the Shea Stadium parking lot and the players saw the new slogan, the entire team burst into laughter.

Then in *July* and for two and a half months, the team began to win and climbed to fourth place. But after Swan and a raft of other players became injured, the team went on a 3–24 losing streak, and finished the season 67–95, in the cellar.

In mid-September when Nelson Doubleday was asked how he was doing, he replied, "We've got a few things going: Gay Talese, Irving Stone, and a paperback edition of *Shogun*." His publishing company was doing a lot better than his baseball team. But Doubleday showed he was not an owner with a short fuse. He would be patient and await results. He told a reporter, "We realized [when we bought the Mets], it was a scruffy club that would take a lot of rebuilding. We realized they weren't winning all those games by 10–1. They were struggling every time."

Doubleday promised that the Mets would be active in both the trading and free-agent markets. He concluded, "It's not over until the fat lady sings. When we get to the top, we want to stay there a long time."

The next day the future of the Mets suffered a blow when one of their few marquee players, Claudell Washington, who had become a free agent, signed with the Atlanta Braves. Ted Turner gave Washington, who had spent half the 1980 season with the Mets, a five-year deal worth a guaranteed $3.5 million. With bonuses he stood to earn another million. Turner's Braves would be a thorn in the side of the Mets for the next twenty years.

★ ★ ★

In the winter of 1980, Frank Cashen began shuffling the cards. He acquired infielder Bob Bailor from Baltimore, former Cy Young Award winner Randy Jones from San Diego, and he signed two free agents, Rusty Staub and Mike Cubbage, a Minnesota third baseman. In February he brought back Dave Kingman, who had hit 48 home runs for Chicago in 1979, but had been hurt most of 1980 and hit only 19. Cashen signed Kong to a five-year contract.

The spring of 1981 saw manager Joe Torre and general manager Cashen arguing over whether to promote minor-league phenom Tim Leary, the second pick overall in the 1979 June draft. In 1980 Leary had been the MVP of the Texas League. "Another Seaver," is what scouts said about him. Torre wanted Leary's 96-mile-an-hour fastball and biting curve badly. Cashen, leery about bringing up Leary, always preferred to leave young players in the minors until he was absolutely sure they were ready.

Torre got his way. In his first start on April 12, 1981, Leary pitched in forty-six degree Chicago. He faced seven batters, striking out three. When his elbow stiffened, Torre took him out of the game. Four days later Leary went on the DL, done for the season. He won one game for Tidewater in 1981, sat out 1982, and then spent three seasons in the minors. A series of doctors could not figure out what was wrong. He was traded away for practically nothing in 1985.

Only after 1986 did he begin to win in the majors, pitching for six ball clubs over the next nine seasons. Cashen never forgave himself—or Torre—for what happened to Leary.

In May, Cashen traded Reardon and Norman to Montreal for Ellis Valentine. Ellis had had a personality conflict with management in Montreal. In New York, he had trouble hitting the ball. That deal never panned out for the Mets.

By the end of May 1981 the Mets were a dozen games out of first, but Doubleday, Wilpon, and Cashen all went out of their way to say nice things of Joe Torre, a stark contrast to the manic hiring and firing by George Steinbrenner across the river with the Yankees.

On June 12, 1981 the players went on strike. Doubleday and Wilpon, who saw a 50 percent rise in attendance since buying the team, both suffered financially as well as emotionally. On July 1, they were so desperate for baseball that they accompanied Frank Cashen to watch their Tidewater Triple A farm team play.

"There is a tremendous void in my life," said Wilpon. "This has become a big part of life for me and my family. I like being out at the ball-park. It's a big disappointment to me that things happen that can't be recovered, the games missed, the opportunities lost."

He concluded, "It's like this: If I have an apartment that's vacant, I can never recover the value from it. It's idle."

Finally, on August 10, the owners and players made up, and play resumed. The Mets, led by rookie center fielder Mookie Wilson, contended in the second half until Randy Jones sprained his ankle and Tom Hausman developed bone chips in his elbow. No Met pitcher won more than seven games.

One of the pitchers brought up to the Mets in 1981 was a short, stocky side-armer by the name of Terry Leach. A native of Selma, Alabama, Leach had starred at Auburn University. He and his 93-mile-an-hour fastball helped get the Tigers into the College World Series in 1976. As a sophomore Leach had a 9–0 record with a 1.30 era, and his pro career looked bright. But, that summer he injured his elbow and shoulder and he never threw as hard again.

He signed with an independent professional team called the Baton Rouge Cougars, and after the team folded, Leach was given a tryout with the Atlanta Braves, signed for not a lot of money, and was sent to Green-wood, Mississippi, Kinston, North Carolina, and Savannah, Georgia, where he compiled a 5–1 record. Among the pitchers on the staff were Steve Bedrosian, Tim Cole, Craig McMurtry, Ken Dayley, and Jim Acker, the last three all number-one-draft picks. Leach, who threw sidearm and featured an outstanding slider and change-up, but whose fastball topped out at 80 miles an hour, became the odd man out.

"They were top draft choices. I came from a tryout," says Leach. "Who do you let go?"

Eddie Haas, his manager, asked the Atlanta front office to find Leach a job, and learned that the Mets' Double A team in Jackson, Mississippi, was fighting to make the playoffs and was looking for a veteran pitcher. Leach, twenty-six, pitched the final month of the 1980 season for Jackson and compiled a 5–1 record.

In 1981 Leach again played at Jackson, this time for manager Davey Johnson. Leach again went 5–1 and was promoted to Tidewater, where he won 5 more games. After the big strike, and after Jones and Hausman went down with injuries, the Mets needed a pitcher. Leach was having a great year, and so up he went. Leach came to appreciate the way Joe Torre integrated the newcomers into the team.

★ ★ ★

Terry Leach: "One thing I liked about Joe, when they brought you up to him, he didn't sit you. Some managers will keep you on the bench for a month and never use you. And then you get sent back, and he has no idea whether you can play or not.

"As soon as you arrived, you better be ready to be in the game, cause Joe was going to put you in. And I liked that. Even though you were new, you were one of the twenty-five. He trusted you.

"When Ron Gardenhire came up, I said, 'Ron, you better be ready to play tonight. He'll have you in there.' And sure enough, he was. He wanted to get your feet wet and get you acclimated.

"And I did very well. I pitched in twenty-one games, and I was only there for 58. I pitched almost every other day, and I did not give up any runs at Shea Stadium."

In 1981 Leach compiled a 2.57 era in the 35 innings he pitched.

One of the Mets players Leach got to watch up close and personal was Dave Kingman. In 1981 Kingman hit 22 home runs. Like everyone else, Leach stopped what he was doing whenever King came up to hit.

Terry Leach: "The first day I got called up, I had to meet the team in Chicago. Coming off the plane, I was late to the ballpark, and when I arrived in the clubhouse, oh, man, I looked like trash. I had old jeans on. I was off a a ten-day road trip, had no money, no clean clothes, I needed a haircut. I was looking pretty bad.

"They put me in a locker right next to Dave Kingman. He was real quiet, a somber kind of guy. I felt bad about interrupting his space.

"But he ended up being a nice guy. He always was nice to me. He had these exercises that he'd do with a bat, and I'd do some with him.

"He was interesting to me. I used to love to watch him swing. Talk about somebody coming out of his shoes to hit a ball! Every pitch he'd be swinging. You have to be ready to swing at every pitch. You had to be ready to stop if it's a bad pitch. What was funny to me was what happened when he didn't swing. I would watch him, he wore those big old hightops, and when he'd start to swing and then stop, his whole body would shake all the way down to his shoes.

"I saw him hit some mammoth blasts. During spring training at Stengel-

Huggins field—that's a huge park—he hit them over the center field fence. He was awesome to watch.

"But, when he'd get into a slump, get into a period where he'd strike out quite often, the pitchers would throw him breaking balls and just have his number. Well, he could run pretty good, and so he'd drop down a drag bunt and beat it out for a hit and get himself going again.

"One time we were in Cincinnati and had the bases loaded, and he came up to bat, and I was sitting there, and I said, 'I know it sounds dumb, but if I was them, I'd walk him.' Rather than have him hit a home run, it just made sense to go ahead and walk the run in. About that time he crushed it for a grand slam. I said, 'Told you. It may have sounded dumb, but you have to think about it.' Dave lived to hit.

"Dave didn't like to do too much with the press. I know he had troubles with that, but he always was very nice to me."

Terry Leach

★ ★ ★

Teammate Pat Zachry was another who liked him as well.

Pat Zachry: "The star of our team was Dave Kingman. He once hit a long home run off of me in Chicago. I actually thought it was foul, but they didn't have enough foul pole. He hit it so high, it was curving foul, and I went running over to the line standing behind home plate. It was a two-run homer, and that was the only game I ever lost in Chicago.

"I enjoyed playing with Dave in New York. He always gave me a hundred percent. I knew darn well he was a gamer. He was going to be there on the field, off the field, whatever it took. At least I felt that way.

"I got along with him. Some of the stuff he did with writers and reporters, I understood some of it, and some of it I didn't understand. I didn't concern myself with it. It wasn't my business.

"I always thought he was brilliant and humorous, but somewhere along the line somebody sure pissed him off. There were some people he didn't like, and he let them know it in no uncertain terms. A lot of people got down on him. They accepted it as generalities rather than specifics."

Before the midsummer strike, the Mets played bad baseball. But after play resumed in August, the team stayed in contention through much of September despite that fact that Ellis Valentine hit .207, Lee Mazzilli .228, and Dave Kingman only .221.

Terry Leach: "We were in second place right up at the end, doing pretty well, and had a shot at going ahead. I remember our catcher, John Stearns, said something in the papers about the veterans having to try harder.

I went in the clubhouse, and his whole locker was trashed. They took his stuff and threw it out onto the floor while he was on the field. And John didn't say a word. He knew it was coming. He just picked everything up. I guess he figured he had to say what he had to say, to shake some people up and get their attention.

"We ended up close but never in striking distance."

The Mets finished the second half of the 1981 season with a 24–28 record, in fourth place, five-and-a-half games behind the Montreal Expos.

On the final Sunday of the season Joe Torre asked to meet with Frank Cashen. Torre had a year left on his contract. His coaches didn't. Torre asked Cashen where his coaches stood. Cashen told him that they stood with him—out of work.

In four-and-a-half years Torre had a 286–420 record. The next year Torre would be hired by Atlanta, and he would lead the Braves to a division title. Torre would also win four World Championships, including three in a row with the New York Yankees in 1996, 1998, 1999, and 2000.

To replace him, Frank Cashen hired Baltimore buddy George Bamberger, formerly Earl Weaver's pitching coach. Like Torre, Bamberger [who had managed Milwaukee from 1978 through 1980, when he retired after suffering a heart attack] was a congenial, kind man.

Terry Leach: "George was pretty quiet and laid back. He came in during a tough time. It seemed the Mets were just thrown together, nothing real solid jelling there, and he had a tough situation to come into. George was a very nice man. I enjoyed playing for him."

While Lou Gorman, Al Harazin, and Joe McIlvaine built the minor-league system, Cashen continued making deals. He sent a message to Mets fans everywhere that the team would spare no expense to bring a winner back to Shea Stadium when he traded three players to Cincinnati for George Foster, a home-run hitter who once had been an important member of Cincinnati's Big Red Machine. This was the Mets front office's way to prove to the fans that the team was serious about competing for a pennant. To get Foster, the Mets paid him $1.6 million annually for five years plus a $1 million signing bonus and another $1 million if the Mets failed to exercise an option beyond the original five years. (The Mets in the spring had offered Dave Winfield $12 million, but the Yankees had offered him $10 million more.)

Foster had helped the Reds to four division titles, three National League pennants, and back-to-back World Championships in 1975 and 1976. His league-leading 52 home runs and 149 rbis in 1975 wowed everyone. In 1981 he batted .295 and hit 22 home runs. Cashen knew that at age 34 his skills were eroding, but he felt he needed a big name to show he was serious about building a winner.

Frank Cashen: "I was looking for cosmetic things to try to make the Mets look decent until I could rebuild them. The first guy I got to give me an infusion of power was Dave Kingman. I had seen George Foster in 1979. I had taken two teams of All Stars, one from the American League and the other from the National, to Japan for twenty-one days. I was in the commissioner's office, and I was on that trip to solve problems. Foster was just awesome on that trip. And he had an awesome year in 1981, although it was shortened by the strike. He had a really awesome year, and we made the trade after that.

"And as it turned out, we really didn't give up anybody who really helped them. They wanted Alex Trevino. They also got Jim Kern and Greg Harris, two players I thought we could afford to give up."

Then on April 1, 1982, Cashen made a trade nobody liked. He sent Lee Mazzilli, the Italian Stallion, a handsome, outgoing outfielder of limited skills who was adored by the fans, to Texas for two minor-league pitchers, Ron Darling and Walt Terrell.

When Mazzilli heard about the deal, he wailed, "For two minor leaguers?" He couldn't believe it. But Cashen knew the Mets needed pitching, and Darling and Terrell were two of the best pitching prospects in the minor leagues. Still, Cashen felt the backlash.

Frank Cashen: "It was a trade that was widely criticized in New York, because the Italian Stallion was the closest thing we had to a superstar at the time, and to give him up for two guys who never played in the major leagues, no matter how much you tell them about promise, it doesn't cut it. New York is a different town to have to work in than any other club. New York is a *now* town. What are you going to do for me today? The whole star system, Broadway, that's the way the city is, and I had to do some things I had to do, even if they were unpopular, and trading Lee Mazzilli was one of them.

"Lou Gorman and some of our scouts had seen Darling pitch for Yale, and we had talked about drafting him number one the year he came up in the draft. The biggest scouting response we had on Terrell came from Davey Johnson, who had seen him in the Texas League and liked him. He liked Darling, too. He was a roving scout, and he liked them both."

Terry Leach: "Maz was a New York boy. They love their hometown heroes. But Lee could not do the things those two guys could do to help a team. Lee was a decent hitter but a very average defensive player. Walt Terrell and Ron Darling could definitely pitch. The Mets figured one of the two had to succeed, and it ended up with both of them being big pitchers."

★ ★ ★

In 1982 the Met pitching rotation was bolstered by the return of Craig Swan. It seemed impossible that he could pitch again. Swan had suffered from a rotator cuff injury that no pitcher had come back from before. But Swan was lucky. Team doctor Jim Parkes had recommended rest rather than an operation, and while sailing down in Florida during the 1981 season, Swan met a practitioner of a treatment called rolfing. After a year of work on his shoulder, he was able to return to the Mets in 1981, a miraculous comeback.

Craig Swan: "I took a look at some of the operations they had performed on the rotator cuff, and I saw that no one ever came back from it. Nobody. Because they had to cut everything to get to the rotator cuff. It was functional and arthritic when you got older—you could play golf. You just couldn't pitch.

"So Dr. Parkes said to me, 'Swannie, let's not do the surgery. Don't pick up a ball. Don't do anything. No physical therapy, nothing for nine months. Let the tissue knit over the muscle again.'

"I was twenty-nine years old. I said, 'Nine months? Holy shit.' And I just didn't do anything. I did a little bit of sailing. That wasn't too strenuous. And while I was down in Florida sailing my seventeen-foot catamaran off the beach, drinking Heinekens and eating raw oysters at Treasure Island, I found my profession after baseball.

"I was sailing, and a beach bum friend of mine said to me, 'Why don't you try rolfing for that shoulder?' I said, 'What's that?' He made a motion with his fingers like he was pushing on something, and he said, 'And they teach you things.' I asked him for details, but he really couldn't explain it. He put me in a van and took me to Tampa to his rolfer who had fixed his ankle that still had pins in it. After rolfing, he didn't limp any more.

"Turned out rolfing has the same effect as pounding a gavel on a piece of meat. It stretches it out and softens it. And that's what I went through in 1980. I know that without it, I never would have returned to pitch.

"I went through my first rolfing session, and immediately I felt better. He taught me a few things about breathing technique, how to carry my shoulders, and I was able to make the seventeen movement cues that he gave me and I applied them all to pitching, and it changed the way I used the musculature of my body. Plus the actual physical manipulation filled in the hole in my arm. He was milking the connective tissue in the muscle toward the rotator cuff, and I was able to come back from that.

"While I was rehabbing in Florida, George Bamberger was there for me. He played catch with me almost every other day. And he would talk to me as I threw the ball as far as what he saw in my delivery. He would never let me throw hard. He would just make me lob it. We had a nice connection. I had a special, special feeling for him.

"I came back late in '81. There was a players strike in June, and everyone stayed out until August, and I came back soon after that. I started throwing long relief and had a few starts. That's why I became a rolfer. I met my fate. I'll be rolfing much longer than I played baseball.

"In '81 Mookie Wilson came up to the Mets to stay. I loved him. Mookie took everything in stride so well. Here he was a young guy, and he had this ability to handle things that most people his age couldn't.

"I had heard that his father was a sharecropper, that he came from a family where if he wasn't in school or playing sports, he worked. Mookie seemed to be one of the most gentle, kind people I met in baseball. He had unbelievable speed and he had power, and he was nice to have around.

"In '81 we also got Hubie Brooks on the team playing third. Hubie had gone to Arizona State, so we had a nice connection right away. Hubie was an outgoing kid, just full of life and fun to be around. He was a lot more outgoing than Mookie.

"Ellis Valentine also was on the team in '81. I really liked Ellis. I had no trouble with him. I think he expected too much of himself. Maybe it was the pressure of playing in New York. I noticed that he had a little attitude with some of the opposing players, maybe from run-ins in the past. He never had any problems with anyone on the Mets that I knew of."

The Met's most expensive acquisition, George Foster, had difficulty adjusting to the pressures of playing in New York. In 1982 he would hit only 13 home runs.

Craig Swan: "That year Frank Cashen signed George Foster to show the fans the Mets were trying to win, but George flopped. George was a nice guy, but he swung at balls in the dirt all the time. *All* the time. I would think, 'Oh, God, there are two strikes, here comes one on the plate. Ooow. George missed again.'

" 'George, hit the plate with your bat!'

"I don't know why he wasn't better. The pressure, I guess. Cincinnati is different from New York. They paid him all that money . . . and when we started getting big money, it was the first time, and nobody was used to it. In fact, when I signed for $3.2 million in 1980, it was probably the worst thing for my arm, because I started overthrowing. That's probably how I tore my cuff. I was trying too hard."

Terry Leach: "George and I would talk, and he was friendly to me. He had his own opinions about how to play the game. He did not want to dive for balls, because he felt if he got hurt, he could not keep producing for the team, which was a logical reason. His contract was for something like $2 million a year for five years. I can see how a player can think like that, but my problem was, when I'm pitching, I want everybody to dive for balls. I need them to do that. I'm going to be diving for balls. I need the other guys to be diving, too.

"That got to a lot of people. But, I liked George. I know it was getting toward the end of his career and he didn't produce as much. And maybe it was because of the pressures of playing in New York.

"It's different playing in New York. Bobby Bonilla was a star in Pittsburgh, but when he came to New York, Bobby told reporters he intended to keep the smile on his face. I said to myself, You shouldn't have said that. I knew that made him a target right there. And he had a tough time, and he didn't produce either.

"Tim Leary was one player who never made it with the Mets. But when he played in LA, he became a star. Some people can't handle the attention, because they expect so much of you. Or you think they expect so much of you, so you try to do more than you are capable of, and that's not good. Everybody has a comfortable point to work at to do their best, and when they try to go harder than that, they usually don't do as well. You have to find your comfort zone. And that's what happened to Tim Leary in New York. He was young, it's hard to cope with.

"The pressure is on in New York. There is way more publicity, much more attention. I would go down to South Street Seaport and my wife and I would spend the morning visiting the shops on the pier, and I'd be eating lunch at a crowded place, and people would recognize me and come over and talk and ask for autographs. Out of thousands of faces, they'd pick me out. Imagine if I had been Dwight [Gooden] or Darryl [Strawberry] or Gary [Carter].

"When I went from New York to Kansas City, I didn't know what to expect. The Royals had a beautiful ballpark, and the guys were great, and I sat in my locker before the game, and there was one radio guy and one newspaper guy! I was standing there thinking, Does anyone know we're playing tonight? In New York you almost couldn't get dressed for all the press in there. You almost needed to go into the hallway.

"Later I went to Minnesota, and I played in the '91 World Series, and I was staying at a hotel in Minneapolis, and it was raining, so I took a cab to get to the park to get ready for batting practice. The cab driver said, 'You're going kind of early, aren't you?' I said, 'Yes, I have to go in and get ready.' He asked, 'Do you play?' I said, 'Yeah.' He said, 'I'm a big Twins fans. Are you on the other team?' I said, 'No, I'm with the Twins. My name is Terry Leach.' He said, 'Are you new?' I said, 'No, I've been here for two years.' I had pitched in about a hundred games. This guy was a *big* fan! That wouldn't happen in New York.

"You don't know what it's like until you're in New York and you come in at four in the morning on the team bus, and there are two or three hundred people at Shea Stadium waiting for you. Or when you go to play in Philadelphia, and they have to block off a corridor in the hotel because there are so many New York fans you can't get through. In St. Louis we'd come out of our rooms to go to the ballpark, and the elevator doors would open into the lobby, and the lobby area would be wall-to-wall with New York fans.

"It was everywhere we went. It seemed there were more Mets fans than San Francisco fans at Candlestick Park. We'd go to Montreal, and there'd be tons of people waiting for us. New York fans follow the game so much more closely. You don't know what it's like until you play big league in New York. That *is* the big leagues."

As late as June 21, 1982, the Mets were three games over .500, in third place. Attendance was on the rise again. But the pitching staff was being held together with glue and Band-Aids. Charlie Puleo, Randy Jones, Mike Scott and Pete Falcone were ordinary. Only Craig Swan was winning. He won 11 games to lead the staff.

Craig Swan: "In '82 I had a very good year. George Bamberger was the manager. He had been a pitching coach, so he gave us a lot of advice about pitching. Bambi kind of nursed me along. I picked up one or two wins in long relief, and about a third of the way through I started. I was happy with that year. I was pitching, and my arm wasn't hurting that bad. I had lost a little, but I still was able to get up to 91 or 92 and spot it. That's how I survived."

★ ★ ★

The glue came from Neil Allen, who had developed into one of the top relievers in the game.

Craig Swan: "That year Neil Allen was great in relief. He was a happy-go-lucky guy, a party guy. He was easy going, seemed to like everybody, didn't have any judgments going, just seemed real happy."

On June 14, 1982, Allen had 15 saves. When he was felled by tendonitis in early August and missed a month, the Mets went on to lose fifteen games in a row.

Ron Gardenhire was a rookie on that 1982 Mets team. He remembers what it was like playing with vets who were playing out the string.

Ron Gardenhire: "When I came up in '82, George Bamberger was the manager, and he started off in spring training with a meeting in which he said, 'Boys, if we can play .500 ball, I'll be happy.' Any time you start off like that you get the feeling right away that, Geez, he doesn't look to win. He looks for a .500 season. I thought that was bad.

"Maybe George had been successful with veterans in Milwaukee, but with the Mets situation, that wasn't going to work. In '82 we still had the older guys, who, to me, were just playing out the season. Once we got past the early part of the season, it was over with. By the midway point, guys didn't seem to really care what went on just as long as they could do their own thing and then get out of the ballpark after the game.

"It came out in the papers that Dave Kingman didn't care about anything but his boat, but I don't believe that. When Dave went out on the baseball field, he was serious. He didn't work hard at taking ground balls at first base, but he hustled out on the field. What more can you ask?"

"I thought one of the greatest guys I ever met was Dave Kingman. I could see how the press used to bug him. They knew he wasn't going to give an interview, but they would come over and say, 'Dave, how about today?' That was agitating, though, I didn't think it was right for Dave not to talk to the press. I think he owed it to them, but it's his life. Dave was the one in '82 who made me enjoy the season, because I was thrilled every time he went to the plate and hit one of those long bombs. He kept me going, so I have nothing bad to say about Dave Kingman. I enjoyed being around him.

"Most of our pitchers were older guys, and I think we'd have been bet-ter off with the young arms we had in the minors, pitchers who should have been in the big leagues. For instance, at the end of the '82 season, Terry Leach pitched a ten-inning, one-hit shutout for the Mets [against the Phils]. In '83 he didn't even get a chance to make the team. He got sent down right away. He *didn't* get a chance, and I heard it was because Jimmy Frey didn't like him. You wonder about things like that."

On the final day of October 1982 baseball commissioner Bowie Kuhn was thrown out of office by a group of owners who felt that the role of com-missioner had outlived its usefulness. They let him stay on through March of 1984, when they chose a successor.

In the past the commissioners, including Kuhn, had acted on behalf of both the owners and the players. In the future, a minority of the baseball owners decided, the players had enough clout that they didn't need an impartial commissioner to help them. The owners intended for any new commissioner to represent the owners and the owners only.

"There are some clubs that just don't want any restrictions, or disci-pline," said Montreal President John McHale, who was among the eigh-teen teams that voted to keep Kuhn in power.

Kuhn won the vote 11–3 in the American League and 7–5 in the National, but under the rules needed a 80 percent majority to be retained. The owners who voted for Kuhn were furious that their man was axed. From the vote everyone could see that the power had shifted away from the likes of Peter O'Malley of the Dodgers and Edward Bennett Williams of the Orioles.

Among the eight owners who pushed Kuhn out were George Stein-brenner of the Yankees, John McMullen, the Houston owner and an ally of Steinbrenner, Texas owner Eddie Chiles, Gussie Busch of the Cardinals, and Nelson Doubleday of the Mets, who agreed beforehand to vote as a bloc with the Yankees. These owners insisted that the new commissioner be a businessman first. The question was, Who would take such a job under such conditions?

Said Angels president Buzzy Bavasi, "No self-respecting man would accept this job after the abuse Bowie Kuhn has taken. For the last 50 years in baseball, our own worst enemies have been ourselves. Looks like it's not going to change."

Bavasi was prescient. After picking a businessman, Peter Uebberoth, a college president, Bart Giamatti, and then naming his assistant, Fay Vincent, the owners finally picked the man they should have gone to right away, one of their own, Milwaukee Brewers owner Bud Selig, to be "acting" commissioner. The restructuring would lead to a vicious conflict between the owners and the players and bring about the most destructive work stoppage in sports history. With the battle lines still drawn, the future of the game remains up in the air.

On December 16, 1982, Frank Cashen endeared himself to Mets fans everywhere when he engineered a trade to bring Tom Seaver back to the Mets. With Cincinnati, Tom was a magnificent 14–2 during the strike season of 1981, but then in '82 he got the flu and developed back and shoulder problems. He finished the year 5–13 with a 5.50 era. The Reds let Cashen know Tom Terrific was available. Cashen sent Charlie Puleo and two minor leaguers to retrieve Seaver.

Cashen also acquired veteran pitcher Mike Torrez, who had worn out his welcome in Boston. The Beantown fans had never forgiven him for throwing the home-run pitch to Bucky Dent to lose the American League pennant in a one-game play-off in 1978. Cashen gave up a minor-league infielder who never made it.

Opening day of 1983 was a happening. More than 48,000 fans packed Shea Stadium to witness the return of Tom Seaver. PA announcer Jack Franchetti announced the starting position players while Seaver waited in the bull pen. Then he intoned, ". . . and pitching, number 41 . . ." and as the roar drowned out the announcement of Seaver's name, the still-boyish pitcher trotted in from the bull pen to take his warm-up pitches before starting the game.

Craig Swan: "For the '83 season the Mets brought Tom Seaver back to New York. I was really happy to have Tom back. I was living a few miles from his house. When I signed my big contract in '80, my agent actually *told* me to move to Connecticut because of the tax laws.

"Tom and I had seen each other in the off-season. We played golf at the country club. He was back with his club, and it was good for him. It felt good. Tom was happy. It was a little different now because there was new ownership. For some reason I felt there was something between Tom and the owners. I don't know what it was. I could never pinpoint it, but it was something, like he was from the *old* Mets, and they were from the *new* Mets.

"I remember opening day at Shea in '83. Gosh, he was back. Tom Seaver. Forty-one was back. Most years we had 50,000 people opening day, no matter what, then it dipped down to two thousand the next day. This year was different, because we had Tom back. He was Mr. Met—without the big head, if you remember Mr. Met.

"His reception was heartfelt. The fans were happy to have him back. He was ecstatic to be back, and there was great energy, the hometown boy coming home. I was just happy for Tom, the fans, and myself."

Seaver shut out the Phils for six innings, and after he came out reliever Doug Sisk got the win in the 2 to 0 victory.

Craig Swan started the second game and beat the Phils.

Craig Swan: "I went out and won the second game with an arm that I had already damaged in spring training in a game against the White Sox. It was a strange injury, kind of ironic. In rolfing I had worked on strengthening my fascia—the white tissue that covers the muscles and become tendons. I tore the fascia off my tricep muscle, and it really wasn't that painful. The next pitch I threw against the backstop. And I blew out my arm. That was the injury that finished me. I pitched the rest of my career with that injury. It was a strange one, because it wasn't painful.

"What happened, the covering had dropped itself over the nerve that ran down the rest of my arm, so the covering kind of balled up around this nerve, and after I threw 50, 60 pitches I would lose about ten miles an hour and I would have a tingly numbness that went into my hands. But, because it wasn't painful like the other injuries, I kept trying. But, nothing was happening, I couldn't get out of the third or fourth inning."

The Mets stopped winning when Swan couldn't get anyone out and Allen's alcohol addiction began to surface. The first clue that Allen had a problem surfaced in St. Louis when he and teammate Mark Bradley got in a brawl over a woman in a bar after curfew. Then at the end of April Allen failed to show up at the ballpark for two days.

When Marty Noble of *Newsday* finally reached him at his home, Allen admitted he had a drinking problem. It was the beginning of the end of his career as a closer. Neil Allen would be remembered for being the first of a distinguished cadre of New York Mets ballplayers felled by drink or drugs.

t h i r t y - t w o

Darryl and Keith

In May of 1983, George Bamberger felt he needed more hitting and he knew just where to find it. Down at Tidewater was a tall, gangly twenty-one-year-old left-handed slugger who everyone was calling either "the next Willie Mays" or "the black Ted Williams." His name was Darryl Strawberry, a lanky outfielder who could hit the ball over buildings.

Strawberry was born on March 12, 1962, in Crenshaw, a suburb of Los Angeles. His father, Henry, gambling addict and drinker, was either absent or abusive. Henry had once been a star baseball player himself, but he never had time to play catch with his son. Darryl soon realized that his father was more committed to his addictions than he was to him, and Darryl was never able to forgive him for that.

From the time Darryl was eleven there was always tension in the Strawberry home. His mother constantly nagged her husband, complaining that he was gambling away whatever money he made and that the family needed it to eat.

He would scream back, "I make it. I can spend it any way I wish." Night after night they would fight. Darryl would hear them and cringe in fear.

Some nights the father would come home drunk, and he would whip Darryl and his brother with an extension cord. Sometimes he had to watch his mother take a beating.

When Darryl was thirteen, he and his two brothers grabbed weapons— a bat, a frying pan, and a kitchen knife—and ordered the father to leave. He did, and so did part of Darryl's childhood. Darryl knew he had done the right thing, but all his life he felt empty, angry, and guilty about sending his own father packing.

The night his father left, Darryl was trapped in such a state of panic, he felt he didn't deserve to have a future. To quell the pain, he played baseball, and like his father, he was extremely good at it.

Darryl was a baseball prodigy, but he could also be tough to deal with. A moody adolescent, he would sometimes act out—or act up. For kids like Strawberry negative attention is better than no attention, and the teenaged Strawberry acted up plenty.

His junior year he quit the high school baseball team in midseason after the coach yelled at him for not putting enough effort into his game and for being disrespectful. Without him Crenshaw High made it to the city championship at Dodger Stadium, but lost in the finals. He returned senior year. His team again made it to the finals and lost to Granada Hills' pitcher John Elway, but he hit a long home run, and the scouts began drooling.

The Mets had the very first pick in the amateur player draft in 1980 and they selected Darryl. He received a $200,000 signing bonus, their biggest pay-out at that time, and guaranteed he'd make the big leagues in three years.

Though Strawberry performed well every step along the way, he always started slowly and had to be coaxed to reach his potential because he always felt he was playing catch-up to the hype that preceded him. Early on he came to resent the sports reporters who alternately praised him and wondered in print when Darryl would fulfill his promise.

After a rookie year at Kingport, Tennessee, he was sent to Lynchburg, Virginia, where his teammates were older and wiser, and the fans shouted racial epithets. He was overwhelmed and wondered whether he should have gone to UCLA and played basketball instead.

Then the next year he played in the deeper South, Jackson, Mississippi. Here he felt at home and he had a tremendous season, driving in 97 runs. He was voted the 1982 MVP of the Texas League and was promoted to Tidewater.

Frank Cashen intended for him to play the entire 1983 season at Tidewater, but after Strawberry put together an impressive spring, a desperate manager George Bamberger begged and begged for him, and on May 5, 1983, Cashen gave in and brought him up to the Mets.

Frank Cashen: "I brought up Darryl Strawberry with a lot of fear and trepidation. And I will go to my grave feeling that if I hadn't succumbed to

Darryl Strawberry

the pressure of bringing him up and let him have that full year at Triple A, he would have been a better ballplayer than he turned out to be.

"But George Bamberger was there, and the season was going down the drain, and it was only May, and they got off to a horrible start. I really did expect that we were going to start to turn the corner in that year, and he wanted to bring him up, so I finally allowed him to bring Darryl up. And Strawberry came up and he struggled for a while and he really would have been better off if he had had more time at the Triple A level."

Even so, when he arrived it was predicted that Strawberry would be as big a star as ever played in New York City. Craig Swan saw the talent. He also saw something else: Darryl lacked the confidence of most superstars. When little kids like Darryl grow up scared, they became scared adults.

★ ★ ★

Craig Swan: "In May of '83 we started poorly, and Darryl Strawberry was called up. He was twenty-one. His abilities were unbelievable. He could do everything. Just watching him that year, I felt, He's a sure superstar.

"But Darryl always seemed real shy and insecure. He was a nice guy, a good teammate, but just real shy. And he never seemed to lose that. I don't think he ever lost that. I saw him in an interview after the first couple bouts with drugs and cancer, and he didn't seem like he had lost it yet.

"He was abused as a child. Those kind of things can affect you. When those kind of things occur, the energy in the household twenty-four-hours-a-day, seven days a week, is even more powerful than the physical harm. He must have suffered through that, and he was just scared to death. Frightened all the time. And so you see it. He's still frightened. He has to get that it wasn't his fault, and that's very hard to process."

Strawberry's insecurity surfaced immediately. The media pressure on him was intense—one reporter announced that if he turned out as great as predicted, he would be the first black superstar to begin his career in New York. Most of the earlier greats, Jackie Robinson and Willie Mays included, had begun in the Negro Leagues. Before Reggie Jackson was a Yankee star, first he was an Oakland Athletic. Though the youngster didn't tell anyone, he had a great deal of difficulty handling the buildup.

No one told him how the media game was supposed to be played and what he was supposed to do once he was crowned the Mets' savior. "To me that meant I could only go *down* from there," said Strawberry. "Was I supposed to walk across the East River next? Actually that would have been easier than reading every day in the papers about the miracles I was expected to perform any minute now." At nights he would lie in bed and say, "Mother, get me out of here." He was absolutely paralyzed by fear.

Affected strongly by the hype, Strawberry tried to hit every ball out of the stadium. By mid-June he was sitting on the bench. Coach Jim Frey took him in hand and explained to him the mental game of hitting.

Strawberry became selective and he began to hit. By the end of July he was dominating the league. In 122 games he hit 26 home runs and drove

in 74 on route to being named National League Rookie of the Year. Even
after he won, Strawberry didn't think he deserved it. Instead he credited
the power of the New York press with winning him the honor.

Darryl Strawberry: "I knew, when I accepted the award, that had I been
playing for Kansas City or Minnesota or even for Pittsburgh, my performance might have been praised but never awarded. New York sportswriters made me into an intimidating hitter, a threat to every team we faced. I
helped by hitting 26 home runs, of course, but it was more than the actual
hits, it was the threat of the hit. That threat was manufactured in the New
York papers. I remember reading the papers and saying to myself that I
was casting a much bigger shadow over the league than any rookie should
have been. It was that the shadow was coming from New York that made
it so big and not because it was Darryl Strawberry's shadow. Part of what
Willie Mays said was coming true. 'The Media can make you much bigger than you are. They can re-create you. They can also tear you down.'"

A month after George Bamberger pressured Frank Cashen into bringing
Strawberry up to make his job a little easier, he suddenly stepped down as
manager. Bamby had tried leaving twice before, but each time Frank
Cashen had talked him out of it. With a record of 16–30, Bamberger was
sure the tension and pressure that went with working in New York would
cause him to have a heart attack and die. He wanted out.

Craig Swan: "Bambi always seemed fragile. He used to get so upset. New
York makes everyone take things too seriously. I was frightened for him
for health reasons. He's a nice, nice guy. I always loved that man.

"But I could see the strain was taking its toll. It was just the look he had.
You could see it was getting to him."

Cashen asked Bamberger to stay one more day. He agreed while Cashen
begged Earl Weaver, who had led the Baltimore Orioles to six division
titles and four World Series appearances, to take the job. Weaver had quit
a fifteen-year managerial career the year before. He told Cashen he preferred to play golf and live the easy life.

As a stopgap, Cashen promoted bench coach Frank Howard to finish
out the year. Howard, whose six-foot-eight frame may appear intimidating, is one of the nicest men in the game. He had a sixteen-year career as a

power-hitting outfielder for the Los Angeles Dodgers and the Washington Senators. He led the league in home runs with 44 in 1968 and 1970. He also knew something about the game. Howard, says Craig Swan, was savvy enough to realize that he was no longer effective enough to start.

Craig Swan: "Frank Howard took over for the rest of the year. Frank called me over and let me know. He said, 'Swannie, look at your numbers here. We got to get you out of the starting rotation.'

"I said, 'Yeah, they stink, Frank. My arm hurts.'

"I hadn't told anyone about my arm problems before. I had just kept plugging through. I would have said something if it would have mattered."

In one of his first moves, on June 15 Howard decided that Jesse Orosco, whom the Mets had acquired for Jerry Koosman, should become the team's closer. The move would make Orosco a star. In '83 Orosco would win 13 games and save 17 more.

Craig Swan: "Jesse threw the way I always pictured that Satchel Paige must have thrown, with that whipping left arm that had so much movement on the ball. He was a loosy-goosy left-hander, so he was perfect for the job. He didn't seem to think too much, and that was good.

"Gosh, Jesse was great."

That same day, June 15, 1983, Cashen bolstered the team by pulling the trigger on another trade. This one was not of his making. It came out of the blue, initiated by Whitey Herzog in St. Louis. Herzog had clashed with his All-Star first baseman Keith Hernandez once too often. Herzog didn't like Hernandez doing crossword puzzles in his locker before the game; he didn't like it that Hernandez didn't always run out ground balls; and he didn't like hearing that Hernandez was using cocaine. When Herzog tried to trade him to Houston, Hernandez threatened to quit first.

An angry Herzog decided to fix Hernandez' wagon and ship him off to the Siberia of National League baseball: the cellar-dwelling Mets.

It would turn out to be one of the few personnel mistakes that Herzog would make. Hernandez admitted later that he used cocaine every once in a while, but back in 1983 so did a lot of people. The jet-setters and burgeoning Yuppie upper-middle class began to use it until it became an epidemic. For a lot of hip young men and women with money, coke was it.

But Keith Hernandez was no drug addict, and he would turn out to be one heck of a first baseman and team leader. Herzog and Joe McDonald asked the Mets for Neil Allen and minor-league pitcher Rick Ownbey in return. In a heartbeat Cashen said yes. Ironically, Neil Allen's drinking problem would turn out to be far more debilitating than any problems Hernandez ended up having.

Frank Cashen: "I would like to tell you I initiated this whole thing, but I didn't. Joe McDonald, who used to work for me, called. He said, 'Frank, if you'll talk about Neil Allen, we'll talk about trading Keith Hernandez.

"I had offered Allen to the Cardinals in a previous trade for Leon Durham, and he knew I was not as high on Allen as they were. I didn't think he'd be the kind of pitcher everybody thought he'd be in New York. And I said, 'Yeah, okay, I'll talk about it,' and they said, 'It's not going to be enough. We need something else.' He wanted either Rick Ownbey or Jeff Bittiger, our choice, and we sent them Ownbey. The whole thing took maybe ten minutes, and it was done. He had to go back and talk to his people, but we settled on the thing.

"You're always curious why a general manager wants to make a deal, probably more today than ever before. I did know there was some unhappiness in the clubhouse there, and I did know Whitey was the kind of guy when he wants to get rid of somebody, he'll dump him quick and go on. I guess I was surprised more than anything that they would trade Keith, because I felt he was one of the quality ballplayers in the National League.

"[As for the drug rumors] I checked around to make sure he was relatively clean. Hell, none of us know who the Saturday nighters are—but what you have to look for is someone who has a dependency, and I was convinced Keith didn't have a dependency. That's why we made the deal."

Keith Hernandez, high-strung and often wound a little too tightly, was also a player who thrived on his nervous intensity. A perfectionist, in St. Louis Hernandez clashed with most of his managers. It wasn't always Hernandez' fault. In 1975 manager Red Schoendienst's batting coach, Harry Walker, wanted him to hit everything to the opposite field. When he didn't hit well, he was benched. He was sent to Triple A Tulsa, where Ken Boyer mentored him and got him back on track. He would just miss winning the Triple A batting championship.

In June, Hernandez blasted general manager Bing Devine, manager Schoendienst, and coach Walker. Devine called him, and they argued.

"Did I receive a fair chance?" Hernandez asked him. Devine admitted he had not.

He hit well in 1976 and thought he had won the first-base job, but then Schoendienst was fired after the season, and Vern Rapp was named manager. Rapp announced he wanted the first baseman's job to go to Roger Freed, Player of the Year in Triple A. Freed had played for Rapp in Denver. Hernandez had to prove himself again, which he did, when he hit four home runs in the first ten games.

In 1978 Hernandez was second in the league in hitting, but was furious when he didn't make the All Star team. Sulking, he had a subpar second half. Rapp was fired after 19 games in '79, and Hernandez's friend Ken Boyer took over.

In 1979 he was hitting .232 in April. He was feeling insecure and jumpy about his job when Boyer took him aside and told him he would play first no matter how he hit. Happy and secure, Hernandez went on to win the batting title at .344, drove in 105 runs, scored 115, and shared the Most Valuable Player Award with Willie Stargell.

Whitey Herzog came in 1980. Herzog, a "my way or the highway" kind of manager, demanded that his players race down to first as hard as they could every time they hit the ball. Hernandez, who preferred to conserve his energy on balls that were obviously going to be outs, refused. To him, it didn't make any sense.

Keith Hernandez: "I hustle like hell when I need to. When I'm clearly out at first on a grounder, no, I don't sprint across the bag to break the tape. If Pete Rose wants to do this, fine, but my legs and ankles are sore enough, and I have miles to go before I sleep at the end of the season.

"Besides, who are these gung-ho guys fooling? I've been called a ballplayer's ballplayer by managers, writers, and announcers I respect, and I'm proud of that designation; not a fan's ballplayer or a management's ballplayer but a player's player. They're the ones who know."

Another habit of Hernandez' that Whitey hated was his practice of sitting in his locker or in the trainer's room before games working on the daily crossword puzzle.

Keith Hernandez

Keith Hernandez: "This harmless and beneficial pastime of mine wasn't appreciated by Whitey. I worked the puzzle in the clubhouse before games, while he thought I should be paling around with teammates, providing leadership. I never bought it. Leadership on a team is 80 percent on the field and in the dugout. The other 20 percent is critical, but it's not an everyday, rah-rah thing. This isn't high school. We're not boys."

Then there was the cocaine charge. Herzog heard it and was convinced that the reason Hernandez loafed as much as he did stemmed from drug use.

Whitey Herzog: "His practice habits were atrocious. He'd come out for batting practice, then head back to the clubhouse to smoke cigarettes and do crossword puzzles. We got on him a couple of times, so he'd do better for a few days, and then he'd go back to his lazy ways. I asked a couple of my coaches to get after him, but he'd ignore them. It was getting to the point where I was getting fed up with him. A couple of my coaches even told me, 'You better get rid of that guy. He's poisoning the whole club.'"

But it was not the cocaine, says Hernandez, that was causing him problems so much as it was a messy divorce.

Keith Hernandez: "I've used cocaine. I don't anymore. I was not, by any stretch of the imagination, a junkie. I could not have hit .321 and almost won the batting title in 1980 if I had been using large amounts of any drug. I hit at least .300 every month of that season."

At the All Star game in 1980, Hernandez and his wife separated. He was second in the league in hitting that year. "In 1981, I gave out." The first players' strike interrupted the season. "It was a tough grind, especially after we came back from the strike."

In 1982, he hit .299 with 94 rbis and the Cards won the pennant and then the World Series against Milwaukee.

Despite his production and his fine defense, Whitey Herzog still got rid of him. Hernandez is convinced it was because he didn't kowtow enough to what he considered Herzog's arbitrary code of conduct.

Keith Hernandez: "In fact, the White Rat got rid of me because he didn't like me. I didn't behave as he thought his ballplayers should, and I wasn't going to change for him. Whitey got rid of all the independent thinkers on the club. Jim Kaat and Gene Tenace, clear winners, but guys who wouldn't march to Whitey's drummer: They were the first to go after the World Series of 1982."

In June 1983 Whitey Herzog attempted to trade Hernandez to the Houston Astros for Ray Knight and Vern Ruhle. But Hernandez didn't want to play in Houston because his mother's family lived nearby. He knew how hard it was to play in front of family. He told the Astros that if the trade went through, he would finish out the year and become a free agent. That killed the deal.

An angry Whitey Herzog then shipped him to the worst team in the National League, the Mets.

★ ★ ★

Keith Hernandez: "I wasn't hitting at all. Whitey is a sharp judge of his personnel. Those little-town blues, They were eating me alive. I can't really blame Herzog for trading me.

"But to the Mets? That's another matter. At the time, it was an insult.

"He wanted Neil Allen, a major error of judgment as it turned out. By offering me, he knew the trade would be made."

When told of the trade Hernandez cried. He wanted to retire, but his agent said he didn't have enough money. The agent encouraged him to meet the Mets in Montreal.

"Welcome to the Stems," said Tom Seaver (that's Mets backwards). Dave Kingman told him, "Keith, you're my ticket out of here." Keith took Kingman's job at first base.

Hernandez turned out to be the complete opposite of what Herzog felt he was in St. Louis: in New York he would inject a renewed purpose into the lackadaisical Mets.

Craig Swan: "In June, Keith came over from St. Louis and just with his own energy had the team thinking like winners. You could see it in the way he played. He was so intense, some guys just seemed to follow that. It just seemed to catch on.

"He was always in the game. He never let down. He had come from St. Louis, where he had been doing well, and he had a thing with Whitey, and so he was traded over here. When he first came I went over to Keith and I said, 'Jesus, I'm sorry you came to the Mets.' And he looked at me, and I'll never forget that look. He was contemptuous when I said that. He had the look of a winner to me.

"Keith was in every game. I wish I had had a little better arm for him, because I loved him as a teammate. He would come to the mound and suggest the type of pitch to throw. He was like a general out there. 'Keep it away from this guy now, Swannie.' 'Okay, Keith.' He'd run over to the mound all the time.

"He was so intense. I never did mind. I always listened to everybody, and if I felt good about what they said, I would use it. If I didn't, I would throw it out."

thirty-three

Davey and Doc

The Mets finished the 1983 season with a 68–94 record, 22 games out of first place. Frank Cashen needed one more important piece to the puzzle before the Mets could move toward respectability: a manager who was tough, decisive, knew the game, wasn't afraid to take chances—someone who wanted to win more than life itself. He had only to reach as far as his Tidewater farm team to get his man.

On October 13, 1983, the Mets announced the hiring of former Baltimore Orioles and Atlanta Braves second baseman Davey Johnson as their new manager. Most Mets fans weren't that impressed. It had been almost ten years since the Mets were decent, and though in 1973 Johnson broke Rogers Hornsby's record for most home runs by a second baseman with 43, there was really no reason for the fans to think Johnson, who had never managed in the big leagues before, would do any better than the veterans who had come before him.

But Cashen, who built two top-notch organizations in Baltimore, and then in New York, picked the right man for the job, someone who could judge talent and who could motivate and manage men.

Frank Cashen: "Back when we were trying to put our organization together after I took over, we were looking for people to work in our minor-league system, and his name came up. Both Lou Gorman and I had known him.

"We were looking for minor-league managers, and I had been in the commissioner's office when Davey was managing a team in the Inter-American League—there was a team in Miami, and the other teams were in Venezuela—Caracas and Maracaibo—Puerto Rico, the Dominican Republic, and Panama, and we had trouble with that league on almost a daily basis. Davey managed the Miami team, and I knew he had done a good job there, and I knew him, because he broke in with the Orioles in '66, which was my first year in Baltimore. I knew he was a real student of the game and a rugged individualist, and the kind of guy I was after.

"So we hired him, and he worked in our minor-league system, and the thing about Davey is he's always been a winner. He's always done what he's had to do to make himself a winner as a ballplayer, and we saw the same kind of things when he was managing in the minor leagues.

"He managed at Jackson and won the pennant there, and he didn't want to go back there, so we let him be a roving instructor for a year, and that was fortuitous because it gave him a chance to see all the people in our system, and then he took that knowledge the next year and went to Triple A with Tidewater and won the Governor's Cup there.

"When I went looking for a manager for the Mets I felt we needed a change of pace. We had had three fraternal managers—Joe Torre for all his macho image was kind of a paternal kind of father-type to the guys, and so was George Bamberger and so was Frank Howard, who managed after George left. I just felt we needed somebody different, preferably someone younger, who could communicate a little better with the ballplayers. That's why we selected him."

Johnson managed for two years in the Mets organization. In 1981 he led Jackson, Mississippi, to a Texas League championship, and in 1983 Tidewater, the Triple A club, won the playoffs and championship under his leadership.

Second baseman Wally Backman, shortstop Ron Gardenhire, and third baseman Clint Hurdle, starters at Tidewater, recalled how Johnson had resuscitated their careers by showing confidence in them when no one else seemed to care. Here was a minor-league manager who didn't just write their names in the lineup and leave them to fend for themselves. Because the man took a genuine interest in them, worked with them to become better players, and guided them back to the big leagues, Backman, Gardenhire, and Hurdle all felt a gratitude and affection toward Johnson, feelings most managers never earned.

★ ★ ★

Wally Backman: "In '83, when I got demoted, Brian Giles got hurt, and he didn't play that much in the spring. Supposedly whoever had the best spring was going to play, and Brian wasn't able to, so I ended up playing just about every game in spring training and had a hell of a spring. Both of us made the team and the most disappointing thing was that on opening day we didn't know who was playing second base. And that, to me, was not right. Your players have got to know what their roles are.

"Then I was sent down and I was furious. I let them know how I felt, told them it wasn't right, that in '82 I thought I had proven myself worthy of still playing for the Mets. To have the job taken away without really losing it was why I was upset.

"So when I arrived at Tidewater, I wasn't happy at all, and Davey was the one who kept me playing the way I always had played in the past. He's the one who made me realize . . . or I could have been a basket case. I could have just said, 'I got screwed. This isn't for me.' But Davey was the one who kept my head level.

"Davey was a no-nonsense guy. He was a guy whose one rule was, 'Don't embarrass the ball club or me.' You give him everything you got. I felt that I did that for him all the time. That's why we had the relationship we had. That was his style, to play to win. Do what it takes to win. Losing was never a part of it, even though there are so many games. I have the utmost respect for the man. He's the one who gave me the opportunity to do the things I was able to accomplish. When other people sent me back to the minor leagues. . . ."

Ron Gardenhire's story was similar.

Ron Gardenhire: "At the start of the 1982 season they said in the papers I was holding the Mets shortstop job until Jose Oquendo was ready. So I went out to try to prove something. I hit .240, and I made 29 errors but I made 10 of them in the first 19 games, so I felt I did okay the rest of the season.

In '83 I didn't get a chance. George Bamberger preferred Oquendo, and the Mets sent me down, which turned out to be a blessing, because I had developed a bad attitude sitting on the Mets bench in '82. I was glad to get out of there because I needed to get my confidence back.

"When I went down to Tidewater, I was disgusted, frustrated, Davey

Davey Johnson

said, If you want to get back to the big leagues, the way to do it is to work
your ass off here.'

"Davey was the kind of guy who let us go out and play. He didn't over-
manage, and it was one of his assets. He'd show you some things, but he
was the kind of guy who did nothing but put confidence into you. That
was the key. Bamberger never really said a whole lot. He was more of a
pitching coach than a manager. But Davey coached [teams] and he knew
all parts of the game.

"At Tidewater we had a stretch where we lost something like 13 games
in a row, and you would think Davey would be uptight, but he wasn't. He
never once lost his composure. One day, I remember, we picked a lineup
out of a hat. He put in all the names, and we drew for what spot we were
going to hit in. It didn't work, but it was his way of saying, 'Don't worry
about it. We're going to win.'

"He instilled confidence in us. He made Wally Backman and me feel really good, because like I said, we were both sent down at the same time, and we both felt we should have been playing in the major leagues. He took us and put us in his lineup and told us he felt we should have been up there also. And when someone says that . . . you'd think as a Triple A manager he would go with what the Big Man says, but that wasn't his feeling. He felt we should have been in the big leagues, and he told us that. Not too many managers would do that.

"Davey didn't show his anger often. He would get mad, but I never saw him blow up. I remember a game we played against Columbus. We were getting our asses kicked, and I hit a ground ball, and I was running to first base. Brad Gulden was the Columbus catcher, and he ran to first to back up the play, and I got thrown out, and he said to me, 'I beat you to first. You're getting slow in your old age,' and I started laughing.

"After the game Johnson had a meeting, and he buried us. He got all over my ass. He said, 'I don't mind us getting our ass kicked, but when you start laughing about it, that's when you're going to have to meet me.' He was really mad. And that was the last time I laughed on a baseball field.

"When Davey talked to us, he came out and said what he wanted to say, didn't pull any punches, and he got through to you without screaming.

"Davey was a tough customer and that's the way we played. We were in Columbus in '83 in the playoffs, and we were beating them 11–1 after four innings. Gil Flores was on first and I was at the plate, and Gil stole second. The next pitch, of course, hit me in the head, knocked me flat. And I was out.

"A big brawl broke out. Kelvin Chapman took out their pitcher, nailed him, and when I finally came to, I could see Davey arguing with the umpire. The umpire pushed Davey, and then Wally Backman started swinging at that umpire. He said, 'I'll kick your ass if you touch my manager.'

"That was typical of Wally. Wally was a little red ass. When I first signed he was the number one pick at shortstop. I saw a quote in the paper one time where Keith Hernandez said, 'If I had to have someone in my foxhole, I'd want it to be Wally Backman.' Pound for pound, Wally was as strong as anybody on our team.

"Anyhow, I was lying on the ground, half-dazed, and there was Wally, swinging at this umpire, and Davey was holding him.

"Chappie got thrown out of the game, and so we had no more infielders left except Wally and me. Wally had gotten hit the night before, and his hand was really swollen. Wally started ripping off the bandage saying, 'Give me my glove.' We were laughing.

"I was dazed, in the ozone, but Davey said to me, 'Gardie, you have to play.' I said, 'All right, all right.' And we proceeded to really beat the shit out of them.

"The Columbus team had great talent, but we had experience. Our whole infield had been in the major leagues—Gary Rajsich, Wally, me, and Clint Hurdle—and our outfielders had been up and down. We hadn't played great baseball until we got down to the last two weeks of the season.

"We were in fifth place, and you had to finish in the top four to get into the playoffs, and we turned it on to get into the fourth spot, and when we got into the playoffs, we just blew everybody out of the water. We felt no pressure. We just kicked their butts. We won it all, and it was a great feeling. It was 'Take this, Mets,' because that's the way we felt down there. 'Take this, Mets. Watch *us* play.' "

Clint Hurdle, a Kansas City Royal phenom who once adorned the cover of *Sports Illustrated*, was released by the Cincinnati Reds and out of work at age twenty-six. He had offers from the Mets, the Orioles, and the Indians to come to training camp in 1983, but chose the Seattle Mariners, because they seemed to want him badly and because they were a lousy ball club. He figured it was his best shot to get back to the big leagues.

The day before the season started manager Rene Lachemann called him in and told him he had made the team. "If we hadn't gotten Steve Henderson," Lachemann told him, "you'd have been my starting left fielder."

The next day, opening day, the Mariners released him. General manager Danny O'Brien overruled his manager and cut Hurdle loose.

When the Mets saw he had been released, they contacted him and asked him to go down to Tidewater. With nothing to lose, Hurdle and his wife drove cross-country to Virginia. When he arrived, his reception was less than cordial. But by the end of the season Davey Johnson had breathed new life into his career, to Hurdle's everlasting gratitude.

Clint Hurdle: "Davey had handpicked his team, had filtered out who he didn't want, and all of a sudden they drop a bomb on him: by the way, we just picked up Clint Hurdle. And I don't think Davey was real receptive to the idea. He's not one to enjoy surprises. But the one thing about him, even though he had these feelings, he allowed us to develop a relationship from day one. We shook hands and said hello, and that's one thing I will always be thankful for: There was none of that, 'You could have been,' or 'You used to be,' or 'What happened to you?' Not one time.

"It was, 'This is the way it can be. You *can* do this. Why don't we work on this? Why don't you work harder to add to your game?' Or, 'Forget about trying to do this. Go out there and have some fun.'

"The biggest thing he did for me was to establish some self-confidence. I was in a really rocky situation, twenty-six years old, in Triple A, just released from the two worst clubs in baseball, the Cincinnati Reds and the Seattle Mariners, within a period of six months.

"When I arrived, Davey told me I was going to be the team's designated hitter—for a National League team. I was a first baseman, and the Mets had sent down Gary Rajsich to play first, a move no one had anticipated, so I got caught in the line again.

"I went to Davey and I said, 'I'll do what I need to get it done. But if the situation arises where I can get in some work, think of me.' He said, 'I understand you. I feel for you, but there's nothing I can do right now. I got Rajsich at first, I got Strawberry, Marvell Wynne, and Rusty Tillman in the outfield.'

"He said, 'Clint, re-evaluate your situation. You're coming to a new organization. They don't have anything invested in you. You're going to have to hang with it for a while. Can you play anywhere else?'

"Mike Bishop, our third baseman, was called up to the Mets for a week when John Stearns got hurt. Davey came to me and asked if I would play third, a position I had never played before. In my mind I couldn't do it. He thought I could, and we built on that.

"He told me the pros and cons. He said, 'You play first and the outfield like quite a few other guys. What you need to do is catch someone's attention. If you learn third, you're going to make yourself that much more attractive not only to the Mets, but everybody else.' And he added, 'I think you can do it.'

"He threw me right in there. We decided during the day, and that night I played third base. There was no getting acquainted.

"My first night I made two errors. I was so nervous. I wasn't acclimated to third base. I was too close to the hitter. But then, I asked myself, How badly do you want to get back to the big leagues? What sacrifices are you willing to make? You've swallowed your pride. How much more are you willing to swallow? I thought about it, and I said, 'Why not?'

"I didn't know Davey well. In the past I had put my eggs in other people's baskets, and they had dropped them. But I figured, What the heck, I have nothing to lose. I'm going to believe in this guy. I'll walk with him and have faith in him.

"When Mike came back down, I was hitting well. I got hot, and Davey said, 'Maybe he can drive in more runs than he'll let in.' He left me there, and I played in 115 games at third. It was something I had never anticipated.

"And Davey worked with me a lot. I'm sure I pained him quite a few games out there, but through the season and with the help of other infielders on the ball club—Rajsich, Wally, and Gardenhire—toward the end of the season I felt adequate.

"I pulled it off.

"We had a melting pot of deflated egos at the start of the year. They had some guys—Tillman, Wynne, Mike Fitzgerald, and some of the pitchers—who had led the team to the [International League] championship and had to come back to Tidewater again, which is not a savory situation for a ballplayer.

"Then we also had some former major leaguers—Gary Rajsich, Backman, Gardenhire, and myself.

"I came first, and then Gary came, and Gary was down, disappointed. We talked. Shoot, we can either feel sorry for each other or we can strap it on and go out and have some fun.'

"And then Gardenhire showed up, and he was down, and Gary talked to him, and I talked to him, and now there were three of us, and then Backman was sent down, and the three of us talked to him. We played upon each other's emotions. My role was to make them feel better. They knew what had happened to me. They asked, 'How do you stay strong? How do you continue?'

"I said, 'I have nothing else to do. This is what I want to do. I like to have fun playing the game, and I don't care if I'm in A ball or in the big leagues.'

"That club had a great pitching staff—Darling, Gorman, Leary, and Leach—and through the course of the year I've never had as much fun in baseball as I had in 1983 in Triple A with those guys. We were all committed to winning, and we were all committed to each other, and when you have that, there is an unbelievable amount of strength on the team. You're able to do just about anything.

"We didn't have the greatest record. We backdoored into the playoffs in fourth place, but we ended up winning the whole thing.

"The camaraderie was excellent. There were *no* petty jealousies—racial, ethnic, salaries, or anything—the first time in pro ball I played on a team that didn't have that.

"I make a joke about Davey. I say he is the type of guy who will eat a quarter and spit up three dimes. And it's because he always prepares himself. I really believe one of his greatest assets is his preparation, and that year, when you look at the players who came down, he had four guys who could have been a lot of trouble—Rajsich, Gary, Wally, and me—but he took each one of us aside and explained to us what we needed to do to get back to the Mets.

"[He said,] 'If you want to do it, fine. If you don't, fine. I want to win. Do you want to win?'

"And he would always work with you. He was always available to talk baseball, to physically help you, and to visually help you. He is expert in having relationships with players.

"And it was really special to see a manager in Triple A who cared so much. I think in the back of his mind he didn't agree with some of the decision making up there, and he was going to do what he thought he needed to do in case he was a in a sitatuon where he'd be managing up there. That's what I mean about preparation.

"I believe as soon as he took that Tidewater job, he was preparing himself for advancement, and he was trying to form a little nucleus of spots he thought the club needed working on. He developed Wally as a second baseman, and Gardy and me as utility players.

"Davey's so committed to people. He's committed to the organization and he's committed to winning, but it's a big pie, and there is a piece for everybody. I don't think anyone on that team could say they didn't like him or he wasn't fair.

"With the contracts floating around, the manager has to juggle to keep everyone happy. But he was the type to throw the ball back in your court. He'd say, 'Hey, let's be realistic. Look at the picture. Here's who I have to work with. Here's what you can do.' Most of the time you end up agreeing with him. He would present the picture realistically and make you be a man about it. 'Here it is in black and white.'

"It was surprising [that] he knew as much about pitching as he did. He could discuss situations with the pitchers. Halfway through the season we weren't even in contention, but he said, 'We will win it *all*.' I thought, 'Geez, who is this guy?' Because I had heard he had done the same thing at

Jackson in the middle of the season. He had written on the blackboard, WE WILL WIN THE CHAMPIONSHIP. And they were in last place.

"The whole year Davey and I kidded back and forth. I'd say, 'Isn't this going to make the script that much better when we win it all?' And he would just look at me with that gleam.

" 'That's right.'

"And we jelled at the end. We had a complete club, and once we got into the playoffs, we blew everybody out of the water."

Johnson, for his part, had no doubts he was the right man for the Mets job. He had prepared. He was ready.

Davey Johnson: "Frank had been hiring paternal, older managers. Every player's dad. Cashen decided to go to a younger manager. He decided he wanted someone decisive and outspoken, someone who wasn't afraid to make a decision, who wasn't afraid to gamble. I knew in my own mind that I was the man for the job. I won as a player with the Orioles and in Japan and I managed three years in the minors and won all three years. I was sure that if anybody could turn the Mets around, I could."

While vacationing in Hawaii, Johnson had dinner with Wally Backman. He told Backman that if he got the Mets job, he would be calling the shots.

Wally Backman: "I didn't realize at the time that he had put in for the job. He said, 'If I get that job, you're going to get an opportunity.'

"And he said that if he got the chance to manage in the big leagues, the only way he would do it would be his way. Davey does things his way, and by doing it his way, he's proven his success. And that might explain some of the problems that have happened to him."

But from the start Johnson and Cashen clashed. Cashen was shy, reserved, and cautious, Johnson outspoken and cocksure. One major issue they adamantly disagreed on throughout Johnson's seven-year reign concerned the manager's responsibility to police his players. Cashen wanted Johnson to baby-sit them and make sure they behaved. Backing Cashen's approach was minority owner Fred Wilpon, a moralist who wanted his players walking the straight and narrow.

Johnson could not have disagreed with them more on the issue. As a player, he never wanted managers telling him how to lead his life off the ball field. He didn't care how his men behaved off the field as long as they performed for him on it. In truth, Johnson liked his men out on the town together drinking and carousing. The cameradie, he knew from his own playing days, built friendships and made a team tight-knit.

Johnson and Cashen's other philosophical differences were minor in comparison. Johnson believed in telling the truth as he saw it. Cashen believed in being circumspect and playing your cards close to your vest. Johnson, who chafed against authority and against the banality of PR equivocation, sometimes would deliberately infuriate Cashen with his outspoken public opinions.

For example, one spring Johnson made the remark, "I expect us to go out and dominate our division." Cashen hated when he crowed. He wanted the more common diplomatic platitudes.

Johnson got a memo on his desk: "How could you say that?" A reporter once commented while covering the Mets at the time, "Davey loved that. It meant he'd made the little white-haired GM a little crazier than the day before."

Cashen in turn upset Johnson even before the first game was played. Cashen had miraculously reacquired Tom Seaver, who had finished the 1983 season 9–14 with a bad ball club. Seaver who was now thirty-nine and Cashen had to decide whether to protect him on the forty-man roster and lose one of the minor leaguers or to protect the kids and risk losing Seaver. Cashen was sure Seaver was a safe risk because of his age, and he chose to protect the kids. When Seaver was snapped up, Johnson fumed.

Davey Johnson: "In retrospect there were a couple of kids who had no chance of making it to the majors. But Frank was higher on them than I was, and he opted to keep the kids on the roster rather than Seaver. He figured no one would take Seaver. Frank was wrong. The White Sox grabbed him. Bye-bye to Tom Seaver from New York.

"What bothered me was that I was not privy to Frank's list. We all could have used Seaver in '84."

Wally Backman: "Tommy was coming to the end. He'll be a fan favorite forever, so he was a tough guy to lose. Though it hurt some of the players, we realized what the front office was doing, because there were a lot of young guys coming up, and they were rebuilding. The only part I don't understand is why we didn't get any compensation for Tom. [The White Sox got a draft pick—Seaver—as compensation for pitcher Dennis Lamp being drafted by Toronto.] They could have traded him and gotten someone for him.

"It was frustrating to lose him at the start—until you realized what they were trying to do, to get a core of players together and make the changes they did."

Cashen also made a trade that Davey didn't like at the time. To bolster the Mets pitching staff Cashen made a deal with the Los Angeles Dodgers for a young, wild, fireballing left-hander from Hawaii by the name of Sid Fernandez. In exchange he gave up two players, Carlos Diaz and Bob Bailor, who Johnson felt he could have used. But Cashen, who, like Johnson, believed that a team is built around strong, young arms, felt Fernandez soon would be ready for the majors.

Davey Johnson: "In the end it turned out for the best, but in the short run, it handicapped me. My roster was weakened right from the start, but Frank figured correctly that sooner or later this hard-throwing left-hander, Fernandez, would be extremely valuable."

Cashen must have felt just a little guilty about losing Seaver, because he was more open than usual when, during spring training, Johnson kept telling Cashen to "keep an open mind" about bringing up to the team a nineteen-year-old phenom pitcher from Tidewater by the name of Dwight "Doc" Gooden. In 1982, the Kingsport manager, Ed Olsen, was late reporting and Johnson filled in until he arrived. Gooden was seventeen, and Johnson fell in love with his live arm and incredible poise. The next year Gooden was promoted from Lynchburg up to Johnson's Tidewater team late in the season, and Johnson gave him several starts. The kid won a playoff game and a Championship Series game. It was then that Johnson vowed that if he became the Mets manager the following year, Gooden would be up there with him. (John McGraw was remembered for bringing up seventeen-year-old Mel Ott, Leo Durocher did the same for Willie Mays, and Johnson would always be remembered as the manager who gave nineteen-year-old Dwight Gooden his baptism.)

Davey Johnson: "I knew he was ready for the Mets, my Mets. Dwight was to be my stopper in the rotation. I had to have him. Doc was a luxury Bamberger didn't have. You didn't have to be a genius to see that this kid was going to star in the big leagues. I had to have him.

"I worked with Doc for about three weeks when he first broke in at Kingsport in the Appalachian League in 1982. He had been the Mets number one pick in the amateur draft. I remember him throwing on the sidelines. As I stood next to him as he worked out, I asked him how he gripped his fastball.

"He said, 'Cross-seams if I want it to go straight or ride up, and with the seams if I want lateral movement.' I was thinking, 'Jeez, he has some poise.' He was firing bullets, his curve broke three feet, and every pitch was a strike or close to it. What control he had. I said to myself, 'This kid is seventeen years old, and the catcher isn't jumping all over the place for the ball. Wow!'"

But first, Davey Johnson would have to convince Frank Cashen. Against his better judgment in 1981 Cashen had allowed phenom pitcher Tim Leary to come up early when Joe Torre and pitching coach Bob Gibson begged for him, and Leary had ruined his Mets career. He had allowed Darryl Strawberry to come to the Mets earlier than he thought prudent, and Cashen would rue that move until his dying day. Here was another impatient manager pushing him to promote another young phenom before his time.

Davey Johnson: "I started working on Frank for Dwight. I would say to him, 'Let's have an open mind going into the spring.' Every time I brought it up, he'd pick up his beer and say, 'Here's to the ladies,' trying to change the subject. Frank said, 'More ballplayers are hurt by bringing them up too quickly than for any other reason. You have to allow youngsters to mature sufficiently in the minor leagues.'"

Cashen would throw Tim Leary up at Johnson and also bring up the case of Strawberry, who was immature and struggled his first season, as most rookies do.

Davey Johnson: "Doc, I was convinced, was different. It became a ritual. I would bring Gooden's name up and Frank would try to change the subject. But I was persistent enough so that I knew when we went into the

spring, Frank would have an open mind. Frank also was aware that it is easier for a pitcher to make the transition to the big leagues than it is for an
everyday player."

Frank Cashen: "With Davey you have discussions and dialogue. He is
single-minded and believes what he believes. Sometimes there is a difference of opinion. I feel that more ballplayers are hurt by bringing them to
the major leagues too quickly than are hurt by lack of talent. We should not
be so desperate as to not give players time to really mature on the major-
league level. And the first year Davey had some thoughts particularly about
John Gibbons, a young catcher, and about Dwight Gooden. He asked me
to keep an open mind on it, and I did. Gooden, of course, was a phenom,
and you really have to wonder if we hadn't lost Tom Seaver in that ill-fated
draft to the White Sox, we might never have brought Doc along that
quickly, although it is easier for a pitcher to come quicker than it is for an
every day player. An every day player has to face some old hands. It's easier
for a pitcher because, all the same stuff you throw in the minors, you throw
up here."

Davey Johnson: "In the spring Doc had back spasms and a torn fingernail
on his pitching hand, but he still was very, very impressive. About a week
before the team broke north, I said, 'Frank, well, how's your open mind?'
    "He said, 'I'll let you have him.'"

Bringing Gooden to the Mets was the single most important player move
Davey Johnson made in 1984. But Johnson wasn't satisfied with inserting one
rookie into the starting rotation. His intention was to bring up two others,
Ron Darling and Walt Terrell, as well. Craig Swan recalled the three youngsters who were threatening to take his, and the other veteran pitchers' jobs.

Craig Swan: "I remember in the winter of '84 the Mets didn't protect
Tom Seaver, and the White Sox took him. I didn't quite understand what
happened. It was weird. That was *so* weird. What happened to Tom? What
was that?
    "But the pitcher who replaced him was awesome. The first time I saw
Dwight Gooden he drove up in his Camero with 'Dr. D' stencilled on the
door. It was classic.
    "When Doc threw I noticed he had a great fastball but a better curve-

ball. His fastball was up there, but there were a lot of guys with his fastball. But not with that curveball.

"I thought, 'God, if I could have had that curveball I could have really won some games.' I would look at that curve and think, 'My God, that thing breaks down and hard.'

"He was awesome.

"Another pitcher Davey brought up was Ron Darling. He was from Yale. The one thing I remember about Ron that I thought was kind of strange was that he used to warm-up in the bull pen, come in and blow dry his hair to get it perfect to go to the mound to open up the first inning. That wasn't what we did in the 60s and 70s. I would think to myself, That's unusual. He's blow drying his hair *after* he's warmed up to get the sweat out of it.

"Ronnie was a smart guy. He was always nice and kind without a lot of stuff going on. A nice guy.

"Davey also brought up Walt Terrell. Walt was a hardnosed guy, threw a heavy sinker, kind of a bulldog, a walrus guy with a gruff attitude, but not a mean guy. You might get two words out of him, 'Rrrr, rrrr.' 'How's it going?' 'Rrr, rrrr, all right.' He was one of those mumblers."

In early May 1984 Johnson decided he would rather go with talented young arms than the vets he had, but didn't trust. Among the vets to get their pink slips were Dick Tidrow, Swan, and a month later Mike Torrez.

Craig Swan: "I started the '84 season in the bull pen, but it wasn't long before Davey got rid of me, Mike Torrez, and Dick Tidrow. It was, 'All three of you old guys, get out.' Yeah, he was cleaning house.

"It was hard for me because the Mets were the only team I'd been with. I was definitely affected, but I knew it was coming."

Swan would pitch only five more innings in the majors. After a tryout he signed with the California Angels, and Gene Mauch let him go. Swan retired and then studied at the Rolfing Institute in Boulder, Colorado. He is currently writing a book on the practice.

The promotion of rookies Gooden, Darling, and Terrell said a great deal about Davey Johnson. For him, winning was more important even than keeping his job. What solidified his philosophy to play the best players, regardless of age, came after a conversation Johnson had with former Baltimore Orioles and Chicago White Sox manager Paul Richards.

Davey Johnson: "One day when I was playing in Atlanta I ran into [Richards] in a coffee shop. He and some of his buddies were talking about the Atlanta ball club. He said to me, 'Dave, if I had a one-year contract I would play you and Mike Lum,' meaning two veterans. 'But if I had a two-year contract, I'd play Marty Perez and Frank Tepedino,' two younger players. I swore to myself at the time, if I'm ever a manager I'll never let the length of my contract make any difference as to who I play.

"When you play veterans, you may lose more games with them than if you had played talented young kids coming up, but your chances of getting rehired improves drastically because you can never be second-guessed by the front office or blamed by the press. If you take what appears to be a gamble—and you're wrong, you're gone. Especially if you're a contender. You also forfeit your chance of developing any talent.

"You prostitute your baseball beliefs when you start making decisions based on the length of your contract. There can be only one answer to the question of who should play. When Richards tied whom he would play to his contractual status, it confirmed something I had suspected all along: For a lot of baseball people, protecting themselves is top priority, more so even than winning."

Cashen, at Johnson's urging, promoted young pitchers Brent Gaff and Tommy Gorman from Tidewater, and he traded three minor leaguers to Cincinnati for fireballing Bruce Berenyi. Johnson then moved youngster Ed Lynch from the bull pen to the starting rotation.

Davey Johnson: If I did nothing else in '84, I am most proud of having established the young arms in the pitching rotation. It was certainly a gamble, but an educated gamble. If they had failed, I would have failed, but in truth I never really was worried. I've always said, 'You can't be afraid to play the kids.' "

When Johnson put "the kids" out there, they responded. Dwight Gooden won 17 games, Ron Darling won 12, Walt Terrell 11, and Sid Fernandez 6. Lynch won 9 and Berenyi won 9 in half a season with the team. Tom

Gorman even went 6–0. Johnson handled the young pitchers gingerly. By the end of the year he had a very strong pitching staff.

But it was young, tall, handsome, poised Gooden with whom the entire baseball world fell in love.

Wally Backman: "Doc was awesome. That's the only word you could use for Dwight when he first came up. He was flat-out *awesome*. He over-matched quality major-league hitters. One guy who sticks out in my mind who hated to face Doc more than anybody was Ryne Sandberg.

"I was a good friend of Dwight all the time, and I still consider myself a friend. Some of the problems Dwight had was because he was so young, he was put into situations and people took advantage of him. He got into some bad situations with some bad people. But, Dwight was a great player and a very, very nice person. Dwight's a great guy.

"I can remember in one of his first starts in Chicago, he walked the bases loaded and then struck the side out, Sandberg, [Andre] Dawson, and Keith Moreland. He had to face the heart of their order, and he over-matched three hitters in a row. He made them look *bad*. You just knew there was something special there."

For the fans, he was a God.

David Brownstein: "My involvement was never as great as it was with Dwight Gooden. For Gooden, I created a new religion. I gave up Judaism entirely. I prayed to Good. We were very involved. I began to understand the concept that God is black. This guy was clearly black and he was clearly God. I don't think there is any question about it and I dare anyone to dispute it. He could do anything he wanted. He was young. He had everything. He was making a million a year, he was good-looking; he wasn't too articulate, but he didn't have to talk to anyone if he didn't want to. If he chose not to snap off ninety-mile-an-hour curveballs, he didn't.

"I once had seats right behind the screen at Shea Stadium, first row, watching Gooden pitch, and that was a religious experience. Watching the breaking ball snap off was just incredible. I realized there was a God on this earth, and that it was Dwight Gooden. During the season, the Mets lost four in a row, and I figured, 'It's Good's way.'"

thirty-four

Darryl and Keith II

The on-field leader of the Mets team in 1984 was Keith Hernandez. One of the reasons for that was, at age thirty he brought maturity and experience to a very young team. Wally Backman recalled the qualities that made "Mex" so invaluable.

Wally Backman: "Keith was a general on the field. He didn't go to the mound just to go to the mound. He knew what to say to the pitchers when he went to the mound. He went there with intention. Keith was one of the most intelligent players I ever played with. He knew the game and everything about it. I was happy to play beside Keith for all those years because he helped me a lot, too.

"He had so much range to his right, and I learned to play off him. I also learned how to play the hitters, instead of just going out and playing the position. They say the game is eighty percent mental, and Keith was mentally prepared for every situation, and not only for himself, but for the rest of the team.

"We were all young around Keith, especially the infield. Rafael Santana was there, myself, and Hubie Brooks. Keith was the guy. He talked a lot. He helped us, and he didn't have to do that. You worry about yourself and do the things you're capable of doing. But Keith tried to help us, to make us better."

Manager Davey Johnson came to respect Hernandez greatly both for his bat and his stellar defense. The two developed a mutual admiration society.

Hernandez credited Johnson's "party hearty" attitude with bringing the Mets together as a team.

Keith Hernandez: "[In 1984] Staub asked [Davey] in spring training what his policy on the hotel bar would be. He said, 'It's open to everyone.' The players started hanging out together, coming together as friends and therefore as a team."

Johnson returned the compliments.

Davey Johnson: "There are few players who compete with the intensity of Keith Hernandez. He brings an enthusiasm and a killer will to win. Out in the field, Keith keeps the players on their toes. He never stops talking, reminding the infielders how many outs there are, constantly telling the young pitchers what a particular batter likes to hit, going to the mound when a pitcher needs a boost or a kick in the butt. It's like having a coach out on the field.

"Through the tail end of the '83 season Keith wasn't really happy, but he made the best of it, played hard, and it didn't take the fans long to fall in love with him. In '84 I fell in love with him as well."

As Johnson explained, Hernandez was his coach on the field. During the game his first baseman knew the strengths and weaknesses of every hitter, and he would constantly be making suggestions to pitchers. In the clubhouse he could be a harsh critic. If a player didn't hustle, he heard about it from Keith. Darryl Strawberry who was moody and sometimes didn't play all-out, in particular rankled at Hernandez' habit of criticizing teammates in the press.

Darryl Strawberry: "Keith had a particularly nasty habit of telling the press what he wanted another player to know. It was indirect and almost always hurtful, but Keith knew how to play the media for all they were worth. He seemed to like to show the other guys on the Mets that they had to be nice to him if they wanted him to use his leverage with reporters to get them 'good press.'

"The press lapped it up because they liked conflict, dirty laundry, raw emotion, mano-a-mano stuff, and it always appeared in the paper the next day. Team solidarity? Loyalty? Fuhgeddaboutit!"

On the very first day of spring training in '84 the twenty-two-year-old Strawberry decided to mark his own territory in a frontal challenge to Hernandez's leadership. Darryl grandly announced that he would not be afraid to speak up if criticism was needed. Strawberry then went on to say that a lot of the Mets players hadn't cared about winning in '83. He added that he intended to lead the team to victory.

But, having said that, Strawberry was still too young and immature to become a team leader, and the end result of making his leadership challenge was to anger some of the veterans, who felt he was out of line. Wally Backman remembers the young Strawberry as being too diffident to be a leader.

Wally Backman: "Darryl and I never were very close. When he first came up, Darryl was pretty quiet. He didn't associate himself with the players very much. That was why Keith was such a tremendous influence on a lot of players, because we could sit in the clubhouse after the game and talk about the game for hours. And Darryl was usually not part of that.

"I thought Darryl had the most power that a person could be blessed with when I first saw him. If Darryl would have done a few things differently in his life, you'd see a guy who hit close to 600 home runs already. He had that kind of ability. If he would have changed a few things in his life. But, unfortunately for him, he didn't. Or couldn't. And that's the sad part."

In September 1984 Hernandez and some of the veterans got back at Strawberry. When Strawberry began to slump, Hernandez was quoted in the papers saying that Strawberry didn't give one hundred percent effort because he was so "down on himself."

Hernandez hated the way Strawberry would laze through batting practice. After holding his tongue much of the season, Hernandez finally blew up. He went to the papers and called his teammate a slacker in an effort to shock him out of his lethargy.

Keith Hernandez: "Darryl is the most frustrating man I have ever played with. In batting practice he'd sometimes give up and take lazy, worthless swings. BP puts a player into more slumps than any other factor. We get about forty swings, so a bad habit can establish itself quickly. It's vital to work on cultivating the smooth, level, disciplined swing; everything a line drive or, at worst, on the ground.

"I never try to hit a home run. A slugger like Darryl might, at the end of a BP session, try to poke a few. Last year, he sometimes tried to hit all of them out. While the early-bird fans 'Ooooohhed' and 'Aaahhed,' I cringed. Several times I stepped in and said, 'Straw, they don't pay you to hit home runs in batting practice.'

"Too often, Darryl was either swinging for the fences or not swinging at all. When a player has so much talent, teammates care. The opposition cares. Around midseason Bill Madlock of the Pirates came to me and asked, 'What the fuck is wrong with Strawberry?'

"It's not that I'm a saint. It's that Straw should have cared more about his talent. He should have cared more about the team.

"Watching him became a drain on me. I took it personally. I, too, had a lot of trouble breaking into the big leagues, but I never quit. Put it this way: I'll quit before I quit. And to see Darryl pissing away his talent, I had to do something.

"Finally, in September, after biting my tongue for a month or more, I decided it might be best to shake him up. I went public and told the reporters after a game that Darryl had quit on himself and his team."

Hernandez had the decency to tell Strawberry that the story would be coming out the next day. That night Hernandez couldn't sleep. And on some level Hernandez regretted having said it. Hernandez told Strawberry he hoped he wouldn't take it the wrong way. Strawberry, who didn't accept his rationale, was furious.

Darryl Strawberry: "He was pulling the same shit that he had pulled the year before. Who made him the manager of the Mets? What right did he have criticizing other players to the press as if he were the public affairs officer or something?"

But for the rest of 1984 Strawberry was a different player. He hustled, improved his hitting, and led the team with 97 rbis. Strawberry later admitted that he never should have let Hernandez affect him as much as he did, but because of his absent-father issue, he had fashioned Hernandez into a father figure and gave him far more sway over his emotions that he should have. He appreciated Mex's advice and leadership, but at the same time resented his stinging criticism.

★ ★ ★

Darryl Strawberry: "I realize now that I was laying the burden on other people instead of dealing with it myself. Sure I came around after the Keith Hernandez story in the paper when he said that I gave up on myself in crisis situations and that I was lazy when I should have been tough. That's partly what makes me so mad. I'd invested so much in what Keith had to say that even though it was insulting, I still responded. It gives me a cold chill not only to realize that, but to realize what the papers said after I pulled out of my slump.

"The newspaper reporters said that I 'woke up,' came around, and started working again. It burned me that they thought that something Hernandez said had that much effect."

Making it worse, in Strawberry's mind, was that Hernandez was white and Strawberry was black.

Darryl Strawberry: "If you're black, when you're in a hitting slump you're just plain lazy. Black players can't have slumps just like they can't have injuries. When you finally pull out of a slump it's because someone— usually someone in a whiter shade of pink or an acceptable variation thereof—has booted you the hell out of the slump. What an insulting thing to read about yourself."

The Darryl–Keith psychodrama would play out for another six years.

thirty-five

The Kid

The Mets were in first place on July 31, 1984, but the Chicago Cubs, led by Jim Frey, who had been a Mets coach the year before, compiled one of their finest seasons, winning 96 games and the Eastern division championship. The Mets, the surprise team in the National League, won 90 games, six-and-a-half games behind. Part of the reason the team did so well was its closeness.

Wally Backman: "We had such a tight unit of players. If the guys were going out to have cocktails, it wouldn't be one or two guys. It would be fifteen guys going out. That makes up part of the chemistry."

The Cubs were a team of vets, featuring Ryne Sandberg, Ron Cey, Larry Bowa, Leon Durham, Keith Moreland, and Gary Matthews. Rick Sutcliffe led a veteran pitching staff. The Mets, on the other hand, were a bunch of little-known kids who came close, but fell just short.

Wally Backman: "Our team was real young, hadn't been there very long, and faltered because of the pressure of the pennant race and our inexperience. We stayed pretty close, but there was so much hype in New York City, it put a lot of pressure on a lot of players. It was the inexperience that cost us that year. The Cubs were a veteran ball club and they just stayed up there and kept grinding it out, while we faltered a little bit."

★ ★ ★

Despite winning 90 games, no one was satisfied.

Wally Backman: "We weren't happy because we thought we should have won, and we didn't. That was the makeup of the ball club. During the successful years we had, we never expected to lose. We were cocky, arrogant. If we had a three-or four-game series, we knew we were going to win the series, on the road or at home. And when we lost a game, we took it personally."

Wally Backman

General manager Frank Cashen felt the same way. He had no intention of standing pat. On December 10, 1984, Cashen pulled a blockbuster deal, trading four youngsters with great potential, third baseman Hubie Brooks, starting catcher Mike Fitzgerald, outfielder prospect Herm Winningham, and pitching prospect Floyd Youmans, to Montreal for perennial National League All Star–catcher Gary "The Kid" Carter.

Along with Andre Dawson, Tim Raines, Warren Cromartie, Tim Wallach, and Al Oliver, Carter was one of a group of star performers from baseball's nastiest dysfunctional family. For all its talent, the Expos could not win a pennant, though they came within one game in 1980 when the Phils' Mike Schmidt hit a home run off Stan Bahnsen in the eleventh inning to beat them on the second-to-last day of the season. In 1981, they lost the division in the fifth game of the playoffs when Rick Monday of the Dodgers homered off reliever Steve Rogers. In 1982 and 1983 they finished third. During this whole time there had been whispers among the team and reporters, accusing Carter of being too concerned with his own stats and not being "a winner."

At the end of the 1983 season Expos owner Charles Bronfman called Carter in for a meeting and during a two-hour tete-a-tete ripped into him, charging that at $2 million a year he should have done more and that he was the reason for the Expos not winning the pennant.

Carter, his pride hurt badly, was mystified that Bronfman could feel that way; he had had one of his best years in 1984, hitting .294, with 27 home runs, and he coled the National League in rbis with 106. But, that year the sniping Expos finished fifth and Bronfman decided to shed Carter and his megasalary.

Carter didn't want to play where he was no longer wanted. He was so hurt by the owner's assessment of him that to escape the Canadian north, Carter even agreed to waive his no-trade clause and a $250,000 buy-out clause.

Gary Carter: "Charles was a funny guy. He was a pioneer bringing baseball into Canada. He took over the organization in 1969 and got it going. [Quebec is] a multilingual province, and they were thinking they were going to draw big crowds, and mind you, during some of the big years, we did draw well, drew over 2 million fans, but in 1982 I signed a seven-year extension for $2 million a year, and at that time it was big money.

"Charles was very upset with the way baseball was going. And then, in 1983, I got severe tendonitis in my elbow. Although I had a decent season, I had 17 home runs, 79 rbis, and hit .270. As a catcher with 37 doubles, I was very productive, and yet Charles was upset because he didn't think I was earning my money, that I wasn't giving enough back to the city. Even though I went to a Berlitz course and learned how to speak French and began working to raise money for leukemia.

"But when I met with Charles during spring training in 1984, I had no idea he was going to rip me. I thought if anything he was going to give me a pep talk.

"He asked me to meet him at his condominium in Palm Beach, and to begin with he showed me his place, and then he got down to the brass nuts. He started by saying, 'I was very disappointed in your performance this past year. I don't think you are earning your money. You're not giving anything back to the community. And there are jealousies on the team creating friction.' And it went on and on. He said, 'Whenever you get up in key situations, I go to the bathroom.'

"And I walked away with my head between my legs thinking, What have I done to get this man so upset to think I'm not giving my all? I had a bad elbow, but I still caught over 140 games. I led the league in games caught for six consecutive years. That's probably why I've had eight knee surgeries. But I was flabbergasted at his approach. As we left, I said to him, 'Charles, I'm going to go out and have my best year for you, and if that still is not enough, then I don't know what it's going to take.'

"And during the course of the '84 season I was hearing some rumblings, and then at the end of the year [president] John McHale, who had always been in my corner, said the board of directors—Charles was the main board member—was thinking of trading me. And I said to John, 'I don't want to just go anywhere.' I gave him some favorites. The Dodgers, Atlanta, and I said, 'Maybe the Mets,' though I didn't think he'd trade me to a contending team in the same division.

"When the trade was announced, I had the right to veto it. But I told John, 'If it's time to move on, I'll accept the trade.' And there was a $250,000 buyout clause that I just basically wrote off. I had just built a home in Montreal, and they agreed to pay 75 percent of the loss, and I lost over $150,000, so they helped me somewhat. But whatever I lost I felt I made up for when I went to New York."

Carter had been an Expo for eleven seasons, an All Star in seven of those. Behind the plate he was an ironman. He would catch more than 2,000 games before he was through, third in history behind Carlton Fisk and Bob Boone, despite knee injuries, bruises, and constant pain almost every day.

And he was a crowd pleaser. He was called "The Kid" because of his boyish enthusiasm about life and about the game of baseball. But his sunny demeanor and apparent willingness to please created resentment among some of his Expo teammates—mostly, but not all—black players. An extrovert with a ready smile, Carter honored almost every media request for an interview or a photograph. In large part because of that, he earned many thousands of dollars doing print and TV ads—Gillette, 7-Up, Chrysler, Dominion Textile, Sasson designer jeans, and Warner Lambert—while the black players, many of whom either resented or avoided the press, rarely got the ink he got and generated almost no outside income. Behind his back, they called him "Camera Carter." Warren Cromartie mockingly called him "Teeths." They questioned his sincerity and hatefully whispered it was all an act designed to ingratiate himself with the media and the public.

But they were very wrong. It was no act. Gary Carter was, and has been, one of the genuine nice guys in sports. Like Darryl Strawberry he had faced adversity as a child and had been humbled by it. When he was 12 his mother had died of leukemia.

The hole in his heart was healed, says Carter, who is not shy about discussing his faith if asked, when he was Born Again some years later. Adding to his saintly ways, he enjoyed talking to the media, and it would gladden him to make a young child's face light up after signing an autograph. Carter, moreover, *loved* playing baseball and it showed, every day.

What further separated him socially from many of his teammates was his refusal to haunt the bars at night. He has always been devoted to his wife and children, and he neither drank nor fooled around. The drinkers on the Expos, who were in the majority as they are on most teams, thought him square and didn't trust him, something that commonly occurs in baseball.

The jealousy and resentment on the part of his teammates also was understandable in that the Montreal fans loved him more than them. Carter truly enjoyed meeting the fans. Most of the other players looked upon the fans as parasites. But what could Carter have done differently? Be less friendly and accessible? Carter heard the criticism and was deeply hurt by it.

Gary Carter: "I was criticized at times for being too accommodating to the press, but I felt it was part of the job. A lot of guys would duck into the trainer's room to avoid the press, but I felt those guys were there to report on the games. I got the nickname 'Camera Carter' and 'Teeths' because I was always smiling. There was a lot of backstabbing going on, and yet, the way you turn those things to the better, you hit them with kindness. If they were badmouthing me, I would say, 'Hey, how are you doing? Great to see you,' and I would just let it go."

Mets general manager Frank Cashen didn't care about the jealousy directed at Carter. When you build a championship team, you build your strength through the middle and surround it. To win, you need a quality catcher.

When Cashen looked at Gary Carter, he appreciated all that the big catcher brought to a ball club. Now the Kid with the infectious grin was his.

Frank Cashen: "I had initiated the discussions with John McHale probably two years before the trade was completed. I told him if he was ever going to give up his catcher that I would be very interested in talking about that. I touched base with him the last series of the '84 season when we were playing Montreal in Shea Stadium. He told me then they were going to do something with the ball club, going to break it up. They had had the same group of people playing together, and they had infinite promise but had never made it, and he said the time had come to make some changes, which I agree with. I thought it took a lot of guts to do what he did.

"John called me and said, 'That player who we talked about, I think they will think about trading him.'

"At the time he was trying to get out of the day-to-day operation of the general managership and turn it over to Murray Cook, so I began discussions with Murray Cook.

"I said, 'Would you trade him?'

"'Yeah, if I can get what I want for him.'

"'What do you want for him?'

"Cook said he wanted an infielder who could hit and he wanted some other people. He kept writing names down and taking them out. The only player who was consistently in was Hubie Brooks. He was the top guy. We talked about a couple of different center fielders. We had Mookie Wilson and Herm Winningham, and he liked the younger of the two, Winningham, which kind of surprised me. And then he wanted a catcher back, and we did that [Mike Fitzgerald], and the big discussion was over who the fourth player should be. He wanted a young pitcher. I turned him down on about five or six guys, including Roger McDowell and Calvin Schiraldi, and finally we agreed to give him Floyd Youmans in the trade."

Gary Carter

★ ★ ★

Once he knew he was going to make the Carter trade, Cashen knew he was going to lose Hubie Brooks and would need another third baseman.

Frank Cashen: "Ray Knight had had an operation, and I wasn't sure about him, so I needed to get some protection at third base. Our people liked Howard Johnson, thought he was going to be good, and we went and traded with Detroit to get him. We had been talking to Detroit for a couple of years about that. Detroit wanted pitching, and the pitcher they wanted was Walt Terrell, and I didn't want to give him up so I didn't make the trade, but when I got Carter and I knew I had to give up Brooks, then I had to go make the trade Terrell for Johnson.

"I had given up Terrell and Youmans, and I made up my mind I was not going to give up any more young pitching. And I turned down a couple of trades during the season because they involved young pitching. I felt I could afford to give up the people I gave up, but not any more."

★ ★ ★

When the trade was announced, the New York writers recounted all the stories of Carter's supposed selfishness. Manager Davey Johnson took offense.

Davey Johnson: "When the media began spreading stories about how self-centered Gary is, I said, 'Great, I like selfish players, because they strive for perfection.' In fact, I tell my guys, 'Take care of number one. Get your rest at night. Play as good as you can. Work as hard as you can. Worry about yourself and I'll worry about everyone else. Let me worry about fitting all the pieces together.'"

Gary Carter: "Davey realized my talent and what I meant to the ball club, especially that the main reason I was brought to New York was not so much because of my offense, because we had an offensive ball club, but to handle the young pitchers. I'm sure the rumblings went on in spring training about the jealousy and what had gone on in Montreal, but I think the Mets players found out in a big hurry that, 'Hey, this guy is not a bad guy.' And Davey made a comment, 'Frank Robinson was perceived the same way,' and he said that Frank Robinson was a guy you loved to hate, but you loved having him on your team. And the players then accepted me, because they realized I was genuine. I wasn't a fake guy. When I go to card shows, people say to me, 'You're the nicest guy who comes to these shows.' And I say, 'You are paying me to come in and be part of this, and I want you to enjoy it and make it worth your while.' Why would I be abrupt and rude to these people because they ask for a kindness like an autograph? That's just the way I've been. But Davey made a point of it right away. He said, 'We've got something special here, and I think we need to go out boys and just play and not be concerned with all this other stuff going. Forget about who's better than who, and who's making money. Let's play baseball.' And that's the way it went."

Others who knew him and liked him wondered why Carter had taken such a beating in Montreal.

Ron Swoboda: "Gary Carter was a kid who read the history of baseball. He knew its history going in. Gary's a very interesting fellow. He got a bum rap, because he was so positive. People took it the wrong way. There was a current of resentment, and you wondered, Why? Gary played hard, he played hurt. He talked to everyone. But he understood the history of the game and respected it.

"When we'd come in for Old Timers games, Carter was the guy coming around to get you to sign stuff and spend some time with you. Roger McDowell would come and he always had time for you. Through that period in the 1970s, you didn't see a whole lot of other guys."

Above all, Gary Carter was talented. Of the catchers in his generation, only Johnny Bench rated in his league.

Wally Backman: "I played against Johnny Bench at the end of his career, and all the things people have said about him, you have to say the same about Gary. Gary took a young pitching staff and he was the boss out there. He called the pitches, talked to the pitchers, continued to build their confidence, and he took a young pitching staff and turned it into a championship a year later. To me that says a lot about Gary.

"They always called him 'Camera Carter,' because he wanted to be in front of the media, but in my opinion, if someone didn't like Gary, it was because of nothing but pure jealousy. There were times we'd get on Gary, because he was a guy who would be standing by the bus when we were trying to get to the airport and keep signing autographs—but that doesn't make you a bad person.

"I never, never, never heard Gary say a bad word about anyone. And that's a fact. If there's one individual who never said a bad thing about any player, it would have been Gary Carter."

With the acquisition of Carter and Howard Johnson, Davey Johnson was upbeat about his chances. He had a player of unlimited potential in Darryl Strawberry, a great field-general in Keith Hernandez, a top catcher in Gary Carter, one of the fastest players in the game in Mookie Wilson; a slugging veteran, George Foster; a young, talented pitching staff led by twenty-year-old phenom Dwight Gooden, and a potentially fine bull pen led by Jesse Orosco and the erratic Doug Sisk.

For the fans there would be something for everybody.

Despite the riches, a soap opera would run during the entire season. An early drama revolved around Keith Hernandez having to testify at the trial of a man accused of supplying ballplayers with drugs. In March 1985, Keith and six other players would admit publicly that they had used cocaine. Keith had been a St. Louis Cardinal at the time. The players worried that Keith might be suspended.

Wally Backman: "There was a concern, because we knew he had to go to the trial. What was going to be the outcome? Keith Hernandez' value to the ball club was tremendous.

"I don't think Keith never talked about it. His feeling was that whatever happened, happened, and it was over and done with, and it was time to get back to baseball. Because on the field Keith was all business. That's where he wanted to be, on the field."

By now Johnson saw how valuable Hernandez was to the team. He could not figure out why in the world Whitey Herzog had traded Hernandez away for Neil Allen. He was quoted as saying, "I know there was talk Keith was involved in drugs, but I have seen no evidence since he joined us. All I know is that Keith Hernandez is a fine man, hits over .300, is a great first baseman, and he will give you everything he's got, day in and day out."

Fortunately for the Mets, Hernandez was put on probation and didn't miss any playing time. In New York his past transgressions were quickly forgiven. The only place he would face fan disapproval would be in St. Louis, largely because in two short years he had become one of the Cardinals' fiercest opponents.

The Mets opened the 1985 season by winning eight out of nine games, many of them nail biters. If Davey Johnson didn't end up with ulcers by the end of the year, he would be surprised.

The opener at Shea was against the St. Louis Cardinals, a team bolstered by the addition of slugging first baseman Jack Clark. Dwight Gooden pitched brilliantly, but the Cards tied it in the bottom of the 9th inning against Doug Sisk, a husky reliever with a knack for walking the bases full and sometimes getting the side out. When Sisk failed to save the game and Johnson came to the mound to take him out, the Shea fans booed both Johnson and Sisk.

Wally Backman: "Little Dougie was wild. Dougie had so much movement on his fastball that he couldn't control it. There were times when he couldn't throw the ball over the plate.

"When he could control it, which was from time to time, he would be unhittable. They tried to get him to throw the ball down the middle of the plate and let it move. Sometimes he could do that, and sometimes he couldn't. Was it the pressure of pitching in New York? I don't know. It was just Dougie's makeup."

Keith Hernandez said of Sisk, "He wears me out, too. I yell at Doug the whole time he's pitching, 'Come on, throw the sonofabitch over.' Two innings of Sisk and I'm exhausted, but sometimes he responded to this harrassment."

The game was tied going into the bottom of the tenth when Cards reliever Neil Allen—who replaced the departed Bruce Sutter as the Cards' closer—gave up a long home run to Gary Carter in a 6–5 Mets win.

Gary Carter: "Coming to a new ball club that had the potential to win was a new beginning for me. When I left Montreal, I realized I was going to be looked at as the missing piece of the puzzle to get us to the World Series. I tried to play that down and emphasize how important all the rest of the guys were. Darryl Strawberry was Rookie of the Year in 1983, Doc Gooden came off a Rookie of the Year season in 1984, Keith Hernandez was a great first baseman, and we had a lot of other talent there.

"As spring training progressed, we could tell we had a pretty special ball club. On opening day it was cold and bitter in New York against the Cardinals. Joaquin Andujar started, and during the game he hit me in the same elbow that bothered me in '83. My arm went numb, and I thought, 'Gosh, I wonder if I can even continue in this game.' I put some ice on, but the feeling never did come back all game long. And after grounding out, I finally broke through with a double.

"We went into extra innings, and I hit a home run off Neil Allen, an ex-Met, and I mean to tell you, right then and there, I endeared myself to the fans. They chanted my name, 'Ga-ry, Ga-ry' as they left the Shea Stadium exits. It just made me feel so good, because I could remember so many great games I had in Montreal—one game I hit three home runs, and I barely got a curtain call.

"But that's just the difference between fans. Montreal fans were good fans, but they really weren't baseball fans. They were more hockey fans. So when I came to New York and that happened, it was a breath of fresh air. I thought, Gosh, this is great. I could understand when they tell about meeting the needs of the New York fans, how they welcome you, how the fans can be your tenth man on the field. So that's how it all started for me."

Wally Backman: "It gave the fans an idea of [Gary's] value to the ball club. As players we knew he was going to be valuable. But when you trade popular players away like Hubie Brooks, players the fans really like, for a guy like Gary to be able to come in there that first game and have an impact, that made a difference."

The second game against the Cards also went into extra innings and Mets rookie reliever Roger McDowell retired Jack Clark, Darrell Porter, and Terry Pendleton, the heart of the Cardinal lineup, in the eleventh while in the bottom of the inning Neil Allen walked Danny Heep with the bases loaded to lose the game.

In the season's third game Gary Carter's home run off Mario Soto beat the Reds 1–0. In the fifth game Dwight Gooden pitched a shutout and Carter hit yet another home run to beat Cincinnati.

Darryl Strawberry: "Gary Carter was our first hero [in '85], getting late-inning and tie-breaking hits that turned around the first five-or-so games. His enthusiasm and raw energy seemed to make things happen from right out of nowhere and infected the entire team with a spirit. It was *fun* to be on the Mets now."

The next time out Gooden pitched another shutout, this time against the Phils, but Steve Carlton matched him inning for inning, for eight innings. In the ninth, Backman was on third with two outs and left-hander Don Carman on the mound when Hernandez hit a single over first base to win the game. This Mets team was colorful as well as exciting.

Once again Hernandez had shown his ability to hit in the clutch. On defense, Hernandez set up the infield and kept the Mets pitchers on their toes. With Gary Carter behind the plate and Hernandez on first, pitchers had a lot of expert assistance.

Terry Leach: "When I pitched to Gary, I didn't have to do anything. I walked out there, and he told me everything I needed to know. He knew everything going on in the game. He wasn't one of those catchers who were just in there for his bat. He played both sides of the field, and he was very into it. He hated not to play.

"I remember every Sunday morning, even though he had caught the night before, it was like a ritual, like he and I going to church; he'd be in Davey's office trying to talk him into letting him play. Davey wanted to give him a day off, and Gary was trying to get back in the game.

"Gary called a great game and caught a great game. Some people got on him about his throwing. As far as I was concerned, Gary threw fine. The major-league average is about 35 percent, and he threw out about half my runners. And I was not extremely quick. We had guys like Dwight and Sid Fernandez who had big leg kicks, so it wasn't Gary's fault when runners stole. Runners would have three steps on him. You can't make up for that.

"It was like [having] a big ol' chair back there. I loved working with Gary. Gary was so intense, he was excited to be in the game. He didn't get bored with it, so his level of play never dropped. Same with Keith Hernandez. When I had both of them out there on the field with me, they protected me working on the hitters with Gary, and Keith working the defense, Keith would even come in and tell me about the hitters. He'd say, 'This guy hasn't been hitting the inside pitch at all.' Okay, here we go. Swing through and miss. Swing through and miss. Swing through and miss. I'd wave to Keith, 'Thank you very much.'

"Those two guys were true leaders to me. They didn't just talk the game. They played it hard. They were very positive.

"When things were going bad, they'd come over. 'You're doing all right. We'll get this guy. Just go after him. Come on, T.L., let's go.'"

The fans also could not get close enough to see that Hernandez had a brilliant baseball mind and a sharp tongue. Teammates had to answer to him for less-than-stellar play.

For instance, there was a game against the Cubs in 1985 in which the bases were loaded. Chicago manager Jim Frey brought in Chris Speier to bat for Larry Bowa. The fans were going crazy. Keith Hernandez analyzed what happened next.

Keith Hernandez: "A bunt is a possibility, so I watch Jim Frey before every pitch to Speier. I don't know the Cubs' signs, but I don't need to know them. *Any* sign will be the squeeze sign in this situation, except with the count two- or three-balls or with two strikes. First pitch, second pitch, third pitch: Frey sits on the bench with his arms folded across his lap, he doesn't move. Now, with the count two-and-one, he touches the bill of his cap with his right hand. No preliminaries, just the artificial movement. What else can it be? I don't need to watch Don Zimmer relaying the signs from the third-base box. The squeeze is on. I ease in. Davey motions me back. I signify 'negative' with a shake of the head, but still retreat a step. I can't call time for a conference. That would clue Frey that I've picked up his sign.

"Speier drops his bat for a bunt. When Hebner on third base breaks for the plate, third baseman Knight automatically breaks. I'm breaking in, too, and cleanly field the bunt—a good one—but nevertheless I don't have a play at home. I wheel and throw to first. But Wally [Backman] has vapor locked, the base is open and my throw is headed for right field—until it hits Speier on the back of his helmet. Cey follows Hebner across the plate, but if the ball hadn't hit Speier, Davis would have scored from first and Speier would have ended up on third, pretty much putting us out of the game.

"The play is a sequence of good sign-stealing by myself, bad brain-work by Backman, good fortune on my throw. Davey and I are probably the only ones in the park who know that if I had held my ground before the play, instead of moving back that one step, I would have had Hebner at the plate."

Hernandez had analyzed the play, explained what happened, and while doing so jumped down the throat of Wally Backman and chided Davey Johnson for not trusting him. It was a microcosm of what it was like to have Keith Hernandez on your team. You had better play smart, or one way or another you were going to hear about it. And if you didn't want to hear it, well, too bad.

One move that Johnson made early that season was to start youngster Lenny Dykstra in center field to replace Mookie Wilson, who had undergone a shoulder operation and was still having trouble throwing. Johnson asked Backman to move from leadoff to the second spot in the order so that Dykstra could leadoff. Backman obliged.

Wally Backman: "When Lenny first came up, Davey took me on the side, and he asked me if it would bother me if I hit second. And I said, 'No.' Davey told me that Lenny had always led off and that he felt I could make the adjustment from first to second, instead of taking a guy they were just bringing up and putting him in a different position in the order and making him do something he hadn't done before.

"I was doing him a favor, but I did it, because I owe a lot of my career to him."

In Davey Johnson's clubhouse other players weren't so tranquil. Doug Sisk was getting booed unmercifully and it was getting to him. The outspoken Ray Knight was not happy platooning with newcomer Howard Johnson. Unhappy with the starting rotation, Hernandez kept bugging Davey to push Cashen to bring up Sid Fernandez from Tidewater to bolster the starting staff so Roger McDowell could return to the bull pen. Ed Lynch, meanwhile, was complaining that Davey didn't leave him in the game long enough. It was a typically chaotic and boisterous Davey Johnson clubhouse.

The manager, himself outspoken, allowed his players the same leeway. As long as they played hard, he forgave them their outbursts in the papers. It made for lively reading in the dailies every morning.

The 1985 Mets were one of the more boisterous ball clubs in baseball's annals. The ringleaders of this Wild Bunch were the relief pitchers, Jesse Orosco, Roger McDowell, Doug Sisk, and Tom Gorman, and position players like Danny Heep, Wally Backman, and Dykstra, plus the towering presence of Keith Hernandez.

Joe Sambito pitched for the Mets during the spring of 1985. A former All Star cut by the Houston Astros after the '84 season, Sambito was returning from arm surgery. A native of Bethpage, Long Island, the lefty jumped at the chance to play back home. Though he was only with the team a short time, he never forgot how wild this team was.

Joe Sambito: "One thing I remember, and this was a normal occurrance, [was when] we'd go on the road, and [if] we were on the bus between the ballpark and the airport, or once we landed and gotten on the bus to go to the hotel, everything was fair game. I mean, insults started flying like you wouldn't believe. *Everything* was fair game. Nothing was sacred from your mother to your sister to your wife to your grandma. I had been a major-league veteran, but I was new on the team, so I wasn't getting involved in this. I thought, 'This is out of my league.'

"So I would sit there and listen and laugh and just cringe at times at some of the things that were said.

"One of the main guys and the favorite target was Tom Gorman, the left-handed relief pitcher. He was also an instigator. Doug Sisk was also a good one and Orosco, and McDowell. Bull pen guys spend a lot of time together, and there are a lot of bonds that are formed. That was part of it. And Wally Backman and Danny Heep. And Keith Hernandez was real good at this. And they had a nickname for the group. They called themselves 'The Scum Bunch.' The back-of-the-bus group.

"All these guys had been around, and they were very comfortable with each other. The things they'd throw at each other! They would be screaming and yelling at each other, and you'd think they'd be coming to blows, but it never got close to that. And when the bus would pull into the airport or the hotel, all of a sudden, silence and everybody applauded. And I thought it was the strangest thing. It was almost like, 'We're done guys, good job. Way to go.'

"They were a wild group and I certainly was not a drinker like they were. I could drink a little bit, but not like them."

The beer drinking on the flights was a constant. On one flight from Los Angeles to New York, the plane had to stop in St. Louis to refuel at six in the morning. Half the team was asleep, but the Scum Bunch was still drinking beer.

Another time the Mets had to fly from Philadelphia to Montreal after a night game. The plane landed about two in the morning, and after the players carried their bags through Canadian customs, the bus arrived at the hotel around three in the morning. Not fifty yards away from the hotel was the Chez Paris, an upscale topless club. The players stepped off the bus, and many of them, instead of heading for the hotel and some needed sleep, made a beeline for the strip club.

Davey Johnson had wanted his players to hang together. And hang together they did!

Joe Sambito: "What I remember best, the bunch of guys who were playing there, it was almost like we were a fraternity. It was like *Animal House*. Everybody got along. And when we went into battle, we went into battle together, and that was good. But it was wild like I had never seen."

On May 11, 1985, Keith Hernandez got his wish when Sid Fernandez came up from Tidewater to start and Roger McDowell returned to the pen. In his first start El Sid, as he was called, went six innings and allowed one hit in a 4–0 victory. McDowell got the save.

Wally Backman: "For us to be able to have a left-handed starter in our rotation, Sid made us that much stronger. It just changed the whole perspective to the opposing team, giving them a different angle. Sid was a power pitcher, and he had a great breaking ball. Sid was quality.

"Roger McDowell and Jesse Orosco in the bull pen were as good a combination as there was. You had both those guys who could close a game, and Davey would play the percentages. He used them against teams and batters he knew they pitched well against. Dave was into percentages, but he had his own percentages as well. Davey took a lot into the game."

In 1985, Davey Johnson had the luxury of knowing that every time twenty-year-old Dwight Gooden was on the mound, his team would win and the fans would be entertained. At Shea the cardboard Ks would hang all over the stadium. In 1985 Gooden finished 24–4, and a 1.53 era, the best in the majors, and won the Cy Young award. He led the league with 16 complete games and 268 strikeouts. Far behind him in Ks were Mario Soto, Nolan Ryan, Fernando Valenzuela, and in fifth place, Sid Fernandez.

Terry Leach, Gooden's teammate in the minors, was as impressed with the youngster's makeup as with his arm.

Terry Leach: "I was with Tidewater in '83 when Dwight came up from Single A. Dwight was young and very quiet. I could tell he was nervous. He came up for the playoffs and the Triple A World Series. The first day he got there it was a rainy day. We went out to do our running, and I was telling him what he was going to have to do, how to pay the clubby, and where to go to do this, that, and the other, and how to take care of himself a little bit. I must have done a good job, because the next year he was in the big leagues, and I was still down in Triple A.

"Dwight didn't try to overdo it. He did what he could, and it was *way* more than anybody else had. He had that nasty fastball, serious gas, and it had good movement. He also had a very good breaking ball. And back then he was throwing a change-up.

"We were at the Triple A World Series playing some pretty good teams, and he was throwing gas and a couple of breaking balls, and then he'd drop a change-up in there, and those guys would screw themselves into the ground.

"I said, 'That's not fair. That's not real.' And even though he was nineteen years old, he was very confident. And he was so quiet and humble about it. Dwight was never cocky, never popped off about things. It was what he was supposed to do, what he had always done. Why should he change now?"

Gary Carter had the privilege of catching Doc Gooden. According to Carter, as talented as Gooden was, what was special about this Mets team was that the rest of the young, talented staff were almost as good.

Gary Carter: "After Doc's rookie year being so successful, a lot of the baseball magazines and the baseball people were saying he was on his way to the Hall of Fame. He was so dominant and so quick to adapt to the major leagues as a rookie, and then in 1985 he was 24–4 with a 1.53 era. Every time he took the mound he had no-hit stuff. He threw 80 to 85 percent fastballs, and he threw what we called his 'Lord Charles,' the big curveball. He was so dominant with the fastball that he could win games with just the fastball. That's how overpowering he was. It had a little rise to it, and he came right over the top, and it was mid-90s every pitch. He had his confidence going and he could paint the outside corner if I put my glove there. He was fun to catch. He really was.

"The staff also had Ron Darling, Sid Fernandez, Rick Aguilera—all young pitchers. Roger McDowell, Jesse Orosco, and Doug Sisk were in the pen. All I tried to do was provide them with leadership to ensure their confidence. I told them, 'Hey, let me call the game, and you just throw.' And Doc very seldom called me off. And I loved that part of the game. I've been out of the game eight years, and I still miss it. It's the thing I miss most. It was fun to catch those guys, because they were around the plate most of the time.

"Ron Darling liked to philosophize a little bit. That's the Ivy League mentality. He went to Yale. Shoot, the guy was an intelligent man, a good-looking guy who obviously endeared himself to New York. He had the perfect name. He was the darling of everybody. And once Ronnie learned to master the split-fingered fastball, he really matured as a pitcher. Mel Stottlemyre taught it to him, and it became his number-one pitch. He had a good fastball, a good curve, a little slider but not much, but boy, when he came up with that split-finger, that became his out pitch.

"Sid Fernandez threw 95 percent fastballs, and he threw a curveball that no one ever swung at. It had a tight spin, he hid it so well that there were a lot of called strikes. It was the greatest thing in the world. He'd start it outside, and the batter would quit on it because they thought it was a rising fastball away, and it would stop and drop over.

"What I would do, I'd hold up my glove, and I'd call him 'Dukey,' after Duke Kamehameha from Hawaii, and I'd say, 'Dukey, just throw it like you're throwing it into a basket.' And he got really good with it.

"And the other thing about it, Sid would average ten strikeouts a game but he would not top 91 miles an hour. He had a little zip and because he had a wide body, he hid the ball well.

"The pitching staff was fun to catch, primarily because they didn't overwork me. The one pitcher who beat me up a little was Bruce Berenyi, who was a big part of our staff in '85 until he got hurt in July. He'd throw one great game and then in another he'd be all over the place.

"I'll never forget one game in St. Louis, I put on my chest protector and my shin guards, and I put another chest protector on and shin guards on my arms, and I said to him, 'Okay, Double B, I'm ready for you now.' He had such good stuff, but sometimes he would work me like you wouldn't believe. He'd throw balls in the dirt and I'd have to block about ten a game.

"Ron Darling would bounce a splitter every once in a while, too, and Roger McDowell had a nasty sinker. It was a fun staff to catch. It really was."

On May 11, 1985, the Mets' right fielder Darryl Strawberry hustled after a sinking blooper hit by Juan Samuel, dove for the ball and when he hit the ground jammed his right thumb back into his hand. He suffered torn ligaments in his thumb. The throbbing pain came instantly. He would be out seven weeks.

Darryl Strawberry: "At the time I was heartsick because I knew we had the Eastern Division right in our hands. It was ours; we knew it and the rest of the teams in the East knew it, too. But, when they took me off the field, the other teams licked their chops."

Fortunately for the Mets, Frank Cashen had stocked the team with more than adequate backup, Danny Heep, who Cashen had acquired from Houston for pitcher Mike Scott.

★ ★ ★

Wally Backman: "If you look at the record, we played real well when Darryl wasn't in the lineup. We were able to overcome losing Darryl, which is one of the hardest things to do. Danny Heep, who never got much credit, did a hell of a job. Heep didn't put up the power numbers Darryl would have put up, but he produced. He did the task in front of him. Trying to fill Darryl's shoes was next to impossible, and he did it as well as anybody could have."

The Mets faced yet another setback when their talented third-base coach, Bobby Valentine, left the team to manage the Texas Rangers. Valentine, who had a strong following among the players, would be missed. Once again, Frank Cashen had a backup in the wings: former shortstop Buddy Harrelson.

The one player who was not carrying his own weight was left fielder George Foster. He was making almost two million dollars a year and hitting under .200. Some of the players would laugh ruefully because game after game Foster would fail to produce and still remain in the lineup.

Wally Backman: "Everyone remembered the years he had in Cincinnati. Frank got him as a publicity thing. I would say when George came, they started drawing more people, put more fans in the seats, and that's what it's all about. But everyone knew George was coming to the end when he came here. How many more good years were you going to get out of him?

"He didn't give them what the Mets expected. And in '85, he didn't hit. But, he continued to play and the reason was obvious. At that time you didn't bench a guy making two million dollars a year. He was one of the three highest paid players in the game, and you're not going to take someone like that and put him on the bench. That was crazy."

On May 30, 1985, Dwight Gooden pitched a six-hitter against the San Francisco Giants, striking out 14. He then went on a fourteen-game winning streak, including a stretch when he went 31 innings in a row without allowing a run. In a game on June 4 Gooden and L.A. Dodgers star Fernando Valenzuela hooked up in a 1–1 pitchers' duel. The two pitching greats provided fans with some classic moments.

★ ★ ★

Wally Backman: "They were great matchups. That's why they were Game of the Week. Dwight was in his prime. Fernando hadn't been there very long, and no one knew how old he was. The only way you were going to win was if a mistake was made."

In one inning the Dodgers loaded the bases with nobody out. Gooden then struck out Greg Brock, got Mike Scioscia to foul out on the first pitch, and fanned Terry Whitfield.

In the ninth inning the Mets wonderkind came up to the plate and drove in a run with a hard hit single. The Mets would win the game 4–1.

Wally Backman: "I had seen Doc strike out the side with the bases loaded a year earlier in Chicago. He had that kind of ability.

"And Doc was a complete player. Not only could he pitch, he could hit. That was always one of the big things with the young pitching staff; they wanted to hit better than each other. In those years the staff hit damn well."

On June 7 the Mets were five full games ahead of the St. Louis Cardinals. But Whitey Herzog's Cardinals won three of four in a series the Mets needed to win.

Wally Backman: "Whitey was tough to beat. The Cards were a team built completely around speed, and they just beat us in so many ways. Tommy Herr drove in 110 runs with only 8 home runs.

"They had so much speed, it was tough. They were able to steal off all our pitchers. They had Vince Coleman, Andy van Slyke, Willie McGee, Ozzie Smith, and Terry Pendleton. It was almost like we were snake bit against them."

The low point of the 1985 season came on June 11 when the Mets lost to the Phils 26–7, the worst defeat in Mets history. Tom Gorman, a last-minute starter, gave up eight runs, and only got one out. Calvin Schiraldi relieved and gave up eight runs in an inning and a third. And then Joe Sambito came in, pitched three innings and allowed ten runs, eight earned. Even though Sambito could joke that his era was low on the staff that day, he was sent back to the minors, ending his tenure in New York. (He would resurface in Boston the following year.)

But, the Mets rebounded quickly after that and won twelve of fourteen. During this period Keith Hernandez provided the tabloids with headlines as he battled his ex-wife in an ugly divorce suit. During the ordeal, Hernandez hit well and often.

Wally Backman: "He talked about it. But, he played through it. It upset him, but he still would go four for five."

A potential derailment to the Mets' pennant hopes were rib, ankle, and knee injuries to Gary Carter. It was so bad he skipped the All Star game to get treatment. Upon his return, Carter stayed in the lineup and played with the pain for the rest of the season.

Gary Carter: "At the end of 1984 I was coming off knee surgery where I had a lateral miniscus flap tear which was getting caught in the joint. Yet, because it didn't break off, it wasn't severe.

"Just before the All Star break in '85 we were in Houston, and I got a base hit up the middle and got to first base, and I could barely run.

"The next day I woke up, and I could barely get out of bed and barely walk. The knee had swelled up. I went to the Mets' trainer and asked what the deal was. He said, 'You might have some torn cartilege.'

"I flew back to New York, and Dr. James Parkes took some fluid out and shot me up with cortisone. He said, 'The smartest thing you can do is rest during the All Star break. It gives you three full days of rest.'

"I was obviously disappointed. I had to watch Terry Kennedy, who was filling in for me, help the National League win in Minnesota that year. I sat and watched the game at home, and I had my glove with me, and I was just so angry this happened, and I spent the game sitting there pounding a ball into my glove.

"When the season started back up, that's when I started taping my knee full-time. Bob Sykes, the assistant trainer, took tape and cut it and overlapped it, and he would pull it real tight and lock the loose side in, and it would hold that piece of loose cartilege. I needed to alter my swing. I stepped a little bit further away from the plate.

"Even so, I had a tremendous September. I ended up being the Player of the Month and ended up having my biggest home-run production for a season with 32 and I drove in 100 runs. It's amazing, because my knee bothered me and yet I was still able to get through it.

"We were in a pennant race, so there was no way I would say, 'Let's have surgery.' I waited until the end of the year.

"I could deal with the pain. And because I played injured, and the people knew I was playing with torn cartilege, there was more of an appreciation for what I went through. See, a uniform always camouflages injuries. My leg was taped from midcalf to midthigh, and I had both my ankles taped from an injury I received in a collision at home plate in Houston in '84 when Tony Scott slid into me and fractured my ankle.

"So I played the rest of '84 with a fractured ankle, and I played in '85 with torn cartilege in my knee.

"It's the position we play. One of those things you have to accept."

Wally Backman: "If you saw how Gary got ready for a game, how they taped him up every day, it was clear his knee was bothering him. You knew he had to be hurt. You knew he wasn't taping it just to tape it. He played with a lot of pain.

"He taped that knee every day and sometimes both knees. I don't know how many surgeries Gary ended up having, but I know he played more than half of his career in pain. That shows you what kind of an individual he was.

"He didn't want any rest. Gary had that young pitching staff, and he was proud of its accomplishments. They had a lot of ability, but their accomplishments early in their career have to be pointed toward Gary. I've seen pitchers with tremendous ability early in their careers have subpar years with a catcher who's not that quality, as opposed to our guys having great years."

Darryl Strawberry returned in June, but didn't start to hit well until July. It took the team until August to get rolling again as efficiently as it had in the spring. On August 5 Strawberry hit three home runs and had 5 rbis in a 7–2 win against the Cubs in Chicago as the Mets regained first place. New York National League fans went wild.

thirty-six

Edged Out

The Davey Johnson Mets could have taken their place in history had one of the writers given them a memorable nickname a la the Gashouse Gang—they could well have been ticketed as the Lunch Bucket Gang or the Wild Bunch or something equally colorful, because this Mets team was every bit as pugnacious, hard drinking, rough, and raucous as the old St. Louis Cardinal Gashouse Gang of the 1930s. That gang had had some legendary fighters like Leo Durocher and Pepper Martin. This team had Ray Knight, a former Golden Glove boxer, and Darryl Strawberry, an L.A. ghetto kid who could turn mean when pushed too hard. Keith Hernandez could fight, too, and so could another of Davey Johnson's proteges, Wally Backman. This was a team that would squabble among themselves, but if pushed by the opposition would quickly start throwing punches.

Unfortunately, one of the side effects of on-field fights is that sometimes a player could get hurt, and that's exactly what happened on September 7, in a game against the Los Angeles Dodgers. Ed Lynch was pitching, and he struck out Mariano Duncan on a change-up.

Duncan, angry, yelled out at Lynch, "Throw something hard."

Lynch, taunting him back, hollered, "Grab some pine."

Duncan cursed at Lynch. Eddie cursed back and signaled for Duncan to come on out and fight him.

Duncan charged the mound and came at Lynch. Ray Knight grabbed Duncan, and the benches cleared.

★ ★ ★

Keith Hernandez: "Lynch was truly angry with Duncan, who was bush all the way. It was no secret; Eddie was sensitive to the charge that, for being such a big guy, he didn't throw very hard. He would have fought Duncan, gladly, if Knight hadn't intervened."

The Mets lost that day 7–6. During the melee, in which no punches were thrown, Lynch suffered a bruised right hip and a serious back injury. He was ineffective the rest of the year, pitching poorly in his next six consecutive starts. Lynch never told Johnson of his injuries, and, by the time Johnson had to resort to starting untested pitchers Wes Gardner and Rick Aguilera, the Cards had stolen the division title.

Wally Backman: "Eddie was all finesse. He was not a power pitcher, and, if he couldn't hit his spots, he could be hit hard. And with a nagging injury like that, it definitely had an effect on him. And yeah, that hurt, but the way the team was, to point a finger at Eddie . . . we couldn't do that.

"Eddie tried to keep the injury to himself, no question about it. He was hurt. Pride takes over a lot. He didn't want to come out of that rotation. I don't blame him for that. If you don't tell somebody you're hurt, they might not know you're hurt, and you can sometimes get through it. That's what Eddie was trying to do, get through it and be part of us trying to win."

On September 10, 1985, the Mets and the Cards had identical records, 82 and 53. The two teams met in New York. Howard Johnson hit a grand-slam home run in the first inning to win the series opener, and then John Tudor and Dwight Gooden pitched nine scoreless innings in the second game, after which Cesar Cedeno, whom the Cards had acquired from Cincinnati on August 29, homered off Jesse Orosco in the 10th inning.

Before the third game, which the Mets and Orosco won 7–6, Darryl Strawberry scratched himself from the Mets lineup, complaining that his thumb was really hurting him. His teammates tried to talk him into playing, but he refused. Keith Hernandez, Wally Backman, and other teammates were furious that Strawberry wasn't in the game regardless.

Wally Backman: "We were in such a tight race. Everyone felt that sixty percent of Darryl Strawberry in the lineup was going to make us a better team. With Darryl at sixty percent, if someone threw him a cookie down the middle, he was still going to hit it four-hundred-fifty feet. And as a team as a whole, we felt he let us down when we *really* needed him. My thought was that even if Darryl was hurt like he said he was, his presence in the lineup would have had a big impact for the ball club. And guys weren't happy with him.

"I'm sure Keith tried to talk to him. I didn't, because I was so pissed off about it, just like a lot of other players were. And it probably carried over onto the field with some of the players. I'm not blaming Darryl for us not winning that year either, but his presence could have made a difference, or it could not have made a difference, but at least we would have had our best players out there.

"When you see Gary Carter taping up his knee the way he did and Ray Knight taking cortisone shots in his hands so he could play, and you see these guys doing everything they could do to get themselves onto the field at almost any cost, and one guy doesn't, you tend to get a little upset.

"Gary was from the old school. Darryl was not from the new school, but getting to the new school. The old school was, 'You go out and play every day as long as you can walk,' as opposed to the new school, 'You don't play when you're injured, because you're going to hurt yourself on the field, and it's going to affect your salary.' Players were starting to listen to that."

Terry Leach: "You only have twenty-five guys on the team, and you don't pull up lame unless you just gotta. And that's the way Gary and Keith played it. If they were dying, okay, then they wouldn't be in there. They were so intense, and they found it difficult to put up with someone, especially a young player, saying that he couldn't go out and play."

Gary Carter: "The biggest thing about Darryl is that everybody knew he was blessed with tremendous talent. And when Darryl asked out of the game, everybody was upset because Darryl meant so much to the lineup. He was an intimidating factor at the plate. He made Keith and me better because of where he hit in the lineup. Keith batted third, I batted fourth, and Darryl batted fifth. If I didn't knock the runs in, he did. The top of the lineup was Wally and Mookie, and then Lenny and Wally. They were the tablesetters.

"Darryl was the type of guy, if you looked at his body, it was chiseled out. Everyone would look at his physique, and if he dogged it in the outfield, didn't hustle, there was disappointment, because you didn't think he was giving his all. If there was a lack of intensity and desire, it was like he had mistakenly hit 35 home runs or mistakenly driven in over 100 runs.

"It's unfair, but certain guys are blessed with more talent, and that was what made the guys furious at Darryl. We'd think, What if this guy *really* turned it on? What kind of stats could he put together? You'd think about it and say, 'My God, this guy could have been phenomenal.' Darryl Strawberry could have had the same type of career as Ken Griffey Jr. But then he'd bugger out of a game here and there.

"We didn't know what was going on off the field with him, though we are hearing more and more about it now. It's unfortunate, because all he did was take a Hall of Fame career and basically throw it away.

"Did he end up with decent stats? Yeah. You could say they were respectable for the talent he was given, but as far as what he could have accomplished if he really had had a burning desire to play. . . . He said his problems stemmed from the pressures of New York. Bullshit. Just play. That's all you need to do. Pressure is brought from within, and the way you avoid that is to just go out and play and hustle.

"I wasn't blessed with the greatest talent, but I made the most out of what I had. And the fans appreciated it when I gave that little extra, sliding into first base when the play was close. The fans appreciated my style of play because I played hard. That's all. That's all you need to do."

The Mets were a game behind the Cards. Eddie Lynch, who had lost four in a row, had to come out in the fifth inning, and when Davey Johnson replaced him with rookie Wes Gardner, he, too, was knocked out. [The Cards scored a run in the ninth to tie the game, but the Mets won it on a single by Keith Hernandez.]

Wally Backman: "Davey's hands were tied. By now we knew Eddie was hurt, but when you get into a race like that, you want to pitch the veteran. You can ruin a rookie's career by putting him in a situation where 'We gotta have this game,' as opposed to a veteran who knows what it's about, what the consequences are.

"The next day Davey pitched Rick Aguilera, who was also a rookie, and he beat the Pirates. He pitched very well down the stretch.

"Gary Carter, who had a big September, won the next two games against the Pirates with home runs."

★ ★ ★

The entire season came down to three games in St. Louis, a team that was hard to beat because of its great speed and fine pitching.

Terry Leach: "The Cards hit very few home runs, but what they could do was just run you to death. If you were in a tight game, which we always seemed to be in with them, you had to face Willie McGee, Vince Coleman, and Ozzie Smith, who all could run. If you walked one of them, they'd bunt him to third and hit a fly ball and score. They could manufacture runs. They didn't have to hit home runs. And they had pretty good pitching, so they were tough to beat. Those were gut-wrenching games."

The Midwest was energized. Before the first game Keith Hernandez called in the troops for some inspiration.

Terry Leach: "In St. Louis they had a slogan, 'Pennant drive in '85.' When the St. Louis fans go to a game, they are all dressed in red and white, and they carry flags, and it's an event, like a football game. At the malls, the fans were just wired. And being against the Mets and being so close, it was a big, big series.

"I remember attending a team meeting in Keith Hernandez's room before the first game. He called us all up and got us into a room together, trying to rally us all up. And everybody came. 'Guys, we gotta do this. We gotta put this together against these guys right here.'"

In the opener Ron Darling was masterful. In nine innings of work he didn't allow a run. John Tudor, meanwhile, pitched ten innings of shutout ball.

It was 0 to 0 in the top of the eleventh inning when left-hander Ken Dayley stood in against Darryl Strawberry, whose thumb still hurt from his injury but whose 29 home runs in less than 400 at bats established him as one of the league's top home-run threats. Strawberry recalled his emotions as he went to bat against the big left-hander.

Darryl Strawberry: " 'Dayley, you're meat!' I screamed to myself. Then the jerk tried to smoke me. Smoke me!

"KA-BOOM. The ball wouldn't stop flying. On and on it went, deep into right center field. Up and up it soared, high over the bleachers. The entire stadium went to its feet as the ball bounced high on the scoreboard [against the clock] and disappeared somewhere in the superstructure of the stadium.

"We were two games out of first."

Terry Leach: "I happened to be in the dugout when he did it. I had to go to the bathroom, and I was in the dugout getting ready to go back to the bull pen when he hit that clock. I mean, that thing got out of there in a heartbeat. It just darted that clock! Boom! He crushed that thing. That was a *very* hard hit ball."

Dwight Gooden then beat the Cards 5–2 to run his record to 22–4 as George Foster hit home-run number 21. The Cards scored a run in the ninth inning and put the tying run on base with Tommy Herr up to the plate. Herr hit a shot—right at Wally Backman. The Mets were now one game back with four games to go.

The season came down to the series finale pitting Denny Cox against Rick Aguilera. The Mets scored a run off Cox in the first and had the bases loaded with only one out. A base hit would have finished Cox and the Cardinals.

But George Foster hit a grounder to third, and Terry Pendleton threw Hernandez out at the plate.

Wally Backman: "We had the bases loaded, one out, a 3 and 0 count on George, and he had a take sign, and he swung and hit a ground ball. I remember the take sign was on. I was on base, and I watched him get the take sign. And George swung away and grounded out, and *that* was what hurt us the worst. Because if we'd have won that game, we'd have had a chance to win the division title.

"We'd have been on a high, and they'd have been low with their backs against the wall. We were young enough to know we were there, because we were supposed to be there now, and you are more relaxed. I remember that *very* well.

Gary Carter: "George was given the take sign and swung away and grounded out, and that created a problem in the dugout. Everybody was upset about that. But George wanted to come through in a big way. Those who know George: he's a different kind of guy, but you know what? He's a good guy. He really is. And that was just a mistake on his part, and he came to New York with a lot of history, with great years in Cincinnati, and unfortunately he didn't live up to those expectations."

With two outs Howard Johnson, who had hit a grand slam against Cox three weeks earlier at Shea, grounded to third baseman Terry Pendleton, who stepped on third to end the inning, the rally, and the Mets' chance at the pennant. The game ended 4–3 Cards when with Hernandez on first, Jeff Lahti got Gary Carter to fly out to right.

Gary Carter: "That was so disappointing because I was so hot in the month of September. If I could hit a home run, I had a chance to tie the game. And that's what I was trying to do. At the time I was so grooved in at the plate, and I tried to get a little extra. I was probably trying too hard. Rather than just try to get on base, I was trying to hit a two-run homer, and all I needed to do was get on base. Jeff Lahti threw the ball in on me, jammed me a little bit, and I hit a slicer to right center for the last out."

Terry Leach: "After we lost [the Cox game] we knew we didn't have a chance. It was a serious letdown. I was really disappointed, because I felt I was lucky to be there, and I didn't know if I'd ever see a playoff game."

Wally Backman: "If we could have won that game, we could have left there with a one-game lead playing the Expos, instead of being behind by one game.

"We flew home to play the Expos, and we won one of three against them, but the Cards kept winning. We were eliminated on the second to last day of the season."

On October 6, 1985, in the final game of the season against the Expos, the Mets and their fans held a love-in. On the scoreboard was flashed the highlights of a wonderful season.

Darryl Strawberry: "We knew that in that moment, Frank Cashen loved his Mets, and we loved him, too. Shea was suddenly alive with feeling. This was the way baseball was supposed to be. Glory, but I was glad to be a Met that night.

"We stood up in the dugout watching the scoreboard while the fans were cheering for us. I couldn't believe it. We were almost there, almost into the playoffs, but the fans were still cheering their New York Mets. I started to cry. Then a few of the guys acknowledged the cheering fans when they ran out on the field and started waving to the stands. The fans went crazy. More of us went out and began tipping our hats to our wonderful, wonderful New York Mets fans. The whole of Shea Stadium was alive with love. It was warm. It was happy, it was like one giant 40,000-person family all wishing the season would continue but thanking each other for what they had."

Terry Leach: "We gave the fans a good show all year long. It was an exciting team, a personable team. We had future stars coming up, and the Mets fans were hungry for something to happen, because when I first came up in 1981, there would be only 14,000 people in the stands because we weren't winning. But even then, they were rabid fans. They were into it, and they could just see us getting better and better, so they were wanting it.

"This team had evolved. We had a lot of homegrown ballplayers who the Mets had drafted and who had come up through the minor leagues, and they liked watching them grow up. The fans were into it, the players liked it, and it was very easy to get along there."

Then Wally Backman, who loved the Mets fans, threw his hat into the stands. Anyone who was there will never forget it.

Darryl Strawberry: "The whole Shea Stadium crowd came alive. People were screaming, 'I love the Mets,' and then Keith threw his hat into the stands and then we all threw our hats into the stands. There was even more cheering. There were tears. The team was crying on that October night in New York City. We thought the whole place would explode in love. The fans loved us. We loved our Mets fans, loved them with all our hearts."

Wally Backman: "I just did it. I don't know why. We had a great year. We knew we had played well. We were frustrated that we didn't get to where we expected ourselves to be. We had the second-best record in the National League, and not to be able to go to the Championship Series was frustrating, and then to watch the Cardinals win the Series when we thought we were a better ball club. In the long haul the Cardinals were two games better, but I and a lot of the other players felt that we were the better ball club.

"If we could have done a few things a little differently, we could have won a few more games."

After being eliminated by the Cardinals with only two days left in the season, Davey Johnson contemplated the future. He recalled the year his Orioles had lost to the Mets in the World Series, and how he felt then. He vowed that for his Mets, 1986 would be different.

Davey Johnson: "I remembered in 1969, when the Orioles were beaten by the Mets. Everyone on our team at the time made a silent vow: Hey, okay, so we got beat. Let's come back next year and go all the way wire-to-wire, And that's what happened. We won the division, beating Minnesota in the playoffs 3–0 and then in the World Series we beat Cincinnati four games out of five. And that's what I want to see happen to us next year.

"As I told the players the day before the season ended, 'I want you to make up your minds we're going to win it next year, that nothing is going to stop us, that we're going to win it next year.'

"After the meeting, I went back to my office to be alone for a while. I swore to myself: Next year, by God, nothing is going to stop us."

thirty-seven

A Runaway Pennant

From the first day of spring training in 1986, Davey Johnson boasted to anyone and everyone, "We're not only going to win, we're going to win *big*. We're going to blow the rest of the division away." He was confident, and he was certain. When Frank Cashen heard Johnson's pronouncements, he hit the roof. Davey didn't care. He had the horses. If everyone stayed healthy, he knew, there wasn't a team in the National League, including the Cardinals, that could stop them.

When St. Louis began its season 4–1, the Mets were only 2–3, including a loss to the Cards, and the writers once again asked their favorite question in bold headlines, WHAT'S WRONG WITH THE METS?

The answer was that *nothing* was wrong, as they won their next five games and flew into St. Louis to play a four-game series.

Before the Cardinal series in late April, Davey pointed to the schedule. He told the players 'You win it all right here.' 'Numbers are numbers and we make them work for us right here. We break the Cardinals at home, we own them for the rest of the year. Other teams will know that we're taking back what should have been ours last year.'

When Davey Johnson told reporters the Mets would win three out of four against the Cardinals at Busch Stadium, his prediction turned out to be too conservative.

The first game was tied when the Mets scored two runs off Todd Worrell in the ninth inning and another in the tenth to win. Doc

Gooden won big in game two, and in game three Wally Backman made an impossible game-ending double play to help win 4–3. Bobby Ojeda, a crafty left-hander acquired during the off-season to bolster the starting rotation, won the 5–3 finale easily while the hitters beat up John Tudor for five runs.

When they left town, the Mets were four-and-a-half games ahead. It was only April, and the pennant was theirs.

Gary Carter: "We went into St. Louis at the very beginning of the season. We had lost out in '85, and Davey said, 'If there is a time to prove yourself, it's now.' We went into St. Louis, and we swept them four games. And that buried them right then. Davey said, 'Whitey will recognize this, too.'

"I give Whitey a lot of credit for keeping his players motivated. He was one who didn't tolerate any of the drugs or dissension or craziness on a team, and if so, he got rid of him. He just flat out got rid of him. And Whitey had a lot to say about what transpired in St. Louis and that's what Davey wanted and didn't get. The scenario was Davey battling Whitey. All in all, it seemed like every year we battled the Cardinals for the Eastern Division.

"We were like a long-distance runner who gets out ahead of the pack early, and who looks, at times, as if he can be caught, but who knows he won't be, because today is his day. His lead may not be enormous, but it is comfortable because he is equal to anyone trying to catch him. When this happens, self-confidence takes over, and it lifts and carries you like a wave."

Bobby Ojeda, the most important new square in the Mets quilt, was a left-handed pitcher who was acquired from the Boston Red Sox with three minor-league pitchers for Calvin Schiraldi, Wes Gardner, and two minor leaguers, John Christianson and Lashelle Tarver. Gary Carter recalled his role in making Ojeda a better pitcher.

Gary Carter: "Once Bobby left Boston and came to New York, I really tried to get him to work inside, to throw more fastballs inside. Everyone is so reluctant to throw inside at Fenway Park, because you know if the batter hits a pop-up to left field, it's going to be a home run. What really improved Bobby when he came to the Mets was that he started throwing those inside fastballs, and he had a great change-up, probably the best change-up of anyone I ever caught."

Wally Backman recalled how easily Ojeda meshed and remembered how badly the Mets players wanted to avenge losing the division title the year before.

Wally Backman: "When we got Ojeda, he fit right into the chemistry of the ball club. He ended up coming over and being a huge part of it, not just because of his success, but what he brought to our ball club, a soft-throwing left-hander who was as fierce a competitor as anybody. He wanted to shove it up the Red Sox butts.

"We were still mad from the year before. We didn't want to have the third-best record in baseball and not go to the playoffs again. We were determined to do what we thought we should have done the year before."

Which is what they did. The Mets won 21 of their first 26 games, while demonstrating a swagger that trumpeted their self-confidence. As the season wore on, opposing players began to bitch and moan about the Mets taking curtain calls after home runs. Gary Carter, in particular, was in the habit of jubilantly bounding out of the dugout and pumping his fist several times in the air after homering. The Mets players thought the criticism was mostly sour grapes.

Gary Carter: "Opposing players complained that we were rubbing it in, showing them up. They called us arrogant. It was said that we were the most hated team in the game. My name kept popping up. Some said that of all the Mets I was the worst offender, the biggest showboat, the most hated.

"I thought it was confidence. I don't think it was really cockiness.

"Whitey [Herzog] is one of those who disliked our style. The fists in the air, the celebrating. Ozzie Smith, their fabulous shortstop, griped about our style. Some of us weren't crazy about *his* style, either—the handstands and cartwheels as he took the field."

The other teams fought the Mets like it was war. The Mets and Pirates had a big brawl on the field in June after Mets first-base coach Bill Robinson accused Pirate pitcher Rick Rhoden of doctoring the ball. Pitchers often threw at Mets batters, runners cut down Mets fielders, and fans booed them everywhere. The Mets fought back even harder. They were an intimidating group. And they beat you.

Darryl Strawberry: "A team on the march to the championship that develops this attitude is no longer a team—it's more like a gang. You hang together, you chill together, you go to war together. You play kick-ass baseball until you're the only ones standing on the field. The machismo builds until you're no longer human, you're like a Terminator."

Part of what binds a winning team together is its closeness, and in 1986 few teams were knit quite so tightly. Mets players hugged and celebrated and shook hands and high-fived at every opportunity. Opposing teams hated the Mets for their shows of affection.

Gary Carter: "The Mets were close and we touched, and the touching grew as the season went by. Touching is a ritual, part of celebrating. I wonder now if it had something to do with the perception that we were arrogant—if our closeness made us seem as if we looked down on everyone else. People did love to beat us. And so there were bean balls and hard words, and fights."

The Mets third brawl of the season came on July 11, 1986, at Shea Stadium against the Atlanta Braves. David Palmer, a former member of the Dawson/Raines Montreal clique, started on the mound for the Braves. In the first inning Carter hit a three-run home run off Palmer.

With the next pitch Palmer hit Darryl Strawberry on the hip. He charged the mound, but Hernandez tackled the pitcher first.

At the end of the inning Strawberry was on third, when Palmer asked him if he wanted to fight. Straw said he did, but third-base coach Buddy Harrelson broke it up.

In the second inning Palmer loaded the bases, and Carter came up. He hit a grand-slam home run over the left-field fence.

Carter came out for a curtain call, and while the Mets celebrated, the Braves fumed.

On July 19, 1986, in the early-morning hours, the Mets reputation for brawling reached national proportions during a series against the Astros. This time the altercation took place not on the field, but in a Houston country-and-western shit-kicker bar called Cooter's.

All of Houston resented the Mets after Gary Carter had accused pitcher Mike Scott of cheating by scuffing up the baseball several weeks earlier. Houston cheered when four Mets—Tim Teufel, Ron Darling, Rick Aguilera, and Bobby Ojeda, were arrested after a fight with a couple of off-duty policemen. Their arrest was further proof that bad boys will be bad boys.

Darryl Strawberry: "You have to do that, too—march into somebody else's city and raise a ruckus at a bar on his turf. Let him know you have no respect for his territory. Piss on him if you have to, but, stomp away having swept the series."

Strawberry, who had been with the four but had left before the fisticuffs broke out, recalled the booze that flowed and the gunslinger atmosphere of the place.

Darryl Strawberry: "Here we are in Cooter's after being shutout, drinking and toasting, and toasting and drinking, and drinking and drinking and drinking. The music's loud; the sawdust tickles our throats and makes them drier; we're in first place; I look around me at the faces of the other people in the bar, as our little group—Timmy, Ron, Bobby, and Rick—gets louder and rowdier. 'I may be tough,' I think, as I check out the slack-jawed mugs on these countryboys, 'but I'm not a masochist.' These guys are looking to size us up for a whupping. I said, "Sorry, fellas, I gotta go. Got a big game tomorrow. Maybe y'all should be thinking about packing in tonight, too. It's been real. We must do this again sometime. See ya.'
    "That's all she wrote, and I hit the hay."

At five o'clock in the morning Tim Teufel, with his beer in his hand, followed the crowd across the sawdust toward the door, where he was stopped by two bouncers who later turned out to be off-duty patrolmen. In dispute was whether they told Teufel they were off-duty patrolmen.

Gary Carter: "Tuff had tried to walk out of the bar with a half-drunk beer, and a couple of off-duty cops had ordered him back inside. It turned ugly. Aggie, Bobby, and Ronnie were trying to protect Tuff, to steer him out of there. Whatever Tuff did to the cops, he'd gotten more than he'd given. They beat him up. He spent the night in jail, bruised and cut.

"Roger [McDowell] got to the clubhouse early the day after. He got a roll of adhesive tape from the trainer's room, blackened the tape with a Magic Marker, and stuck it in vertical rows down the fronts of Tuff's, R.J.'s and Bobby O's, and Aggie's dressing cubbies. Black bars, miniature jail cells. Tuff, with his swollen purple face, wasn't very amused. The other guys were able to laugh. 'I should have known you'd do something,' R.J. said."

A few nights later Davey Johnson announced that he was going to play rookie Kevin Mitchell and Danny Heep in left field and that George Foster, who had stopped hitting, was going to be benched. Though Foster was making $1.8 million in '86, his low production had made him a liability, and after playing him in '85 and suffering with his lack of productivity, Davey decided that it was time for Kevin Mitchell and Danny Heep to take his place.

Then on July 22, the Mets got into a vicious brawl against the Reds. In the 10th inning Pete Rose singled, and Rose, who was managing the Reds, sent Eric Davis in to pinch run. Davis stole second, and as he was stealing third, he bumped into Ray Knight with his forearms. Neither would move, and Knight said something to Davis. When Davis said something back, Ray—a former Golden Glove boxer—hit Davis square in the jaw with a short right-hand punch.

Ray Knight turned out to be a fixture at third base during the 1986 season, but before the season began, there had been a question whether he would even be on the team.

Davey wanted him. Frank Cashen didn't. Ray had not hit well in 1984 and 1985. He had played ten years and Cashen figured he was finished. After '84 Knight had bone chips taken out of his throwing elbow and he'd had shoulder surgery.

"I want Ray Knight," Davey kept proclaiming. And finally, he got him. At first, Davey only played him against left-handers.

On April 21 against the Pirates, Knight started against a lefty. Late in the game he was scheduled to hit against right-hander Cecilio Guante. He stood in the on-deck circle, expecting to be pinch hit for. Ray looked at Davey, who nodded to him to hit. Knight hit the ball out of the park. From that moment, he was the every-day third baseman. There were periods when he was banged up and shouldn't have been in the lineup, but Knight took cortisone shots and taped himself up, refusing to come out.

Knight's gritty competitiveness provided a role model for the Mets younger players. His teammates sometimes joked to his face that he wasn't as famous as his golfer wife, calling him Mr. Nancy Lopez, but they only did it if he was in a good mood. They knew there were few players in all of baseball as tough as he. That Knight would punch a player in the jaw when provoked surprised no one on the Mets.

Ray Knight

When Knight slugged Eric Davis, the dugouts emptied. While his teammates fought the Reds, George Foster stood by himself in the Mets dugout, a lone figure. After the umpires broke up the fight Ray Knight and Kevin Mitchell were thrown out of the game along with Davis. With HoJo in the game at shortstop for Raffy Santana, Davey Johnson had to come up with a fill-in third baseman. Johnson tapped Gary Carter, who became the eightieth Met to play third base. Ed Hearn caught, and Roger McDowell played right field.

The Mets won in the 14th inning when Howard Johnson hit a three-run home run. McDowell came in from the outfield to get the save. For the Mets it was like a sandlot game, improvised and a lot of fun.

But after the game all the talk was about the behavior of George Foster. Gary Carter, a gentle man, tried to figure Foster out. As much time as he spent with Foster, which was considerable, it wasn't easy.

Gary Carter: "George Foster was a mystery to most of us. I couldn't see inside the man very much and I couldn't make out his moods and changes on the surface. He was a quiet guy, a loner, I think; he would sit by himself on a bus or plane and think his own thoughts, and I never really knew what they were. He seemed to have a chip on his shoulder; he had a hard stare. He could challenge you with that stare. He could make an opposing pitcher furious.

"George was mostly silent, but he had a sharp tongue. He would make remarks, kind of joking, kind of not; little barbs that he would flick at you across the clubhouse or around the batting cage. I heard some things like that from George when I first arrived to play with the Mets, in spring training in '85. Jokes, but with a sharpness to them. The sort of stuff I'd gotten in Montreal, except it had been personal then, and had real poison in it. I know George didn't mean to be nasty. He was the same way with the other guys. He looked at you from a distance, wouldn't let you come close. I never had a heart-to-heart with George Foster.

"There are things to admire in George, besides his greatness as a player. He's a devoted family man and a devout Christian. I've never heard George swear. Never. He used to read his Bible on the planes. I'll always remember George sitting alone, reading the Bible.

"George never quite came up to expectations in New York. His first two years [1982 and 1983] were huge disappointments. He was much more productive in '84 and '85, but he had left the great years behind him. But, he was in New York where everybody notices. It must have been hard for this proud man.

"The way George played was also a mystery to us. He had a reputation for never getting his uniform dirty. It was said that he never dove for a ball in the outfield, and that he shied away from collisions with walls. Running into a wall is nobody's idea of fun, but an outfielder has to now and then if he's going to catch a ball. It was said that George wouldn't do it. There was some truth in it, as if George had disdain for crash landings, as if that was for lesser ballplayers. Was this pride? It should have had the opposite effect, we thought.

"1986 was the final year of George's contract, and even before the season began, it was a good guess that he wouldn't be around the next season. The Mets were paying him for the kind of years he'd had in Cincinnati, and weren't getting them. And George was getting on as a ballplayer. Still, we expected him to have a decent year, like the last two, and to help us win.

"But George wasn't his old self. He got hot in May for about ten days, but other than that he wasn't much of a presence in our lineup. Every now and then he'd slug one of his mammoth home runs, but on the whole he was pretty quiet. Meanwhile, Kevin Mitchell and Danny were warming the bench, and so was Mookie, who's lost his job to Lenny. Davey had three good, hungry ballplayers waiting in the wings. George was batting in the .220s.

"After the All Star break, Davey began using Mookie and World [Kevin Mitchell] in left field, which meant benching George. And George was miserable. He turned more silent, withdrew deeper inside himself than ever. On July 22, we were in a big and wild brawl with the Reds in Cincinnati; both benches emptied, and it went on for a while. George did not leave the dugout. It's a question of standing by each other."

Wally Backman: "It was time for us to try to find another guy for left field. We couldn't trade him. Nobody would touch him. And then in that game when George Foster stayed on the bench, that was the end of Foster. George lost all the respect from his peers. He was upset because Davey wanted to play Kevin and Danny Heep, but that was a piss–poor excuse. That shows you right there the guy was not a team player at that time. I'm sure he was a team player when he was in Cincinnati, having the good years, but if you have a player who won't back up the other players, that has a huge effect on a team. If there is a fight, everybody has got to back up everybody else, no matter who's wrong. That was the type of players we had. And by not doing that, George was cutting his own throat."

Around the end of July the Pirates released Lee Mazzilli. Frank Cashen signed him to a contract and sent him to Tidewater. Mazzilli's signing further threatened Foster, who was already on ground that was beginning to give way.

★ ★ ★

Gary Carter: "From the beginning George had been ungracious about being benched. He'd sulked. Almost within earshot, he'd talked disgust-edly about Mookie's, Danny's, and World's abilities. He said right out that he was better. And I think he sealed his own fate.

"George was miserable and bitter and no fun to be around. He made Davey uneasy. He made all of us uneasy. And yet we felt for him, too, a man who not so long ago had hit 52 home runs, and been feared. About the time the Mets acquired Mazzilli, George started muttering about racism.

"He told a reporter that he was probably going to be released and replaced by Mazzilli, and that he smelled racial prejudice in the move. Next day, his statements were in the papers. Frank was furious."

So were his teammates.

Wally Backman: "When George accused the Mets of racism, that was George's problem. It wasn't anybody else's problem, because that wasn't the case at all. George's lack of production was obvious. You look at the numbers, and it was obvious it was time to try something else. Did I disre-spect Davey for the time I hit .320 and the next year I only hit .250 and lost my job and he started Tim Teufel? He felt the guy could help the ball club more than I did in the previous year, and so I had to re-earn my respect with Davey as a player. But do I have anything bad to say about Davey? No. I wish he had given me a little more of an opportunity at the start and not been so quick to pull the trigger, but that was his decision, and I respected him, and I just knew I had to work harder.

"When you start throwing out racism, that is *not* a factor in sports. I have never seen that be a factor in sports. I saw someone trying to use racism, and it wasn't right.

"Not long afterward we were in Chicago, and they got rid of him. He was hurting the team."

Gary Carter: "On August 6, we had played the Cubs in Chicago, and before the game George was nowhere to be found. He wasn't in the club-house, and he didn't take batting practice. The guys were wondering if he'd been let go. No one knew. The game began and after a while, George came out in his uniform. On that afternoon Mookie didn't start, came in the game late, and drove in the winning run with a single in the twelfth inning. George pinch hit, his final act as a New York Met.

"The next day, the papers carried more of George's talk about racism among the Mets. It was now inevitable: George was going."

The next afternoon Foster called the players together and apologized to them. "I just want to say . . . if I've caused any problems, if I've hurt anybody, I'm sorry. I apologize."

Ray Knight followed George to his locker and began to challenge some of the accusations he had made. As Foster talked, he began to cry. Foster left the ballpark, and he was never seen at Shea again.

What made Foster's behavior seem even worse was the contrast to the way Mookie Wilson had behaved after he had lost his center field job to Lenny Dykstra earlier in the year.

In the spring of 1986 the Mets were practicing rundowns. Carter, who had had knee surgery, was playing first base. Rafael Santana was at the other end of the rundown. Mookie was running. Raffy whipped a ball that hit Mookie right in the eye.

The ball broke his glasses, and he dropped. An edge of the lens had cut him above the eye. Bits of glass were *in* his eye, and there was internal bleeding. For ten days Mookie had to sit out. On Opening Day he was on the DL. He joined the team in mid-April.

When he returned the outfield of Foster, Dykstra, and Strawberry was solid. Mookie, now a part-time player, never complained, didn't sulk, and didn't ask to be traded. Mookie waited patiently while George Foster self-destructed.

Lenny Dykstra: "George cut his own throat, with that racial shit he said in Chicago. I mean, he could have stayed with us the whole year and been part of a World Series. But, he shot his mouth off. It seemed like Davey was just looking for an excuse and George gave him one."

An angry Wally Backman buried George Foster in the papers after his release saying, "Good riddance. We should have done it long ago. You don't bury your teammates and act like he acted the last few weeks and then call yourself a teammate."

On August 16, 1986, it looked like the Mets injury-free string had run out. After Gary Carter fell on his left hand making a play at first base in the second inning, his thumb was swollen and throbbing. Thinking it was broken and fearing his season was over, Carter was in a state of panic. His National League rbi lead was in jeopardy. That inning he had made three stellar plays, but in the dugout the pain overwhelmed the congratulations.

On the way to the hospital Dr. Parkes examined him and told him it wasn't broken. The thumb was put in a cast for a week, and he was out fifteen days. Not wanting to miss anything he traveled with the team. He drove Davey and the players on the bench crazy as he watched Philadelphia third baseman Mike Schmidt take the rbi lead from him for good.

Gary Carter: "I was playing first base, and Ozzie Smith ripped a one-hopper to me, and I landed on my thumb, and I really thought I had broken it, because I had broken it back in '76 and had two pins put in it. And I threw to second to get Mike LaValliere for the first out of the inning.

"My thumb was hurting like crazy, yet I didn't come out of the game until the inning was over. On the next play Greg Matthews bunted over by our dugout, and I went over sliding and made the catch, and so I also made the MetLife play of the month. And then after the inning was over, I came in and told Steve Garland, our trainer, 'I think I broke my thumb.'

"He said, 'Let's get Dr. Parkes down here,' and he looked at it and fooled with it, and I said, 'Please don't put me on the disabled list.'

"Dr. Parkes examined it, and there was still enough ligament holding that it wasn't completely torn. We had a meeting of the minds, and Frank Cashen convinced everyone, 'Let's cast him,' and I was extremely disappointed, but they didn't say it was fractured, and they didn't say the ligament was torn. I was supposed to rehab and then come back and play.

"I was reinstated the first part of September when the rosters expanded, but I had to have my thumb taped. Bob Sykes taped it, held it together, and I played that way the rest of the season.

"I came back and had a decent September, and breaking my thumb probably cost me the MVP. I ended up third. Mike Schmidt won and Glenn Davis was second. I had 20 home runs and 80 rbis at the end of August, and I ended the season with 105, which tied the Mets record with Rusty Staub.

"But what happened, when the Mets went to the West Coast without me, they ended up 11–3 with John Gibbons and Ed Hearn, and the team played so well, and the press jumped on it and said, 'This team is so good it can win with or without Gary.' And yet other people believe I was MVP that year. But because I was out those fifteen days, it probably cost me the award."

When he returned the Mets fans cheered him, GA-RY. GA-RY. Darryl Strawberry, meanwhile, was in an 0–47 slump at home, and on August 31, 1986, at Shea, the hometown fans began to boo their sensitive right fielder. Lenny Dykstra couldn't understand how the fans could be so fickle and said, "Why do they boo him? They're not helping him? I tell ya what I would love to do sometimes—the next time they get on Darryl real loud. I wanna go up to the press box, grab the microphone from the guy on the PA, and just scream at those assholes: 'Will you people shut the fuck up and let this guy play?' "

Gary Carter: "It comes as a surprise in your own ballpark. I know it affected Straw. He began putting pressure on himself, which never helps a hitter. The fans, I guess, expected big things of him. The press, and our noisy city, built him up as a potential Mays or DiMaggio, a kid of such breathtaking talent that he ought to hit forty home runs and bat .300 as a matter of course. I've even heard it said that he had the talent to hit fifty home runs. The expectation was a heavy burden to carry."

As Davey Johnson had predicted from the start, the season was a rout. The magic number was two when the Mets went into Philadelphia on September 12 to play a four-game series. They led the Phils by 22 games. Thousands of Mets fans drove the length of the New Jersey Turnpike to watch the games. It was almost like playing at home for the Mets players. The Phils swept them.

They flew to St. Louis, where they lost a thirteen-inning game. The next night, September 16th, Rick Aguilera won, and Jesse Orosco saved it. The Mets had clinched a tie and returned to New York.

Doc Gooden pitched against the Cubs and won 4–2. The last out was fielded by Wally Backman. By the time the ball reached first base, a mob had swarmed onto the field and had surrounded the players. The fans knocked Rick Aguilera down, and someone jumped on his shoulder, injuring him badly enough that he missed a start. Doc Gooden found himself trapped, and Davey Johnson sent the police out onto the field to bring him back safely. Mookie Wilson had to escape through the visitor's bull pen.

The field was destroyed.

Gary Carter: "You've heard of bat day and cap day? September 17 was Turf Day. Thousands of people went home with hunks of grass and sod. I wonder if they planted it in their backyards. Think of it: Shea Stadium grass sprouting all over New York, New Jersey, and Connecticut."

Wally Backman: "It was a thrilling moment. We finally accomplished what we hadn't accomplished the year before. And we did it quick. It wasn't like we won by three or four games. We won by a lot. Whitey Herzog had already conceded the race to us at the All Star break, but we still had something to prove, and we just kept winning. We didn't want to fall short like we did the year before."

Gary Carter: "We won 108 regular-season games. That wasn't matched until the Yankees won 114 games in 1998. Anything over a hundred wins is a great year. We won the pennant by twenty-one-and-a-half games. We had a *great* year."

thirty-eight

Drama in Houston

The Houston Astros, winner of the National League West in 1986, had two former New York Mets in its starting rotation. One was Nolan Ryan, finishing his twentieth season at 12–8. The second, Mike Scott, who had toiled in mediocrity for the Mets, was sent to the Astros for Danny Heep in December of 1982. In four years with New York, Scott had been an ordinary 14–27.

Wally Backman: "Scottie and I did instructional leagues together [with the Mets]. Scottie was an average major-league pitcher, maybe even a little below average, .500 at best."

In his first two years in Houston Scott had 15 wins and 17 losses. When in 1985 his record jumped to 18–8, Scott credited Roger Craig with teaching him the split-fingered fastball and making a new pitcher out of him.

In 1986 Mike Scott proved his stardom was no fluke. He again won 18 games, led the league with a 2.22 era, and struck out a league-high 306 batters. The night the Houston Astros became Western Division champions, Mike Scott pitched a no-hitter against the San Francisco Giants in the Astrodome.

The Mets were certain that Scott's success came because he cheated. What he called his split-fingered fastball didn't do what everyone else's splitter did. A splitter comes to the plate and drops. Scott's came to the plate and jumped unpredictably—up, down, or sideways. The Mets were certain that Scott was scuffing the ball—using a rough material, like sand-paper, a file, or an emery board—to affect its surface so that it came to the plate and darted—somewhere. When Leon Durham of the Cubs found a shard of sandpaper on the mound after a game Scott pitched, the certainty grew.

Wally Backman: "We all questioned whether it was really a split-finger what with the way the ball was scuffed. What I was told was that he had an emery board. They found it. He put it on his glove hand and glued it onto his finger. He'd pull his finger out of his glove and rub up the baseball."

No matter. The umpires couldn't catch him and refused to call him on it. With his "splitter," in 1986 Scott was close to unbeatable. Assuming a seven-game playoff series, the Mets would have to face him three times: in games one, four, and seven. The prospects were daunting.

In the visitors clubhouse in the Astrodome before the first game Davey Johnson convened his troops to explain his strategy. He said, "No seventh game. You win games two, three, five, and six. Simple as that." He was conceding games one and four to Scott.

As expected, Scott started against the Mets in game one in the Astrodome, and during Gary Carter's first at bat, the Mets catcher asked plate umpire Doug Harvey to check the ball for scuffing. Down reigned the boos. Carter then struck out. The noise was loud.

During the game Carter and Harvey talked about Scott.

"Son, I've umpired behind the plate with Scott pitching five or six times, and I've never found anything."

"I just don't believe it."

"I've never found a thing, son," said Harvey.

Dwight Gooden, the Mets' wonderkind who had won 17 games during '86, pitched for the Mets. He made only one bad pitch—to Astro slugger Glenn Davis—who homered in the second inning. Scott showed no weaknesses at all.

Gary Carter: "He got tougher. And tougher. Guys would come back to the dugout dragging their bats, scrunching up their faces, amazed. 'He's unhittable,' they'd say. We were all saying it."

★ ★ ★

Scott struck Carter out a second and third time. Keith Hernandez struck out three times. In all Scott K'ed 14 Mets, matching a League championship record.

In the ninth inning Carter went up to bat trying not to strike out. He hit a tapper to third. The Astros won 1–0.

Gary Carter: "In game one, when Mike Scott struck out 14 batters, he K'ed me three times, and I barely touched the ball. When I made a little dribbler to third base for my fourth out, I was happy I didn't get the Golden Sombrero. That's how unhittable he was."

During the game, under instructions from Frank Cashen, the Mets collected a group of game-used discarded baseballs.

Wally Backman: "We grabbed some baseballs that we all thought were scuffed—we had a big bucket of them—you bet that had a big effect on us. It had an effect throughout the game. It got into our heads more than anything. We could have manufactured a couple runs, but we were bothered by what we thought was happening. We let that bother us too much."

After the game Keith Hernandez boldly promised everyone the Mets would beat Nolan Ryan in the next game.

Ryan, 39, left game two after five innings down 5–0. Carter drove in the first run in the fourth with a line drive off the right-center field wall for a double. A Darryl Strawberry sacrifice fly scored another run. In the fifth inning three singles and a triple by Hernandez—making good on his promise—scored the other three.

Wally Backman: "We were a fastball-hitting team, and Ryan was a fastball pitcher. We had quite a bit of success against fastball pitchers."

Bobby Ojeda, who went 18–5 with a 2.57 era in '86, started game two for the Mets and gave up but one run in a 5–1 victory. Ojeda, a pitcher of quiet intensity, never really got the ink he deserved.

Wally Backman: "He was 18–5 in '86. Why didn't he get his share of the credit? It might be because he just came [to the Mets] that year. And he wasn't a power pitcher like Gooden, but a high-intensity pitcher, a really excellent fielding pitcher. He won a lot of close games. He wasn't getting ten runs a game. He wasn't getting cheap wins. Bobby deserved as much credit as anybody on that pitching staff. His record speaks for itself."

Game three, played at Shea Stadium, pitted Bob Knepper, a junkballing right-hander, against Ron Darling, who fell behind quickly when the Astros scored two in the first and two in the second. Darling came out after five.

In the sixth inning Kevin Mitchell singled, Keith Hernandez singled, and Gary Carter hit a roller that went under shortstop Craig Reynolds' glove for an error, allowing Mitchell to score.

An upset Knepper then threw Strawberry a fastball that Darryl hit out of the park. The game was tied.

In the seventh inning the Astros' Billy Doran walked, and Billy Hatcher hit a bouncer to Ray Knight at third. Knight bobbled it and then threw it over Hernandez' head for an error. Doran went to third and then scored the go-ahead run on a grounder to second.

Leading by a run going into the ninth inning, the Astros' fireballing Dave Smith came in to close it. Wally Backman, who came into the game late, bunted down the first-base line. Glenn Davis, the Astros first baseman, tried to tag the hustling Backman, who eluded him.

Gary Carter: "In my opinion the whole series turned on that bunt by Wally Backman."

Wally Backman: "I bunted the ball down the line, and I dove to the outside of the bag, and they wanted everybody to think I got out of the baseline. I've seen it on tape, and it kind of looked that way.

"[Astros manager] Hal Lanier was pissed off. That really bothered them."

After Backman went to second on a passed ball, Lenny Dkystra, who had also come into the game late and who had surprising power for a little guy, hit a long home run over the right-field fence and into the bull pen. The Mets were 6–5 winners. Backman leaped high in the air. So did Lenny and 55,052 Mets fans. The noise washed over everyone.

Mike Scott started for the Astros in game four, but it was Frank Cashen's intention to get him thrown out before he even threw a pitch. About a dozen baseballs with discolored scuff marks were delivered to

National League president Chub Feeney. The Mets waited to hear Feeney's ruling, hoping Scott would be suspended, but nothing was said about the baseballs and the game started as though it wasn't even an issue.

Wally Backman: "They didn't want the controversy. They are not going to question a player, because they [would] end up with some huge lawsuits. It was obvious the balls were scuffed up. You'd have to be crazy not to see what everybody saw and not think somebody did something to them. There were big scuffs on those balls. That was just the way Feeney dealt with it."

As a result Scott, pitching on only three days rest, did not allow a hit until Ray Knight hit a two-out single in the fifth inning. Danny Heep's sacrifice fly scored the only Mets run. Scott allowed the Mets a total of three hits as he beat Sid Fernandez 3–1.

Two of the Astros' runs should not have scored. With runners on first and second and two out—both strikeouts—Fernandez got Alan Ashby to pop up down the third-base line. It appeared that Knight would have caught it, but Rafael Santana thought he had a better angle, and called him off. The ball dropped into the first row. On the next pitch Ashby hit a long home run to make it 2–0 Astros.

Jim Deshaies had been scheduled to pitch game five at Shea Stadium, but it rained all day Monday, and the next day Hal Lanier instead gave the ball to Nolan Ryan. If the Mets lost one of the next two games, they would have to face Mike Scott in game seven.

For nine innings Ryan was in top form. He allowed but two hits and struck out twelve. The run he gave up came in the bottom of the fifth inning when Darryl Strawberry, once again the offensive hero, pulled a pitch against the right-field foul pole. A foot to the right, and the Astros would have won the game.

Dwight Gooden was also brilliant pitching ten innings and giving up but one run. It came in the fifth. With runners on first and third and one out, Bill Doran hit a grounder to Wally Backman, who flipped to Rafael Santana, and when they just missed the double play, the run counted.

Charlie Kerfeld, who came in after Ryan went out for a pinch hitter, and Jesse Orosco, who replaced Gooden, were perfect in the eleventh inning. In the twelfth Kerfeld was still on the mound when with one out, Wally Backman slashed a single off Walling's glove at second. Wally took a big lead, and when Kerfeld tried to pick him off, the throw bounced, and Backman went to second.

Kerfield walked Keith Hernandez intentionally. Gary Carter was up next. To get his adrenaline flowing, Darryl Strawberry said to Carter, "Don't let 'em do this to you, Kid. Don't let 'em do it.' Carter became angry at the insult, though he knew the Astros were doing what any team would have done in that situation.

Kerfield threw Carter three balls. Carter who was 1–21 hitting in the series, could well have sought a walk. The last time the Astros walked Hernandez to pitch to him, Carter had hit into a double play.

Carter took a strike, then fouled back a pitch. Then he hit another foul. And another.

The next pitch was low and away, and Carter hit a one–hopper through the middle to score a sliding Backman with the winner.

Wally Backman: "Gary was in a slump at the time, but we still expected him to drive in those big runs. He had shown he could do it throughout the year. The first day he became a Met he hit a last-inning home run to win a game. That was the start of our expecting him to do that. His hit might have been the turning point of the Houston series."

Gary Carter: "It was one of the biggest, most welcome hits of my life. It was one of the very finest games in the history of these playoffs. The next day we played the greatest ever."

The teams had to fly to Houston for game six. But before the Mets played it, Darryl Strawberry became caught up in a melodrama that had already been consuming him. His wife, Lisa, from whom he was separated, had returned to New York to try to patch things up with him. She demanded Darryl's attention, while Darryl wanted to be left alone so he could concentrate on beating the Astros. Lisa insisted Darryl repent his ways. She accused him of failing as a husband, of drinking too much, of not paying attention to her, of fooling around. Strawberry begged her to leave him alone until the end of the season. She refused and continued to badger him.

According to Strawberry the result went something like this: "'You confronting me?' he asked her.

"I'm distant, drinking, and downright ugly mean. Now she wants a confrontation. I'm out of control. *KA-BOOM*." In a rage, Strawberry lost his grip. He swung and hit Lisa in the face, breaking her nose. But when he arrived in Houston for game six, you never would have known Strawberry had just beaten his wife and sabotaged his marriage.

Darryl Strawberry: "I put it all behind me—my marriage as well—when I got to the Astrodome for game six."

Bob Knepper started for the Astros, Bobby Ojeda for the Mets. Ojeda allowed three runs in the first inning, while Knepper kept the Mets off-stride all game long, allowing two harmless singles in eight innings. With the score 3–0 Houston in the ninth inning, the Astro fans, on their feet, waiting for the end, were celebrating, secure in their knowledge that Mike Scott waited in the wings for game seven.

Teams don't usually come back from such large deficits, especially in big games. One run, maybe. Two runs, possibly. Three runs? Never.

To start the Mets' ninth Davey Johnson sent Lenny Dykstra to pinch-hit for Aguilera, who had pitched three innings of one-hit relief after Ojeda.

Gary Carter: "Davey told Lenny just two minutes before that he was going to lead off the inning. Knepper was throwing a two-hit shutout against us, and we're thinking, 'Gosh, if we lose this game, we're going to have to face Mike Scott in game seven.' So Lenny started it off with a triple. He hit it into the right-center field gap, and Mookie Wilson then drove the run home with a single to right field just out of Bill Doran's reach.

"Kevin Mitchell hit a slow grounder to third. Mookie was running on the pitch so Denny Walling had to throw to first. One out. Keith Hernandez was next. Knepper threw a high fastball, and Hernandez doubled past Billy Hatcher in right-center as Wilson scored a second run. It was now 3–2 Astros, with Hernandez on second. There was still only one out.

"Knepper was pulled and they brought in Dave Smith, and he walked me, and then he walked Darryl to load the bases. Smith needed a strikeout. Ray Knight, the batter, needed a long fly ball. Ray hung tight, fouling off pitcher after pitch. Knight then hit a long fly ball to right-center deep enough to score Hernandez with the tying run."

Wally Backman: "Ray was a competitor. He didn't want to lose. As a kid he was a Golden Glove boxer. I used to watch Ray take cortisone shots in his hands just so he could play. Ray would do everything and anything it took."

★ ★ ★

The game was going into extra innings. That they were still in the game was a miracle.

Gary Carter: "So now we're tied, and we go into extra innings. All I could think about was, 'We have a new life.' And this was the character of that ball club. I was just thankful that, 'Hey, we have a shot here.' Again, we realized that if we didn't win this game, we were probably going to lose the series because Mike Scott was so dominant.

"But the way we came back and came back, it was unbelievable."

The high drama didn't let up. Roger McDowell pitched one of his best games, allowing just one hit in five innings. Larry Andersen matched zeroes for the Astros.

Gary Carter, leading off the fourteenth inning against Aurelio Lopez, singled to right and Darryl Strawberry followed with a walk. Ray Knight bunted but Lopez threw Carter out at third.

Wally Backman was next and he yanked a single to right. In right field Kevin Bass picked up the ball and threw home as Strawberry streaked for the plate. The throw went over Ashby's head, and Knight took third, Backman second. The Mets had the lead.

Gary Carter: "When we scored one in the fourteenth inning, we said, 'Oh, man, this is it.' Wally was going to be the hero of the playoffs."

Wally Backman: "I was trying to hit the ball hard, and I hit it to right, which I didn't do very often. I thought that was the game. We all did. We were all excited. After tying it up, I had come into the game late, and I got into a situation where I could drive in the run to win the series. At that moment I thought I was going to be the series hero. Even though everybody was a hero, I thought. The Mets only needed three outs to win it."

Jesse Orosco was on the mound for the Mets. He struck out Billy Doran. He went 3–2 on Billy Hatcher and threw him a fastball that Hatcher hit for a home run. The score was tied again. The Astrodome fans were ecstatic, and Backman's heroics would be forgotten.

★ ★ ★

Gary Carter: "It turned out that Billy Hatcher hit one against the foul screen or the fair screen and tied it in the fourteenth inning. We went into the sixteenth, and that's when all heck broke loose, and we were able, fortunately, to score three runs."

Darryl Strawberry was the first hitter in the sixteenth. Davey Johnson told his team, "The numbers don't lie, fellas. We may be in extra innings, but they're your extra innings. We've pulled out almost every extra-inning game this year."

He shouted into Strawberry's face, "Now, Darryl, you hear? Numbers, Darryl."

Strawberry saw right-fielder Billy Hatcher moving back and thought to himself that no matter how far back he moved, it would not be far enough. But on the first pitch Lopez fooled the Mets slugger. Strawberry was looking for a fastball and got a screwgie instead. He hit a short squib to short center. Hatcher lost it in the Dome haze and was late getting to it. Strawberry, hustling all the way, charged into second standing up.

Ray Knight drove a single to deep right, and Strawberry scored easily. Bass' throw was high, and Knight hustled into second.

Astros manager Hal Lanier brought in lefty Jeff Calhoun. The Mets saw Calhoun as a pitcher of last resort. They knew it was their game now.

Switch hitter Wally Backman turned around to hit righty. Calhoun threw a pitch down and in that sailed past the catcher for a wild pitch and Knight moved to third. Calhoun walked Backman and when he threw another wild pitch, Knight scored. The Mets were now two runs ahead.

Jesse Orosco dropped a bunt down the third-base line, moving Backman to third. When Dykstra singled off first baseman Glenn Davis' glove, Backman scored to make it 7–4 Mets.

Mookie Wilson hit into a double play, but no one cared. With Orosco on the mound, the three runs should have been enough. A team should not be allowed to come back from a three-run deficit.

Though Jesse was tired, he was a fearless competitor. Orosco could be a cutup—even a clown—off the field, but on the mound he was cocky and fierce. The first batter, Craig Reynolds, struck out. But Orosco then walked pinch hitter Davey Lopes on four pitches and allowed a single up the middle to Bill Doran. Denny Walling, the tying run, came to the plate. The left-handed Walling pulled a shot at Hernandez. Mex threw to Santana at second base for out number two.

Glenn Davis, the Astros' one legitimate home-run threat, was the hitter. He had struck 31 dingers in '86, big numbers for a hitter playing in the Astrodome. Orosco threw him a slider on the wrists, and Davis blooped a single to center in front of Dykstra as Doran scored to close the gap to 7–6.

With the Astrodome crowd in bedlam, Doug Sisk grimly warmed up in the Mets bull pen. Orosco was out of gas. A base hit would tie the game. A double would end it. Davey Johnson, unwilling to risk a bad Sisk outing, stayed with Orosco.

Kevin Bass was the hitter.

Gary Carter: "I'm sure you remember Houston had the tying run on second base in the likes of Denny Walling with Kevin Bass at the plate. They had gotten a couple of runs off Orosco to score two, so we were ahead 7–6, and all I could think of was that Kevin was a great fastball hitter.

"I intended to go with nothing but breaking balls, a steady diet of them."

Orosco did as he was told, throwing Bass slider after slider. With the count 3–2, Orosco threw one more slider. He swung through it, and when the ball thwacked into Carter's glove, one of the great games of playoff history was over.

Wally Backman: "Jesse just reached back with everything he had. I thought Jesse struck him out with a high fastball. I don't think it was a strike. It was a pitch a little out of the strike zone. As tired as Jesse was, and everybody knew he was tired, he got the job done. It wasn't pretty, but he got it done."

Gary Carter: "When Jesse struck him out, I was so ecstatic, but so exhausted, because I caught all sixteen innings. In fact, I caught every inning, every pitch of the League championship and the World Series. There wasn't a pitch I didn't catch."

The Mets were National League champions.

After the game Gary Carter kept yelling to reporters, "We're going to the World Series!"

Wally Backman: "After the last out we mauled Jesse. It was so exciting. Keith was the only one of the Mets players who had started in a World Series before. The excitement . . . the World Series is the ultimate goal for a major leaguer. You don't get that many opportunities.

"It's been fourteen years, and I still remember the emotions. There is nothing like it. It's the best high anybody could ever have. And the biggest low for the guys who lost."

On the charter back from Houston the Mets players and wives partied. They chanted 'Lets Go Mets,' and sang and danced. They then started throwing food and ripping up seats. The drunken rampage continued through most of the flight.

Dwight Gooden: "To say we caused damage is a pristine way of putting it. It was a scene out of *Animal House*; food fights, heavy drinking, loud music, openly groping our wives and girlfriends, who were allowed on this one trip. At one point the partying was so out of control, the lavatory door accidentally flew open and there was one of my teammates, his face in front of lines of cocaine.

"I wasn't shocked that he was using; I was shocked that he was so high; he didn't even realize the door was open.

"As for the rest of the Mets, they continued treating the plane like it was a fraternity house with wings, which is why, days later, the front office received a bill from United for $20,000."

Wally Backman: "It was fun. We celebrated to the extreme by drinking on that airplane trip. I was in the back of the plane, and I didn't see the seats ripped out but it was my understanding that the wrecking of the seats wasn't done by the players but by the wives. I think the wives were pissed at Frank Cashen. He wouldn't let the wives fly with the players going to the series unless we won. But I understand what he was trying to do. He wanted the players to be together and not change anything, let the players do what they wanted to do on the airplane and not get their minds somewhere else. I didn't see one player tear a seat out. But I do know that three of them were very screwed up."

★ ★ ★

Gary Carter: "I remember the celebration. All the wives were there, and on the flight home some of them got a little rowdy. I just think there was a craziness of excitement, jubilation, celebration, whatever you want to call it.

"I was in the back of the plane playing cards. My wife was sitting next to me. And because there was so much damage done to the plane, we ultimately paid part of it out of our paychecks. Oh, yeah. It was about ten thousand dollars worth of damage, and I can't imagine that, but we had to agree to pay it.

"I wish I could tell you what went on. I mean, I saw some food being thrown around and some wine and champagne was probably spilled, and some beer cans were tossed around, but that was a normal flight. And yeah, guys used to get a little rowdy on planes, especially when we flew from coast to coast. I remember other planes that seemed a lot more trashed than that one. I really don't know what went on and I was so exhausted. I don't remember whether I napped, I was just so awed that we were going to the World Series. This was my twelfth-year playing, and I was finally going."

When the players got back to Shea Stadium, Frank Cashen informed the players that United Airlines had sent the Mets a bill for ripped upholstery, broken seats, and to replace the interior that had been drenched in beer. Cashen was furious at the damage done by the players. United, moreover, informed him that the airline would never take another Mets team anywhere ever again.

Davey Johnson also was furious—not at his rampaging players but at Frank Cashen, who, he felt, should have been grateful for their efforts on the field and who should have just gone ahead and paid the bill.

Dwight Gooden: "Frank Cashen, our general manager, handed the airline's letter to Davey Johnson, obviously expecting that we, the players, would come up with the cash.

"Davey's response? In front of us all, he tore up the piece of paper and said, 'Fuck 'em, if it wasn't for us, there wouldn't have been a reason to celebrate. Let Frank pay for it.'

"That's why we loved Davey so much; he was a renegade, just like us, and in the years when we enjoyed a talent gap over the rest of the National League, he was the perfect manager."

The players, whether they knew it or not, ended up paying, according to Carter.

Gary Carter: "We had a meeting about it, and Frank Cashen was incensed, and then we had a meeting of our own in which Davey said, 'The best way to reconcile this whole thing is for us to pay for it.' And each of us had five hundred dollars taken out of our paychecks. I was just sucking it up, because I had been as quiet as a churchmouse on that flight, playing cards, and I was oblivious to even knowing what was going on."

Wally Backman: "We had fun together, we played hard together, and we probably drank too hard, but it kind of went with the game then. Davey liked his players to stay together off the field. That is part of your chemistry. When you can stay together and do things off the field together, that's what builds chemistry. Davey was able to get that type of player and to keep them together, because in the minor leagues the players are tight, but usually once they reach the majors, they start to separate, even though they might have played together in the minors. Davey tried not to let that happen.

"That was one of Davey's philosophies, even if by doing that he had a falling out with the front office. Like I said, Davey wanted to do things his way. He was a talented manager, and he had success doing things his way, and he didn't want that success affected by having someone else tell him what to do [even if that person was the general manager]. And I didn't see anything wrong with that. I'm sure the front office might not have appreciated some of the things he did, but Davey had to have the respect of the players, and that's what Davey got. And that's what made Davey successful. He needed the support of his players. If he didn't have management's support, that wasn't good for him, and yet, he won. You can't get rid of a winner. And that was part of it. The problem Frank Cashen had was that Davey kept on winning."

For the rest of his days with the Mets, Davey Johnson knew he would keep his job as long as the team could keep winning. It was really no different from what most managers faced. The difference was that even if Johnson won 90 games a year season after season, if just one spring his team faltered, he knew, he would be gone.

thirty-nine

Miracle of Miracles

W hen the Mets flew from Houston to New York to open the 1986 World Series at Shea Stadium against the Boston Red Sox, the players were exhilarated but at the same time so drained they were too tired to feel the pressure of playing in the World Series for the first time.

Gary Carter: "We'd beaten Houston. The worst was over. We'd been through fire. We'd earned our way into the World Series, and no one doubted we were there. When a dream comes that hard, you have no trouble believing in it.

"We were exhausted from the Houston series. Fatigue may have hurt us, and it may have helped us: in a strange sort of way we were too tired to be terribly nervous. As the Series wore on, the fire rose in us, and then we started feeling the tension."

It was a cold Sunday night in Queens and the large crowd was subdued. Ron Darling started for the Mets against Boston's Bruce Hurst, a cagey left-hander. The Mets were in a foggy state. Davey Johnson knew his troops were pooped and kept muttering about a "bad moon on the rise," a line from a Creedence Clearwater Revival song. Johnson's premonition turned out as he had predicted. Hurst, with Calvin Schiraldi's help in the ninth, shutout the Mets on four hits.

Darling was almost as good. He allowed three hits and one run, and it was a cheapie. Jim Rice walked and went to second on a wild pitch in the dirt. The wild pitch was costly. Dwight Evans then hit back to Darling, who held Rice and threw to first. Had Rice been on first, it would have been an inning ending doubleplay. Had Rice been on first, Teufel probably would not have missed Gedman's ground ball hit his way. But when Teufel took his eye off the ball to find Rice, it rolled through his legs into right field, and Rice scored the winner.

Schiraldi, the former Met who had taken over from an overworked Bob Stanley as Boston's top closer, pitched the ninth. He struck out pinch hitter Danny Heep to end the game.

Wally Backman: "The World Series, to us, was an anticlimax. We got to where we wanted to go, and for the first few days we suffered kind of a letdown. We were just happy to be there. And we weren't thinking about the winning as much as we should have focused on it."

Davey Johnson, who made player moves based on his numbers and his intuition, rolled the dice when he decided to start the younger Howard Johnson at third base instead of the veteran Ray Knight, who had played every game since May. Roger Clemens was pitching for the Red Sox, and Johnson decided to start two lefties, HoJo for Knight, and Danny Heep in place of Mookie Wilson, against the hard-throwing right-hander.

Knight, an intense competitor, was furious. He took the benching personally and complained loudly about it.

Wally Backman: "Everybody knew Ray was pissed. I tried to understand why Davey did it. I kind of think he did it because he didn't want to ruin HoJo. HoJo was the future for us. And Clemens was pitching, and Howard hit right-handers so well, even though he was struggling during the playoffs. It was a confidence thing for him. Both of those guys helped us win. But Davey looked at the matchups and just thought Howard would play better."

Gary Carter: "HoJo, meanwhile, was a little hurt because Ray was acting like his, HoJo's, playing third base was the end of the world. Ray and HoJo didn't speak to each other before the game. Ray didn't get much batting practice, so he had plenty of time before the game to answer reporters' questions about being benched.

"Ray didn't hold back. He said he didn't like it, and he said he thought Davey was wrong.

"Ray was our main guy, but Davey decided to change it up a little bit, and it might have motivated Ray to have the last couple of games that he did."

The predicted pitchers' battle between Roger Clemens and Dwight Gooden turned out to be a Red Sox rout as eighty million TV viewers saw the Red Sox pummel Gooden.

The Mets trailed 6–3 after six innings, and then in the seventh inning Mets rookie pitcher Rick Aguilera allowed singles to the first five Sox batters in a row. Most of the hits were bloops and bleeders, but two more runs counted, and when the Red Sox scored another run off Sid Fernandez in the ninth, the game ended Red Sox 9, Mets 3. Boston had a two-game lead and was threatening to win its first World Championship since 1918. The arrogant, but emotionally challenged Boston fans were so confident they began talking sweep, much to the dismay of the Mets players.

Darryl Strawberry: "It was a disaster. Everything we'd accomplished all season was unraveling right before our eyes."

Wally Backman: "Through that whole series, we didn't hit well. We didn't play well. The Red Sox played well. I thought that was the worst seven games in a row that we played all year long."

The game ended late, and the players went to bed even later. Everyone had to meet at Shea at 9:45 the next morning for the short flight from La Guardia to Boston. Johnson cancelled the afternoon workout at Fenway Park. He told the players that he was sure they were going to hit Oil Can Boyd and win the game. He ordered them to stay in their rooms and not to come out. He told the press, "They don't need practice. These guys are bone tired. With a day's rest, they'll clean up."

Wally Backman: "We were just exhausted. Mentally, it went back to the Houston series. We needed the day off to rest our minds."

Johnson was criticized for his actions in New York and Boston. The New York writers asserted it was another example of the Mets arrogance. The

Boston writers accused the Mets of skipping practice to avoid having to answer for their lackluster performance of the first two games.

Wally Backman: "Absolutely not."

Gary Carter: "No, we were not afraid to face the music. We were *tired*."

According to Carter, Johnson giving his players a day of rest was a key decision in the Series.

Gary Carter: "We had been picked to win the Series. We lost game one 1–0 and we got crushed 9–3 in game two when Dwight Evans had a big game. Boston had their heads pretty high thinking they've left Shea, they've beaten us in our own ballpark, and they were going home.

"I remember Davey saying, 'Hey, I know you guys are exhausted. You guys have come a long ways. You've had a great season. Let's don't lose our aggressiveness. Let's don't lose what our incentive has been.'

"And he said, 'I want none of you to come to the ballpark on the day off.'

"And that to me was the turning point, because when my wife and I got to the hotel on the off-day we took a nap, and when we got up, we had room service. We never left the room.

"My family was there, but we never saw them. We stayed in the room the whole time. We watched a movie on TV and slept in, and the next day I felt refreshed. I really did.

"I got into the clubhouse and it was like, All right, we're back at it again. This is it, guys."

Johnson was right about the Mets hitting Oil Can Boyd often and early. On the third pitch of the game Lenny Dykstra hit a home run into the right-field stands. It was the Mets' first extra hit of the Series. Wally Backman and Keith Hernandez followed with base hits, and after falling behind 0–2, Gary Carter doubled off the Green Monster to score another run as Hernandez went to third.

Wally Backman: "Boyd had a pretty good change-up, not a bad breaking ball, and an average fastball. The one thing he could do; he threw strikes. He had pretty good command of his pitches, but that day he didn't have the command he wanted to have. He kept the ball up in the strike zone, gave us quite a few opportunities to hit balls hard. Even when he was ahead in the count, he would try to make a pitch, and he'd make a bad pitch, and we'd get a hit in a key situation."

Darryl Strawberry was still suffering from the distraction of his failing marriage. He was feeling contrite and wondering whether his wife would ever forgive him and take him back. Against Boyd, he struck out.

Ray Knight, back in the lineup after what he saw as his one-game demotion, then bounced a ball slowly to Wade Boggs at third. In a rundown Hernandez slid head-first safely back into third, so Carter had to run back to second. Boggs threw over to second, and when Spike Owen looked over to third to check on Hernandez, who had been faking a dash home, Carter slid back in safely. Everyone was safe, and the bases were loaded. The Red Sox fans were in a state of shock.

Wally Backman: "It wasn't a tag play and instead of just trying to get the out, they were concerned with us scoring too many runs in that inning. It ended up a big rundown between home and third and then second and third, and they didn't get anyone."

Danny Heep, inserted in the lineup by Johnson as the designated hitter, lined a shot over second base into center to score Hernandez and Carter and make the score 4–0 Mets.

Wally Backman: 'What I remember most vividly about that game was the first inning. We set the tone. We had Bobby on the mound and I always felt that if we could get three or four runs, the game was pretty much sewed up. And it came to pass that way."

With two outs in the seventh inning and the bases again loaded, Carter drove in two more runs with a soft line drive to left. Ojeda, the beneficiary of this largesse, only allowed one run in seven innings, and Roger McDowell pitched two perfect innings. The final score was Mets 7, Red Sox 1.

Gary Carter: "When we won game three, we figured, Okay, we're back on track, one game behind them. We knew how important it was to win game four, because if you fall back three games to one it's almost over at that point."

There was some controversy before game four, and for a change it involved the Red Sox. Boston manager John McNamara decided to give Roger Clemens and Bruce Hurst another day's rest and to pitch journeyman Al Nipper instead. Most of the writers and Boston fans thought McNamara should have pitched Clemens and Hurst on three days rest. Ron Darling was the announced starter for the Mets.

Wally Backman: "The thing about Nipper, he pitched similar to Boyd. He wasn't a power pitcher either. He was a control pitcher, and if he didn't hit his spots, he was going to get hit hard."

The game was scoreless through the first three innings, and then in the fourth inning with a runner on second, Nipper threw Carter an inside fastball that Carter pulled over the Green Monster and into the high screen for a two-run home run.

Carter didn't stop there. He led off with a double in the sixth, and in the eighth inning against Jim Crawford, he hit a hanging curve out of sight for his second dinger of the game to help the Mets win 6–2. Carter's heroics was the realization of a dream he had had since he was a boy.

Gary Carter: "As a kid growing up, I was a huge fan, and even today, after playing eighteen years, I'm still a fan. I love the game. When we were growing up, I remember in grade school and in seventh and eighth grade, there were a lot of day World Series games, and we would be able to bring our radios or watch them on TV during PE, and I remember seeing The Mick. Mickey Mantle was my fave, and he played in just about every series, as did Yogi Berra, who has the most hits in World Series history, and when we made it into the World Series, I was in such awe.

"And then in the series I got a hit, and then I got a double, and in Game three I had three rbis off Oil Can Boyd, and I came back and had three rbis in game four, and a lot of people thought I was the MVP of the series.

"In game four I hit a home run against Al Nipper. There was a cameraman up on the screen [above the left-field wall]. This was NBC's way of showing the game in a different perspective, and he got me that first home-run ball.

"The second home run was a breaking ball that I hit not only over the Green Wall but into the parking lot across the street. That was a bomb. Some kid scrambled and got that ball.

"That was such a thrill."

The Series was tied two games apiece, and the Mets seemed to have the momentum as the Boston media lambasted McNamara for choosing to pitch Nipper.

Gary Carter: "We had new life. Again."

Doc Gooden started game five for the Mets against Bruce Hurst. Every time Gooden pitched, everyone expected brilliance and was disappointed and surprised when he pitched less than his best. Against the Red Sox, Gooden never showed his best form. On this night the Red Sox waited on Gooden's fastball and lit him up. Johnson had to relieve him in the sixth inning with nobody out. The Mets would lose the game, 4–2 as Hurst scattered ten hits and allowed single tallies in the eighth and ninth.

Gary Carter: "Dwight didn't have his real good stuff. I really don't know why. Maybe the cold weather affected him, because I know he didn't like to pitch in the cold. But he was not very effective.

"Later we learned Dwight used drugs, and I asked Doc, 'You were sweating pretty profusely on a very cold night. Were you using drugs?' And he said, 'No.' So I don't know what went on. I can't really say. All the Red Sox had were two starters, Hurst and Clemens, and if you got by them you were going to go pretty deep. But Doc, I don't know, Hurst kind of outpitched him. Simple as that."

The Boston fans were gleeful. The last time the Red Sox had won a World Series was in 1918 when Babe Ruth and Harry Hooper led Boston over the Chicago Cubs four games to two. Generations of Red Sox fans had gone to their graves without seeing their heroes win in the World Series. After sixty-eight years it appeared that "the Curse of the Bambino" would finally be broken.

Spontaneously, the Red Sox fans opted to take their hostility toward the

Mets out on Darryl Strawberry. Somehow they sensed he was vulnerable and like pit bulls, attacked him.

When Strawberry, who was mired in a slump, was called out on strikes in the sixth inning, he glared at plate umpire Ed Montague. The Boston fans began booing him. When Strawberry fouled out in the eighth, the boos again rained down. When he returned to right field, the Red Sox fans began the (now famous) mocking chorus of 'Dar-ryl, Dar-ryl.' Strawberry lifted his hat high over his head in acknowledgment as the chanting continued.

Wally Backman: "They picked on Darryl because he was such an impact player for the ball club. So many times he would either tie a game or put us ahead with one swing of the bat. They were trying to do anything they could to wreck his concentration. The fans sensed they could get to him easier than get to Gary or Keith. They might have seen him as a softer person. But Darryl did the opposite of what they wanted to see happen."

Gary Carter: "The fact that the fans felt comfortable enough to tease him told me that they figured their team had the Series won. When will people learn?"

Down three games to two, to win the Series the Mets would have to win both games six and seven.

Wally Backman: "When we were going to Boston, we knew we had to win both games, and we did that. Once we won those first two games in Boston, I don't know if it was a letdown, but we knew we'd be going home and playing on our own field in front of our own fans and have all that support. We felt good about being able to go home for games six and seven."

Though they would have the home-team advantage playing at Shea Stadium, they would have to beat soon-to-be-Cy Young Award winner Roger Clemens—24–4 with a 2.48 era— both league bests—and Bruce Hurst—13–8 with a 2.99 era. Few thought they could do it. The Mets looked flat. After Davey Johnson crunched his numbers, even he didn't like what he saw. Frank Cashen came down to the clubhouse and gave the team a pep talk. He told them, "The outcome of this Series depends on your fortitude, your endurance, your perseverance, and your stout hearts."

"We can still do it," Johnson added.

The players weren't so sure.

After Clemens buzzed through Dykstra [strike three looking], Backman [strike three looking], and Hernandez [fly out] in the first inning, the Shea faithful were quieted when the Red Sox scored single runs in the first and the second innings off Bobby Ojeda, who settled down after a rocky beginning.

Early in the game a parachutist came floating down onto the infield. The skydiver just materialized out of the night, toting a big flag that said, 'Let's Go Mets.' The crowd roared. The skydiver landed near the first-base line, where the police were waiting for him. The cops led him away through the Mets' dugout. It was the highlight of the early part of the game.

Wally Backman: "He scared the shit out of me. I was kind of standing there, and everybody was screaming and yelling, and the next thing I knew, this guy came right over my head. He landed, and the police got him. It was a big deal for him. He had to have the biggest thrill of all. And with the level of intensity out there, I think he relaxed us, because it became a joke."

In the bottom of the fifth inning Strawberry walked, and with Ray Knight up, stole second. Darryl had done the same thing in the second inning.

Wally Backman: "Darryl had some speed, and he wasn't a bad base runner. When you have a guy like Clemens on the mound, he's a pretty easy guy to steal off of. Easier than most. Most big power pitchers like Clemens or Gooden are not as quick to the plate as most."

Ray Knight hit a single to center and Strawberry scored the first Mets run. Mookie Wilson hit a liner that Dewey Evans almost caught, then dropped, as Knight ran to third.

Rafael Santana was up, and Davey sent Danny Heep up to bat for him.

Wally Backman: "By Davey pinch hitting for Rafael, it didn't hurt the ball club because we had Kevin Elster come off the bench for us and play shortstop. So defensively we didn't lose anything, and we might have gained some offensive power. Heep was much more of a threat than Raffy. I thought it was a good move, even though he hit into a double play."

★ ★ ★

On the play, Ray Knight was able to score to tie the game. The run allowed Bobby O. to stay in the ball game.

In the seventh inning Johnson brought in Roger McDowell. Marty Barrett walked, and on the first pitch he took second on a grounder hit by left-handed batter Bill Buckner, the Sox number three hitter in the lineup despite an ankle that was killing him. Buckner, who was a gamer and was still a potent bat, wore high-top sneakers and hobbled when he ran.

Jim Rice grounded to Ray Knight, who threw wild to first. A grounder by Dwight Evans to Kevin Elster got a force out as Barrett scored. When Gedman singled to Mookie Wilson in left, everyone figured Jim Rice would score because of Mookie's bad shoulder, but the Mets outfielder made a terrific throw to Gary Carter, who made the tag.

The Red Sox led by a run.

McNamara let Clemens pitch the seventh, and he retired the side.

In the eighth inning the Red Sox loaded the bases with two outs. Davey took Roger McDowell out and brought in lefty Jesse Orosco to face left-hander Bill Buckner, who flew out harmlessly.

In the Mets eighth, Clemens was forced to leave because of a blister, and McNamara brought in Calvin Schiraldi. Johnson sent up Lee Mazzilli to pinch hit for Orosco.

On Schiraldi's first pitch Maz pulled a fastball to right field for a base hit. Dykstra, trying to sacrifice, bunted right back to the mound. Schraldi grabbed it and threw—too late—to second and both runners were safe. Wally Backman also bunted toward the pitcher, but this time Schiraldi threw to first for the out as the runners moved up. McNamara ordered Hernandez walked intentionally to load the bases.

Gary Carter was the batter. Calvin threw three balls. Davey let him hit away. Schiraldi threw and Carter pulled a line drive to deep left right at Jim Rice. After the catch Mazzilli trotted home. They were even again.

Strawberry, who the fans were counting on to win the ball game, swung and missed twice and then flied lazily to center field. Strawberry was still suffering the depths of domestic relationship hell. The crowd at Shea cared only that he had failed them. Tickled by Boston's chant of "Dar-ryl, Dar-ryl," the Shea faithful adopted it as their own and booed him as well. To add to his humiliation, after the at bat, Davey Johnson made a double-switch because the pitcher was due to hit the next inning.

Davey chose to take Darryl out of the game and put Lee Mazzilli in. Darryl felt humiliated and angry. Davey brought Aguilera in to pitch and placed him fifth in the lineup in Darryl's spot.

Wally Backman: "Darryl felt hurt because it was the first time in his career that he was used in a double-switch. I can see him feeling that way, but I can also see the other side of it. You use a double-switch because you don't want the pitcher leading off the next inning. Darryl wasn't coming up to hit, so the move was the right move. Davey could have taken out either Darryl or Keith, and there was no way Keith could come out of the game. He was our leader. Unfortunately, it was Darryl who had to come out."

Gary Carter: "Davey took Darryl out on a double-switch, and he was pissed about that, too. He sulked and went into the clubhouse, and as soon as the game was over, he was dressed and he was gone. After the great win of game six, he didn't even stick around. He was gone."

Rick Aguilera had to face Jim Rice, Dwight Evans, and Rich Gedman. He K'ed Rice. Evans hit a grounder to Elster at short that the rookie bobbled, but when Gedman bounced to Backman, the Mets had an easy inning-ending double play.

The Mets had the hammer. A run would have won it, but they did little in the bottom of the ninth. The game went into extra innings.

Aguilera was a rookie who had shown signs of brilliance throughout the pennant race. But he was still a rookie, and he had never faced this much pressure before. It was a tough situation for any pitcher, never mind a youngster.

The first batter in the tenth inning was outfielder Dave Henderson, the hero of the American League division series against the California Angels. Henderson hit a long home run to put Boston in the lead. The Red Sox mobbed Henderson when he came into the dugout.

Wally Backman: "I figured it gave the Series to the Red Sox. That feeling was going through the dugout quite a bit."

Aguilera struck out Spike Owen and Schiraldi, but Wade Boggs, the future Red Sox Hall of Fame third baseman, doubled into left-center and then

Marty Barrett, who the Mets rarely got out, lined a single to center to score an insurance run. The Red Sox 5–3 lead looked insurmountable.

Schiraldi was on the mound for the Red Sox when the Mets came to bat in the bottom of the tenth. Backman led off.

Wally Backman: "I had played with Calvin, and I knew what type of pitcher he was. He was a decent pitcher. But when I came to bat, sometimes you can see when a pitcher is . . . 'scared,' is not what I am looking for, but what you see is a different look in his eyes. And I thought he had that look."

Perhaps Schiraldi was feeling the pressure, but when Backman and then Hernandez both flew out harmlessly, it appeared to everyone that the dreaded "Curse of the Bambino" was about to be broken. There was no way any team, even the accursed Red Sox, could blow this game, it seemed.

Gary Carter: "In the bottom half of the tenth inning of the sixth game, with two out, none on base, and the Red Sox ahead by two, the operator of the Diamond Vision screen pressed the wrong button, and for a few seconds congratulated Boston on winning the World Series. In the Red Sox clubhouse, somebody was pulling corks out of champagne bottles."

Wally Backman: "When I made the first out and Keith made the second out, all that was running through my mind was that we had played as bad as we could have played and we still had an opportunity to win, and it didn't look like we were going to. After the first two outs, the thought of us being able to win that game was that it wasn't going to happen.

"We felt such a letdown, because, God, the feeling was, 'We played so well during the season, and we've played as poorly as we could have played, and here we were going to lose this game and lose the Series.'"

Lenny Dykstra: "We were an out away from wasting a whole fucking season. They had the champagne in their clubhouse—they borrowed it from us. They had all the TV cameras in their clubhouse. They were ready to show the whole country what a Red Sox World Series celebration looked like.

"I was ready to get sick. Mex was ready to go on an all-night, forget-everything drunk."

Wally Backman: "The Red Sox were on the field. They were *on the field*, off the top step."

Gary Carter: "After Wally led off the tenth inning, flying out down the left-field line, Keith then hit one to left-center for the second out. He bee-lined it right into the clubhouse, grabbed a beer, went into Davey's office, and watched it on TV.

"In the meantime Bob Costas and the NBC gang were putting the plat-form up in the Red Sox locker room and putting up the plastic over the lockers, and Oil Can Boyd was already in there popping champagne when I got to the plate.

"Everybody thought it was over. God, yes. Everybody at Shea had basi-cally left the ballpark. Only the diehards were still there. Davey had kind of slunched back into his seat. Everybody thought it was over.

"When I came to bat, Kevin Mitchell was in the clubhouse half undressed, and Keith was in Davey's office drinking a beer.

"When I went up there, I thought back to the time I flew out against Jeff Lahti to end our chances in '85. I said to myself, A home run is not going to do it here. I just wanted to get on base. That's all I wanted to do. And I *knew*, one way or another I was going to do that. Cause I knew a little bit about Calvin Schiraldi, because he had been with us the year before, and what I knew was that he was gutless. And the reason I knew that was an incident that occurred during the 26–7 game the year before when the Philadelphia Phillies lit him up. I was catching and I remember he kept looking over to the dugout. He wanted out of the game. I walked out to him, got in his face, and I said, 'Don't you ever give up. I don't care what the score is. I'm out here, everyone else is out here. Don't you ever give up.'

"And I could just see the timidness in his face, and I knew right then and there, if I was ever going to face him in a tight situation, he was not going to get me out. I just felt that. He looked like a scared puppy. Yeah, he was. I didn't think he was capable of closing the door.

"And so when I got my base hit, I said, 'Hey, we got life here. We got life.'

"Kevin Mitchell was called out of the clubhouse to pinch-hit for Aguilera. He was undressed in the clubhouse when Davey called for him. He came out and he was putting himself together, threw his batting gloves on, went up to the plate, and Mitchell one time had told Schiraldi, 'You better not try to throw me a fastball, because you'll never get me out that way.' And so Schiraldi threw him a breaking ball and hung it, and Mitch hit it into left field."

Wally Backman: "We didn't think much of anything until we got two men on base. After Mitch lined a single to center, the fans started to stir, because we had a chance to tie or win the ball game."

Gary Carter: "Ray Knight was the batter, and I was on second giving him encouragement and after Schiraldi got two strikes on him—we were one strike away from losing the series—he battled his way, got his hit over Marty Barrett's head into right field, and I scored. Mitchell went to third, and that's when John McNamara made his change. And that's when he should have also brought in Dave Stapleton to replace Buckner at first base.

"There was something in the air now, electricity, magic; we knew it, and so did they. They were beginning not to believe what was happening, you could see it in their faces. You could see it in John McNamara's stony Irish face as he took the slow walk to the mound to get Schiraldi."

McNamara called for the veteran Bob Stanley, who had not given up a run in the Series. Mookie Wilson was the batter. The Shea fans were screaming, "Moo-kie, Moo-kie." The stadium was in an uproar. The situation was desperate.

In the dugout Lenny Dykstra said to Wally Backman, "Relax, it's over. We've won."

Backman replied, "Who showed you the ending?"

Lenny Dykstra: "Once we got a run in, they were dead. I think they knew it. I would have bet anything that we were going to win. I didn't know how. No one ever could have guessed."

Stanley threw a strike. The crowd tensed. Then he threw a pitch inside that just missed hitting Wilson in the thigh. The Mets left fielder nimbly jumped back. The ball was catchable, but Boston catcher Rich Gedman reacted too slowly, and when the ball darted past him toward the back-stop, Wilson frantically waved Mitchell home from third to tie the game.

The Mets say it wasn't Stanley's fault but Gedman's.

Wally Backman: "It wasn't that bad of a pitch. The pitch was catchable and Gedman missed it. It was a pitch that could have been handled. Why didn't he handle it? I can't say. There was a lot of pressure in that situation."

Gary Carter agreed. But, rather than place blame, he instead credits Mookie Wilson for making the play happen.

Gary Carter: "Mookie's at bat—one of the most famous in baseball history—was vintage Mookie Wilson. What happened next was compelled, *created* by Mookie's cleverness and speed—a hitless at bat that had wizardry to it.

"The pitch was sailing; Mookie had to know it might get away from Gedman. Dodging that ball was crucial.

"Turned out that Stanley threw what they called a wild pitch, but it could have just as easily have been a passed ball. But the ball did something different from what Stanley was accustomed to throwing. He threw a sinker, and this was a riser or a cutter, and so it got by Gedman and Mitchell scored, and just like in game six against Houston, we tied it up and had new life again. And I thought, 'This is God's way of saying we have another chance.' Because we were almost out of it."

As Kevin Mitchell scored the tying run on the wild pitch, Ray Knight, the winning run, moved into scoring position at second. Bob Stanley, showing poise, bore down and threw strikes, but Mookie kept fouling off pitch after pitch, including one that he chopped off his foot.

Mookie Wilson then hit one of the most famous ground balls in baseball history. The ball bounced slowly down the first base line toward the gimpy Bill Buckner, who was playing behind the bag. Not only did Buckner have to pick the ball up but he also had to beat the fleet Mookster to first. Stanley, figuring Buckner would make the play, failed to cover first base.

Buckner, who played twenty-two years in the big leagues, awkwardly bent for the ball and, with a look of horror, came up with air. The ball skipped past him, rolling down the right-field line. Ray Knight, running all the way, came around third and scored the winning run before anyone could retrieve the ball.

Buckner was never forgiven by the Boston press or public for missing Mookie Wilson's ground ball. According to the Mets, even if he had fielded it cleanly, he would not have retired Wilson on the play.

Wally Backman: "Mookie was just too fast. Buckner wasn't going to beat Mookie to first base. He was *not* going to beat Mookie to first base. Had he caught it, there would have been runners on first and third, and it would have brought up another batter.

"But, when he missed the ball, we all went nuts. We thought it was our destiny."

Gary Carter: "Buckner knew who was flying down the line, and he was thinking about fielding the ball and racing Mookie to the bag. He was distracted [by that] and the ball jumped his glove, and was gone. McNamara was criticized by Red Sox fans for letting Buckner play the tenth with that bum ankle. The ankle never affected his glove, but because of it, he may have been worrying about Mookie's well-known speed."

Dwight Gooden: "The question for the ages was: Even if Billy Buckner had caught it, would he have beaten Mookie to the bag? I doubt it. I think we would've beaten the Sox even without The Error, although we'll never know, because the last image of game six was the ball whispering through Buckner's legs and the look of horror on Buckner's face when he realized. that we'd just scored three runs with two outs.

"People ask me, what was my favorite, all-time Met memory, and it's exactly that: seeing Ray Knight landing on home plate and the riot that followed."

Gary Carter: "It took us and 55,000 fans a second to comprehend. The Red Sox were sitting like statues over there. They had to be astonished. We were amazed ourselves."

Wally Backman: "The celebration was pretty intense. A lot of guys were hugging each other. It was a *very* happy clubhouse. But we handled it well. It didn't go to our head. What it did was give us life for a seventh game. And we knew by having life, we had to focus on the seventh game."

★ ★ ★

Gary Carter: "After Mookie hit that slow roller to Buckner, and the ball rolled through his legs, and we won, I *knew* then, with that tremendous comeback, we were going to win game seven. There was no holding us back."

Darryl Strawberry was awash in emotion. He was elated that the team had come back and won and at the same time couldn't quell his dark feelings of humiliation after being taken out of the game.

Darryl Strawberry: "I let the magic of the night before wash over me. You'd have to be made of stone not to feel that magic. Sure I felt that I'd messed up. I felt I'd been cheated of glory. I felt humiliated. I said to myself that bitter wounds were opened up that night that would still remain long after the World Series. Part of me, the part that wanted the world to go my way always, no matter what, was as mad as could be at Davey for putting me on my ass on the bench the night before. I gnashed my teeth and said I'd never forgive him for humiliating me. But then there was this family thing. At the very moment I'd been told to sit myself down in front of millions of fans around the world, I couldn't deny the part of me that wanted to see the Mets win because I had made them into my surrogate family. So I said to myself I would give it all another try."

It rained on Sunday, and the seventh game had to be postponed until Monday. A lot of the Mets players spent the day in the clubhouse under Shea Stadium playing cards.

Oil Can Boyd would have pitched, but with one more day of rest, Red Sox manager John McNamara switched to Bruce Hurst, his ace.

Wally Backman: "Hurst was a good pitcher. He was a lefty and it took away from our left-handed hitting lineup. Offensively we were a much better hitting ball club when we faced right-handed pitching. It turned Mookie around, Lenny had to face a guy he didn't swing the bat so well against, it took me out of the lineup, and Keith and Straw weren't as effective. Darryl didn't swing the bat as well against left-handers. So the advantage went to Hurst."

Ron Darling pitched for the Mets. Darling had allowed one unearned run in his last fourteen innings, but on this day he didn't have it. Dwight Evans homered in the second inning, and so did the next batter Rich Gedman. Wade Boggs drove in a third run with a single.

With two outs and a runner on second in the fourth inning, Davey Johnson pulled Darling and brought Sid Fernandez in to pitch. Except for a walk to Wade Boggs, the first batter he faced, in two-and-one-third innings, Sid was perfect.

Wally Backman: "Sid did exactly what he had to do to give us a chance to play catch-up and score some runs."

Gary Carter: "When Davey handed him the ball, the game—the World Series—was settled. It was over for the Red Sox when he started pitching. It wasn't just that he held them off; he overwhelmed them. They couldn't catch-up with his climbing fastball. It soared high when they swung at it. They hacked at his floating curve ball, missing."

The Mets tied the game in the sixth inning. After Hurst got Rafael Santana on a ground ball, Davey lifted Fernandez for Lee Mazzilli, who singled to left. Wilson, starting against the lefty pitcher, also singled to left. Tim Teufel, who was playing instead of Backman, walked.

Hernandez, in one of the most important appearances of his career, batted with the bases loaded. Hurst threw two strikes past him. He then threw a fastball in and Hernandez drove it into left-center, scoring Mazzilli and Mookie.

Wally Backman: "Keith was a very smart and very intense player, and when the game was on the line he was always able to keep his emotions from getting involved in the situations. I played fourteen seasons in the major leagues and Keith was the best clutch hitter I ever played with."

The Mets were still down, 3–2, with runners on the corners. Carter, who was 1–10 against Hurst, was the batter. He needed a long fly ball to bring home the tying run. He hit a soft liner toward Dwight Evans, who dove and rolled. The ball disappeared under him. Evans emerged, picked it up and threw to second before Hernandez could get there. The run scored, but Hernandez, who was called out at second base on the force play, was furious with right-field umpire Dale Ford for not signaling whether it was a catch or not. The play was also important for Carter. Had Hernandez made it into second, Carter would have hit .310 for the Series and probably would have been named the Most Valuable Player. But with the hit taken away, his final average was only .276 and it became easier to overlook him.

A Strawberry liner ended the inning when left-fielder Jim Rice made a diving catch. With the score now tied, Roger McDowell pitched the seventh inning without incident.

Wally Backman: "The tempo had changed, because we knew what we had done in the past, and the Red Sox were still thinking about what had just happened a couple days before! We had a great bull pen. We had Jesse and Roger. The game was starting to play into our hands."

Boston manager John McNamara pinch hit for Hurst, who had to come out of the game, and Calvin Schiraldi came in to pitch for the Red Sox in the bottom of the seventh. Ray Knight, the first batter he faced, struck a long home run over the fence in left, perhaps the biggest home run of his illustrious career.

Wally Backman: "Ray was looked up to in a lot of ways. He did whatever it took to get on the field to be able to play. He was a guy who was not going to take himself out of the lineup at any cost, unless he couldn't walk, and there were times when he could *barely* walk, and he played. He was very intense. Very intense."

Lenny Dykstra hit for Kevin Mitchell and singled to right.

Gary Carter: "Shea was rocking; everyone was beginning to smell it."

Schiraldi threw a wild pitch past Gedman, allowing Dykstra to run to second. When Rafael Santana hit a soft ground ball to right, Lenny scored and the Mets led by two.

Wally Backman: "Raffy hit the ball soft, but he got his hits and he was very solid. He was another guy who didn't come out of the lineup very often. Davey had a lot of guys who *wanted* to play and who didn't want to come out of the lineup."

Pitcher Roger McDowell batted and sacrificed Raffy to second. Joe Sambito, who had been released by the Mets at the end of the '85 season, then came in to pitch for the Red Sox and walked Mookie Wilson intentionally to load the bases and set up the double play.

When Keith Hernandez hit a long fly ball to score another run, the Met lead had swelled to three runs.

John McNamara didn't want the lefty Sambito pitching to the right-handed Gary Carter, so he brought in Bob Stanley. As Stanley was warming up, Darryl Strawberry went over to his catcher and told him that in his opinion he should be the Most Valuable Player of the Series, and that he should go up and add to it. Carter was thrilled by Strawberry's kind remarks. After Carter grounded out easily to end the inning, the Mets led 6–3.

In the eighth inning the pesky Red Sox rallied. Bill Buckner singled to left, and Jim Rice hit a line shot up the middle, a long single. Dwight Evans hit a double to right, driving both runners in. Suddenly the score was 6–5, and the Mets' lead was down to one. A runner was on second with no one out.

Davey Johnson called time, pulled McDowell, and brought in Jesse Orosco.

Wally Backman: "Jesse and Roger scratched each other's backs. Those two guys worked so well together. Both had a lot of saves, and it was all based on situations, and if one guy wasn't sharp, Davey could go to the other guy."

When during the season Jesse slumped, Davey went to McDowell more. But Orosco developed a tricky change-up, a fork ball, retained his edge, and returned to Johnson's good graces.

Orosco was brilliant. Rich Gedman hit a slider softly to Backman. Dave Henderson struck out. Don Baylor, hitting for Spike Owen, grounded out easily to Raffy.

The Mets still led 6–5 when McNamara brought in Al Nipper to pitch the eighth. Strawberry, who had continued to seethe over being taken out of the previous game, and who was convinced manager Johnson had done him wrong, led off.

Johnson knew how emotional his temperamental star could be, and all through game seven Johnson had tried to calm Strawberry, telling him to keep his head clear. Strawberry desperately wanted to be part of winning this championship, and he was grateful that Johnson hadn't kept him on the bench and that his manager was taking time to try to soothe the ruffled feathers of his troubled outfielder.

Darryl Strawberry: "He knew I was dealing with problems, but he was helping me postpone them until after the game by showing he understood. Just the knowledge that Davey understood I was in trouble was support enough. I could handle my problems knowing I had just a little bit of emotional support. It's a bad, bad feeling when you're out on a limb all by yourself and can't turn to anyone for help. Davey made me feel part of the family instead of just a troubled kid who'd been told to stand in the corner."

Nipper threw Strawberry two strikes. Straw then hit a tremendous shot *way* over the right-center field wall. He ran the bases slowly, savoring the roar of the crowd, certain the Mets would win now that they had a two-run lead. When Strawberry crossed home plate, Knight told him to go shake hands with Johnson.

Davey stood out front as Strawberry came in and dutifully grabbed his hand. Unfortunately, even this home run would not prevent Strawberry from having to live with his demons after the game and the series were over.

Ray Knight singled to center, his third hit. When Lenny Dykstra grounded out, Ray took second. The Red Sox walked Santana intentionally, but Orosco fooled everyone when he singled up the middle. Knight scored from second, and the Mets led 8–5.

Gary Carter: "The excitement grew and grew. It felt inevitable, like counting down the minutes on New Year's Eve."

McNamara brought in Steve Crawford, who got the final two outs to end the inning.

It was the top of the ninth, and it was up to Jesse Orosco. When Orosco took the mound to start the inning, all of New York was on the edge of its collective seats.

Ed Romero, Wade Boggs, and Marty Barrett were the batters. Romero was in the lineup because earlier McNamara had pinch hit for Spike Owen. Romero, a weak hitter, popped out to Hernandez in foul territory.

When Boggs pulled a ground ball to Wally Backman, there were two outs. A smoke bomb went off in left field, throwing up red smoke and delaying the game. Policeman began ringing the field by the wall.

Marty Barrett stood in. Had the Red Sox won the Series, Barrett stood to be the Most Valuable Player. But with two outs in the ninth the air had gone out of Boston's balloon. The Sox had nothing left. Orosco threw a strike and then another. He threw a fastball, high and inside, and Barrett swung and missed. Strike three. Game and Series over.

Orosco threw his glove in the air, then fell to his knees and shot his arms up in a V. The players in the infield, Hernandez and Backman, then Carter and Knight, all gathered in a heap on the mound. Strawberry, Dysktra and Wilson ran in from the outfield. The pile kept growing as the police kept most of the crowd away.

Dwight Gooden: "Ah, that last out will last a lifetime in my memory bank: Jesse striking out Marty Barrett, flinging his glove into the air and dropping to his knees, his fists raised to the sky. It was the greatest moment of my career, and the best team—on and off the field—that I ever knew.

Gary Carter: "We hugged, jumped on each other, wrestled, fell down, got up, and laughed till we wept."

Lenny Dykstra: "Hey, they can hate us, they can resent us, I don't give a fuck. We got what we earned. We got what we deserved. We were the best. The good guys won."

Darryl Strawberry: "It had taken four full seasons for the Mets to build themselves into a World Championship ball club. We almost made it to the top in '84. Almost again in '85. And now in '86 we had gone all the way. We had shown that we were made of better stuff than most of the other teams in the National League."

Wally Backman: "We went from being so depressed in game six and then being so high in the end after being able to come back and win. After first the Houston series and then the Red Sox series, every player was mentally drained. It was the hardest two series back-to-back that I can think of.

"The Houston series was well-played. The games went back-and-forth and were so close. But I really felt that we played some of the worst games we [ever] played against the Red Sox. I really felt that. During the season we'd eat up teams and beat them up pretty consistently. We never had a mental breakdown for a seven-game period. When we went into the Red Sox series we were mentally fatigued. Nothing against the Red Sox—they played a good Series—but we didn't play near the Series that we possibly could have played. For us to be able to win the championship was a thrill."

Ron Swoboda: "I am a Mets *fan*. That's my organization, ever since '86. I had drifted away. I was doing sports in New Orleans. I was aware they were trying in '84 and '85. Frank Cashen was there, and Davey was the manager, and I thought, This team knows what it's doing. So they got my attention.

"In '86 I was let go from my TV job in Phoenix, and I worked freelance in New York for Channel 2, and I followed the playoffs and the World Series. As an observer and a Mets fan, that '86 team will always be my team. That will always be the greatest baseball I ever watched back-to-back-to-back, playoffs and World Series. The greatest. It was played so well, so intense. It was dramatic to the extreme. I can't image anything surpassing that in the quality of the baseball that was played and the dramatics that came with it."

Wally Backman: "We only won one World Championship but I still consider that we had a dynasty. When you can put together a team that can win 90 games a year for five years in a row, you've got something special.

"The way I look back at it now, it was different than it is today. In 1985 we won 98 ball games, but there was no wild card. If there had been a wild card, we might have been in the Series the way the 2000 Mets were. It could have been that way [the] other years as well. It probably would have. We had a team that *should* have been there more than once. But when you win 98 games in a season, you can't be depressed about that, because you've had a very successful season. So we had a dynasty there. We were consistently one of the teams people were shooting for, trying to beat. We knew we were one of the best teams in baseball. I just wish it would have been the same as it is today. That's all I can say."

But if the 1986 World Series was the apex, the only way things could go was down. A black cloud was coming. Dark days were on the horizon. Who could have guessed that Davey Johnson's triumph in 1986 would never be repeated? Who would have predicted that mixed with success would be heartbreak and recriminations.

For Darryl Strawberry, it was the kind of season any youngster would dream of. There was a ticker-tape parade and a key to the city from the mayor. But his personal demons were dancing in his head.

Darryl Strawberry: I was feeling strangely empty, dangerously hungry, needy, and unfulfilled. I could already feel the pain that was waiting for me in California. [His wife was threatening divorce.] I knew that my triumph would soon dissolve into loneliness and anger. I knew that this celebration would only be a small envelope in time, and I tried to hold on to it even as I felt it slipping away with the slow-motion whooping and wailing of my teammates on the Mets. They were my summertime family, but the winter was closing in.

"I didn't like it, but I could spot it. Evil was at work, throwing long shadows across my triumph, like the coming of night."

forty

Rum and Coke

According to Casey Stengel, there are two types of ballplayers: the drinkers and the milkshake men. Some of the greatest baseball teams, including the St. Louis Cardinal Gashouse Gang of 1934 and both Stengel's and Billy Martin's Yankees were made up mostly of hardnosed drinkers, a reflection of their managers. Many of Davey Johnson's 1986 World Champions also loved to go late into the evening at watering holes around the league.

The Championship season had been a blur of heavy drinking, on-field fighting, and constant partying by many of the Mets players, and when the players and wives damaged the charter flight after beating Houston in the playoffs, both owner Fred Wilpon and general manager Frank Cashen, his bow tie always in place, wanted it to stop. To end it, they decided that what they needed to do was put a muzzle on their manager and trade away some of the badder boys. The weeding-out process would take several years.

The first to go left not because of his habits but because he wanted too much money for too long a period of time. Ray Knight, a stubborn, proud warrior was demanding a two-year contract at $1 million each to play. But the MVP of the World Series was thirty-four, and his best years were behind him, and Cashen didn't want to give him two years. For the one year he offered $800,000. Knight turned him down. The Mets even declined to offer him arbitration. When he tested the market, the best offer to come his way was a two-year deal at $475,000 plus a possible $150,000 in incentive bonuses from Baltimore.

Some players thought not re-signing Knight was a mistake.

Lenny Dykstra: "I don't think the front office realized how important he was to us winning. We could have had another guy hit for the same average with the same homers and RBIs and make the same plays at third. It would have been different, though. The front office underestimated what he did for us.

"Everyone respected Ray and wanted him back—even HoJo. But Ray thought the front office didn't like him and what he gave to a team—any team."

Other players were sorry to see Knight go but like Cashen felt that it was time for the younger talented, Howard Johnson to take over at third base.

Gary Carter: "Ray had a great year in '86. He was very much a part of the reason for our success. I think Frank was thinking that Howard Johnson was going to be the incumbent, which he did become. HoJo did far more than Ray Knight ever thought about doing. He was a 30-home-run—30-steal guy two or three times, so Howard really did come into his own.

"When Ray left the ball club he was adamant about getting a two-year contract. Cashen offered him one year and lowballed him. So he took a two-year deal with Baltimore for less money, faltered there, went to Detroit and retired. So maybe Frank saw the writing on the wall that he didn't have a whole lot left in him. It wasn't like we missed a beat with Ray gone. That was not demoralizing."

The next to go was Kevin Mitchell, who, along with Ray Knight had been a key motivator on the team even though he was only a rookie. The Met ownership was concerned that Mitch was too volatile in his private life and on the field, and one day might bring opprobrium to the ball club.

When sober, Mitchell was tough but fun. According to Dwight Gooden, who was admittedly one of the drinkers, when drunk the player Gary Carter nicknamed 'World' could be out of control and dangerous.

★ ★ ★

Dwight Gooden: "Drinking allowed me to commune with Darryl and
Kevin Mitchell, who was funny, but very wild and sometimes a very
dangerous guy. I liked Mitch, but I knew better than to ever fuck with
him. I'd heard stories about his background in San Diego, some of
which included rumors that he'd hurt some people in gang-related vio-
lence. I don't know about that, but I got to witness, firsthand, Mitch's
temper.

"He was so good with his fists, I saw him beat up Strawberry during a
pickup basketball game in spring training. Darryl liked to think he was a
pretty good hoops player, and actually, he was. But one day in St. Petersburg, he and Mitch were on the same team and they got into an argument
about who was taking too many shots and who wasn't passing the ball. The
usual stuff.

"Out of nowhere, bam, Mitch slugged Darryl right in the face. Then he
hit him again and knocked Straw down. It took a couple of us to pull him
off, and I swear I never saw a punch that connected so cleanly. As much as
I hated to see it, Mitch really did beat the hell out of Darryl.

"Later that year, in 1986, we were in the middle of a bench-clearing
brawl with the Pirates, and amid all the minifights, I saw Mitch overpower
Pittsburgh's shortstop Sammy Khalifa. He took Khalifa down, got on top
of him, and applied a choke hold. I couldn't believe my eyes, because
Mitch was doing more than just trying to beat up Khalifa. [It looked like]
he was attempting to kill him.

"Indeed, Khalifa's eyes were wide and unseeing, and it suddenly
occurred to me that he was being strangled to death. Several players,
including a few Mets who saw what was going on, pulled Mitch off him.
What was so scary is that later on, when we asked why the hell he wanted
to kill Khalifa, Mitch couldn't remember anything about the fight."

Later that summer Gooden and a civilian friend went to visit Mitchell at
his home unannounced. According to Gooden, when they arrived
Mitchell appeared drunk and was acting crazy. He was fighting with his
live-in girlfriend and holding a foot-long knife in his hands. When
Gooden and the friend turned to leave, Mitchell made it clear if they didn't
sit down, he would hurt them. He said he was sure the two had been followed by the police and that the cops were outside staking him out.

Gooden and the friend, afraid for their lives, barricaded the door to try to quiet Mitchell's paranoia about the police. But when Gooden and the girlfriend tried to calm Mitchell down, he only got angrier.

Dwight Gooden: "[His girlfriend said,] Kevin, stop acting so crazy, these people are your friends. With that, Mitch turned to her and raised his anger to yet another level. Still holding the knife in his right hand, he grabbed his girlfriend's little cat, who had the misfortune to be walking near his feet at that very moment.

"In one awful sweep of his hand, Mitch pulled the cat's head back, exposing its throat.

"You think I'm kidding when I say don't ever fuck with me?' he shouted. Before the girl could answer, Mitch took the knife to the cat, and cut its head off. Clean."

Gooden and the friend were ordered to sit on the couch and not move, and they sat stock-still for the next two hours, with no one saying a word. For everyone in the room, time seemed to standstill and terror hung in the air. Finally whatever was affecting him wore off, and Mitchell returned to sanity. He told them, "You can go."

The next day at the ballpark Gooden approached Mitchell and asked him whether he was all right.

Mitchell replied, "Yesterday never happened."

They never mentioned it again.

What bothered the Mets management was that Kevin Mitchell hung out with Dwight Gooden and Darryl Strawberry. In order to rid itself of what they perceived to be his influence on their two young stars, on December 11, 1986, Mitchell was traded to the San Diego Padres. In exchange the Mets acquired another Kevin, a bloodless, phlegmatic white guy named McReynolds, whose passion, his teammates say, was duck hunting, not baseball.

With the departure of Ray Knight and Kevin Mitchell and the coming of Kevin McReynolds, the team had changed. According to Wally Backman, some of the great team chemistry of the '86 team was lost.

Wally Backman: "The chemistry in the clubhouse had started to change after we lost Ray and Mitch. Ray Knight was a fighter. Kevin Mitchell had big game after big game playing four different positions for us all the time. So we lost the depth we had with Mitchell.

"We got McReynolds, a very quiet guy. He was different, more laid back, opposed to how the team was in '86 and '87. So the team changed directions a little bit, away from the wildness. Not that Ray was wild, but he was very vocal, a very hard-nosed player. He was a good guy for the young players to look up to. Cause he played the game so hard. We lost some of that, so it wasn't the same team.

"On paper the team should have been as good, if not better, but that's where chemistry comes into effect. The chemistry in '87 wasn't as good."

Carter, who says he never saw Mitchell's dangerous side, was surprised when Cashen traded the young outfielder away. Carter had been impressed with Mitchell's talent. Carter, who did not go out at night and who was unceasingly faithful to his wife, hadn't known anything about the drinking and drug-taking that was consuming the Mets.

Gary Carter: "Kevin Mitchell grew up in the San Diego area where there was a lot of gangs and drugs. He grew up basically with a gang. But, to be honest, I never saw Kevin's bad side. All I saw was his talent on the field. I gave him the nickname 'World,' because he could do everything. He was a big guy and yet he could play shortstop. He could play any position, except perhaps catcher.

"He was multitalented, and I just can't imagine what Kevin might have done to anger the Mets, other than the notion that things were going on off the field the Mets didn't like, and they felt Mitch might have been pulling down some of the other guys, and so Frank Cashen felt he needed to trade him.

"I remember Frank once made the comment, 'A team that stands pat cannot win. You need to make at least one change.' And he made that change with Mitchell for McReynolds in '87.

"Like everyone else, I felt Kevin was in line to be the number one guy in left field in '87. Cause he had proven himself. He played the whole '86 season and played so well. But he wasn't a regular. And McReynolds was a proven veteran.

"But even though Kevin McReynolds had great talent, my God, he could have cared less about anything. He'd show up in just enough time to throw his uniform on, go out and take batting practice, come in and as soon as the game was over he was already dressed and ready to leave by the time I had packed up all my catcher's gear and come up to the clubhouse! You know how they said Cool Papa Bell was so fast if he turned out the light, he could be in bed before it got dark. Kevin McReynolds was that way. Honest to God, I never saw a guy leave the clubhouse as quick as him. I think what was happening [was], the team was losing its desire for the game. I used to love to hang around and talk baseball. A lot of these guys couldn't wait to leave and go and do their own thing. Especially on the road. These guys would want to go out and do their stuff, and I'd rather sit there and talk baseball. Cause all I was going to do after the game was go back to my room, and I wanted to key down a little bit, and I *loved* those times. Those were the *best*. Oh, I loved those times. I miss those times, to sit with Wally and Keith and have a beer and talk. And that was the time to do it. You're talking baseball and knowing what other guys were doing around the league. I used to follow everybody and watch games on TV, and we'd come into the clubhouse and want to know what the other team was doing. But, in '87 the guys had more and more desire to do other things than concentrate on what we had."

If the Mets had wanted to protect Dwight Gooden, they would have been better off keeping their young star away from his longtime hometown Tampa buddies than trade Mitchell.

Two nights after Mitchell was traded away, Gooden, driving his fancy Mercedes 500SL, was stopped by a cop in Tampa after a dinner at Chili's. In 1986 the Tampa police routinely stopped blacks without legitimate probable cause, especially those driving expensive cars. In the back of their minds if a black was driving an expensive car he had probably stolen it, and if he owned it, he didn't deserve to own such a vehicle. Stereotyping and racial profiling were products of a still-racist South that went unchallenged.

At least ten times in the past Gooden had been hassled by white police officers on his way home from Tampa across the bay to south St. Petersburg. Sick of it, when the cop asked for Gooden's license and registration this time, he turned belligerent.

"Now you're going to jail," the cop said. When the officer went for his handcuffs, Gooden foolishly went to grab his hands to stop him. At this moment fifteen squad cars of fellow officers pulled up. Using the rationale that Gooden was going for the arresting officer's gun, they pounced on him, knocked him to the ground, and began to beat him a la Rodney King.

They knew who he was, and his celebrity seemed to infuriate them. According to Gooden, one cop shouted, "Break the arm. Break the fucking arm." He was beaten and choked. To get them to stop, Gooden pretended he was dead.

The cops then handcuffed *and* shackled him, and drove him to the parking lot of a local dog track. Gooden was sure he was going to be murdered. Instead he was met by an ambulance and taken to jail.

Gooden, guilty only of DWB (driving while black) was lucky he didn't end up in jail for life—or worse—when after his arrest he and six friends from the 'hood coldly plotted revenge against the Tampa Police Department.

Carrying automatic weapons, they went out the next night intent on assassinating the first white police officer they saw. For thirty minutes they drove the streets of downtown Tampa at eighty miles an hour, hoping a Cracker cop would stop them. Luckily for all involved, none did. Had a white officer seen them and pulled them over, that officer may well have been killed, and Gooden and his revenge-crazed buddies would likely have faced "Old Smokey", Florida's antiquated electric chair.

But after riding around for an hour Dwight's right-mind returned and he asked out of the car. He called his mother, who came and picked him up.

Though Gooden was lucky that time, his luck was about to run out. The cause of his trouble this time would be the drug of choice in the 1980s, cocaine.

According to Gooden, on March 25, 1987, three weeks into spring training, he and two unnamed Mets teammates got high in Tampa. The next day the Mets demanded he take a drug test, something his new contract allowed them to do. Because this was the first time such a test was requested, Gooden speculated that his teammates had ratted him out after he had crossed them by going home earlier than they had wanted him to. Whatever the reason for his being asked to take the test, when he took it, he failed.

Wally Backman: "We were all getting on the bus to play the Pirates in Bradenton and he was supposed to pitch, and we were waiting for him. He wasn't on the bus yet. We didn't know what was going on. They called Dwight on it, and I believe that's when the Mets called him in to tell him the test was positive.

"They had questioned Dwight about it and he got mad and said, 'You go ahead and test me,' and they did. That was my understanding. I don't

Dwight Gooden

know if Dwight realized how long drugs stay in your system. He probably didn't do very much and didn't think it was going to stay in his system.

"Dwight was still very young, and he got with the wrong group of people, especially in Tampa."

Gary Carter: "On April 1, we found out about Dwight's drug use. He had taken a random test that the Mets gave. He didn't know what it took, because before that he did use cocaine, and it showed up in his urine. He said he thought if one day passed, it wouldn't show up. But I guess it stays in your system. That's where he got caught."

When Frank Cashen told him of the results, Gooden put his head on the desk and cried.

He was sent to the Smithers Alcoholism and Treatment Center in Manhattan. He was still only twenty-two years old, but he had already given up his status as a pitcher extraordinaire. Like so many players before him who had succumbed to the temptation of illegal drugs, Dwight now would be labeled a druggie by some fans, and no amount of success on the mound could win back their loyalty.

Gooden had become another victim of America's war on drugs the result of which, saw thousands of nonviolent offenders end up arrested and often in jail. Although he wasn't jailed, in an attempt to protect him from himself, Gooden's reputation was instead ruined by the Mets organization. Having forced him to be tested, the Mets then blew the whistle on him when he failed the test.

The argument for doing this, of course, was the usual one: they were trying to save Gooden from himself the only way they knew how—humiliate him publicly and shame him into being clean. Why couldn't they have called him in, sent him to Smithers under a cover story and let him come back with his reputation intact? Why is it that society treats drug addicts like criminals rather than illness sufferers? One could argue that the cure is worse than the disease, but, at the time, no one criticized the Mets' action. Teammates had seen how general manager Frank Cashen had always treated Gooden with kid gloves. They surmised that Cashen did what he did—despite the harm to the team—in order to straighten out the young pitcher's life.

Wally Backman: "Were they trying to help him or hurt him? That's a good question. Frank Cashen is the only one who can answer that. I'm assuming it was to help him.

"I think they understood this might cost us a pennant, but on the other hand, Dwight was so young and Dwight was a *huge* part of the Mets future. I think the front-office people of the Mets looked out for Dwight pretty well. I think that they did."

Terry Leach: "Maybe it was Frank Cashen's way of trying to take care of Dwight, because he was young and Frank didn't want him to get caught up with the wrong people, which is very easy to do. People trying to con you seem like your friends. That's how they get to you. If they were acting like jerks, you wouldn't mess with them. But they are going to be friendly and get you to do things, and maybe that was Mr. Cashen's way of trying to look after him and catch him early, have a little penalty, make Dwight see that this is not going to work, and then that little bit of fear keeps you out of trouble.

"I always thought Mr. Cashen looked upon Dwight and Darryl as sons. They had Jay Horowitz look after them. These guys were young, and the Mets tried to protect them. But you can get into a lot of trouble if you aren't very careful. You really have to surround yourself with good people.

"I believe Mr. Cashen was doing his best to take care of them. Darryl would get mad at him. In his book Darryl complained that Mr. Cashen wouldn't give him another chance. I thought to myself, Darryl, they gave you all sorts of chances. You're just blinded. You don't see it. You're seeing it *way* too one-sided here."

For the hard-ass Mets fans in a society that sentences drug users to unconscionably long terms even under the most benign circumstances, he had become tainted goods.

For his Mets teammates, losing Gooden was a hard blow.

Terry Leach: "It was pretty crushing losing your number-one starter. We knew Dwight was coming back and that we had to hold the fort until he could come back and take up the slack. Fortunately, we were talented enough and deep enough.

"But, unfortunately [on March 30], Roger McDowell had to have a hernia operation and didn't come back for a while [May 14], and Sid Fernandez had some problems, and during the season David Cone got hit by a pitch trying to bunt and broke a finger. [He was out May 27 to August 13.]

"Everybody went down. We had an unbelievable amount of time lost by pitchers on the disabled list."

Gooden spent twenty-eight days at Smithers Institute, the whole time denying he had an addiction to either drugs or alcohol. During the very first road trip back with the Mets, he says, he began drinking again.

Gooden made his first start in 1987 on June 5 against the Pirates. Dick Young, who had turned even more shrilly right-wing, wrote that before the first pitch every fan should stand up and boo him. Gooden never forgave Young for being the angry, reactionary, and judgmental writer that he had become.

Meanwhile, Gooden, as nice and decent a person as you could meet, was tested frequently and asserts he didn't touch cocaine again for another seven years. Unfortunately, the seven long, hard years of sobriety would not be remembered. Only the relapse.

What was clear was that Gooden's suspension for drug use in 1987 cost the Mets the pennant. Not only did the team not have his services for two months, but his suspension had an emotional impact on the team as well.

Gary Carter: "It all started with Doc Gooden having to go to rehab in April of '87. That was a setback. It was disappointing and shocking, because I really didn't think that Doc was doing that stuff. I can't even imagine that he was pulled into the group that was doing it. So it was a shock to me. Of course I was demoralized by it, Doc was such an integral part of the ball club, and you know, it set the tone for '87. It really did.

"And as the season wore on, even though we finished in second, we just didn't have a real good year. We had spurts when we were good, but spurts when we weren't so good."

"And I asked Doc this last time we got together about the drugs that were running rampant on the team, and he told me, 'You would have been amazed.' And I said, 'No!' And he said, 'Yeah, there was quite a bit of that going on.' And he named some names. And I was clueless. I had no idea. I've never touched the stuff. I had no idea. Doc said, 'People who don't know what it's like will never be able to figure it out.'

Something was clearly missing for the Mets during the 1987 season. The commitment and work ethic of some of the players had lessened, which often happens the year after a team wins the World Series.

Meanwhile, Darryl Strawberry was himself in terrible emotional trouble. Throughout the winter of 1986 Strawberry drank heavily, in large part because his wife Lisa refused to see him or let him see his son. He was distraught over the likelihood of his son growing up without a father, as he had. As Strawberry put it, "I was trapped in a script I couldn't rewrite."

Strawberry, whose ego was fragile, could not forgive Davey Johnson for lifting him in game six of the World Series. His feelings of humiliation would not go away as he reported for spring training in 1987.

An alcohol-besotted Darryl Strawberry became convinced that for the team to win he would have to carry the load, a role he took upon himself and at the same time resented deeply.

Meanwhile, as Darryl's role became more grandiose in his own mind, Strawberry became convinced that Davey Johnson was picking on him. Strawberry complained that when other guys slacked off, Johnson would say nothing, but when he messed up, Johnson always was hard on his case. It infuriated him.

Darryl Strawberry: "These guys didn't have their hearts in it at all, so I had to carry the team. These guys felt like they were the World Champions and the team to beat. Let the other teams work hard. The Mets had already won it. Now I was feeling that I was being made to carry the burden of the entire club and that I would get punished if I slacked off.

"Like most of the other players on the Mets, I had lost my edge. Like many other players, I was trying to put my life back together from out of hundreds of jigsaw puzzle pieces scattered around my room. And I had no set of instructions, no picture of the finished puzzle to guide me.

"I was the fall guy because it was my fault that the team was in such trouble. Why was I the only guy in the clubhouse who had to go out and play under the worst circumstances, when there were guys sleeping on the locker-room benches."

But all his teammates saw was a player whose self-importance was greater than the reality. They knew Darryl wasn't a bad guy. They just wished he'd keep his opinions to himself, do as he was told, and hustle.

Terry Leach: "I liked Darryl. He was a good guy, but at the time, he made Davey bat him fourth even though he wasn't producing that much. Gary had been doing that and it probably upset him that he didn't have that job anymore, because Gary's a proud man, but he was getting older and we had a young stud coming up.

"You can have a lot of talent, but you still have to work. Now Straw worked, but he didn't work as hard as he could have. He could have been great. He was real good, but he could have been great. Kirby Puckett was great. Kirby didn't have the attributes that Straw had, but he worked at it and made himself the best. Puck overall was the best. Straw could have done that, but a lot of guys who are good have the tendency not to work as hard, because they are already better than most people. They don't understand that no matter how good you are, there is still more; you can always be better. And that's what you gotta try to work for. But Straw definitely could play.

"In his book, when Darryl started talking about how important he was . . . I couldn't even finish reading his book. There was too much whining going on for me. I read about half of it, and I had to put it down. The way I saw things going on wasn't anywhere close to what he said it was. It was like, 'Oh, poor me. Oh, poor me.' Darryl should have been on top of the world. Take advantage of it. Don't be brought down by it. He should have *owned* New York and he could have. Darryl got with people who made him think different ways.I could see the effort not being there some days. He knew he was good, but you need to try to be better. You need to try to be the best, not just good."

In 1987 the players noticed how dark Darryl had turned. As for his charge that the rest of the players were pulling him down, their only response was, "That's Darryl."

Gary Carter: "It's hard to believe he could say that we were bringing the team down, but Darryl had his opinion, and if that's the way he felt, God bless him. To be honest, I felt like we did everything we could to keep Darryl on the straight and narrow, but we could only say so much about how he lived his life. I talked to him until I was blue in the face. I'd say, 'You can't do this.' "

"In '87 Darryl changed. We'd go on team buses and it was like he was constantly angry. Instead of needling with humor, it was becoming more malicious. Guys were recognizing that more and more.

"I always sat in the front of the bus. I avoided all that stuff. I wouldn't think of going to the back of the bus. That way if Darryl said something and it was pointed toward me, it just went in one ear and out the other. We said what most of New York said, 'That's Darryl. Just let it go.' "

Strawberry's teammates listened to his litany of complaints about them and shook their heads. It was Strawberry, they felt, who too often didn't hustle and who rarely worked at the game to become the best he could be.

Gary Carter: "In Darryl's case, all I wanted him to do was give it his all. I looked at other guys with a lot less talent who would go out and play their hearts out, the way Mookie or Wally would play, and Rafael Santana, guys who didn't have anywhere near the talent that Darryl had, and there would be days he'd go out there, and it looked like he wasn't even trying.

He'd have good games, but other days his lack of effort would show. And I think that's the unfortunate thing about Darryl's career. I really believe he could have had a *very* productive and successful career and maybe make the Hall of Fame. To me, he pretty much wasted a lot of it because of his lack of desire."

After Johnson fined Strawberry for showing up late to practice, Strawberry decided he would no longer speak to Johnson.

Darryl Strawberry: "There was nothing more I could say to the man that would have made any sense."

When teammates like Keith Hernandez, Wally Backman, and Lee Mazzilli expressed their disappointment when Strawberry refused to play hurt or was lazy, Strawberry turned on them with a vengeance.

There was a logical reason for this. Strawberry's marriage had fallen apart, and the Mets had become, in his mind, his substitute family. When Strawberry was a kid, he and his brothers fought every day, and then they would make up. He tried the same role-playing with his teammates. Unfortunately, as Strawberry would learn, his teammates were not his brothers. Instead of seeing his criticisms as brotherly advice, the other players took his jibes personally and held grudges. When Strawberry realized his teammates not only weren't blood, but that they weren't even his friends, he was devastated.

Darryl Strawberry: "I said it back then that those guys were a bunch of asses who would really miss me once I was gone. I really didn't want to play with a bunch of backstabbers and mean-spirited individuals who sniped at one another and at the only person who was winning games for them. I felt like I was a horse pulling the entire partying Mets team behind me on a cart, and if I paused to rest my back for a second or to get a drink of water, they'd scream that I was dropping them off a cliff. I was bitter, hateful, loathsome, angry, and mostly drunk."

What was most amazing about Darryl Strawberry in 1987 was that despite his drinking and his paranoia and his feelings of grandeur alternating with sinking feelings of self-worth, the man was the best pure power hitter New York had seen since Mickey Mantle. When he came to bat, everything stopped, and everyone watched. And when he uncoiled and met the ball

squarely, he would hit long, majestic home runs that have not been dupli-
cated since by a Met.

In 1987, despite his demons, Darryl Strawberry had a tremendous season, hitting .284 with 39 home runs and driving in 104 runs. He also stole
36 bases. But for all his production he felt painfully alone—unloved and
unappreciated.

The 1987 Strawberry-led Mets lost the division title by three games to the
St. Louis Cardinals. A chastened Dwight Gooden finished the year 15–7
with a 3.21. If he had only started the season with the team, instead of in
the Smithers drug clinic, the end result might have been different. Howard
Johnson, a regular for the first time, in 1987 had a breakout year, hitting 36
home runs and driving in 99 runs. Kevin McReynolds, the object of scorn
because of his silence and blandness, finished the season with 29 homers
and 95 rbis.

Terry Leach: "I thought it was good that Mac was quiet, because by not
talking he wasn't putting extra pressure on himself. He just went about his
business. He did what he did when he was in San Diego, and it was good.
He played good defense, good offense, and he could run the bases. He
could do a lot of things, hit for average, had a little power.

"I would watch him, and he'd look real bad on one swing, and then
he'd make an adjustment and just crush one. He was a smart hitter.

"Kevin didn't like being in the limelight, even though you don't make
as much money that way. He knew it was better for him to just get in and
get out."

The surprise performer on the Mets in 1987 was Terry Leach, the pocket
side-armer who compiled a stunning 11–1 mark. Whenever Davey Johnson needed a reliever or was stuck for a spot starter, Leach got the call.

Terry Leach: "I remember during the '87 season we didn't have a lot of
pitchers left. Wally Backman and I were shaving, and he said, 'Terr, they
are going to have to throw you out there. You throw a gem every time
you walk out there.'

"I said, 'They have to hit the bottom of the barrel before throwing me
out there.' And sure enough, the next week I was out there.

"My first start was against Fernando Valenzuela in California. I had thrown six out of seven days, Davey gave me two days off, and when I started I went into the seventh, and I was fine, but Davey figured, 'We've ridden this horse long enough. Let's get somebody else in there.' They took me out, and we won 5–2.

"Another time he started me against Cincinnati and the Reds were very hot at the time. They had Dave Parker and they were the hottest hitting team around, and I threw a shutout, only gave up four or five hits, and I was heading off the field, and Keith Hernandez came by and said, 'I'm glad I'm not hitting against you.' It was working. I had a great feeling, and I went with it, and I was hitting corners, the ball was moving, I was having a great time.

"Unfortunately I developed knee problems, and I needed an operation, but I wouldn't do it during the season because I didn't want to miss time. It got to where I couldn't drive off my right leg anymore, and my arm was dying. I bet I was topping out at 75 miles an hour.

"I was starting one game against the Cubs at Wrigley Field, and as I was warming up a lady in the first row said, 'Is this guy a pitcher?'

"So Davey took me out of the rotation, put me back in the bull pen— he was being good to me, tried to protect me and help me—he told me, 'I will not warm you up unless you are going into the game. I don't want you to throw on the side ever.'

"So the only time I pitched was when I warmed up and went into the game. And that gave my arm a chance to strengthen, so even with a bad knee I could still be effective. And I finished the year doing very well in relief.

"Davey liked me because he could abuse me. He could pitch me every day and I could go and not be affected the next day. I could go and go and go and go.

"I finished the season 11–1, and in fact, I had chances for two more wins into the ninth inning, and Randy Myers had a couple of blown saves. I kidded him about them. Randy didn't do that often. So I could have been 13–1. That would have been real cool.

"In 1987 we almost got to the playoffs again. We played very well."

The Mets, despite all the Sturm and Drang, were still a powerhouse.

Gary Carter: "In '87, despite everything that went on, we still managed to win 92 games, because we still had guys who could play the game. Even the Mitchell–McReynolds trade worked out. It turned out to be a much better trade for the Mets than we thought, because McReynolds came into his own. Mitch had his troubles in '87, and McReynolds had a *very* big year.

"We had a good pitching staff, guys who wanted to play, and even when they didn't want to play they still came through."

forty-one

A Division Title

During spring training of 1988 Darryl Strawberry came to camp like a player possessed. He was determined to be *great*, to lead the team to the pennant. But, with his improved performance came a concomitant rise in expectations from the press and the public. Darryl had energized himself into the role of superstar. But Darryl was emotionally unsuited for stardom. He had been much happier in a supporting role. As the spotlight once again turned toward him, Strawberry became resentful of the added pressure, especially when he wasn't performing like Superman.

In April 1988 Strawberry let it all hang out to journalist Mike Lupica, who wrote an article in *Esquire* airing his neuroses and complaints.

Strawberry accused teammates of suffering from a victim complex. He accused them of having the attitude that they didn't have to win games to be the top team in New York. He said they were content just earning their salaries.

In the article Strawberry said he wanted to be on a winning team, but that his teammates didn't. He named names. He accused Gary Carter and Keith Hernandez of not contributing. He accused Davey Johnson of coddling Hernandez and at the same time trying to bury him, the great Darryl Strawberry, all year long.

He charged that Wally Backman, Lee Mazzilli, Lenny Dykstra, and others could have produced more but didn't. All, of course, had criticized Strawberry during the previous year. The article was Darryl's payback.

It was very much like the article in which Reggie Jackson had been quoted in a *Sport* magazine article in the spring 1977 saying, "I'm the straw that stirs the drink." The difference was that this Straw didn't have that straw's gift of gab.

The result, however, was identical. Like Jackson, Strawberry became the object of pity and/or derision. For others, like Backman, Darryl's remarks rolled right off their backs.

Wally Backman: "I never let Darryl really bother me. I never tried to talk to him. He wasn't a guy I would have been able to communicate with very well. Not at that time. I know the more veteran guys, Hernandez and Carter, sat and talked with him. That was really their spot, because of who they were and what their importance was to the team. They could sink something into Darryl.

"What's happened to Darryl is so sad. It's real sad."

Backpedaling when the article came out, Strawberry accused Lupica of taking some of his remarks out of context. Few bought his alibi.

Carter didn't learn about the *Esquire* article until years later. He admits that 1987 had been an off-year for him, but not because of any lack of effort. Rather, his tired legs were beginning to give out. What he saw was Davey Johnson, far from trying to bury Strawberry, often bent over backward to accommodate the moody slugger, who insisted on hitting fourth even though his teammates felt it made more sense for him to bat fifth considering the players the Mets had.

Gary Carter: "I hit 20 home runs in '87 and had 83 rbis, and that was an off-year for me. It was my thirteenth season, and my body was beginning to break down quite a bit. I knew that things were not going the right way, although I worked very hard in the off-season. That was also when Darryl was going through his trials and tribulations with his own self.

"And that's when Davey dropped me from the number-four spot to the number-six spot without telling me. Joe Durso came to me and told me. And it was to appease Darryl. He did it to get Darryl to play. Because Darryl felt like he was better, God bless him, but Darryl didn't want to realize the way the lineup was set to have Keith, a lefty, batting third, and fourth being a right-hander, fifth a to a left-hander, and sixth a right-hander. If McReynolds was better than me, then put him there, but don't put Darryl there. Leave him five. You want to go left, right, left, right. And yet Davey had to do it because Darryl had this thing about batting cleanup.

"I don't know where Darryl got that. If anything, he should have looked at his own self in the mirror. I didn't know that article was written. If he ripped on me, so be it. I'm not going to lose any sleep over it.

"I can't understand half the stuff that came out of Darryl's mouth anyway. I really can't. He would talk before he ever thought, and that's what got him in trouble a lot of the time. There were so many things that came out of his mouth that didn't make any sense, or he was totally off-the-cuff because he didn't know any better. All I would do was shake my head. I wouldn't even comment when the writers came and asked me about it. I'd just say, 'I'm not going to get into it. That's Darryl, and he's entitled to his own opinion.' I wasn't going to create friction on the ball club by battling back in the press. I just let it go."

On opening day of 1988 in Montreal, Darryl Strawberry made a lot of people forgive him for his words when he hit two long home runs—one that went over 600 feet. By June the Mets were in first place by four-and-a-half games.

One reason the team dominated was its still overpowering pitching staff. In addition to Dwight Gooden and Ron Darling, David Cone had been acquired from Kansas City before the '87 season. Cone turned out to be one of the best pitchers in baseball. In 1988 he compiled a 20–3 record with a 2.22 era. Not only was Coney—as he was called—a great pitcher, but he fit in perfectly with the Wild Bunch.

Wally Backman: "David Cone was a hell of a pitcher. Coney did his business on the field. You knew what you were getting when he went out there.

"He was a wild guy. He would have fit into the mix of players we had in '86. He was a good fit for the ball club. The pitching was strong, no question about it."

Terry Leach: "We were winning every day. When we went to the ballpark, we were supposed to win. The guys got along well. They played well together. Davey was happy and he was easy to get along with. So, it was a great team to be on. I did not get any starts that year, but I threw 92 innings in relief. Davey was not afraid to throw me out there. That was a very good team."

Dwight Gooden: "We ran away with the Eastern Division. In fact, we won 31 of our first 43 games, all but clinching things by June. Still, there was a strange lethargy in the clubhouse; we weren't nearly as explosive or magical as we'd been two years earlier. I'm sure it was a bad omen, but we never, ever regained that sense of invincibility that existed in '86."

Part of the reason the magic seemed to have vanished was the strain in the relationships between Strawberry and many of his teammates. Although racing out to a big lead helped ease much of the clubhouse tension. Even Strawberry was more relaxed than he had been in a long time because he and his wife had reconciled and they had a second child. He flew to California for the birth of his daughter and came back the next day to hit another long home run to beat Pittsburgh.

In 1988, Strawberry continued to drink but he had at least stopped feuding with his teammates.

Darryl Strawberry: "It looked like the team had the spirit and the attitude of two years earlier. It looked like the team that would go all the way to the World Series, not like the team that had folded the year before."

The team won even though Gary Carter appeared to be at the end of his productive years offensively. After hitting seven home runs, driving in 15 rbis and hitting .322 in the month of April, his right knee became so bad that he was playing on guts alone. Behind the plate he was still doing his job, but the last five months of the season showed a serious drop in his batting numbers. He hit only four more home runs, including number 299 on May 17 and number 300 on August 10, and finished the year with only 11. In '88 he hit only .242 with but 46 rbis.

Despite an early division title, the year did not end smoothly for the Mets as a team. In September the Mets called up 21-year-old switch-hitting infielder Greg Jefferies, a kid with huge potential. The Minor League Player of the Year two years running, he was the organization's best young prospect.

But, Jefferies was viewed by many of his teammates as a selfish jerk, dedicated to himself, not to the team. His arrogance and egotism were so obnoxious that some of his teammates quickly came to despise him. They felt the kid single-handedly destroyed any cohesiveness the team might have had.

In the minors Jefferies had been in the habit of cursing loudly, a trait that embarrassed manager Mike Cubbage. When Cubbage asked him to stop, he refused. When he came up to the Mets, Jefferies refused to take counsel from batting coach Bill Robinson. He said he would only listen to his father.

What made the situation worse was that Davey Johnson loved Jefferies' hitting ability and appeared to coddle him, hurting team morale badly. It's also possible that Johnson was championing Jefferies at the behest of the Mets' front office, who felt they needed a new fan idol.

Wally Backman: "Greg's a hell of a player, but one of the things that happened that hurt Greg with teammates was in spring training of '88 they let him do a lot of crazy things like he was an important veteran. Supposedly they let him go home early so he could swing a bat in the pool. Things like that didn't set well with the other players. They gave him a lot of room to do things that others couldn't do.

"He pretty much set his own agenda, though not completely. But he could do a lot more than other people could. I could be wrong, but I don't think this was Davey's doing. Davey's not a guy who would give other people those type of . . . I think Davey had people telling him how to run him. Jefferies was the new era that hadn't gotten there yet. You know?

"The things he was able to do rubbed a lot of players wrong. The first day he stepped into the clubhouse, there weren't a lot of happy people.

Former icons, Dwight Gooden and Darryl Strawberry, had had their run-ins with the law, Gary Carter had slowed, and Keith Hernandez was also reaching the end of his tenure. Jefferies was picked to be the next big deal.

Dwight Gooden: "We needed a better-looking poster boy, and from a distance, Jefferies had the perfect résumé. He was polite, skilled, stable, not likely to ever get in trouble. The problem with this buildup, of course, was that Jefferies simply didn't know how to act around older, more hardened players.

"Keith and Darryl took an instant dislike to him, as did Roger McDowell, who once sawed all of Jefferies bats in half. It was wrong to do that, but Greg brought it on himself, as he insisted that his bats be packed and shipped separately on road trips, as if they were somehow better than everyone else's.

"One time Straw decided he'd had enough of Jefferies' self-absorption. He took the bats out of [equipment manager Charlie] Samuel's hands and dumped every one of them in the garbage. We all laughed; making fun of Jefferies was a popular thing to do.

"Jefferies was a terrific hitter; he finished with a .321 average and proved he was a match for any major-league pitcher. But it was also obvious what a baby Jefferies was. He'd been catered to his whole career, first by his father and now by the Mets, who were looking for new superstars to take them into the nineties."

Gary Carter: "The Mets were really promoting Greg Jefferies. There was a lot of jealousy on the ball club. The guy was a good hitter. And he started out at shortstop, and then they tried to play him at second, and he was taking Wally's job away and Wally was a ringleader of the gang, and that didn't sit very well.

"He had a smile that kind of rubbed you the wrong way, and after the game he would take all his bats and put them in his locker. Everybody else kept their bats in the bat rack. I don't see anything wrong with taking care of your bats. They are your livelihood. But I guess the manner in which he did it didn't sit very well with the guys.

"The biggest thing was that Greg came up with a lot of accolades and he was very egotistical. He was saying, 'I have my sights on Pete Rose's hit record.' He had torn up the minor leagues and he felt he was going to do the same thing on the major-league level. But he was not very good in the field, and after he left the Mets he floated from ball club to ball club, Kansas City, St. Louis, Philadelphia, and Detroit.

"I tried to take care of him. Not that I took him under my wing, but I tried to talk to him and direct him in the right way. I think it did some good. I didn't treat him as horribly as some of the guys did.

"Davey took his side and that didn't help him with some of the players. It became very sided. But the fact of the matter was, the guy played pretty good, and he did help us, but he might have been one of the reasons we didn't win it all in '88. Davey put him on third in the playoffs against the Dodgers. When Jefferies was given that opportunity, there was a separation on the team. Especially since the guy hadn't played [there] all year long. We go into the playoffs and he's the starting third baseman."

Terry Leach: "Greg did very well. It seemed like he hit a double every other time he came to bat. He was crushing it. The only problem was that we had a ranking of order. You had Mex and Kid, older guys, and Straw and Dwight, and you had your levels of players, and in New York that's pretty important.

"Wally and Teufel were our second basemen, and everybody liked the way they played, how hard they played, and it's tough to sit back and watch when management says, 'We're going to make a change. Get this kid in.' And Greg was a very average fielder. He could make a good play every once in a while, but then he'd boot one. I thought Wally was a much better second baseman. But, Greg had a lot of offense and they wanted more pop in the lineup. And when he came in and hit, it helped.

"But, you had Greg Jefferies coming in, very young, a little cocky, maybe even more than a little, and just the talk and attention he was getting, some of the things he said and his agent was always around, and it just didn't sit right.

"If he had come in, stayed quiet, learned what was going on before opening up his mouth, things would probably have been fine, but he had already started doing this in the minor leagues and it was just the way he was. Greg was a good guy, but he didn't know any better. He just didn't sit that well. He was an irritant."

"One time we were on a road trip and somebody who I won't name but who used to like to play a lot of practical jokes, went into the locker room during the game and took Greg's dress shoes and left him these big green-and-gold saddle oxfords that looked like clown shoes. And that's all he had to wear home on the plane.

"He took it pretty well. He put the shoes on and wore them. If he had bitched and moaned, it could have been trouble, but he pretty well took it in stride. When you're a rookie, you better. Guys are going to play with you a little bit."

Wally Backman: "Greg Jefferies was their minor-league guy. He was supposedly their big future. They were going to build the ball club around him.

"Everybody in the world knew he couldn't field, but he was going to get every opportunity to mess that up, as he did. He's an awesome offensive player, a *very* good offensive player, from both sides of the plate, but he's a designated hitter is what he is. That's as liable as somebody can be when they're in the field.

"I liked Greg. I never had any problem with him. But Jefferies was the reason I asked to be traded in '89. I talked with Joe McIlvaine. I didn't want to be there and be the guy whose job was taken by this guy. I saw that it was going to affect my playing time, because they wanted to make him a second baseman. I'd heard everything and that's when I went to Joe and asked him to trade me. I wish I wouldn't have done that, after the fact. Cause I wasn't the first guy on the trading block in the winter meetings that year. Howard Johnson was. But when they couldn't make a trade for Howard, they traded me."

Though the promotion of Greg Jefferies became a distraction, the Mets still won the Eastern division by fifteen games. In the playoffs the Mets faced the Los Angeles Dodgers, a team they had beaten ten out of the eleven times they had met in 1988. The series was a cliffhanger.

Game one pitted Dwight Gooden against Orel Hershiser. The Dodgers led 2–0 in the eighth inning. With one out and Gregg Jefferies on second, Strawberry doubled into the gap. It was the first run scored off Hershiser since August 30. Lasorda brought in Jay Howell to pitch. He walked Kevin McReynolds, then struck out HoJo for the second out. Gary Carter then hit a bloop double to right-center. Two runs scored and the Mets were winners.

Gary Carter: "I guess I thrived on situations like that. I was just trying to do my part and it was nice being able to come through against Howell. He threw me a breaking ball. John Shelby was playing deep on me, and I hit a ball that dropped in front of Shelby and McReynolds scored from second and barreled into Scioscia for the game-winner.

"I credit Kevin McReynolds for bowling over Mike Scioscia— McReynolds got banged up on that play, but he scored the winning run. I appreciated his effort on that."

Darryl Strawberry: "I will probably go to my grave with one nagging doubt: We might have won the 1988 National League playoffs had we not made one tiny mistake after the first game. We shot off our mouths!"

★ ★ ★

David Cone was the main culprit. Cone told reporters that they hadn't been lucky, but that they won because they were *good*. Cone was quoted as saying, "Hershiser was lucky. Doc was good." He also derided the way Jay Howell pitched to Gary Carter. Cone made it personal, angering Tommy Lasorda and his Dodgers.

Gary Carter: "David Cone was writing a column for a newspaper, and he made an off-the-wall comment. He said that Jay Howell was a Little League pitcher, given that he threw a lot of breaking pitches. He wondered how he could have thrown me a breaking ball. And when it came out, Tommy Lasorda turned it around and made Coney look bad.

"And when he pitched that second game, he was so nervous. Because of the comment and the Dodgers making such a big deal about it.

"I could tell he was nervous. I said, 'Coney, you got to let that go. Just blow it off. That's Lasorda, trying to pump the guys up.' But he was really concerned he had hurt their feelings. Some guys would say, 'Screw it. It doesn't matter,' but Coney was concerned.

"And I know it affected him in that game. They racky-tacked him."

Tim Belcher held the Mets to three runs while the Dodgers scored five runs off Cone.

Game three, held in New York, became known as "the pine-tar game." Ron Darling and Orel Hershiser battled to a 3–3 tie after seven innings. Jay Howell took the mound for the Dodgers in the eighth.

Davey Johnson had complained about Howell's pitches, accusing him of doing something to the ball a la Mike Scott. Johnson told the other players and coaches to keep an eye on Howell while he was pitching. Third-base coach Bill Robinson noticed that Howell kept tugging at the strings of his glove.

The Dodgers were leading 4–3 in the bottom of the eighth with the count 3–2 on Kevin McReynolds. Howell was on the mound and Johnson called time. Johnson went to umpire Joe West and asked him to inspect the ball. It was found to have pine tar and Howell was thrown out of the game. The glove was taken to commissioner Bart Giamatti.

The Mets fans began chanting, "Cheaters."

Alejandro Pena came into the game in relief, completed the walk to McReynolds, and the Mets rallied for five runs.

In game four the Mets could have won the Series had they held a 4–2 lead going into the ninth inning. Gooden was unable to retire the side in the ninth. He allowed a walk and a home run, and just like that, the game was tied.

Dwight Gooden: "I'd devastated the Dodgers for the first eight innings. They were mine and those last three outs were so close, I could feel them. Even the walk I issued offered no hint of a collapse. I still had good velocity and felt like I was in control of the at-bat.

"That's why Davey left me in the game, because throughout the year I'd slithered through many similar tight spots.

"Unfortunately it was the wrong decision."

Gary Carter: "We were up in the game by two runs in the seventh, and John Shelby led off and walked, and then Mike Scioscia came up. I knew he was notorious for liking to take the first pitch. We always knew when Scioscia was taking and you could just lay it in there, and he was not going to swing. All I was thinking about was trying to get ahead of him. With the first pitch we were trying to hit the outside corner, not trying to throw one right down the middle.

"But after walking Shelby on four pitches, Doc grooved one to Scioscia, and he knocked it out of the park."

Shea was silent, everyone was so shocked.

The Dodgers went on to win 5–4 in twelve innings when with two outs Roger McDowell gave up a long home run to a gimpy Kirk Gibson.

The next afternoon the Dodgers trounced Sid Fernandez. Tim Belcher won again, beating the Mets 7–4 with his overpowering fastball.

Gary Carter: "Sid was the type of guy, if he had it going, he could be unhittable. But if you got to him early and he got rattled a little bit, he would have a bad game."

David Cone won game six 5–1 behind a two-run home run hit by Kevin McReynolds off Tim Leary.

Gary Carter: "When Coney came back to pitch game six, he was a totally different pitcher. He said to whoever needed to hear it that he was not going to do the column anymore, not going to make any more comments and I think that's when David Cone came of age. He's a very articulate young man and I've always appreciated the way he's handled himself since. He's really done quite well for himself in the major leagues."

Davey Johnson faced a dilemna before game seven. It was Ron Darling's turn to pitch, but Dwight Gooden let him know that he could go with two days rest if he was needed. Johnson chose to start Darling, who didn't get out of the second inning. At least one teammate, in hindsight, wished he had started Doc instead.

Wally Backman: "The only thing I can tell you about the '88 playoffs, I do know this: Ron Darling lost game seven, and I do know Dwight had said he could pitch—it was the day Dwight was supposed to throw on the side—he could go five or six, and we were facing Hershiser and Dwight would have been our best pitcher. That's one thing in my mind and it's always after the fact, cause it's easy to second-guess, but knowing Dwight being the best pitcher we had, I would have liked to have seen him give us those five innings. Maybe the game would have turned out a little different.

"Ronnie fell behind real fast. It was frustrating, because we had beaten this team so many times. We had beaten the Dodgers 10 of 11 times in the regular season. Ronnie was a hell of a pitcher, too, but I thought Dwight was our number one guy. He had been for the last few years.

"There was a lot of frustration, because we knew how bad we had beaten them throughout the season. I know I was frustrated that we didn't beat them, and most everyone else was, too."

When Darling came out in the second inning, Johnson then brought in Dwight Gooden, used in relief for the first time since high school. When he came in he was roughed up. At the end of the second inning, the Dodgers had a 6–0 lead. The Mets were never in the game. The relievers were upset Johnson had used Gooden in relief of Darling instead of one of them.

Terry Leach: "To get beat out by the Dodgers . . . we beat them ten out of eleven games during the season. We had one rainout. And then to go to the playoffs and get beat in seven games . . . the Dodgers got hot right at the end, and we didn't put it together. We weren't scoring very much. Our pitchers were a little shaky at the end. The Dodgers lit up Ronnie for a run in the first inning, and they scored five in the second against Darling and Dwight. Using Dwight in relief was the only questionable decision. Dwight's a great pitcher, but he's not a reliever. It's a different game. It's easy to be a reliever and start a game. But, it's hard to be a starter and try to relieve. It took Dwight ten minutes to get loose. It took Roger and me about one minute, and we could be in for the next hitter. So neither of us could understand Davey doing that. It's a thing managers do. They go to their number-one man. But, the way I saw it, you get through all year long with your relievers, you don't change around. You use them in their role.

"I remember in the seventh game I threw two shutout innings. I said, 'Come on, guys. We're wasting my life here. We gotta win this game.' But we couldn't pull it out. We couldn't get it going against Hershiser. He was almost untouchable that year. He had a great season.

"The Dodgers then went on to win the World Series. That was the Series when Kirk Gibson hit that home run and limped around the bases."

Orel Hershiser, who would go on to win the Cy Young Award, only allowed five hits in the finale.

Darryl Strawberry: "For nine innings on the night of October 12, Orel Hershiser was the toughest pitcher I had ever seen in my life. He seemed to draw a power from somewhere and frustrated us completely."

Gary Carter: "That was the year Hershiser broke Don Drysdale's record for consecutive scoreless innings. Drysdale had 58⅔ innings, and Hershiser had 59. He was masterful that year. He threw curveballs two and oh, three and one. He threw change-ups. He had a sinking fastball. He had all his pitches working. He threw a masterful game in game seven. We knew we had our backs to the wall, but it wasn't like Orel was unhittable. But that year he had it going. He was the Cy Young award winner. He was the league champion MVP, and ultimately he was the Series MVP. So he won all the awards. It was one of those great years and then the Dodgers rewarded him with a $3 million contract.

"In '88, we should have won the pennant again. We had beaten the Dodgers eleven out of twelve times we played them during the season, and they beat us in the playoffs.

"I was totally, totally disappointed."

★ ★ ★

Darryl Strawberry, on whose broad shoulders the fate of the Mets rested, was inconsolable.

Darryl Strawberry: "After the game I sat down in front of my locker and cried like a baby. Nothing anybody could say could ease my feelings of failure at having lost the National League championship right in front of my own mother, brothers, and sisters.

"I just wanted to get into bed and not come out of it again, we played so bad.

"Worst of all, I didn't want it for the Mets. I wanted it just for me. And just for me."

And at the end of the series Strawberry had an old thought: "I want to be a Dodger." He told a reporter from the *LA Times* that he had dreamed about playing with the Dodgers. He complained that whenever he was in a slump the New York fans were merciless.

Darryl Strawberry: "I felt like I was vanishing as a real person, even in my own eyes, in the late fall of 1988 and turning into the creature the press had created. So I continued to drink, letting the human being called Darryl Strawberry become so completely absorbed into what the media were calling Darryl Strawberry that all I had left was the marriage I was trying to put back on its feet and my two little kids."

The constant beating he was taking in the newspapers was also taking its toll on his already tentative relationship with his teammates.

On the long plane ride home Strawberry became angered when some teammates were loudly talking about their winter plans and laughing.

". . . better shut their fucking mouths," he snarled. "Anyone have any problem with that?"

Darryl was no person to mess with when angry.

Dwight Gooden: "The bad feeling on the plane carried over into 1989."

forty-two

The End of An Era

Though Davey Johnson's Mets only won one pennant and one World Championship, the Mets players are convinced that his teams deserve to be remembered as having been much more dominating. Had they played during the era of the wild card, they say, the likelihood is that they would made the playoffs as often as the Atlanta Braves and would have appeared at least a couple of times more in the fall classic.

Wally Backman: "Everybody looks at that team and says we should have won more than we did and we probably should have, but if you put it into the context of today's baseball, if there had been a wild card that team would have been in the playoffs in '84, '85, '86, '87, and '88. Because of the number of games we won each year. That's six years that team would have been in the playoffs and had a chance at the World Series. If you'd have given us ten extra years to the 90s, we would have been in the playoffs every year, like the Braves are now."

Backman's last year with the Mets was the 1988 season. When he saw that Greg Jefferies had been knighted by the Mets front-office choice to take his job at second base, the veteran asked for his walking papers and got them on December 7, 1988.

Wally Backman: "One of the front-office people had called me anonymously and told me that Howard [Johnson] was the one on the block. He said, 'Wally, if something doesn't happen with Howard, you'll be on the block the next morning.'

"Then he called me back and he said, 'Wally, they made a deal with the Dodgers, and you're going to be called pretty soon.'

"When Joe McIlvaine called me, I told him I knew about it. I was excited. If I was going somewhere I wanted to go to a big market team, and I definitely was glad I was staying in the National League.

"When he called he asked if I was sitting or standing, and I said, 'I'm standing. I already know you've traded me.'

"He said, 'Yes, we did.'

"I said, 'You traded me to the Dodgers.'

"He said, 'No,' and then I about fell down.

"When he told me I was going to Minnesota, I was upset. I don't have many good memories of Minnesota except for playing with Kent Hrbek and Kirby Puckett and some of those guys, great guys to play with, but going from New York with the media and the hype to a place where they had one newspaper and one radio station, it was a terrible fit for me after all those years in New York. I didn't like it at all. If there was one year I could have done without, it was the year in Minnesota.

"After that I went to Pittsburgh and that was the year we lost to the Reds in the playoffs. Paul O'Neill jumped over the wall and took a home run away from Bobby Bonilla. That cost us going into game seven.

"That was a fun year. I would have liked to have finished my career with Jim Leyland. They wanted to re-sign me and they didn't because my agent wasn't quick enough to do it, and I ended up going to Philadelphia for a couple of years. I was with Atlanta in spring training in '93 and I ended up with Seattle playing for Lou Piniella. Lou was the Cincinnati manager when they beat us in the playoffs in '90. He made a lot of unbelievable strategic moves, killed our left-handed hitting lineup with the moves he made. He was a very, very smart manager, I thought.

"And after I retired I managed four years in the minors in an independent league and I've just signed with the White Sox to manage in their system. I would have liked to have come back to the Mets—in fact, that's the first place I sent my résumé. But, the whole front office has changed except for Jay Horowitz and Jim Plummer, great guys who'll never leave. The rest have changed and one of the problems is that they [think] we were wild. We kicked people's butts on the field and we ran the streets hard. But, times and people change. I know all of us have slowed *way* down. But I think the new front-office people still look at us like the way we were as players, and not what we can give the organization in return. It's a shame, because that's where I wanted to go. Maybe one day down the road. I'd love to be back in New York, yes.

"Playing in New York [makes] you the best you [can] be. The atmosphere is so different in the big cities. I'll tell you what, my years in New York were by far my best years and liking the game the way I liked the game. New York to me is the greatest place to play baseball."

By 1989 the Mets camaraderie was about gone. In the spring Strawberry asked for a contract extension. Though his contract had another year to run, he had had an outstanding season in '88, and he and his agent felt it was only fair that the Mets rework his contract to pay him more money in '89 and add a year in '90.

When Cashen turned him down cold, Strawberry became belligerent. He told Cashen that if he didn't sit down with his agent, Eric Goldschmidt, he would walk out of camp, play out '89 and leave the Mets at the end of the season.

Keith Hernandez, savvy in the ways of the media, was in the habit of criticizing teammates to reporters, letting them know what was going on in exclusive interviews so long as the reporter kept his name out of the story. Hernandez' made unattributed comments in the newspapers attacking Strawberry for his stand. Hernandez looked upon Strawberry as a malingering malcontent. Darryl, who looked to Hernandez for his approval, felt betrayed.

When the issue became public and Strawberry didn't show up for spring training on time, the writers also made Strawberry sound like an ingrate.

Like Hernandez, teammates were furious with him for disrupting training camp.

Terry Leach: "By Straw not coming in to spring training he was disrupting the team, not doing his work. He was looking after himself instead of the team.

"And my thought of it—I kept my nose out of it—but I thought it was ridiculous. I thought, 'When you signed that contract, you were happy with it.' And if you got hurt, you expect them to pay you. They expect you to play until this is over and when it's over *then* you renegotiate. If you don't like the way the long-term contract goes, then go year to year. Put your money where your mouth is. Play every year.

"When I was with the Royals Jeff Montgomery did that. He was a young kid. He never had much money. Boom, they offered him a three-year deal. He turned it down. He got a one-year deal and did real good and got even more. He said, 'I'm betting on myself.' So he did it year after year for a while, and that's the way everybody figured. 'If you think you're that good, put it on the line, otherwise play for what you sign for, do your best, and when it's over, then re-do it.' Like Kirby Puckett. He wouldn't renegotiate. He could have, but he said, 'When my contract's through, *then* I'll get the money.' And he was the best. He'd say, 'My time will come. I signed for this, and I'll play for this.' Kirby was a very honorable man."

Gary Carter was also quoted criticizing Strawberry for wanting to reopen contract negotiations.

Gary Carter: "One time I said to Darryl, 'Why don't you get it? Why don't you understand? If you just play and forget about everything else and keep your nose clean, one of these days you'll make three times the money that Keith and I ever thought of making.' And wouldn't you know it, in 1991 the Dodgers signed him to a four-year, $20 million contract. I said, 'Darryl, see what I told you.' And he said, 'You were right, Kid.'

"I would try to talk sense into some of these guys to make them understand that [their time in] baseball is very short-lived and our lives are basically short, and it's a matter of what kind of legacy do you want to leave? I feel very good and very proud of what I accomplished in my lifetime. I feel good that I didn't cheat anybody. I didn't cheat my teammates. And that's something Darryl can't say. He'll look back on this whole thing and know he cheated not only himself but his teammates a lot, too."

On Picture Day during spring training Strawberry walked up to Keith Hernandez and Gary Carter and complained to them saying that he wasn't discussing their contracts and they shouldn't be commenting on his.

Also bugging Strawberry was that he learned from a reporter that the year before Hernandez had actively campaigned for Kevin McReynolds to be the National League's Most Valuable Player, and had bad-mouthed Strawberry. The Dodgers' Kirk Gibson ended up winning it with 272 votes, but it's certainly possible Strawberry (second with 236 votes) might have won had Hernandez not been so outspoken against him.

When the photographer placed Hernandez and Strawberry side by side for the team picture, Darryl said out loud, "I'm not sitting next to any backstabber." Punches started flying. Strawberry, angry at management *and* his teammates, walked off the field, left camp, and didn't show up for practice the next day. When he returned, he reiterated to Davey Johnson that he would play out the season and go elsewhere.

Gary Carter: "The fight mostly transpired between Keith and Darryl. I pretty much tried to remove myself. It was done in a belligerent way, and the press was all there, and they built it up."

Terry Leach: "Straw and Keith ended up having words. While they were taking the team picture Keith was sticking little knives in Darryl. Darryl was sitting right next to me. They were quipping back and forth, and then all of a sudden Straw snapped.

"But Straw didn't want to fight. I pulled him out of there way too easily. I picked him up and moved him a little bit. He should have been throwing me around. He's much bigger than me. So I was holding Darryl, pulling him out of it, and it was one of the few times I ever got my picture in *Sports Illustrated*.

"I moved him out of there because Straw didn't want to be there. Like we said, Straw had a good heart, but sometimes he wasn't the brightest guy in the world. He'd let other people—his agents and all—lead him too much sometimes. I think this must have been his agent's idea. Darryl was hearing something he wanted to hear, so he was going along with it. But, you gotta do more than just look out for yourself. You gotta take one for the team sometimes. He was going to make money. If you're good enough, you're going to make money. Take your time. Pick your spots. That's what Keith was saying. And Darryl went after him."

The next day against the LA Dodgers, the St. Lucie fans booed him fiercely. Strawberry acted quickly. He ran over to Keith Hernandez at first base and planted a wet kiss on his cheek. On his next at bat he hit a long home run.

Darryl was back in the good graces of the fans, but he couldn't stop thinking about the unfairness of it all.

★ ★ ★

Darryl Strawberry: "As long as I was hitting home runs, driving base runners home, and giving the fans a show, I was entitled to my share of the accolades. But, just as soon as I stepped out of line, I was no good."

Darryl's problem was that he desperately needed unconditional approval and very few athletes get that from the fans and teammates.

In 1989, Strawberry began to frame his problems in racial terms. White players, he sensed, got away with things black players couldn't. White players, like Keith Hernandez who had admitted to drug use, were quickly forgiven, but black players weren't. The fixation further infuriated Strawberry.

Strawberry, like other black players, came to believe the Mets management preferred white players to blacks. In 1989 Strawberry and Gooden were the only black regulars. Kevin Mitchell, Mookie Wilson, and Hubie Brooks had all been dealt away. Strawberry noticed that black minor leaguers such as LaSchelle Tarver and Terry Blocker never made it with the Mets while all sorts of lesser white players like Clint Hurdle, Ron Gardenhire, and Danny Heep played or sat on the bench. Race will always be an issue that divides white and black. The blacks are sure they are right. The whites disagree.

Gary Carter: "For Darryl to say that, I just feel sorry for him. I don't know if it was said out of spite or what. I don't hold it against Darryl."

Strawberry complained bitterly that Frank Cashen would not sit down with him and renegotiate his contract. He resented that Cashen never praised him for his past work, never made him feel part of something.

Darryl Strawberry: "If he would have only said *once* that he wanted me to remain with the Mets, but that renegotiating my contract would have meant renegotiating all the contracts, I would have understood that, too. Had I been in his position, I would have taken the time to let that player know how much he meant to the organization but how the organization had to adhere to certain bargaining principles with all players, regardless of their race or background, I would have bought that hook, line, and sinker, because I was *looking* for that kind of communication. I needed the support of the Mets family. I craved it. I wanted to stay on the Mets.

"But at that time in 1989, they put out all the signals to me that they didn't want me to stay on the team, and that's still the hardest thing in the world for me to accept."

After two weeks of the 1989 season, the Mets were in last place. There was trouble between Davey Johnson and Frank Cashen. On instructions from the front office to crack down on the players, Davey announced that golf and cards would be banned from the clubhouse. Cashen wanted more discipline from Davey, and this was to part of the new get-tough policy.

Two days later Davey told the players that if they wanted to play cards or golf, they should do it quietly and out of sight of Cashen and the reporters. The players noticed Davey's isolation from the front office. They also saw that he wasn't the same easygoing, damn-the-torpedoes leader he once had been.

Terry Leach: "A lot of things had changed about Davey in '89. Davey got where he didn't talk to the guys as much as he used to. Part of it was the press. Every time his door was open, which was always, his office was full of press, always trying to get something, get something, and it got to where he just didn't want to talk anymore. It got to be work and he was stressed. He used to be laid back and easygoing and it to got to where it didn't look to me that he was enjoying it as much.

"He used to always sit around and talk with guys, but he got to where he was very quiet, and even a little hard. I just don't think he was enjoying it much.

"And part of it was the pressure he was under from management wanting him to do exactly what they wanted him to do, despite his having his own ideas about how things should go. He wasn't getting to do things he thought he needed to do and that just took the fun out of it.

"I know Davey used to make Mr. Cashen mad. He would almost say just the opposite of what Mr. Cashen would say. 'Don't worry about this. We're going to do it like this.'"

By May the Mets had climbed into first place, but injuries slowed their march. On May 10, 1989, Gary Carter scored a run from third base in Cincinnati on the AstroTurf, and the next day his knee blew up. He went on the disabled list and missed two-and-a-half months after undergoing a knee operation.

Darryl Strawberry's back stiffened and Tim Teufel popped an ankle while jogging.

Then Keith Hernandez crashed into Dodgers second baseman Dave Anderson and broke his right kneecap. With both Carter and Hernandez out and Strawberry doubled up in back pain, the Mets were hurting badly. Making Strawberry's travails harder, Lisa Strawberry filed for divorce in May, sending Darryl into a deep depression.

On June 5, David Cone and the Mets lost 15–3 to the Cubs. The next day the Cubs beat up Bobby Ojeda 8–4. They split the final two games. Then Pittsburgh beat them two out of three.

The front office, in one of the stranger deals the Mets ever made, traded two of their leaders, Lenny Dykstra, and Roger McDowell, to Philadelphia for Juan Samuel.

Lenny was a handful. He was an inveterate gambler. He was obsessed with money. He could be a flake. But no one played harder. Dykstra could no longer stand being platooned with Mookie Wilson. He wanted the center field spot to himself. Cashen sent Lenny and the effervescent Roger McDowell packing in a really terrible trade.

Why they paid so dearly for Samuel was a mystery. He was a second baseman and they already had Jefferies. The Phils had tried him in the outfield and when he arrived in New York, Samuel was put in center field, a position he rarely had played. Why they didn't trade for a pure center fielder perplexed everyone.

What galled the Mets players and fans was that Dykstra became a star in Philadelphia and McDowell became the Phils' stopper.

Gary Carter: "Why did the Mets do some of the things they did? They traded Roger McDowell and Lenny Dykstra? What was that? For Juan Samuel? That did nothing for us."

Johnson expressed his frustration to Carter over Cashen making trades without consulting him.

Gary Carter: "Around the time Lenny and Roger were traded, I said to him, 'Skip, what's up?' And he said, 'God, they never tell me anything. All

I want to do is be a part of this and know what's going on and who we're getting. . . . '

"All hell was breaking loose."

In July 1989 the Mets pulled within two-and-a-half games of the Montreal Expos but injuries continued to haunt the team. On July 1 Doc Gooden was sidelined for the rest of the season with a muscle tear in his side. In a game against Montreal, Kevin Gross hit Darryl Strawberry on the foot with a pitch and broke his right toe. Even with Hernandez back in the lineup, the Mets began to slip.

With Gooden out, on July 31, 1989, the Mets strengthened their starting staff when Frank Cashen traded much of the Met's pitching future— Aguilera, David West, Kevin Tapani, and three other minor leaguers to the Minnesota Twins—for Frank Viola, who had won 24 games and the Cy Young Award the year before. The Mets were giving up a great deal, but it was hard for Cashen to pass up a top starter like Viola.

Gary Carter: "There was some adamancy that Aguilera was promising, but we needed another starter and Frank Viola had been a Cy Young Award winner, and the Mets needed to do something to shake things up a bit. So we traded five for one. Frank turned out to be pretty important."

But then Cashen upset everyone when he traded Mookie Wilson to Toronto for middle reliever Jeff Musselman. Wilson would have been a free agent at the end of the season and the front office decided that since they had Samuel, they would rather get a body for Wilson, even if only a middle reliever, rather than let him go at the end of the season for nothing.

Mookie, though quiet, had been a spark plug through his hustle and speed. But by 1989, Mookie struck out too much to lead off and didn't hit average enough to hit lower in the order. They gave him away. A middle reliever seemed way too little in return.

Gary Carter: "I couldn't understand that one, because Mookie was one of the guys who should have been a lifetime Met. He's one of the nicest guys in the entire world.

"When they traded Lenny, we thought Mookie was going to have the everyday job, and then they traded him. I didn't understand it. And Juan

Samuel didn't last very long. He went to LA and became their second baseman.

"But, it doesn't surprise me some of the things that have transpired in the game. When you think you know it all, something else pops up. When you've got it somewhat figured out thinking how a team stays together, they break it up. And you don't understand why. To this day I will never figure it out. I don't second-guess or hold grudges, I just shake my head and ponder and wonder why things happen."

Meanwhile, Carter and Hernandez were getting old and the resentment against Jefferies remained. An injury to Gooden, still only twenty-four, limited his appearances. And there were rumors Johnson was on the way out. Players began to see that Cashen was calling the shots and that Johnson no longer had much authority. He was no longer even picking the starting lineup. Rather, like a dutiful foot soldier, he was stoicly taking orders from the bully-boy front office.

After Carter injured his knee and had it operated on, Johnson pushed him to return. Because Davey had asked him to, Carter came back a week early. But then, once the Mets called him up, Johnson only played him sporadically. As it turned out, the front office had ordered Johnson to keep the aging Carter on the bench and play his successors, Mackey Sasser and Barry Lyons. Carter learned firsthand that Johnson was no longer his own man.

Gary Carter: "The first part of the '89 season, I had 79 at bats and hit .114. I was hurting, but the Mets were doing everything they could to keep me playing. But, obviously I had a problem with my knee.

"They corrected it and I came back early for Davey. I went down to Tidewater, played a couple games. I was on first base, and a ball was hit down the right-field line and by the time I got to third base I was limping, and the third-base coach sent me home, and I got thrown out by fifteen feet, and I didn't slide, and the fans booed me. I'm thinking, How come this was created? I didn't even want to go to Norfolk, for crying out loud. And I knew I wasn't ready. I'm thinking, What the . . .

"On July 25th, my first at bat back with the Mets, I pinch hit and grounded into a double play and I got booed. So I'm thinking, 'Why did I come back?'

"And in those last two months I ended up with fewer at bats than I did the first month and ten days. I had 74 at bats in those last two months. There was one game in Philadelphia I was 4 for 4 and had a big game, won it, and then we came home to play the Cardinals in a doubleheader, and I didn't start either one of those games. But I ended up getting a hit in one and a sacrifice hit in the other, and I had a streak going where I had seven straight hits. And yet, I wasn't playing.

"The writing on the wall became more and more obvious—especially coming from our announcer, Tim McCarver, who kept saying, 'He's done. He shouldn't be playing.' On and on and on and on.

"I raised my average from .114 to .183. I hit 2 home runs and had 15 rbis the whole year, but I only had 153 at bats. So was it disappointing? Absolutely it was.

"The next year I asked Davey why he had bothered to bring me back early. He said, 'Gary, my hands were tied. My back was up against the wall. I couldn't do anything.' Meaning he was the one who wanted me to come back, but when I joined the club the front office told him not to play me because they were not going to bring me back the next year. So he already knew.

"Davey said, 'I wanted to play you. You were my guy. But they told me, 'No, we don't want you to play him.' Davey had wanted me for the pennant race in '89. It turned out we won 87 games in '89, but we ended up losing to the Chicago Cubs by six games.

"They had the plan that Keith and I were not coming back in 1990. Right at the end of '89 we were playing our last game against the Phillies at home and I hit a double in my last at bat at Shea in a Mets uniform, and the fans gave me a standing ovation.

"And then we went on the road and finished out the year, and when we came back, the Mets set up a press conference for both Keith and me. We walked in and Frank Cashen's last words were that he didn't want the fans to remember Gary Carter on the downside, that he wanted them to remember me in New York for the good things. Same thing with Keith. He thought our skills were diminishing, and it was time to move on.

"I wanted to finish my career in New York. I would have played for a lot less money. I didn't want to move on. I really didn't. I'd have been much happier staying. I should have played another three years in New York. I was just disappointed more than anything. I knew I had an off year and my body was breaking down, but that didn't mean I didn't have the desire to continue to play there. It was very disappointing, but I could see there were some things going on, the Darryl situation with all the press and negativity.

"So many Mets players left disappointed—Wally, Roger McDowell, Jesse, Doc, even George Foster and Lee Mazzilli. Even Tom Seaver, the Golden Boy, was let go. I haven't made my final decision what I will wear when I get into the Hall of Fame, a Montreal cap or a Mets cap. I'm leaning more toward the Mets, because I had five great years there. The bottom line is, I'm very thankful for the eighteen glorious years. It's nothing but fond memories."

Despite the rash of serious injuries to key players, the Mets won 87 games in 1989 and finished second, six games behind Don Zimmer's Chicago Cubs. Once again, the team, despite all the turmoil, came close to winning the division title before losing to a hotter team. In his six full years with the Mets, Davey Johnson's teams twice finished first and four times finished second. They'd have won even more had Johnson and Cashen gotten along.

Cashen, meanwhile, couldn't decide whether the time had come to fire Johnson or not. Davey had bent over backward to accommodate Cashen, but he had refused to clamp down on the players, to make them clean up their act, something Davey wouldn't do because he knew how deleterious it would be on morale.

Dwight Gooden: "That disappointing season more or less ended Davey's tenure at Shea. He and Cashen had grown openly hostile to each other. I know Frank was getting tired of the wild and crazy Mets, and wanted Davey to keep us in check. We heard the most petty complaints from the front office, like not enough of us were on the top step of the dugout during the national anthem.

"And Johnson was just as disturbed by Frank's constant meddling."

Instead of firing Johnson, Cashen fired his coaches, hitting coach Bill Robinson and third-base coach Sam Perlozzo. Johnson was tempted to quit, but didn't. He felt he owed it to his players to stay on.

Gary Carter: "Davey was furious, because Bill and Sam were so much a part of the ball club. Once again, it was a slap in the face. Cashen was going over his head and doing this.

"Why not just fire Davey? But, he didn't and he kept him for the beginning of the 1990 season."

As a counterpoint to the Johnson–Cashen melodrama, the Darryl Strawberry soap opera continued. At the end of the 1989 season Darryl and Lisa again tried to reconcile, but Darryl's occasional drunken debauchery made a long-term relationship impossible. When a St. Louis woman publicly accused Darryl of being the father of her child, he denied paternity. A blood test, however, proved otherwise. When a St. Louis judge upheld the suit against him, his marriage was dead.

Lisa continued to berate him until Darryl finally cracked up and on January 26, 1990, Darryl, drunk and angry, waited for her to return from a night out. By two in the morning his fury had grown. When she walked in the door at three, they called each other names.

The bickering escalated and Darryl smacked her across the face with a right hand that knocked her to the floor. She grabbed a metal rod and whipped it hard across his wrists and side. Injured and furious that she had struck him, he ran to the closet and grabbed his .25-caliber semiautomatic pistol. She kept jamming the rod into his chest when he turned and pointed the gun at her. At that point Lisa's mother came in, saw the confrontation and began screaming.

Her mother called 911 and reported that he had a gun. The LAPD responded immediately. Strawberry was arrested for possession of an unregistered, unlicensed handgun. He was read his rights and taken to the West Valley Division of the LAPD.

He posted $12,000 bail and was released.

When he got home, he faced his wife and he began to sob. He admitted the drinking had ruined so much of what he had. She also began to cry.

Darryl Strawberry: "I could only stare at the hopeless prison that was my future, both as a member of the Mets and—a frightening alternative—as an inmate in the Los Angeles County jail."

When during spring training of 1990 the Mets said they would reopen negotiations with Darryl Strawberry, he was elated. He had gone to Smithers and decided to quit drinking. Strawberry had hit 29 home runs but only hit .225 and drove in 77 runs in 1989 and wanted a five-year contract with the sort of money Don Mattingly made with the Yankees ($19 million) or Jose Canseco pocketed from Oakland. Why not? Strawberry had put up better numbers than either of them.

But, the Mets were only playing with his head. They made him a low-ball offer.

The team started the 1990 season badly and while the front office was criticizing Strawberry for letting the team down, at the same time it was telling him that he needed to step up and shoulder the load. Unable to reconcile the two messages, Strawberry felt bitter and angry.

As the negotiations dragged on and Johnson began to criticize Strawberry in the press, Strawberry came to view his former friend as a front office co-conspirator in an effort to break his spirit and lower his value. Strawberry saw what a puppet of Cashen his manager had become and he was convinced that it was time to flee to hometown L.A. at the end of the year.

Frank Viola starred in 1990, beginning the season with a 7–0 record and a 0.87 era, but the team only played under .500 in April. The Mets players became frustrated at their own ineptness. During one game against the Braves, with runners on second and third, David Cone covered first on a ball hit to the right side, took the throw, and when the first-base umpire called the runner safe, Cone stood there arguing and holding the ball as both runners scored, the latter from second base. The fans hooted. Johnson was disgusted. The next night Ron Darling gave up four home runs.

By early May from the stands the fans were chanting, "Davey must go."

Darryl was hitting .231 and on May 14, Davey dropped him from fourth to fifth in the batting order. Strawberry felt that Cashen had ordered him to do it as a contract bargaining ploy.

Darryl Strawberry: "I could tell that [Davey] had been mentally defeated, but I couldn't help thinking—call me paranoid—that the front office was as much his enemy as anything else. It looked like management was sabotaging its own team. I had the sneaking suspicion that Frank had been after Davey's scalp for two years and now he saw his chance to get it. I was sure my scalp was next, but I didn't know yet how he had planned to take it."

When *New York Times* columnist Dave Anderson accused Strawberry of not living up to his standard, of not being worth $3 million a year, of not even being worth the $1.8 million he was currently making, Strawberry accused Anderson of becoming part of Cashen's negotiating strategy.

In late May HoJo and Bobby Ojeda barred the press and Davey and held a team meeting. The players agreed they had to play more as a team.

The Mets started the 1990 season 20–22. As long as the Mets were winning, Frank Cashen couldn't in good conscience fire Davey Johnson. But in 1990 Cashen felt Johnson had lost control of his players. When the team began to lose, Cashen saw Johnson—not his series of questionable trades or the fact he had emasculated his manager—as the reason why.

Dwight Gooden: "As the years passed and some of us, like Hernandez and Carter, got older, Davey's magic stopped working. Suddenly his anti-authoritarian ways became an irritation to the front office.

"Actually, Davey was always a pebble in Cashen's shoe, but by 1990, the GM was in a position to do something about it."

Johnson's pride and big mouth also contributed to his demise. In 1990 Joe McIlvaine was handling player matters and Al Harazin was handling the business side. Johnson, on the defensive, wondered aloud to a reporter about Cashen's role. He remarked, "Just once, I'd like to have a job description for Frank Cashen. I mean, what does he do?"

The next day, May 29, 1990, Frank Cashen convened the players and accused them of being underachievers. He told them he was firing Davey Johnson and replacing him with third-base coach Buddy Harrelson.

Terry Leach: "How do you figure it? The man was averaging 95 wins a year. Something had to be right."

Darryl Strawberry: "When management turned him into just a shell before blaming him for the decisions that they had made themselves, it convinced the players that Davey had gotten a raw deal. The front office was making the press happy and the press was running the ball club. Once that happened, Davey couldn't rely on his team. When management saw that he couldn't rely on his team, they got rid of him and blamed him for the whole thing.

"Frank finally had his revenge on Davey. Frank, it was said, had had it in for Johnson even during the early years in 1984 and 1985.

"We assumed that Frank had used the team's stumbling as an excuse to get rid of Davey. Yet we knew that even though Davey had his problems, Cashen had taken the team away from him through all the disastrous trades. Now Davey was taking the fall, not only for the entire team but for mangement as well."

Davey Johnson was hustled out of the hotel in Cincinnati without even getting the chance to say good-bye to his team.

Darryl Strawberry: "Davey looked out for his players. That kind of bare-knuckles management works, of course, as long as the team wins and stays in contention. But when you're an 'almost' for three years after you won all the marbles, the fellas upstairs start to get nervous. Then when you start to fail and the team gets shaky under you, they call your number."

Dwight Gooden: "When Davey got fired early in '90, I went home and cried. And I remember Davey saying, 'I'll never come back here.'"

The feeling must have been mutual: Davey Johnson has never been invited back to Shea stadium for Old Timers Day.

Ten years after his firing Johnson was still feeling the pain. Davey and I had been close. We had collaborated on *Bats*, his first-person account of the 1985 season. When I called to ask if I could come over to talk about the rest of his Mets career, he was hesitant.

"I don't really want to go back over that shit," he said. "I really don't."

I reminded him that things had been said about him, and that he owed it to himself to defend himself.

"If you have done any homework at all and know anything about Cashen, then this conversation is moot," he said.

"But, I really don't," I said. I had interviewed Cashen once in 1985 and he had been cooperative and answered my questions.

Johnson replied, "What do you know about lawyers? What do you know about newspaper people who couldn't make it there or in the law profession? What do you know about people who are small? All those things. You know what I mean?"

He continued, "I mean, you are opening real deep wounds as far as I'm concerned. You are talking about a person . . . I was my own agent. This was a person I was dealing directly with. You're talking about . . . he only remembered things the way that made him look good. That's the only way he remembered things. He didn't remember them as they were. When you made a deal, he didn't remember it that way.

"At the end of the [1989] season they had a big press conference, right before the playoffs and they said they weren't going to renew Keith Hernandez or Gary Carter. And Frank was asked, 'What about Johnson's status?' And Frank said, 'I've made up my mind what I'm going to do, but I can't talk about it because I haven't talked to Davey about it.' So everybody assumed I was going to get fired, and he *knew* what the reaction would be.

"When they were all naming my replacement at the start of '90, I said, 'You might as well finish it, Frank. You told everybody what your intent is.' And he said, 'I'm not going to.' He waited 42 games into the season and he hired Buddy Harrelson. I knew I was gone when Buddy and him both had bow ties on and were sitting together at the Opening Day dinner in '90.

"That's all I want to talk about. That's it."

forty-three

Darryl Twists in the Wind

From the start of Buddy Harrelson's tenure as manager many of his players were skeptical about his abilities. When he told them that the sportswriters were the enemy that type of insecurity and paranoia would haunt the former Mets star during his two-year reign.

Nevertheless, during Harrelson's first season the Mets almost rebounded to win the Eastern division title. With a star-studded pitching staff of Frank Viola, Dwight Gooden, David Cone, Sid Fernandez, Ron Darling, and Bobby Ojeda, the Mets usually were in the ball game. Scoring runs, historically a bugaboo, was also not a problem in 1990, as Darryl Strawberry, Howard Johnson, Kevin McReynolds, and cornerman Dave Magadan led the offense.

In early June, led by Strawberry, the Mets went on a tear. On June 9, Sid Fernandez pitched a two-hitter against the Pirates and Strawberry hit two home runs. The next night Straw hit another home run.

The Mets then went to Wrigley Field, where they won three out of four as the team caught fire. The Mets were seven games behind the Pirates when they went into Pittsburgh and won two out of three. They had their eye on first place. After beating the Cards twice, the Mets were now only four games out.

They then flew to Philadelphia to play Lenny Dykstra and the Phils. Frank Viola won the opener. The lead was down to three. The next night Strawberry homered to win. Two and a half back.

Everything was looking up when on June 27, Jose Canseco signed with

Oakland for $23.5 million for five years. Suddenly Strawberry's salary demands, which the Mets and the press had been pooh-poohing as being outrageous, didn't seem so crazy anymore.

But, as though scripted by the Mets front office, no sooner had Canseco signed than stories began appearing in the New York papers accusing Strawberry of being ungrateful and unreasonable in his negotiations.

The Mets were a game out and Strawberry was leading the charge, but Cashen nevertheless went out of his way to publicly accuse Strawberry of playing only for himself.

On June 29, the Mets climbed into first place as Strawberry hit a 450-foot home run against the Reds. By July 1990, Strawberry was among the top-ten hitters in the National League.

Even so, Strawberry was haunted by the realizations that no matter how much he did for the team—and his contributions were substantial—the front office didn't want to pay him the type of money Canseco was getting and the press didn't respect him.

Then during the week of July 12, while the Mets were playing the Reds for the pennant, Strawberry learned from his boyhood friend Eric Davis, who read it in the papers, that Frank Cashen had broken off contract negotiations with Eric Goldschmidt. Strawberry was crushed.

The Mets lost the series to the Reds.

The writers, despite Strawberry's raw numbers—he hit 37 home runs and drove in 108 runs—hoed Cashen's company-line. They cited reasons why Cashen shouldn't pay him the same type of money Canseco was making. He was "spoiled," "pouted," "sulked," "would never fulfil his potential," and was "mediocre." Cashen's bottom line: Strawberry wasn't worth it.

Cashen closed down negotiations and at the same time tried to publicly humiliate his star hitter. Why would a general manager run down his best player?

Darryl Strawberry: "If getting you at a good price is more important than getting the pennant, then your boss is showing the world he knows how to 'manage' people."

Darryl Strawberry cried. He knew his ten-year love/hate affair with the New York Mets was at an end.

There was still half a season to play, but Strawberry's heart was no longer in it. He was not about to bust his hump for a team that didn't care about him. He felt abandoned and unwanted. And when Strawberry went to Bud Harrelson to talk about his situation, he found that Harrelson sought to avoid him.

Darryl Strawberry: "When Buddy Harrelson turned against me in August 1990 after the Mets' management broke off negotiations, he told me, in effect, 'I don't care about Darryl Strawberry the human being.' All that mattered was what I could produce for the team. He cast me off into the darkness when I had come to rely on his friendship."

The Mets remained in contention throughout the month of July and Darryl Strawberry played all through the summer with a broken heart. Strawberry relished playing with Ron Darling, Mackey Sasser, and his other friends. He wanted to stay a New York Met, but knew he would be leaving, as had Carter and Hernandez the year before.

Darryl Strawberry: "The intensity of the race for the championship had turned us into friends playing baseball together on a team that had the potential to go all the way. If only management had believed in us as much as we believed in ourselves. But we were fighting our own leadership and we knew it."

At the end of August, the Pirates had a two-game lead, but the Mets caught them again in mid-September. Strawberry starred in a double-header win over the Pirates on September 12 and 13. He threw a runner out at the plate and hit a long home run off Doug Drabek.

Darryl Strawberry: "I wasn't putting on a show for the fans just to justify my contract demands. I was simply saying that I wanted the pennant, wanted it more than I wanted anything else that September. Poor, dumb Frank Cashen never realized that I really did love the Mets, New York, and baseball after all. He never figured that out."

In 1990, Dwight Gooden had begun the season 3–5 but then won 16 of his last 18 decisions. With two more starts he could have won twenty.

Frank Viola also was attempting to win his twentieth. Viola asked Harrelson for an extra shot at 20 and he gave him Gooden's spot, allowing Viola to win 20 and keeping Gooden from the goal.

The Mets had lost the meat of their lineup to bad trades. They had a rookie manager who made mistakes. And yet in 1990, led by Viola and Gooden, the Mets finished the year 91–71, only four games behind the Pittsburgh Pirates. Though Kevin McReynolds played without fire, he still managed to hit 24 homers and drive in 82 runs. HoJo's 23 homers and 90 rbis also contributed greatly. Strawberry, despite any off-the-field troubles, had another huge season.

At the end of the season Frank Cashen had to decide whether or not to sign Darryl Strawberry. The front office worried about his heavy drinking and they also were upset about the way Strawberry had treated Greg Jefferies. The front office learned of the bat dumping incident and weren't happy about it. But Strawberry was a crowd pleaser who rarely turned down an autograph request, while Jefferies rarely rewarded a young fan with even a smile.

Toward the end of October the Mets finally made Strawberry an offer, $15.5 million for four years. Cashen told Eric Goldschmidt that was the only offer he would make. Take it or leave it.

Strawberry rejected it and left the Mets.

Dwight Gooden: "All the old warriors had been phased out. Ray Knight had left after the '86 season. Mitch was traded away, Lenny was with the Phillies, Mookie was with Toronto, and Darryl was on his way to the Dodgers via free agency.

"Little by little they'd been replaced by talented-but-less-inspired players.

"What Fred Wilpon and Nelson Doubleday, along with Frank Cashen, never understood is that we won because we were so damn cocky."

Darryl Strawberry could only shake his head. What he called his "eight-year nightmare" was over.

Cashen predicted the Mets would be better without the top-run producer in Mets history. "We'll be a better team without Darryl in two years," Cashen proclaimed on the day Strawberry signed with the Dodgers. But he was very wrong. The Mets would sink like a rock without the Straw-man.

★ ★ ★

Strawberry, back home in L.A., had an excellent season in 1991, hitting 28 homers and driving in 99 runs. But then in 1992 he suffered a back injury and underwent surgery for a ruptured disk. It was the start of a downward spiral that continues to this day.

He missed most of the 1993 season and the depression that followed led to a serious drug problem. While forced to sit out Strawberry began drinking heavily again, and he started using cocaine.

Strawberry met Charisse Simon at Eric Davis' birthday party in May of 1990 and when Strawberry learned she was pregnant, they married on December 3, 1993.

In March of 1994, the IRS accused him of tax fraud. Though he had hired a team of tax advisors, he had not declared his income from card shows to the tune of $300,000 and the IRS decided to make an example out of him.

In 1994 Tommy Lasorda, who Darryl considered a "fake and a phony," who once called him "a dog," told Darryl he better "get going. We're paying you a lot of money."

Darryl responded by going AWOL for three days. When he returned he confessed his drug problem and he went on the DL. Shortly thereafter, on May 26, 1994, the Dodgers released him. On June 19, 1994, he signed a contract with the San Francisco Giants. In February of 1995 he pleaded guilty to tax evasion. He spent 100 hours doing community service and paid a $350,000 fine.

The IRS scare pushed him to continue his heavy drinking. He wanted to quit, he says, but he couldn't control his cravings. In a panic, he checked himself into the Betty Ford Clinic in Palm Springs.

He failed a drug test and Major League Baseball suspended him for 60 days, beginning at the start of the 1995 season, once the long player strike was settled. On February 28, 1995, he was released by the Giants.

He went back to the Betty Ford clinic, where he entered a Twelve-step program and began attending meetings regularly. Agent Bill Goodstein got Darryl a contract with the New York Yankees, but he played and did little in 1995.

After much reluctance a broke Strawberry signed a contract with the St. Paul Saints in the independent Northern League. The pay was low, but agent Bill Goodstein convinced Darryl that if he did well, he would earn his ticket back to the big leagues. Not long afterward, on January 14, 1996,

Goodstein, in his 50s, died unexpectedly of a heart attack. At the funeral Darryl sobbed. He kept staring at the casket. Goodstein had loved him and taken care of him. And now he was gone.

His problems mounted. Two weeks later he was accused of the misdemeanor charge of "wilfully failing to provide" for his former wife Lisa and their two children. The court was seeking $370,000 in back child support.

Back home, his mother, Ruby Strawberry, was suffering from breast cancer. She kept the pain to herself. Only when she died on February 25, 1996, did the family know she had had the disease. She was only fifty-five. At her viewing, Darryl sobbed without stop. After the burial, he wasn't sure he could go on. She represented all that was important in life to him, he said.

Strawberry lay in bed for two weeks. He rarely ate.

At St. Paul in 1996 he earned $2,000 a month, but he rediscovered his love for the game. He began hitting long home runs. The scouts came running. On July 3, he hit his eighteenth. During the game the Yankees re-signed him. He flew to Columbus that night. The Yankees needed him. But he never should have gone back to New York. He should have played in Minnesota or Kansas City or some other small city where the pressure to win and perform and shine and lead and be a star would have been so much less.

In 1996 he hit 11 home runs and drove in 36 runs in the 63 games he played. Two of those home runs were hit in the final game of the ALCS against the Baltimore Orioles in Camden Yards to help clinch the American League pennant for the Yankees. Darryl was once again on top of the world.

But because of injuries to his left knee, he missed most of the '97 season. He recovered in '98 to become one of the Yankees top power hitters and team leaders. That year he hit 24 home runs and drove in 57 as a part-time player. But during the season Strawberry experienced stomach pain. He lost apetite and began passing blood.

In mid-September Darryl sought out longtime friend Eric Davis. Davis had contracted colon cancer in 1997 and underwent surgery. Strawberry told Davis about his pain, and Davis told him to see a doctor immediately.

The pain in his stomach worsened and ten days later he went to see the Yankee team doctor. After an examination, Strawberry, still only thirty-six, learned he too had colon cancer.

On October 3, 1998, he had surgery. Surgeons removed 36 lymph nodes. George Steinbrenner was there during the entire four hours. After surgery Darryl contracted an infection in his colon and remained in the hospital for two weeks. Months of chemotherapy lay ahead.

Before game one of the American League Championship Series against the Cleveland Indians, while Darryl was still in the hospital, Charisse Strawberry threw out the first ball. The players all wore Darryl's number, 39, embossed on their hats.

Darryl came home from the hospital on October 16, the first day of the 1998 World Series. The Yankees beat the San Diego Padres and Darryl once again rode in the victory parade down Broadway.

In November 1998 Darryl began getting in shape to play ball in 1999. He had three-and-a-half months to prepare. Everything was going fine until a morning in early January when his stomach began to hurt. A build-up of scar tissue had formed knots around Darryl's intestine, almost blocking it. He needed another operation. It took only 45 minutes to remove the knots.

Five days later Darryl was working out, preparing for spring training. He ate well and regained his playing weight. But when the season began, Strawberry flew to Tampa for a rehabiliatation assignment. The pressure built. He began to suffer from depression. When he didn't make the team, for the first time in four years he took a drink.

On April 14, 1999, Darryl was arrested in downtown Tampa charged with soliciting prostitution (from an undercover cop). He had a small amount of cocaine in his wallet. He was jailed and let out on bail in an hour. He pleaded no contest and was sentenced to eighteen months probation.

His cancer, meanwhile, continued to eat away at him. In mid–August 1999, he had his left kidney removed during surgery. After eleven days at Columbia-Presbyterian hospital he returned home to Tampa.

Despite the operation, Strawberry was able to rejoin the New York Yankees in September and hit with authority.

In September 2000 Strawberry was involved in a minor traffic accident. He had blacked out after taking a sleeping medication while en route to a meeting with his probation officer. After the accident, he left the scene.

He was sentenced to two years of house arrest. Two months later Strawberry, depressed over his house arrest, his cancer, and his lack of finances, slipped out of his in-patient treatment center in the middle of the night to smoke cocaine with a lady friend.

Monitored by a tracking device, Strawberry's four-hour disappearance was noticed immediately. When his drug test came back positive, he was arrested and jailed. In court, he told the judge that he had stopped his chemotherapy treatments because he had lost his will to live. He spent 30 days in the county jail and was then sent home to complete his two years of house arrest. His teammates have followed his ordeal. They are sympathetic, though not entirely understanding. They certainly wish him well.

Gary Carter: "When he said he didn't have any desire to live anymore, that's heavy stuff. I can't imagine why. He said he's been in a living hell for all these years. I never saw that. He wasn't a real happy, jovial guy, but I didn't realize there were all these problems. He said the only reason he now has a desire to try and turn his life around is for his kids sake. He has five, two from his first marriage, two with Charisse, and an illegitimate one.

"Darryl said it all comes from having been abandoned by his father when he was thirteen. I lost my mother when I was twelve. It was a void in my life also. But you've got to move on. You can't blame anyone. You have to grasp [the] life that's been given to you. It's sad. It is. And I hope he can come out of it, but I just don't know."

Darryl Strawberry's prognosis is not good. The cancer is spreading. I mourn him already.

To me, he will always be remembered for his ready smile, his willingness to sign autographs, his kindness to people, and, of course, his dramatic home runs. His curse was to develop a drug addiction he couldn't shake. Darryl Strawberry was the King of the Mets for almost a decade. He too was human, and should be beloved and remembered for his contributions— even though he has suffered from a drug addiction. It seems only fair.

forty-four

Free Fall

In 1991 Frank Cashen retired. Joe McIlvaine, one of the brightest of young baseball executives, should have taken his place. But Cashen had insisted on staying through the 1990 season and McIlvaine, who was a fine judge of talent, became impatient and left for the general manager's job in San Diego. By default, Al Harazin got the job. His first trade was a great one: Jefferies, McReynolds, and Keith Miller to Kansas City for two-time Cy Young Award winner Bret Saberhagen and infielder Bill Pecota. It turned out to be beginner's luck.

On April 13, 1991, Harrelson left Doc Gooden in the game too long on a cold, damp day in a 5–3 victory. He struck out 14 and defeated Pedro Martinez. The next day he could not raise his arm high enough to brush his teeth. His pain lasted almost a week.

Dwight Gooden: "[Buddy] should have known better. He should've looked out for me, instead of getting caught up in a pitchers' duel. I guess Buddy was so intent on proving that he could change the Mets' fortunes—remember, we'd finished second two years in a row—he forgot how long the season really is."

Gooden, whose record in '91 was 13–7 with a 3.60 era, made his last start on August 22. He won 6–0 but pitched only five innings. There was something seriously wrong with his shoulder. Two weeks later he had surgery to repair his labrum and his rotator cuff. The operation marked the disappearance of his dominating fastball and ended his Hall of Fame chances. Dwight Gooden's gravy days were over.

Dwight Gooden: "That surgery turned out to be a dark landmark for me. I never had another winning season for the Mets. Part of the reason was because the teams I played on from 1992 to 1994 were awful—mystifyingly so because we had so much on-paper talent. But, I was also pitching so poorly and my arm hurt so much, I was seriously considering retiring."

In 1991, the Strawberry-less Mets fell to earth. They won only 77 games, 20½ games behind the Pittsburgh Pirates. A week before the end of the season Buddy Harrelson was fired. Third-base coach Mike Cubbage finished out the season.

Dwight Gooden: "That was really the official end of the Mets' golden era. I only wish the Mets front office would recognize us, the '86 Mets, for the love affair we had with New York.

"To this day, we haven't been formally invited back to Shea. The most beloved team in franchise history remains invisible to management, for reasons I can't understand. In fact, the Mets recently gave away my old number 16 to Hideo Nomo, which is further proof that the organization doesn't really appreciate us, or me."

At the end of the 1991 season, the Mets finally found bats to replace the departed Darryl Strawberry by signing Eddie Murray of the Dodgers and Bobby Bonilla of the Pittsburgh Pirates. The cost—$40 million. Strawberry would have been a bargain.

Both Murray and Bonilla were sullen, neither performed, and the team sank like a stone.

In 1992 Jeff Torborg replaced Buddy Harrelson as manager. The Mets' old cast, with the exception of Doc Gooden and Howard Johnson, was gone; a new group had taken its place. Eddie Murray played first base, Bobby Bonilla was in right, and the speedy Vince Coleman was in center field. That spring Coleman, outfielder Darryl Boston, and Doc Gooden, were accused of rape. The case was never pressed because of lack of evidence, but the accusations were enough to damage the team's reputation.

On the field things were just as bad. The starting rotation had both David Cone *and* Bret Saberhagen, Cy Young Award winners, but the 1992 team was terrible. No one performed well. The chemistry was terrible.

Gooden nevertheless thought a great deal of Torborg.

Dwight Gooden: "I thought Jeff did a great job. He was the most prepared and organized man I ever played for. He was the first manager to have hitters' and pitchers' meetings; the opposing team was thoroughly scouted, and before each series, we went over their strengths and weaknesses. So, what was wrong with preparation?"

Torborg was the antithesis of Davey Johnson. The Mets wanted a milkshake drinker to lead the troops and Torborg was their man. When Torborg refused to let the players drink on the flights, they were royally pissed off.

Torborg, moreover, had an uneasy relationship with the press and his players followed his example. The Mets' two hitting stars were the worst offenders. Bobby Bonilla fought with the press. Eddie Murray, as he had most of his long and illustrious career, refused to even talk to them.

In September 1992, Vince Coleman went out of his way to make Torborg look weak. Vince had been thrown out for arguing a checked-swing called third strike and was ejected. Torborg interceded and he tried to push Coleman back into the dugout.

Coleman shouted at him, "What the fuck are you pushing me for?" And he shoved Torborg back—hard.

When Torborg demanded an apology, Coleman told him to "Go fuck yourself." Coleman was suspended for two games.

Coleman was gone after the 1993 season. Torborg didn't last that long.

After a 13–25 start in 1993, the Mets front office swung the ax and fired Torborg. Dallas Green, who had led the Philadelphia Phillies to a World Championship in 1980 and a division title in 1981 was hired on May 19.

When Green came in, he saw he had a bad ball club and he immediately let it be known that the team's performance would not be his fault. Gooden was 12–15 in '93. He felt Green went out of his way to embarrass him, and some of the younger players as well. Gooden came to hate him.

One time Green told Jeromy Burnitz he was tired of his "stupid, fucking mistakes," and Burnitz told him he was tired of listening "to his shit."

Green challenged him to a fight. Burnitz was twenty-four, Green sixty. But when Green kept his door closed, the players snickered at his tough-guy image and never saw him the same way again.

In September 1993 the Mets were in last place. After losing six of seven on a road trip, Green angered everyone when he tipped over the food table after the game, sending the repast flying.

After Green's rampage, Dwight Gooden and pitcher Pete Schourek grabbed the food off the floor and ate anyway.

The team finished the 1993 season with a 59–103 record, good for last place in the National League East. Al Harazin was fired as general manager. The roller coaster had reached the bottom of its ride.

The start of 1994 appeared to bring more of the same. The trio of Coleman, Bonilla, and Murray offended everyone with their churlishness and lack of performance. Coleman was injured all the time, Bonilla seemed angry more of the time, and Murray couldn't wait to get out of New York.

The Golden Boy of the Mets was Doc Gooden, no longer the phenom he once was, but his good looks and winning personality continued to endear him to the Mets fans.

But on Opening Day of 1994 Gooden, still only twenty-nine, broke his right big toe. He went on the DL for six weeks.

It was during this period that his seven years of cocaine abstinence came to an end. While on his rehab assignment in Norfolk, he noticed that Major League Baseball had neglected to take a urine sample. Gooden wondered if just this once he could get away with snorting a little cocaine.

At about two A.M. on June 2, he was in a Manhattan nightclub and a bartender offered to share some cocaine with him. He had turned down dozens of such offers in the past, but this time he agreed, even though he knew he had a drug test coming up.

When the tester didn't show up in Binghamton, he was relieved. But on June 5, 1994, when he joined the Mets in Cincinnati, he was approached by the drug tester. Gooden wanted to run, but he couldn't.

He took the test and waited. Day after day, he heard nothing.

When the Mets arrived in Atlanta in late June, he was busted. Gooden was summoned to New York, and automatically suspended for sixty days.

The Mets asked him to pitch and told him the suspension would begin the next day. The Pirates beat him up. He told his friends on the club, Saberhagen and John Franco, what had happened and then dressed and left.

On July 1, Gooden flew home to St. Petersburg. He was unemployed, frustrated, and bored. He began to drink, heavily, and on July 4 admittedly began to use cocaine regularly. He kept getting tested and he kept failing. Finally, Major League Baseball ordered him to the Betty Ford clinic.

When he got out, he went to AA meetings regularly.

When the players called a strike on August 12, 1994, fourteen days short of reinstatement, Gooden was crushed.

After getting out of Betty Ford, he returned to Florida—and relapsed that night. He went out to see friends, drank beer, and snorted coke. For two months he drank and used coke at least once a week. One time his heart raced so fast, he checked into a Tampa hotel because he didn't think he could get home without having a heart attack.

On September 15, 1994, the Mets announced that Gooden had had one positive test—though there had been many. They announced that he would not return to the Mets in 1995 and he was given his unconditional release.

Gooden failed more tests in September and October 1994, as his self-destruction got worse. He drove at high speeds in the hopes he would be taken to jail.

On November 4 he got a letter from acting baseball commissioner Bud Selig saying that he had flunked so many drug tests that baseball was suspending him for the entire 1995 season.

Gooden went into his dresser and found his nine-millimeter automatic. He loaded it full, unlocked the safety, and put the gun to his head. He considered squeezing the trigger . . . but he decided that first he should write his wife Monica a note. Then he decided to leave her a voice message instead. After changing his mind, he again picked up the gun. He spent an hour trying to decide the best spot to place the barrel of the gun.

When his wife walked in on him, the gun was pointed at his temple. It took a while, but his wife and his mother talked him into giving them the gun.

That was the low point. Finally, he was able to admit to himself that he had a drug dependency. He decided to clean himself up for good so he could pitch again.

After sitting out the entire 1995 season, Gooden was signed by the Yankees' George Steinbrenner, the saver of lost souls. Joe Torre was there and so was Mel Stottlemyre, who had been Davey Johnson's pitching coach with the Mets. Fortunately for Gooden, Torre and Stottlemyre stuck with him as he struggled during the early part of the '96 season and after a spring training where he went 0–3 with an 8.88 era. His first starts of the regular season resulted in an 0–3 record with an 11.48 earned-run average. The Yankees front office put him on waivers, preparing to send him down to Columbus, a move Gooden would have refused. Torre gave him a week to work exclusively with pitching coach Stottlemyre.

Torre's faith and a lot of luck kept Gooden in the big leagues. David Cone, another ex-Met teammate, was diagnosed with an aneurism in his right shoulder, Torre chose Doc to take his place in the rotation. When he started against the Twins on April 27, he pitched a six-inning, one-run, seven-strikeout performance.

Then on May 14, 1996, against the Seattle Mariners, Gooden pitched one of the greatest games of his career, a sparkling no-hitter. In the ninth inning his fastball was clocked at 95 miles an hour. His rise, fall, and rise again was the stuff of movies.

It was to be Gooden's only complete game all season. His arm tired, and he finished the year 11–7 with a 5.01 era. He did not pitch in the postseason as the Yankees won the World Championship. He re-signed with New York the following year and he went 9–5 with a 4.91 era, but an incident in Texas in midseason hurt his relations with the Yankees.

While in Dallas, Gooden went to a strip club, broke curfew, and got in a fight with a cabbie, who called the police after he refused to pay the $5 on the meter. The matter ended up costing Gooden more than $100,000, but it also soured him with Torre, who angered Gooden when he forced him to room next to him when the team flew to Boston. When the Yankees chose not to renew his option at the end of the season, Gooden blasted Torre, bringing down a roar of criticism on himself in the press.

In 1998, Gooden signed with the Cleveland Indians. He finished the year 8–6 with a 3.76 era, but failed to win in the postseason. Against the Red Sox in the second game of the division series, he started and made only 22 pitches. After a Red Sox runner was called safe at the plate on a close play, he threw a tantrum and was thrown out of the game by plate umpire Joe Brinkman along with manager Mike Hargrove. He started game four of the American League Championship Series against the Yankees, giving up three runs on three hits, and walking three in four innings, extending his winless postseason streak to eight games.

In 1999 his record dropped to 3–4 with a 6.26 era. In 2000 he was signed and released by two teams who were desperate for pitchers, The

Tampa Bay Devil Rays and the Houston Astros, before once again signing with Steinbrenner, Torre, and company in New York. He returned a finesse pitcher whose 4–2 record with a 3.36 era with the Yankees caused baseball fans everywhere to marvel. He owes a lot to George Steinbrenner.

Before the 2000 Subway Series against the Mets, Dwight Gooden told reporters, "I just look at this whole situation for myself. The fans in New York, the support I've gotten. I've been at my best and also I've been at my lowest, and the fan support has never changed.

"As a player I've done everything that I can possibly do; this year, getting to pitch at Shea Stadium as a Yankee coming back after being released by Tampa, it was like the ultimate. This is unbelievable. I still have to pinch myself. You can never imagine this. This is too good to be true. Things like this just don't happen."

Gooden was asked whether, in fact, he was still a Met at heart.

He smiled.

"I'm a New Yorker at heart," he replied.

forty-five

Bobby

When all of baseball went on strike in August 1994, the Mets were in third place, 19 games behind the Montreal Expos. The team was bland and lifeless.

The strike was the ugliest in the history of the game. The owners attempted to shove a salary cap down the throats of the players as their predecessors had in 1890, when the players formed their own league, and brought ruin to everyone. In 1994, history repeated itself. That there was no World Series was unthinkable, and many baseball fans across the country, especially the older ones who were around when you could sit in the best box seat at Shea Stadium for $6, were resentful of the high salaries and soaring ticket prices. Many swore off America's Pastime for good.

When baseball resumed on April 28, 1995, in the fourth inning of the home opener against the St. Louis Cardinals at Shea Stadium, three men wearing "Greed" on their T-shirts ran out onto the field and began throwing hundreds of one-dollar bills at the Mets players. They then stood at second base and raised their fists in a defiant salute as the fans gave them a standing ovation before the gendarmes dragged them off. Another protester pulled third base out of the ground and tried to run back into the stands with it but was caught. Only 26,636 fans showed up for the game, the lowest Opening Day attendance in Mets history.

Toward the end of June, it was clear that there would be precious few ovations in '95. The Mets' record was 21–37. The team was 17 games behind the Greg Maddux–John Smoltz–Tom Glavine Atlanta Braves.

Said manager Dallas Green, "We may have overevaluated what we had. We were basing that largely on the performance of our guys last year." He observed that the nine months of inactivity "really hurt our players." By the end of July the Mets were in the cellar.

In late July and early August, the Mets' new general manager, Joe McIlvaine, who had returned from San Diego and replaced Al Harazin, traded away Bobby Bonilla, Bret Saberhagen, and Brett Butler, veterans with large salaries but with little to show for it, and replaced them with youngsters Bill Pulsipher, Jason Isringhausen, Carl Everett, and in September, Butch Huskey. The performances of the kids saved the sixty-one-year-old Green's job.

McIlvaine boasted that when a group of talented minor-league prospects including starting pitcher Paul Wilson, shortstop Rey Ordonez, a Cuban defector, and outfielder Jay Payton, reached maturity and came up to the Mets, the team would return to their winning ways.

When the team finished the year 44–31, after their terrible start, McIlvaine looked to be prophetic.

But in 1996 the Mets' three young blue-chip pitching prospects, Bill Pulsipher, Paul Wilson, and Jason Isringhausen, healthy at the start of the season, all came down with season–ending arm miseries. By the end of June, their combined record was 7–15. Mets' co-owner Fred Wilpon felt he had to do something to shake up the ball club.

At the start of the season Green had predicted success for his young pitchers, but he was singing a different tune by summer. On August 20, he told reporters, "They don't belong in the big leagues. That might sound harsh and negative, but what have they done to get here?"

On August 26, 1996, Wilpon, over the strenuous objections of general manager Joe McIlvaine, fired Dallas Green and replaced him with his Norfolk manager, Bobby Valentine. Dwight Gooden, for one, was glad the Mets had made the change.

Dwight Gooden: "Green never did have a bag of magic tricks, after all. He ended up being no better than Jeff Torborg and in fact, a lot less sincere. Finally, it seems, the Mets made a great choice in promoting Valentine from AAA, and I'm sure the front office's only regret about Valentine is that he wasn't around sooner."

When he took over the team, the self-confident Valentine told the players he would keep an open mind about them and asked them to keep an open mind about him. He told the players, "Give me a chance and I'll show you how to get there."

As a boy growing up in Stamford, Connecticut, Bobby Valentine was the finest schoolboy athlete the city had ever seen. Playing football for Rippowam High School, Valentine scored 53 touchdowns during his three-year career. He was the only football player in the history of the state of Connecticut to be voted All American three years in a row.

In baseball, he was more amazing. Fast and agile, when he was an eighth grader attending Burdick Junior High School he was the starting shortstop on the high school varsity team. The city, which has a rich baseball tradition, celebrated him. The sports staff of the *Stamford Advocate* helped make him a statewide hero.

Valentine could have gone to the University of Southern California and replaced O. J. Simpson at tailback, but he chose instead to sign with the Los Angeles Dodgers as their number-one draft choice of 1968. He was the fifth pick in the country.

He was eighteen when Tommy Lasorda, his rookie-league manager at Ogden, Utah fell in love with his drive to succeed. Said Lasorda, "He was insufferable, but in a good way." Kinda like his manager.

In 1969 both Valentine and Lasorda were promoted to Triple A Spokane, and in 1970 Valentine won the batting crown, hitting .340, and was named the Pacific Coast League Player of the Year. Then in 1971 after playing most of the season with the Dodgers, shuffling between short, third, second, and the outfield, he got hurt.

Valentine, who knew only to play whatever game he was playing at full speed without regard for life or limb, blew out his knee while playing intramural football at Arizona State. The injury slowed him enough that he could no longer perform as a top shortstop.

In 1972 he hit .274 in 119 games. Dodgers manager, Walter Alston, who preferred veterans to undeveloped kids, chose to trade the twenty-two-year-old Valentine, along with Frank Robinson, Bill Grabarkewitz, Bill Singer, and Mike Strahler to the California Angels for Andy Messersmith and Ken McMullen.

Valentine should have familiarized himself with the sad tale of Pete Reiser, the Brooklyn Dodgers hell-bent-for-leather outfielder who destroyed a Hall of Fame career by continually running into outfield walls.

Playing center field in his second game for the Angels on May 17, 1973,

Valentine "pulled a Reiser" when he ran at top speed chasing a home-run hit by Dick Green until he met the unpadded outfield fence. He suffered a compound fracture of his leg. The bone of his leg stuck out hideously. Those who saw it felt like vomiting.

The broken bone was set wrong. His stride was thrown off so seriously that when he returned to try to play, he sometimes would trip and fall while trying to run. Today, the leg has a baseball-sized lump protruding from it.

Valentine quickly went from prospect to suspect, bouncing from the Angels to San Diego to the Mets in 1977 and 1978. While with the Mets he became close friends with teammate Tom Grieve, who noted how Valentine never missed a pitch, or a trick, during the game. Valentine left the Mets and signed with Seattle, where he retired after the 1979 season at age twenty-nine.

For the next two years he served as the minor-league infield instructor for the San Diego Padres, and in 1981 was hired by the Mets in the same capacity. In November 1982 George Bamberger picked him to be his third-base coach. He served under Bamberger, Frank Howard, and Davey Johnson until 1985.

After Tom Grieve became the Texas Rangers' general manager in 1985, he hired his former teammate to manage his hapless team.

Within two years Valentine lifted the Rangers to a second-place finish. In his eight years as manager he won more games than any other in franchise history up to that time, though he was never able to bring home a division title.

Throughout his reign, he was controversial. He was accused of demanding much of the attention of the press. He stood much of the game on the top step, badgering umpires and razzing opposing players. His detractors saw this as a sign of his vanity. He once taunted Kansas City pitcher Joe Beckwith so incessantly from the top step that Beckwith threw a series of wild pitches. The Royals manager, Dick Howser, gave his pitchers permission to throw beanballs—at Valentine. He angered a lot of people along the way.

But the man closest to him, GM Tom Grieve, ignored the criticism. Grieve once called Valentine "the most knowledgeable baseball man" he had ever met. He also called him the finest judge of talent he had ever seen.

Said Grieve in 1997, "The bottom line is that [Bobby] was the principal reason we went from a laughingstock to the championship franchise that Texas is now."

Bobby Valentine

After he was fired on July 9, 1992, no other team hired him to manage. In 1993 he worked in the Cincinnati Reds organization as an advance scout. When Davey Johnson took over as Reds manager in '93, he again became Johnson's third-base coach and infield instructor.

In November 1993 he was named the manager of the Mets' top farm club, the Norfolk Tides.

He was making $65,000. At the end of the 1994 season, the Chiba Lotte Marines, the worst team in Japanese baseball, offered him a two-year contract at $600,000 a year to become the first American in twenty years to manage a Japanese team. For ten years in a row, the Marines had finished in the second division of the Pacific Division of the Japanese League.

When Valentine came to Kobe, Japan, he learned the local traditions and sometimes flouted them. In Japan, baseball players traditionally stay apart from the fans. The outgoing Valentine spent as much time out in public as he could. He rode his bicycle along the beach, took the train to work, posed for thousands of photos, and signed autographs for anyone who asked.

He continued to create a lot of controversy by always demanding his team do things his way, even if it was not the Japanese way. He banned smoking while in uniform, which the older players resented. Japanese players are expected to take four hours of batting practice every day, including game days, as a show of manhood. Valentine cut practice *way* down to conserve the energy of his players. In Japan starting pitchers were supposed to complete games, even if it took 200 pitches to do it. Valentine ended that by instituting a pitch count.

Valentine began hearing the word "chigaimasu." It means three things, "change," "different," and also "incorrect." Valentine discovered early on that the Japanese don't like chigaimasu.

The team started 4–12 but by June began winning regularly. To ingratiate himself with his players, he underwent the ritual that called for him to field 1,000 ground balls. It took him three-and-a-half hours, but he did it.

He led Chiba Lotte to a 69–58–3 record, good for second place, the best finish in eleven seasons. He earned himself a $200,000 bonus.

General manager Tatsuro Hirooka, the former Japanese star who hired him, came to resent that Valentine was more popular than he was. It caused him to lose face, which in Japanese society borders on the tragic, and Hirooka did the only thing he could do under the circumstances: he fired his manager at the end of the season, citing as the excuse Valentine's upsetting chigaimasu—his changes—including the pitch count and the cut-down practices.

When 14,000 Marine fans heard he might be fired, they signed a petition begging Hirooka not to do it. Akira Ejiri, a former Japanese star, took his place anyway. Japan isn't much different than the United States when it comes to baseball power struggles between the manager and general manager—the manager almost always loses.

On the day he flew back to his home in Arlington, Texas, from Japan, the Mets offered Valentine his old job back managing Triple A Norfolk. He took it, gladly.

When Joe McIlvaine fired Dallas Green as Mets manager, it was against his wishes. Co-owner Fred Wilpon, asserting himself, decided his new manager would be someone he had wanted for quite a while—Bobby Valentine.

Joe McIlvaine might have been Valentine's boss but Valentine, hired by Wilpon, didn't treat him that way. Most employees act discreetly when talking about a superior, but Valentine was never known for his tact. As with one of his mentors, Davey Johnson, there was only one way—his. If things weren't done his way, he would let you know about it, even if you were the guy with the power to hire and fire.

In 1996 the Mets had finished fourth. Todd Hundley had become a superstar, hitting 41 home runs to break Roy Campanella's record for most homers hit in a season by a catcher. Valentine wanted Joe McIlvaine to acquire another hitter to go along with Hundley plus pick up a couple more middle relievers to shore up the staff.

When during the winter break McIlvaine failed to sign any free agents, Valentine suggested out loud in the papers that the Mets change their policy. It was the sort of thing Johnson used to do to Frank Cashen. But in this case Valentine had Wilpon's ear and McIlvaine had to put up with Bobby's outbursts.

On December 20, 1996, McIlvaine acquired the sort of hitter Valentine was looking for, when he swapped pitching prospect Robert Person to the Toronto Blue Jays for first baseman John Olerud.

Valentine was pleased, but stopped short of saying he was satisfied. "I don't want to say anything is over, but this makes our lineup more complete."

When he arrived to start spring training in 1997, Valentine carried a stack of computer printouts in his arms, the daily schedule for each of the 45 days of preseason practice. One of his goals, he said, was to establish an "organizationwide look and philosophy." The players were impressed. They also felt comfortable enough with their new manager that after Todd Hundley and John Franco presented him with a huge cake inscribed "Happy Valentine's Day," they pushed his face into the icing.

Valenting, laughing, told reporters, "Another rule: no cake in the face."

The Bobby Valentine era of fun and games had begun.

f o r t y · s i x

Al and Mike

Mets general manager Joe McIlvaine was a believer in building a franchise the old-fashioned way, nursing the minor-league franchises, nurturing the homegrown prospects until they were ready for the Big Show and disdaining the open checkbook to buy expensive free agents.

Pursuant to his philosophy, McIlvaine spent a lot of his time observing each of the teams in the Mets minor-league chain. It didn't leave him a lot of room to schmooze with his manager and owners, upsetting both Bobby Valentine and Fred Wilpon. Valentine would come up with suggestions to better the team, but when he would call around to try to find McIlvaine, too often he was on the road and no one knew where.

McIlvaine's cause was also hurt as a result of serious injuries to some of his best prospects, including Wilson, Isringhausen, Pulsipher, Wallace and Payton. When he gave $1.9 million to 1995–1996 draftees Ryan Jaroncyk and Robert Stratton, the former a high schooler who quit soon after taking the money, saying baseball didn't interest him anymore, and the latter another high school prospect who proved a bust, his stock dropped a little farther.

McIlvaine's position was weakened when Valentine proved himself capable of turning around the franchise almost single-handedly. Valentine had been unable to find a satisfactory batting order, no matter how he designed it. There was little speed in the lineup and no natural number-two hitter. Other players, moreover, were balking at having to hit low in the order.

His solution was ingenious. Valentine decided that the best way to keep everyone involved and happy was to post a different lineup every day, shuffling the players up and down in the order. Before any game, few players knew in which spot in the lineup he would hit. Speedy outfielder Lance Johnson led off, but behind him Valentine tried John Olerud, Rey Ordonez, Bernard Gilkey, and Carlos Baerga in the second spot. For the players, this was something different, but soon they got used to it, and before long no one was complaining about their spot in the order. That they could hit from any spot became a badge of honor. Valentine's strategy, and his insistence on playing everyone on the roster, contributed to team unity.

Veteran Carlos Baerga said, "He made everyone believe that everyone was important on this team, even the bench guys. At the beginning we said, 'Hey, what is he doing with all these guys? Why not play the regular lineup?' But it worked."

Added John Franco, "Some of the things Valentine does, some of his lineups, make you scratch your head. But it all seems to work, so you go with the flow. He's kept everyone involved and everything positive. We have a great attitude and you have to give Bobby credit for that."

Valentine's enthusiasm was contagious. Before every game, just after the National Anthem, Valentine would yell out, "Hey, this is a really big game."

One or two of the Mets players would respond, "Why the heck is it?"

He'd reply, "Because it's the only one we're playing."

By the end of June, Valentine was being touted for Manager of the Year as his Mets boasted a 42–32 record. For the first time in almost a decade, the Mets were being touted as a playoff contender.

As trading deadline approached that year Wilpon decided that for the team to contend for the pennant, the Mets would have to make a couple of blockbuster trades and sign a couple of big-name free agents during the off-season. Everything was in place. The only problem he saw was McIlvaine's disdain for the signing of free agents. Wilpon had to make a tough decision.

On July 16, 1997, Wilpon, with Nelson Doubleday by his side, announced that McIlvaine no longer would be the Mets general manager. Wilpon put him in charge of minor-league development, which Wilpon said, was "what he is happiest doing." Wilpon named thirty-four-year-old Steve Phillips, McIlvaine's assistant, as the Mets' new general manager. At the press conference Wilpon made it clear that Phillips was now McIlvaine's boss. The kid was calling the shots.

McIlvaine, Wilpon said, spent so much time watching the minor leaguers, he was never around to talk to him or to Valentine, an organizational freak who became frustrated whenever he needed to talk to McIlvaine and he wasn't around.

"This change was made to improve the team not only in the next few years but this year as well," said Wilpon prophetically.

By the middle of August the Mets continued to sport a patchwork starting rotation led by Rick Reed who had been a replacement player for six weeks with the 1995 Mets. When the team went into a miniswoon, Mets fans were hoping there wouldn't be a late-season collapse. Catcher Todd Hundley's 5–46 slump wasn't helping. Bobby Valentine decided to shake up his team by getting on his catcher a little.

When on August 20, reporters asked Valentine about Hundley, he replied, "I think he doesn't sleep enough. He's a nocturnal person. He needs to get more rest. He has a real tough time getting to sleep after games. I think he needs to change his ways." He made it clear he didn't consider Hundley a carouser but suggested Hundley should stop smoking, a bone of contention between them all year.

When Hundley heard what Valentine had to say about him, he was furious. He insisted he got plenty of sleep. He was upset some fans might think he was a boozing, bar-hopping night owl.

Said Hundley about Valentine, "I don't get paid enough to be friends with that guy." He added, "Did I get arrested at four in the morning? Did someone in a bar say I was out all night? What did I do? I didn't do anything."

Valentine would later apologize, and Hundley would go on to hit 30 home runs, but their relationship would never be the same.

As a result of the incident, reporters began dredging up old stories of how much Valentine had been hated in Texas as a result of the manipulation of his players. The writers talked of how he had alienated Buddy Bell and Larry Parrish, and wondered whether he would do the same in the Mets clubhouse. Some of the goodwill Valentine had brought to the team was lost.

Nevertheless, a week later the Mets made it clear that Valentine was firmly in control. He signed a three-year $2.1 million contract extension through the year 2000.

John Franco, for one, applauded the move. "For years, you pretty much used to hate to get in your car and drive here," he said. "Now we have an opportunity to do something."

By mid-September the surprising Mets were still in contention for the Wild Card berth. It was a team that never quit. In a game against the Montreal Expos on September 13 at Shea, the Mets were losing 6–0 going into the bottom of the ninth inning. With a runner on first and two outs, Butch Huskey and Carlos Baerga singled. Roberto Petagine hit a two-run single, and then Luis Lopez and Matt Franco had back-to-back singles. Carl Everett, who along with his wife had been accused earlier in the year of abusing his two children, and whose tenure with the Mets was about to end, then hit a long home run off Ugueth Urbina for a grand-slam home run to tie the game at 6–6.

In the bottom of the eleventh inning Bernard Gilkey pinch hit for John Franco and drilled a Steve Kline fastball into the seats in left field to win it with a three-run homer.

It was just one of their league-leading 47 come-from-behind wins that year. The Mets finished the 1997 season with a 88–74 record, third in the National League East behind the Atlanta Braves and the Florida Marlins— who would go on to defeat the Cleveland Indians and become the first Wild Card team to win a World Series.

On February 6, 1998, Phillips and Wilpon made a move that elevated the Mets to a higher plateau when they traded three rookies, including Robert Stratton, to the Marlins for Al Leiter, one of the aces of the Florida rotation.

Despite winning the World Series, Florida owner Wayne Huizinga decided his losses didn't warrant spending what he shelled out for players, and with the trade of eleven other players plus Al Leiter he shed almost $30 million of his $53 million payroll.

The acquisition of Leiter signaled a change in direction from the conservative build-from-within step-by-step method of franchise improvement to a back-up-the-Brinks-truck-and-shell-out-for-the-best-money-has-to-buy approach.

But for such an approach to work, the purchaser must select wisely and Steve Phillips proved a master at doing just that. Leiter was a modest, talented left-handed pitcher who featured a 96-mile-an-hour fastball. With a

60–53 record and a 4.01 lifetime era, the knock on Leiter was his sometime lack of control.

Leiter, though, had smarts and a lot of heart. He was a baseball purist who believed in working hard and learning something new every day, and who put the team above personal achievements.

On May 11, 1996, he threw the first-ever no-hitter for the Florida Marlins against the Colorado Rockies. He is prouder of the fact that he was able to help lead, first the Toronto Blue Jays in 1993 and then the Florida Marlins in 1997, to the World Championship.

A local boy, Leiter grew up in Toms River, New Jersey, where his whole family rooted for the Mets.

Al Leiter: "I remember watching the '69 World Series on a black-and-white TV in the upstairs part of my house on the Jersey shore. I was five years old. I remember my father absolutely loving the Mets, because of Casey Stengel, and also my dad was of the underdog mentality. The Yankees were winning every year, and here come the lowly Mets, and he just fell in love with them. As did my older brothers, John, Carl, Curt, and Mark. They all started liking the Mets. Then Tom Seaver came along, and we all started watching Tom, imitating him and Jerry Koosman, and we just became Mets fans. We kept it on WOR and you didn't turn to WPIX unless you heard that Phil Rizzuto was saying some really goofy stuff. We watched WOR TV and listened to Lindsay Nelson and Bob Murphy on the radio.

"When I was ten, eleven, twelve, my most impressionable time before I became a teenager, they stunk. They were the years of Mike Vail and George Theodore, and Lee Mazzilli came, and it was fun watching how crummy they were.

"In my memory I was always watching the Mets playing a day game and it always seemed the Cubs were on, and it was at Wrigley. We lived an hour and a half from the stadium and didn't go to that many games—we did go to opening day in 1970 when they lifted the World Championship flag. We played Pittsburgh, and I have a picture of all the boys on that day. We were all wearing different types of caps, I was six years old—a cute memory.

"In '83 I was a junior in high school, Tom Seaver did an appearance for the baseball coaches of New Jersey down at the Cherry Hill Hyatt. My high school coach invited me to listen to Tom talk and I remember Seaver on the stand doing his thing, and he had this big weight, which I thought was heavy, ten pounds, and he was showing all the coaches what he used [to train] and I was just looking up to him in complete awe. Years later Tom did a little TV with the Yankees—very seldom did he come down to the clubhouse—but I was thrilled. And right now as a mature thirty-four-year-old man, here's Tom, and we talk pitching and we sit and chat on the road, and we've had a glass of wine. He's into wine now.

"I won my one hundredth game and he wrote, 'Congratulations, Al. All you need is 213 more.' Tom always has to get that little dig in. He's the great Tom Seaver, which is cool. On the plane I'll come up and bother him. I'm the goofy left-hander and I don't care, and I'll sit with him and ask him, 'What kind of shitty wine do you have there?' And I stop and pinch myself. I say to myself, I can't believe this is little ol' me.

"I was in the American League all those years with the Yankees and Blue Jays, and then the Marlins, and finally as a Marlin I got to play in Shea Stadium as a visiting player, and I remember a few times I would stay a little longer, and after everybody left the stadium I would walk across to the home dugout with a beer and sit in the Mets dugout. I'd look out and just think about the Mets years [when I was a kid]. And the Marlins bus would leave, and I'd take the train back to Grand Central.

"Most recently we had an Old Timers game, and John Franco and I were the only two players who came out. I was looking out and seeing all these old names and thinking, I remember these guys. A year later Ron Swoboda came over and said, 'I was impressed with you, because you and Johnny were the only two guys who came out to watch this Old Timers game.' It was fun for me to watch it.

"In the no-hitter against the Rockies I remember batting in the first inning, grounding out to the first baseman and making the last out, which kind of took away the suspense about whether we were going to win the game.

"I also remember in the second inning walking a batter and then hitting Ellis Burks. Larry Rothschild, my pitching coach, kind of got in my face a little bit. 'What the heck are you doing?' Basically, to get my head out of my ass.

"After that I don't remember a hell of a lot. When you see no-hitters, usually the meat of the order comes up in the seventh inning, and if you get through the seventh, you have a shot at not facing the middle of the

order, two, three, four, again. You get the bottom of the order and hopefully you end up with the leadoff guy, which is how I did it.

"Charles Johnson and I threw all fastballs the last couple of innings. I got
a batter named Owens and there was a pinch hitter, McCracken. I didn't
know them, and I got them out, and the last batter was Eric Young, the
leadoff. He fouled a bunch off and I struck him out on a fastball away.

"And even though I'm a pitcher who gets all fired up, the accomplishment was mine because I did it, but, of course, not with a selfish thought,
when it was over, I didn't know how much I should show my excitement.
When you win a World Series, everybody is all fired up. But basically, we
won a ball game. And yes, I threw a no-hitter, but it wasn't a team thing.
The guys who are out there are happy you've thrown it. But how fired up
are they? I didn't think anybody else was really all that interested. Maybe it
was my modesty.

"C. J. and I ended up hugging, like no big deal, like a spring-training
win. It was out of my not wanting to make a big scene out of it. He ran
out, I ran to him, we looked at each other, and we hugged. After I joked
with him. I said, 'If I ever throw another no-hitter, I'm going to jump
around like an idiot.'

"Then about five days later Doc Gooden took away my thunder with
the Yankees when he threw a no-hitter against Seattle in Yankee Stadium.
Who do you think got the week's praise, the guy from the Marlins or the
one pitching for the Yankees?

"I started game seven of the 1997 World Series against Cleveland.
Overall when I think of that game, I think of that World Championship
ring. I'm most proud of that. I had an off-year—I was 13–13 with a 4.
era—I got some crap from Jim Leyland off and on during the year—I don't
know if that was his way of trying to fire me up or not—some of his psychology I question, but so be it. What I remember most, I didn't pitch well
in Cleveland in game three. We ended up winning the game, but it was a
poorly pitched game.

"We lost game six with our ace Kevin Brown. Basically [for game
seven] the joke internally was—nobody would say it to me, but Leyland
said it later—'Who the hell else am I going to start?'

"And the feeling of going out and nailing that son of a bitch and helping the team win the championship when basically everyone wrote us off
and said, 'No way Leiter is going to get out of the second inning.' It was
more of a real satisfying competitive thing that I felt. [It was] basically,

'Fuck everybody'. And not in the martyr sense. Among my friends I thought, 'This is *really* satisfying after hearing my manager joke, "Who the hell else am I going to start?" '

"So it was good that I did my part. I remember the 70,000 fans—the Marlins sold every ticket—and it was really, really exciting. [It was in] my previous World Series experience in Toronto—the Toronto fans are great, but they are very quiet—it was a tremendous experience playing the Phillies in that World Series.

"I honestly believe I would rather have a poor year and win a championship than have a great year and not win. Having a good year means something, but you know what, ultimately its championships.

"I didn't really care when Mr. Huizinga started breaking up the team. It's his business. He's a wealthy man, very successful in business. He got into baseball and we had a strike, and here's a guy who deals in the business world and he basically looked at the other owners with mockery and couldn't believe people like this were running the game. He became very disenchanted with the whole thing. Had he realized what he was getting into, he never would have bought the team.

"His key people told him, 'Wayne, sell the team. Put it up for sale, and you'll be removed, and they'll get a stadium. You're a rich billionaire, and nobody is going to pay for your stadium.'

"But he was foolish, because after he committed to selling, everyone rallied behind the Marlins. We ended up with 2.4 million in attendance and the people were really fired up. I think he missed the boat. He was ill-advised.

"Not a week after the World Series Charlie Johnson and several other Marlins players went to his office in downtown Miami where he had his Blockbuster headquarters and pleaded with him to keep the team together. And from talking with the guys who were there, he started to really buy into it.

"Well, Don Smiley, who was the president at the time, got on the phone and told all the players if they wanted to keep the team together to give some money back on their contracts. This is where that was going. Now you open up a whole other can of worms. Open up your true books and become a public company, and we'll find out what the *real* numbers are. Then you know what you're getting into.

"I didn't care. I knew I was getting traded. I heard the Cubs mentioned a lot. Pat Gillick was the Orioles GM—he was with me during my Blue Jays days—and I heard I was getting traded to the Orioles for a couple of players, and that year the Devil Rays ended up drafting one of the players in the deal, so the way it turned out, I got traded to the Mets and I was thrilled. I think of my career as a dream and it continues to be a dream."

On May 22, 1998, Steve Phillips made his most spectacular acquisition to date, trading Mookie Wilson's stepson Preston and two minor-league pitchers to the Florida Marlins for the best-hitting catcher in baseball, twenty-nine-year-old Mike Piazza.

Only several days earlier, the Marlins had gotten Piazza and third baseman Todd Zeile in a trade with the LA Dodgers for Gary Sheffield, Bobby Bonilla, Charlie Johnson, and Jim Eisenreich, after Piazza demanded a seven-year, $100 million contract. The Marlins made the trade with the Dodgers in order to shed millions of dollars in megasalaries earned by veterans, some past their prime, and to acquire a blue chipper with which to make another trade for cheaper prospects.

That Piazza ended up with the Mets surprised everyone, because the day before the trade, Fred Wilpon told the media he wasn't interested in the All Star catcher. The Mets would wait for catcher Todd Hundley, who was on the DL, to get well, Wilpon said. A day later, Piazza became a Met. Al Leiter, for one, couldn't believe it.

Al Leiter: "I remember talking to my friends on the phone when it first went down, and my comment to them was, 'We have Mike Piazza!' In a fanatic, fan sense. I was thinking about it totally as a Mets fan. I have ten years in the big leagues, and I'm thinking, 'Can you believe it? We got Piazza!' It was definitely surreal and one reason why I was surprised was that 'Mike and the Mad Dog,' the radio show on WFAN in New York was pushing the Mets ownership: 'You have to get that guy.' You hate to think radio personalities influence owners, and I don't know if they would ever admit it, but I think how badly Mike Francesa was berating the Mets, saying, 'How the hell can you *not* sign this guy?' Todd Hundley was hurt, this guy was available, and it was like, 'What are you guys doing?'

"The day before the trade, Fred Wilpon was on, and he was justifying how we didn't need him. 'Todd will be back . . . ' saying what he was supposed to be saying for someone who doesn't want Piazza.

"And literally twenty-four hours later, we got the guy, so something happened. I don't know whether he got with Nelson [Doubleday] or what. So that's what made it even more surprising.

"I had pitched against Piazza. Oh, yeah. I always joked that I never wanted to face him. I'd pitch around him and go after Karros and Zeile behind him. Until this year [2000] Karros wasn't doing anything against me. Now he's made up some ground. But Mike is one of those devastating guys in the lineup.

"So we got him, he flies in, and I'm pitching that day against Milwaukee. It was a midweek day game. He didn't even get there until game time. He didn't even go over any scouting reports. Piazza just showed up and I was a little intimidated. I have a new guy catching me. You look in and see a new mask, a new face, and this guy is giving me signs. This guy doesn't know dick about what kind of a pitcher I am, except that he's faced me. And I threw a four-hit shutout! It was so fitting.

"I threw my best game. And Piazza got all the thunder. The whole next day it was, 'Piazza's here! Piazza's here! And oh, by the way, Al Leiter threw a three-hit shutout. Christ, couldn't I have done it the *next* day? Michael Kay, an old friend of mine, used to say, 'If you're ever going to pitch a great game, don't do it on the West Coast.' Because of the deadlines. It never gets into the morning papers."

With Piazza behind the plate and Leiter in the rotation, Bobby Valentine's Mets made a strong run to make the play-offs. It was clear this team had a special closeness.

Al Leiter: "One of the things that have gone on with my tenure here as a Met: We have a lot of quality guys who get along. On most teams there are three or four guys you can go out with, and the guys will be segregated into different groups. But that has not been the case with the Mets. On any given night you'll see a handful of guys together, it's the whole pulling [together] thing, the chemistry. A lot of people say, 'The chemistry? Who cares?' But there is something to be said for it, and a lot of the credit has to go to Steve, because he not only gets good players, he gets good people, and it's not cliché crap. I've been really impressed with a lot of his decisions to bring in quality people as well as good players. Robin Ventura comes to mind. Todd Zeile is a quality professional athlete. Mike Piazza, for a superstar guy, could be way more of a prima donna than he is. He understands he's the mouthpiece and he has to do his nightly interviews, even though he really just wants to be left alone. A few times he'll say, 'Do you think it's all right if I don't come out and stretch?' or ' . . . if I fly home early on an off-day?' Trivial stuff. Of course, it's all right. You can do anything you want. You're the man.

"Mike's a good guy, and it starts with the big-time player and it filters down. If there are some wise little assholes who are young, they see guys like Johnny, Robin, myself, Lenny Harris, who is a good guy to have around."

By mid–September 1998, the Mets began to play win-one, lose-one ball. On September 20, Al Leiter started against his old team, the Florida Marlins, before 52,000 fans at Shea Stadium. In the second inning he got an out, the next two hitters singled, and Bobby Valentine came out to the mound to talk to him. Valentine's message to Leiter hit home and the lefty flamethrower got the final out of the inning and went on to shut out the Marlins by the score of 5–0. Leiter, a big fan of Valentine, gave his manager the credit for appearing on the mound exactly when he needed to.

Al Leiter: "The Marlins came in when we were tailspinning. It was one of those times when we needed to win to stop all the bullshit. It was the second time I faced the Marlins since I was traded. I didn't have a terrible relationship with Jim Leyland, but there were some things I didn't care for, like most players, and I think Bobby sensed some of this.

"Mark Kotsay got a base hit and then Cliff Floyd got a base hit, and normally the pitching coach, Bob Apodaca, would have come out, but this time it was Bobby. He said to me, 'Look, what are you doing?' I knew what his motive was. Bobby's not a guy to get in your face and start yelling, but he did make it pretty clear he was pissed off. Basically it was, 'What the heck are you doing? Get your head out of your ass. Let's go.' That kind of thing.

"Maybe it looked like I was not being aggressive and he fired me up. He pissed me off enough to say, 'He's right. What am I doing here?' And it was a *good* thing. That was a day he got into me a little bit, as much as Bobby Valentine gets into somebody. To me, he's pretty harmless when he tries to get in your face.

"I like Bobby a lot. He leaves me alone and never really fucks with me."

The Mets led the race for the Wild Card playoff spot, but in late September, all at once, the hitters stopped producing, and the Mets went into a late-season swoon. After beating the Marlins, the Mets lost two games to lowly Montreal. In the finale the Mets were shutout by youngster Carl

Pavano. Al Leiter understood too well the psychology behind lesser teams beating the big boys down the stretch.

Al Leiter: "You can talk to the Braves, to any team in contention and it happens every year. The lowly Expos have talented young players who want to stick it up your ass. I have a theory about that: When you go in to play a team late, they actually can play better against you than the team with superstars. There is absolutely nothing to lose, the manager generally will take more risks because who cares? Why did you hit-and-run such and such? Why not? The attitude is freer and also, a young team knows full well, whether we win or lose the game tonight who cares? Let's just go out and have fun and wouldn't it be great to kick the Mets' ass? That's the feeling.

"It happens every year. The Mets are coming down the stretch, they have three games against the Marlins and six against the Expos; it looks easy. Bullshit. A team like that gets fired up coming in for the Yankees, the Braves, the Dodgers, the Mets, and you know those teams are going to give you a tough time. Pavano to me is a pitcher with great stuff who just has to learn how to pitch. That was a night he stuck it to us."

The Mets, now tied with the Cubs for the Wild Card spot, had to go to Atlanta to play three games. They had to face Bruce Chen, Denny Neagle, and Greg Maddux. The Mets had the bases loaded twice in the opener but only scored once. Rookie Jay Payton got thrown out at third base for the third out to end one inning. They lost, 6–5.

In the second game, Al Leiter started against Denny Neagle, and the Braves won 4–0. The Mets were running out of steam after a long season.

Al Leiter: "I can't explain it. What happened that year, whether Mike likes to believe it or not, as Piazza goes, so we go offensively. That year John Olerud was a force, and Edgardo [Alfonso] was coming into his own, but I got the feeling . . . we rely on a guy who relies on the tools of ignorance, and he's a strong man, but whether he believes it or likes it or thinks it is not, it's a tiring position, and maybe Mike does get tired at the end of the year. I'm not sure how the numbers went, but I know it was pretty tough to score runs. The Mets were shut out a couple of times the last couple of weeks.

"In my game I gave up a home run to someone to ruin it, and Glavine just sailed. In my mind, with those guys, if you give up one or two, you got a shot. If you give up three, you lose. And that's what happened."

★ ★ ★

In the 1998 season finale Bobby Valentine asked Hideo Nomo to pitch. Nomo, who had been acquired by the Mets during the summer, told Valentine that other pitchers deserved to start more. As result Bobby started Armando Reynoso, who got clobbered within two innings, and the Mets lost 7–2. Nomo came in in relief and pitched four shutout innings.

Al Leiter: "Hideo had been pitching very poorly, and in his eyes, he felt he didn't deserve it. I think Hideo was saying, 'Look, for the good of the team, I stink right now. Give it to Armando.' I don't think he was being cowardly about it. He really honestly thought we had a better shot with the other guy. Armando was rested, and he was throwing the ball well. A start or two before that, he had pitched a gem.

"Hideo went in in relief and pitched four scoreless innings. So what? I know the mind-set of a pitcher. If you go into a game and you drop an early lead and now all of a sudden the reliever throws five or six scoreless innings, well, there was no pressure. The game has already been lost. Gee whiz, he thinks, maybe I can get a few scoreless innings here and lower my era. He relaxes and his stuff is effective, and he gets guys out. Conversely, the hitters have a big lead and they kind of go to sleep. Don't assume that if Hideo had started the game he would have pitched a shutout."

The season ended with the empty-handed Mets being edged out by one game for the Wild Card spot by the Chicago Cubs. Had they won any one of the last six games, they'd have been in the playoffs for the first time since 1988. Not to get in was devastating for everyone.

Al Leiter: "It was bad, because we let what little lead we had completely slip away by our poor play. Even though in the heart of hearts you dream of being a world champion, I knew we weren't that caliber of a team. We blew a chance to be in the postseason cause we gave the lead away. We tailspinned, and it didn't seem that there was a degree of giving up, but it definitely seemed that the focus was not where it was needed to be, with a tenacious, aggressive 'we're going to go out and kick your ass' feeling. If you lose that way, I always feel I can stand in my locker and face the press. 'I left my balls out there.' And I didn't get the feeling we were all doing that."

★ ★ ★

At the end of the 1998 season both Al Leiter and Mike Piazza had to decide whether to re-sign with the Mets or become free agents and see what the market might bear. Leiter, the lifetime Mets fan, wanted to stay in New York, and he personally let Steve Phillips know what it would take to keep him in New York.

Al Leiter: "My decision was so simple. It was easy because I knew I was living out a Mets dream. I came over and had one of my best years, was the best pitcher on the Mets, yada, yada, yada, and all I knew talking to my agent—it was silly to even have an agent at the time. I had a very easy, relaxed relationship with Steve and now in my old years I'm not afraid to talk with a general manager.

"You hear rumblings of what teams might be interested and how much they'd be interested in offering [two teams wanted to give him $45 million for five years]. I didn't want to file [for free agency] because what kind of ass would I be if I signed for $13 million less with the team that I love, knowing I had a bird-in-the-hand, supposedly for more money. But, money wasn't an issue. I can't believe what I get paid now. I didn't want to blow the Mets gig, because I love it here.

"Basically I was looking for Alex Fernandez money. I knew he had signed for five years. During the World Series I was doing some work for ESPN, and I was staying at the U.N. Plaza hotel. I went to see Steve, and I said, 'With respect to where I stand, the number should be this and if you get this, then go back to Fred and Nelson, and I'll sign. But,' I said, 'it has to be x.'

"Sometimes agents do their job and they make it seem like the players are a lot more aggressive than the numbers they actually want. You know the game.

"It all worked out, and I was thrilled that I was able to get the four-year deal. So far, it's been great."

Piazza stayed, too. He signed a seven-year $91 million deal to finish out his career in New York. With his signing, Mets fans now understood that Doubleday and Wilpon would do whatever it took to bring the Mets a World Championship, that it was just a matter of time.

forty-seven

Playoff Bound—Barely

After the 1998 season, the Mets impressed their fans when they re-signed Al Leiter, Mike Piazza, and reliever Dennis Cook for big bucks. It presaged a new era. No longer would the Mets be content with bringing up prospects while watching George Steinbrenner over in the Bronx spend millions signing the best free agents available.

In December 1998 the Mets put out notice that anyone the Yankees wanted, the Mets wanted, too. The Mets even tried to acquire Roger Clemens, a Yankee whose contract had run out. (Clemens re-signed with the Yankees.) Then came a brace of expensive signings: future Hall of Fame outfielder Rickey Henderson, arguably the finest leadoff hitter in the history of the game (Henderson had 66 steals in 1998; The Mets team had 62); Japanese phenom pitcher Masato Yoshii, All Star third baseman Robin Ventura, and slugger Bobby Bonilla, a failure with the Mets the first time around.

After failing to reach the playoffs by one game in 1998. Msssrs. Wilpon and Doubleday were giving Phillips carte blanche to make certain that did not happen again. Including Piazza and Leiter, in all the Mets spent $168.9 million to acquire their new players. Ted Turner's similarly unlimited budget had helped make his Atlanta Braves perennial division champs.

On December 1, 1998, Steve Phillips orchestrated one of his best trades. He sent Todd Hundley to Los Angeles for catcher Charlie Johnson and outfielder Roger Cedeno. He then swapped Johnson to the Baltimore Orioles for flamethrowing reliever Armando Benitez.

The Mets' breathtaking expenditures, along with the boldness of Steve

Phillips' moves, put Mets fans on notice that the Mets were finally serious about catching Atlanta.

Al Leiter: "Think about the dynamics in New York through the years. I lived it as a Yankee in the late 80s when it was a Mets town and George was pissed he wasn't getting the back page. And then there was a period where they both were kind of floundering, and then George started picking it up, and there was a period—I don't know Fred or Nelson that well, and I don't know if they'd ever admit it, but through the days when they thought Pulsipher, Isringhausen, and Wilson were going to be the next Seaver, Koosman, and Gentry—they started saving some dough. They still had the $47 million TV package, and after '92, when they had Bobby Bonilla the first time around, when Klap [Bob Klapisch and John Harper] wrote, 'The Worst Team Money Could Buy,' in '93, '94, '95, and '96, they were going with a pretty lean team. I imagine they were saving up their war chest to get to where they felt they were ready to go for it.

"And Steve Phillips got a team that turned it around, and you have to include Bobby Valentine in that turnaround. Dallas Green was kind of wasting the time of many. So yeah, it all came into place, and I was fortunate to get in there, and as soon as we got Piazza, clearly the alarms went off. You're not going to bring on Mike and sign him to be a mediocre team. Cause why have a $13 million-a-year player on your team if you're just planning on being .500?"

But spending so much money on players has its down side. It raises everyone's expectations—the fans, the press, and ownership alike. The pressure ratchets upward. Money, after all, is supposed to buy success. But baseball is a funny game, and no matter how much you pay a player success can only be achieved through performance, and after June 5, 1999, the Mets were floundering, losing eight games in a row dropping their record to 27–28.

The Mets front office, feeling a need to act, didn't fire Bobby Valentine. Instead, on June 6, 1999, general manager Steve Phillips fired the three coaches closest to him, Bob Apodaca, Randy Niemann, and Tom Robson, who had worked closely with Valentine for ten years including in Japan.

Valentine and Phillips had sharp words. The manager considered quitting, but decided to stay, predicting that the team would turn around. If it didn't, he said, he would resign.

Said Valentine, "I'm not worried about my job. I believe, though, that if in the next 55 games we're not better, I shouldn't be the manager."

Said Phillips, "He'll pull things together with a new staff."

Leiter, who saw the strain between Valentine and Phillips, knew why the front office did what it did.

Al Leiter: "At the time things were pretty tense between Bobby and Steve—it was obvious. In New York, nothing is hidden, unless you're the kind of guy who is completely oblivious, who only shows up, puts on his uniform and gets out to the field. I don't know what their internal decision-making process was. Maybe their communication fell off. I don't know, but under the basic agreement you have to pay everybody. You can't fire all the players or send them home, so you get rid of some coaches or the manager. It's obvious anytime you get rid of coaches or the manager, you're putting everyone on high alert that 'we're not happy with the way the game is being played.'

"If you look at the guys Phillips fired, they were supposedly Bobby's guys. [Coach] Mookie [Wilson] wasn't Bobby's guy. Cookie [Rojas] wasn't Bobby's guy. And of course, the three men they brought in, Dave Wallace, Al Jackson, and John Stearns, *weren't* Bobby's guys.

"The next day there was some talk in the papers—Mike Keegan, a writer with the *Post*, wrote, 'Al Leiter has blood on his hands,' for the firing of Apodaca, which is a bunch of shit. Because I had said some things casually, saying, 'Apodaca's personality is a little bit on the quiet side. You never really knew where this guy was coming from. He really didn't communicate that well.' That's all. There was absolutely *no* problem between Bob and me. I thought the work we got done on the side and his rationale on pitching was good. Other than that, he wasn't a guy you sat with over a glass of wine or beer and talked about life. It just wasn't there. And I had made casual comments about that and it was viewed that Dennis Cook and I didn't like the guy. And it was a bunch of shit.

"And I have to say, Wallace and Jackson did help me. Really, the wake-up call was, 'Look, get back to being aggressive. Forget about everything else.' It's more in-the-head stuff. Yeah, absolutely Wally and Al helped me with that. It was, 'What are you doing?'

"When Apodaca was there, whenever you struggled, Bob was very good at breaking down the mechanics, and I felt that my problem had to do with my mechanics. Most pitchers do. But your problems aren't always with your mechanics. If you're a healthy pitcher and you're good enough to pitch in the big leagues, your problems are between the ears. I'm so convinced of that. Oh, absolutely. Mechanics is sometimes a bunch of crap, somewhere for a pitcher to hide and say, 'I have a bad release point.' Bullshit. You get the little white ball and you throw it to the catcher, and you get them out. How you do that is with balls and heart.

"You see guys with lesser stuff over the years and they win, and you ask yourself, 'How do *they* win?' They win with what it takes internally. The reason the great pitchers, like Greg Maddux, do it year in and year out, is they have such command and such ability to believe in themselves and execute a quality pitch, and they do it more often than the others.

"I felt that when Dack was there, it was always back to the drawing board. You started to think, 'Where's my arm? Where's my leg?' What the fuck? You were thinking about everything but, 'Get the ball, look in to Piazza, and throw it.' And I had kind of gotten to that point.

"And, what happens, you go out and have a good game, feel good about yourself, and the next five days your chin gets a little higher, and then you go out and nail another one . . . all right! And that's what happens."

The day after the coaches were fired, Al Leiter ended the Mets' eight-game losing streak. He beat Roger Clemens and the Yankees 7–2 in front of 56,294 fans at Yankee Stadium. Mike Piazza hit a mammoth home run and Bobby Bonilla drove in two runs in a crucial situation.

Al Leiter: "I pitched the next night at Yankee Stadium, and we beat Roger Clemens. I pitched a great game. And supposedly turned our season around.

"Roger had won 20 games in a row, and I stopped Derek Jeter's on-base streak [at 53 games in a row]. A lot of good stuff happened that night and I nailed it. It was another one of those good feelings like I got from game seven of the World Series. Up to that point I was having a floundering year. It was my first year under the new contract and stuff was being said in the papers about that, and I really let the signing affect me in a negative way, because I was thinking about stuff I wasn't supposed to be thinking about.

"What happens is, it's like anything else in life, you start out and think you have a good game plan, but when I started pitching, I got behind the eight ball. I had some bad starts, and in New York that isn't a good thing.

I had three or four bad outings, and all of a sudden it was, 'Al Leiter, the $32 million pitcher . . . ' and for as much as I told myself, Don't read it. Don't listen, it's difficult, and now it's your start again, and you have those little gremlins in your head telling you that you suck. And it's a catch-22 of going out and nailing some performances and elevating your confidence and self-esteem. Like most players who go in and out, I wasn't feeling good about myself, and it looked like I was letting the season get away from me.

"But from that point in June, my numbers completely turned around, and I actually turned what looked like would be a really shitty year into a pretty good one."

On June 10, 1999 against Toronto, Bobby Valentine was thrown out of the game for arguing a call. He returned in the bottom of the twelfth inning, standing at the edge of the dugout wearing sunglasses and a fake mustache. TV cameras caught him in the act. The commissioner's office fined him for returning to the dugout after being tossed from a game.

The writers came down on Valentine like he had committed murder. The manager tried to tell everyone he was just fooling around, but few accepted his explanation or thought the antic funny.

Al Leiter: "Bobby is a misunderstood man who is perceived as a guy who doesn't listen to others and is kind of a know-it-all, and he rubs people the wrong way. When I was pitching for the Marlins late in 1997 and he was managing the Mets, and I didn't know him, he rubbed me the wrong way. I was standing on the mound, and I heard this voice over from the visiting dugout at Pro Player Stadium. 'He ain't gonna make the fifth inning. . . . ' I'm listening, and I thought to myself, 'If I didn't know any better, that sounds like the manager over there.' So while I was looking in at Charlie Johnson, I'm peeking glances over to the dugout to see who it is. Cause if it was a regular player, I would have stuck one in his ear. And I looked over, and sure enough, it was Bobby, because he has that high squeaky voice, and he said later that he was trying to fire up his team.

"He was yelling out at me, but I pitched a great game, nailed the bastard, and in the postgame on one of the New York radio stations, I said, 'I want to thank the Mets manager for firing me up.'

"Bobby does stuff like that, but do you know what? Now that I'm on his side, I see that he's a smart guy, a nice guy, a charitable guy, definitely misunderstood. If anybody needs a PR person, it's him. His knowledge is dangerous, because Bobby is a smart guy. He's got a lot of neat ideas, New-age stuff, which are a little different.

"He likes to be noticed. He likes to be The Guy. Most recently I read a quote where Mike Piazza endorsed Bobby, which I completely do endorse him. I like Bobby a lot. He defuses a lot of the bullshit that goes on in New York, like the way Billy Martin used to. And it's a good thing. Again, Bobby is smart enough to know that. He doesn't care if an opposing manager has to sit in the utmost corner of the dugout so Bobby can't look at him. I've heard that from opposing managers. Well, Bobby doesn't care. If he's going to put on sunglasses and a beard and come out there and do his thing, or whatever he does, he has fun. The guy is fun. He really enjoys the game and sometimes he doesn't realize—maybe he does realize—that he's being watched all the time. He stands there in the middle of the game and he'll sing a little tune, or dance. You're in the opposing dugout, and you look and think, What's up with this guy? Or he stands on the top step— they call him 'Top Step Bobby.' To me, why not? It's not World War III. We're not trying to kill the opponent. It's a baseball game. Here's a guy who's thrilled to be a big-league manager—resurrected. He's come back, and he's having the time of his life, and if you have a problem with the way that looks, tough.

"Bobby makes things easier for the players. He knows when he's needed and he becomes kind of a lightning rod. And maybe he doesn't even realize he's doing it. I don't know, but I sense a few times when he does something when everyone scratches their heads and say, What's he doing now?' Maybe he's smarter than you think, and he's doing it for a reason.

"I like the guy. I heard amazing stories about him. Robinson, the famous football coach at USC, said that Bobby Valentine was the next best running back since O.J. Simpson. Men praise the kind of athlete he was. And he has a big heart. He does the right things. He's very political, and he's confident. I guess Lasorda helped him out with that. Last year [1999] I went to the *Sports Illustrated* Sportsman of the Year dinner and there was a preparty. I was there and I was intimidated by some of the celebrities standing around. Bobby yells, 'Al, get over here.' I came over and he said, 'Meet Donald.' And Donald Trump turned around. Bobby was palling around him, patting him, and doing the political grab ass. He's a confident guy, and he feels comfortable with all that."

★ ★ ★

In his next start, Leiter defeated the Boston Red Sox 4–2. Benny Agbayani, the rookie outfielder from Hawaii who Valentine had brought up to Norfolk from Double A when everyone else was ready to give up on him, hit a long home run, as did John Olerud. Observers said it was Leiter who was bringing the Mets out of their slump. Leiter reveled in the role.

Al Leiter: "Guys would say, 'Who's pitching tonight? Leiter. Ah, good.' Nothing against your teammates, but you know on a certain night who's pitching for you. 'Him. We've going to have to bang out some runs.' That kind of thing. You know the pitchers who are going to nail it. And I took pride in that. I started doing well. I don't know if one guy can carry a team to a championship, but if you get a starter—I believe this about about good pitching staffs and bad—it's contagious. You look at the Braves' staff. They have good pitchers who believe in themselves and they follow one another, and they start feeding off that in friendly, good-natured fun. I had it with Kevin Brown my first year with the Marlins. We had internal games between each other. Good stuff. When you see your fellow starter doing his thing, you want to do it, too. It carries over and all of a sudden it becomes contagious. Also, it's good if you have a quality starter or two so you have a chance to talk pitching. There has to be a reason why a team will have bad staffs year after year. Because it becomes contagious. You look at the guy next to you and say, 'He went five innings and gave up three runs. That's not so bad. I went six innings and gave up four. I guess I'm as good as he is.' That breeds mediocrity. And somehow you have to get rid of it."

By the end of June 1999, the Mets were in the hunt for the division title, a game ahead of the San Francisco Giants in the race for the Wild Card spot. In the month of June the Mets infield of John Olerud, Edgardo Alfonzo, Rey Ordonez, and Robin Ventura made just two errors. Ordonez was staking his claim to being the best-fielding shortstop in baseball, an honor considering the competition, A-Rod, Jeter, and Nomar.

Al Leiter: "It's one of those things, like anything else in life, when you have it, you don't appreciate it until you lose it. We really had it in 1999, until Rey broke his arm in May. It was unbelievable to see some of the play Rey made at shortstop. I've seen thousands of pitches and thousands of innings. You throw the ball, and you know the velocity of the ball on the ground, where it was hit, and before you turn around, you have the feeling, 'It's a base hit.' And the amazement of watching Rey Ordonez do what he does and pick up the ball and throw it and get them out—you're the one who has to perform and get the next pitch going, and you just stand there amazed. You want to see the replay.

"It's saying a lot about Rey, [that I'm] talking as much as I am about him, because Robin is a Golden Glover, Fonzie got screwed again he should have won it. He is very solid at second and Olerud is a guy who's six-foot-six, who completely spoiled those guys throwing the ball, balls that normally would get away. He did a fabulous job.

"Look, you win with pitching and defense."

In July 1999 the Mets went on a 12–3 tear, and to bolster the rotation, on July 23, the Mets acquired left-handed starter Kenny Rogers. "The Gambler," as he was called, was a quiet, hard-working guy with an extraordinary curveball. Al Leiter, for one, learned from him.

Al Leiter: "Kenny was kind of a quiet guy. He was a nice guy. Nothing really stood out about him. He was vanilla; not bad, not good. He had a great curveball and while he was with us, I learned some things from him. He had his routine, his program, and it worked. He liked to throw on the side, like Tommy John.

"There was always this touchy-feely on his breaking stuff, and what he taught me was to have a firm frontside, stay closed as long as you can, and spin your curveball.

"I have tried to pick up something from every single pitcher I have ever played with, especially left-handers. Even Glendon Rusch—he's a great kid who wants to learn, and in turn, while I'm helping him, there are numerous times when I'm asking him, 'What did you do on this? What did you think about that?' If he had a good change-up, the next day I'd ask him how he held it. It's a constant learning thing.

"I remember in '88 when I had Tommy John on my team. I was twenty-one, and he was forty-five. He had twenty-five years in the big leagues. He was constantly tinkering and touching and feeling and throwing. He had 286 wins by the end of '88. I asked him, 'What the hell can you learn?' He said, 'Are you kidding me? You learn constantly.' And it kind of stuck. I remember some guys vividly. David Cone would always talk about,

'Get your glove, get your shit, run out there, get on the mound as fast as you can, and be ready. Have the umpire call to the hitter, "Get in the box. Let's go.' He said, 'The umpires appreciate that.' Dave Stewart was an advocate of, 'Believe in your strength and stay with it until they prove they can hit it.' You pick up things over the years. That's how you learn.

"I'll tell you, guys like Maddux and Glavine, especially Maddux, I read any article that's written on him, and I read every one of his quotes. I want to know why this guy with good stuff—not great stuff—and great command is one of the best pitchers in the history of the game. The thing I get from him, all he ever talks about is executing a quality pitch. You start living by it.

"You know, he's got a point. The only thing you can control is where you throw the ball. Harvey Dorfman is a sports psychologist who worked with Oakland and with the Marlins when I was there. He helped me out a great deal. He made me realize in the transition after the two surgeries on my arm that the game is very mental, and that's the way you win the game. How do you explain the guy who look like Adonis, is in great shape, can run, has great stuff, and he sucks? Because he has two cents between his ears, and he doesn't listen, and he doesn't know what the fuck he's doing out there."

After Valentine's proclamation to "see how we do over the next 55 games," the Mets did extremely well, compiling a 40–15 record. They led the Braves for the National League East Division title and held a four-game lead over the Cincinnati Reds. It looked like Valentine would finally make it to the playoffs for the first time in his twelve-year major-league managerial career.

Al Leiter: "We all got a wake-up call. We kicked ourselves in the asses, we were embarrassed that we weren't playing better than we were. We got on a nice roll. and we started playing good baseball."

But, for the second year in a row, the Mets had a devastating late-season swoon. During the last week of September they lost seven games in a row—even worse than the 0–5 debacle of the year before. Once again, the wolves were howling for Bobby V's scalp.

After falling two games behind the Reds, the Mets trailed in the Wild Card race by two games with only three to go. A couple of the Atlanta Braves players had the temerity to declare the Mets to be finished for the season.

But in their final series of the season, the Mets beat the Pittsburgh Pirates in all three games, while the Reds lost two of three to the Brewers. Once again, it was back in the Mets' collective hands whether they'd make it to the playoffs or not.

On the final day of the season the Mets won their game at Shea when, with the bases loaded in the bottom of the ninth inning, Brad Clontz bounced a pitch that went to the backstop.

The Mets, winners of a remarkable 96 games, led the Reds by half a game. The question was whether the Milwaukee Brewers could beat the Reds and give the Mets the Wild Card spot or whether the Mets and Reds would have to face each other in a one-game playoff.

Al Leiter: "We played the last game, and we won it on a wild pitch with Mike Piazza up. We were waiting to find out the score of the Cincinnati–Milwaukee game.

"We went up to the Diamond Club and we had dinner with our families, because we knew we were either flying to Cincinnati or we're flying to Arizona. And lo and behold, Milwaukee lost—Cincinnati won—so we had this team family dinner. I was getting all psyched up for it. As soon as I found out we were playing the Reds, I began focusing on the Cincinnati lineup and what I had to do."

Ordinarily, if you win 97 games, you are a lock to get into the playoffs. Not in 1999. The Atlanta Braves won 103 games that year, and the Reds final win gave them 97 to finish the season, necessitating a one-game preplayoff playoff for a chance to play the Arizona Diamondbacks in the National League Wild Card Series.

Technically, the Mets had made the playoffs for the first time since 1988, but the players didn't want to have to be satisfied with playing one game. They wanted to beat the Reds and go on to play Arizona. Al Leiter started, and he pitched a sensational two-hitter en route to a 5–0 shutout win. It was a highlight in a career featuring more and more memorable performances.

Al Leiter: "To be honest, I was thrilled when the game was over, but I didn't even realize it was a two-hitter. The game was over and I knew I had pitched a good game; that we had won. Rickey Henderson and Fonzie hit homers in the first inning and we had a 2–0 lead. In my career I pitched well against Cincinnati, but that year I pitched particularly well, and I knew they weren't feeling all that comfortable facing me. I don't know. It just worked out. And I nailed it."

And so it was on to Arizona.

forty-eight

The Cardiac Kids

By "nailing it," Al Leiter may well have saved Bobby Valentine's job, his career, and his reputation. But, even winning and moving on to the 1999 National League playoffs, Valentine found himself in another awkward situation. During the final days of the regular season, when it looked to Valentine that the Mets were not going to catch the Reds, he had opened his heart to *Sports Illustrated* writer S. L. Price, who like Valentine (and the author of this book who remembers a pint-sized Valentine as a Burdick Junior High eighth grader starting at shortstop for the Rippowam High School varsity) hails from Stamford, Connecticut. In the article Valentine talked about his life in baseball, and when he analyzed why the Mets looked like they were not going to make the playoffs, he spoke with bitterness about several of his players.

Said Valentine, "You're not dealing with real professionals in the clubhouse. You're not dealing with real intelligent guys for the most part. A lot can swim, but most of them just float along, looking for something to hold onto. That's why, I'm sure, they're having a players' only meeting. Because there's about five guys in there right now who basically are losers, who are seeing if they can recruit. They actually think there's some accomplishment and some reward in being the BMOC. They don't know that, looking back at it five years from now, that will mean nothing."

When the magazine hit the stands with Bobby's inflammatory comments, some of the players—and Steve Phillips, Fred Wilpon, and Nelson Doubleday—were furious with their outspoken manager.

Al Leiter: "There was a lot of tension from Steve and ownership and everybody. Oh, yeah. It was the bad timing of the article. After tailspinning at the end of the season in the Braves and Phillies series, he talked about what happened. He said those things when it looked like we were going to do the same thing we had done in 1998.

"Had we not made the playoffs, the article would have been on the newsstand when we were in our respective homes. But because we came back and won, we were still together at Shea Stadium when it came out, so we were reading this *SI* story, and it wasn't good. The article was written by Valentine's friend and it really came across bad. He referred to the team's 'five losers.'

"There was no apology. Bobby felt the way he felt about the players he pointed out. He didn't mention any names, but everybody on the team knew who they were. So, after that, it was kind of bittersweet.

"Maybe that's why people don't like Bobby. But, depending on how you say things and when you say them, I'd rather have someone be honest than lie.

"He does have his eyes in a lot of places. He does pay attention. As long as he sees that you work hard and you have a good program and improve, and you care about winning, he leaves you alone. The guys who stray from that, who stop working hard, and maybe who do things that *don't* make them the best they can be, he's not afraid to say something. And that pisses guys off.

"There are guys who are having a poor season who need to be coddled or hope they can hide under their locker and nobody will say anything. And he brings it to the forefront and *that* pisses people off. But, I'm one who will admit when he sucks and one to know and cherish this job, and I think I work hard, and I try my best, and therefore I don't have any problem with a guy like Valentine."

The first playoff match-up was against Randy Johnson and the Arizona Diamondbacks, a new team that had spent millions on marquee players including shortstop Jay Bell, third baseman Matt Williams, and outfielder Steve Finley. But the player the Mets feared most was the Diamondback's six-foot-ten pitcher, Randy Johnson.

★ ★ ★

Al Leiter: "I never batted against him, thank God. Look, anybody who throws in the mid-to-upper 90s is intimidating already, and then you've got a guy who's six-foot-ten, who's got a little bit of an unorthodox herky-jerky motion, left-handed, and who occasionally airmails one up onto the screen: he's intimidating.

"Before the game I sensed that the general feeling was that we weren't as cocky and confident as we should have been for a team that easily could have swept them. Our feeling was, 'Oh, gosh, we're facing Randy Johnson in one of the two games, and we'd better win one of them. But then Edgardo hit a big grand slam off reliever Bobby Chouinard and it certainly felt like a rout. Then Todd Stottlemyre shut us down 7–1 in game two, and we had to play the rest of the series without Mike Piazza. His thumb had been bent back and it was jammed. I remember during my game against Cincinnati that I pitched, I banged him up pretty good with my cutter, which is a boring slider that's pretty hard to catch. That kind of messed him up. He played game one against Arizona because he's a great player and we needed him in the lineup. But he was pretty sore, and by the third game he was very sore."

In 1999 Mike Piazza hit .303 with 40 home runs and drove in 124 runs. Observers wondered if the Mets could succeed in the playoffs without him. Todd Pratt, a journeyman who his teammates called "Tank," filled in.

Game three was played at Shea Stadium. Rick Reed, pitching to Pratt, worked six strong innings. Rickey Henderson had three hits and stole his sixth base of the series as the Mets won 9–2. At age forty, the future Hall of Famer still had a lot of life left in him.

Al Leiter: "Rickey had a hell of a year. But the substory which helped us win was Rickey's influence on Roger Cedeno. Roger was a young Latin player who had a lot of tools but maybe not the baseball moxie he needed, and Rickey gave that to him, took him under his wing. Roger stole a lot of bases in the first half. He kind of fell off the second half, I don't know why. But Rickey really worked with Cedeno and that was a big, big boost for us.

"Rickey never got good press. He usually said things that kind of put his foot in his mouth. Or maybe he didn't say things as they were intended. He got to the point where he was such a celebrity, a star figure, there was a perception of what people thought he was and also what he perceived himself to be, that he really didn't give a shit what people were writing or saying about him. He would pontificate with a group of beat writers, and I just thought of it as one big comedy routine. He was just jerking them around. He was having fun with it. He'd talk about himself in the third person. 'Rickey Henderson . . . ' He was having fun.

"Rickey is a Hall of Fame ball player. Absolutely, first ballot. Look, I enjoyed Rickey tremendously, and I've played with a lot of great players, and he will go down in my career as one I'll remember. I'll be able to say, 'I played with Rickey Henderson.'"

Leiter should have been the winner of game four. He had a 2–1 lead over the Diamondbacks when Armando Benitez allowed a two-run double to Jay Bell to take a one-run Arizona lead. But after Cedeno's sacrifice fly tied the game and sent it into extra innings, Pratt, a most improbable hero, was able to come up and hit a home run in the bottom of the tenth inning to eliminate Arizona and send the Mets to the next round of the playoffs against Atlanta.

Al Leiter: "I pitched that game, and I pitched great. We were up 1–0 when Greg Colbrunn hit a solo home run off me in the 5th. I went seven and two thirds.

"We blew it in the eight. Armando blew the game and I'm not saying this meanly or facetiously, but it's funny how things work out and heroes are created. It was the tenth inning. Todd Pratt came up and hit a home run to win it.

"It cost me a postseason win, which has still eluded me, but it also created a hero out of a guy who's been a backup. And the irony of the whole damn thing is that you'd have figured the hero to have been Mike Piazza, but the hero turned out to be Todd Pratt. Looking at it as a fan, I refer to the quote, 'That's baseball.' It was refreshing to see Todd end up being the hero.

"Todd is an excellent catcher. He's in a great position as the Mets' backup. Mike arguably is one of the best catchers ever and Todd fills in nicely when needed. By all rights he could be the starting catcher on many big league ball clubs. He's great defensively, has a great arm, and calls a great game. He's a great catcher. And periodically he'll get in streaks. The year Mike got hurt in Montreal and was on the DL, Todd filled in and won some games and really filled in great. Good for Todd.

"I think of Ron Swoboda, who certainly wasn't a great player, but what people will forever remember him for is the catch he made in right field with Tom Seaver on the mound. He's a hero. But if you look at his career numbers, he doesn't have hero numbers. That's refreshing. Here's Swoboda, one of the heroes of '69, and you think of Todd Pratt in '99, and albeit we didn't get into the World Series, but he *was* a hero."

The Atlanta Braves were winners in 9 of their 12 meetings against the Mets for the second season in a row. When Greg Maddux beat Masato Yoshii 4–2 and Kenny Rogers lost to Kevin Millwood 4–3, on Eddie Perez' home run, the numbers got worse. In the first two games John Olerud, Mike Piazza, and Robin Ventura were 1–21. The Braves seemed to have the better of the Mets and no one seemed to know what to do about it.

Al Leiter: "As the new Mets players came aboard—Mike and myself— the Braves [had been] pretty much kicking the Mets ass for a good period of time. New York, with its seven beat writers and all the media attention, begins calling them our nemesis and say the Braves are the team to beat, and the question is asked repeatedly, 'How come you can't beat the Atlanta Braves?' It becomes a mental nuisance more than anything else.

"So you go to the series and you don't feel inferior to them, but collectively you look around and you start doubting, 'Hey, can we beat these guys?' And then it's reinforced after you lose the first game and every beat writer asks you why you can't beat them. And it's a snowball that continues to roll, and somehow, some way, you have to stop it. How you stop it is [to have] some lucky, good, miraculous baseball thing happens, that turns it around, and in the second game it didn't happen. Then you start believing the press, you start believing the stories being written. You think, 'Maybe we *can't* beat these guys,' and then you're defeated before you go out there. You look at the club and say, 'Geez, we're just flat.' It looks like we're waiting to lose, yada, yada, yada, and sure enough, you lose."

The series went back to Shea Stadium. Al Leiter started against Tom Glavine. Leiter again was brilliant. He allowed but one cheap unearned run in the first inning. Glavine was better, and the Mets lost 1–0. The Mets were down 3 games to 0. A sweep seemed inevitable.

Al Leiter: "I started game three, and anytime you pitch against those guys, you know you have to nail it and I did, and the whole irony of this is—no, there was no irony, it just plain sucked—in the first inning of the game, I walked Gerald Williams. Bret Boone hit a ball back to me and I threw it away from Olerud, and it went down the right-field line, and he got to third base. Williams scored when Mike overthrew second trying to catch Boone, I got out of the inning, and I threw seven scoreless after that. We lost 1–0, on that wild throw to first.

"But, we didn't hit, and Glavine was Glavine. You know, I never understood how hitters become so mental when it comes to the pressure of the game or of one singular at bat. You see it a lot of times when teams press. No doubt about it, teams press, lineups press. You rely on your three, four, and five guys, and they don't do it, and now you're relying on six, seven, and eight, and they are guys you don't normally rely on, and the opposing pitcher is sitting in the dugout, and he's getting away with garbage because the batters are swinging at shit they have no right to be swinging at. You saw it when Bobby Jones pitched his one-hitter against the Giants. We went up 4–0 after the fifth inning and they were *done*. Cincinnati was done in the one-game playoff after we went up 2–0. Hitters just do that. Obviously, when you're the starting pitcher and you're watching this unfold, you want to yell or do something. That was my feeling in this game. When they won 1–0, the Braves were ahead three games to one, and it seemed that everything was turning out the way the experts said it would because we couldn't beat them. It was that way for two or three years."

The win gave the Braves their 12th out of 15, and 21st in the last 27 games. And yet, the Mets never quit. In game four the Braves led 2–1 after a pitchers' duel between John Smoltz and Rick Reed and were four outs away from sweeping when, in the eighth inning with two outs, closer John Rocker, who had to dodge plastic bottles and cups thrown from the Shea Stadium stands before entering the game, allowed a two-run single by John Olerud to give the Mets a 3–2 victory. Olerud, who was 0–9 against Rocker with five strikeouts, had homered earlier in the game off Smoltz. Said Bobby Valentine, "John has been a big hitter all his career. He's just a talented guy who goes unnoticed."

Al Leiter: "I've had the pleasure of playing with John off and on since he came on the professional scene in 1989 through my tenure with the Blue Jays up through '95. John's a great player with a great swing, a great first baseman, quiet. As far as teammates hanging out, he's not really interested in having a beer with anybody, which is fine. He's a great guy. I think of him as the ultimate consistent player, not Tony Gwynn caliber but very, very good. He hits .290, .300 every year, has very few cycles of ups and downs, and you can count on him. He was the glue that year. Mike, like most power hitters, has streaks. Robin had a great year. Ole has great eyes and you knew he was going to get on base. A great player, and the fact he doesn't say a whole lot lets him go unnoticed."

Game five of the Braves series was one of the great games in Mets history. Greg Maddux pitched for the Braves. Bobby Valentine gave the start to Masado Yoshii.

Al Leiter: "I don't know what turns guys on, but there was a point earlier in the year when the Mets were considering not only demoting Masado to the bull pen, but they were thinking about releasing him. And then at some moment in May or June, after having been demoted to the pen for a start or two, he just kicked it in, and he was our best pitcher in August. He just got real aggressive, got some balls, just got tough. I saw a different pitcher. He really got fired up. I liked it.

"He would get mad. He was so different from Nomo. You didn't know what Nomo was thinking. Yoshii would come in, pound his glove, punch his fist. Valentine said that was unusual for Japanese players. It was refreshing for me to see it. He really turned it around and he had a hell of a second half and really helped us out in the postseason."

In this game, though, Yoshii gave up the tying runs after John Olerud's two-run homer in the first inning. Valentine brought forty-one-year-old Orel Hershiser in to relieve in the fourth inning. Hershiser shut the door, allowing the Braves one harmless hit in the three-and-a-third innings he worked.

Al Leiter: "I loved having Orel on the team. Orel was so studious and cerebral about the game. He was another pitching coach. He wanted to talk about pitching and he could talk in depth, and he really, really cared about the guys. On numerous occasions he got a handful of us together, and we'd go out for dinner. We'd go to Morton's, a steakhouse, and it was fun. He was forty-one. He had kids almost in high school. [He'd say,] 'Hey guys, let's go.' You'd think he'd go back to the room and read a book, but he knew and understand the importance of camaraderie, and he wanted that kind of relationship. I loved him. I thought he was great.

"I enjoyed the fact that when we had side days—every starting pitcher has a day in which he throws on the side—Orel was always down there, and you'd have Dave Wallace, the pitching coach help as well. Orel was into mechanics. If Wally said something, Orel might interject, and we would all talk about what we thought. It was really, really helpful.

"In that game against the Braves, Orel totally stifled them. It was really great to see. I'm sure he doesn't put his performance up there with his great moments, but for me to see a guy who was 13–12 come in and do that, it kind of changed his whole season which had looked kind of mediocre into 'Wow, he really helped us!' "

In a game played through a steady rain in which both managers used a record 45 players, the score was still tied 2–2 in the thirteenth inning when the Braves' Keith Lockhart was waved around third on a double by Chipper Jones. Defensive replacement Melvin Mora, playing right field, threw a bullet to Alfonzo, who threw to Piazza at the plate for the out several steps before Lockhart arrived. The play allowed the game to continue.

Al Leiter: "Every year you see teams that make it and go on to win who have that no-name, unsung player who plays solidly over a short period of time. When Melvin got called up, nobody knew who he was. He came up, Maddux threw a fastball in there, and he hit a home run in Atlanta, and he went from there.

"On every team I've been on, there is always that guy. Pat Hentgen in '93. Livan Hernandez in '97. For us, Melvin was it. He was a spark plug, and he helped. Certainly that was a frozen moment of this guy's skill as a baseball player, because it was a flawless, well-executed relay that ultimately helped us win the game."

The Braves took the lead in the top of the fifteenth inning on a two-out triple by pesky Lockhart. Then in the bottom of the inning against a kid reliever by the name of Kevin McGlinchy, the Mets Shawon Dunston battled before singling sharply up the middle. Pinch hitter Matt Franco walked and Alfonzo moved the runners up with a sacrifice bunt.

McGlinchy walked Olerud intentionally to load the bases. He then walked Pratt unintentionally to tie the game and bring Robin Ventura, who was mired in a 1–18 slump, to the plate.

Ventura swung and sent a long drive into the right-field stands for what should have been a grand-slam home run. Dunston ran home with the winning run. Pratt, thinking the ball had caromed off the wall, touched second, ran back toward first and embraced Ventura. When they hugged, Ventura was called out for passing Pratt. None of the other runners were allowed to score.

The Mets had won 4–3. Pratt had cost Ventura his grand salami and three rbis, but the wackiness of the scenario sent it into the history books as one of the great moments in Mets history. Had Ventura not won the game, Leiter would have been the fifth Mets starting pitcher to go into the game. He was warming up in the bull pen when the ball was hit.

Al Leiter: "Robin was playing that game injured. I knew that, because right after the season both of us went in and had knee surgery. We were both kind of gimping around. Robin being the true professional he is, wasn't going to complain about it, because nobody wants to hear it. You are either going to play or you don't play. If you're going to play, shut up and play. I understand that, he understands that. We knew that.

"What really stunk for me, we were down to no more pitchers. I was in the bull pen throwing with Rick Reed. Bobby had Reed and me throwing, albeit I was supposed to throw easy. I hadn't warmed up in the bull pen since '93. Valentine came down and said, 'Can you go down? We don't have anybody left.' I said, 'Of course.' You put your balls on the line and give it all you got, because this is it. If we don't win, we're going home.

"Reed was slated to pitch game seven and me six, so I guess they figured he had another day or two to recuperate, so he was going to be the pitcher had Robin not gotten a hit in the sixteenth. But I remember warming up and Rick and I are getting hot, and Robin roped it. I was looking through the bull pen at Shea, and we knew it was a home run. Everybody else thought it was a ground-rule double. It went to the right of us, and I remember sprinting out from there and running down to congratulate the team.

"Robin should have had a grand-slam home run, but Todd obviously didn't know the ball was over the fence. I guess his only concern was that it automatically scored the winning run, and who cares about Robin's home run? Look, Tank didn't see the ball go over the fence, and Tank's a real fired-up guy who's got a bit of the football mentality in him. All he knew was that we had won the game, and he was excited.

"I think Robin was a little upset, because hell, I'd want a grand slam in the LCS rather than a single. He lost a grand slam and three rbis. But, deep down, I'm sure Robin didn't care."

After two heart-stopping, game-ending comebacks, the Mets now trailed the Braves three games to two. No team had ever come back from a 3–0 deficit. Al Leiter started game six, played in Atlanta. The Braves led 5–0 before he could catch his breath.

In a game where Leiter was unable to get a single out, the Mets once again showed their ability to bounce back, only to lose the game in the bottom of the tenth inning on a bases-loaded walk by pitcher Kenny Rogers. It was a hard ending to a brilliant season.

Al Leiter: "I had played ten years in the majors and had experience pitching in the World Series, and you always know when it's going to be a bit of a struggle. Warming up that night, the aches and pains were a lot more apparent as I threw. I kind of figured this was going to be one of those games where I'd have to figure out some moxie to get them out, cause it was not going to be on sheer stuff. And that's a negative thought, a lack of confidence going in. But, I wasn't thinking I wasn't going to get an out. If I remember correctly, I hit the first guy, walked the next guy, and then hit Chipper, and then I had a ground ball go past Robin. It was bing, bing, bing, bing, and I'm out of there."

But, the plucky Mets came back, powered by a Mike Piazza home run off John Smoltz, pitching in relief, and New York even went ahead in the ninth and tenth inning. Both times, however, the Mets bull pen was unable to hold on, and the Braves came back to tie the score in another incredibly memorable postseason contest.

Al Leiter: "After Bobby took me out, I went up to the clubhouse for a couple of innings. I put my dry clothes on and came back down. How exciting! Cause Smoltz is a guy who has been Mike's nemesis. Mike never did anything against him careerwise. And when Mike hit that home run to tie up the game, I thought for sure we had it.

"And we went up twice, in the eight and again in the tenth, so, even though I know I was one of the reasons we lost, we had the opportunity to win twice, and that made my winter a *little* bit better, but still not great. Obviously, baseball is a team game and all of that, but if Millwood would have shut us out 5–0, I would have felt *really* crappy about what went on."

In the bottom of the eleventh inning, with the scored tied at 9, Rogers allowed a double to Gerald Williams. Bobby Valentine then ordered Rogers to intentionally walk Chipper Jones and Brian Jordan, hoping for a force at the plate. Andruw Jones, the young Braves star, was up next, and Rogers, pitching ever so carefully, ran the count to 3–2 before missing by a hair with a change-up just off the plate. Williams came home and the Braves were 10–9 winners. Said Bobby Valentine after the game, "We gave everything we had. There's not a lot left out on that field."

Al Leiter: "Look, you think, he's a major leaguer getting paid a lot of money, he ought to be able to throw a strike, but you know, it's not that easy. I felt bad for Kenny. You hope for anything but a walk. You want a guy to earn his way. But it happens. Kenny got crucified for it, but I don't know why.

"It's really unfair to Kenny, because he got us five wins. He was a very good pitcher, a very good acquisition. He helped us get to that point. It was just one of those things.

"But the press made a big deal of his not flourishing with the Yankees, and here during a moment of unbelievable pressure, he didn't do it, so they wrote, 'We told you so.' There weren't a lot of Kenny Rogers fans. Oh, well. People said to me, 'How was your winter?'

"I looked at it that it was great to have gotten to that point. We were one pitch away from going to game seven, and I know the Braves didn't want to have to play us in that game. Tommy Glavine was quoted as saying, 'I didn't want to have to start game seven,' because the momentum clearly was turning. If we had won game six, that would have been games four, five, and six, and if I were in Tommy's shoes, I wouldn't have wanted that either. We were feeling really good about ourselves.

"I look at our team and I feel that year we didn't overachieve. I don't think we were better than the Braves and we certainly made a series out of it.

"The series ended in Atlanta and some guys actually left for home right from Turner Field. Mike drove back to Philly. Kenny got in a rental car and drove right to Florida. It was a sad moment."

forty-nine

Wild Card Winners

The first season of the new millennium opened with the Mets playing against Sammy Sosa and the Chicago Cubs in Japan as baseball began tip-toeing toward international play (not counting Canada). In Japan the Mets discovered the talents of a powerful new outfielder, Benny Agbayani, who like Mets pitcher Sid Fernandez before him, was a native of Hawaii.

Al Leiter: "I was in Port St. Lucie while the team was in Japan. I started opening day at Shea against San Diego. I wasn't going to pitch in any of the games in Japan, wasn't going to get any work so there was no reason for me to be jetlagged for game one at home. So I stayed back.

"Before the trip there was a handful of players who were excited about going, another handful begrudging having to go, and a small group pissed off they had to go. But when everyone came back to New York, I heard great stories from every single player. They all loved the experience. They had a great time. They wore out Rapungi, the English-speaking section of Tokyo, a fun area where there was a Hard Rock Cafe and a Tony Roma's.

"In the second game in Japan, Benny Agbayani, who was picked by the Mets in the thirtieth round of the draft in 1993, hit a grand-slam home run. I didn't know Benny that well—he was up a little bit the year before—but talking to the guys who played with him in the minors, they told me, 'This guy can flat out hit.'"

Agbayani was a backup to Rickey Henderson, but on May 13, the Mets released Henderson, who was embroiled in a contract dispute, and turned the job over to him. Manager Bobby Valentine made the big Hawaiian the leadoff batter in his lineup.

Al Leiter: "For a big guy, Benny can run. He was a running back in college. He was fast and he just put on a lot of muscle."

Two weeks later, on May 29, the Mets suffered a terrible loss when acrobatic shortstop Rey Ordonez broke his left forearm and was out for the season. Ordonez, considered the best-fielding shortstop in the league, if not all of baseball, would be difficult to replace. Rookie Melvin Mora was given the job temporarily. Steve Phillips, needing better defense and desiring a veteran at the position, by the end of July traded Mora to the Baltimore Orioles for an excellent fielder, Mike Bordick.

Al Leiter: "I started the game in which Rey was hurt. It happened on a ball hit to first. Todd Zeile, who replaced John Olerud at first in 2000, threw the ball to Rey, and as he was coming across the bag he hit the runner's helmet, cracking him in the arm and breaking it. That was obviously devastating. Melvin filled in until we traded him to Baltimore for Mike Bordick.

"Melvin was doing all right, but the thing was, when you lose Rey Ordonez, you realize that defensively you're missing a great deal. At the time, Bordick was going to be a free agent at the end of the season and he was having a hell of a first half, made the All Star team, and Steve traded for him. It was a perfect fit.

"When Mike came over he hit the first pitch he saw off Andy Benes, a home run. We all thought, 'Wow, this is going to be great.' Mike is one of the true professionals in the game. What a great, great guy! He didn't hit as well as he did in Baltimore, but he was steady defensively."

A highlight of the 2000 summer for Mets fans came in June when the Atlanta Braves came to Shea for the first time. The previous December, Braves closer John Rocker had been quoted in *Sports Illustrated* as saying he found New York "depressing."

He went on, "Imagine taking the 7 train . . . looking like you're in Beirut next to some kid with purple hair, next to some queer with AIDS, right next to some dude who got out of jail for the fourth time, right next to some twenty-year-old mom with four kids."

In short, a taunting Rocker, crowing over Atlanta's dominance of the Mets, was rubbing the city's nose in its diversity. Rocker, displaying bravado, told reporters he intended to take the subway to the game. After being warned against it by Mayor Rudy Giuliani, he instead took an unmarked town car. When he arrived, he found that the mayor, a law-and-order devotee, had assigned more than 500 of New York's finest to make sure nothing untoward happened to him at Shea. When Rocker arrived, he found a full house waiting for him. Every seat was taken. Some seats bought from scalpers went for as high as $435 for a pair at field-level.

Al Leiter: "That was a complete sideshow, *his* show. We could care less. What we did care for was the safety of our fans and the players. I envisioned that there was going to be a fan or two who would bring something into the game and try to reach [Rocker] to hit him with something. I thought, 'The guy who has the battery in the upper deck, and doesn't quite have John Rocker's arm who whips the battery and hits a little girl in the eighth row instead, and then what do we have?'

"But the New York police handled it. It was overkill. They brought in 500 cops. They had SWAT teams. They envisioned some serious stuff. And luckily, nothing happened.

"I was glad Bobby Cox got him out there right away. He came in, got the save, and that was it. From that point on, it was no big deal.

"All the stories were written and nothing happened."

The next day the Braves were whipping up on the Mets by the score of 8–1 when the Mets scored ten runs off Atlanta starter Kevin Millwood and a couple of relievers. The capper was a three-run home run by Mike Piazza off Terry Mulholland. It was an important, memorable midseason win that really lit a fire under the Mets. The Mets, with a 45–32 record, were now only two games behind the Braves.

Al Leiter: "I was driving home during that inning and I could not get out of my car. The reason I left was because whenever there's a day game following a night game, especially if there's a big crowd, the starting pitcher for the following day leaves a little early to beat the crowd, and also to get home at a reasonable hour. We were down by seven runs and I left Shea in that inning. I usually sit for seven innings and then shower and get out before the end of the game so I could beat the crowd and get home before midnight.

"But I'll never forget it, because I enjoyed it. I was listening to Gary Cohen and Bob Murphy—who I love to listen to anyway, cause I grew up on his voice—and the picture was painted so beautifully. I understand why people prefer to listen to a baseball game rather than watch it on TV—they did such a great job, and I was a fan. I was no longer a teammate. I was truly a fan, listening to this inning develop, and Mike hit the home run, I was sitting on Eighty-third Street and First Avenue just screaming, imagining what it must have looked like.

"My garage is underneath my building, and I could not get out of my car, because I was afraid I'd miss the signal and miss what happened. So I sat in the car outside my apartment building hearing Fonzie hit a ground ball, and then a walk, and then Piazza had a long at bat before homering. That's what I remember. I enjoyed it."

In July 2000 there was another exciting sideshow. The Mets had been rained out of a game at Yankee Stadium earlier in the year, and so the Yankees and Mets scheduled a doubleheader—the first game was played at Shea, the second at Yankee Stadium. The players thought it a gimmick. Fans sold out both games.

Al Leiter: "George [Steinbrenner] wanted his gate, and we owed them a rain-out from a Sunday night game earlier in the year, and they thought it would be a neat thing, something that hadn't happened in a a hundred years. The guys were behind it. I thought it was kind of a nuisance. It was okay."

In the second game Roger Clemens of the Yankees beaned Mike Piazza and gave him a concussion. Leiter, who himself has hit batters, was contemptuous that he did it, but he stopped short of accusing Clemens of trying to bean the Mets star.

Al Leiter: Because I'm a pitcher and I've hit my share of batters in my career—never, ever was any of them intentional other than one time, and I didn't hit the guy in the head. I was told by a manager to flip him, or knock him down, and it was a while back, not with the Mets.

"Mike was wearing Roger out. He hit a home run off him, and the year before hit a couple off of him. Mike had his number, so to speak, and I think Roger was going to establish himself early, and he came high and tight.

"Now the difference between coming high and tight and hitting a guy in the head is the difference between releasing in front of your ear or one or two inches to the right of your ear. After the fact I think it was kind of cheesy, not a good thing, poor judgment on Roger's ability to throw the ball effectively inside wild. Especially if you're trying to knock a guy back.

"I throw inside a lot and I'll hit guys, but honestly, the thought is not to try to hit him or even think about knocking a guy back. But, when you're thinking, All right, I have a purpose here. We, as major league [pitchers] have the ability to find that window, that release point, and know it's going to be somewhere around the chest, the midsection, the armpit. And Roger missed. So, I don't know. Even with all that said, I don't see Roger trying to hit Mike in the head.

"The real amazing thing is that Mike has a history of being a hitter who never ever swings at the first pitch. Therefore, if you know you're taking, you have no intention of stepping toward the plate or being aggressive at all. And that was Mike's thing. Either the pitch just shocked the hell out of him and was too fast for him to get out of the way, or it was just a straight laser right at his head. But you watch, Mike never swings at the first pitch. At least 95 percent of the time he doesn't swing. So, factoring that in and Roger still able to pop him in the head, that was something.

"Mike was out a few days with a slight concussion."

By September 2000 the Mets were still in the hunt, led by a solid pitching staff and perhaps the finest bull pen in baseball. One reason the pen was so good was that John Franco, the Grand Old Man of the team, agreed to cede his closer's role to youngster Armando Benitez without throwing a tantrum or demanding a trade. Franco, who like Leiter was a Mets fan as a child, was told by manager Bobby Valentine that though he was no longer closing, his value had not diminished.

By September 1, the thirty-nine-year-old Franco, who had 420 saves, only 58 shy of the career record set by Lee Smith, had pitched in 23 straight games without giving up a run. Benitez, tall and strong, had 36 saves going into September.

★ ★ ★

Al Leiter: "We call John the 'Godfather' for many reasons, starting with his Italian descent. I was very lucky to have played against Johnny and then to get an opportunity to play on his team, and to have such a great teammate.

"Earlier, I was talking about Orel and the way he organized get-togethers. John is *the* organizer. He makes it a point to get everybody together somewhere, somehow. He really is *the* clubhouse leader. He's vocal enough to speak up, and he has the respect of everyone.

"When they made Armando—a great thrower with great stuff, closer stuff—the closer, it was only because John was getting up in age, not because of heart or ability. When Bobby made that decision, Johnny wasn't happy about it. Here he was, second all-time in saves to Lee Smith, the number-one left-handed closer—certainly when you get that close to those great numbers, you think about being in the Hall of Fame. That's something John dreams about. But Johnny didn't bitch. He knew it wasn't healthy to be disruptive and start complaining. 'Here's another kid living out his boyhood dream of playing for his team, the New York Mets. He was a big Mets fan growing up in Brooklyn. His dad used to take him and his brother to the games. We talk fondly about the times we got to Shea and did all the things fans did as kids.

"Armando, meanwhile, racked up 36 saves by September 1. He's got top closer stuff and like any young closer, there's the constant learning curve. He's learning and he'll continue to learn. Every pitcher should feel that way. I feel that way after thirteen years. Tommy John felt that way after twenty-six years.

"But clearly, Armando has superior stuff, a 95-mile-an-hour-or-better fastball. He has a slider that hitters think is a split—just nasty—and he's an imposing figure on the mound at six-four with legs and arms flying all over the place. He's very intimidating."

On September 2 the Mets, sporting the best record in baseball, climbed into first place ahead of the Atlanta Braves, the first time the team was in first since September 1990. The media made a big deal over it. The players were less impressed because the Braves, nipping at their heels, were still the Braves.

Al Leiter: "We didn't celebrate. Not at all, because, look, the Braves weren't going anywhere. Of course not. We didn't feel we were going to overtake them and put on the afterburner and they'd be in the rearview mirror. The reality was that it would be tooth and nail right to the end. We couldn't assume anything. And it was short-lived."

The Mets proceeded to lose seven of their next eight games, going into a third-straight September swoon. The lone win was by 3–2. One of those losses was 2 to 0 to the Philadelphia Phillies. Mets starter Mike Hampton, acquired in a trade from Houston after winning 22 games in 1999, allowed a two-run home run in the eighth inning to Scott Rolen. When Bobby Valentine took him out, he was upset he had to come out of the game. He went into the dugout and tried to tear up the place.

Mike would prove a valuable addition to the Mets, but he would leave the Mets at the end of the season, yearning for a quieter place where he could hunt and fish and not have to answer questions from eleven metropolitan dailies.

Al Leiter: "He pitched a great game against the Phillies. He was pitching a shutout and late in the game Rolen hit a two-run home run, and right after that, Bobby took him out. To add insult to injury, Mike was thinking, 'If I'm good enough to get to that point, and then I blow it by giving up the home run, you're not going to give me a chance to win this game after I put my balls on the line for nine innings?' When Bobby yanked him, he completely lost it.

"I got very friendly with Mike and Connie, his wife. He was a great teammate and a good guy. Look, here's a guy from the northern Florida town of Brooksville, gets drafted by the Mariners, makes it to the big leagues with Seattle, a small-market club. But he didn't establish himself. He went to Houston, Texas, a southern cowboy town, not big at all—I think there's only one daily paper down there—so the media attention and coverage isn't great. He gets very comfortable and then he gets traded to big, scary New York, where the media attention can be overwhelming. In New York, Mike was a big story, and if you don't feel like talking to some beat writers or do some bullshit story every day, it becomes a nuisance.

"He came on as the new ace of the staff, or at least ace/1a, and he started off on a bad note, putting more pressure on himself, and free agency was looming at the end of the year, and you find yourself getting a little nastier, and he internalized some things, and I'm saying all this as speculation—he never told me these things. I can paint the picture, because I've been there. And that was it. He left.

"The mistake he made was getting an apartment in Manhattan. I love the city. But his apartment was on Central Park West, and if you know the city, you have to go crosstown and hit the FDR Drive and then go up the drive to the Triborough Bridge. My apartment is on 84th Street on the upper East Side and I go up to 96th, boom, boom, boom, I'm at Shea Stadium literally in fifteen minutes. For Mike there were times going crosstown when it might take him an hour.

"It got to the point where his wife didn't like it, yada, yada, yada, and it was disappointing because we are friends, and I would have loved for him to come back, because he's a great pitcher, and he's going to continue to be a great pitcher."

The next day the Mets again lost to the Phils. The loser was the wild-and-wacky reliever Turk Wendell, known for chewing licorice during ball games and brushing his teeth between each inning. After this game, Wendell took his glove and throw it into the stands. He told reporters, "It was like if you were dating a girl and not having a good time. You dump her and get a new one."

Al Leiter: "Turk's a good-hearted guy, and he means well, but he's definitely a couple of cards short of a full deck. Somebody might say, 'That's the pot calling the kettle black,' cause I can get pretty fired up and goofy out there, but from his habit of eating licorice and brushing his teeth to having a tooth from every animal he's ever killed on a chain around his neck, he's definitely the wackiest guy I ever played with.

"With all that said, it's a term of endearment. I do like him, he's a great teammate, and he's great with kids. He's just wacky. He's a wack job. I'll walk by him, and our salutation to each other is this: I'll say, 'Hey, weirdo,' and he'll say, 'Hey, freak.' As for his throwing his glove, that was part of the show, too. He wanted to get on the ESPN highlight clips."

On September 10 Al Leiter proved his value as a stopper as he shutout the Phillies 3–0 on five hits. Before the game he told pitching coach Dave Wallace he wanted to go nine. During the game Robin Ventura, given the day off, entertained his teammates with imitations of Steve Phillips, Bobby Valentine, and some teammates, and during the game Valentine added to the merriment when he donned his wig-and-sunglasses disguise that had created such a fuss earlier in the season. Leiter was duly impressed with Ventura's abilities as a mimic and Bobby's ability to keep the team loose.

Al Leiter: "The first time we played the Yankees at the Stadium, we had a long rain delay and Robin dressed up like Mike Piazza and ran around the infield in the rain, like what Rick Dempsey did years ago. He loosened up the guys during that first Yankee series. He dressed up in Mike's uniform 31, put a fake mustache on, and ran around the bases. It was hilarious.

"Mike Kay, who does the Yankee broadcasts, was talking during the rain delay, and he said, 'I can't believe what an idiot Piazza is. He can get hurt. Why is he doing this? This is so foolish.' Kay actually thought it was Mike goofing around. All the Yankees were laughing. We were saying, 'George would never allow them to do that.'

"But because Bobby does his thing, guys feel comfortable and at ease to do stuff on their own."

After losing the opening game of the series with the Milwaukee Brewers on September 12, the Mets eighth loss in ten games, the vets held a team meeting the next day before going out against the Brew Crew. Leiter was one of those who led the meeting.

Al Leiter: "Sometimes the time is right for players only to articulate their feelings. Whenever you put coaches, the manager, trainer, or anybody else in the room, there may be that one guy who is afraid to get something off his chest. So we prefaced it very, very carefully, and sensitively to Bobby that, 'Look, it's nothing against you. Nothing against the staff. It's clearly for us to have good dialog.' And he certainly was fine with it, and a few of the veterans, Johnny, myself, Piazza, Edgardo, and Lenny Harris, spoke up, and we just said the basic stuff all major leaguers know. 'Let's get back to it, stop thinking about the negative things. Do your share. You're 1/25th of this club.' Just basic shit you'd say to advise someone to be all they can be.

"The team was very, very close. Since I've been a Met, [the team is] the closest it's ever been. The '97 Marlins team was very close, too."

After the meeting the Mets went out and stomped the Brewers by the score of 10–2. The next day outfielder Jay Payton starred, leading off the ninth with a double and eventually scoring the tying run, and then hitting a three-run home run in the tenth inning to win it. Before that at bat, Leiter called the free-swinging rookie aside for some advice.

"Be patient," Leiter told him.

The first pitch was a slider. Payton hit it over the left-center field fence.

Al Leiter: "It's not me saying anything as a hitting coach, per se, but the angle I was coming from—I talk a lot to the players about a lot of different things that could help and try not to be overbearing. Hopefully a guy will respect and appreciate that I'm actually trying to help him and some good will come of it, and he'll be helped. That's what's great about a team. That's what's great about a coaching staff and a manager who's not insecure and doesn't mind a player helping, like Orel Hershiser or me giving advice. All I did was tell him to be more selective. Then he hit it out."

Despite the team's fine play, the Mets could not catch the Braves. After losing two games to Atlanta in Atlanta, on September 20, Bobby Valentine again opened his mouth without thinking—Fred Wilpon had warned him in spring training to keep away from controversy.

He told two dozen reporters, "If we don't make the playoffs,' said Valentine, "I will gladly take Fred off the hook," meaning he'd resign as manager. But, this time no one was even considering such a move. Valentine, realizing he was being defensive for no real reason, quickly retracted his words, apologizing for talking without thinking. In New York, though, public utterances cannot be taken back. For better or for worse, the Mets manager was becoming Billy Martin without the booze. The headlines were his, whether he wanted them or not.

Fortunately for Valentine, Leiter pitched one of his greatest games against the Braves. He had a perfect game going through the sixth, as Piazza, Zeile, and Alfonzo homered. The win gave the Mets a five-and-a-half game lead in the Wild Card race. There was no question about the Mets making the playoffs this year.

Al Leiter: "That [game] was really, really good. Hell, every game I go out, my whole thought process the last few years of my career is to just try to go out and execute a quality pitch. I try to stay aggressive and do the things a major- league pitcher has to do to try to make outs.

"At the time when I was through six innings, I started thinking, Hey, who knows? Maybe I'll be the one to throw the first no-hitter for the Mets. And since I've already pitched a no-hitter for Florida, it's no longer a dream. Like anything else in life, you think, 'Not me.' I could never do it. And then when you finally do it, you realize it's a real possibility. So yeah, I was going for it. We had the lead against Millwood, and that was nice.

"And then Robin made an error between his legs. Hell, Robin is one of the best third basemen the Mets have ever had. And then I had a real tough time with that Furcal guy. He fouled off at least seven or eight, and then he just rapped one to left. I was disappointed, because I really felt that had I gotten through that inning, who knows? But it didn't happen, so I'm still hoping to either be the first Met to do it or at least to witness it."

In the next game, played against the Phils in Philadelphia, Mike Piazza, who hails from Morristown, just outside the City of Brotherly Love, brought everyone Philadelphia cheese steaks before the game. He then went out and hit two home runs to win the game. One couldn't help notice the connection between Piazza home runs and Mets victories.

Al Leiter: "Look, anytime you've got a guy who's as explosive and as great as Piazza is, and he's the center of your lineup . . . the whole theory of lineups and the mentality of the hitter kind of plays off each other. Certainly when your big guy is producing, it makes the Jay Paytons and other guys down the line that much more comfortable and less pressured and yada, yada, yada. They relax, and they perform.

"Mike's very, very aware of that. He *knows* that. Sometimes our lineup relies on him more than he would like, but he handles it, and has certainly come through for the Mets."

On September 27, 2000, the Mets clinched the Wild Card spot with a 6–2 win over the Atlanta Braves at Shea Stadium. It was the first time in Mets history that the team made back-to-back appearances in the postseason.

There was a great deal of commentary about the fact that the Mets had such a hard time winning games against the Braves. The Mets players knew that to win the National League pennant, they would either have to beat their nemesis, or someone else would have to knock Atlanta off for them. Few in the press thought it would happen.

★ ★ ★

Al Leiter: "Hearing all the talk about the Braves didn't anger us, if any-thing, it gave us an anxious feeling, or the feeling of stress and concern that a) you have to field these questions, and b) you have to look at the reality of it, and the reality was that we didn't beat them. They kind of had our number. So, in some way, everyone tries to do their own little voodoo-type way to switch the luck, or change the formula to win, not think about it, think about it, don't talk about it. . . . It was a concern."

Said John Franco, "Come Sunday, there will be 22 teams going home. We'll still be playing. That's an accomplishment in itself. Once you're in, anything can happen."

fifty

A Pennant—At Last

The first-round playoff opponents would be the San Francisco Giants, led by star outfielder Barry Bonds. In the third inning of game one the Mets chances dimmed considerably when Bonds hit a drive off pitcher Mike Hampton toward the right-field wall of Pac Bell Park. Veteran Derek Bell fell awkwardly going after the ball and badly sprained his right ankle. He would be lost for the rest of the playoffs. The hit fell for a triple and Hampton seemed to have lost his composure. Two batters later Ellis Burks hit the foul pole for a three-run homer and a 5–1 victory.

Valentine surprised the experts when he chose to play little-known outfielder Timo Perez in Bell's place. He had two veterans, Darryl Hamilton and Bubba Trammell, the latter acquired on July 28 from the Tampa Bay Devil Rays, but instead opted to play a rookie who had been with the Mets only a month.

Al Leiter: "Surprise? Yeah, a little bit. The safe bet would have been to stick with a veteran guy, a guy like Hamilton, who had a track record and a history in postseason, and you don't have to worry about a young player who may succumb to the pressures of the postseason.

"But from what we heard—the scouting reports came in saying that Timo Perez via Japan and wherever the heck else he was playing, the guy was terrific. I remember Darryl Hamilton coming back from rehab saying, 'This guy can be and might be a star.' I said, 'Really?' He said, 'For a little guy, he has power, he has a great arm, he plays terrific defense, he's got speed. Basically, he kind of has it all.'

"I said, 'Great?' I wondered what was he doing playing in Japan? Maybe he just turned it around. Bobby went on what he heard from the scouts and the player development people. He figured, 'Why not?' And what the Mets have gone to since I've been here is clearly that pitching and defense is more important than offense. So long as you have a guy like Piazza who can bang out a three-run home run, Bobby's thing is, let's have a good, strong defense, and clearly, Timo was better defensively than Hambone or Bubba.

"Nothing against Darryl, I like him a lot, but this guy has a great arm, and speed. He's really good!"

In game two against the Giants Al Leiter started and as he has done so often in the postseason, he pitched brilliantly but failed to get the win. He was leading 4–1 going into the last of the ninth inning when Valentine brought Armando Benitez into the game in relief. Benitez allowed the Giants' J. T. Snow to pinch-hit a three-run home run to tie the game.

In the tenth inning, though, the Mets won when Hamilton, out much of the year with a toe injury, doubled with two outs. Jay Payton, who much of the year took his place in left, then singled him home.

Timo Perez also had a great game. He had three hits, all with two outs, in his first postseason start. His two-run single in the second inning would have made him the hero if Snow hadn't tied the game in the ninth. Though Leiter didn't get the win, he didn't hold it against Benitez. He was just glad the Mets got the win.

Al Leiter: "I hadn't run out of steam, but I *had* thrown a lot of pitches. With a three-run lead and a high pitch count, knowing Bobby, I had hopefully three or four more starts, and it was clearly the right move. Armando was well rested. He hadn't pitched the day before.

"Look, I never, ever say anything bad about a reliever blowing games. I know Armando and I talked to Johnny Franco about it, and Johnny had talked to Armando about it. It got to the point where, for whatever reasons, a starter will get in the head of his own closer, because for whatever reason he's blown a few saves for the starter, and then it comes into his own head, and basically Armando expressed that after the game.

"He said he felt bad and he was sorry, the usual stuff. It was, 'Gosh, I'm sick of blowing your games.' Cause he had done it before. I totally understand it. It's part of the game, and yeah, it was upsetting, but it turned out okay. J. T. got the homer, tied the game up, and we proceeded to win it rather dramatically in the tenth, so hell, we won the game.

"I know so much has been said—I've now broken the record for the most career postseason starts without a win, but aside for a game or two, I've been pretty good. I still believe, and I continue to believe, I could care less if I don't get *any* wins as long as I get the ring that says 'World Champions.' That's all that matters to me."

For game three the series moved to Shea Stadium. The Mets trailed 2–1 in the eighth inning when with Lenny Harris on second, Edgardo Alfonzo singled him in to tie the game.

Al Leiter: "Outside of Mike, Alfonzo gets the big press play because of his superior power and his physique, and his being an intimidating force consistency-wise. If I were an everyday player, I would even appreciate more of what Edgardo Alfonzo brings to the table, because everyday players— not only our players but opposing players—view him as a really, really terrific ballplayer.

"He's a great hitter. He's probably the most consistent that we have, especially since Olerud left. You know he's going to give a good at bat. He doesn't go into too many valleys and peaks. He's really, really steady. He's turned out to be a big force in our lineup and one of the better players in the league."

For the second night in a row, the game went into extra innings. With one out in the bottom of the thirteenth, Benny Agbayani, one of Bobby Valentine's reclamation projects, ended the five-and-a-half-hour marathon when he hit a long drive over the left-center field wall off Giant reliever Aaron Fultz.

More than 56,000 fans began chanting his name, "Benny, Benny, Benny." Agbayani had not been expected to start the season with the Mets. Said manager Bobby Valentine after the game, "I don't know where we'd be without him."

Al Leiter: "That really is a tribute to Valentine. Because Bobby is a little controversial and really could care less about what people think, he kind of does things that are untraditional and not the safe bet. He had Benny at

Norfolk when Benny turned his career around, and he believed in him just as he believed in Rick Reed. It's really a tribute to Bobby not to give up on a guy like that, and to give a guy like Timo Perez an opportunity to play."

In game four Bobby Jones, the Mets ace back in '95, but in June demoted to the minors only to return with a renewed sense of purpose, clinched the series against the Giants with a remarkably easy one-hitter. The only hit was a line-drive double by Jeff Kent that grazed the top of third baseman Robin Ventura's glove. If Ventura could have jumped two inches higher, Jones would have had the Mets' first no-hitter. Ventura more than made up for it with a two-run home run in the first inning.

Al Leiter: "What was most memorable was at the final out, you look back and you realize Bobby was one out away from throwing the first no-hitter in the history of the franchise.

"It was kind of uneventful. It wasn't very exciting. They didn't lay down, but we went up early, and for me the most exciting thing that came from it, Bobby deserved so much praise and credit because we won, but he lost a little bit of it from all the talk about our going on to the championship series.

"What really made me happy for Bobby was that earlier in the year and since my tenure with the Mets, he kind of lost his place as the Mets ace, and here was a quality pitcher, an All Star, who had basically become an afterthought. And for him to step up and have big balls and go out there and be aggressive and do what he had to do to dominate, it was something. He would have to tell you, but I'm sure he would say it was very, very satisfying in his career, because not only was it, 'I pitched a great game,' but 'fuck everybody who thought I sucked.' I sensed that. And good for him.

"And that's what happened. He came back from the minors. There were a lot of questions about his arm. He definitely lost his fastball somewhere, and he stepped it up, and what I always perceive as pitchers getting after it and having some balls—like what I said about Masado earlier and Glendon Rusch, you try to have that demeanor and that look that, 'I'm coming at you,' even if it's only an 84-mile-an-hour fastball. Bobby picked it up and really pitched well when he came back."

The Mets' next opponent would not be hated Atlanta, but rather the red-hot St. Louis Cardinals, led by Jim Edmonds and Will Clark. But Mark McGwire, their superstar home-run hitter, was injured so badly he would not be able to do much more than pinch-hit twice. When the Redbirds swept the pain-in-the-ass Braves, the Mets players rejoiced.

Al Leiter: "It absolutely made everyone's job easier. I felt like, heck no, I didn't want to have to prove we could beat the Braves to go into the World Series. Screw that. The Cardinals were good. They whipped the Braves' pretty handily, swept them. So we knew we were facing a real hot team. They were really hitting the ball well. Will Clark stepped up and Jim Edmunds had a great year. They were really getting it together.

"We knew they wouldn't be pushovers, but I felt with their left-handed dominant lineup, with me, Hampton, and Rusch, I thought we had a good shot at the Cards. And it turned out that way."

Mike Hampton threw seven shutout innings en route to a 6–2 win in the series opener in St. Louis. In game two Leiter got the start. He allowed but three runs in seven innings and had the lead, but this time Franco blew the save before the Mets won it on a single by Jay Payton.

The Cards won game three behind Andy Benes, but the Mets rebounded to win 10–6 in game four behind the fine relief pitching of Rusch. Hampton got the call in game five and it was clear early on that the Mets were going to win it. No Cardinal runner reached second base. Throughout the game, Shea Stadium was loud and boisterous and shook like it was hosting a rock-and-roll concert.

Al Leiter: "We had come from St. Louis, where it was unbelievable how much the fans were into it. Their sound system was so loud it was intimidating at times. When I was on the mound, you felt the fans.

"If there is one thing about a visiting player coming into New York, especially playing against the Mets for some reason, they don't like coming to Shea. It's not the prettiest stadium, it's not the best facilities, the clubhouse is old, and then you have to deal with the New York fan. As we know, he can be obnoxious. That all works to our favor.

"When we got back to New York, Johnny Franco and I complained to the front office. We were talking to Mark Bingham [Senior Vice-President of Marketing and Broadcasting]. We told him we wanted to see this place rock, and he brought in rock-concert speakers for the Cardinal series, right over the center-field fence, and they just rocked it. Yeah. No doubt about it. And it was great.

"We liked it. We thought it had an intimidating effect on the opposing team. Who knows? But it was definitely a fired-up atmosphere."

The Mets jumped out to a 3–0 lead, and when Todd Zeile smashed a two-run double in the fourth, it was all but over. Hampton shut out the Cards, 7–0, in a laugher, and the New York Mets were National League champs for the first time in fourteen years. The ease of victory took away some of the excitement for the players.

Al Leiter: "It was almost uneventful, again, because of how we won. I've been part of two World Championship teams that won in heroic fashion. In 1993 [with Toronto], we were definitely heading for game seven. Everyone was biting their nails. We thought, We might lose this thing, and whammo, two outs, Joe Carter hit a three-run homer off Mitch Williams to win the son-of-a-bitch. Talk about that feeling of wanting to yell and scream and dance. And then in '97, same thing with Florida. We lost game six, and I start game seven, and we had a hell of a game, and then Renteria got a base hit up the middle, and we won in extra innings.

"Against the Cards, we were up three games to one, and it wasn't that you felt you were going to win it for sure, but we felt pretty good about it. We took an early lead, and it was a big cushion for Hampton. And the opposing lineup—like what I talked about in the one-game playoff against Cincinatti—even though it was only 2–0, I felt like it was a pretty big lead.

"Mike had a six-run lead by the fifth. So, it was over, and the last few innings you were just waiting for the inevitable. It happened in New York. And we didn't have to go back to St. Louis. Not to diminish the fact it was the first time in fourteen years that the Mets got into the Series and that I was actually part of the team that got in, *my Mets team*! What a great feeling!"

All the New York Yankees had to do was win one more game against the Seattle Mariners and there would be a Subway Series. Already the ghosts of Jackie Robinson, Willie Mays, Ralph Branca, Bobby Thomson, Duke Snider, Roy Campanella, Gil Hodges, Whitey Ford, Billy Martin, Mickey Mantle, Don Larsen, Sandy Amoros, and Johnny Podres were beginning to reappear.

Thomas Boswell commented, "This city may be twenty-four hours from needing 20 million sedatives."

fifty-one

A Subway Series

Through the month of September the back pages of the New York tabloids usually were filled not with Mets exploits but with those of the crosstown New York Yankees. Would the Yankees threepeat as champions? Would they continue their sudden September collapse and fail to even make the Series? The media obsession was with the Yankees, Yankees, Yankees. The Mets had won 94 games but they hadn't been to a World Series in fourteen years. Reporters were used to covering Yankee success, and they had not anticipated that the Mets would play as well as they did.

But when the Yankees wrapped it up against the Mariners, all of New York took sides. In one of the more humorous essays, John Leo in *U.S. News & World Report*, explained why he was rooting for the Mets against the Yankees.

John Leo: "One of the teams represents truth, justice, the American way, and underdogs everywhere. The other represents George Steinbrenner.

"Ridiculously rich people who live in Manhattan root for the Yankees. When they hear about a coming 'Subway Series,' they scratch their heads and ask their doormen, 'What's a subway?' The Mets are located in Queens, where real people predominate. Yankee fans don't even know where Queens is. Luckily, their chauffeurs do, or Yankee fans would never be able to reach either city airport.

". . . The Yankees are the team of HMOs, Big Oil, and Big Tobacco. When not chortling over a Yankee demolition of some harmless American

League opponent, Yankee fans spend a lot of time worrying about the unfairness of death taxes on estates as small as $10 million.

"Mets fans, on the other hand, are members of 'working families.' Lacking the foresight to inherit trust funds, they have actual jobs. They don't go to work in pinstripes, and they don't send their baseball team out in them, either. Unlike Yankee fans, they don't expect to win every year, and they don't throw tantrums or complain bitterly to their butlers in those off years when they don't win the pennant."

After comparing Yankee stars such as Joe DiMaggio to Mets stars such as Marv Throneberry, Leo then pointed out the scruffiness of their playoff heros, Benny Agbayani and Timo Perez.

Leo concluded, "When the Yankees faltered in July, they simply went out and ransacked other teams, buying seven or eight more zillionaire ballplayers. That's the Yankee way. The Mets do it by producing improbable heroes like Timo and Benny. So who are you going to root for? Real people like Timo or Benny, or Yankee automatons and Steinbrenner's wallet?"

Al Leiter: "I had been in New York and knew all those guys. I had played for the Yanks. It does get a little sickening and nauseating that you have to watch those guys win every year.

"A lot of reasons I used to watch the World Series as a kid was to watch everybody go nuts. But the Yankees—after they won in '98—swept the San Diego Padres and danced around a little bit, kind of exciting, but it was ho hum, another World Series. And the following year, '99, after they swept the Braves, they acted like it was no big deal and I know there are players who have never even been in a World Series, and you see these guys acting like it's just another ball game? So it kind of bothers you a little bit. Maybe there's some jealousy. You wish it was you.

"The fact that I was part of history on a team playing in a year that hasn't seen a Subway Series in forty-four years, I absolutely wanted that. I was with the Moyers at a Garth Brooks function in Vegas, and Jamie Moyers' wife came up to me and playfully hit me. She said, 'I read about your quotes on ESPN. You didn't want us [the Seattle Mariners] in the World Series.'

"I said, 'Look, I wanted *you* in the World Series. I wanted to see Olerud. But I didn't want to have to get on a plane and fly six hours for game one and possibly game six. That was the only reason.' I told her, 'I love Seattle coffee, and I think Pike's Peak is cool, but I like the idea of staying in my apartment and just taking the car over to Yankee Stadium.

"For that reason, and also, it was really cool to be playing the Yankees. It was exciting."

Game one proved one of the more memorable in World Series history. The *New York Post* called it "Baseball Nirvana." At Yankee Stadium, Don Larsen, who fashioned the only perfect game in World Series history in 1956, threw out the first ball. Yogi Berra, his catcher that day, dropped it.

For twelve innings the Mets and Yankees scrapped and battled. Al Leiter started against Andy Pettitte. Leiter had the lead late in the game, but Armando Benitez again couldn't hold it. The game ended at 1:04 Sunday morning when Jose Vizcaino, a former Met who came to the Yankees from the Dodgers in June and who was starting because he was hitting over .500 lifetime against Leiter, singled in the winning run for the Yankees in the bottom of the twelfth inning off Turk Wendell to win the game 4–3.

Al Leiter: "Jose started because his batting average against me was almost .600. Albeit most of the hits couldn't blacken your eye, they were still hits. I knew that, because it was written about. Chuck Knoblauch Dhed. And Jose didn't actually get a hit off me until the sixth inning. It was his second at bat.

"It was 0–0 in the sixth. Jose was the first batter of the inning. I looked over, and I'm thinking, He's already oh for one. I looked at Robin, and I said, 'Robin, move in,' because he's laid bunts down on me, too. 'Robin, move in.'

"Sure as shit, the guy hits what would have been a three hopper to the third baseman, but Robin's up on the grass, so the ball scoots by him. And it just pissed me off, because there have been articles about this guy hitting well against me, Joe [Torre] was making this great move, and I was conscious of it, and wanted that guy to go oh for.

"He got three more hits later, but I'm glad I at least stopped him early on. Oh, well. Yeah, Jose had a great game, and his hit in the twelfth to win it was a big moment.

"I kind of root for the underdog. I like the fact Todd Pratt or whoever who doesn't get his due—I like it when they come through. Unfortunately, it was for the enemy this time."

Game two was another rough-and-tumble game, a 6–5 win by the Yankees. Roger Clemens, the five-time Cy Young Award winner, had pitched in the famous game in the 1986 World Series in which Mookie Wilson grounded through Bill Buckner's legs to win it for the Mets. In a way, this could be looked at as his revenge.

In the first inning he was clocked throwing at 99 miles an hour and before he was done for the day, he held the Mets to two singles by Todd Zeile in eight innings. But at the end of the game no one was talking about the score. Rather, they were discussing Clemens' moment of what appeared to be madness when during Mike Piazza's first at bat in the first inning, the big catcher swung and broke his bat, with the fat end rolling out toward the pitcher's mound. Clemens shocked everyone when he picked it up and hurled it end over end back at Piazza, who had to duck away. It was the first meeting of the two future Hall of Famers since Clemens beaned Piazza back in July.

What everyone wanted to know was, "Did Clemens throw it at Piazza on purpose." Clemens denied doing so, and then made the cryptic comment, "I thought it was the ball."

Leiter, for one, was following the Piazza–Clemens wars. Leiter wondered whether the Yankees would have the guts to pitch Clemens in a game at Shea, where Clemens would have to bat and face retaliation. They didn't.

Al Leiter: "The hype was that this was the first time since Clemens had beaned Mike. The question was, was Joe [Torre] going to pitch Roger in Game 1 and possibly pitch him in game five at Shea, where one of us might have maybe knocked him or hit him as a result of what he did to Mike [in July.] Joe elected to go two and six, keep him in Yankee Stadium, so Roger didn't have to bat, which was probably a smart move.

"Everyone was watching Mike's first at bat. I didn't think there was going to be another knockdown. Who the hell would have dreamt this possibly could have happened? Mike breaks his bat on the first pitch, and it sails right back at Roger.

"And look, I'm about as fired up and goofy as the next guy on the mound, and maybe Roger does things to get himself all hyped up, so maybe he was really, really fired up and he got the bat—and I think part of Roger's game is to intimidate anyway. He's a big guy and he throws hard, and he gets the reputation after a while that you're not afraid to knock somebody down on their ass, so maybe he had an opportunity to put another little thing in Mike's mind, to keep him off when he throws a slider. I don't know, but the quote was awfully funny when he said he thought it was the ball. So? If he thought it was the ball, he should have whipped it to Tino at first and not at the bat boy.

"Whatever. Look, it made good theater.

"And it worked. The guy stuck it up our butts. So, I don't know, who was the joke on?"

In game two the Yankees led 6–0 going into the ninth inning. The Mets then staged a fierce rally to close the gap to 6–5 before expiring. Mike Piazza's two-run homer off the foul pole ignited the rally.

Al Leiter: "Our reputation preceded us as a team that never gave up, all through the time I've been there. We have always figured out a way to get back at it.

"We were down two games to none. After the first game everyone said we could have won the game, and then here we didn't lay over and die. We made it to a foot or so away from Todd Zeile tying up the game. Cause we were one run away, and he hit a ball that almost went out."

The Mets now were down to the Yankees two games to none. For the Yankees, this wasn't surprising. They had swept the Padres in '98 and swept the Braves in '99. The ten in a row was a record for a franchise that was trying to win its twenty-sixth World Championship over the course of the twentieth century.

The Mets fought back. They won game three by the score of 4–2. Robin Ventura homered in the game and Benny Agbayani drove in the go-ahead run in the eighth with a double. Bubba Trammell's sacrifice fly drove in run number four.

But in game four Derek Jeter homered off Bobby Jones' first pitch, and the Yankees appeared to have things sewn up with a 4–3 win in a game in which Mike Piazza's long two-run home run off Denny Neagle left the Mets a single run short.

Al Leiter, who boasted a 16–8 record in 2000 with a 3.20 era, started Game 5 against Andy Pettite, and as he usually did in the postseason, he pitched brilliantly, allowing seven hits in eight-and-two-thirds innings.

Al Leiter: "For whatever reasons, I've been able to focus on what matters and not get all too hyped up and hyperventilated over the Big Game, and it's worked for the most part. I've thrown pretty well in the Big Game.

What I did was, I didn't want myself to be distracted by anyone, so my wife and kids left. My mom was with me and I didn't field any phone calls, and I just kind of internalized everything and thought about what mattered and what was important, and that's executing a quality pitch. It's all I thought about all day, and I was pretty relaxed and happy-go-lucky.

"In fact I was more excited about getting to the park and find out where Bruce Springsteen was going to sit. I'm a big fan of Bruce Springsteen. His guy called me and told me he was taking the helicopter. Bruce wanted to give me a heads up, but then someone from Bud Selig's office called to say the weather was a little gray, and he was nervous about the helicopter, so he said he wasn't going to come in and later I went to a family Halloween party that Bruce invited me to, a big thrill.

"So, forget about the nerves of pitching in the game that could possibly have ended the season and the series. I was all excited about Bruce coming to watch up close and personal.

"I knew it was going to be low-scoring. I figured Andy Pettitte would be on. The guy always has been in the postseason."

In game five Leiter allowed but two runs, solo homers by Bernie Williams and Derek Jeter, plus two unearned runs in the ninth. Once again, it wasn't good enough to win. Pettitte allowed only two Mets tallies as the Yankees won their third straight World Series by the margin of four games to one. The 4–2 loss gave the hardluck Leiter his tenth-straight postseason appearance without a victory, a streak that began in 1993. In four of those games the bull pen sabotaged his efforts. In this game, manager Bobby Valentine left him in the game to the bitter end.

Leiter recalled both home runs against him and the disastrous ninth in torturous detail.

Al Leiter: "Bernie hadn't had a hit up to the point when he hit the home run. He fouled a couple of pitches off, and the count went to 3–2. He was looking for my cutter and of course, I threw it. He got some good wood on it, and he hit a legit, nice home run to left.

"What upset me about the second run I gave up in the sixth inning, I had gotten Jeter out twice, on a curveball in the dirt and in his second at bat I jammed him. In this third at bat, I just kind of fucked my own mind.

"Mike called for a slider in and then a fastball in, and I shook him, and I shook him. I wanted to get to a change-up, because periodically, as much as I throw inside, I know everyone in the park and everyone watching knows I throw inside, and I wanted to throw a change-up. And I threw a good one and it was down and away for a ball, and I said to myself, If I could duplicate it, I envision Jeter pulling off a little bit and hitting a nice little grounder to short.

"So, Mike gave me two other signs, and I got back to the change-up, and instead of throwing it with the conviction you need to throw it with, I babied it, and it ended up being a shitty nothing ball that actually did cut at about 82 miles an hour, and Jeter launched it. Ugh, I just totally served it up for him. And that pissed me off.

"But hell, I would take two runs through eight innings going into the ninth for the rest of my career and probably win eighty to ninety percent of the time.

"I went out for the ninth with the score 2–2. I was excited to be in there. I struck out Bernie Williams to end the eighth, and struck out Tino and Paul O'Neill to start the ninth. So I got two outs and it looked great.

"Posada gave me a tough at bat. On a 2–2 pitch, I thought I had him struck out, but he probably wasn't. Maybe I was begging a little. He fouled off a couple of pitches and I walked him. And then Brosius came up and he hit a little base hit to left, and runners are on first and second with Luis Sojo coming up to bat.

"I've made a lot of pitches. But two days before, when Bobby came around the pitching bucket during batting practice, I said, 'Just remember, Bobby, if you get a chance, when in doubt, I'm telling you now, Leave me in there. I don't care if I have 150 pitches.'

"So it was my hope if there was a shadow of a doubt, Bobby would have the confidence to keep me in there, and he did. As Bobby said, 'Here was a guy who left his balls out there, pitching his heart out, and it was either him against Sojo or Johnny Franco.'

"A lot of times just witnessing a game, I prefer to let the tempo and the guy who's been doing it all night long try to get the guy out. And look, Luis stepped out, and he hit what amounted to about a ten hopper up the middle.

"We had [shortstop Kurt] Abbott playing in the hole—had he been playing straight up he definitely would have knocked the ball down—if you look at the positioning of the middle infield, you got Alfonzo [at second] shaded to pull—I basically play everyone shaded to pull—and the ball just went past me, and ah, well, what the hell are you going to do?

"And Posada scored [the winning run], and it was upsetting. I was very,

very upset after that when it happened. But time goes on, and it was an opportunity and a frozen moment in my life, and it was a thrill."

After Posada scored and Luis Sojo scored on an error, Valentine brought Johnny Franco in to get the final out in the ninth. The Mets still had a chance to bat in the bottom of the ninth. The fandom at Shea continued to be hopeful. But at exactly the stroke of midnight, Mike Piazza hit a long fly ball into the Queens night that at first looked like it might go out, but settled into the glove of Yankee center fielder Bernie Williams, and the first Subway Series in forty-four years was in the record books. Once again, the Yankees were the victors.

Al Leiter: "Obviously I was disappointed by the way it finished, because I certainly felt we were every bit as good. And with an 'oops' here and a 'maybe' there and a 'what if' here, we would have been the World Champs.

"It was harder because it was the Yankees. Not for me personally, but I just think now playing in New York three years, during the time when the Yanks have been the most dominant baseball team during this period, you want to beat them. You want to come in and beat them. And we didn't and then you have to deal with your own fans, just as they have to deal with their friends who are Yankee fans, and that whole fun scenario, where it pans out that everybody is pissed off at everybody else.

"Have we become the old Brooklyn Dodgers having not beaten the mighty Yankees? Yeah, maybe. We'll see. Maybe we'll get another chance in 2001."

On October 31, 2000, just four days after the final game, the Mets rewarded general manager Steve Phillips and manager Bobby Valentine with multiyear contracts. Both agreed they needed to work more closely with the other. Mets fans everywhere will watch closely to see if they do. The Steve and Bobby show—otherwise known as "The Odd Couple"— are contracted to run the Mets for at least another three years.

Al Leiter: "Hopefully this will give us some consistency and continuity from a front-office perspective—so the decision makers will be on the same page. It's pretty much been a winning formula the last few years I've been there. Steve Phillips has done a great job, and Bobby has done a great job, and it's my hope ownership continues to believe in us and tries to keep putting the little pieces of the puzzle together until we become World Champs."

notes

one: *The Original New York Metropolitans*

p.1   "of meager reputation." Frank Graham, *The New York Giants*, page 4.

p.3   "The Southest field, where the Gothams played, was fancy . . ." Jerry Lansche, *Glory Fades Away*, page 40.

p.3   "go down for a grounder and come up with six months of malaria." David Nemec, *The Beer and Whiskey League*, page 50.

p.3   "Mets players had to resort to stealing." Ibid, page 50.

p.4   "so he reinstated Radbourne and gave him a raise." *Glory*, page 36.

p.5   "the Metropolitans played like children." *The Beer and Whisky League*, page 58.

p.5   "The Metropolitans lost $8,000 . . ." *Glory*, page 40.

p.7   Aided by the Metropolitans' best players, the duplicitous Charlie Byrne's Brooklyn Bridegrooms won the 1889 American Association pennant. Then in 1890 the players revolted against a strict and odious salary cap mandated by the owners and started their own league, called the Brotherhood or Players League. The war was so costly that the Brotherhood folded after only one year, and with both the American Association and the National League losing money at a fast rate, the owners decided the only way they could survive was to combine and run a single powerful league. As a result four American Association teams were folded into the twelve-team National League. In 1901 another rival, the American League was formed. The New York Highlanders, which later became the Yankees, began play in 1903.

two: *The Emotions of the Giants Fans*

p.8   "The real manager and leader on the field was Buck Ewing." Graham, *The New York Giants*, page 6.

p.8   "Many were displayed behind the many saloons of New York." Ibid, page 7.

p.9   "These are my big fellows! These are my giants!" Lee Allen, *The National League Story*, page 61.

p.11   "coarse, vain, arrogant, and abusive." Graham, *The New York Giants*, page 19.

p.11   "in a bleak Bowery tenement . . ." Nemec, *The Beer and Whiskey League*, page 52. Day died in 1925 in Cliffside, New Jersey.

p.13 "Where are we going to get the players?" Graham, *The New York Giants*, page 241.
Interviews with Larry Ritter, Stan Isaacs, Joe Flaherty, Bobby McCarthy, Bill Reddy, and Donald Hall.

three: *Yonkel! Yonkel!*
Interviews with Jack Lang, Joel Oppenheimer, Donald Hall, and Ray Robinson.

four: *Leo Switches Sides*
Interviews with Charles Einstein, Jack Lang, Ray Robinson, Stan Isaacs, Larry Ritter, and Joel Oppenheimer.

five: *Willie Mays and Other Miracles*
p.37 "Do you think you can hit two-fucking-seventy for me?" Charles Einstein, *Willie's Time*, page 25.
p.38 When he was brought up to the Giants, Mays had a 16-game hitting streak at Minneapolis.
p.38 ". . . Mays' home run off Warren Spahn." Mays was 0–12 before hitting the homer off Spahn and then went fourteen more at bats before getting his second major-league hit.
p.44 "We got the shit kicked out of us . . ." Willie's Time, page 52.
Interviews with Jack Lang, Bill Reddy, Stan Isaacs, Ray Robinson, Charlie Einstein, and Joel Oppenheimer.

six: *New York's Golden Age*
Interviews with Jack Lang, Ray Robinson, Stan Isaacs, and Joel Oppenheimer.

seven: *Rumblings, Departure, and the Void*
Interviews with Stan Isaacs, Harold Parrott, Jack Lang, Joel Oppenheimer, Irving Rudd, Horace Stoneham, Ray Robinson, and Lou Larosa.

eight: *Bill Shea Performs a Miracle*
p.67 ". . . he got in—and gradually took over." *New York Daily News*, August 6, 1959.
p.67 ". . . became his enemy the day Walter O'Malley decided to go to California without his consent and his knowledge." Bill Shea letter to James Tinsley, August 18, 1983.
p.68 Clinton W. Blume pitched for the New York Giants, compiling a 1–0 record in 1922 and a 2–0 record in 1923.
p.70 The Long Island Indians folded because of World War II. Once the war started, the team didn't have enough players to continue. Bill Shea, who owned the Long Island Indians football team, hired Jim Thorpe, the legendary Carlisle football star, to be the team mascot. Says Shea's daughter, Kathy, "I have pictures of him wearing an Indian headdress. Isn't that pathetic? He was in bad shape in those days, had nothing to do, and dad wanted him to have a job so he wouldn't starve to death."
p.76 ". . . We know that it will take a lot to make it go." Harry Wismer, *The Public Calls It Sport*, page 65.
p.77 George V. McLaughlin was commissioner of the Triborough Bridge and Tunnel Authority since 1934. McLaughlin had always voted as Robert Moses asked. McLaughlin also was a major stockholder in the Equitable Life Assur-

ance Society. Moses and the Authority bought insurance from Equitable. When in 1963 McLaughlin announced he would no longer be a rubber stamp, Moses changed policies to the Hartford Life. McLaughlin left the authority in 1965. He died in 1969.

See *The Power Broker*, by Robert Caro, Knopf, NYC, 1974.

Interviews with Kathy Shea Alfuso, Kevin McGrath, Jack Lang, Stan Isaacs, Bernard Fishman, Judd Gould, and Arthur Richman.

nine: Mrs. Payson Hires George Weiss

p.87 "Okay, Let's Go Mets." Lindsay Nelson, *Backstage at the Mets*, page 54.

p.88 "he asked for the moon . . ." Robert Creamer, *Casey Stengel*, page 295.

p.97 "Where would you like them?" Nelson, Backstage at the Mets, page 29.

p.99 The first day Arthur Richman went to work for the Mets, he slipped on the ice outside of Shea Stadium and fell. The *Daily News* headline the next day read: NEW PROMOTION DIRECTOR A FLOP.

Interviews with Charles Hurth III, Jack Lang, Hazel Weiss, who I interviewed in 1973, a few years before her death; Bob Mandt, and Arthur Richman.

See also my book, *Dynasty*, Prentice Hall, 1975 for more on George Weiss.

ten: The Return of the Old Perfessor

p.107 "It's a great honor for me to be joining the Knickerbockers." Creamer, *Casey Stengel*, page 297.

Interviews with Jack Lang, Stan Isaacs, and Robert Lipsyte.

eleven: A Shortage of Talent

p.114 "It really was robbery in the daytime." Jimmy Breslin, *Can't Anybody Here Play This Game?* page 62.

p.115 ". . . So what do they do? Why, rob her?" Ibid, page 63.

p.115 "You have to have a catcher . . ." Creamer, *Casey Stengel*, page 297.

p.116 ". . . But usually it happened inside his head." Leonard Shecter, *Once Upon the Polo Grounds*, page 56–57.

p.117 "I don't know when they're going to learn." Ibid, page 46.

p.118 ". . . Skowron is the only one I know turns his head and hits the ball anyway." Ibid, page 73–74.

p.118 "That Zimmer's the guts of the club . . ." Ibid, page 46.

p.118 "We're in Philadelphia after finally winning our first game . . ." Ira Berkow and Jim Kaplan, *The Gospel According to Casey*, page 17.

p.118 ". . . Then you can go back to school." Shecter, *Once Upon the Polo Grounds*, page 82.

Interview with Stan Isaacs.

twelve: Hot Rod

Interview with Rod Kanehl.

thirteen: Ron Hunt

p.138 "I wanna say that the Mets fans has been marvelous . . ." Nelson, *Backstage at the Mets*, pages 131–132.

p.139 "But you didn't play well in any of them." Shecter, *Once Upon the Polo Grounds*, page 101.

p.139 "Marv got the good guy award mixed up with the most valuable player award." Nelson, *Backstage at the Mets*, page 129.

p.140 "We're still a fraud." Shecter, *Once Upon the Polo Grounds*, p.140   ". . . I notice he's playing the players I hollered at." Ibid, page 28.

p.141   "I don't think we can catch the Dodgers—until we play winter ball." Ibid, page 134.

p.141   "I told you they were mahogany and we're driftwood." Maury Allen, *You Could Look It Up*, page 232.

p.141   "The way you're pitching, that right-field section will be gone already." Nelson, *Backstage at the Mets*, page 112.

p.145   "It's young ballplayers like Ron Hunt . . ." Ibid, page 146.

p.145   "He's still gonna knock in twenty-seven runs for you." Shecter, *Once Upon the Polo Grounds*, page 101.
        Interviews with Rod Kanehl and Ron Hunt.

fourteen: *Kings of Queens*

p.153   "There's a housing project . . ." Shecter, *Once Upon the Polo Grounds*, page 140.
        Interview with Rod Kanehl.

fifteen: *Soboda*

p.172   "Whatta ya mean, can I still manage?" Allen, *You Could Look It Up*, page 258.

p.175   "When I go home this fall, I hope to leave a young team." Nelson, *Backstage at the Mets*, page 145.

p.175   "I've been going home to California for a long time . . ." Ibid, page 145.

p.175   "If I can't run out there and take the pitcher out, I'm not capable of managing." Allen, *You Could Look It Up*, page 262.

p.176   "I hope they don't put a mummy in a glass case." Creamer, *Casey Stengel*, page 312.

p.176   "I've been fortunate in being able to watch some of you men on television . . ." Leonard Koppett, *The New York Mets,* page 112.
        Interview with Ron Swoboda.

sixteen: *Bing*

        Bing Devine also was involved in making two unfortunate first-round draft picks, selecting pitcher Les Rohr in 1965 and catcher Steve Chilcott, who was chosen over Reggie Jackson, in 1966. Both Rohr and Chilcott were injured before they could reach the Mets.
        Interview with Bing Devine.

seventeen: *Tom Terrific*

p.186   "he was six-foot-one and weighed one-hundred-and-ninety-five pounds." Tom Seaver and Dick Schaap, *The Perfect Game: Tom Seaver and the Mets*, page 12.

p.188   "And the name is, the New York Mets." Tom Seaver, *The Inside Corner*, page 24.

p.188   "you can either accept what we agreed to give you, or you can wait until the next draft." Seaver and Schaap, *The Perfect Game*, page 33.

p.188   "The main thing is to get to the big leagues." Ibid, page 33.

p.188   She flew in and the next day they were married. Seaver, *The Inside Corner*, page 25.

p.190   "I never did find defeat particularly amusing." Ibid, page 35.

p.190   "it was definitely there when I first joined the club." Ibid, page 29.

p.190   "Hey, boy, would you get me a beer?" George Vecsey, *Joy in Mudville*, page 138.
        Interviews with Bing Devine, Ron Swoboda, and Jack Lang.

eighteen: *Gil's Kids*

p.194   To get Gil Hodges, the Mets traded Bill Denehy and $100,000. Denehy, who lives in Orlando, finds that his biggest claim to fame is that he is the other player on Tom Seaver's 1967 Topps rookie card.

p.198   "His biggest plus, perhaps, was his willingness . . ." Jack Lang, *The New York Mets*, page 66.

p.199   "When [Devine] left the Mets, they made John Murphy the general manager . . ." Whitey Herzog, *The White Rat*, pages 81–82.

p.200   "The only real problem in working with the Mets . . ." Ibid, pages 79–81.

p.203   "As a kid he was an attention seeker . . ." Tug McGraw, *Screwball*, page 19.

p.203   "he did a flip from a hayloft . . ." Ibid, page 73.

p.203   "The teammate thought he was kidding." Ibid, page 83.

p.204   "My first impression was that he was shorter . . ." Ibid, pages 90–91.

p.205   "But I thought it was horseshit." Ibid, pages 120–121.

p.205   "Mickey Mouse was off-limits . . ." Ibid, page 121.

p.205   McGraw apprenticed at a barber shop on the Bowery. Ibid, page 132.

p.206   "Why don't you just leave him alone?" Ibid, page 50.
         Interviews with Bing Devine, Rich Wolfe, Ron Swoboda, Jack Lang, and Jerry Koosman.

nineteen: *1969*

p.215   "I'd change doctors, that's all." Vescey, *Joy in Mudville*, page 165.

p.221   it was because it "wasn't a fair pitch." Seaver, *The Inside Corner*, page 227.

p.222   ". . . We felt we could win." Seaver and Schaap, *The Perfect Game*, page 47.

p.222   "We knew that our best days were in front of us . . ." Ibid, page 50.

p.227   "Tom could pitch a no-hitter tonight." Vescey, *Joy in Mudville*, page 182.

p.228   "It was like being in a dream." Ibid, page 182.

p.229   "Someday I'll pitch a perfect game." Seaver and Schaap, *The Perfect Game*, page 137.

p.229   "No, those were the real Mets today." Stanley Cohen, *The Magic Summer*, page 124.
         Interviews with Ron Swoboda, Jerry Koosman, Amos Otis, and Bernie Levy.

twenty: *Amazing*

p.230   "You're intelligent enough to do something else if you have to give up baseball." Seaver and Schaap, *The Perfect Game*, page 59.

p.239   "Our team finally caught up to our fans." Vescey, *Joy in Mudville*, page 209.
         Interviews with Ron Swoboda and Jerry Koosman.

twenty-one: *Champions*

p.243   "The Mets really are amazing." Lang, *The New York Mets*, page 97.

p.243   "We ought to send the Mets to Vietnam." Ibid, page 97.

p.243   "In the eyes of the Orioles . . ." Ibid, page 97.

p.243   "Okay, bring on Ron Stupid." Vescey, *Joy in Mudville*, page 223.

p.244   "On the second pitch I came inside with a fastball . . ." Seaver and Schaap, *The Perfect Game*, page 15.

p.246   Upon reflection, he felt "cheerful." Ibid, page 15.

p.252   "All right. A little tired, but nothing serious." Ibid, page 143.

p.252   "Let's go with my strength." Ibid, pages 143–144.

p.256   "I don't want to go back there either." Ibid, page 168.

p.262   "I still don't know how we won the World Championship . . ." Herzog, *The White Rat*, pages 82–83.
Interviews with Ron Swoboda and Jerry Koosman.

twenty-two: Vietnam
Interview with Ron Swoboda.

twenty-three: Gil's Untimely Demise
p.267   "These guys in the Ohio National Guard were no different from me and my teammates . . ." McGraw, *Screwball*, page 153.
p.268   "I went in to Gil . . ." Ibid, pages 154–155.
p.273   "Their affinity for the game brought them that much closer together . . ." Lang, *The New York Mets*, page 114.
p.274   "We really thought we had a chance to win the pennant if we could get a third baseman . . ." Ibid, page 115.
p.275   "One night, as he strolled through the back row of the press box . . ." Ibid, page 216.
p.275   "Watch the cigarettes." Ibid, page 117.

twenty-four: Yogi Takes Over
p.278   "For some reason Grant always thought a former Yankee or Dodger should manage the club." Herzog, *The White Rat*, page 86.
p.279   "We made a terrible deal with Montreal . . ." Ibid, page 84.
In 1972 the Mets hit .225 as a team. They scored 528 runs, compared to the 691 runs scored by the Pirates and 685 runs scored by the Cubs. The Mets' rbi leader that season was Cleon Jones with 52. Rusty Staub was injured much of the season and only drove in 38 runs that year.
Interview with Jon Matlack.

twenty-five: Willie's Returns
p.292   "In the first inning, he walked . . ." Joel Oppenheimer, *The wrong season*, page 71.
p.293   "I guess I learned as much from Willie Mays as anybody . . ." McGraw *Screwball*, pages 175–176.
p.296   "At first, I remember we'd come to the park every day and everything was cheerful . . ." Ibid, page 162.
p.300   "In baseball, you hear guys horsing around . . ." Ibid, page 15.
p.301   "Aw Carm, don't say that." Lang, *The New York Mets*, page 125.
Interview with Jerry Koosman, Ken Samuelson, Felix Millan, and George Theodore.

twenty-six: "Ya Gotta Believe"
p.302   "Grant could not get Scheffing to go along with him . . ." Lang, *The New York Mets*, page 128.
p.303   "I didn't have any feel for the baseball at all . . ." McGraw, *Screwball*, page 22.
p.303   "foggiest idea what in hell to do." Ibid, page *22*.
p.304   "The only way to do that," Badamo kept saying, "was to *believe* in yourself." Ibid, page 23.
p.304   "There's nothing wrong with the Mets . . ." Ibid, page 25.
Interviews with Jon Matlack and Jerry Koosman.

twenty-seven: *The Miracle Mets*

p.308   "There's no question he was beneficial to us . . ." Seaver, *The Inside Corner*, page 140.

p.309   "Fine with me." Einstein, *Willie's Time*, page 336.
When Willie Mays went into the Hall of Fame in 1979, he went in as a Met, not as a Giant, even though he had played most of his career with the New York/San Francisco Giants. At the press conference announcing his election he was asked who he thought was the greatest player.
"I thought I was," he said, then added, "I hope I didn't say that wrong." Ibid, page 346.

p.309   "We stopped being restrained . . ." McGraw, *Screwball*, pages 18–19.

p.310   "Koosman grabbed the intercom . . ." Ibid, page 39.

p.313   "Jerry Grote realized that right away . . ." Seaver, *The Insider Inside Corner*, page 69.

p.315   "Some of the guys wondered why we pitched Seaver in the sixth game . . ." McGraw, *Screwball*, page 173.

p.316   "Ninth inning, the A's had us, 5–1 . . ." Ibid, page 177.

p.317   "But then Garrett popped a litle fly behind shortstop . . ." Ibid., page 178.
Interviews with Jon Matlack and Jerry Koosman.

twenty-eight: *The Seaver Fiasco*

p.318   "A baseball team is like an organism . . ." Herzog, *The White Rat*, page 84.

p.324   "Grant had simply misread his personality." Lang, *The New York Mets*, page 146.

p.327   "One day I decided to speak to McDonald, face-to-face . . ." Ibid, page 150.

p.331   "I want out. The attack on my family is something I just can't take." Ibid, page 157.
Interviews with Jerry Koosman, Jon Matlack, and Lenny Randle.

twenty-nine: *Into the Abyss*

p.340   "I feel terrible talking about Dick Young . . ." Dick Young, who always berated players who wanted to renegotiate a contract and was always exhorting players to honor their contracts, broke his own contract when he jumped from the *New York Daily News* to the *New York Post*. The switch from the *News* gave the players yet another reason to lower their estimation of Young even further.
In 1978 Kingman eventually signed a five-year $1.375 million contract with the Chicago Cubs. He returned to the Mets in 1981.
Interviews with Jerry Koosman, Lenny Randle, Pat Zachry, Steve Henderson, and Jon Matlack.

thirty: *Swannie*

p.348   Craig Swan held the college career record with 47 wins. Since his graduation in June of 1972, the record holders have been Don Heinkel, Wichita State, 51; Richard Wortham, Texas, 50; David Haas, Wichita State, 49; Doug Little, Florida State, 49; and Kendall Carter, Arizona State, 47. Swan got his 47 wins in 67 games. He finished with a 47–9 collegiate record.
Interview with Craig Swan.

thirty-one: *Doubleday and Wilpon Rebuild*

p.359   "Couldn't we take the used balls and wash them?" Lang, *The New York Mets*, page 172.

p.361   "There are still a lot of National League fans in this town . . ." *New York Times*, June 29, 1980.

p.361   "Sports teaches you something about competition . . ." Ibid, November 21, 1981.

p.362   the entire team burst into laughter. Keith Hernandez and Mark Bryan, *If At First*, pages 8–9.

p.362   "We realized it was a scruffy club . . ." *New York Times*, September 14, 1980.

p.364   "It's like this: If I have an apartment that vacant . . ." Ibid, July 1, 1981.

p.375   "There are some clubs that just don't want any restrictions . . ." *New York Times*, November 1, 1982.

        Interviews with Terry Leach, Pat Zachry, Frank Cashen, Craig Swan, and Ron Gardenhire.

thirty-two: Darryl and Keith

p.379   He felt guilty about sending his own father packing. Darryl Strawberry with Art Rust, *Darryl*, page 89.

p.379   he felt he didn't deserve to have a future. Ibid, page 94.

p.381   "I wasn't prepared for the hype . . ." Ibid, page 134.

p.382   "I knew, when I accepted the award, that had I been playing for Kansas City or Minnesota . . ." Ibid, page 141.

p.382   Two years after Earl Weaver rejected Frank Cashen's offer in June 1983, he returned to the Orioles. He would manage the Orioles in 1985 and 1986 and then retire for good.

p.385   "Did I receive a fair chance? . . ." Hernandez and Bryan, *If At First*, page 51.

p.385   "I hustle like hell when I need to . . ." Ibid, pages 69–70.

p.386   "This harmless and beneficial pasttime of mine wasn't appreciated by Whitey . . ." Ibid, page 8.

p.387   "His practice habits were atrocious . . ." Herzog, The White Rat, page 149.

p.387   "I've used cocaine. I don't anymore . . ." Hernandez and Bryan, *If At First*, page 2.

p.387   In March 1985 Keith Hernandez and six other players—Dave Parker, Lonnie Smith, Dale Berra, Jeff Leonard, Enos Cabell, and Joaquin Andujar—testified at a trial in Pittsburgh that they had used cocaine supplied to them by the defendant of that trial. Hernandez testified that "cocaine's a demon, that you can really get stuck on it." Lenny Dykstra with Marty Noble, Nails, page 24.

        The players feared they would be suspended. Commissioner Peter Uebberoth announced that each of the players would be suspended a year unless they agreed to be tested the rest of their careers and pay fines. Hernandez was fined 10 percent of his $1,350,000 1986 salary.

p.387   "In fact, the White Rat got rid of me . . ." Ibid, pages 292–293.

p.388   "I wasn't hitting at all . . ." Ibid, pages 71–72 and 293.

p.388   "Welcome to the Stems . . ." Ibid, page 9.

p.389   "In 1983, it wasn't easy being the Mets . . ." Ibid, pages 8–9.

p.389   "[In 1983] the Mets had little leadership . . ." Ibid, page 29.

p.390   "I was uncertain, despite my public pronouncements . . ." Ibid, pages 10–11.

        Interviews with Frank Cashen and Craig Swan.

thirty-three: Davey and Doc

p.401   "Davey loved that . . ." The Worst Team Money Could Buy, page 50.

p.406   In addition to promoting his young pitchers, Johnson also brought catcher John Gibbons up from the minors early in 1984. But in a game during the last week of spring training Joe Lefebvre of the San Diego Padres rounded third and tried to score. Gibbons went up the line to tag him, and Lefebvre smashed

him in the cheekbone with his elbow and put him on the disabled list. By the
time he could play again, he was returned to Tidewater.
Interviews with Frank Cashen, Wally Backman, Ron Gardenhire, Clint Hurdle, Davey Johnson, Craig Swan, and David Brownstein.

thirty-four: Darryl and Keith II

p.409 "[In 1984] Staub asked [Davey] in spring training what his policy . . ." Hernandez and Bryan, *If At First*, page 74.
p.409 "Keith had a particularly nasty habit . . ." Strawberry and Rust, *Darryl*, page
       144.
p.410 "Darryl is the most frustrating man . . ." Hernandez and Bryan, *If At First*,
       pages 15–16.
p.411 "He was pulling the same shit . . ." Strawberry and Rust, *Darryl*, page 161.
p.412 "I realize now I was laying the burden on other people . . ." Ibid, pages
       163–164.
p.412 "If you're black, when you're in a hitting slump . . ." Ibid.
       Interviews with Wally Backman and Davey Johnson.

thirty-five: The Kid

p.423 "He wears me out, too . . ." Hernandez and Bryan, *If At First*, page 6.
p.424 "Gary Carter was our first hero . . ." Strawberry and Rust, *Darryl*, page 168.
p.425 "A bunt is a possibility, so . . ." Hernandez and Bryan, *If At First*, pages
       231–232.
p.431 "At the time I was heartsick . . ." Strawberry and Rust, *Darryl*, page 171.
       Interviews with Wally Backman, Gary Carter, Frank Cashen, Davey Johnson,
       Ron Swoboda, Terry Leach, and Joe Sambito.

thirty-six: Edged Out

p.437 "Lynch was truly angry with Duncan, who was bush all the way . . ." Hernandez and Bryan, *If At First*, page 288.
p.440 "Dayley, you're meat . . ." Strawberry and Rust, *Darryl*, pages 177–178.
p.442 "We knew that in that moment, Frank Cashen loved his Mets . . ." Ibid, pages
       179–180.
p.443 "The whole Shea Stadium crowd came alive . . ." Ibid, page 180.
       Interviews with Wally Backman, Terry Leach, and Gary Carter.

thirty-seven: A Runaway Pennant

p.445 "Davey set the tone just as the season started . . ." Strawberry and Rust, *Darryl*,
       page 188.
p.446 "We were like a long-distance runner . . ." Gary Carter and John Hough Jr., *A
       Dream Season*, page 76.
p.447 "Opposing players complained . . ." Ibid, page 25, 71.
p.448 "A team on the march to the championship . . ." Strawberry and Rust, *Darryl*,
       page 190.
p.448 "The Mets were close, and we touched," Carter and Hough Jr., *A Dream Season*, page 124.
p.449 "You have to do that, too . . ." Strawberry and Rust, *Darryl*, page 191.
p.449 "Here we are in Cooter's . . ." Ibid, pages 191–192.
p.449 "Tuff had tried to walk out of the bar . . ." Carter and Hough Jr., *A Dream
       Season*, page 61.
p.454 "On August 6, we had played the Cubs in Chicago . . ." Ibid, pages 113–115.
p.455 "George cut his own throat . . ." Dykstra and Noble, *Nails*, page 73.

p.455 "Good riddance . . ." Ibid, page 151.

p.457 "Why do they boo him? They're not helping him . . ." Ibid, page 166.

p.457 "It comes as a surprise in your own ballpark . . ." Carter and Hough Jr. *A Dream Season*, page 161.

p.458 "You've heard of bat day and cap day? . . ." Ibid, page 166.
Interviews with Gary Carter and Wally Backman.

thirty-eight: *Drama in Houston*

p.460 "No seventh game . . ." Strawberry and Rust, *Darryl*, page 196.

p.460 "I've never found a thing, son." Carter and Hough Jr., *A Dream Season*, page 15.

p.460 "He got tougher . . ." Ibid, page *15*.

p.462 "In my opinion the whole series turned on that bunt by Wally Backman." Ibid, page 28.

p.464 "It was one of the biggest, most welcome hits . . ." Ibid, page 44.

p.464 "You confronting me? . . ." Strawberry and Rust, *Darryl*, page 216.

p.465 "I put it all behind me . . ." Ibid, page 203.

p.467 "Now, Darryl, you hear? Numbers, Darryl." Ibid, *Darryl,* page 208.

p.469 "To say we caused damage is a pristine way of putting it . . ." Dwight Gooden with Bob Klapisch, *Heat*, pages 46–47.

p.470 "Davey's response? In front of us . . ." Ibid, page *47*.
Interviews with Wally Backman and Gary Carter.

thirty-nine: *Miracle of Miracles*

p.472 "We'd beaten Houston. The worst was over . . ." A Dream Season, pages 93–94.

p.473 "HoJo, meanwhile, was a little hurt . . ." Ibid, pages 110–111.

p.474 "It was a disaster . . ." Strawberry and Rust, *Darryl*, page 221.

p.474 "They don't need practice . . ." Ibid, page 222.

p.475 "No, we were not afraid to face the music . . ." Carter and Hough Jr. *A Dream Season*, page 122.

p.479 "The fact that the fans felt comfortable . . ." Ibid, page 161.

p.479 "The outcome of this Series depends on your fortitude . . ." Strawberry and Rust, *Darryl*, page 229.

p.483 "We were an out away from wasting a whole fucking season . . ." Dykstra and Noble, *Nails*, page 210.

p.485 "Ray Knight was the batter, and I was on second giving him encouragement . . ." Carter and Hough Jr., *A Dream Season*, page 177.

p.485 "Who showed you the ending?" Dykstra and Noble, *Nails*, page 211.

p.485 "Once we got a run in, they were dead . . ." Ibid, page xx.

p.486 "Mookie's at bat—one of the most famous in baseball history . . ." Carter and Hough Jr. *A Dream Season*, page 178.

p.487 "Buckner knew who was flying down the line . . ." Ibid, page 179.

p.487 "The question for the ages was . . ." Gooden and Klapisch, *Heat*, page 49.

p.487 "It took us and 55,000 fans . . ." Carter and Hough Jr. *A Dream Season*, page 179.

p.488 "I let the magic of the night before wash over me . . ." Strawberry and Rust, *Darryl*, pages 236–237.

p.489 "When Davey handed him the ball, the game—the World Series—was settled . . ." Carter and Hough Jr. *A Dream Season*, page 197.

p.490 "Shea was rocking; everyone was beginning to smell it." Ibid, page 199.

p.492 "He knew I was dealing with problems . . ." Strawberry and Rust, *Darryl*, page 240.

p.492 "The excitement grew and grew . . ." Carter and Hough Jr. *A Dream Season*, page 201.

p.493 "Ah, that last out will last a lifetime . . ." Gooden and Klapisch, *Heat*, page 49.

p.493 "We hugged, jumped on each other . . ." Carter and Hough Jr., *A Dream Season*, page 203.

p.493 "Hey, they can hate us . . ." Dykstra and Noble, *Nails*, page 215.

p.495 "This was the kind of year that any young baseball player looks forward to . . ." Strawberry and Rust, *Darryl*, pages 244–245.

Interview with Wally Backman, Gary Carter, and Ron Swoboda.

forty: Rum and Coke

p.497 "I don't think the front office realized how important he was to winning . . ." Dykstra and Noble, *Nails*, page 90.

p.498 "Drinking allowed me to commune with Darryl and Kevin Mitchell . . ." Gooden and Klapisch, *Heat*, pages 34 and 35.

p.499 "Kevin, stop acting so crazy . . ." Ibid, page 36.

p.502 "He called his mother, who came and picked him up." Ibid, pages 68–69.

p.506 "I was trapped in a script I coldn't rewrite." Strawberry and Rust, *Darryl*, page 250.

p.506 "These guys didn't have their hearts in it at all . . ." Ibid, pages 257–258.

p.509 "There was nothing more I could say to the man that would have made any sense." Ibid, page 259.

p.509 "I said it back then that those guys were a bunch of asses . . ." Ibid, page 261.

p.509 "I was at times ungrateful . . ." Ibid, page 263.

Interviews with Gary Carter and Terry Leach.

forty-one: A Division Title

p.516 "We ran away with the Eastern Division . . ." Gooden and Klapisch, *Heat*, page 80.

p.516 "It looked like the team had the spirit . . ." Strawberry and Rust, *Darryl*, page 275.

p.517 "We needed a better-looking poster boy . . ." Gooden and Klapisch, *Heat*, page 80–81.

p.520 "I will probably go to my grave . . ." Strawberry and Rust, *Darryl*, page 276.

p.522 "I'd devastated the Dodgers for the first eight innings . . ." Gooden and Klapisch, *Heat*, page 82.

p.524 "For nine innings on the night of October 12 . . ." Strawberry and Rust, *Darryl*, page 280.

p.525 "After the game I sat down in front of my locker and cried like a baby . . ." Ibid, pages 281–282.

p.525 "I want to be a Dodger." Ibid, page 282.

p.525 "I felt like I was vanishing . . ." Ibid, page 283.

p.525 "The bad feeling on the plane carried over into 1989." Gooden and Klapisch, *Heat*, page 84.

Interviews with Wally Backman, Gary Carter, and Terry Leach.

forty-two: The End of An Era

p.531 "As long as I was hitting home runs . . ." Strawberry and Rust, *Darryl*, page 291.

p.531 "If he would have only said *once* that he wanted me to remain with the Mets . . ." Ibid, pages 295–296.

p.537 "That disappointing season more or less ended Davey's tenure at Shea . . ." Gooden and Klapisch, *Heat*, page 85.

p.538   "I could only stare at the hopeless prison . . ." Strawberry and Rust, *Darryl*, page 17.

p.539   "The team was in such a mess under Johnson's lack of leadership . . ." Ibid, pages 35–36.

p.540   "I could tell that [Davey] had been mentally defeated . . ." Ibid, page 39.

p.540   "As the years passed and some of us . . ." Gooden and Klapisch, *Heat*, page 47.

p.541   "When management turned him into just a shell . . ." Strawberry and Rust, *Darryl*, pages 46, 43.

p.541   "Davey looked out for his players . . ." Ibid, page 174.

p.541   "I'll never come back here." Gooden and Klapisch, *Heat*, page 47. Interviews with Wally Backman, Terry Leach, Gary Carter, and Davey Johnson.

forty-three: *Darryl Twists in the Wind*

p.544   "If getting you at a good price is more important . . ." Strawberry and Rust, *Darryl*, page 57.

p.545   "When Buddy Harrelson turned against me . . ." Ibid, page 113.

p.545   "The intensity of the race for the championship . . ." Ibid, page 65.

p.545   "I wasn't putting on a show for the fans just . . ." Ibid, page 67.

p.546   "All the old warriors had been phased out . . ." Gooden and Klapisch, *Heat*, pages 86–87, 93.

p.546   "his eight-year nightmare." Strawberry and Rust, *Darryl*, page 69.

p.547   He missed most of the 1993 season, and the depression that followed led to a serious drug problem. Gooden and Klapisch, *Heat*, page 133.

p.547   "While forced to sit out Strawberry began drinking heavily again, and he started seriously using cocaine." Darryl Strawberry, *Recovering Life*, page 64. Interview with Gary Carter.

forty-four: *Free Fall*

p.551   "[Buddy] should have known better . . ." Gooden and Klapisch, *Heat*, page 89.

p.552   "That surgery turned out to be a dark landmark for me . . ." Ibid, page 89.

p.552   "That was really the official end of the Mets' golden era." Ibid, page 86.

p.552   "To this day, we haven't been formally invited back to Shea . . ." Ibid, pages 49–50.

p.553   "I thought Jeff did a great job . . ." Ibid, page 90.

p.555   "[Gooden] put the gun to his head." Ibid, page 137.

p.557   "I just look at this whole situation for myself . . ." *New York Times*, October 19, 2000.

forty-five: *Bobby*

p.559   "We may have overevaluated what we had . . ." *New York Times*, June 30, 1995.

p.559   "Green never did have a bag of magic tricks . . ." Gooden and Klapisch, *Heat*, pages 106–107.

p.561   Howser told his pitchers to throw at Valentine. *Los Angeles Times*, July 22, 1997.

p.561   "the most knowledgeable baseball man." Ibid

p.561   "The bottom line is that . . ." Ibid

p.562   The first manager in twenty years to manage in Japan. In the 1970s Don Blasingame managed the Hanshin Tigers and Nankai Hawks. *The Virginia Pilot*, May 11, 1996.

p.563   "I don't want to say anything is over. . . ." *New York Times*, December 21, 1996.

p.564   "an organizationwide look and philosophy" *New York Times*, February 15, 1997.

forty-six: *Al and Mike*

p.566 "He made everyone believe that everyone is important . . ." *New York Daily News*, Sept. 28, 1997.

p.566 "Some of the things Valentine does. . . ." *Los Angeles Times*, July 22, 1997.

p.566 "what he is happiest doing" *New York Times*, July 17, 1997.

p.567 "This change was made to improve the team . . ." *New York Times*, August 22, 1997.

p.568 "Now we have an opportunity to do something . . ." *New York Times*, August 29, 1997.

Interview with Al Leiter.

forty-seven: *Playoff Bound—Barely*

Interview with Al Leiter.

forty-eight: *The Cardiac Kids*

p.590 "You're not dealing with real professionals in the clubhouse . . ." *Sports Illustrated*, October 11, 1999, S.I. Price, "His Legion of Critics Reveled in his Late-Season Misery, but Mets Manager Bobby Valentine, Play-off Bound, Has the Last Laugh."

p.595 "John has been a big hitter all his career." *Los Angeles Times*, October 17, 1999.

p.606 "We gave everything we had." *The Washington Post*, October 20, 1999.

Interview with Al Leiter.

forty-nine: *Wild Card Winners*

p.608 "It was like if you were dating a girl . . ." *New York Daily News*, September 10, 2000.

p.612 "Once you're in, anything can happen." *New York Post*, September 28, 2000.

Interview with Al Leiter.

fifty: *A Pennant—At Last*

p.618 "This city may be twenty-four hours from needing 20 million sedatives." *The Washington Post*, October 17, 2000.

Interview with Al Leiter.

fifty-one: *A Subway Series*

p.619 "one of the teams represents truth, justice, the American way . . ." *U.S. News & World Report*, October 30, 2000.

Interview with Al Leiter.

index